The Mexican War

1846-1848

The
MEXICAN WAR
1846-1848

K. JACK BAUER

Introduction to the Bison Book Edition
by Robert W. Johannsen

University of Nebraska Press
Lincoln and London

Copyright © 1974 by K. Jack Bauer
Introduction copyright © 1992 by the University of Nebraska Press
Manufactured in the United States of America

First Bison Book Printing: 1992
Most recent printing indicated by the last digit below:
10   9   8   7   6   5   4   3   2   1

Library of Congress Cataloging-in-Publication Data
Bauer, K. Jack (Karl Jack), 1926–
The Mexican war, 1846–1848 / K. Jack Bauer; introduction by
Robert W. Johannsen.
p.   cm.
Originally published: New York: Macmillan, 1974.
Includes bibliographical references and index.
ISBN 0-8032-6107-1 (paper)
1. Mexican War, 1846–1848.   I. Title.
E404.B37   1993
972'.05—dc20
92-13927   CIP

This edition is reprinted by arrangement with Macmillan Publishing Company, a
division of Macmillan, Inc.

∞

FOR
Dodie

Contents

☆

☆　☆

List of Maps

☆

☆　☆

Standard Abbreviations Used in Notes

AF	Office of Naval Records & Library, Area File
AG	Adjutant General
AGGO	Adjutant General, General & Special Orders
AGLG	Adjutant General, Letters to Generals in the Field & to State Governors
AGLR	Adjutant General, Letters Received
AGLS	Adjutant General, Letters Sent
AHR	*American Historical Review*
AMLB	Army in Mexico, Letter Book
AO	Army of Occupation
AOGO	Army of Occupation, Orders
AOLB	Army of Occupation, Letter Book
AOLR	Army of Occupation, Letters Received
AOSO	Army of Occupation, Special Orders
BL	Secretary of the Navy, Letters from Bureaus
BLB	Letter Book, Commanding General, City of Mexico
BLUC	Bancroft Library, University of California
BOB	Maj. Gen. W. O. Butler, General Orders
CHS	Chicago Historical Society
CHSQ	*California Historical Society Quarterly*
CLB	Commo. David Conner, Letter Book
CMCLB	Commandant of the Marine Corps, Letter Book
CO	Commanding Officer
COB	Brig. Gen. Caleb Cushing, Order Book, Cushing Papers
Conner(FDR)	David Conner Papers, Franklin D. Roosevelt Library

Conner(LC)	David Conner Papers, L.C.
Conner(NY)	David Conner Papers, NYPL
Conner(Yale)	David Conner Papers, YWA
DAB	*Dictionary of American Biography*
Desp. Mex.	Diplomatic Despatches from Ministers to Mexico
2DivOB	Army of Occupation & 2d Division Order Book
ELB	Secretary of the Navy, Executive Letter Book
GO	General Order
HAHR	*Hispanic American Historical Review*
HQMCO	Marine Corps Orders
HSL	Home Squadron Letters
HSSCP	*Historical Society of Southern California Publications*
HSSCQ	*Historical Society of Southern California Quarterly*
JMLB	Brig. Gen. T. S. Jesup, Military Letter Book, Jesup Papers
KLB	Brig. Gen. S. W. Kearny, Letter Book
LB	Secretary of the Navy, Letters to Bureaus
L.C.	Library of Congress
LNA	Secretary of the Navy, Letters to Navy Agents
LO	Secretary of the Navy, Letters to Officers, Ships of War
M.C. Cons.	Despatches from U.S. Consuls in Mexico City
MCL	Secretary of the Navy, Marine Corps Letters
MCM	Marine Corps Museum
MCO	Secretary of the Navy, Letters to Marine Corps Officers
MHS	Massachusetts Historical Society
MLB	Cdr. J. B. Montgomery, Letter Book
MoHS	Missouri Historical Society
Mont. Cons.	Despatches from U.S. Consul in Monterrey
MVHR	*Mississippi Valley Historical Review*
N.A.	National Archives
NAL	Secretary of the Navy, Letters from Navy Agents
NMHR	*New Mexico Historical Review*
NYHS	New York Historical Society
NYPL	New York Public Library
PHR	*Pacific Historical Review*
PLPB	J. K. Polk, Letter Press Book, Polk Papers
POB	Maj. Gen. G. J. Pillow, Order Book
PSL	Pacific Squadron Letters
RCL	Secretary of the Navy, Record of Confidential Letters
RG	Record Group
SLB	Commo. R. F. Stockton, Letter Book
SO	Special Orders
SW	Secretary of War
SWHQ	*Southwestern Historical Quarterly*
SWLG	Secretary of War, Letters to Generals in the Field

SWLR	Secretary of War, Letters Received
SWMA	Secretary of War, Letters Sent, Military Affairs
SWML	Secretary of War, Miscellaneous Letters & Orders
SWUL	Secretary of War, Letters Received, Unregistered Series
UHQ	*Utah Historical Quarterly*
USMA	United States Military Academy Library
USNIP	*United States Naval Institute Proceedings*
UTA	University of Texas Archives
UTLA	University of Texas, Latin American Collection
V.C. Cons.	Despatches from U. S. Consuls in Veracruz
V.C. Orders	Department of Vera Cruz, Orders
1VolBrigG&SO	1st Volunteer Brigade, General & Special Orders
1VolDivLB	1st Volunteer Division, Letter Book
WLB	Brig. Gen. J. E. Wool, Letter Book, Wool Papers
WOB	Brig. Gen. J. E. Wool, Orders, Wool Papers
YWA	Western Americana Collection, Yale University.

Introduction

by Robert W. Johannsen

In 1974, when K. Jack Bauer's *The Mexican War, 1846–1848* was published, Americans were preoccupied with events in southeast Asia. The year before the last American combat troops were withdrawn from Vietnam; several months after the book appeared, television viewers witnessed the chaotic evacuation of the American embassy as North Vietnamese tanks rolled into Saigon. The longest, least popular and most controversial war in American history finally ended, but its legacy was to be felt for many years afterward. Its impact on the study of American military history was apparent, according to Peter Paret, for it "stimulated fresh, more encompassing inquiries into the nature and development of American political society—and thus into the martial side of American history." That the "new military history" enjoyed its most significant development during the troubled years of the Vietnam intervention is no coincidence. The focus shifted "from the battlefields to military institutions, society, and thought, and how they fit in the currents of their times"; the military was viewed as a "projection of society at large," and war became a clue to national character. The series of which Bauer's book was a part, Macmillan's *Wars of the United States*, edited by Louis Morton, was itself a product of the late 1960s, the Vietnam years.[1]

No past war seemed more appropriately linked to the Vietnamese conflict than the war with Mexico. The decade preceding the appearance of Bauer's history saw the publication of an unusually large number of books relating in one way or another to the Mexican War, more than in any previous comparable period. Why, asked one reviewer, "has there been so much writing on the Mexican War of late?" The answer seemed obvious.

"A probable explanation is that we are looking to the past for a reasonable concomitant to the internal arguments which raged in the 1960's and early 1970's over the war in Viet Nam." The "most likely candidate," he concluded, was the "Mexican encounter."[2]

Historians found analogies that seemed to bind the two wars together. Both wars "provided cases in which the president was unable to convince an overwhelming majority of Americans that war was either advisable or imperative." A strident, albeit highly partisan, opposition to the Mexican War appeared to be comparable to the widespread protests against Vietnam. In one of his more vehement outbursts, Abraham Lincoln declared the war with Mexico to be both unjust and unnecessary, and called President Polk a liar, in words reminiscent of the 1960s. Abolitionists who were persuaded that the conflict had been deliberately provoked by the Slave Power cast charges of moral transgression against the nation's leaders; and a prominent Ohio senator openly supported the Mexican enemy while characterizing the war as organized thievery and its perpetrators as robber chiefs.[3] The Mexican War, concluded a recent historian, was the "most reviled in American history—at least until the Vietnam war of the 1960s," and another suggested that if television cameras had been on hand, the Mexican War "might have developed into another Vietnam." One writer went further when he found in President Polk's policies toward Mexico the pattern of Lyndon Johnson's action in the 1960s. The Mexican War was somehow responsible for Vietnam, for "our troubles today [1974] can be traced back to that time."[4]

Yet analogies can be deceptive. Apparent similarities often have a way of becoming significant differences. A recent study of dissent during the Mexican War has pointed out that opposition to the conflict never assumed the "consuming activist" character of the protests against the Vietnam War. The Mexican War was popular with large segments of the American population, and for others response to the war was strikingly ambivalent. Even some of the staunchest expansionists of the 1840s deplored the war and found it contrary to the purposes of the republic. Many of those who opposed the war, like Abraham Lincoln, who waited until it was over before denouncing it, gave their support to the needs and demands of the conflict while it was being fought. The question of the Mexican War's popularity will no doubt be debated for some time to come, but one conclusion is clear: it in no way mirrored the Vietnam intervention. The 1840s were not the 1960s. "More than just a century and simple geography separates these two foes of our military forces."[5]

There is little doubt that the Vietnam experience provided Bauer with a perspective on the Mexican War that enabled him to analyze the war policies of the Polk administration more clearly and more meaningfully, but more importantly he brought to bear on his work an expertise derived from a long and intimate involvement in the study of American military

history. A doctoral graduate of Indiana University, Bauer filled a long-ne-
glected gap with his dissertation on American naval operations in the
Mexican War, a study that was published under the title of *Surfboats and
Horse Marines: U.S. Naval Operations in the Mexican War, 1846–1848* (1969).
He served in the historical branches of both the Marine Corps and the
Navy, held a visiting professorship at the United States Army Command
and General Staff College, and for twenty-two years taught military history at Rensselaer Polytechnic Institute in Troy, New York. Following his
publication of *The Mexican War,* Bauer edited the Civil War diary of Rice C.
Bull, and in 1985, just two years before his untimely death, he published
his highly praised biography of Zachary Taylor, the best up-to-date study
of the Mexican War's greatest hero.[6]

Bauer's study of the Mexican War is focused almost exclusively on military operations, for it is here that his expertise is concentrated. He gives
less attention to the war's origins, does not second-guess the motivations
of the nation's leaders, and resists the temptation to chide them for not
adopting alternative lines of action. In other words, he wisely and carefully avoids the pitfalls of presentism, into which so many others have
fallen. Although he acknowledges the value of Justin H. Smith's pioneer-
ing two-volume compendium on the war (1919), as most students of the
Mexican War must, Bauer has rejected Smith's one-sided interpretation in
favor of a more judicious and balanced account. The strength of Bauer's
book is in its objectivity. The war, he declares, was unavoidable, considering the rigid mind-sets of each adversary. Neither side really understood
the other. Bauer's exhaustive research in government documents, manuscript collections, and contemporary accounts provide his work with an
authenticity that sets it apart from previous efforts to relate the story of
the Mexican War.[7]

Although he is most concerned with military affairs, Bauer is aware that
wars do not happen in a vacuum, and that they have significance beyond
the campaigns and battles. "In few places," he wrote, "does a national
character show more clearly than in a society's response to war."[8] It is in
the failure to heed this response that much of what has been written about
the war falls short. The Mexican War, like all wars in their times, was a part
of the cultural milieu of the period in which it was fought. The conflict was
a product of America's romantic age, in its own right an important cultural episode in the young life of the United States. Its meaning to midcentury Americans was derived from the assumptions of popular romanticism and from the challenges that those assumptions faced in the 1840s.
The war came at a critical moment in the country's development, when a
rapidly changing social and economic environment brought profound
changes in the lives of the people. An expanding industrialism, stimulated
by technological advances, a prosperous and far-reaching commerce, the
growth of cities and the influx of immigrants all threatened existing social

relationships. The sweeping sense of unlimited progress and optimism, of republican virtue and national mission of earlier years, seemed to be under siege before the forces of a new materialism.

For a time and for many Americans, the war with Mexico offered reassurance that the beliefs undergirding American romanticism still held meaning. The extraordinary rush of volunteers to the colors in the early stages of the conflict, the popular demonstrations of support in small towns and large cities, the bonfires, booming cannon, and illuminated buildings with which the victories were celebrated gave vent to an outpouring of patriotic fervor that seemed to legitimize long-held convictions of mission and destiny. An excited Walt Whitman observed in the columns of his newspaper, "There is hardly a more admirable impulse in the human soul than *patriotism*." The Mexican War was even compared with the American Revolution, its heroes with those of 1776. The Sword of Washington, exclaimed the eccentric popular novelist George Lippard, blazed forth over Mexico to demonstrate to the world that the "American People, are in arms for the freedom of the Continent." To an even more widely read novelist, James Fenimore Cooper, the war was a great moral stride in America's "progress toward real independence and high political influence." The *New York Herald* was among the first to announce a new role for the nation: laying the "foundation of a new age" and a "new destiny" that would ultimately affect "both this continent and the old continent of Europe."[9]

The Mexican War touched American lives more intimately and with greater immediacy than any event to that time. The war coincided with what has been called the "print explosion" of the mid-nineteenth century, of which the penny press was only one manifestation. Fast steam presses, innovative techniques in news gathering, the employment of war correspondents for the first time (including many volunteers who reported the war for their hometown newspapers), the use of the new magnetic telegraph, and the rapid proliferation of books and periodicals—all combined to carry the war into people's lives on an unprecedented scale. The episodes of the war, the experiences of its combatants in camp and on the battlefield, even the intentions and feelings of the enemy, were reported in greater detail than in any previous war, anywhere in the world. The public's eagerness for information was insatiable, and the nation's presses struggled to keep up with it.

The war entered the stream of American popular culture in a variety of ways. All the elements of moral drama, romantic pathos, and gushing sentimentality were present: great clashes between rival armies, poorly trained citizen-soldiers outnumbered by the professional army of a military nation, patriotism and selfless devotion, individual heroism, death on the battlefield, the separation of loved ones, the sorrow and grief. The conflict was commemorated in poetry and song, in paintings and lithographs, and in great national dramas performed on the stage. Battles were reenacted by circuses, and described visually to the accompaniment of stirring piano music at panoramic exhibitions. Tales of Gothic romance with Mexican War settings flooded the book market. Publishers raced against time (and their competitors) to put histories of the war and biographies of its leaders before the reading public. The war literature, complained a critic of the conflict, "is so diffused, that it enters every nook and corner of the land." To opponents of the Mexican War, struggling to get their arguments to the people, the popular response was discouraging indeed.[10]

Mexico was but dimly known before the 1840s. To Americans, it was a land of antiquity, strange and mysterious, still clinging to vestiges of the feudal past so dramatically described by Sir Walter Scott. It was the closest they could come (actually or vicariously) to the Old World, without leaving American shores. Mexico was a land of contrasts; its tropical climate and exotic vegetation, its deserts and barren mountains, and its craggy, snow-capped peaks evoked feelings of awe and wonder. For the soldiers who marched into Mexico, curiosity vied with the spirit of adventure. The war expanded their horizons, and through their letters and published diaries (many of them appearing before the war was over) and the detailed reports of the correspondents who accompanied them, the war expanded the horizons of those at home as well. For the first time, Americans were exposed to a culture not their own, to a people with unfamiliar and strange ways who differed in language, customs, and heritage. The effect was as educational as it was startling. The soldiers experienced what could not be acquired in books, a first-hand knowledge of the land and its people. The veterans, suggested one historian at the time, would long remember the "delicious land, amid whose valleys and majestic mountains" they had learned not only to appreciate the "sublimity of nature" but also to accept the differences of other people in other lands.[11]

Popular interest in Mexico had been aroused three years before the war began, in 1843 when the New England historian William Hickling Prescott published his monumental *History of the Conquest of Mexico*. No single individual did so much to kindle the flames of the war spirit as did Prescott, an ironic distinction for a devoted antislavery Whig who opposed the war as "mad and unprincipled." Nonetheless, through Prescott's work, Americans became familiar with the titanic struggle between Cortez and Montezuma, and when the Mexican War began the example of sixteenth-century Spain's conquest of Mexico, with all the drama and romance that Prescott gave it, was fresh in the American mind. By describing "the past Conquest of Mexico" so eloquently, it was said, Prescott had "foretold the *future* one."[12] Volunteer soldiers read and re-read it and many of them carried copies with them into Mexico. For the soldiers in the army of Winfield Scott, marching along the route of Cortez from Vera Cruz to the Mexican capital, the book served as a guide. With only a small imaginative leap they saw themselves as successors to the sixteenth-century conquistadors. Prescott himself, with a grudging admiration for their victories, suggested that the volunteers reflected the best in the American character.

There was another side to the war with Mexico, as the expectations of the soldiers gradually gave way before their actual experiences. The realities of combat, the hardships of the march, the disease-ridden camps, the bad water and the strange and inadequate food, and (as one soldier put it) the "myriads of crawling, flying, stinging and biting things" with which they had to contend, all tended to dispel their visions of glory in an exotic paradise.[13] The citron groves and perfumed bowers became hot sandy plains covered with scrub chaparral. Medieval villages gave way to filthy adobe hovels. Boredom, yellow fever, amoebic dysentery, and diarrhea took their toll. Most sobering of all was the carnage of the battlefield—the jumbled masses of discarded equipment, broken guns, battered cannon, the dead horses and mules, and the bodies of the fallen soldiers, torn and mangled. The volunteers summed up their experiences in a popular phrase of the time—they had "seen the Elephant." The "elephant" stripped the war of its romantic veil.

As the war dragged on and a peaceful settlement of the conflict seemed as elusive as ever, many Americans became more ambivalent in their attitude. War, as they had always been told, was out of place in a republic. A remnant of barbarism, it was employed only by monarchies and absolutist governments, while republics, where government rested upon the consent of the governed, were dedicated to the arts of peace, to the worth and dignity of human beings. Yet even in their ambivalence, they drew a line between war as an abstraction and the war that was then being waged against Mexico. As much as they disliked war, and opposed it as an instrument of national policy, they saw benefits for the United States resulting from this one. Outspoken critics of the conflict felt the war would show the world that a people devoted to peace could vanquish a military people governed by military despots. Europeans who had scoffed at America's republican pretensions, who thought republics to be inherently weak, would now have reason to change their minds. America would enjoy a new prestige abroad. Some activists in the peace movement believed the war with Mexico would actually strengthen their cause, for they could no longer be charged with seeking the outlawry of war because their country was incapable of fighting one. The war, others were convinced, not only reflected national character but would also strengthen it. It was clear to Walt Whitman, for example, that "whatever may be said of the evil moral effects of war," the victories in Mexico "must elevate the *true* self-respect of the American people to a far higher point than heretofore." His words were echoed by the historian Prescott. Whatever might be thought of the expediency or justice of the Mexican War, he wrote, the spirit with which it was conducted was "proof of the indomitable energy of our people, and their capacity for the highest and most difficult scenes of action." But, Prescott added, "the patriot would rather see us go ahead by the arts of peace than war, as better suited to the permanent prosperity of the republic."[14]

To midcentury Americans, the Mexican War seemed to win a unique place in history for their experiment in democracy. The campaigns in Mexico, it was predicted, would stand proudly beside those of Marlborough, Frederick, and Napoleon; and the names of Buena Vista, Cerro Gordo, Contreras, and Churbusco would be forever impressed into the American memory. Yet, the war is virtually unknown to the American public today, perhaps because it was so soon overshadowed by the Civil War. For this reason as well, the war has often been viewed simply as an episode in the coming of the Civil War, setting in motion a train of events that carried the American people into that larger, more dramatic conflict. As an event worthy of study in its own right, it has suffered an undeserved neglect. The war with Mexico was an extraordinarily complex stage in the development of the nation, closely interwoven with the national culture. It cannot be isolated from its time without seriously distorting its meaning. As a cultural event, it can tell us much about the ideas, assumptions, and popular behavior of romantic America, and in doing so it may offer clues to an understanding of the troubled pre–Civil War generation.

NOTES

1. Peter Paret, "The History of War," *Daedalus*, 100 (Spring 1971), 376–96 (quotation, 385); Edward M. Coffman, "The New American Military History," *Military Affairs*, 48 (January 1984), 1–5 (quotation, 1); Russell F. Weigley, ed., *New Dimensions in Military History: An Anthology* (San Rafael, California, 1975), 11.

2. Archie McDonald, review of John Edward Weems, *To Conquer a Peace: The War between the United States and Mexico*, and K. Jack Bauer, *The Mexican War, 1846–1848, Civil War History*, 22 (March, 1976), 81–82.

3. John H. Schroeder, *Mr. Polk's War: American Opposition and Dissent, 1846–1848* (Madison, Wisconsin, 1973), x; Abraham Lincoln, speech in United States House of Representatives: "The War with Mexico," January 12, 1848; Roy P. Basler and others, eds., *The Collected Works of Abraham Lincoln* (9 vols., New Brunswick, N. J., 1953), 1: 431–42; Robert W. Johannsen, *To the Halls of Montezumas: The Mexican War in the American Imagination* (New York, 1985), 276.

4. Norman A. Graebner, "The Mexican War: A Study in Causation," *Pacific Historical Review*, 49 (August 1980), 405; Harry L. Coles, "The War of 1812 and the Mexican War," in Weigley, ed., *New Dimensions in Military History*, 324; Robert Sherrill, "That Old Cup of Forebearance," *The Nation*, 219 (August 17, 1974), 121.

5. Schroeder, *Mr. Polk's War*, xiv; McDonald, *Civil War History*, 22: 82.

6. *Surfboats and Horse Marines: U.S. Naval Operations in the Mexican War, 1846–48* (Annapolis, Maryland, 1969); *Soldiering: The Civil War Diary of Rice C. Bull* (San Rafael, California, 1977); *Zachary Taylor: Soldier, Planter, Statesman of the Old South-*

west (Baton Rouge, 1985). For Bauer's obituary, see *New York Times*, October 1, 1987.

7. For the historiographic tradition into which Bauer's study fits, see Thomas Benjamin, "Recent Historiography of the Origins of the Mexican War," *New Mexico Historical Review*, 54 (July, 1979), 169–81.

8. Bauer, Review of Robert W. Johannsen, *To the Halls of the Montezumas: The Mexican War in the American Imagination, New Mexico Historical Review*, 61 (January, 1986), 74.

9. Walt Whitman in the Brooklyn *Eagle*, April 16, 1847, in *The Gathering of the Forces* (eds. Cleveland Rodgers and John Black, 2 vols., New York, 1920), 1: 84; George Lippard, *Legends of Mexico: The Battles of Taylor* (Philadelphia, 1847), 53; James Fenimore Cooper, "Introduction," *The Spy: A Tale of the Neutral Ground* (New York, 1848), vii–viii; *New York Herald*, May 13, 1846.

10. Abiel Abbot Livermore, *The War with Mexico Reviewed* (Boston, 1850), 229. For the popular cultural response to the Mexican War, see Johannsen, *To the Halls of the Montezumas*.

11. Brantz Mayer, *Mexico, Aztec, Spanish and Republican* (2 vols. in 1, Hartford, 1851), 1: 1–2.

12. Roger Wolcott, ed., *The Correspondence of William Hickling Prescott, 1833–1847* (Cambridge, 1925), 645, 648, 658.

13. *Niles' National Register*, 71 (September 26, 1846), 55.

14. Whitman in the *Brooklyn Eagle*, April 3, 1847, in *The Gathering of the Forces*, 1: 82; Wolcott, ed., *Correspondence of William Hickling Prescott*, 658.

Errata

Page	For	Read
15, fn. 17, l. 8	MBS	MHS (Mass. Hist. Soc.)
29, fn. 3, l. 9	Taylor	Tyler
53, 2nd par., l. 13	10th and 6th Infantry	1st and 6th Infantry
60, 2nd par., l. 6	Captain William W. Mackall	Captain McCall
60, 2nd par., l. 8	Mackall's	McCall's
64, fn. 13, l. 7	193–94	293–94
64, fn. 16, l. 15	119–25	109–25
65, fn. 23, l. 14	Theodore	Theophilus
68, l. 3 from bottom	Alexander J.	George M.
79, fn. 11, l. 1	Kriedbery	Kriedberg
158, l. 18	a paymaster	Paymaster Charles Bodine
163, fn. 41, l. 2	Theodore	Theophilus
229, fn. 35, l. 1	Taylor to Wool	Taylor to Wood
229, fn. 41, l. 8	*ibid.*,	AGLS, XXIII
270, 2nd par., l. 19	June 6 and 7	May 6 and 7
273, 3rd par., l. 6	August 8.	July 8.
433	Rodenbough, Theodore F.	Rodenbough, Theophilus F.
444	Dallas, Vice Pres. Alexander J.	Dallas, Vice Pres. George M.
452	entry on Strategy, U.S.	(Added page numbers) 70, 71, 85, 119, 127–29

☆
☆ ☆

Preface

IF AMERICA EVER fought an unavoidable war, it was the conflict with Mexico over the delineation of the common boundary. The whole thrust of America's physical and cultural growth carried her inexorably westward toward the setting sun and the Great Ocean. Thrust in the way of this movement were three sparsely settled and inadequately protected Mexican provinces: Alta California, New Mexico, and Texas. If the inexorable demands of destiny drove the United States onto Mexican lands, similar demands of nationalism and self-respect prevented Mexico from parting with those areas except to overwhelming force. This book is a study of the application of the irresistible force by the United States in that situation.

The story of the application of that force by James K. Polk, like that of America's recent experience in Vietnam, depicts the dangers inherent in the application of graduated force. It is the story of an American administration which wished to live in peace with her neighbors but edged closer and closer to the abyss of war because it did not understand that the logic which it perceived so clearly was not equally evident in Mexico City. Polk and his advisers believed at each step that the application of a little more pressure would convince the Mexicans that the United States was serious in her demands and force the start of serious negotiations. The Americans did not understand mid-nineteenth-century Mexico and failed to realize that the Mexicans would not countenance the loss of territory unless it was forced upon them by the destruction of their capacity to resist. Indeed, Mexico underwent the shattering of her army, the seizure of her capital, and the threat of a total and possibly permanent occupation of her territory before any government would negotiate a settlement.

As in Vietnam, much of the diplomatic story of the conflict swirls around failure of the efforts of the American government to initiate negotiations to bring the war to a close. Through much of the period, those efforts took place against the background of a guerrilla war, a war at which nineteenth-century Americans proved themselves more adept than their twentieth-century descendants. In 1846–48 as in 1964–72 the growing disenchantment with the war by vocal segments of the American populace reflected as much frustration over the inability of the national leadership to bring the conflict to a close as it did any deep disagreement with the objectives that led the nation into the war.

In telling the story of the clash of national interests and objectives I have gone back wherever possible to the original sources. While I have attempted to read all the major published studies of the war, American and Mexican, I have tried to form my own conclusions independently of them. Primarily I conceived of the history as a story of the impact of pressures, events, and personalities upon the American activities. Therefore, I have not searched the Mexican material as exhaustively as I have the American. In part this was a philosophical decision and in part it was one forced by the limits of time, distance, and volume.

One thing is very clear. Little material on the war has passed into the public domain which was not seen by Justin Smith during research for his classic *The War with Mexico*. The only important exception is the papers of General John E. Wool at the New York State Library. These are a major addition. In one area I have made no effort to revisit the ground trod by Smith. His exhaustive coverage of the American and foreign press, the results of which fill volumes in the Smith Transcripts at the University of Texas's Latin American Collection, cannot be improved upon, and I have not tried. Why then have I trespassed upon Smith's preserve? This book grows out of the truism that every generation must reinterpret history in the light of its own experience. The reader will find that Professor Smith and I disagree on the interpretation and stress of events as well as the weight to be accorded different aspects of the war.

The primary base for this study is the voluminous collection of reports and orders housed in the National Archives. Without the sage advice and dedicated assistance of such men and women of its staff as Dr. Robert W. Krauskopf, Elmer O. Parker, Harry Schwartz, and the late Mary Johnson this study could not have been written. To list those in other institutions and repositories to whom the author is indebted is too formidable a task, and indeed too often the very people to whom I owe my greatest debt are anonymous. However, I cannot fail to thank publicly here Paul R. Rugan at the New York Public Library, Chester V. Kielman at the University of Texas, Mrs. Francis H. Stadler at the Missouri Historical Society, Mrs. Marie T. Capps at the Military Academy; Archibald Hanna and Joan Hofmann at Yale; and Mrs. Wanda M. Randall at Princeton. Special thanks must be reserved for Mrs. Rebecca R. Gould of the Interlibrary Loan Section of the Rensselaer Polytechnic Institute. She found the obscure titles which I wanted!

To Professors Harwood P. Hinton, Harold E. Brazil, and David L. Porter go my thanks for reading and commenting extensively on various chapters. The manuscript has benefited from the careful and penetrating comments of Professor Louis Morton, the overall editor of this series, and of Michael Denneny, its editor at Macmillan. The errors, however, remain mine. My wife, Dorothy, has been a pillar of support and remains one of the most careful and effective of editors. Mrs. Bettie Tomblin, Mrs. Betty Ohanian, and Mrs. Nan Hadley joined my wife in typing the manuscript.

This study was prepared in part under a research grant made available by Rensselaer Polytechnic Institute.

K. JACK BAUER

Troy, New York
December 1973

I: Imperial America

AMERICA'S FOUNDING FATHERS were inspired dreamers who conceived of the new nation which rose from the clash of revolutionary battle and the heated deliberations of the Constitutional Convention as a beacon to lead mankind to a better world. They were children of the Enlightenment who believed that the sheer power of America's example would awaken the peoples of the world and lead them on the path to the new era. This did not occur, although the United States herself prospered and grew. Pragmatic leaders used Europe's preoccupation with the wars of the French Revolution and Napoleon to gain concessions disproportionate to America's power. Many Americans were unwilling or unable to evaluate realistically their country's role, and assessed the successes of their diplomats as proof of American sociopolitical superiority.

The War of 1812 hastened the growth of a nationalism which warped the American view of her role into a divine mission to evangelize the rest of the world with her one true way. In the second quarter of the nineteenth century that concept came to embrace imprecisely many factors, including the worship of progress, the common man, and practicality.

From the beginning of the nation American leaders had cultivated the myth of democratic egalitarianism, and naturally this concept became the cornerstone of the new national religion. Had not the Minute Men, like Cincinnatus, sprung to the defense of their homes in 1775 and administered a crushing defeat to the professionals of the British army? Had not other parttime soldiers taken the measure of other professionals at Saratoga, Yorktown, and more recently at New Orleans? Had not unspoiled American diplomats like Benjamin Franklin, John Adams, and John Jay proved to be the equals of any powdered European statesman? Where in Europe were the equals of American inventors like Eli Whitney and Robert Fulton?

America, Americans believed, represented the wave of the future and the hope of mankind. Her mission was to carry the gospel to the rest of the world, especially to those nations suffering the plague of autocracy. The initial evangelizing area was Latin America, since the new states emerging from the ruins of Spain's New World empire had the good sense to copy many of their political institutions from the American model. Predictably, these new republics attracted the enmity of the autocrats of Europe, and it fell to the United States to spread that umbrella of protection which was the Monroe Doctrine. Likewise it was clearly America's obligation to overspread the continent from the Atlantic to the Pacific. Only under the American Way could the trackless wilderness be brought into blossom.

Whether this ultimately involved placing the entire area between Baffin Land and Tierra del Fuego under the Stars and Stripes was a practical issue which really stirred only newspaper editors and the penmen of political tracts. For example, when Texan-Americans, disenchanted with Mexican rule, established a government on the American model there was no unanimity among Americans as to the desirability of adding the Lone Star to the celestial cluster on the blue field.

The hostility toward European powers was augmented by the common but basically invalid belief that Europe had acquisitive designs on Texas, Oregon, and California. Whether these threats were realistic or not is unimportant, because American leaders and the public believed they were. Indeed the famous passage in which John L. O'Sullivan coined the term "Manifest Destiny" concerned frustrating foreign intrusions into the continent.

These were the views of a large segment, possibly a majority, of the American populace in the middle years of the decade of the 1840s. That the factual bases were scarcely discernible in many instances and that other factors in American political life were being entirely overlooked is clear. But is this not normally true of any generation's conventional wisdom?[1]

The most significant factor, completely ignored by the champions of Manifest Destiny, was the emergence of the all-pervading issue of sectionalism. The South had entered the revived union of 1789 with every expectation of maintaining control of the nation. Her population lacked but 7,000 of equaling that of the North and the alignment of states gave her at least an even split in numbers. But the commercializing and industrializing North experienced a surge of population and an acumen which enabled it rapidly to establish its economic and political hegemony.

Nevertheless, the southern states were able to secure the admission of a new slave-holding commonwealth into the union for each free one admitted. Consequently, although the South lost control of the House of Representatives, her equality in the Senate prevented passage of laws detrimental to her interests. But geography played a dastardly trick. After Arkansas became a state in 1836 the only area remaining south of the Missouri Compromise line was that reserved for Indians being moved west of the Mississippi. Hence the possibility of acquisition of the Lone Star Republic and its division into three or four states had an obvious appeal to many southerners. For similar reasons it had the opposite effect on many northerners.

Slavery was involved in the question of the acquisition of Texas, but it was more an emotional issue than a substantive one. Slavery as an institution was a central but not critical factor in the way of life which the southerner was trying to preserve. While abolitionists saw the sectional fight in terms of slavery, most southerners like John C. Calhoun viewed it as protecting the section's broader interests. These embraced low tariffs; the right to create and maintain a unique culture without harassment; liberal land laws; and a decentralized banking system.

Even in the North the abolitionists stood outside the acceptable political spectrum and possessed little political power. What influence they did possess rested on their ability to stir up trouble, complain loudly, and petition Congress incessantly.[2]

If many Americans saw their country's messiah role clearly and were ready to play their part, many Mexicans viewed it with equal clarity quite differently. Prior to the Texas Revolution, Mexicans had tended to admire the United States and many believed that the adoption of American institutions and methods would be beneficial. However, the obvious American support of the Texan revolt, whether officially inspired or not, confirmed latent Mexican fears that intrigue and force were standard American procedures.[3]

Distrust of the United States and its objectives therefore became a fact of Mexican political life. The acceptance by most Mexican political leaders of the notion that the public would not countenance any concessions further complicated relations. This conviction, which suggested a more clearly definable public opinion than Mexico possessed, grew into an almost oriental obsession with "face-saving" and led nearly all aspiring Mexican politicians to adopt an unreasoning opposition to any settlement with the United States.

Just as she possessed no discernible public opinion, Mexico lacked organized political parties. Her political life revolved around shifting groups which swirled about individual leaders or special interests. In 1844 control of Mexico passed to a coalition of Federalists whose only common interest was to strengthen the power of the states at the expense of the central government. The coalition shattered upon the question of the response to the American annexation of Texas. A small group of *moderados* like José Joaquín de Herrera recognized the absurdity of war with the United States and hoped to negotiate a settlement. A larger group of *puros*, led by Valentín Gómez Farías, preferred losing a war to the ignominy of parting with Texas without a struggle.

There was also an unholy alliance of Centralists and opportunists who were opposed to any government in Mexico except their own. They drew much of their strength from the large landowners, the monarchists, the church, and others who viewed a stabilized centralized government as the best hope to protect their interests. Skittering from one group to another as it served their purposes was a large group of military officers who found in the continued struggle between factions an excuse to maintain a sizable army with its appurtenances of power and prestige. The situation was still further complicated by the inevitable large group who were chiefly concerned with personal advancement. There were others who, although able and dedicated, retained a particularistic outlook. The tragedy was that Mexican leaders were able to agree only on resistance to the United States—and that policy was a foundation too fragile to establish a stable government.

Texas displayed neither sufficient natural wealth nor strategic significance to be settled early and it lay too far from the center of life in Spain's New World empire to benefit from natural expansion. It remained so until the middle of the seventeenth century when settlement began as a defense against the growing French power in

Louisiana. Spain's interests in the region declined sharply following her acquisition of Louisiana in 1763.

The Connecticut-born, St. Louis land speculator Moses Austin secured permission in 1821 to settle 300 families in Texas. Before the plans could be implemented Spain had been evicted from Mexico. Austin's son Stephen, however, secured Mexican concurrence. Other Americans followed Austin; so many, indeed, that the Mexican government feared they would innundate the area.

In 1829 the Mexican government officially abolished slavery in Mexico and in the following year prohibited further American settlement in Texas. Neither law was enforced but the threat hung like a massive boulder over the Americans already on the scene. This uncertainty, coupled with a growing suspicion of the intent of the central Mexican government, caused the Texans to support a federal organization of the nation. Consequently, when centralization triumphed during 1834 in the person of General Antonio López de Santa Anna the Texans refused to accept his new constitution.

Following a series of incidents during 1835 and 1836 the Texans established a provisional state government. Santa Anna countered by taking the field, whereupon the Texans proclaimed their independence. Throughout the ensuing revolution American popular sympathy rested with the Texans. Many Americans, enticed by promises of cheap land, Manifest Destiny, or the simple love of adventure, hastened to Texas. Lax enforcement of the neutrality laws greatly facilitated the movement but poor communications and the pro-Texan sentiments of the border population would not permit effective enforcement.

The United States government, however, was neutral and where possible attempted to live up to its obligations as the activities of the Navy in the Gulf of Mexico demonstrate. Despite the nearly total reliance of the Mexican forces in Texas upon supplies from New Orleans, American naval forces refused to intervene, even surreptitiously, to assist the Texans. Indeed, American warships kept the Mexican lifeline open, seizing Texas vessels which attempted to sever it.[4]

Despite the lack of official United States support, the Texans easily won their independence on the battlefield beside the Rio San Jacinto on April 21, 1836. Although Mexico refused to recognize that independence, Britain, France, and the United States did. Over the next nine years Texas maintained her sovereignty with little difficulty despite loud Mexican threats.

Although the Texans from the start had indicated interest in annexation to the United States, the issue was politically too explosive for any administration to raise before 1843. Then John Tyler and Secretary of State Abel P. Upshur began discussions with the Texans. Although Upshur died before he could finish negotiations, John C. Calhoun completed the assignment and signed a treaty of annexation on April 12, 1844.[5]

As early as mid-February, William J. Murphy, the American Chargé, had requested that American troops and warships be sent to defend Texas. Calhoun assured both Murphy and the Texas representatives in Washington that this would be done.[6] On April 15 Secretary of the Navy John Y. Mason ordered the able commander of the Home Squadron, Commodore David Conner, to concentrate his force in Mexican waters to deter any Mexican attack. Conner not only collected his vessels at Veracruz but in early May he visited Galveston in his flagship, the *Potomac*.[7] In a companion move the Adjutant General on April 23 assigned Brevet Brigadier General Zachary Taylor to command of the 1st Military District at Fort Jesup, Louisiana, on the Texas frontier. On the twenty-seventh broadened orders authorized Taylor to march a "Corps of Observation" to the Texas boundary.[8] These orders were so secret that Taylor's immediate superior, Brigadier General Edmund P. Gaines, was not informed. As commander of the Corps of Observation, Taylor was not responsible to Gaines but reported directly to Washington.

Taylor's selection for the very sensitive command illustrated the problems of command which beset the Army. A good but unimaginative field leader, he had won a brevet brigadier generalcy for his success in the Battle of Lake Okeechobee during the Seminole War. He projected the image of the successful commander who still retained identity with his plebeian origins. In reality he was not what he appeared. He was the son of a Kentucky plantation owner and politician who sprang from one of the leading families of Virginia. His boyhood was spent near Louisville when that city was the Kentucky frontier. Nevertheless, the roughness and excitement of frontier life left an indelible stamp. After a rudimentary education Taylor in 1808 secured a commission in the Army. His steady rise in rank reflected more perseverance and luck than brilliance. Yet no better qualified officer could be assigned the command without forcing a major shake-up within the Army. Major General Winfield Scott recognized Taylor's limitations and assigned Captain William W. S. Bliss as his adjutant general and chief staff officer. Bliss, in the opinion of most of his contemporaries, possessed the brightest intellect in the Army and was its most promising junior officer. He would guide Taylor discreetly into the best decision and his skillful pen would compensate for the limitations of Taylor's literary style. Scott's choice proved to be sagacious, for "Perfect" Bliss became Taylor's intimate and later his son-in-law. Taylor reached his new post on June 17 and immediately notified Sam Houston, the President of Texas, that the United States was honoring its commitment to protect the infant republic. This information was welcome news indeed because General Adrian Woll, Mexican commander on the Rio Grande, had warned Houston that he had received orders on the nineteenth to resume hostilities.[9]

When Calhoun's annexation treaty reached the Senate for ratification it encountered strong opposition. Many senators genuinely feared that annexation would create insurmountable difficulties. That anxiety grew from twin roots. One was an intense sectionalism which already showed symptoms of becoming the cancer that nearly proved fatal in 1861. The second was an uncertain ideological base which caused the Whigs to fear the havoc that sectionalism and abolitionism threatened to work within their ranks. As a result the treaty lost by the overwhelming vote of 35 to 16 on June 8.

The unexpected defeat threw the administration into gloom but it passed quickly as President Tyler and his advisers settled upon a new strategy. This called for annexation through joint resolution. Although the resolution would have to pass both houses, the administration believed it could muster the simple majorities required in each.

Even before the new strategy could be tested, Texas became the critical issue in the presidential election. Martin Van Buren, the leading Democratic candidate, and Henry Clay, the permanent Whig contender, both issued carefully designed statements opposing annexation in a vain hope of excluding the divisive issue from the campaign. As a result of Van Buren's statement the southern delegates vetoed his candidacy and forced his replacement by the dark horse James Knox Polk. Polk injected the question of Texas directly into the campaign by insisting on the "Reoccupation of Oregon and the reannexation of Texas." That tactic forced Clay to modify his stand in order to hold some of his southern votes. This in turn alienated sufficient abolitionist, antiannexationist voters in the Northeast to enable Polk to carry New York State and with it the presidency.

Annexation had carried the day. Therefore President Tyler's recommendation of annexation by joint resolution was anticlimactic. Administration Democrats held sufficient majorities in both houses to permit them to override Whig and dissident Democratic opposition. The House heard some spirited debate but the administration had sufficient votes to prevent any major amendments and the resolution passed the Senate by a vote of 120 to 96. The long, bitter fight hinged on two points. One was Senator Thomas Hart Benton's proposal to admit Texas half free and half slave. It furnished the abolitionists a point of departure for their oratory but otherwise drew little support. More significantly the Missouri senator introduced a measure to require the negotiation of a new treaty. This was important because it would allow him to save face while voting for annexation and at the same time would serve to salvage the Senate's prerogatives in foreign policy. Senator Robert J. Walker, soon to become Polk's secretary of the treasury, proposed to permit the President to choose between negotiating a new treaty and requiring Texan acquiescence in the terms of the House resolution. The Senate's acceptance of the Walker Compromise on the next to last day of February cleared final impediment to passage. The initial tally showed a 26 to 26 tie but Whig Senator Henry Johnson of Louisiana shifted his vote to make the final count 27 to 25. The House agreed to the compromise by a 132 to 28 vote on the twenty-eighth and President John Tyler signed the resolution on March first. He gave the gold pen with which he signed it to his wife who wore it "around her neck like the Distinguished Service Medal it was" in recognition of her lobbying efforts on behalf of the legislation.[10]

Many if not most of the legislators assumed that the choice of method would rest with incoming President James K. Polk. The Benton supporters believed that they had a commitment for the treaty option. John Tyler upset those plans. On March 3, after consulting with Polk and the cabinet, he offered annexation under the House plan because he did not consider it advisable to negotiate the terms.[11]

Polk's inaugural address on the following day dealt only fleetingly with Texas and then largely in terms calculated to smooth Mexican feelings:

> I regard the question of annexation as belonging exclusively to the United States and Texas . . . [but] the world has nothing to fear from military ambition in our Government. . . . Foreign powers should therefore look on the annexation of Texas to the United States not as the conquest of a nation seeking to extend her dominions by arms and violence, but as the peaceful acquisition of a Territory once her own. . . .[12]

A week later Polk and his cabinet formally accepted the plan marked out by Tyler. This decision naturally led to accusations of bad faith from Benton's supporters. Whether Polk had deliberately misled them is uncertain, but the best evidence suggests that he allowed them to read what they wanted into his statements.[13] Undoubtedly the decision to follow the House plan was the wisest. It was both quicker and more certain at a moment when the fluid situation in Texas made haste desirable.

The instructions issued to Chargé Andrew Jackson Donelson following the cabinet meeting stressed speed. He reached Galveston on March 27 where he heard rumors, substantially correct, of English moves to secure Mexican acceptance of Texas independence. The American hurriedly set out for the Texas capital of Washington and laid the American proposals before President Anson Jones on the first day of April. Jones complained about the terms but called his Congress to meet in a special mid-June session. On May 5 he also called a popular convention to meet in Austin on July 4 to act on the American offer.[14]

When he learned of the British efforts to forestall annexation, Polk dispatched former Postmaster General Charles A. Wickliffe to organize a countermove. In order to increase American leverage in the negotiations and to dissuade Mexico from any military moves, Commodore Conner in late March again received orders to concentrate his vessels in Mexican waters. In April Commodore Robert F. Stockton with a small squadron scheduled for a visit to Europe and the Near East was diverted into Texas waters as temporary reinforcement of Conner's force during the period of negotiation.[15]

The British moves had been initiated by Foreign Minister Lord Aberdeen upon learning of the signing of the annexation treaty. His first effort, an Anglo-French guarantee of both Mexican integrity and Texan independence, foundered on French indifference. He persisted and his Minister to Mexico, Charles Bankhead, in January 1845 secured in principle a Mexican acceptance of a treaty recognizing Texas's loss. Charles Elliot, Britain's representative in Texas, secured her agreement and on March 29 President Jones agreed to delay action on annexation pending receipt of the actual document. The agreement was finally initialed in Mexico City on May 17 but by then time was running out for the British.[16]

During May Stockton and Wickliffe, impatient over Jones's seeming inactivity, allied themselves with a group of Texans in a scheme to force the issue by means of an attack on the Mexican forces along the Rio Grande. The plan collapsed when Jones refused to participate. Despite Stockton's claims to the contrary, the Americans undoubtedly acted without presidential authorization. The plan was in keeping with Stockton's character but ran counter to Polk's policy.[17]

From the American standpoint the key individual in Texas politics was Sam Houston. Indeed, Donelson received his appointment in large part in hopes that he would enlist Andrew Jackson to employ his powers of persuasion on Houston. The Texan had initially been cool to annexation but by early May had been won over. "Without his aid," Donelson reported, "the party opposed to annexation cannot hope to muster one tenth of the voting population."[18] As a result, when Congress met, the British offer of independence with guarantees had little support. Even that vanished when the members learned that Mexico had refused to reciprocate President Jones's June 4 unilateral proclamation of a truce between the two countries. The Congress at once voted unanimously for annexation. The popular convention which met at Austin on July 4 immediately put its stamp of approval on the acceptance. Texas was now a part of the United States. On December 22 the American Congress agreed to the joint resolution which made Texas a state.

Ralph Waldo Emerson gave voice to the thoughts of many in the United States when he commented in his journal that: "The annexation of Texas looks like one of those events which retard or retrograde the civilization of ages. But the World Spirit is a good swimmer, and storms and waves cannot easily drown him."[19]

Texas was not the only—and in some American eyes scarcely the most important—source of friction with Mexico. The United States had a long-standing quarrel with Mexico over the settlement of claims by American citizens for losses incurred during Mexico's frequent revolutions or as a result of arbitrary actions by Mexican officials. In 1837 the United States formally presented fifty-seven cases totaling $6,291,605 for redress. At Mexico's request they were submitted to an international tribunal which in 1842 awarded $2,026,149. Another $3,334,837 was not considered. In 1843 Mexico agreed to pay the award with interest over a five-year period. In 1844, after four quarterly payments, she defaulted.[20]

It was the duty of the American government to press for a resumption of those payments or for new, acceptable alternatives. Since Mexico was broke many people, notably those impregnated with Manifest Destiny, found that alternative in the exchange of Mexican territory for American assumption of responsibility for the payments.

Land was indeed about the only commodity which Mexico had not mortgaged to one or another of her creditors.

The Joint Resolution was imprecise about the boundaries of the new state of Texas. In 1836 the Lone Star Republic had claimed a western boundary along the Rio Grande River and had held to it ever since. Moreover, Texas authorities claimed to have established customshouses, post offices, post roads, and election precincts west of the Nueces River. They even laid out an entire county, San Patricio, reaching to the Rio Grande. The claim was more fancy than fact, since very few inhabitants lived in the area and most of them were Mexicans living near the Brazos Santiago in the Rio Grande valley.[21] Considerably more significant, but generally overlooked by the Texans, was the directive issued by Minister of War José María Tornel y Mendivil to General Woll on July 7, 1843, to withdraw to "the line under your command," the Rio Grande.[22] This acknowledged that Mexican authority stopped at the river. Mexico's claim to the area from there to the Nueces rested on the traditional boundaries of the state of Tamaulipas which put them in the same category as those of Texas. The area in dispute was a no-man's land to which neither side had an overriding claim.

Polk pressured Texas to insist on the Rio Grande boundary and to occupy at least some of the territory below the Nueces prior to annexation. He viewed possession as a weapon to force the Mexicans into a general boundary and claims settlement. Although Polk never spelled out his diplomatic strategy, we do know that he wished to acquire California above all else and hoped less fervently for New Mexico and the Rio Grande boundary. If his public insistence on that boundary is viewed as a bargaining stance, the rest of his diplomatic maneuvers with Mexico fall into place. The occupation of the disputed area and the concentration of American naval forces at Veracruz and Mazatlán served as a means of upping the ante in the diplomatic poker game. Since this strategy called for a negotiated settlement, Mexican intransigence forced Polk to grab for nearly any opportunity, no matter how unlikely, which might lead to the start of the talks that were necessary if hostilities were to be avoided or ended. Polk wanted a peaceful, diplomatic settlement. That desire permeates all of the public and private utterances of the administration, as George Bancroft wrote in mid-1845:

You are quite right in supposing the disposition of this government towards Mexico to be of the most conciliatory character. . . . I hope war is permanently out of fashion in the civilized world; but at least I hope and trust that that savage custom is not to intrude itself into the relations of American republics with each other.[23]

A similar policy of public brinksmanship won Polk a monumental victory in the Oregon dispute. The tactics did not work during the Texas negotiations because his opponent was insecure, faction-rent Mexico, not worldly and haughty Great Britain. It was Polk's shortcoming that he, like most of his countrymen, did not understand the complexities of Mexican character.

With the completion of negotiations with Texas over the annexation, Polk shifted priorities in foreign policy to give primacy to the peaceful acquisition of California. Throughout nearly all its Spanish and Mexican periods Alta, or Upper, California was a fringe area too distant and difficult to reach to be governed effectively by the series of weak administrations in Mexico City. In practice they exercised only nominal control over California's 15,000 white and 24,000 Indian inhabitants. To many foreigners, Americans, Britons, and Frenchmen, the area's obvious richness[24] demanded acquisition by a strong power.

To the American exponents of Manifest Destiny, California had an attraction like that of a crowd for a politician. For them it was the natural western limit of the country, a great commonwealth connecting America's heartland with the wealth of the Orient. Moreover only through the application of the American Way could the riches of the area be successfully exploited. These men also worried that the acquisition of California by Britain would isolate the American settlements in Oregon. In their fear of Britain, which verged on a national obsession, they overlooked obvious indications that Britain had no such ambitions.[25]

Although American vessels had traded on the California coast since 1822, not until the following two decades did significant numbers of Americans visit the area. American vessels worked the hide trade along the coast; California harbors became favorite stopping places for whaling ships in the north Pacific; and a growing number of Americans like Thomas O. Larkin, Abel Stearns, and William Leidesdorff settled there as merchants and landowners. As a result of the growing American presence there the Navy's Pacific Squadron in 1839 received orders to send a vessel to California.

The American interest in securing California was so clear that when in September 1842 Commodore Thomas apCatesby Jones decided the United States and Mexico were on the verge of war, he rushed his squadron north from Callao, Peru. After occupying Monterey, California's chief port, on October 19, he discovered that war had not developed. Jones promptly restored the town to its Mexican authorities with full apologies and ceremonies. The incident cost the Commodore his command but proved the ease with which the California ports could be secured. Although Jones acted on his own initiative without specific orders, his actions were in accord with national objectives as envisioned by many, if not most, Americans.[26]

In late 1842 the Mexican government attempted to strengthen its control over California by dispatching General Manuel Micheltorena as governor. Micheltorena's administration so irritated the Californians that they drove him out in February 1845. The Paredes revolt in December 1845 forced cancellation of an expedition which had gathered at Acapulco preparatory to reasserting Mexican authority. As a result the central government was forced to recognize the insurrectionary regime under Pio Pico as the legal administration in the state. That act signaled Mexico's effective abandonment of her efforts to control the area.

By the end of 1845 California was ready for any movement which would assure it peace, tranquility, and a stable government. Although most of the intensely proud and independent Californians would not have accepted the forcible annexation of their country by a foreign power, a growing number recognized the advantages of protection by one of the great powers or the United States. All of this was being regularly and incisively reported to Washington by the able Consul at Monterey, Thomas O. Larkin. Those reports convinced Polk that California was ripe for a peaceful conquest through infiltration and subversion. Such a program undoubtedly strongly appealed to the devious-minded Polk. It also fitted the conditions in California.

NOTES

For key to abbreviations used in Notes, see page xi.

1. The classic exposition of America's concept of her divine role to overspread the continent is Albert K. Weinberg, *Manifest Destiny* (Chicago, 1963), chs. iv, vi; and of her mission, is Frederick Merk, *Manifest Destiny and Mission in American History* (New York, 1963), chs. i–ii.
2. Good summaries of the development of the sectional struggle can be found in Roy F. Nichols, *The Stakes of Power* (New York, 1961), chs. i–iii; Charles S.

Sydner, *Development of Southern Sectionalism, 1819–1848* (Baton Rouge, 1948); and Glyndon G. Van Deusen, *The Jacksonian Era, 1838–1848* (New York, 1966), chs. vii–x.

3. This change is well documented in Gene Brack, "Mexican Opinion and the Texas Revolution," *SWHQ*, LXXII (Oct. 1968), 170–82, and in Frank A. Knapp, Jr., "The Mexican Fear of Manifest Destiny in California," in Thomas E. Cotner and Carlos E. Castaneda (eds.), *Essays in Mexican History* (Austin, 1958), 192–208.

4. This issue is discussed at greater length in K. Jack Bauer, "The U.S. Navy and Texas Independence: A Study in Jacksonian Integrity," *Military Affairs*, XXXIV (April 1970), 44–48.

5. The Texas annexation is discussed extensively in Justin H. Smith, *The Annexation of Texas* (New York, 1911); George Lockhart Rives, *The United States and Mexico, 1821–1848* (2 vols., New York, 1913), I, 585–617; Eugene Irving McCormac, *James K. Polk* (New York, 1965), 309–15, 355–71; Charles Sellers, *James K. Polk Continentalist 1843–1846* (Princeton, 1966), 208–29.

6. Calhoun to Murphy, April 13, 1844, to Isaac Van Zandt and J. P. Henderson, April 11, 1844, in William R. Manning (ed.), *Diplomatic Correspondence of the United States: Inter-American Affairs, 1831–1860* (12 vols., Washington, 1932–39), XII, 71–72.

7. Mason to Conner, April 15, 1844, to Taylor, April 27, 1844, *S. Doc. 341, 28th Cong., 1st Sess.*, 76, 78–79; Conner to Mason, May 27, 1844, *HSL*.

8. AG, Memorandum to SW, Oct. 7, 1845, *AGLS*, XXI, 1019.

9. William S. Henry, *Campaign Sketches of the War with Mexico* (New York, 1847), 8–9; Ethan Allen Hitchcock, *Fifty Years in Camp and Field*, ed. W. A. Croffut (New York, 1909), 185; Brainerd Dyer, *Zachary Taylor* (Baton Rouge, 1946), 148; Woll to Houston, June 19, 1844, J. C. Hays to G. W. Hill, June 21, 1844, and Anson Jones to T. A. Howard, Aug. 6, 1844, *Cong. Globe, 28th Cong., 1st Sess.*, XIV, app. 2. Commodore Conner assured the government from Veracruz that any such movement was unlikely. Conner to Mason, June 25, 1844, *HSL*.

10. *Cong. Globe, 28th Cong., 1st Sess.*, 16–372 *passim*; 5 *U.S. Stat.*, 797–98; Oliver Perry Chitwood, *John Tyler, Champion of the Old South* (New York, 1939), 359–60; Thomas H. Benton, *30 Years View* (2 vols., New York, 1856), II, 619–24, 631–38. The quotation is from Robert Seager II, *And Tyler Too* (New York, 1963), 283.

11. Calhoun to A. J. Donelson, March 3, 1845, Manning, *Diplo. Corres.*, XXII, 83–85.

12. James D. Richardson (ed.), *The Messages and Papers of the Presidents* (20 vols., New York, 1897–1922), V, 2230.

13. For differing interpretations of Polk's supposed duplicity, see McCormac, *Polk*, 315; Sellers, *Polk Continentalist*, 215–19; and Benton, *30 Years View*, II, 636–37.

14. Jones, Proclamations, April 15, May 5, 1845, *S. Doc. 1, 29th Cong., 1st Sess.*, 54–55, 63–64.

15. Buchanan to Wickliffe, March 27, 1845, Manning, *Diplo. Corres.*, XII, 85–90; Bancroft to Conner, March 20, April 22, 1845, to Stockton, April 22, 1845, all in *RCL*, I, 108–9, 115.

16. The British moves are treated at length in Ephraim Douglas Adams, *British Interests and Activities in Texas 1838–1846* (Baltimore, 1910), 168–218; Rives, *U.S. and Mexico*, I, 705–10; George Lockhart Rives, "Mexican Diplomacy on the Eve of the War with the United States," *AHR*, XVIII (Jan. 1913), 277–78; Ramon Alcaraz, *et al., The Other Side*, trans. Albert C. Ramsey (New York, 1850), 27. The American consul at Veracruz, F. M. Dimond, relayed frequent status reports on the subject to Washington. See Dimond to Buchanan, April 12, 29, May 8, 1845, *V.C. Cons.*, V.

17. The attribution of such a conspiracy between Polk and Stockton forms the basis of Glenn W. Price, *Origins of the War with Mexico* (Austin, 1967) and Richard R. Stenberg, "The Failure of Polk's Mexican War Intrigue of 1845," *PHR*, IV (March 1935), 36–68. It is dealt with more objectively in Sellers, *Polk Continentalist*, 222–25; Smith, *The Annexation of Texas*, 447–48, and Frederick Merk, *The Monroe Doctrine and American Expansion 1845–1849* (New York, 1966), 150–51. See also Stockton to Bancroft, May 27, 1845, George Bancroft Papers, MBS.

18. Donelson to Buchanan, May 6, 1845, *S. Doc. 1, 29th Cong., 1st Sess.*, 56–57.

19. Bliss Perry (ed.), *The Heart of Emerson's Journals* (Boston, 1926), 212.

20. The claims question is treated at length in Clayton Charles Kohl, *Claims as a Cause of the Mexican War* (New York, 1914), and John Bassett Moore, *History and Digest of the International Arbitrations to Which the United States Has Been a Party* (6 vols., Washington, 1898), II, 1209–59. Lowell L. Blaisdell, "The Santangelo Case: A Claim Preceding the Mexican War," *Journal of the West*, XI (April 1972), 248–59, studies a single claim.

21. The Texas claims are put forth very strongly in John S. Jenkins, *The Life of James Knox Polk* (Hudson, New York, 1850), 251, and Z. T. Fulmore, "The Annexation of Texas and the Mexican War," *Quarterly of the Texas State Historical Association*, V (July 1901), 28–48. A balanced summary and evaluation appears in Seymour V. Connor and Odie B. Faulk, *North America Divided* (New York, 1971), 26.

22. Tornel to Woll, July 7, 1843, *S. Doc. 341, 28th Cong., 1st Sess.*, 84.

23. Bancroft to Henry Wikoff, May 12, 1845, Mark Anthony DeWolf Howe, *The Life and Letters of George Bancroft* (2 vols., New York, 1908), I, 288. See also Louis Martin Sears, "Slidell's Mission to Mexico," *South Atlantic Quarterly*, XII (Jan. 1913), 14–15.

24. The 1846 exports included 85,000 hides, 1.5 million lbs. of tallow, 16,000 bus. of wheat, 1 million board feet of timber, 20,000 beaver and otter skins, 1000 bbl. of aguardiente and wine, and 200 oz. of gold. Thomas O. Larkin, "Description of California Prior to the Year 1846," *Mont. Cons.*

25. Nathaniel W. Stephenson, *Texas and the Mexican War* (New Haven, 1921), 183. Particularly good discussions of American interest in California are in Norman A. Graebner, *Empire on the Pacific* (New York, 1955), 83–102, and Rives, *U.S. and Mexico*, II, 22–52. See also Sister Magdelen Coughlin, "California Ports: A Key to West Coast Diplomacy," *Journal of the West*, V (April 1966), 153–72.

26. The reports covering the seizure of Monterey are in *PSL*. The more important ones are reprinted in *H. Doc. 166, 27th Cong., 2d Sess.*, and Charles Roberts Anderson (ed.), *Journal of a Cruise in the Pacific Ocean, 1842–1844, in the Frigate United States with Notes on Herman Melville* (Durham, 1937), 78–99. The best general accounts are George M. Brooke, Jr., "The Vest Pocket War of Commodore Jones," *PHR*, XXXI (Aug. 1962), 217–34, and James High, "Jones at Monterey," *Journal of the West*, V (April 1966), 173–86.

2: The Failure of Graduated Pressure

Mexican reaction to the annexation of Texas was predictable. On March 6, 1845, Minister General Juan N. Amonte penned a scalding note to Secretary of State John C. Calhoun. The annexation, he asserted, "is an act of aggression, the most unjust which can be found recorded in the annals of modern history." Mexico, he continued, claimed the right to recover her lost territory, and as an exclamation point he requested his passports. The bellicose reaction set back President James K. Polk's hopes for a negotiated settlement. Nevertheless, Secretary of State James Buchanan attempted to calm the situation with a conciliatory and amicable letter while refusing to discuss annexation.[1]

Polk wished to avoid giving the Mexicans or the antiannexationist group in Texas pretext for claiming that the United States was applying military pressure. His reaction appears in the March 20 orders to the Home Squadron. These directed its concentration at Veracruz but charged Commodore Conner to friendly relations with the local officials while being prepared to protect American persons and property.[2]

Rumors emanating from Mexico City indicated that the newly installed government of General José Joaquín de Herrera would be willing to negotiate if it could do so without appearing to bow before American pressure. Therefore, in late March Polk undertook an unorthodox maneuver designed to start the negotiations he so earnestly desired. Polk chose Dr. William Parrott to arrange discussions. Dr. Parrott was a dentist whose practice was less than thriving and whose reputation for honesty left much to be desired. Nevertheless, he had the advantage of having many years' residence in Mexico and presumably was aware of the shifts in political thought. If, in his opinion, Mexico was ready to renew diplomatic relations, he was authorized to inform the Mexicans that all questions, with the exception of Texas, were open for discussion "in a liberal and friendly spirit."[3]

Parrott reached Mexico City on April 23 and filed the unwelcome report that all factions were united in preferring war to acquiescing in the loss of Texas.[4] To most knowledgeable Americans, forgetting their own countrymen's actions in 1775 and 1812, the position appeared ludicrous. Mexico was bankrupt, her army unpaid and on the verge of mutiny, and her government near collapse. Probably half a dozen would-be dictators waited for the propitious moment to launch their revolt. It was in their inability to recognize that Mexican public opinion considered acceptance of the loss of Texas a shattering of national honor and dignity that the American leaders made their greatest mistake. They failed to recognize the depth of what the Consul at Tampico called "the most stubborn and malignant feeling . . . in the mind of every Mexican against the United States."[5]

Consul John Black at Mexico City made as concise a statement of the administration's position as any of its spokesmen in Washington could have enunciated when he wrote:

> It is not known what course Mexico will take in respect to the question of Annexation of Texas. . . . No doubt she will make some noise . . . but I do not think that the present Government (or the opposition) has any serious idea of carrying on any other kind of war against us.[6]

One of the few Mexican leaders to recognize the stupidity of fighting the United States over Texas was President Herrera, but he could do little to deflect the tidal run toward suicidal war promoted by his opponents. So great were those pressures that he had to make public motions in support of war measures. On June 4 he reiterated Mexico's claim to Texas and her intention to maintain it by arms if necessary. At the same time he called all state as well as federal armed forces into service. Later in the month, after putting down a premature pro-Santa Anna uprising among the Mexico City garrison, he called the Congress into special session to consider constitutional reforms and to decide upon actions to be taken in regard to Texas.[7]

The bellicose cries uttered in the exhilarating atmosphere of the

Mexican capital impressed distant listeners in Washington. On May 23 Donelson was instructed to assure the Texan officials that a 3,000-man army would march at the moment annexation was accepted. General Zachary Taylor's directive to prepare for such a march followed six days later. The War Department's initial plan envisioned Commodore Robert F. Stockton's squadron carrying Taylor's men from the mouth of the Sabine River to a healthful position "on or near the Rio Grande well suited to repel any invasion."[8]

The orders reached Taylor at Fort Jesup on June 29, 1845. Ignoring the administration's plan, he sent his infantry by way of New Orleans and his cavalry overland to Corpus Christi at the mouth of the Nueces River. Practical considerations and advice from Donelson dictated the decision to avoid the disputed area. Taylor knew little of the country south of the Nueces; his army was too weak to contend successfully with the large Mexican force reported enroute to Matamoros; and Corpus Christi appeared to be a good base.[9] Taylor's cautiousness filled well Secretary of War William L. Marcy's directive not to disturb the Mexican posts east of the Rio Grande. As Secretary of the Navy George Bancroft wrote to Commodore David Conner, his senior commander in the Gulf of Mexico, "the President reserves the vindication of our boundary, if possible, to methods of peace," and only in the event that Mexico declared war was he to dislodge Mexican troops east of the river.[10]

Taylor and the leading unit, the 3d Infantry (Lieutenant Colonel Ethan A. Hitchcock), left New Orleans on July 24 in the steamer *Alabama*.[11] Rather than wait for the remaining transports, Taylor pushed ahead to Corpus Christi, leaving the sloop-of-war *St. Mary's* (Commander John L. Saunders) at Southwest Pass to shepherd them when they appeared.

The *Alabama* reached Aransas Pass, the entrance to Corpus Christi Bay, about noon on the twenty-fifth but could not enter because the bar had only three feet of water over it. High winds and seas prevented the troops landing on St. Joseph's Island (which many in the army mistook for Matagorda, its twin to the north) until the following day. The steamer's boats grounded about seventy-five yards from shore, forcing the men to wade ashore. Even to the wet men the pretty island with its glistening white beaches and immense live-oak trees was a welcome change from the cramped quarters of the troopship.

Once ashore on St. Joseph's Island the troops faced problems in leaving. Taylor had neglected to order a reconnaissance of the site before drawing his plans. Nor did he consult any knowledgeable seamen in New Orleans regarding difficulties he might encounter. Therefore, he was unpleasantly surprised to discover that the light draft "steam lighter" *Undine* which he had intended to use could not easily navigate the bay. Seven small local fishing craft came to the rescue. The passage must have seemed ignominious to many of the soldiers; nevertheless the mission was accomplished and by the end of the month the whole force and its supplies had reached the mainland.[12]

Taylor's actions were approved on the thirtieth. Secretary Marcy acquiesced in the halt at Corpus Christi, since a move to the Rio Grande and the army's final position "must be governed by circumstance. It is expected that in selecting the establishment of your troops," he reminded Taylor, "you will approach as near the boundary line—the Rio Grande—as prudence will dictate." Some troops, the Secretary insisted, must be stationed beyond the Nueces.[13] These orders ensured an American presence in the disputed territory before the start of any negotiations. They also represented a further increase in Polk's policy of graduated pressure that he expected would force Mexico to negotiate.

In early August an attack of jitters struck Washington. The Prussian minister, Baron Gerolt, relayed a report from Mexico that 3,000 men had been ordered to the Rio Grande with another 10,000 to follow. The administration sent 10,000 muskets to Galveston to arm Texas volunteers.[14] The report proved to contain little fact. A more accurate view was seen from Corpus Christi. By August 12 Taylor knew that the Matamoros garrison numbered but 500 men and the reinforcements numbered only 1,000 soldiers. Nevertheless, Colonel Hitchcock began building defenses at Corpus Christi while Taylor himself hurried over from St. Joseph's Island on August 15, followed by the 7th Infantry. The threat also caused Taylor to cancel plans to station a dragoon garrison in Austin as a protection against Comanche raids. Instead he directed Colonel David E. Twiggs's horsemen to San Patricio about twenty-five miles up the Nueces and borrowed three "indifferent" artillery pieces from the Texans to offset his weakness in that arm. In an order to what he now called the Army of Occupation, Taylor reminded his officers of "the necessity of general vigilance and assiduity in the discharge of their duties, particularly in the careful instruction of the enlisted men" because of the "present state of our relations with Mexico, and the probability of conflict."[15]

The same rumors, given substance by reprinting in the New Orleans press, caused Major General Edmund P. Gaines to request four regiments of Louisiana volunteers and two companies of artillery to assist Taylor. The artillery, formed into a battalion under Major Louis Gally, reached Corpus Christi on August 25 and served with the army until November 4. The four regiments were canceled before their formation.[16]

Gaines's action irritated a War Department struggling to create a respectable force in Texas with the limited resources and funds available. Not only did short-term volunteers have to be paid, equipped, transported, and fed but they had a habit of returning home before rendering any service worth the supplies they consumed. Secretary Marcy wrote Gaines on August 28 reminding him that authority to call out volunteers had to be delegated specifically by the President. Gaines's insistence on viewing the reprimand as an accolade started a long and increasingly acrimonious correspondence with the Department.[17]

Gaines further diminished his standing in the War Department later in the month. He concluded from letters which reached New Orleans from Corpus Christi that Taylor on August 13 had received notice of the Mexican declaration of war. Gaines assured the Adjutant General that he could assemble 250 battalions of mounted men on the Rio Grande by November 10 and that with the regulars enroute to Texas they could capture Mexico City by the end of that month. He did not explain how 125,000 men could be supplied with the necessities of the campaign nor how they could march 630 miles across mountains and deserts in twenty days, fighting battles along the way. Gaines followed this on September 2 with a request for standby authority to call out fifty mounted battalions in case war developed and asked to command them.[18] The War Department ignored both proposals.

Polk and his cabinet did not really believe that the Mexicans were bent on war but they dared not act on that belief. On August 23 Marcy authorized Taylor to call on the governors of Louisiana, Alabama, Mississippi, Tennessee, and Kentucky for troops in an emergency and informed him that ten companies of "red-legged infantry," artillerymen serving as infantry, were on the way to Texas. During its August 29 meeting the cabinet agreed that if Mexico declared war or invaded Texas, Taylor should drive the invaders back across the Rio Grande and seize Matamoros and any other Mexican towns he found expedient. The Navy would cooperate by blockading or seizing Mexico's ports except for those in the rebellious states of Yucatán and Tabasco.[19]

The orders to Taylor have been attacked as unconstitutional, since they envisioned use of the militia outside the country.[20] But that argument overlooks the fact that the occupation of Mexican soil was intended to serve defensive purposes. The dispute centers around two seemingly conflicting sections of the Constitution. Article I, Section 8, under which the legislation controlling the call was made, authorized use of the militia to repel an invasion. On the other hand, Article II, Section 2, which designates the President as Commander in Chief of the militia when it is called into federal service, contains no limiting language.

The war scare was over by early September. Taylor's spy, Chapita, returned from Matamoros on the sixth. He reported that the garrison had not been reinforced although there were vague rumors that 3,000 men were enroute. Another informant reported conversations with General Mariano Arista, the Mexican commander along the Rio Grande, in which the latter reported Mexican willingness to negotiate. Nevertheless, Taylor believed that occupation of one or two points on or near the river would hasten a settlement, although he did not feel at liberty to march to the Rio Grande, since Mexico had committed no overt act! It is an interesting commentary on the state of communications within Taylor's force that it was generally believed at this time that a movement to the Rio Grande was imminent.[21]

Marcy's response to Taylor's uneasiness about moving deeper into the disputed zone was to direct the General to place his army in winter quarters as near the border as prudence and convenience permitted. Before he could carry out the orders Taylor learned of the agreement to reopen negotiations and canceled the move. He did, however, send Engineer Captain John Sanders to reconnoiter the Matamoros route as far as the Arroyo Colorado.[22]

The crisis looked much different to those on the scene in Mexico. Black continued his optimistic reports which confirmed the administration in the correctness of its policy of friendship, firmness, and readiness to negotiate. By mid-July the Consul reported that the Herrera government would not go beyond an undeclared war against Texas. He was wrong in this only in detail, for Herrera on July 21 bowed to political realities. He asked Congress to declare war as soon as the annexation became a fact or American troops entered Texas but he threw out a heavy drag to precipitous action by insisting that Congress find the money to finance the undertaking. Three days later Black reported that action had been postponed until after the August presidential elections and that he did not believe that war would follow, no matter who won.[23]

It was into this highly confused and volatile situation that Dr. William Parrott rode when he reached Mexico City in April. Parrott bided his time before beginning negotiations with the Mexican government because he realized that British and French opposition would stunt the flames of war. On the sixteenth he reported that Herrera, just reelected, had been overheard saying that a minister would be well received. By the end of the month Parrott reported that an envoy would be welcome but that Herrera dared not initiate the move. Parrott was so confident that he assured Buchanan: "An Envoy possessing suitable qualifications for this Court might with comparative ease, settle over a breakfast, the most important national question." The consuls at Mexico City and Veracruz shared his optimism.[24]

Polk laid the matter before his cabinet on September 16. They concurred in his proposal to initiate the reopening of relations as well as his selection of John Slidell as the negotiator. Slidell's task would be to secure Mexican agreement to the Rio Grande boundary and "to purchase for a pecuniary consideration Upper California and New Mexico . . . [although] a better boundary would be the Del Norte from its mouth to the Passo, in latitude 32° North, and thence West to the Pacific Ocean." Such a settlement, Polk estimated, could be secured for fifteen to twenty million dollars, although he was willing to pay as much as $40 million. The next day the President and his advisers received conflicting reports suggesting war preparations as late as August 21. They decided therefore, as a precaution, to ask Consul Black to secure an official statement of Mexican willingness to receive a minister.[25]

Black received the request on October 10. He consulted Parrott and on the following day held an interview with Foreign Minister Manuel de la Peña y Peña. The Mexican asked for the proposition in writing and on the thirteenth Black complied, copying the exact words of his instructions. Peña y Peña replied that Mexico would receive a commissioner empowered "to settle the present dispute." In the course of a meeting at his home during the evening of the fifteenth Don Manuel asked for the removal of Commodore Conner's squadron from Veracruz and the nomination of a negotiator who would be acceptable to the Mexicans. The latter was a thinly disguised request not to name Parrott.[26]

When the news of the agreement reached Veracruz, Consul Dimond forwarded it to Washington with the comment: "I am rejoiced to have the honor to inform you that God has opened the eyes of these people, and they have consented to negotiate rather than fight. . . . Allow me to congratulate you on the prospect of bringing this vexed question to an honorable and speedy close." The

Consul also relayed to Commodore Conner the Mexican request that
the naval force be withdrawn; Conner promptly complied without
waiting for instructions from Washington.[27]

While the Mexican negotiations appeared headed toward a successful and peaceful solution, danger sprang from another quarter.
On October 11 the President received news from Consul Thomas O.
Larkin in Monterey, California. He reported that the Hudson's Bay
Company had offered weapons and money to equip an expedition to
reassert the Mexican government's control over California. When
linked with rumors from Mexico City and Europe concerning the
visionary project of Father Eugene McNamara to settle 10,000 Irish
Catholics in California, the report seemed to spell a British takeover.[28]

The administration's initial reaction was to deputize Larkin as a
confidential agent to oppose the "transfer of California to Great Britain or any other Power." In his instructions Secretary Buchanan clari-
fied the position of the United States vis-à-vis acquisition of the territory: "this Government has no ambitious aspirations to gratify
and no desire to extend our federal system over more territory than
we already possess, unless by the free and spontaneous wish of the
independent people of adjoining territories," and will make no overt
effort to acquire California. It would, however, welcome the area
into the Union "whenever this can be done without affording Mexico
just cause of complaint."[29]

At the same time it was decided to send Larkin an assistant. He was
Lieutenant Archibald H. Gillespie, a marine officer just returned
from a cruise to the Orient. The reasons for his selection are unknown
but probably reflected his availability and knowledge of Spanish.
Gillespie was called to Washington, briefed by Secretary Bancroft
and the President, given a copy of the instructions to Larkin, and
sent on his way. He also carried a packet of letters from Senator
Thomas Hart Benton and his daughter, Mrs. John C. Frémont, to
the explorer who, they expected, would be in California.[30]

On November 8 the cabinet reviewed the final draft of Slidell's
instructions. It was none too soon, for on the following day Parrott
arrived with the Black–Peña y Peña exchange of notes. On the tenth
Slidell's commission was signed and, despite the predictable displeasure which it would cause in Mexico City, Parrott became Secretary
of the Legation. Slidell's commission was as Minister. This was a
mistake caused chiefly by a slight mistranslation of Peña y Peña's note
and the natural desire of the administration to hasten a settlement.

The Mexican foreign minister had said that his country would receive a *comisionado* (commissioner) empowered to settle *la conteinda existante* (the existing dispute). He had not committed his government to receive a minister resident, and Herrera had made explicit statements to that effect to at least two former American ministers.

Slidell's instructions included a graduated set of payments to be made in accord with the boundary secured:

For the Rio Grande line plus the eastern half of New Mexico— assumption of American claims against Mexico;

For the western half of New Mexico—$5 million;

For a boundary giving the United States San Francisco—$20 million;

For a settlement including California north of Monterey—$25 million.

The diplomat was to press hard for a claims settlement and to use them as the basis for the boundary negotiations. The reduced emphasis on California reflected both the hopes for the success of Larkin's intrigues and a desire not to alert Mexico to American activities there. In December, after learning from Larkin that the Californians were ready to accept any flag that was not Mexican, Buchanan told Slidell not to press the California proposals if they threatened the success of his mission.

In a private letter to his negotiator, Polk repeated Parrott's contention that California and New Mexico could be purchased for $15 million. The President observed that in the unlikely event that the mission failed, the United States would have to take the redress of her grievances into her own hands.[31]

Slidell reached Veracruz on November 30. His appearance stunned the Herrera government, which had apparently assumed that the appointment would require Senate confirmation and therefore did not expect him until January. From Herrera's standpoint the timing could not have been worse. "You know," Peña y Peña told Black, "that the opposition are calling us traitors, for entering into this agreement with you." As a result the government asked that the diplomat remain away from the capital at least until January.

Black intercepted his fellow countryman at Puebla, but Slidell decided to continue on to Mexico City and present his credentials. The decision was the only one he could have made, since if he had done otherwise he would have had to admit that the agreement upon which his mission rested was invalid.[32]

On the eighth of December Slidell reached the Mexican capital and immediately requested an appointment to present his credentials. Peña y Peña reiterated his reluctance to receive the American before Congress met in January but agreed to receive the credentials. On December 16 the Mexican pointed out the discrepancy between the wording of Slidell's credentials and that of the October 15 agreement. The question of reception, therefore, would have to be submitted to the Council of Government. In part the reply was an attempt to postpone the question until a propitious moment, but in part it was a legitimate concern. Technically the Mexicans had agreed only to receive a commissioner empowered to settle the Texas question. Acceptance of a minister resident implied restoration of normal relations which under the circumstances would permit the government's opponents to claim acceptance of the loss of Texas. Such an accusation would surely topple the Herrera government, which remained in power largely because no one yet had moved to unseat it.

On the sixteenth the Council decided against receiving Slidell. Peña y Peña in relaying that information suggested that if Slidell's commission was altered to that of a commissioner empowered to settle outstanding differences he would be received. The American replied with a mild note pointing out that the agreement had not limited the discussions to Texas and that he already had authority to adjust all questions in dispute. Although the reply was an attempt to keep the spark of negotiation alive it did not show much understanding of Herrera's political tightrope. While waiting for new instructions Slidell retired to Jalapa, covering his withdrawal with a fusillade of words insinuating Mexican bad faith. This shift of ground obviously stemmed from Slidell's conclusion that his mission had failed and that the case for intervention must be presented in the strongest possible terms.[33]

Herrera's attempt to win public support for his peaceful policy in a December 22 manifesto had little visible effect. But that had little importance, since his remaining days in office were few. A revolt was brewing at San Luis Potosí. There Mexico's largest and finest military force, the Army of the North, waited under the command of the opportunist and intriguer Major General (*General de división*) Mariano Paredes y Arrillaga. It had been sent there in part to move its commander away from the capital, since he led an amalgamation of "aristocratic elements" drawn from the church, the army, and monarchists who feared that the Federalists would reform the church, strengthen popular political institutions, and destroy the military's privileged position.

Paredes feigned allegiance to the Herrera government in order to secure money and manpower, but since August had resisted orders to reinforce Arista on the Rio Grande. He also refused to appear in Mexico City to stand trial for insubordination. On December 14, probably because of fear that the Federalists would control the new Congress, he pronounced against the government for having "admitted a commissioner with whom it was endeavoring to arrange for the loss of the integrity of the republic."

Paredes marched on Mexico City, gaining the support of other commanders as he advanced. On December 29 when he was within twelve miles of the capital, its garrison led by Major General Gabriel Valencia defected. Herrera thereupon abandoned his office and with a few close supporters fled the presidential palace in a hansom cab. Valencia, the legal successor to the ousted president, had undoubtedly embraced the revolution on the assumption that he would succeed to the presidency. He was quickly disabused of this idea when Paredes warned that anyone opposing him, "archbishop, general, magistrate, or anybody else," would be shot. Paredes had himself proclaimed acting president.[34]

Paredes entered the capital on January 2, 1846, and delivered a ringing inaugural address containing an oath to uphold the integrity of Mexican territory as far as the Sabine River. Now the stalemate was complete. Neither Mexico nor the United States would give ground and each believed she was the aggrieved party. Actually either one of them could have modified her position, but they were scarcely likely to because of the political climate in which their leaders operated. The situation paralleled that of July 1941 following the Japanese decision for a confrontation with the United States. Negotiations would continue, but only surrender by one side or the other could prevent war.

Slidell's preliminary reports of the refusal of the Mexican government to receive him reached Washington during the evening of January 12. They were as unexpected as they were devastating. Polk immediately directed Taylor to move to the Rio Grande as soon as possible but not to consider Mexico an enemy until war was declared or Mexican forces attacked.[35]

The record is not entirely clear, but the reason behind the orders appears to have been twofold. "The president was of the opinion," Secretary Bancroft later wrote, "that the appearance of our land and naval forces upon the borders of Mexico and in the Gulf, would deter Mexico alike from declaring war or invading the United States." In addition, if war did come an army on the Rio Grande would be 125 miles closer to Mexican territory.[36] The orders have been attacked as aggressive and provocative but the charges overlook a basic fact. Since the United States did not concede Mexican title to the disputed territory, it was the duty of the President to maintain the American claim through occupation even though the boundary might later be adjusted to less than the full amount.

Some of the Whigs in Congress viewed the orders to Taylor as one element in a complex scheme to force the Mexicans to sell New Mexico and California. They considered enacting a restraining motion but dropped the project when John C. Calhoun refused to join them. Although he was disposed toward the proposal, Calhoun feared that the effect of his participation would be to undercut his efforts to convince the administration to compromise on Oregon.[37]

Buchanan forwarded Slidell's revised commission on January 20. He repeated the administration's desire for peace but concluded that if the Mexicans still refused to receive Slidell, ". . . the cup of forbearance will then have been exhausted."[38] The administration had committed itself to war upon Slidell's final rejection.

While waiting for the Slidell charade to play out, Polk was visited by one of the more shadowy figures of the era. Colonel Alexander Atocha was a Mexican with an uncertain claim to American citizenship and a stronger one to being Santa Anna's confidential agent. He told the President on February 13 that the exiled Mexican strongman would support a settlement with the United States if returned to power. Although Polk suspected the visit was little more than an effort to obtain some money from the United States, he did report it to his cabinet. Atocha returned twice on the sixteenth and finally convinced Polk that the proposal, undoubtedly embellished in the telling, did originate with Santa Anna. The proposal, which called for a boundary line following the Rio Grande and the "Colorado of the West down through the Bay of San Francisco," carried a price tag of $30 million. Since it had to appear that Santa Anna had been forced into the arrangement, Atocha proposed that Taylor invade Mexico; the fleet concentrate at Veracruz; and Slidell make a preemptory demand for payment of the claims from the deck of a warship. This, opined Atocha, would convince the Mexicans that the United States was sincere. If immediately provided with $500,000 in cash, the agent assured the American that Santa Anna could return to power in April or May. Atocha, apparently on his own, also suggested that the northern states of Nuevo León and Tamaulipas had uncertain loyalties to the central government and might prove easy to annex. Polk discussed the proposal with his cabinet. The consensus was that the idea, though interesting, was too uncertain for serious consideration, but that direct, secret negotiations be opened with Santa Anna.[39]

The visit, if indeed it was inspired by Santa Anna and there is little reason to doubt it, was one of a series of steps which the wily ex-dictator took to ensure his return to power. At the same moment he approached the United States he was deeply engaged in negotiations with his ostensible enemies, the *puro* Federalists of Valentín Gómez Farías. To them Santa Anna's agents offered the sword of a soldier who had foresworn any ambition to resume political leadership in Mexico.[40]

Slidell waited until March 1 before asking for reconsideration of his recognition. Foreign Minister Joaquín M. de Castillo y Lanzas consulted with the Spanish Minister, who apparently suggested arbitration by European powers and a strong note to head off direct negotiations. On the sixth the Council of Government reiterated its refusal to receive the American and six days later Castillo wrote *finis* to Slidell's mission. The annexation of Texas, the Mexican wrote, had been a *causus belli*, yet Mexico had agreed to receive a commissioner. Instead of a commissioner the United States sent Slidell with a minister's commission. Needless to say, Don Joaquín continued, Mexico could not accept him. Slidell penned a long rebuttal on the seventeenth, which concluded that "words must now give place to acts" and requested his passports.[41]

While Slidell awaited his passports, Paredes on the twenty-first issued a manifesto which called for war. Taking note of Taylor's move to the Rio Grande, then in progress, he announced the refusal to receive Slidell. It is not the President's right to declare war, Paredes shouted, although I favor it and the United States may do so before Congress can act; the Army will fight, however, to protect the nation even without a formal directive. The same day Slidell's passports were forwarded and he left Jalapa on March 28. Sailing from Veracruz on the last day of the month, Slidell reached Washington on the eighth of May.[42]

Any knowledgeable observer could have predicted that the Slidell mission would end in failure. It was so ordained by the realities of Mexican domestic politics. The fact that the Polk administration embarked upon the project with such high expectations demonstrates how poorly it understood Mexico and the Mexican character. The final irony came with Paredes's attack on the United States for the movement to the Rio Grande, a step seen by the administration as a further means of applying pressure on Mexico to force negotiations.

NOTES

For key to abbreviations used in Notes, see page xi.

1. Almonte to Calhoun, March 6, 1845; Buchanan to Almonte, March 10, 1845, both in Manning, *Diplo. Corres.*, VIII, 163, 699–700.
2. Mason to Conner, March 20, 1845, *RCL*, I, 108–9.
3. Buchanan to Parrott, March 28, 1845, Manning, *Diplo. Corres.*, VIII, 164–65. Good accounts of the background and progress of the Slidell Mission can be found in Rives, *U.S. and Mexico*, II, 53–80; Sellers, *Polk Continentalist*, 230–65, 331–38, 398–404; St. George Leakin Sioussat, "James Buchanan," in Samuel Flagg Bemis (ed.), *The American Secretaries of State and Their Diplomacy* (17 vols., New York, 1927–67), V, 265–76; James Morton Callahan, *American Foreign Policy in Mexican Relations* (New York, 1932), 151–57; Louis M. Sears, *John Slidell* (Durham, 1925), 56–73; and Jesse S. Reeves, *American Diplomacy under Taylor and Polk* (Baltimore, 1907), 268–88.
4. Parrott to Buchanan, April 26, 1845, in Manning, *Diplo. Corres.*, VIII, 712.
5. Franklin Chase to Buchanan, Sept. 26, 1845, in Dispatches from U.S. Consulate at Tampico, RG-59, NA, III.
6. Black to Buchanan, June 21, 1845, *M. C. Cons.*, VIII.
7. Thomas Ewing Cotner, *The Military and Political Career of José Joaquín de Herrera* (Austin, 1949), 130–31, 135; Herrera, Decreto, June 4, 1845, in *V.C. Cons.*, V; John S. Jenkins, *History of the War Between the United States and Mexico* (Auburn, 1851), 43; Black to Buchanan, June 10, 21, 1845. *M. C. Cons.*, VIII.
8. Buchanan to Donelson, May 23, June 15, 1845, Manning, *Diplo. Corres.*, XII, 92–96; Marcy to Taylor, May 28, 1845, Bancroft to Taylor, June 15, 1845, *H. Ex. Doc. 60, 30th Cong., 1st Sess.*, 79–82; Bancroft to Stockton, June 15, 1845, *RCL*, I, 137; Polk to Donelson, June 15, 1845, St. George L. Sioussat (ed.), "Polk-Donelson Letters," *Tennessee Historical Magazine*, III (March 1917), 67–68, authorized the diplomat to call American forces to Texas in case of an invasion.
9. Donelson to Taylor, June 28, 1845, Taylor to AG, June 30, 1845, *H. Ex. Doc. 60, 30th Cong., 1st Sess.*, 801, 804–6; Taylor to K. Rayner, Oct. 30, 1848, YWA; Holman Hamilton, *Zachary Taylor, Soldier of the Republic* (Indianapolis, 1941), 159, 162.
10. Marcy to Taylor, July 8, 1845, *SWMA*, XXVI, 36; Bancroft to Conner, July 11, 1845, *H. Ex. Doc. 60, 30th Cong., 1st Sess.*, 232–3.
11. Conner to Bancroft, July 21, 1845, *HSL*; Hunt to Taylor, July 22, 1845, *AOLR*, Box 1; Henry, *Campaign Sketches*, 12–13.
12. Henry, *Campaign Sketches*, 12–16; Hitchcock, *50 Years*, 194; Ulysses S. Grant, *Personal Memoirs of U. S. Grant* (Cleveland, 1952), 26–27; Taylor to AG, July 25, 1845, *H. Ex. Doc. 60, 30th Cong., 1st Sess.*, 97; Hamilton, *Taylor*, 163.
13. Marcy to Taylor, July 30, 1845, *H. Ex. Doc. 60, 30th Cong., 1st Sess.*, 82–83.
14. Bancroft to Buchanan, Aug. 7, 1845, John Bassett Moore (ed.), *The Works of James Buchanan* (12 vols., Philadelphia, 1908–11), VI, 224–25; Mason to Donelson, Aug. 7, 1845, Manning, *Diplo. Corres.*, XII, 97–98.

15. Henry, *Campaign Sketches*, 27–29; Taylor to AG, Aug. 15, 20, 1845, to Anson Jones, Aug. 16, 1845, *H. Ex. Doc. 60, 30th Cong., 1st Sess.*, 98–103; Army of Occupation, Orders No. 2, Aug. 16, 1845, *AOGO*, I; Twiggs to Bliss, Aug. 18, 1845, *AOLR*, Box 1.

16. Gaines to Jones, Aug. 17, 31, 1845, Western Div., *SO* 28, Aug. 21, 1845, all in *S. Doc. 378, 29th Cong., 1st Sess.*, 23, 26; New Orleans *Daily Picayune*, Aug. 17, 1845; Gov. Alexander Mouton to Maj. Gen. J. S. Armant, Aug. 18, 19, 1845, *Niles National Register*, LXIX (1845), 8; Henry, *Campaign Sketches*, 34, 44; James W. Silver, *Edmund Pendleton Gaines* (Baton Rouge, 1949), 259–60.

17. Marcy to Gaines, Aug. 28, Sept. 13, 30, 1845, Gaines to Marcy, Sept. 3, 20, 24, 1845, Jones to Gaines, Sept. 10, 1845, all in *S. Doc. 378, 29th Cong., 1st Sess.*, 31, 35–44, 47–50; Silver, *Gaines*, 260.

18. Gaines to Jones, Aug. 23, Sept. 2, 1845, *S. Doc. 378, 29th Cong., 1st Sess.*, 25, 27–31.

19. Buchanan to Calhoun, Aug. 22, 1845, Chauncey B. Boucher and Robert P. Brooks (eds.), "Correspondence Addressed to John C. Calhoun 1837–1849," *Annual Report of the American Historical Association for the Year 1919* (Washington, 1920), 302; Marcy to Taylor, Aug. 23, 30, 1845, *H. Ex. Doc. 60, 30th Cong., 1st Sess.*, 84–85, 88–89; Jones to Wool, Aug. 23, 1845, *AGLS*, XXI, 820; Marcy to Govs. Ala., La., Miss. Tenn., Ky., Aug. 25, 28, 1845, *SWMA*, 64, 67; Milo Milton Quaife (ed.), *The Diary of James K. Polk During His Presidency 1845 to 1849* (4 vols., Chicago, 1910), I, 9–10, 12; Bancroft to Conner, Aug. 30, 1845, *RCL*, I, 159.

20. Emory Upton, *The Military Policy of the United States* (New York, 1968), 197.

21. Taylor to AG, Sept. 6, Oct. 4, 1845, *H. Ex. Doc. 60, 30th Cong., 1st Sess.*, 105, 107–9; Henry, *Campaign Sketches*, 35, 39; Hitchcock, *50 Years*, 199; J. D. Marks to Taylor, Sept. 23, 1845; *AOLR*, Box 1.

22. Marcy to Taylor, Oct. 16, Taylor to AG, Nov. 7, 1845, *H. Ex. Doc. 60, 30th Cong., 1st Sess.*, 89–90, 111; AO 50 #36, 46, Oct. 25, Nov. 7, 1845, in *AOGO*, II.

23. Black to Buchanan, July 19, 24, 1845, Manning, *Diplo. Corres.*, VIII, 738–39, 741; Justin H. Smith, *War with Mexico*, (2 vols., New York, 1919), I, 87; Sellers, *Polk Continentalist*, 259.

24. Parrott to Buchanan, Aug. 16, 24, 1845, Jesse S. Reeves, "The Treaty of Guadalupe-Hidalgo," *AHR* X (Jan. 1905), 310–11, Manning, *Diplo. Corres.*, VIII, 746–47.

25. Quaife, *Diary of Polk*, I, 33–36; Smith, *War with Mexico*, I, 91; Buchanan to Black, Sept. 17, 1845, Manning, *Diplo. Corres.*, VIII, 167–69.

26. Black to Peña, Oct. 13, Peña to Black, Oct. 15, Black to Buchanan, Oct. 17, 1845, all in *ibid.*, 761–65.

27. Dimond to Buchanan, Oct. 21, 1845, *V. C. Cons.*; Conner to Dimond, Oct. 23, 1845, Manning, *Diplo. Corres.*, VIII, 769n.

28. Larkin to Bancroft, July 10, 1845, Manning, *Diplo. Corres.*, VIII, 735–36; John Adam Hussey, "The Origin of Gillespie Mission," *CHSQ*, XIX (March 1940), 46–47. Actually the British had no such designs. Ephraim Douglas Adams, "English Interest in Annexation of California," *AHR*, XIV (July 1909), 763.

29. Buchanan to Larkin, Oct. 17, 1845, George P. Hammond (ed.), *The Larkin Papers* (8 vols., Berkeley, 1951–62), IV, 44–47.

30. Extensive correspondence related to the detailing of Gillespie and the arrangements for his trip are preserved in the Bancroft Papers, MHS; *MCO*, V; *LNA*, VII; and Archibald H. Gillespie Papers, University of California, Los Angeles, Library. See also Gillespie's Testimony in *S. Rpt. 75, 30th Cong., 1st Sess.*, 30.

31. Quaife, *Diary of Polk*, I, 92–93, 97; Polk, Letter of Credence, Nov. 10, 1845, *Ex. Doc. 60, 30th Cong., 1st Sess.*, 27–28; Buchanan to Slidell, Nov. 10, 1845, Manning,

Diplo. Corres., VIII, 172–82; Sellers, *Polk Continentalist*, 265; Polk to Slidell, Nov. 10, 1845, Richard R. Stenberg, "President Polk and California: Additional Documents," *PHR*, X (June 1941), 217–18.

32. Black to Buchanan, Dec. 18, 1845, Manning, *Diplo. Corres.*, VIII, 783–84; Sellers, *Polk Continentalist*, 398; Cotner *Herrera*, 143–45.

33. Slidell to Peña, Dec. 8, 20, 24, 1845, Peña to Slidell, Dec. 16, 20, 1845, Black to Slidell, Dec. 15, 1845, Slidell to Buchanan, Dec. 27, 1845, all in *H. Ex. Doc. 60, 30th Cong., 1st Sess.*, 27–37, 39–40; Peña to Consejo de Gobierno, Dec. 11, 1845, Consejo de Gobierno, Dictamen, Dec. 16, 1845, both in Luis Cabrero (ed.), *Diario del Presidente Polk . . . con Numerosos Anexos Relacionados con la Guerra Entre México y Estados Unidos* (2 vols., México, 1948), II, 70–73, 74–81; Slidell to Polk, Dec. 29, 1845, James K. Polk Papers, L.C.

34. José Bravo Ugarte, *Historia de México* (3 vols., México, 1959), III, pt. 2, 191–97; Smith, *War with Mexico*, I, 98–99; Robert Selph Henry, *The Story of the Mexican War* (Indianapolis, 1950), 30–31; Cotner, *Herrera*, 145–49; José Fernando Ramírez, *Mexico During the War with the United States*, ed. Walter V. Scholes (Columbia, Mo., 1950), 30–39.

35. Marcy to Taylor, Jan. 13, 1846, *H. Ex. Doc. 60, 30th Cong., 1st Sess.*, 90. Scott's "projet" for the letter is in William L. Marcy Papers, L.C., XI.

36. Bancroft to Conner, Jan. 17, 1846, *LO*, XXXIX, 145; Quaife, *Diary of Polk*, I, 171. The quotation is from George Bancroft, "Biographical Sketch of James K. Polk," Bancroft Collection, NYPL.

37. Margaret L. Coit, *John C. Calhoun* (Cambridge, 1950), 439–40.

38. Buchanan to Slidell, Jan. 20, 1846, Manning, *Diplo. Corres.*, VIII, 185–86.

39. Quaife, *Diary of Polk*, I, 223, 226–27, 233; Rives, *U.S. and Mexico*, II, 119–22.

40. Wilfrid Hardy Callcott, *Santa Anna* (Norman, 1936), 226; Oakah L. Jones, *Santa Anna* (New York, 1968), 100; C. Alan Hutchinson, "Valentin Gomez Farias and the Movement for the Return of General Santa Anna to Mexico in 1846" in Cotner and Castaneda, *Essays in Mexican History*, 186–87. Numerous letters from both Santa Anna and his agents are in the Valentín Gómez Farías Papers, UTLA.

41. Slidell to Castillo y Lanzas, March 1, 17, 1846; Buchanan to Slidell, March 12, 1846, all in Manning, *Diplo. Corres.*, VIII, 189–92, 814–15, 818–19; Consejo de Gobierno, Dictamen, March 6, 1846, Cabrera, *Diario del Polk*, II, 11–15.

42. Paredes, Manifesto, March 21, 1846, *Niles*, LXX (April 18, 1846), 97–98; Castillo to Slidell, March 21, 1846, Slidell to Buchanan, March 27, 1846, both in *H. Ex. Doc. 60, 30th Cong., 1st Sess.*, 77, 79.

3: Taylor in Texas

T HE MAIN BODY of Taylor's Army of Observation followed its commander to Corpus Christi. The transports reached Aransas Pass during August 2, 1845, and quickly ferried their passengers and cargo ashore to the temporary camp on St. Joseph's Island.

After personally examining the potential campsites, Taylor chose one near the hamlet of Corpus Christi on the southern shore of the Nueces River near its mouth. Few points could better have fitted Taylor's requirements. It was an excellent intelligence-gathering location, yet far enough from the Rio Grande to permit Taylor to organize an effective defense should any Mexican force move against him. The hamlet had grown up around a trading post established there in 1838 by Colonel Henry L. Kinney and now served as the focal point of a clandestine trade with Matamoros. It consisted of twenty or thirty weatherbeaten buildings scattered along a narrow shelf of land like a partially strung necklace. At one end a grassy bluff stippled with scraggly bushes rose a hundred feet toward the hot Texas sun to break the monotony.[1]

As rapidly as they could be freed from other duties, the War Department sent reinforcements to Corpus Christi. Adjutant General Roger Jones wrote Taylor that the administration believed:

Although a state of war with Mexico, or an invasion of Texas by her forces, may not take place, it is . . . proper and necessary that your force shall be fully equal to meet with certainty of success any crisis which may arise in Texas and which would require you by force of arms to carry out the instructions of the Government.[2]

As a result, by mid-October Taylor's command had grown to 3,922 officers and men organized into three brigades.[3] This represented approximately half the total strength of the army and was the largest force assembled since the War of 1812. The concentration left only one regiment to watch the 2,000 miles of border with Canada and but three to protect the 1,500 miles of Indian frontier.[4]

The concentration of regiments and the organization of brigades accentuated problems which the Indian-fighting army was ill-equipped to handle. The army was dispersed in small garrisons which encouraged small-unit training and rapidly seasoned junior officers fresh from West Point but gave field and senior officers, many of whom lacked formal military training, little experience in handling large units in the field and even less experience with staff planning or logistics. Lieutenant Colonel Hitchcock, whose contempt for the older, non-West-Point-trained officers was ill-concealed, claimed he alone among the field officers could correctly drill his command. Self-serving as the comment was, it does illustrate the atrophy of competence induced by the army's fragmentation.

A shortage of senior army officers caused further difficulties. The number of senior line officers was restricted by law to three generals plus one colonel, one lieutenant colonel, and one major for each of the fourteen regiments. Promotion was governed by the vacancies occurring in each regiment. While transfer between regiments was occasionally used to bypass infirm, aged, or inadequate officers, seniority within the regiment generally controlled advancement. Since there were no provisions for retirement or the replacement of officers on detached duty, the regiments were often short of officers, particularly in the field grades. This was partially offset during the war by the addition of a second major in each regiment. As a result few old regular regiments served in Mexico under its colonel. Indeed a regiment commanded by a major was not uncommon, nor by a captain unknown.

Further complicating the command structure was the device of brevet promotion. Intended initially as a means of rewarding officers for meritorious combat service it was used in the stagnating interwar years to honor officers prevented from promotion by the lack of a retirement system. Although normally the brevet rank carried no greater authority and no increase in pay, an officer could be ordered to duty in his brevet rank. For instance, Zachary Taylor took command of the Army of Observation as a Brevet Brigadier General.

When they reached Corpus Christi many units started extensive training programs, since they had so seldom served together. The 5th Infantry, for instance, had not done so in nine years. As a result junior officers tended to forget what they had learned of battalion drill and tactics. Drilling took place on a 150-to-200-acre field hacked out of the underbrush about a quarter of a mile from the camp. The training was so incessant that one participant complained that life became "nothing but drill and parades, and your ears are filled all day with drumming and fifeing." But by mid-September the army could mount a creditable review.[5]

Taylor, whose conception of warfare hardly went beyond marching, shooting, and charging, soon lost interest in the training program. Nor did he spend much time or effort on preparations for future operations. He dispatched a few reconnoitering expeditions up the Nueces and down the Laguna Madre but made no concerted effort to develop intelligence of the area of his potential future operations. He did not send advance warning of his plans to Washington nor did he give his staff quartermaster any indication of future operations which might help that officer arrange the necessary logistic support.

When the salubrious weather of the early fall gave way to the miserable, wet, and unhealthy climate of winter, drill ceased, illness appeared, and discipline nearly disappeared. Taylor, who was accustomed to the conditions and discipline of the frontier, considered his troops healthy, well behaved, and comfortable. The latter they were most assuredly not! The men shivered in leaking tents around which they banked earth to keep out the wind. Taylor himself complained of the cold at the end of November and recorded that the sun did not shine at all during the first two weeks of December. A few of the officers improvised heating stoves but fuel for them was limited. Good drinking water was scarce; most of that available was brackish. Illness, largely diarrhea and dysentery, became widespread. At one time a fifth of the force was on the sick list and half of the others were scarcely able to perform their duties.[6]

The conditions bred a sullen torpor which expressed itself in brawls and orgies. The "outrages of aggravated character" which some of his men committed against the local Mexicans led Taylor to restrict the army to camp at night.[7] The camp also quickly attracted the usual band of camp followers, adventurers, and grog shop proprietors which plague all military posts. By November, Corpus Christi's population had bulged to 1,000 and would double in the following month.

Although most surviving accounts stress the primitive conditions of the post, some officers improvised a few amenities. The 3d Infantry built a large thatched officers' mess which drew heavily from other units as well. Many of the officers acquired mustangs from the herds which grazed nearby or purchased them from Mexican horsesellers who frequented the area. The horse races which naturally followed came to have a major place in nearly all accounts of life at Corpus Christi. At the dragoon camp the Texas Rangers gave lessons in trick riding.

One group of officers led by Captain John B. Magruder organized a theater and built an 800-seat house. Casting presented some problems because of the shortage of females. An attempt to cast Lieutenant Ulysses S. Grant as the daughter of Brabanito in the *Moor of Venice* brought such a complaint from Lieutenant Theodoric Porter who played the Moor that an actress was imported from New Orleans. The theater opened on January 8, 1846 and played to packed houses thereafter.[8]

A further sophistication of the atmosphere came early in 1846. An itinerant Texas printer, Samuel Bangs, in conjunction with two local leaders began publishing the Corpus Christi *Gazette*.[9] It was the first of a series of newspapers which sprang up around American camps in Texas and Mexico.

One of the less productive avocations which the officers at Corpus Christi found to while away the time was to argue the brevet-lineal rank issue. In October Taylor had raised the issue because of the presence in the army of both Colonels Twiggs and Worth. Twiggs was senior to Worth as a colonel but the latter held a brevet as a brigadier general. Whoever was senior would be the second-in-command of the army. General Winfield Scott ruled in Worth's favor but Secretary Marcy took the issue to the President. Without waiting to learn Polk's decision, Taylor reversed Scott's ruling.

This should have ended the dispute, since the President's ruling in March sustained the primacy of lineal rank. Unfortunately, Hitchcock, to whom such matters had much importance, muddied the waters in mid-December by forwarding to the Senate a memorial signed by over a hundred officers asking for legislation to settle the question. The issue came to a head when Taylor ordered a review of the army on February 25. He designated Twiggs as the senior officer, which caused Worth to refuse to participate and ask permission to leave the army. To save appearances Taylor took advantage of a break in the weather to cancel the review.[10]

When the news of Polk's decision reached Texas, Worth's temper got the best of him and he resigned his commission, although he did not leave the army until it reached the Rio Grande. On May 9, when he learned of the developing hostilities, Worth withdrew his resignation. Scott ordered him back to the army, but he missed Palo Alto and Resaca de la Palma.[11]

The Quartermaster Department was partially responsible for the misery at Corpus Christi. For example, most of the tents of the infantry were in such deplorable condition that Colonel Trueman Cross, Taylor's quartermaster, requisitioned sufficient new ones to house 2,000 men. The Quartermaster Department could not purchase sufficient heavy duck and had to substitute a lighter material. This increased the volume of complaints. The men could have built huts or other shelters from locally available material but Taylor insisted on housing them in tents erected on wooden platforms. These had been very successful in Florida, but unfortunately he neglected to consider the differences in climate. Moreover, the flooring did not reach the troops until mid-January, by which time the weather had begun to moderate.[12]

Taylor constantly complained of a shortage of transport. Quartermaster General Thomas S. Jesup had ordered a limited number of wagons in the spring and summer but they were slow to reach Corpus Christi. In mid-September there were only 130 of the 265 wagons needed to move the army to the Rio Grande. Draft animals remained scarce until the supply officers began purchasing oxen locally. Since few wagon drivers could be hired locally and an attempt to use soldiers failed, the Quartermaster hired drivers from as far away as New York City. For the most part, however, they proved to be unreliable or simply incompetent when confronted with a wagon and a team.[13]

Soon after the turn of the year Taylor faced a complicated politico-military problem. During the early weeks of 1846 a group of northern Mexican leaders considered declaring the area independent with General Arista as president. At the end of January one of the conspirators, General Antonio Canales, a shadowy lawyer-politician from Camargo, asked Taylor if the Americans would support such a move in case it proved impossible to restore President Herrera. The proposal was carried by the American-educated Colonel José María Carbajal, who promised Canales's support in case of hostilities if the Americans provided 5,000 rifles, 1,000 pistols, 10,000 muskets, ammunition, and money. Taylor temporized and requested guidance from his superiors. Marcy's response was equivocal but suggested that Taylor make full use of any disaffected Mexicans if war came. That killed whatever prospects the project might have had.[14]

Taylor received Marcy's order to advance to the Rio Grande on February 3. Three days later he alerted the army and sent Captain Ebenezer S. Sibley to reconnoiter the Matamoros Road. Sibley found it passable despite recent torrential rains.[15] On February 24, the day after Sibley's return, Taylor put the army on forty-eight-hour notice. All except Major John Munroe's company of artillerymen would march overland. "It is possible," Lieutenant Colonel William G. Belknap wrote to his wife, "but barely so, that we may have a tussle with the Mexicans." "But fight or no fight," Lieutenant Grant wrote his fiancée, "evry [sic] one rejoises [sic] at the idea of leaving Corpus Christi."[16]

In preparation for the move Taylor established an advance depot on the Santa Gertrudes Creek, near present-day Kingsville. The Santa Gertrudes depot served only as a replenishment point. The bulk of the supplies and the heavy artillery moved by water from St. Joseph's Island. Nevertheless, the quartermaster officers in the last few days before departure purchased horses and mules from Mexican smugglers and horse traders for eight to eleven dollars per animal. Yet this was sufficient only to permit each company to take a single wagonload, 1,500 pounds, of baggage overland.[17]

The orders for the march appeared on March 4. After specifying the order of march, Taylor directed: "Persons not properly attached to the Army will not be permitted to accompany the troops nor to establish themselves in their vicinity on any pretense whatsoever." Four days later, as the leading elements prepared to depart, Taylor issued explicit orders to govern relations with the Mexicans. He had it translated into Spanish and sent ahead to the Mexican communities on the Rio Grande.

> The Army of Occupation of Texas being now about to take a position upon the left bank of the Rio Grande, under the orders of the Executive of the United States, the general-in-chief desires to express the hope that the movement will be advantageous to all concerned; and with the object of attaining this most laudable end he strictly enjoins all under his command to observe, with the most scrupulous regard, the rights of all persons who may be found in the peaceful pursuit of their respective avocations, residing on both banks of the Rio Grande. No person,

under any pretence whatsoever, will interfere in any manner with the civil rights or religious privileges of the people, but will pay the utmost respect to both.

All goods purchased, he promised, would be paid for at the highest market price.[18]

The dragoons and Ringgold's battery started on schedule at ten o'clock on Sunday morning, March 8. The three infantry brigades followed on successive days. Taylor and his staff departed with the final elements.[19]

The route to Matamoros covered about 150 miles. Most of the way it crossed an uninhabited flat prairie offering few waterholes. The distance between waterholes usually determined the length of a day's march. Luckily for the Americans the weather stayed dry and relatively cool, although sultry, through most of the march. In some places the troops could enjoy carpets of wild flowers, while in others cactus and cochineal abounded. Ducks and geese, rabbits and deer were as common as the centipedes, tarantulas, and rattlesnakes. The immense herd of mustangs which grazed the prairie lost a few of its members to some of the more athletic American officers, who took them for their personal mounts.[20]

The route of march took the army up the Nueces, across Hogwallow Prairie, the Agua Dulce and San Fernando rivers to the Santa Gertrudes depot. From there it marched into the live-oak region with its deep sandy soil and then through a desert into the mesquite areas north of the Arroyo Colorado.

On March 14 Twiggs's advance guard came upon five or six Mexicans who set fire to the prairie and then fled. The following day Lieutenant Fowler Hamilton's six-man advance party met Mexican Lieutenant Ramón Falcon and a detachment from the Auxiliary Company of Bahía who demanded to know the American's mission. Hamilton replied that they were enroute to occupy the left bank of the Rio Grande. Falcon replied that he would so report to his superiors but warned that Mexico would fight should the Americans advance further. Twiggs temporarily checked his advance to await further word from the Mexicans, but none came.[21]

As the army moved closer to its destination, Taylor ordered the brigades to close up to supporting distance in order to meet any opposition. He planned to concentrate the entire force prior to crossing the Arroyo Colorado. The decision was a wise one, since General Francisco Mejía, the commander at Matamoros, intended to dispute its passage. The sluggish and brackish stream was little more than a hundred-yard-wide, four-foot-deep salt lagoon, but its timber-lined banks dropped too steeply for teams to cross easily. Taylor's advance units camped about three miles from there on March 19. Scouts reconnoitering the crossing learned from Mexican pickets that any passage would be resisted. This seemed substantiated by the volume of bugle calls issuing from the Mexican bivouacs hidden in the chaparral.

Taylor prepared to force a crossing on the twentieth under the cover of Ringgold's and Duncan's batteries. While the Americans moved into place and working parties cut down the banks to facilitate passage, Captain José Barragan of General Mejía's staff delivered a copy of his superior's March 18 proclamation. It called the inhabitants of the frontier to arms to oppose the "degenerate sons of Washington." Barragan reiterated the Mexican intention to contest the crossing, to which Taylor replied that his army would cross immediately. At 10:30 A.M. Colonel Worth and his staff, along with four light infantry companies under Captain Charles F. Smith, sloshed through the muddy water and after struggling to the top of the south bank caught a glimpse of a few Mexican horsemen taking their hasty departure. They and their bugles represented the ruse by which Mejía hoped to stop the American advance.[22]

The army encamped just beyond the Arroyo to await the train and the 3d Brigade. It resumed the advance at 7:00 A.M. on the twenty-third, "prepared at all moments to repel an attack." Taking advantage of the flat, open country, Taylor moved his force in four parallel columns. On the twenty-fourth the Americans reached the junction of the roads from Point Isabel and Matamoros. Taylor left Worth and the infantry there while he proceeded to the coast with the dragoons. Enroute, Taylor received a strongly worded note from the Prefect of the Northern District of Tamaulipas announcing the start of hostilities. At the same time the Mexicans set fire to the little village of Frontón de Santa Isabela on Point Isabel. In Taylor's eyes this was a definite evidence of hostilities; and in the eyes of the dragoons who had to put out the fires, a definite nuisance. About two hours before Taylor appeared, the transports and their escort arrived from Corpus Christi. Taylor garrisoned the base with two artillery companies under Major Munroe and ordered work started on a fort to protect the supplies.[23]

Taylor and the dragoons rejoined the main body at Palo Alto some ten miles from the Rio Grande during the twenty-seventh. The next morning the columns resumed their march and by midmorning came into the view of the curious inhabitants of Matamoros who thronged rooftops and other vantage points. The Americans established camp in a plowed field opposite the Mexican town. Within about an hour they had raised a flagstaff and run up the Stars and Stripes.[24]

Taylor sent Worth to assure Mejía that the advance was peaceful. Mejía refused to see any American except Taylor but sent his second-in-command, the courtly Brigadier General Rómulo Díaz de la Vega, to receive the message. The two conversed under a tree on the Mexican bank of the river in very difficult circumstances. None of the Americans present spoke Spanish and none of the Mexicans were conversant in English. Worth's English was translated by one of his officers into French and then into Spanish by one of the Mexicans. Worth explained that the American advance to the river was not hostile in intent nor an invasion of Mexican territory. When not allowed to deliver Taylor's letter in person he withdrew it but read the contents to la Vega. The Mexican also refused, on instructions from Mejía, to permit Worth to consult with the American consul although he insisted that the two countries were still at peace.[25]

Beyond his lack of orders to test arms with the Americans, the relative weakness of his army gave Mejía a more practical reason to maintain the peace. He had less than 2,000 men and only some twenty pieces of artillery, the heaviest of which was a 12-pounder. At the start of April the 6th Infantry Regiment, the Battalion of Tampico, and a battalion of the *Guardacosta de Tampico* arrived. Following the arrival of the Americans, Mejía hastened to erect the fortifications he had scorned earlier. Just upstream from Matamoros and commanding the Las Anacuitas ferry crossing, he started an earthwork large enough for 800 men. Two redoubts were positioned about 700 or 800 yards from the American camp to place it under a crossfire. The locations of the Mexican works were well chosen but their effectiveness was diminished by the lack of heavy guns.[26]

In view of the Mexican hostility, Taylor asked the War Department to hasten shipment of recruits to bring his regiments up to full strength.[27] He also ordered sites selected for a permanent camp and batteries to command Matamoros. The principal work was a star-shaped earthwork for 800 men designed by Captain Joseph K. F. Mansfield. Once the work started, young American soldiers no longer would have time to watch young señoritas come down to the river, disrobe, and plunge in for a frolicsome swim. Some of the anguish was undoubtedly reduced by Taylor's order to issue a gill of whiskey to each man "engaged on Engineer fatigues."[28]

The Americans were nervous in their unfamiliar surroundings. At tattoo on the night of March 29-30 a report arrived that 600 Mexican horsemen had crossed the river. The men slept that night on their arms while dragoon patrols scoured the country between Point Isabel and the river. The following morning Taylor sent the wagon train under escort of the 7th Infantry (Captain D. S. Miles) to fetch supplies and the siege battery from Point Isabel. There were no Mexican cavalry north of the river. Actually the relations between the opposing forces were correct and more friendly than the superficial record would indicate. Taylor asked for, and received, the return of two of Twiggs's dragoons who had been seized by Mexican patrols. The American General further reminded his officers of the "necessity of observing proper courtesy and dignity in their intercourse with the inhabitants . . . [since] our attitude is essentially pacific and our policy conciliatory."[29]

Almost as soon as he reached the river Taylor faced a problem of desertion of soldiers who swam the river to the Mexican side.[30] Although much has been written about the deserters, most of it is based upon conjecture rather than evidence. The initial deserters were not enticed by the Mexicans. They were simply taking advantage of the proximity of a haven to escape from the rigors of their life. Regimented military life did not appeal to the freesoaring spirit of most Americans. Nor did military life represent a socially acceptable or economically viable career except for officers. Therefore, the few native American enlisted men tended to be individuals who could find no other job or did not possess the ability to try their hand at a new life on the frontier. Immigrants, on the other hand, often found in the army a solution to their problems. Frequently less concerned by the regimentation, less attractive to the factory-hiring boss, less aware of the relatively low pay scale, and less capable of reaching the frontier on their own, they were attracted by the prospects of service. The result was an army of enlisted men who by and large viewed their service as a distasteful alternative to the life they wished to lead and who therefore had few scruples about leaving it when the conditions outside appeared attractive.

It has been suggested that the bulk of the deserters were Irishmen. This stems from Mexican attempts to recruit the deserters into a unit which came to be called the Battalion of Saint Patrick, or *Batallón de San Patricio*. It was commanded by a Florida native, Major Francisco Rosendo Moreno, and had as its highest-ranking deserter John Reilly (also given as Riley and O'Reilly), who served as acting major. It seems to have been officially called the Legion of Foreigners (*Legión de Estrangaros*). Actually most of the deserters were not Irish, although a majority were probably Catholics and immigrants. The best evidence indicates moreover that the bulk of the San Patricios were not deserters.[31]

This does not mean that the Mexicans did not attempt to foment desertion. On the contrary, they did so whenever possible. As early as April 2 Major General Pedro de Ampudia, the commander of the Division of the North, issued an appeal to foreigners in the American service to desert. While the number of men who deserted is uncertain, most contemporary accounts of life in the American camp speak of daily firing on deserters. The Matamoros *Gazette* on April 11 claimed that forty-three deserters and six runaway slaves had crossed the river. As an inducement the Mexicans on April 20 offered 320 acres of land to any deserter who would assume Mexican citizenship. At the end of that month Major General Mariano Arista confidently predicted that 1,500 "Irishmen and Frenchmen" would desert; on May 4 General Mejía expected most of the 7th Infantry to decamp, since it consisted largely of Irish and Germans.[32]

Taylor's view of the general situation was interesting. When the scare over the Mexican cavalry proved unreal and his relations with the Mexican commander continued correct if cool, he concluded that the crisis had faded. He assured Governor J. Pinckney Henderson of Texas that he did not expect the Mexicans to "attempt any offensive operations," although three days later he warned that the quiet might last only until General Ampudia arrived.[33] The latter assessment proved to be more realistic.

On April 4 Minister of War and Marine General José María Tornel y Mendivil, bowing to the realities of northern Mexican politics, ordered General Arista to resume command of the Division of the North. The same directive ordered an attack on the American invaders. Arista alerted Ampudia but stressed the need for secrecy.[34] More important was the manifesto issued in Mexico City on the twenty-third by President Paredes. After recounting a long list of grievances against the United States, he declared a defensive war because hostilities "have been begun by the United States of America, who have undertaken new conquests in the territory lying within the line of the Departments of Tamaulipas and Nuevo León while troops of the United States are threatening Monterey in Upper

California." The document was not given wide distribution. Two days after its issuance, Consul Black still had not seen a copy and branded reports of its existence "nothing but a piece of humbug" to distract the Mexican populace.[35]

NOTES

For key to abbreviations used in Notes, see page xi.

1. Taylor to AG, Aug. 15, 1845, *H. Ex. Doc. 60, 30th Cong., 1st Sess.*, 99–100; Henry, *Campaign Sketches*, 17–19.

2. Jones to Taylor, Aug. 6, 1845, in *H. Ex. Doc. 60, 30th Cong., 1st Sess.*, 83–84.

3. 1st Brigade (Brevet Brigadier General William J. Worth): 8th Infantry (Worth) and Artillery Battalion (Brevet Lieutenant Colonel Thomas Childs). 2d Brigade (Lieutenant Colonel James S. McIntosh): 5th (McIntosh) and 7th Infantry (Major Jacob Brown). 3d Brigade (Colonel William Whistler): 3d (Lieutenant Colonel Ethan A. Hitchcock) and 4th Infantry (Whistler). The field batteries of Captain Samuel Ringgold and Lieutenants Braxton Bragg and James Duncan along with 2d Dragoons (Colonel David E. Twiggs) and John C. Hays's Company of Texas Rangers reported directly to the commanding general. AO Orders #14, 15, Sept. 26, 28, 1845, *AOGO*, I; Hamilton, *Taylor*, 163–64.

4. Henry P. Beers, *The Western Military Frontier 1815–1846* (Philadelphia, 1935), 167–68; *S. Doc. 1, 29th Cong., 1st Sess.*, 193.

5. Hitchcock, *50 Years*, 198–99; John P. Hatch to sister, Oct. 28, 1845, George Winston Smith and Charles Judah (eds.), *Chronicles of the Gringos* (Albuquerque, 1968), 26; Meade to wife, Nov. 3, 1845, George G. Meade, *The Life and Letters of George Gordon Meade* (2 vols., New York, 1913), I, 35; Cadmus M. Wilcox, *History of the Mexican War* (Washington, 1892), 13; Barna Upton Letter, Aug. 31, 1845, William F. Goetzmann (ed.), "Our First Foreign War," *American Heritage*, XVII (June 1966), 87.

6. Taylor to T. W. Ringgold, Dec. 16, 1845, Zachary Taylor Papers, L.C.; Henry, *Campaign Sketches*, 45–47; Hitchcock, *50 Years*, 207; Beers; *Western Military Frontier*, 168; Hamilton, *Taylor*, 105–7; Smith, *War with Mexico*, I, 144; Edward J. Nichols, *Toward Gettysburg* (State College, Pa., 1958), 20; Louis C. Duncan, "A Medical History of General Zachary Taylor's Army of Occupation in Texas and Mexico, 1845–1847," *Military Surgeon*, XLVIII (1921), 77–80.

7. AO Orders #1, Jan. 2, 1846, *AOGO*, I.

8. Hatch to sister, Oct. 14, 1845, Smith and Judah, *Chronicles of the Gringos*, 25–26; James Longstreet, *From Manassas to Appomattox* (Philadelphia, 1908), 20; Cochran to parents, Sept. 27, 1845, R. E. Cochran Papers, UTA; Henry, *Campaign Sketches*, 47; James Love to A. S. Johnston, Sept. 1845, William Preston Johnston, *The Life of Gen. Albert Sidney Johnston* (New York, 1878), 131. Darwin Payne, "Camp Life in the Army of Occupation: Corpus Christi, July 1845 to March 1846," *SWHQ*, LXXIII (Jan. 1970), 326–42, is a detailed study of conditions.

9. Lota M. Spell, "The Anglo-Saxon Press in Mexico, 1846–1848," *AHR*, XXXVIII (Oct. 1932), 20–21.

10. Jones to Taylor, Nov. 14, 1845, *AGLS*, XXI, 1150; Churchill to Scott, March 2, 1846, *SWUL*; Marcy, Regulation, March 12, Childs to Jones, Feb. 2, Worth to Taylor, Feb. 24, 1846, *AGLR 46*, C-69, M-84, W-119; AO, After Orders and

Orders #21, Feb. 24, 25, 1846, *AOGO*, II; Edward S. Wallace, *General William Jenkins Worth* (Dallas, 1953), 69–71; Quaife, *Diary of Polk*, I, 284–85.

11. Worth to Bliss, April 2, 1846, *AOLR*, Box 2; Worth to AG, April 2, May 9, 1846, *AGLR'46*, W-160, 162; Jones to Worth, May 9, 1846, *AGLS*, XXII, 610.

12. AO, Orders #8, Jan. 19, 1846, *AOGO*, I.

13. The best discussion of the logistics problems is in Erna Risch, *Quartermaster Support of the Army* (Washington, 1962), 241–42.

14. Canales to Taylor, Jan. 29, Carbajal, Memorandum, Feb. 6, to Taylor, March 4, Taylor to AG, Feb. 7, 1846, all in *AGLR'47*, T-51; Marcy to Taylor, March 2, 1846, *H. Ex. Doc. 60, 30th Cong., 1st Sess.*, 92; Henry, *Campaign Sketches*, 49; John R. Kenly, *Memoirs of a Maryland Volunteer* (Philadelphia, 1873), 64; Connor and Faulk, *North America Divided*, 138–40; Justin H. Smith, "La Republica de Rio Grande" *AHR*, XXV (July 1920), 662–65. See Clarence C. Clendenen, *Blood on the Border* (New York, 1969), 18, in this series for a later equally abortive attempt by Carbajal to establish an independent north Mexican republic.

15. AO, Orders #13, SO #18, Feb. 6, 1846, *AOGO*, I, II; Sibley to Taylor, Feb. 23, 1846, *AOLR*, Box 2.

16. AO, Orders #20, Feb. 24, 1846, *AOGO*, I; Belknap to wife, Feb. 24, 1846, William Worth Belknap Papers, Princeton University Library; Grant to Julia Dent, March 3, 1846, John Y. Simon (ed.), *The Papers of Ulysses S. Grant* (Carbondale, 1967), I, 74–75.

17. AO, SO 29, Feb. 29 [*sic*], 1846, *AOGO*, II; Taylor to AG, March 8, 12, 1846, *H. Ex. Doc. 196, 29th Cong., 1st Sess.*, 104–5; Grant, *Memoirs*, 31, 38; Hamilton, *Taylor*, 171; Risch, *Quartermaster Support*, 245.

18. AO, Orders #26, 30, March 4, 8, 1846, *AOGO*, I.

19. Taylor to AG, March 11, 1846, *S. Doc. 337, 29th Cong., 1st Sess.*, 110.

20. Grant, *Memoirs*, 31; Smith, *War with Mexico*, I, 146–47; Henry, *Campaign Sketches*, 52–61; Emma Jerome Blackwood (ed.), *To Mexico with Scott* (Cambridge, 1917), 23–24; Cochran to wife, March 25, to parents, April 6, 1846, Cochran Papers.

21. Twiggs to Bliss, March 15, 1846, Justin H. Smith Transcripts, UTLA, XI; Emelio del Castillo Negrete, *Invasión de los Norte-americanos en México* (2 vols., México, 1890), I, 114; Henry, *Campaign Sketches*, 58.

22. Taylor to AG, March 21, Mejía, Proclamation, March 18, 1846, both in *H. Ex. Doc. 60, 30th Cong., 1st Sess.*, 123–29; Wilcox, *Mexican War*, 35; Henry, *Campaign Sketches*, 59–60; Grant, *Memoirs*, 40–41; Blackwood, *To Mexico with Scott*, 29–30.

23. AO, Orders #35, 80, 40, March 22, 26, 1846, *AOGO*, I, II; Jenés Cardenes to Taylor, March 23, Taylor to AG, March 25, 1846, both in *H. Ex. Doc. 60, 30th Cong., 1st Sess.*, 129–32; Henry, *Campaign Sketches*, 61–62; *Niles*, LXX (April 18, 1846), 112.

24. AO, Orders #37, March 27, 1846, *AOGO*, I; Henry, *Campaign Sketches*, 63.

25. Taylor to Mejía, March 28, 1846, *H. Ex. Doc. 56, 30th Cong., 1st Sess.*, 393. The minutes of the interview are in *H. Ex. Doc. 60, 30th Cong., 1st Sess.*, 122–28. It is described in Blackwood, *To Mexico with Scott*, 34; Henry, *Campaign Sketches*, 55–57; George A. McCall, *Letters from the Frontiers* (Philadelphia, 1868), 439; Rhoda van Bibber Tanner Doubleday (ed.), *Journal of the Late Brevet Major Philip Bourne Barbour* (New York, 1936), 17–20.

26. Bravo Ugarte, *História de México*, III, t. 2, 198; José María Roa Bárcena, *Recuerdos de la Invasión Norte-americana* (3 vols., México, 1947), I, 61; J. P. Hatch to sister, April 3, 1846, Smith & Judah, *Chronicles of the Gringos*, 60; Ramsey, *Other Side*, 36–37.

27. Taylor, to AG, March 29, 1846, *H. Ex. Doc. 60, 30th Cong., 1st Sess.*, 132–33. The best that could be done was to send about 300 recruits and four companies of the 1st Infantry. Jones to Taylor, April 20, 1846, *ibid.*, 96–97.

28. AO, Orders #39, SO #41, 45, March 29, April 6, 1846, AOGO, I, II; Blackwood, *To Mexico with Scott*, 34; Hamilton, *Taylor*, 175.

29. Doubleday, *Journal of Barbour*, 21–22; Hitchcock, *50 Years*, 218; Henry; *Campaign Sketches*, 68; Taylor to Mejía, March 30, Mejía to Taylor, March 31, 1846, *H. Ex. Doc. 56, 30th Cong., 1st Sess.*, 393–95; AO, Orders #38, April 1, *AOGO*, I.

30. Bliss, Description of Deserters supposed to have been shot in attempting to cross Rio Grande, May 31, Taylor to AG, May 30, 1846, *H. Ex. Doc. 60, 30th Cong., 1st Sess.*, 302–3.

31. G. T. Hopkins, "The San Patricio Battalion in the Mexican War," *U.S. Cavalry Journal*, XXIV (1913), 179–84; Richard B. McCornack, "The San Patricio Deserters in the Mexican War," *The Americas*, VIII (Oct. 1951), 131–42; Edward S. Wallace, "The Battalion of Saint Patrick in the Mexican War," *Military Affairs*, XIV (Summer 1950), 84; S. G. Hopkins to J. H. Smith, June 1, 1917, and unidentified letter dated Oct. 17, 1847, enclosed, Justin H. Smith Papers, UTA; Detmar H. Finke, "Organization and Uniforms of the San Patricio Units of the Mexican Army, 1846–1848," *Military Collector and Historian* IX (Summer 1957), 36–38.

32. Ampudia, Proclamation, April 2, 1846, John Frost, *Life of Major General Zachary Taylor* (New York, 1847), 48–49; Arista, Proclamation, April 20, 1846, John Frost, *The Mexican War and Its Warriors* (New York, 1848), 25; Arista to Ampudia, April 30, Mejía to Arista, May 4, 1846, both in papers captured with General Arista's baggage, RG-94, NA, 1-b-15, I-b-58; Henry, *Campaign Sketches*, 74.

33. Taylor to Henderson, April 3, 1846, in Henderson Family Papers, UTA; Taylor to AG, April 6, 1846, *H. Ex. Doc 60, 30th Cong., 1st Sess.*, 133.

34. Tornel to Arista, April 4, 1846, Smith Transcripts, XI, 224–25; Arista to Ampudia, April 10, 1846, Pedro de Ampudia, *El Cuidadano General Pedro de Ampudia Ante el Tribunal Respectable de la Opinión Publica* (San Luis Potosí, 1846), 15–16.

35. Paredes, Manifesto, April 23, 1846, Rives, *U.S. and Mexico*, II, 141–2; Black to Buchanan, April 25, 1846, *M.C. Cons.*, IX.

4: The Roar of Guns
Along the Rio Grande

O N APRIL 10, while Taylor's army dug in opposite Matamoros, Colonel Trueman Cross, the army's chief quartermaster, failed to return from a horseback ride. Search parties could not locate him and Mexican authorities disclaimed knowledge of the disappearance. His body was found on the twenty-first stripped of everything valuable. The Americans assumed he probably had been waylaid by one or more of the bandits in the area. Suspicion fell on Ramón Falcon. Two young infantry officers, Lieutenant Theodoric H. Porter and Lieutenant Stephen D. Dobbins, received permission to lead patrols in pursuit of Falcon. Dobbins found nothing and returned safely, but Porter led his force into an ambush during which he and one man were killed. Since Porter, the son of the Navy's distinguished Commodore David Porter, was a very popular and promising officer, his death had an even more profound effect upon the army than Cross's disappearance.[1] The two incidents added to the tension between the two armies, since there lingered in American minds a belief of official Mexican complicity in the deaths. In all probability there was none.

The day following Cross's disappearance, the clanging of bells and a 21-gun salute announced the arrival in Matamoros of Major General Pedro de Ampudia, the commander of the Division of the North, and his 200-man light cavalry escort. They had ridden the 180 miles from Monterrey in four days. Three days behind them marched the rest of Ampudia's force, 2,200 men under Brigadier General Anastasio

(46)

Torrejón.[2] The new commander at Matamoros was a different personality from the irresolute Mejía. At the upriver market town of Reinosa he had given the American residents twenty-four hours to retire to Victoria, the Tamaulipas capital. Upon reaching Matamoros he issued a similar order. That was followed by a strong letter to Taylor demanding that the Americans withdraw to the Nueces or face the start of hostilities. Taylor refused on the grounds that his orders would not permit a withdrawal. Accepting the Mexican statement that this meant war, he ordered the mouth of the Rio Grande closed in order to cut Ampudia's supply line to New Orleans from whence came the bulk of the Mexican supplies.

A storm having driven the *Lawrence* (Commander Samuel Mercer) and her consort the small schooner *Flirt* (Lieutenant Arthur Sinclair) to sea, Major Munroe chartered the merchantman *Alert*, placed Lieutenant Francis B. Renshaw of the Navy on board, and sent her to establish the blockade. On the seventeenth Renshaw warned off the American schooners *Equity* and *Floridian* enroute from New Orleans with flour for the Mexicans. When Ampudia protested the stopping of the two vessels, Taylor replied: "I am certainly surprised that you should complain of a measure which is no other than a natural result of the state of war so much insisted upon by the Mexican authorities as actually existing at this time."[3]

Immediately upon Torrejón's arrival, Ampudia prepared to cross the Rio Grande but halted the operation upon learning that Major General Mariano Arista would supersede him. The change grew out of complaints from the frontier dwellers who distrusted the cruel and marginally competent Ampudia, who remained with the army as second-in-command.[4]

Arista was a forty-two-year-old red-haired native of San Luis Potosí who had lived for some years in Cincinnati. He had commanded the Division of the North before Ampudia but had been displaced because of his failure to support the Paredes uprising. It was Paredes's need to solidify his political position in the northern states that led to his decision of April 4 to bow to the requests that Arista be restored to his command. Arista was not a towering figure in Mexican military history but he did enjoy the trust of his army.[5]

Arista reached Matamoros on April 24. His escort brought the strength of the force there up to about 5,000 men. The new commander immediately began active operations. He notified Taylor that hostilities had commenced, to which the American expressed his regret, since he had hoped that friendly relations could continue until the dispute was settled by the two governments. After a grand review of his army, Arista sent General Torrejón across the river at La Palangana, about fourteen miles upstream from Matamoros. Torrejón's 1,600-man force of cavalry, sappers, and light infantry was to cut the Point Isabel road and isolate the American force from its supply point.[6]

Taylor received a report of Mexicans crossing below him at about three o'clock in the afternoon of the twenty-fourth. He sent Captain Croghan Ker with a detachment of dragoons to investigate. They found nothing. A second report during the evening caused the American general to send Captain Seth B. Thornton with two squadrons to check the upriver crossings. The following morning at the Rancho de Carricitos, about twenty miles from the camp, Thornton rode into an ambush. He tried to fight his way out but lost eleven men killed and six wounded. Most of the rest of his eighty men were captured. Among the prisoners were both Thornton and his second-in-command, Captain William J. Hardee. News of the fight reached Taylor at reveille on the twenty-sixth when Thornton's guide returned. His story was confirmed shortly before noon when a wounded dragoon arrived at the camp in a cart with a note from Torrejón saying that he did not have facilities to care for the man and that the others were prisoners. The dragoon could give few details but clearly established that Thornton had met regulars, not bandits.[7]

Taylor hastened reports of the clash to Washington and New Orleans. To Governor Issac Johnson of Louisiana he sent a call for four regiments of infantry and a request that Persifor F. Smith be named their commander. To Adjutant General Jones went a longer letter reporting the call on Louisiana and the observation that "hostilities may now be considered as commenced. . . ."[8]

After his clash with Thornton, Torrejón continued on toward the Matamoros–Point Isabel road. There on the twenty-eighth one of his patrols under Major (*Commandante de Escuadron*) Rafael Quintero surprised a camp of Captain Samuel H. Walker's company of Texas Rangers, killed five, and took four men prisoner. Shortly afterward Torrejón led his men to the river at the Longoreño crossing, about thirteen miles below Matamoros, to cover the passage there of part of the main body.[9]

News of the attack threw Point Isabel into a state of high anxiety. By arming every available man, including the crews of the vessels in the harbor, Munroe managed to find 500 defenders, but they could not protect the base against a serious Mexican assault. Accordingly, on the morning of the twenty-ninth Munroe sent Captain Walker, who had been absent at the surprise of his camp, to Taylor with a request for reinforcements. Walker reached Taylor that evening without difficulty.[10]

During the last day of April Arista's main body began crossing the Rio Grande. Ampudia's 1st Brigade with four guns crossed first at Longoreño. Since they had only three small scows, the crossing was extremely slow. Arista, with the remainder of the assault force, did not get across until the following day. Walker gave an accurate report of Mexican activities, but Taylor made no effort to contest the crossing from the low ground along the Rio Grande. Instead he channeled his efforts into strengthening Fort Texas, the fortification opposite Matamoros, to withstand a siege. This was sensible strategy, since Taylor could not be sure that Longoreño would be the only crossing.

By May 1 Fort Texas could withstand a short siege, so Taylor prepared to march the bulk of his force to Point Isabel. His objective was twofold: to protect the supply point and to fetch supplies. Taylor left Major Jacob Brown to hold Fort Texas with the 7th Infantry, Captain Allen Lowd's four 18-pounders, and Lieutenant Braxton Bragg's field battery, in all about 500 men. The remaining 2,000 men Taylor consolidated into two brigades under Colonel David E. Twiggs and Brevet Lieutenant Colonel William G. Belknap.

The advance guard, Captain George A. McCall's battalion of light infantry, started the exodus at noon on the first, with the rest of the force about two hours behind. Arista had planned to cut the road ahead of Taylor but was unable to do so because of his delayed crossing. He chased the American column but never caught it. At midnight Taylor halted his men and bivouacked, having marched about eighteen miles. Roused early the next morning the Americans reached Point Isabel at about noon without incident. The troops promptly started strengthening the defenses there.[11]

That work acquired urgency at five o'clock on the morning of the third when the distant booming of guns announced the start of the attack on Fort Texas. Taylor dispatched Walker with instructions for Brown to remain within the fort and to defend it to the last man. The messenger reached the beleaguered fort at 2:00 A.M. on the fourth. He had been escorted part of the way by Captain Charles A. May's dragoons. The Mexican siege lines prevented Walker's party from slipping out of the fort until five o'clock the following afternoon. Walker missed his rendezvous with May, since the cavalryman had waited only until daylight before returning to Point Isabel.[12]

Once he realized that Taylor had taken the bulk of the American forces to Point Isabel, Arista revised his strategy. His new plan was to knock out Fort Texas before Taylor could return with reinforcements. To do so he split up his force. While the main body under his immediate command watched Taylor, Ampudia's brigade, in cooperation with the 1,600 men who had remained at Matamoros under Mejía, invested the fort.

The guns at Matamoros opened the bombardment of Fort Texas at daylight on May 3. The Americans replied with their 18- and 6-pounders, and within thirty minutes had silenced the Mexicans, dismounting two guns. Shortly afterward other Mexican artillery farther down the river assumed the burden with more success. Bragg's light field guns were useless against them and quickly ceased firing to conserve ammunition. The 18-pounders alone proved incapable of silencing the Mexicans. Nor were the heavy guns more successful when Lowd attempted to set Matamoros on fire with hot shot, because the Americans could not heat their projectiles sufficiently. The Mexican batteries secured at 7:30 P.M., while the Americans kept firing until eleven o'clock.

During the fourth the Mexicans emplaced a new, strong battery containing both guns and a mortar on the northern bank behind Fort Texas. The next day Ampudia arrived with four more guns and 1,230 men to complete the investment. From then until the ninth a desultory bombardment and counterbombardment continued, but the Mexicans made no effort to close on the American fortification. Apparently Ampudia had concluded that his artillery was too light to breach the earthen walls. He therefore settled down to a regular siege in hopes of starving the Americans into submission. To prevent supplies from slipping into the fort, he placed Brigadier General Antonio Canales's irregular cavalry astride the Point Isabel road and ringed the fort with infantry. Ampudia's siege benefited the Mexicans very little, since the decisive action would be that between the main bodies. If Taylor's force failed to break through Arista's lines, Fort Texas would quickly be starved into surrender; if Taylor broke through, the fort would be saved. Therefore, Ampudia's only contribution could have been an action which would have eliminated the American position and allowed his men to join Arista before Taylor advanced. That he probably could not have done without crippling losses to his brigade.

At about ten o'clock in the morning of the sixth, Major Brown was mortally wounded and command passed to Captain Edgar S. Hawkins.

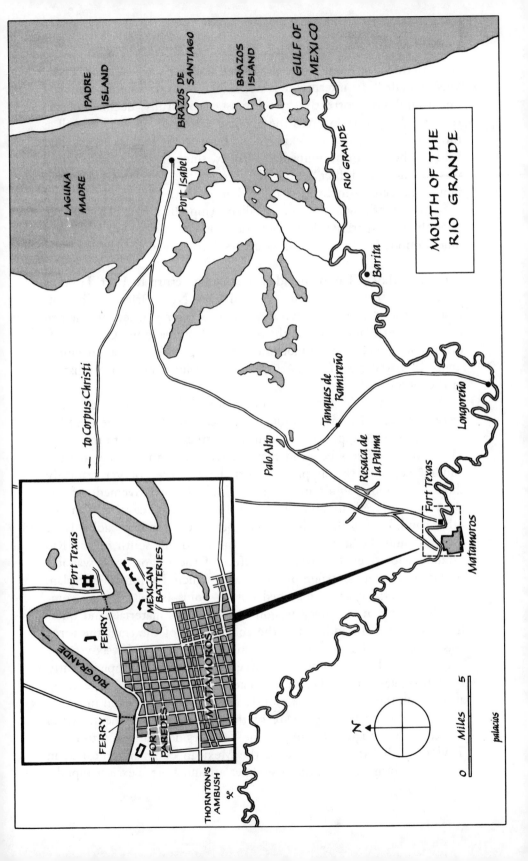

MOUTH OF THE RIO GRANDE

PADRE ISLAND

LAGUNA MADRE

BRAZOS DE SANTIAGO

BRAZOS ISLAND

GULF OF MEXICO

Port Isabel

RIO GRANDE

Barita

to Corpus Christi

N

Tanques de Ramireño

Palo Alto

Resaca de la Palma

Longoreño

Fort Texas

Matamoros

0   Miles   5

palacios

THORNTON'S AMBUSH

RIO GRANDE

FERRY

FERRY

FERRY

Fort Texas

MEXICAN BATTERIES

FORT PAREDES

MATAMOROS

At 4:30 that afternoon Arista demanded the fort's capitulation. Hawkins replied: "My interpreter is not skilled in your language but if I understand you correctly . . . I must respectfully decline to surrender." The bravado fitted the opening action of the war as well as the situation in which Hawkins found himself. As long as his supplies held out he was in no immediate danger, since the Mexican artillery was too light to inflict serious damage on the fort, and enemy infantry showed no inclination toward an assault. The deadlock lasted until the eighth when Arista recalled Ampudia's men. During the siege the fort's garrison lost in addition to Brown one man killed and nine wounded. The Mexican casualties were never determined.[13]

During May 5 Taylor decided to start his return to Fort Texas as soon as some expected recruits arrived from New Orleans. The column set out at 3:00 P.M. two days later. Taylor warned his men to expect a battle and assured them: "The Commanding General has every confidence in his officers and men. . . . He wishes to enjoin upon the battalions of Infantry that their main dependence must be in the bayonet."[14]

One of Taylor's initial decisions subjected him to considerable second-guessing by his subordinates. Instead of clearing the road before moving the supply train, he chose to attach the latter to the army. Many of his officers believed that the train was an unnecessary encumbrance, since the supplies at Fort Texas were not yet critically short. The 200 wagons undoubtedly limited the movement of the army and offered an inviting target for Mexican cavalry. On the other hand, leaving the train behind would mean sending back a large escort should the army fail to force the Mexicans south of the Rio Grande. Moreover, the inhibiting effect of the wagon train was important only in a campaign of movement, which Taylor did not plan.

The 2,228-man army marched out of Point Isabel with its commander riding in "a Jersey wagon of ponderous materials and questionable shape." In addition to the 200 wagons of the train the force was accompanied by a pair of 18-pounders, each hauled by six yoke of oxen. Taylor led his force about seven miles across the open, gently rolling, treeless prairie before bivouacking.[15] The army broke camp at dawn on the eighth and cautiously advanced about eleven miles.

As soon as he became aware of the American movement, Arista moved his army from its camp at the Tanques del Ramireño to block Taylor's path. At the same time the Mexican commander called in Ampudia's brigade from the siege lines around Fort Texas. Ampudia arrived just in time for his men to take their place on the left of the Mexican line near Palo Alto before the battle started. Shortly before noon Taylor's scouts sighted the Mexicans. The American advance guard halted near a small pond to allow the men to drink and refill their canteens while the rear units in the long column reached the field. During the hour it took for Taylor's column to close up, Lieutenant Jacob E. Blake of the Topographical Engineers made a careful reconnaissance of Arista's position.[16]

Arista's left rested on the Point Isabel road at a point where it skirted an expanse of chaparral in which was stationed General Canales with about 400 irregular cavalry. They took no part in the ensuing action, whether as a signal of their willingness to cooperate with the Americans or for other reasons is not certain. Torrejón's cavalry brigade held the road. His men were arranged with the Presidiales on the extreme left, followed (as one moved to the right) by the 8th Cavalry, 7th Cavalry, and the Light Cavalry. To their right stretched a long line of infantry interspersed with artillery batteries. On the left, forming a brigade under Brigadier General José María García, were the 4th and 10th Infantry Regiments separated by a pair of 8-pounders. Then came Brigadier General Rómulo Díaz de la Vega's brigade, consisting of the 10th and 6th Infantry, with five 4-pounders stationed on its right flank. Completing the infantry line were the Tampico Corps, the 2d Light Infantry, and the sapper battalion on whose extreme right stood a lone 4-pounder. The remaining light cavalry under Colonel Cayetano Montero waited between the infantry and a slight tree-covered rise around whose base ran the road to Tanques del Ramireño. The Mexican line stretched about a mile. The nearly flat field between the two opponents was broken by small shallow depressions still water-filled from the recent rains. The shoulder-high, sharp-edged grass which covered the field inhibited movement by unmounted men. The sky was bright and clear.

Taylor's plan was to mass on his right and rely on a bayonet charge. Whether this plan grew out of the comparative weakness of the Mexican left, his conclusion that the ground there was better for infantry, or simply that the road ran there is unclear. As he formed his army, Taylor placed Twiggs's right wing on the road, with its extreme right elements—Lieutenant Colonel James S. McIntosh's 5th Infantry and Ringgold's battery—beyond both the road and the Mexican left flank. The two 18-pounders under Lieutenant William H. Churchill, supported by the 3d Infantry (Captain Lewis N. Morris), held the road, with the 4th Infantry (Captain George W. Allen)

formed to its left.[17] Captain May's dragoon squadron guarded
Twiggs's right flank. Belknap's wing formed with the artillery battalion (Brevet Lieutenant Colonel Thomas Childs) on its right, and
with Duncan's battery between it and the 8th Infantry (Captain William R. Montgomery), which held the American left. Montgomery's
regiment faced the extreme right of Arista's line. Captain Ker's dragoon squadron drew the dual responsibility of guarding the train,
which was parked near the pond, and supporting the American left
wing.

As the Americans advanced in columns at about 2:00 P.M. the
Mexican artillery opened fire at a range of about a half mile. Taylor
halted his force and formed it in a line under cover of the fire of his
batteries. On the extreme left the 8th Infantry was refused to secure
the flank, while Duncan's battery supported by May's squadron
rushed about 200 yards ahead of the line. The Mexican copper cannonballs tended to fall short and ricochet into the American line slowly
enough for the Americans to dodge them. The American artillery
fire, on the other hand, was very effective, notably the shelling of
Colonel José López Uraga's 4th Infantry on the Mexican extreme left
by Ringgold's and Churchill's guns.

Arista seems to have planned a double envelopment of the American position and ordered Torrejón's cavalry supported by two guns
to move through the chaparral and attack the American right, rear,
and train. Torrejón had not reconnoitered the ground and his column
quickly bogged down in a small swale. This gave the Americans time
to react. Taylor's own response was simply to tell his staff to "keep
a bright lookout for them," but someone, probably Twiggs, moved
the 5th Infantry about a quarter mile to the right and rear where
it formed a square behind a small marsh. Torrejón came out of
the chaparral with his men in a column and his poorest troops, the
Presidiales, in the lead. Their ineffectual fire drew a volley from the
square, which did little damage but caused the Mexicans to withdraw
about 300 yards. Torrejón concluded that he could not attack because of the marshy terrain but when Arista insisted he "persevere,"
Torrejón attacked the west face of the square. Once again his men
recoiled from an American volley, this time fired at only fifty yards.
The Mexican cavalry next tried to bypass the square and attack the
parked wagons but abandoned that idea when they sighted the 3d
Infantry and Lieutenant Randolph Ridgely's two guns preparing to
greet them.

While the action on the American right flamed, Ringgold, with
the remaining section of his battery, and the 4th Infantry pushed

forward. The guns barked ferociously and effectively until a burning wad from one of them set fire to the grass which carpeted the battlefield, and the wind drove the flames and smoke across the field nearly parallel to the American lines. The smoke so obscured visibility that fighting ceased for an hour.

During the lull Arista's left pulled back about 1,000 yards, leaving the road open, so Taylor sent the 18-pounders down the road almost as far as the position which the Mexican lancers had held at the start of the fight. On the extreme right the 5th Infantry made a similar advance. The effect therefore was to pivot the axis of the battlefield 30° to 40° counterclockwise. Taylor sent May to turn the Mexican left, but the swashbuckling dragoon found too many Mexicans in the chaparral to do so. As the smoke lifted, the artillery duel resumed. The American fire was fast and effective, opening temporary gaps in the Mexican ranks which closed nearly instantly as the *soldados mexicanos* proved their constancy. Nor was the fight one-sided. The 4th Infantry, which supported the 18-pounders and Ringgold's battery, suffered so badly that it finally had to fall back, and Ringgold himself was mortally wounded by the Mexican counterbattery fire.

Childs's provisional artillery battalion moved into the space between the 5th Infantry and Churchill's guns in order to buttress the American right. There it formed a square to meet Torrejón's horsemen who once again advanced only to be halted by canister rounds from the 18-pounders. Mexican infantry then opened a brisk fire on the square, which responded with such a well-directed volley that it silenced the Mexicans.

Meanwhile Arista attempted to turn the American left, but Duncan, who handled his battery as though it were on a parade ground, frustrated the move. Advancing in conjunction with the 8th Infantry and Ker's dragoons, the battery drove the Mexican right from the field. Although Arista and some of his officers kept the retreat from turning into a rout, their work was complicated by the Mexican cavalry. In an effort to keep the shattered units from bolting after this unexpected turn, Arista ordered a charge supported by the light cavalry. It was lackadaisically executed by already demoralized men who suddenly found themselves enfiladed by Duncan's guns. They fled across the front of the Mexican line, taking all the troops as far as the 6th Infantry with them. Taylor, afraid of overly exposing his train, did not pursue. Since dusk had now fallen, the firing slackened and the two armies camped for the night. The Americans bivouacked on the ground they held, while the Mexicans withdrew slightly into the chaparral behind their position.

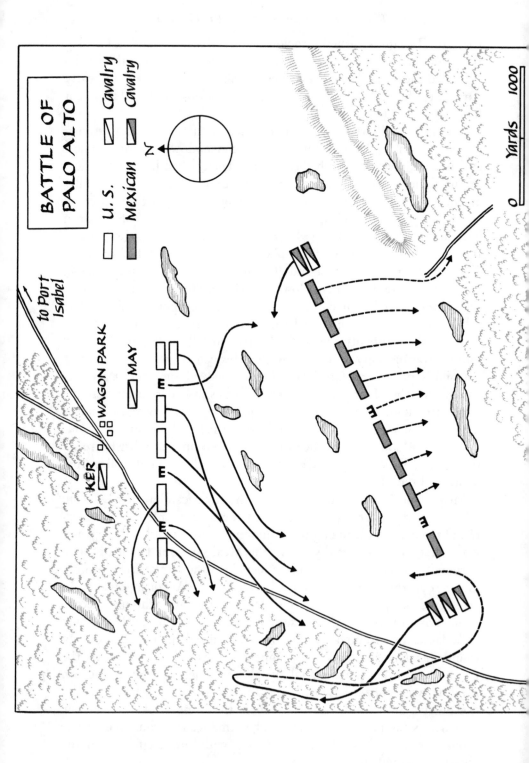

BATTLE OF
PALO ALTO

U.S. ☐ Cavalry ▨
Mexican ▩ Cavalry ▨

N

to Port Isabel

WAGON PARK ▫ MAY ▨

KER

0   1000
Yards

The American success was due to the artillery. Except for the 5th Infantry and the artillery battalion none of the American infantry had directly faced the enemy. The bayonet upon whose dependence Taylor had instructed the army was not used. Indeed, Taylor's own contribution to the victory, aside from the charisma of his personality, was limited. The battle was won by Duncan, Ringgold, and their cannoneers, who accounted for the great disproportion in casualties between the two forces. The Americans lost five killed, forty-eight wounded, and two missing out of a force of 2,288, while the Mexicans suffered 102 killed, 129 wounded, and twenty-six missing from their force of 3,709.

Tactically the fight could be counted an American victory since Taylor's troops slept on the battlefield, but strategically it was a draw. Neither side had accomplished its objective. Taylor had not reopened the road to Fort Texas, and Arista had not destroyed the American force.

Taylor's April 26 calls for emergency reinforcement set in motion an operation so massive that it came to embarrass the field commander. The call reached New Orleans on May 3. General Gaines promptly conferred with Governor Johnson of Louisiana, who immediately secured $100,000 from his legislature to equip the four regiments which Taylor requested. Gaines also called in regulars from Jefferson Barracks and the Pensacola forts and asked the Navy to furnish the big steam frigate *Mississippi* to rush reinforcements to Point Isabel. In addition he called on the Governors of Alabama, Kentucky, Mississippi, and Missouri for troops. Although most of the latter were headed off before reaching New Orleans, the St. Louis (Colonel Alton R. Easton) and Louisville (Colonel Stephen Ormsby) Legions did reach the front.

Despite initial enthusiasm, Governor Johnson had to resort to the threat of a draft to bring forward sufficient men to fill the Louisiana regiments. About 1,200 had signed up for six months' service by the ninth, and nearly 4,500 by the thirteenth. Since the *Mississippi* was not available, Gaines chartered the steamers *Galveston* and *Telegraph* and fitted each with a 12-pounder field gun in case the troops had to fight their way ashore. The leading elements, four companies of the 1st Infantry under Lieutenant Colonel Henry Wilson and two companies of volunteers, reached Point Isabel on May 7, shortly after Taylor left.[18]

On May 11 General Gaines sent the War Department the un-

welcome news that once again he had called for an unspecified number of regiments of mounted men to gather at Fort Jesup preparatory
to marching overland to the front. His requisitions, those of May 3
as well as those of the later call, amounted to fifteen regiments, or
11,211 men. Since it had neither a plan to employ the men nor the
money to pay them, the War Department's horrified response was a
clear and unequivocal directive to cancel the call. Gaines then opened
a long, wearisome correspondence with the Department justifying
his conduct. As a result on June 2 he was replaced as Commander
of the Western Division by Brigadier General George M. Brooke and
later brought before a court of inquiry that found him guilty of
exceeding his authority but recommended no further action. None
was taken and in late August he became Commander of the Eastern
Division at New York.[19]

Other less controversial reinforcements were also on the way to
Taylor. The War Department ordered an additional twelve artillery
companies from eastern coastal fortifications to Texas during the second week of May.[20] Commodore David Conner at Veracruz on May 3
received word of Paredes's April 23 declaration of defensive war and
correctly concluded that orders to attack had been issued to Arista.
Hoping that their presence might somehow forestall that move, he
ordered all his vessels, except the sloop-of-war *Falmouth* (Commander
Joseph R. Jarvis) which remained at Veracruz, to Point Isabel.[21]
Conner with three frigates and a sloop-of-war reached there during
the morning of May 8 but anchored offshore because of the shallow-
ness of water on the bar. Major Munroe immediately requested 150–
200 men to reinforce his garrison but raised it to "a pretty strong
force" after hearing the sounds of action. Conner dispatched Captain
Francis H. Gregory with 500 men who were ferried from the anchorage to the shore on the Army's steamer *Monmouth*.

Expecting to march to the relief of Taylor, the sailors and Marines
found the assignment to a passive role irritating. Their restiveness
increased when a camp follower came in from the army about midnight with a tale of a major defeat and great loss of life. Gregory
then proposed marching to the rescue, but Conner refused. The sailors were untrained for land fighting, and as he pointed out, a single
cavalry regiment could cut them to pieces and cripple the squadron
at the very start of operations. The light of day, in any event, brought
more accurate news of Taylor's victory at Palo Alto. Nevertheless, the
sailors and marines remained ashore until May 13 to help guard the
base against any Mexican raid.[22]

On the morning of May 9 the sun rose in a cloudless sky and quickly burned off the early morning mist which obscured the Palo Alto battlefield. It also revealed the Mexican army slowly moving southward. The Americans ate breakfast, sent their wounded on the painful journey to the uncertain comforts of Point Isabel, and went about their usual housekeeping duties while awaiting the order to resume the action. Taylor called a council of his officers after Twiggs reported that many favored digging in while awaiting reinforcements. The council split, with only McIntosh, Morris, and Duncan supporting Taylor's decision to resume the advance. Even Taylor's resolve seems to have waivered, since he hesitated for nearly two hours until Captain Ker reported that his dragoons had located the Mexicans. Taylor then decided to resume the advance, throwing forward the 220-man light battalion under McCall to feel out the Mexican position. Meanwhile, the rest of the army threw up a temporary breastwork to protect the wagon train.[23]

About a half mile beyond the Palo Alto battlefield the flat open prairie gave way to a dense tangle of chaparral and trees which extended nearly seven miles to the Rio Grande. The gently rolling terrain was cut by a series of long meandering depressions sometimes containing stagnant pools of water (*resacas*) which represented old river courses. At one of these, called Resaca de la Guerrero by the Mexicans and Resaca de la Palma by the Americans, Arista chose to take his stand. It was a strong position about three miles from the river. The *resaca* extended for several miles and at the point where the Matamoros road crossed was about ten or twelve feet deep and 200 feet wide. Both sides of the ravine were thickly forested, while just beyond the south bank was an opening large enough to hold the Mexican camp.

Arista had been chagrined but not disheartened by the events of the eighth. He recalled the remaining forces besieging Fort Texas[24] and slowly led his army the five miles to the new position. By ten o'clock he had his men in position and confidently awaited the coming of the Americans.

His position was a strong one. It effectively limited the role which American artillery could play while severely decreasing the demands on Arista's short supply of artillery ammunition. The Mexican commander placed the bulk of his infantry in the ravine so as to take full advantage of its cover. To the east of the road along which the Americans would advance, he placed the 6th Infantry, 10th Infantry, the Sappers, 2nd Light Infantry, and finally the 1st Infantry. To the west of the crossing he stationed the 2nd Infantry, the Tampico Battalion, and the 4th Infantry. In the rear, covering the flanks were the *Presidiales* along with the light cavalry and the 7th and 8th Regiments of heavy cavalry. A three-gun battery emplaced on the south bank swept the crossing, while a lone gun stood near the middle of the Mexican left wing. The remaining four guns were placed to concentrate on any force breaking through along the road. Skirmishers covered the entire Mexican front.[25]

Taylor left the artillery battalion, the 18-pounders, and a pair of 12-pounders at the old camp to protect the train. This gave him less than 2,000 men to force the Mexican position. About two o'clock the American commander received the first contact reports and set his force in motion. About an hour later he reached the scene of action and conferred with Captain William W. Mackall of the light troops, who sketched the Mexican position for him. After Lieutenant Dobbins and a few men deliberately drew fire to disclose the position of the Mexican guns, Taylor ordered Mackall's skirmishers into the chaparral along the road while Ridgely's[26] battery moved down it. The 5th Infantry and part of the 4th moved to the left of the road while the rest of the 4th and the 3d took to the chaparral on the right. Taylor intended to use the infantry as skirmishers to support Ridgely, but their difficulties in working through the underbrush prevented that.

The firing now became intense and the fighting disorganized, since the density of the chaparral destroyed any semblance of unit integrity. The action became one of small groups of men led by an officer or a noncom who worked their way forward as best they could. There was little coordination between groups. Slowly they pushed the Mexican skirmishers back to the *resaca* but could progress no further because of the enemy artillery. Even without support Ridgely had moved his guns forward, and unassisted they beat off a charge by a detachment of Mexican lancers. The torrent of Mexican fire, however, prevented Ridgely's cannoneers from silencing the opposing pieces, and the Americans in turn were threatened by more Mexican cavalry. The artilleryman asked for help.

Taylor's response was to call forward May's squadron of dragoons and order it to charge the offending battery. When the cavalrymen reached Ridgely's position, May sang out, "Hello, Ridgely, where is that battery? I am ordered to charge it." Ridgely's classic answer was: "Hold on, Charley, 'till I draw their fire and you will see where they are." The two batteries exchanged fire and, before the Mexicans could reload, May's men charged at a full gallop in a column of fours.

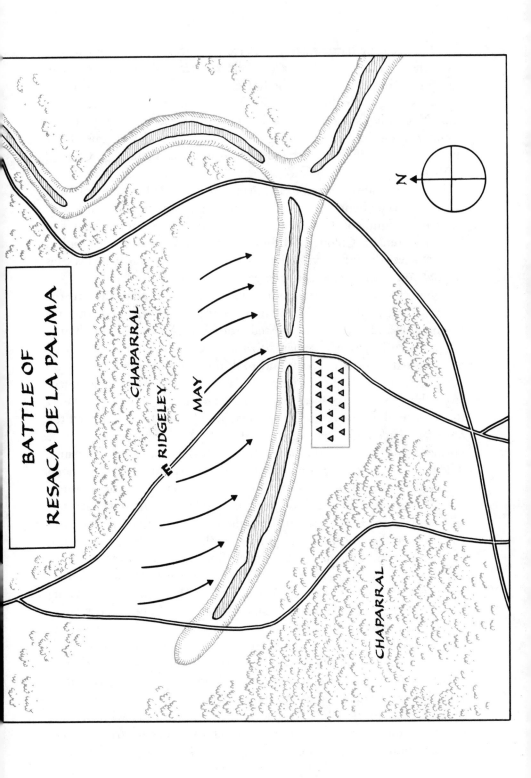

BATTLE OF
RESACA DE LA PALMA

CHAPARRAL

RIDGELEY

MAY

CHAPARRAL

N

They cleared the battery with little loss, but their momentum was so great that it took them a quarter mile farther and exposed them to heavy fire from the flanks. The horsemen lost all semblance of order so that when he finally reined up, May had but six troopers beside him. Not only had the charge been poorly executed, but with no accompanying infantry the dragoons could not hold the guns. They did, however, return with several prisoners, including General la Vega.[27]

Taylor in disgust turned to Belknap and said, "Take these guns and by God, keep them!" The 5th and the newly arrived 8th Infantry drew the assignment. It was a particularly bloody transaction in which both Lieutenant Colonels McIntosh and Belknap were wounded. Nevertheless the infantrymen secured the guns, forcing the Mexicans to abandon their positions to the east of the road.

While this was transpiring, a portion of the light companies to the right of the road, under Captain Robert C. Buchanan of the 4th Infantry, found a trail which passed around the Mexican left. Though Ampudia rushed reinforcements to the threatened point, the Americans pushed across the *resaca* and took the one gun emplacement on the Mexican left. Captain Philip N. Barbour and a small detachment from the 4th Infantry beat off two Mexican counterattacks against the battery. This proved to be the final act of the battle. It turned the Mexican flank and, when combined with the abandonment of the positions on the east of the road, threw the Mexican force into panic. The troops fled, leaving baggage of every description behind. Among the items found by the 4th Infantry when it occupied the Mexican camp was all of Arista's correspondence and his personal silver service.

Taylor ordered the artillery battalion, Ker's dragoons, Duncan's battery, and the 3d Infantry to pursue the fleeing enemy. They picked up a number of stragglers and camped for the night on the banks of the Rio Grande but inflicted little further damage. Mexican soldiers streamed over the river crossing well into the night, many drowning in their panic. Arista himself reached Matamoros about 10:00 P.M.

Of an army of 2,222, about 1,700 Americans were actually engaged. Their losses were thirty-three killed and eighty-nine wounded. Official Mexican casualties were 154 killed, 205 wounded, and 156 missing, but they were undoubtedly low, since Taylor claims to have buried 200 Mexican dead. Among the spoils was a large quantity of official Mexican stationery which provided many Americans with writing paper for their next few letters home, eight pieces of artillery, 474 muskets and carbines, and the colors of the Tampico Battalion.

Arista had clearly been overconfident. He had thought that his position was nearly invulnerable and that the Americans would delay before attacking. After the battle la Vega admitted, "If I had had with me yesterday $100,000 in silver, I would have bet the whole of it that no 10,000 men on earth could drive us from our position."[28]

NOTES

For key to abbreviations used in Notes, see page xi.

1. Henry, *Campaign Sketches*, 73, 77–78; Ampudia to Taylor, April 16, 1846, *H. Ex. Doc. 60, 30th Cong., 1st Sess.*, 147–48; Report of board of officers to examine body of Cross and circumstances of his death, April 23, 1846, *AOLR*, Box 2; Frost, *Mexican War and Warriors*, 18–19; Meade to wife, April 21, 22, 1846, Meade, *Life and Letters*, I, 67–68.

2. Jenkins, *War Between U.S. and Mexico*, 81–82; Roa Bárcena, *Recuerdos*, I, 148; José C. Valades, *Breve Historia de la Guerra con les Estados Unidos* (México, 1947), 115; Isaac I. Stevens, *Campaigns of the Rio Grande and of Mexico* (New York, 1851), 39; Smith, *War with Mexico*, I, 148.

3. Ampudia to Taylor, April 12, 22, Taylor to Ampudia, April 12, 22, Taylor to AG, April 15, 1846, all in *H. Ex. Doc. 60, 30th Cong., 1st Sess.*, 138–40, 144–47; Munroe to Bliss, April 17, 19, 1846, *AOLR*, Box 2.

4. Castillo Negrete, *Invasión de los Norte-Americanos*, II, 112; Ramsey, *Other Side*, 39–40. Ampudia's greatest claim to fame was his execution of General Francisco de Sentamanat and fourteen of his men after their abortive 1844 attack on Tabasco. To discourage others Ampudia had their heads boiled in oil and hung on the walls of buildings. Fayette Robinson, *Mexico and Her Military Chieftains* (Hartford, 1848), 259.

5. Alberto María Carreño, *Jefes del Ejército Mexicano en 1847* (Mexico, 1914), 44–57; Smith, *War with Mexico*, I, 149; Robinson, *Mexico and Her Military Chieftains*, 255.

6. Arista to Taylor, April 24, Taylor to Arista, April 25, 1846, *H. Ex. Doc. 56, 30th Cong., 1st Sess.*, 395–96; Roa Bárcena, *Recuerdos*, I, 62; Bravo Ugarte, *História de Mexico*, III, t. II, 198; Ramsey, *Other Side*, 42.

7. Hardee to Taylor, April 26, Thornton to Bliss, April 27, AO, Orders #74, June 8, 1846, all in *H. Ex. Doc. 60, 30th Cong., 1st Sess.*, 290–92, 491–92; Torrejón to Taylor, April 25, 1846, *AOLR*, Box 2; Torrejón to Arista, April 26, 1846, Arista Papers, I-b-92; Henry, *Campaign Sketches*, 82–5; *S. Ex. Doc. 36, 30th Cong., 1st Sess.*, 15; *The Rough and Ready Annual* (New York, 1848), 37–39; Blackwood, *To Mexico with Scott*, 39, 41–42.

8. Taylor to Gaines, April 26, 1846, RPO File 498773, RG-92, NA; Taylor to AG, April 26, 1846, *H. Ex. Doc. 60, 30th Cong., 1st Sess.*, 288.

9. Torrejón to Arista, April 27, 1846, Arista Papers, I-b-93; Ampudia to Arista, April 27, 1846, Ampudia, *El Cuidadano . . . Antes el Tribunal*, 16–17; Arista to Ministro de Guerra y Marina, April 29, 1846, Castillo Negrete, *Invasión de los Norte-americanos*, I, 167; Walker to Taylor, May 2, 1846, *AOLR*, Box 2; Ramsey, *Other Side*, 44; A. Russell Buchanan (ed.), "George Washington Trahern: Texas Cowboy Soldier from Mier to Buena Vista," *Southwestern Historical Quarterly* LXXVIII (July 1954), 71, is a first-hand account by one of the survivors.

10. Jenkins, *War Between U.S. and Mexico*, 99.

11. Taylor to Jones, May 3, AO, Order #55, May 1, 1846, *H. Ex. Doc. 60, 30th Cong., 1st Sess.*, 289–90, 486, 488; Oficial de la Infantría, *Campaña Contra los Americanos del Norte* (México, 1846), 5; Ramsey, *Other Side*, 43–44; Smith, *War with Mexico*, I, 162–63, 464; Henry, *Campaign Sketches*, 86; Hamilton, *Taylor*, 177. Twiggs commanded the 3d, 4th, and 5th Infantry, three companies of dragoons, and Ringgold's battery; Belknap had the 8th Infantry, the composite artillery battalion, two companies of dragoons, and Duncan's battery.

12. Jenkins, *War Between U.S. and Mexico*, 103–4.

13. Ampudia to Mejía, May 2, Arista to Canales, May 4, 1846, Arista Papers, I-a-8, I-b-17; Arista to CO, U.S. Forces Opposite Matamoros, May 6, Hawkins to Arista, May 6, Hawkins to Bliss, May 10, Mansfield to Taylor, May 12, 1846, all in *S. Doc. 388, 29th Cong., 1st Sess.*, 31–37; Arista to Ministro de Guerra y Marina, May 7, 1846, Nathan Covington Brooks, *A Complete History of the Mexican War* (Chicago, 1965), 135–36; Brown to Bliss, May 4, 1846, *H. Ex. Doc. 60, 30th Cong., 1st Sess.*, 193–94; Requeña to Ampudia, May 31, 1846, Ampudia, *El Ciudadano . . . Entre el Tribunal*, 18; Roa Bárcena, *Recuerdos*, I, 63; Jenkins, *War Between U.S. and Mexico*, 101–6; Niles, LXX (May 23, June 20, 1846), 179, 254–55; Oficial de la Infantría, *Campaña Contra los Americanos*, 7; Ramsey, *Other Side*, 44; *S. Ex. Doc. 36, 30th Cong., 1st Sess.*, 17.

14. Taylor to AG, May 5, AO, Orders #58, May 7, 1846, *H. Ex. Doc. 60, 30th Cong., 1st Sess.*, 292–93, 487.

15. Grant, *Memoirs*, 43; *Rough and Ready Annual*, 18; Smith and Judah, *Chronicles of the Gringos*, 472; Hazlitt to sister, May 14, 1846, Robert Hazlitt Letters, USMA, #1531; Hamilton, *Taylor*, 177–81; Smith, *War with Mexico*, 163.

16. Unless otherwise noted the description of the Battle of Palo Alto is derived from: Taylor to AG, May 16, 17, 1846, with enclosed subordinate reports, *S. Doc. 388, 29th Cong., 1st Sess.*, 6–30; Arista to Ministro Guerra y Marina, May 8, 1846, Robinson, *Mexico and Her Military Chieftains*, 318–21; Mexican reports in Ampudia, *El Cuidadano . . . entre al Tribunal* 17–23; Henry, *Campaign Sketches*, 90–94; Grant, *Memoirs*, 43–45; Smith and Judah, *Chronicles of the Gringos*, 65–67; Ramsey, *Other Side*, 45–50; Doubleday, *Journal of Barbour*, 54–55; Oficial de Infantría, *Campaña Contra los Americanos*, 8–14; Oliver Otis Howard, *General Taylor* (New York, 1892), 106–14; Smith, *War with Mexico*, I, 164–69; Hamilton, *Taylor*, 182–85; Jenkins, *War Between U.S. and Mexico*, 108–12; Roswell Sabine Ripley, *War with Mexico* (2 vols., New York, 1899), I, 116–24; Wilcox, *History of the Mexican War*, 51–58; Brooks, *Complete History*, 125–33; Roa Bárcena, *Recuerdos*, I, 67; *S. Ex. Doc. 36, 30th Cong., 1st Sess.*, 15; *H. Ex. Doc. 24, 31st Cong., 1st Sess.*, 8a; Abner Doubleday, "From Mexican War to the Rebellion," NYHS, 119–25; Duncan, "Medical History," 86–88; Henry B. Dawson, *Battles of the United States by Land and Sea* (2 vols., New York, 1860), II, 447–50.

17. The 3d and 4th Infantry formed a small brigade under Lieutenant Colonel John Garland.

18. Gaines to Marcy, May 3, 15, 1846, RPO File 498773, RG-94, N.A.; Gaines to Latimer, May 3, Memorandum of Maj. W. H. Chase, ca. May 8, Gaines to Wilson, May 9, Jones to Gaines, May 22, 1846, all in *S. Doc. 378, 29th Cong., 1st Sess.*, 52–54, 58, 64–67; Marcy to Taylor, May 23, 1846, *H. Ex. Doc. 60, 30th Cong., 1st Sess.*, 281; New Orleans *Daily Picayune*, May 7, 1846; John Bach McMaster, *A History of the People of the United States* (8 vols., New York, 1883–1913), VII, 442; Silver, *Gaines*, 263.

19. Gaines to Marcy, May 11, Jones to Gaines, May 18, Marcy to Gaines, May 8, Marcy, Order, June 2, 1846, all in *S. Doc. 378, 29th Cong., 1st Sess.*, 50–51, 59–61; Jones to Gaines, June 20, 1846, *AGLS*, XXII, 901½; Gaines to Marcy, June 7,

1846, *S. Doc. 402, 29th Cong., 1st Sess.*, 1–3; War Dept., GO #39, Aug. 20, 1846, Polk Papers; Marcy to AG, Aug. 27, 1846, *AGLR'46*, M-536; Quaife, *Diary of Polk*, I, 480, II, 82–83; Marvin A. Kriedberg and Merton G. Henry, *History of Military Mobilization in the United States Army, 1775–1948* (Washington, 1955), 75; Silver, *Gaines*, 267.

20. Jones to C. Sturtevant, James Bankhead, CO D Co., 2d Arty., F. S. Belton, J. DeB. Walbach, William Gates, D. H. Vinton, May 9, to R. D. A. Wade, May 10, 1846, all in *AGLS*, XXII, 603–9, 611.

21. Conner to Bancroft, May 3, 1846, *Niles*, LXX (May 30, 1846), 197; Conner to Jarvis, Saunders, F. H. Gregory, J. H. Aulick, W. J. McCluney, and D. N. Ingraham, May 4, 1846, all in *CLB*; Fitch W. Taylor, *The Broad Pennant* (New York, 1848), 154–55.

22. Monroe to Conner, May 8, 1846, *Conner (NY)*; Conner to Gregory, May 8, 1846, *CLB*; Conner to Bancroft, May 9, 1846, *H. Ex. Doc. 1, 30th Cong., 2nd Sess.*, 1161–62; logs of vessels involved; Monroe to Bliss, *AOLR*, Box 2; William Harwar Parker, *Recollections of a Naval Officer* (New York, 1883), 51–52; Taylor, *Broad Pennant*, 165–66; Conner to wife, May 29, 1846, *Conner(FDR)*.

23. Unless otherwise indicated the sources for the following account of the Battle of Resaca de la Palma are: Taylor to AG, May 17, 1846, with the enclosed reports of his subordinates, *S. Doc. 388, 29th Cong., 1st Sess.*, 6–21, McCall to Capt. B. R. Alden, June 5, 1846, Alden Papers, #311; Lieutenant George Deas to Brooke, July 22, 1846, Childs to Belknap, May 12, 1846, *AGLR'46*, B-549, C-454; McIntosh to Bliss, Dec. 2, 1846, *H. Ex. Doc. 60, 30th Cong., 1st Sess.*, 1102–4; Mexican reports in Ampudia, *El Cuidadano . . . Ante el Tribunal*, 18–23; Dawson, *Battles of U.S.*, II, 451–53; Doubleday, *Journal of Barbour*, 58–59; Henry, *Campaign Sketches*, 94–100; Samuel G. French, *Two Wars* (Nashville, 1901), 51; Grant, *Memoirs*, 45–46; Oficial de Infantría, *Campaña Contra los Americanos*, 15–20; *Niles*, LXX (June 27, 1846), 265; Howard, *Taylor*, 116–22; Roa Bárcena, *Recuerdos*, I, 84–85; David Lavender, *Climax at Buena Vista* (Philadelphia, 1966), 73–77; Hamilton, *Taylor*, 186–90; Smith, *War with Mexico*, I, 170–76, 467; Theodore F. Rodenbough, *From Everglade to Canon* (New York, 1875), 514–15; Brackett, *History of Cavalry*, 56–59; Ripley, *War with Mexico*, I, 125–31; Wilcox, *History of the Mexican War*, 58–65; Brooks, *Complete History*, 137–47; Ramsey, *Other Side*, 50–55; *S. Ex. Doc. 36, 30th Cong., 1st Sess.*, 16; Abner Doubleday, From Mexican War to the Rebellion, NYHS, 125–33; Duncan, "Medical History," 88–89.

24. Arista to Morlet, May 8, 1846, Arista Papers, I-a-18.

25. Taylor to Thomas Butler, June 19, 1846, YWA argues that Arista's position threw away his superiority in cavalry. This overlooks its ineffectiveness at Palo Alto and the fact that any battlefield which would favor horsemen would also favor artillery.

26. This was Ringgold's battery now commanded by Lieutenant Randolph Ridgely.

27. May claimed to have taken Díaz de la Vega prisoner himself. The actual captor was a bugler, Pvt. Winchell. May was a very colorful figure who became one of the heroes of the war as a result of this mishandled charge. Nothing in his performance at Resaca de la Palma or later in the war dispells the notion that he was one of the least deserving heroes of the conflict.

28. McCall to Alden, June 5, 1846, Alden Papers. See also Guillermo Vigil y Robles, *La Invasión de México por los Estados Unidos* (México, 1923), 18–19.

5: The Declaration of War

PRESIDENT POLK and his advisers had sufficient intimations of probable Mexican hostility not to be astonished at the outbreak of fighting. Since they clung tentatively to their hopes of a peaceful settlement, the decision for war was an unpleasant one. The terminal illness of Polk's hopes began during the evening of April 6 when a letter from Consul Francis M. Dimond at Veracruz warning that Slidell probably would not be received reached the State Department. The next day President Polk discussed the unwelcome development with his cabinet and proposed that he send a message to Congress recommending that the United States "take the remedy for the injuries and wrongs we have suffered into our own hands." That evening Slidell's report of the final Mexican refusal to receive him reached Washington.

The cabinet resumed its discussion of the rejection on April 11 and agreed that no message should be sent to Congress until after Slidell had reported in person. During the wait for the diplomat's return, the President discussed Mexican relations with two of the leading Democrats in the Senate, John C. Calhoun and Thomas H. Benton. Calhoun counseled delaying until the Oregon negotiations were settled before making any decision about Mexico, because he thought that the British would then assist in arranging a settlement. Benton also recommended settling Oregon first. Moreover, he opposed war with Mexico if it could be avoided with honor.

Slidell reached Washington on May 8. After hearing his report, the President concluded that despite the recommendations of Calhoun and Benton the only course now left to the United States was war. Polk arrived at that conclusion with the Oregon question still unsettled and war with Britain a far from remote possibility. If Polk's diary accurately reflects his thinking, he gave the problem scant consideration and, as events proved, he understood well the course of British policy. The cabinet concurred in Polk's decision on May 9. It agreed that any hostile act by the Mexicans at Matamoros should be sufficient cause for war. With Secretary of the Navy George Bancroft alone opposing, it also agreed that the President should recommend a declaration of war because of the refusal to accept Slidell. At six o'clock that evening Adjutant General Roger Jones brought to the White House General Zachary Taylor's April 26 report of the attack on Thornton's command. Polk called the cabinet back into session at 7:30 and it unanimously supported a declaration of war.[1]

Between 9:30 in the morning and five o'clock in the afternoon of Sunday, May 10, Polk, assisted by Bancroft and Buchanan, drafted the war message. During the evening the President conferred with key members of Congress over the tactics to be followed in requesting the declaration of war and the passage of a bill to appropriate $10 million and raise 50,000 volunteers to fight the war.[2]

Calhoun spent the day consulting with his political supporters in an attempt to head off the fatal legislation. He argued that such a step was too dangerous, since the Oregon dispute remained unsettled. Instead of declaring war, he suggested that Congress vote the money to purchase enough supplies to ensure the safety of Taylor's force.[3]

Polk sent his message to Congress at noon on the eleventh. Basically it rehashed the well-known story of the long-standing complaints against Mexico and the failure of the Slidell mission. Taylor's movement to Corpus Christi, the President declared, had been "to meet a threatened invasion of Texas by Mexican forces, for which extensive military preparations had been made." He stressed the inclusion of the disputed area in the American "revenue system" by the Act of December 31, 1845, and justified the movement to the Rio Grande as an "urgent necessity to provide for the defense of that portion of our country." The United States "have tried every effort at reconciliation," he said, yet "Mexico . . . has invaded our territory and shed American blood upon the American soil. She has proclaimed that hostilities have commenced, and that the two nations are at war."[4]

The administration strategy for countering the strong opposition which the war proposal was sure to encounter involved coupling the declaration of war to a law appropriating the money to support Taylor and his men. The critical isssue here, as it would be in the congressional debates of a century and a quarter later, was the power to declare war. Polk, his critics argued, had involved the country in an undeclared war. While they could not refuse to support the men in the field, the President's opponents argued that his actions did not bind them to a declaration of war even if American troops were exposed to unprovoked attacks as a result of his actions. Thus the opposition had the choice of either endorsing the Polk interpretation of events along the Rio Grande or voting against supporting Taylor's imperiled force. The administration's first step was to limit debate in the House to two hours, three quarters of which was spent in reading the President's message and its accompanying documents. When the Whigs and Calhounites attempted to separate the preamble, declaring that war existed by Mexican action, from the rest of the bill, they lost 123 to 76. On the final vote, 174 Congressmen supported the bill and fourteen, chiefly northern antislavery Whigs led by John Quincy Adams, voted nay. Twenty members abstained.

The administration had greater difficulty in the Senate. Calhoun's argument for the separation of the war declaration from the support of the troops in the field won enough converts that on Benton's motion the Senate sent the former to the Committee on Foreign Relations and the appropriations segment to Benton's Military Affairs group. Benton caused the administration real concern, since he had been highly critical of the march to the Rio Grande and vocal in his opposition to an "aggressive war." On the other hand, he had made it clear that he was prepared to vote men and money for defense.

The administration succeeded in winning over the Missourian as both committees reported favorably on the House bill. This caught the antiadministration forces flatfooted. They had not expected such quick or decisive action and lost all their efforts to alter the bill. When the final vote came at 6:30 P.M. on May 13, the war's opponents found themselves impaled on the horns of a dilemma, as Polk had intended. "The Whigs in the Senate," chortled Vice President Alexander J. Dallas, "after struggling hard, for hours, finally almost got upon their knees to beg to be spared from voting on the preamble—

but the democrats were resolved that they should speak out." Few Whigs or Calhounites dared to fail to vote support for Taylor, so the final tally read forty yeas, two nays, and three abstentions. The two negative votes came from Whigs: John Davis of Massachusetts and Thomas Clayton of Delaware. Calhoun, Whigs John M. Berrien of Georgia, and George Evans of Maine abstained.[5]

It is an understatement to suggest that the Whigs felt that they had been duped by a masterful political maneuver. "I think the vote of our Whigs on the war bill," wrote one of the House diehards, "the most unfortunate ever given, so far as party considerations are concerned."[6] Another Whig Congressman stormed:

> It is useless to disguise the fact that we have been brought into this war by the weakness or wickedness of our prest. and his cabinet, and while we must all stand by the country right or wrong it is grevious to know that when we pray "God defend the right" our prayers are not for our own country.[7]

The supporters of Manifest Destiny were elated. Walt Whitman, who had made the *Eagle* of Brooklyn a companion of the eagle of Manifest Destiny, cried: "Let our arms now be carried with a spirit which shall teach the world that, while we are not forward for a quarrel, America knows how to crush, as well as how to expand."[8] A less star-blinded pair of eyes in Lansingburgh, New York, saw the sham in much that followed: "People here are all in a state of delirium about the Mexican War. A military order pervades all ranks—Militia Colonels wax red in the coat facing—and 'prentice Boys are running off to the wars by scores—Nothing is talked of but the 'Halls of Montezuma.'"[9]

The "Act providing for the prosecution of the existing war between the United States and the Republic of Mexico" authorized 50,000 volunteers to serve for either a year or the duration of the war. They were to furnish their own uniforms and, if cavalry, horses, but would be reimbursed for the former and draw forty cents per day for the latter. Otherwise they would be paid the same as regulars. Volunteer officers were to be appointed as provided for in the militia laws of each state. Although there was some difference between states, this normally meant election. Generals and staff officers, however, would be federal appointees. The law further provided that any warships under construction could be completed or others acquired as necessary. The legislation provided $10 million to pay for these war measures.[10]

The law clearly showed its hasty formulation. The year term, while better than the six months suggested by Polk, was too short, although it undoubtedly eased recruiting. The provision for state appointment of officers was undesirable, although there is no assurance that federal selection would have greatly improved the quality of the volunteer officers. It would probably have been better to have enlarged the regular army than supplement it with volunteers, but that was not a possible solution considering the political realities of mid-nineteenth-century America.[11]

Since the Navy already had more large vessels than it could easily man, the completion of vessels on the ways was not pushed except for the nearly completed sloops-of-war *Germantown* and *Albany*. The real need of the Navy, as Commodore David Conner's reports from the Gulf of Mexico stressed, was for small, light-draft craft. Consequently, most of the naval portion of the appropriation went to purchase small steamers, schooners, brigs, and storeships.

The administration began the war with no clear strategy beyond supporting Taylor and initiating operations to seize California. Indeed, Polk and his advisers had an entirely unrealistic view of the war. They expected to win the desired peace without a major military effort. Moreover, they totally discounted the possibility of hostilities with Britain over Oregon. Thomas Hart Benton's analysis was undoubtedly correct:

> [The administration] were men of peace, with the object to be accomplished by means of war; . . . but they wanted no more of it than would answer their purposes. . . . Never were men at the head of a government less imbued with military spirit, or more addicted to intrigue.[12]

At about one o'clock on the afternoon of May 13, President Polk signed the war legislation. Soon afterward Secretary of War William L. Marcy and Major General Winfield Scott called. Although he had strong misgivings, Polk offered the General in Chief command of the army to be raised under the newly signed law. Scott accepted at once and hurried to complete drafting of the plan for the distribution of volunteers among the states.

Later that afternoon, following Madison's precedent in 1812, the President issued a proclamation announcing Congress' action and calling on all citizens to support the war effort. Much more important was the circular that Secretary of State James Buchanan prepared for dispatch to American diplomatic representatives abroad. When the Secretary of State brought his draft before the cabinet that evening, Polk was horrified to find that it contained a nonterritorial aggrandizement statement and a specific disclaimer about California. Buchanan defended the draft by arguing that Britain and France would intervene if the United States did not expressly deny California was a war aim. To Polk's relief the rest of the cabinet stood firm and Buchanan backed down.[13] It was the first crack in a split between the President and his Secretary of State over territorial war aims which would widen as Buchanan grew more interested in the 1848 presidential nomination.

During the evening of the fourteenth the President, Marcy, and Scott again conferred. Polk "gave it as my opinion that the first movement should be to march a competent force into the Northern Provinces" of Mexico, with which the two advisers concurred. In addition the three men decided to send a 2,000-man column against Santa Fe and a 4,000-man column toward Chihuahua. The main body under Scott would occupy the lower Rio Grande and the Mexican interior. This plan required about 20,000 men who were apportioned among Alabama, Arkansas, Georgia, Illinois, Indiana, Kentucky, Mississippi, Missouri, Ohio, Tennessee, and Texas (see Table 1). About 25,000 additional infantry were to be enrolled in the northeastern states but not called into service until later.

At one point in the discussion Scott pointed out that the volunteers would not reach the Rio Grande in any numbers before the first week in August, which coincided with the middle of the rainy season. Even then, he reminded the others, the hooves of their horses and mules would not yet be hardened enough for heavy service. Therefore he recommended that the troops train in the United States before moving to the theater of operations in mid-September. That argument may have been sound militarily but it was poor politics. It did not improve Scott's standing with Polk, who observed that the General in Chief "did not impress me favorably as a military man. He has had experience in his profession but I thought was rather scientific and visionary in his views."[14]

On May 15 Scott issued the instructions necessary to ensure that the arms, supplies, and transportation required by the volunteers were provided. Marcy began issuing the individual requisitions to the states at the same time. The general procedure was for each governor to direct his militia officers or the sheriff to assemble the local military units and call for volunteers. The volunteers were then shipped to the state rendezvous point and organized into units which were then enrolled. Once the regiment was organized and its officers elected,

TABLE 1
Allotment of Troops Called May–July 1846

| STATE | FOOT | | | MOUNTED |
	REGIMENT	BATTALION	COMPANY	REGIMENT
Alabama	1			
Arkansas		1		1
District of Columbia			6	
Florida			1	
Georgia	1			
Illinois	4			
Indiana	3			
Iowa		1[a]	1	
Kentucky	2			1
Mississippi	1			
Missouri	1[b]	1		2
Ohio	3			
Tennessee	2			1
Texas		1		1
Wisconsin			1	

[a] The Mormon battalion.
[b] The St. Louis legion, which served only until August 25, 1846.

the federal mustering officer would accept them into service. The cost of transportation from the points of assembly to the rendezvous had to be supplied from local public, or private, sources because Congress had neglected to appropriate money to pay for it. That oversight would cause much bad feeling between those who bore the expense and the federal government before the summer was over. Another difficulty arose in some of the states where the militia systems had atrophied: long-forgotten laws had to be unearthed in order to determine how officers were elected or appointed.

The regiments had a standardized organization which paralleled that of their regular counterparts with the exception that company sizes were smaller, eighty in foot companies and sixty-four in mounted ones. The actual size of the volunteer regiments ranged from the 691-man, eight-company 2d Tennessee to the 1,182 man, fourteen-company Virginia Regiment of 1847.

Unfortunately, Marcy's call repeated the wording of the May 13 law. The effect was to allow each volunteer to elect to be discharged at the end of twelve months if he so chose. Most did.[15]

In keeping with his desire for a quick military campaign, Polk apparently expected Scott to hasten to lead the freshly raised 20,000 men into Mexico to force an early peace. That such a plan was impossible to execute did not occur to the President, despite Scott's efforts to introduce reality. Polk was imbued with one of the great fallacies of nineteenth-century American political life: the militia myth, which held that in times of peril hordes of gallant young Americans would spring to the colors and decisively whip any army arrogant enough to confront them. That an untrained soldier, no matter what his nationality, was no match for a trained one was a lesson that the United States steadfastly refused to learn.

Winfield Scott without question was the ablest American soldier to appear in America between Washington and Sherman. He was a man of monumental abilities with shortcomings nearly to scale. One of the latter was his inability to understand the political realities under which his civilian superiors lived. He did not recognize the political necessity for some form of immediate military action nor the necessity of using the short-term, six-month volunteers called out by Taylor. Since he considered that it was impossible to start any campaign on the Rio Grande earlier than mid-September and did not wish to supersede Taylor until large numbers of the new troops had arrived, he saw no reason to rush his departure.[16] Moreover, much of the management of the War Department fell on his shoulders, since Marcy was a poor administrator. Polk so distrusted Scott that he interpreted the delay as a political maneuver to embarrass the administration and further Scott's ambitions for the Whig presidential nomination in 1848. This was not so but, had it been, the results would have been no worse, for Scott distrusted the President as much as Polk distrusted Scott.

Almost as soon as Scott was named to command the new volunteer army, the selection came under heavy fire from western and southwestern Democrats because of its political implications. This caused Polk to have second thoughts about the selection, but he could find no excuse to withdraw it. Scott gave him that opportunity. During May 19 Marcy had sought congressional authorization to appoint a major general from civilian life to command the volunteers. This would also permit the administration to retire Scott at the close of hostilities by retaining the new general as senior officer of the peace establishment. Scott learned of the move on the twentieth. He "smelt the rat" and told Marcy he "saw the double trick." The Secretary in turn taxed the General about his dilatoriness in leaving for the front. The attack was unfair, for Scott had been working fifteen to eighteen hours a day handling the administrative details of the mobilization. In white heat he wrote a letter to Marcy complaining of the pressure to leave Washington precipitously, pointing out "that I do not desire to place myself in the most perilous of all positions;—*a fire upon my rear, from Washington, and the fire, in front, from the Mexicans.*" The timing could not have been worse. That very morning the President had seen a letter written by Scott in February complaining that "The proposed [Regiment of Mounted] rifle men are intended by western men to give commissions or rather *pay* to western democrats. Not an eastern man, not a graduate of the Military Academy and certainly not a *Whig* would obtain a place under such proscriptive circumstances or prospects." This was the excuse Polk wanted. On the twenty-fifth Marcy sent the General a long, stiff, well-argued letter informing him that he would not be sent to the front. Francis, the War Department messenger, delivered the bombshell as Scott "sat down to take a hasty plate of soup" at 6:00 P.M. Scott hastened to argue that he had not attacked the President but some of his political advisers and that he had no quarrel with Marcy, but to no avail.[17]

The bill for the additional generals cleared the Senate under Benton's management on May 29. It provided for a pair of new regular major generals and four new brigadiers as well as authorizing the calling up of militia generals to command the volunteers. The Whigs in the House, who suspected that the second major generalcy would go to Benton, cut the number of regulars to one major and two brigadier generals.[18] The regular commissions went to Taylor and Colonels Stephen Watts Kearney and David E. Twiggs. The militia generals were to command the brigades and divisions into which the volunteers had been organized.

To command the 1st Division of Volunteers, composed of those from Kentucky, Ohio, and Indiana, Polk chose a Kentucky lawyer-politician, William Orlando Butler. He had served in the War of 1812 on both the Ohio and the New Orleans fronts. After the war he continued on Andrew Jackson's staff but resigned from the army in 1817. Returning to his native state, Butler became one of its leading Democratic politicians, serving two terms in Congress and losing the governorship in 1844 by less than 5,000 votes. A very personable and well-liked individual, he demonstrated more than a modicum of military ability, although his active service was limited by a painful wound which he received at Monterrey.[19]

Troops from Illinois, Tennessee, Georgia, Alabama, and Mississippi composed the 2d Division, whose commander was the fifty-four-year-old, Irish-born, Pennsylvania Democrat Robert Patterson. Like Butler he had served in the War of 1812 and had left the army following it. He made a considerable fortune as a commission merchant and served as a major general in the state's militia. An overly cautious leader, he proved to be a satisfactory subordinate commander. In Mexico, as during the Civil War, however, his performance as an independent commander was less satisfactory.[20]

The six new brigadier generals appointed from civilian life varied widely in quality. Probably the best was John A. Quitman, a New York native who had settled in Mississippi and had long been the most respected of her militia officers. Another good selection was the Irish-born head of the land office, James Shields of Illinois, who, despite a near fatal wound at Cerro Gordo, achieved a reputation as one of the best volunteer officers in the army. Perhaps the most colorful of the brigadiers was the Hoosier Joseph Lane, an energetic, courageous, and shrewd backwoods lawyer who had a flair for successful partisan warfare. Potentially one of the most promising of the civilian generals was the able and popular Ohio Democratic Congressman, Thomas L. Hamer. His sudden death in December 1846 caused Zachary Taylor to lament, "I have lost the balance wheel of my volunteer army." The Kentuckian Thomas Marshall is the only one of the brigadiers without entry in the *Dictionary of American Biography*, although he stayed in service after the 1846 volunteers went home. Nearly every historian, including this one, has concluded that to say of Gideon J. Pillow that he was the President's law partner was to sum up his military talents.[21]

Scott reopened the question of his field command in mid-September with the observation that the troops were now collecting on the Rio Grande. That merely earned him a one-sentence reply refusing the coveted order.[22]

Despite the outbreak of fighting, Consul John Black remained at his post in Mexico City. There on the evening of May 19 an American confidant recounted a conversation that he had held with a member of the Mexican cabinet to the effect that Mexico would be willing to receive an *ad hoc* minister to settle Texas and other questions. The proposal for the resumption of negotiations, however, would have to come from the United States. Black, whose fingers still smarted from their singeing over the Slidell mission, asked that the proposal be put into writing.[23] While nothing directly came from the approach, it served to fan the hopes in Washington that negotiations could be reinstituted.

The cabinet for the first time discussed territorial war aims at its

June 30 meeting. Their talk delineated the cleavage between Buchanan and Polk. The Secretary of State wished to settle for a line running up the Rio Grande to El Paso and then following the 32nd parallel to the Pacific. He argued that annexation of land below that line would be politically unpalatable to the North because of its potential development into slave territory. Secretary of the Treasury Walker, the cabinet's most outspoken exponent of expansion, wished to run the boundary west of El Paso along the 26th parallel. Although Polk favored Walker's proposal, he was willing to accept the 32° line provided California and New Mexico also passed into American hands.[24]

As if in response, President Paredes reminded the Mexican Congress when it met on June 6 that the time had come to declare war on the invader. He got, instead, authorization to repel the invader. Paredes formally proclaimed the defensive war on July 9 and announced that the clergy would supply $1 million to help pay for it. He genuinely desired to rescue Mexico's national honor, yet he failed to raise significant additional funds or arouse strong support for the war effort among the masses. The Mexican President hoped in vain for British intervention and counted on strong assistance from the monarchists, only to find that they commanded little following.[25] An indication of the lack of unanimity in Mexican support of the war was Commodore Conner's mid-July report that he had confirmation from Consul Black of Mexican willingness to receive an American proposal for negotiations.[26]

Coincident with the reports of increased Mexican willingness to negotiate, the administration opened secret negotiations with Santa Anna. Remembering Colonel Atocha's earlier statement attesting to the willingness of Santa Anna to negotiate and reading the reports of Consul Robert B. Campbell in Havana, Polk decided to open direct negotiations with the dethroned Mexican dictator. The agent was John Slidell's brother, Alexander Slidell Mackenzie,[27] who went to Havana ostensibly to check on privateers. On July 6-7 Mackenzie held two conversations with Santa Anna. In the second of these he informed the Mexican of orders to permit him to pass the blockade. Mackenzie also relayed Polk's proposal that the United States would suspend all active operations except the blockade whenever Santa Anna, having regained power, announced a willingness to negotiate. The American peace terms would be: no indemnity; settlement of the spoilation claims; United States purchase of the disputed territory and New Mexico. Santa Anna responded with a document stating his hopes for peace and his readiness to negotiate. He also offered several good suggestions for American strategy, notably the seizure of Saltillo and Tampico and the suggestion that Veracruz could be taken by landing below it and then investing the town. In the course of the three-hour meeting, Santa Anna told Mackenzie that on returning to power he would govern in the interests of the masses, reduce the power and wealth of the clergy, and embrace free trade. He could scarcely have chosen sentiments which would have been more warmly welcomed. They did not, however, prevent Polk from complaining that Mackenzie had exceeded his authority by writing out and showing the American terms to Santa Anna.[28]

American historians frequently accuse Santa Anna of duplicity, since his actions upon returning to power showed little indication of a peaceful intent. While it would not have been out of character for the Mexican to have promised nearly anything to facilitate his return to power, it may well be that the pressure of events after his return prevented his following the course which he had in mind.[29]

Black's intimation of Mexican willingness to negotiate reinforced this effort to reach an agreement with Santa Anna. If Black's information proved correct, negotiations could start either before or soon after the return of Santa Anna to power. Therefore, on July 27 Buchanan sent a note to Mexico City proposing negotiations either there or in Washington.[30]

Six days after Buchanan dispatched his negotiation proposal, Mackenzie's report reached the President. Polk seized the opportunity to send the Senate a copy of Buchanan's "peace overture" in a confidential message suggesting that a fair price be paid for a boundary including the Rio Grande, New Mexico, California, and possibly some land south of them. He asked for an advance appropriation of unspecified amount, which Buchanan in his testimony before the Foreign Relations Committee indicated was $2 million. The Senate was inclined to cooperate and in a secret session on August 6 agreed to the reopening of negotiations and to the appropriation by a 43 to 2 vote. The Whigs, as a price for their support, insisted upon the President sending a similar confidential message to the House. Polk was reluctant. He feared the resultant publicity. He tried to circumvent the requirement by having Buchanan send confidential letters to the chairmen of the Senate Finance and House Ways and Means Committees but this did not satisfy his opponents.[31]

In actuality the background against which Polk operated as far as Congress was concerned was not nearly as promising as the foregoing would indicate. The Democrats in late July controlled the 29th Congress 30 to 25 in the Senate and 142 to 74 in the House. The administration used those majorities to pass a pair of acts during the summer of 1846 which alienated a broad segment of the manufacturing and banking communities, particularly in the Northeast. The first reduced the wall of tariff protection around many manufacturers and the second, by establishing an independent treasury system, threatened many bankers with a withdrawal of the federal funds they had on deposit. A third insult to local pride, particularly in the strongly Whig Northeast, appeared to be brewing by midsummer when it became clear that Polk was prepared to veto the Rivers and Harbors appropriation bill, so pregnant with local projects. Further complicating the political climate was the unique situation created by the admission of Texas and Florida in 1845: for the first time since the founding of the country the South had a four-seat majority in the Senate.

Conditions were right for a revolt and one soon simmered in Washington's humid heat. The spark was Polk's open request on August 8 for money to assist the peace negotiations. The heretofore secret figure of $2 million proved to many that the President anticipated securing additional ex-Mexican territory. This they interpreted to mean more slave states and a continued southern congressional domination. They did so in the face of an apparent general recognition that most of the territory to be secured from Mexico would be unsuitable for slavery.[32]

When the House adjourned for dinner after hearing the President's message, a small group of northern Democrats met. All feared the impact of the legislation on their constituents. At about seven o'clock that evening David Wilmot of Pennsylvania offered their solution. It was an amendment to the appropriation bill which provided that "neither slavery nor involuntary servitude shall ever exist in any part of said territory, except for crime whereof the party shall first be duly convicted." The amendment passed the House 83 to 64. In the Senate, however, the bill became snarled in the homeward dash. It was finally talked to death by Senator John Davis, who obtained the floor and refused to surrender it until the session ended later in the day.[33] Polk's insistence on secrecy undoubtedly cost him the appropriation just as the seemingly sectional orientation of his policies gave the antislavery forces their long-sought popular issue in the Wilmot Proviso.

NOTES

For key to abbreviations used in Notes, see page xi.

1. Quaife, *Diary of Polk*, I, 319, 322, 327, 337–38, 375, 383, 384–86.
2. *Ibid.*, 387–89.
3. Coit, *Calhoun*, 440.
4. Richardson, *Messages and Papers of the Presidents*, V, 2287–93.
5. Sellers, *Polk Continentalist*, 416–19; McCormac, *Polk*, 415–16; Quaife, *Diary of Polk*, I, 391–93; *Cong. Globe, 29th Cong., 1st Sess.*, XV, 783–88, 791–804; Dallas to wife, May 13, 1846; Roy F. Nichols, "The Mystery of the Dallas Papers," *Pennsylvania Magazine of History & Biography*, LXXIII (July 1949), 378.
6. Joshua R. Giddings to W. G. Howell, June 8, 1846, CHS.
7. John H. McHenry to John Hardin, May 12, 1846, Hardin Family Papers, CHS.
8. The Brooklyn *Eagle*, May 11, 1846, quoted in Archie P. McDonald (ed.), *The Mexican War* (Lexington, 1969), 47.
9. Herman Melville quoted in Marcus Cunliffe, *Soldiers and Civilians* (Boston, 1968), 69–70.
10. *9 U.S. Stat.*, 9–10. The appropriation was split $7,250,000 to the Army and $2,750,000 to the Navy. Bancroft to Polk, May 15, 1846, Polk Papers.
11. Kriedbery and Henry, *History of Mobilization*, 70–71; Charles A. McCoy, *Polk and the Presidency* (Austin, 1960), 119–20. Two minor acts, however, did enlarge the regular forces. That of May 13 increased the number of privates in a company to 100 men for the duration of the war and the second, two days later, added a 100-man engineer company of sappers, miners, and pontooners. More significant was the authorization on May 19 of a regiment of Mounted Riflemen whose approval had been hanging all spring. *9 U.S. Stat.*, 11–14.
12. Benton, *Thirty Years View*, II, 680.
13. Quaife, *Diary of Polk*, I, 395–99; Richardson, *Messages and Papers of the Presidents*, V, 2320.
14. Quaife, *Diary of Polk*, I, 400–1.
15. Marcy to Govs., May 15–29, 1846, *SWMA*, XXVI, 220–40; Scott to Jesup, Gibson, Towson, Talcott, and Lawson, May 15, 1846, *H. Ex. Doc. 60, 30th Cong., 1st Sess.*, 546–47; Marcy, Memorandum, May 18, June 3, 1846, *AGLR'46*, M-204; M-258; *H. Doc. 42, 29th Cong., 2d Sess.*, 3–5; *S. Ex. Doc. 36, 30th Cong., 1st Sess.*, 28–29, 32–33; Kriedberg and Henry, *History of Mobilization*, 75–76. Normally the selection of officers was left to the state but Marcy intervened directly to secure the appointment of Edward D. Baker, Sterling Price, and Archibald Yell as regimental commanders. In Baker's and Price's cases, Illinois and Missouri were allotted additional regiments to ensure their appointments. Marcy to Gov. Thomas Ford, May 27, to Gov. Thomas A. Drew and Gov. John C. Edwards, June 3, 1846, all in *S. Doc. 439, 29th Cong., 1st Sess.*, 2–4.
16. See Scott's May 18, 1846 letter to Taylor, *H. Ex. Doc. 60, 30th Cong., 1st Sess.*, 446, which sketches the plan and asks for advice. He enlarged upon the plan in a memorandum to Marcy, May 25, 1846, *S. Doc. 378, 29th Cong., 1st Sess.*, 10–12.
17. Scott to Marcy, May 21, 25, Marcy to Scott, May 25, 1846, all in *S. Doc. 378, 29th Cong., 1st Sess.*, 5–9; Scott to R. P. Letcher, June 5, 1846, Mrs. Chapman (Ann Mary Butler) Coleman, *The Life of John J. Crittenden* (2 vols., Philadelphia, 1871), I, 244–47; Quaife, *Diary of Polk*, I, 408–9, 412–16, 419, 421, 425; Scott to W. S. Archer, Feb. 6, 1846, Polk Papers; Winfield Scott, *Memoirs* (New

York, 1864), 384–85; Sellers, *Polk Continentalist*, 439–42; Spencer, *Victor & Spoils*, 155; Smith, *War with Mexico*, I, 198–99.

18. 9 *U.S. Stat.*, 17–18; Sellers, *Polk Continentalist*, 435–37.

19. Ellis Merton Coulter, "William Orlando Butler," *DAB*, III, 371; Francis B. Heitman, *Historical Register and Dictionary of the United States Army* (2 vols., Washington, 1903), I, 270.

20. Robert C. Cotton, "Robert Patterson," *DAB*, XIV, 306; Heitman, *Historical Register*, I, 775.

21. Individual biographies aside from those in *DAB* and the entries in Heitman, *Historical Register* include: John F. H. Claiborne, *Life and Correspondence of John A. Quitman* (2 vols., New York, 1860); William H. Condon, *Life of Major General James Shields* (Chicago, 1900); and Sister M. Margaret Jean Kelly, *The Career of Joseph Lane* (Washington, 1947). See also Daniel J. Ryan, "Ohio in the Mexican War," *Ohio Archaeological and Historical Quarterly*, XXI (April–July 1912), 289; Hazard Stevens, *The Life of Isaac Ingalls Stevens* (2 vols., Boston, 1901), I, 221. The relative rank as established by lot on July 7 was: Marshall, Pillow, Hamer, Lane, Quitman, and Shields. Polk to Pillow, July 7, 1846, *PLPB*, J, 580–81.

22. Scott to Marcy, Sept. 12, Marcy to Scott, Sept. 14, 1846, *H. Ex. Doc. 60, 30th Cong., 1st Sess.*, 372–73.

23. Black to Buchanan, May 21, 1846, *M.C. Cons.*, IX.

24. Quaife, *Diary of Polk*, I, 495–96.

25. Manuel Dublán and José María Lozano, *Legislación Mexicana* (6 vols., México, 1876–77), V, 136; Paredes, Decreto, July 6, 1846, Smith Papers, UTA; Smith, *War with Mexico*, I, 212–17.

26. Conner to Bancroft, July 16, 1846, *HSL*.

27. Mackenzie had adopted the surname of an uncle.

28. Mackenzie to Buchanan, June [*sic*] 7, 1846, Reeves, *American Diplomacy under Taylor and Polk*, 299–305; Mackenzie, Copy of Paper drawn up by Santa Anna, July 7, 1846, filed with Mackenzie to Buchanan, Aug. 15, 1846, Polk Papers; Quaife, *Diary of Polk*, III, 290; Calcott, *Santa Anna*, 231–34; Rives, *U. S. and Mexico*, II, 233–36; Jones, *Santa Anna*, 104–5; Sellers, *Polk Continentalist*, 431; Smith, *War with Mexico*, I, 202, 479.

29. See Hutchinson, "Gómez Farías and the Return of Santa Anna," 187–88.

30. Buchanan to Minister of Foreign Relations, July 27, 1846, Manning, *Diplo. Corres.*, VIII, 193.

31. Polk to Senate, Aug. 4, 1846, Richardson, *Messages and Papers of the Presidents*, V, 2307; Quaife, *Diary of Polk*, II, 75–77; Sellers, *Polk Continentalist*, 431–32; McCormac, *Polk*, 442.

32. For example, see John A. Campbell to Calhoun, Nov. 20, 1847, in J. Franklin Jameson (ed.), "Correspondence of John C. Calhoun," *American Historical Association Annual Report 1899*, (2 vols., Washington, 1900), II, 1140.

33. Polk to House and Senate, Aug. 8, 1846, Richardson, *Messages & Papers of the Presidents*, V, 2309–10; *Cong. Globe, 29th Cong., 1st Sess.*, XV, 1210–13, 1217–21; Charles Buxton Going, *David Wilmot* (New York, 1924), 96–98, 117–41; Chaplin W. Morrison, *Democratic Politics and Sectionalism* (Chapel Hill, 1967), 15–20; Richard R. Stenberg, "The Motivation of the Wilmot Proviso," *Mississippi Valley Historical Review*, XVIII (March 1932), 535–41, argues that Wilmot was merely trying to prove his political independence.

6: The Monterrey Campaign

A FTER RESACA DE LA PALMA, Zachary Taylor's army settled down in its familiar campsite at Fort Texas[1] while its commander pondered his next move. Across the river, Arista and his senior officers agreed that they needed at least 7,000 men to defend Matamoros. But beyond that there was no agreement, not even to the conditions under which the town should be abandoned. Following the meeting Arista proposed, and Taylor accepted, an exchange of prisoners. Thus Thornton and his command were exchanged for the men taken at Resaca de la Palma, except for General Díaz de la Vega and his staff.[2] On May 11 Taylor rode to Point Isabel to confer with Commodore Conner. What transpired was comic opera. Taylor, wishing to impress Conner, one of the dandies of the naval service, wore his uniform. It was one of the few times in the entire campaign that he did so. Conner, in deference to Taylor's aversion to uniforms, wore civilian clothes. After the appropriate apologies the two men did agree on a joint operation to cross the Rio Grande near the hamlet of Barita.[3]

The expedition grew out of rumors that Mexican troops were massing there. Lieutenant Colonel Henry Wilson, with a battalion of the 1st Infantry and two companies of Louisiana volunteers, seized the town without any assistance on the seventeenth when heavy seas kept the supporting Navy party under Captain John H. Aulick out of the river. The sailors arrived the following day and spent forty-eight hours at Barita before returning to their ships. On the twenty-second two regiments of Louisiana volunteers under Brigadier General Persifor F. Smith reinforced Wilson's garrison.[4]

The main American crossing took place at Matamoros. It was delayed by a shortage of boats caused primarily by Taylor's lack of foresight, although he naturally preferred to blame the Quartermaster Department. He set the crossing for 1:30 P.M. on May 17.[5]

At noon that day, while Taylor checked the potential crossing points, Arista proposed an armistice to await the outcome of negotiations he reported under way in Mexico City. Taylor, who considered the proposition a ruse to gain time for an evacuation, refused. Arista then offered to surrender all public property, including ammunition, provided Taylor not occupy Matamoros. The American responded: "These are my terms: The city must capitulate; all property must be surrendered; then and only then may the Mexican army march out and retire." Although Arista promised a reply by three o'clock that afternoon, he used the time to evacuate.[6]

The Mexicans moved about ten miles upriver where they threw five cannon and other equipment into the river and abandoned the sick and wounded, along with most of the baggage. From there the force struggled southward for eleven days before reaching Linares on the twenty-eighth. Alternately roasted by parching heat and chilled by teeth-chattering cold, they were plagued by a scarcity of water, food, and medicine. Heavy rains turned the road into a quagmire, while nearly a thousand wives, families, and camp followers added immeasurably to the column's difficulties. Only 2,638 men still answered the roll when the force reached its destination.[7] In early June Arista transferred the command to Mejía, who led the army to Monterrey.[8]

Taylor postponed his crossing until the morning of May 18 because of the discussions with Arista. The light companies then embarked on the few boats which had been gathered or built. They rowed across the river about two miles above Matamoros. They were followed by the dragoons, Walker's Rangers, the 5th Infantry, and Ridgely's battery. White-clad city officials on white horses reported the evacuation and asked for terms. Taylor assured them that private persons and property would be safe, as would the women. He promised to keep Mexican civil laws in effect. The ferries were quickly manned and hauled the bulk of the army across. Thus the United States Army for the first time since Andrew Jackson's invasion of Florida in 1818 found itself in control of foreign territory. Taylor set up his headquarters in the new American camp just outside the town.

During the twenty-second Lieutenant Colonel John Garland, who had pursued the retreating Mexicans, returned to Matamoros with twenty-two prisoners. His small force of dragoons and Texas Rangers had clashed with Arista's rearguard twenty-seven miles south of Matamoros. Each side lost two men killed.[9]

Matamoros became the light which attracted thousands of short-term volunteers. They arrived with no equipment, two left feet, and an innate resistance to discipline. Since the initial units were six-month men called out by Taylor and Gaines, they rendered scant service. The men slept, ate, drilled, held target practice, and spent their too extensive spare time drinking, training donkeys, attending church, monte parlors, or the theaters. One member of a theatrical company which played in Matamoros remembered the audience as "the most motley that ever filled a theater."[10]

The discipline problems with the volunteers were enormous. Their officers could not control them, which made it impossible to halt the plundering of local civilians. Before his men crossed the Rio Grande, Taylor issued a general order threatening courts-martial and discharge for men caught plundering. It had little effect. There were numerous incidents, some involving whole units. The most serious was a riot which erupted among Georgia troops on the last day of August. When Colonel Edward D. Baker and a detachment of the 4th Illinois attempted to quell it, a donnybrook resulted in which one man was killed and several wounded, two fatally. Perhaps the best explanation of the behavior of the volunteers was offered by the *Niles Register*: "The graceless and lawless spirits, being the most difficult to control, join the ranks and carry with them their lawless propensities, as a matter of course."[11]

Since the volunteers knew or cared little about camp sanitation and possessed limited medical supplies or knowledge, sickness was rampant. At the end of July the 900-man Georgia Regiment averaged 127 to 160 men on the sick list. No wonder one professional soldier concluded that a third of the volunteers were sick and the remaining two thirds "not worth a straw."[12]

As the volunteers arrived, Taylor placed them in camps at Point Isabel and along the Rio Grande. The largest was at the north end of Brazos Island, that low-lying sand spit which formed the southern side of the Brazos Santiago. The most infamous one was a patch of dust on the north side of the Rio Grande, between Barita and Fort Brown, known as Camp Belknap. A new supply depot arose at the mouth of the river. There the oceangoing freighters unloaded their cargoes for transshipment upstream on river steamers. This was faster and more efficient than having the relatively deep-draft ocean schooners and brigs struggle across the bar and up the narrow, winding channel to Barita or Matamoros.

The problem of maintaining a satisfactory fleet of river steamers plagued Major Charles Thomas, the Depot Quartermaster at Point Isabel, all summer. As early as May 15 he asked for one or two moderate-sized craft. On the twenty-fourth Taylor raised this requisition to four. Lieutenant Colonel Thomas F. Hunt, the Quartermaster at New Orleans, asked his superiors in Washington for permission to purchase twice the number. By mid-June vessels began moving to Texas, and by July 23 a full dozen craft churned their way through the coffee-colored water of the Great River.

The shortage of wagons which hobbled the movement from Corpus Christi continued to plague the army. As soon as war was declared, Quartermaster General Jesup ordered 700 wagons, but few suitable ones could be acquired. As a result only a handful reached Point Isabel before August. Despite the orders for wagons both Jesup and the President questioned Taylor's reliance on them. They suspected that pack trains were better suited to Mexican terrain. But, as Jesup feelingly complained, Taylor would not even comment on which was the best transportation system. Taylor's failure to provide the information led Polk to the conclusion that Old Rough and Ready "is not the man for the command of the army."

Nearly every contemporary account by a soldier in the field complained of the poor logistic support, but the responsibility is diffused and difficult to assign. The peacetime bureaucracy of the supply departments with their built-in checks on waste and embezzlement clearly did not have the capacity for the rapid expansion called for by wartime conditions. On the other hand, much of the difficulty arose from the field commanders' failure to anticipate their requirements or to provide advance information of their plans. Even so, the support rendered throughout the war was exceptional compared with earlier American experience.[13] The problems were not limited to the army. The navy's supply bureaus faced the same complaints and the same lack of logistic concern among the distant commanders.

An entirely different difficulty faced by Taylor and other American commanders was the intense anti-Catholicism of many of the volunteers. They were products of a militantly Protestant culture which still viewed Catholicism as a misdirected and misbegotten Christian heresy. Although the regulars included a significant number of Catholic enlisted men, the volunteers did not. This strengthened the tendency to ignore the traditional rights and privileges of the church in a Catholic country as well as increase the harassing of that church. Some of the volunteers' acts, like the stabling of horses in the Shrine of San Francisco in Monterrey, so upset the Mexicans that they still merit mention in modern Mexican works.[14]

The American authorities, fearing a Mexican campaign of religious propaganda might turn the conflict into a holy war, mounted a well-conceived campaign to offset the possibility. Polk approached Bishops John Hughes of New York, Michael Portier of Mobile, and Peter R. Kendrick of St. Louis for help in securing some Catholic priests to accompany the American columns moving into Mexico. The prelates turned the problem over to the head of Georgetown College, Rev. Peter Verhaegen. He recommended two fellow Jesuits, Revs. John McElroy and Antony Rey.

Since there were no chaplain vacancies to which they could be appointed, they joined Taylor's army as civilians, although he was directed to treat them as chaplains. Both men accompanied the army during the Monterrey campaign. Father McElroy remained with the army until mid-1847 when he returned home because of ill-health. Father Rey left Monterrey on January 15, 1847, for Matamoros, but near Marín he was murdered by bandits. Bishop Kendrick was supposed to provide a chaplain for the Santa Fe column, but for reasons unknown he never appeared.[15]

Another step in the religious campaign was a proclamation drawn up in Washington for issuance by Taylor. It promised the Mexicans: "Your religion, your altars, and churches, the property of your churches and citizens, the emblems of your faith and its ministers, shall be protected and remain inviolate." Moreover, the Mexicans were reminded, "Hundreds of our army, and hundreds of thousands of our people are members of the Catholic Church. . . ."[16]

On May 21, despite his logistic uncertainties, Taylor requested instructions as to operations after the projected attack on Monterrey. A week later Marcy issued the orders which were effectively the answer: "Prosecute the war with vigor, in the manner you deem most effective." This would have been a good order under normal circumstances, since the administration as yet had no strategic plan and Taylor was closer to the sources of intelligence. Unfortunately, however, the directive overlooked both Taylor's deficiencies as a strategist and his lack of knowledge of the resources to be made available to him.

On June 8 Marcy reported 20,000 reinforcements were enroute

and informed Taylor that he would continue in command of the operations in northern Mexico, including the force being gathered at San Antonio for an expedition to Chihuahua. After suggesting that Monterrey be taken, as Taylor already planned, Marcy defined the aim of operations as to "dispose the enemy to desire an end to the war . . . in the shortest space of time practicable." Would this be best accomplished, he inquired, by an attack on Mexico City or by operations in northern Mexico? Were supplies available locally for an advance inland? What should the proportion of infantry, artillery, and cavalry be in such a force? This was as much direction as Washington was willing to give, although Taylor was authorized to conclude an armistice if a "sufficiently formal and sincere" proposal for peace negotiations reached him.[17]

Because of the long supply line involved, Taylor recommended against an advance on Mexico City from the Rio Grande. Advances on Monterrey and Chihuahua, he believed, might separate the northern provinces from the rest of Mexico. These recommendations crossed a long letter from Marcy which established the political strategy to be followed in the invaded states. It had been worked out in a series of conferences between Marcy, Polk, and Benton. It began with a section, chiefly the work of Benton, which proposed sending agents into the Mexican armies in an effort to persuade the military leaders to negotiate. At the same time all other discordant factions among the Mexicans were to be cultivated. Polk added a section stressing the desirability of promoting independence movements among the provinces. The letter also requested that Taylor advise whether Tampico or Veracruz would make the better base for an invasion of the interior, but it divulged no plans for operations beyond the already authorized one toward Monterrey and Chihuahua.[18]

Taylor's response to the suggestion of subverting the Mexican army was unenthusiastic, since his contact with the Mexican commanders was limited and had proven to be a poor source of intelligence. It was too early, in his opinion, to judge the possibilities of separatist movements, but he had found little support for them. His strategic suggestions scarcely went beyond those he had submitted in early July. If he could collect 10,000 men at Saltillo fifty miles southwest of Monterrey, he might advance against San Luis Potosí, "and I doubt not [it] would speedily bring proposals for peace." If logistics prevented his advance beyond Monterrey, Taylor recommended occupation of the frontier departments and a landing at Veracruz. The Tampico–Mexico City route, he reported, was impractical.[19]

Since he did not have sufficient shipping to send them upriver for the projected Monterrey expedition, the 5,000 short-term volunteers were a liability to Taylor. They complicated his difficult logistic situation and undercut his efforts to develop good relations with the local Mexicans. Therefore he decided to send home those who could not extend their enlistments to a full year and in late July discharged the Louisiana Brigade, the St. Louis Legion, and some Alabama companies. The handful of Louisianians who agreed to stay formed a company under Captain Albert C. Blanchard which they called the Phoenix Company, since it had arisen from the ashes of the brigade. In August a dispute over the length of service caused the Regiment of Texas Riflemen commanded by Colonel Albert Sidney Johnston to leave the army on the eve of the Monterrey campaign. Only about 150 men remained with the army, as did Johnston who became the inspector general of Major General William O. Butler's division of volunteers.[20]

Taylor's first move in the Monterrey campaign developed from a request for assistance. During June 1 the Alcalde of Reynosa, a rather pretty and well-situated settlement of 1,000, requested that Taylor send a garrison to protect his town against Mexican stragglers and other marauders. This Lieutenant Colonel Wilson did on June 10 with four companies of infantry, a section of artillery, and a company of Texas Rangers.[21] Other movements followed as soon as transportation could be arranged. Taylor's plans were to move his force by steamboat upstream to Camargo, establish a depot there, and then advance southward against Monterrey.[22] The plan was sensible, although there is no evidence that Taylor ever considered the practicality of using the river and clearly had no conception of the number of steamers necessary to put the move into effect.

While waiting for the logistics snarl to clear, Taylor in mid-June sent Captain Ben McCulloch and his Ranger company to reconnoiter the Linares route as a possible alternative to the Camargo one. At Reynosa on July 4 the Rangers contributed to the lore of the campaign by consuming two horse buckets of whiskey and eating a feast of pigs and chickens "accidentally killed while firing in honor of the day."[23]

The move to Camargo started at 4:00 P.M. on Monday, July 6, when three companies of the 7th Infantry under Captain Dixon S. Miles embarked on the steamer *Enterprise* at Matamoros. They were delayed for three days at Reynosa by mechanical troubles which forced transfer of a part of the command to another steamer but reached Camargo at 8:50 on the morning of the fourteenth. The rest of the regiment arrived the next day, followed shortly by General Worth and the 5th Infantry.[24]

Taylor now had seven steamers in use, and as their pilots began to master the whims of the river the movement began to gather speed. Nevertheless it was not easy. The Rio Grande valley was still in the grip of the rainy season, which brought flooded land, impassable roads, and a river with such strong currents and uncertain channels as to be nearly unnavigable. Despite the obstacles the 1st Brigade began its move on July 19. Most of the men experienced the frightening ride upstream in the nearly uncontrollable steamers, but the train and artillery with escorting infantry companies marched overland. The 3d Brigade followed as transportation became available. Taylor's concentration on moving the regulars to Camargo forced him temporarily to leave behind such volunteer regiments as the Mississippi Rifles commanded by his son-in-law, Colonel Jefferson Davis. Not until the end of July did Taylor order any volunteer regiments to Camargo. The remainder guarded the supply line.[25]

In early August McCulloch's Rangers checked the road to China, one of the alternative routes to Monterrey, but missed a group of about 115 irregulars who were their main quarry. During the middle of the month McCulloch's men escorted Captain James Duncan on a reconnaissance of the road to Mier and Cerralvo. Enroute they passed through Punta Aguada, which was reputedly General Canales's headquarters. When the Americans entered they discovered not the partisan leader but a fandango in process. Duncan, it was reported, entered the hall with the Texans at his back, ordered the music to continue, led off the next dance with the prettiest girl in the room, and then bade the Mexicans *adios* and rode off to Cerralvo.[26]

Taylor and his staff reached Camargo on August 8. The new headquarters of the Army of Occupation was not an imposing sight. The town of 3,000 persons squatted on the right bank of the San Juan River about three miles above its confluence with the Rio Grande. Many of its houses of unburnt brick were in ruins as the result of a spring freshet. In the words of one American it was simply "a dilapidated-looking town," and to another "the hottest and dustiest place I have ever seen." The complaints were reasonable. The temperature reached as high as 112° and a breeze was nearly unknown, although bugs, ants, tarantulas, scorpions, and frogs were rampant. So was illness among the volunteers, who still had to learn the rudiments of camp sanitation and discipline.[27] Whether Camargo's advantages as a supply point overshadowed its disadvantages is a moot point. In 1846 it had better communications with Monterrey than Mier or Reynosa, although the latter were in more healthy locations.

The bulk of the army reached Camargo in the days that followed. It was a hot, wet, and uncomfortable march for those who came overland and not appreciably better for those who rode the panting steamers from Matamoros. While waiting for his forces to gather, Taylor reorganized the army for the forthcoming campaign.

General Worth's 2d Division left for Cerralvo on the nineteenth to establish a supply depot. The march was nearly as unpleasant as that to Camargo. The road, at times scarcely more than a trail, had to be rebuilt. Nevertheless the column completed its sixty-mile march to Cerralvo about noon on August 25. The picturesque town of 1,800 with its low stone houses and fruit trees was a pleasant change from the river settlement. Here Worth awaited the rest of the army. Taylor and his staff reached Cerralvo on September 9 and the last of General Butler's volunteer division arrived four days later. All told the expedition numbered 6,640 officers and men.

Since the army was still short of transport, Taylor shuttled his 1,500 pack mules and 180 wagons between Camargo and Cerralvo to bring up 160,000 rations. One result of the shortage was another severe limitation on baggage allowances. With good sense Taylor assigned responsibility for the train to the able and knowledgeable founder of Corpus Christi, Major Henry L. Kinney.[28]

Into late August Taylor did not expect the Mexicans to fight for Monterrey. Shortly after his arrival at Cerralvo, he received an accurate report on the defenses there. This, along with other indications, led him to revise his expectations.[29] The Mexicans had early recognized the importance of Monterrey in the American scheme of campaign. General Tomás Requena, the second in command of the Mexican forces in the north, left Linares on July 9 with 1,800 survivors of Arista's army to garrison the Nuevo León capital. The rest soon followed, as did additional troops from Mexico City. The latter were delayed by the political uncertainties in the Mexican capital, so the first units did not reach Monterrey until August 29 and some of the intended reinforcements did not arrive in time to join in its defense.[30]

Santa Anna, now in command of the Mexican army, doubted both the wisdom and the practicality of holding the northern city. He suggested that Ampudia, who had taken command there, withdraw his forces to Saltillo. Ampudia disagreed. He sensed the glory of a successful defense, while General Mejía, who commanded the garrison, believed that it would be dishonorable to surrender the city after expending so much time and effort on its fortification. Furthermore, it would be difficult to retake the mountain road from Saltillo once it passed into American control. Ampudia, therefore, decided to continue to hold his advanced position.

Governor Francisco Morales of Nuevo León threw the state's full support behind the defensive preparations. While the reinforcements marched northward, Lieutenant Colonel Mariano Reyes and Captain Luis Robles, two of Mexico's best military engineers, laid out the fortifications. Ampudia contributed a series of patriotic exhortations. One threatened death to anyone caught trading with the Americans, while another offered inducements to American soldiers to desert.[31]

At Cerralvo on September 11 Taylor ordered the resumption of the march to Monterrey. The pioneers marched the following morning to prepare the road for the divisions which followed at one-day intervals starting on the thirteenth. Each man carried eight days' rations and forty rounds of buck and ball ammunition. The preparations for a battle were well taken, since Ampudia had changed his plans. Heeding the advice of Robles he decided to make the initial stand at Marín midway between Monterrey and Cerralvo, falling back to the former if necessary. He had to abandon his plan, however, because most of his subordinates claimed that their men were not capable of marching there. Ampudia then sent a thousand cavalry under Torrejón to harass the advancing column, but they failed to do so. The only skirmish occurred near the hamlet of Ramos on September 14, when the American advance guard, McCulloch and thirty-five Texas Rangers, handily drove off 200 Mexican cavalry. On September 18 Torrejón and his horsemen returned to Monterrey.

The American advance paused at Marín on the fifteenth to allow the whole force to close up and march in a single mass. The column left Marín on September 18. That night the Texas Division joined. The division, which was really no larger than a brigade, consisted of two mounted regiments of short-term volunteers under Major General and Governor J. Pinckney Henderson. At sunrise on the following morning Henderson's horsemen led the army out of its camp.[32]

At about 9:00 A.M., September 19, Taylor and the Texan advance guard rode out onto the plain before Monterrey. Mist still shrouded the spires of the churches and obscured the surrounding heights. As the sun warmed the air, the mass of the city, the bishop's palace atop

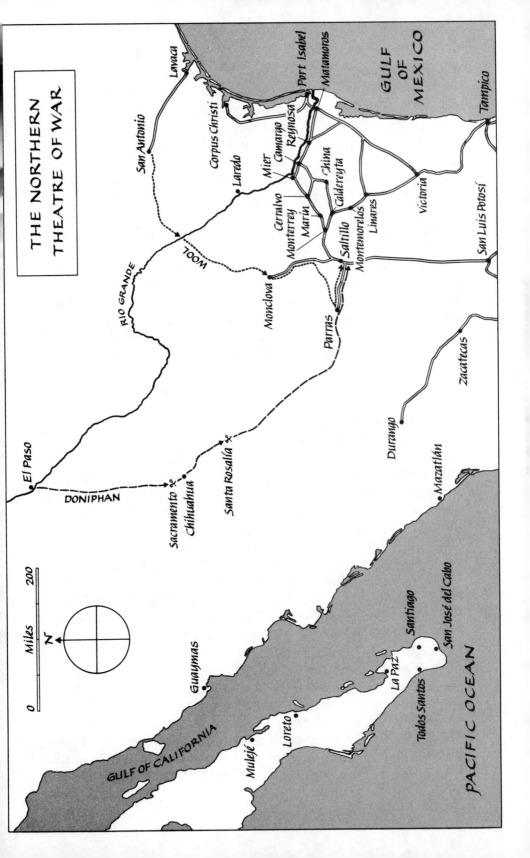

its hill, and the dark walls of the citadel took form. When they had ridden to within about three miles of the citadel, the riders were greeted by the flash and boom of artillery firing and the thud of cannonballs striking the ground nearby. If any hopes had lingered that Monterrey would fall without a fight, they now disappeared. Taylor ordered the army to camp in the Bosque de San Domingo, a lovely grove of oak and pecan trees containing a number of springs inexplicably called Walnut Springs by the Americans.[33]

While the army made camp, a group of engineer officers under Brevet Major Joseph F. K. Mansfield reconnoitered the impressive Mexican defenses. Monterrey, a city of about 10,000 inhabitants, nestled on the north, or left, bank of the Rio Santa Catarina, a tributary of the San Juan, in the shadow of the eastern ramparts of the Sierra Madres, which formed a seeming wall of rugged and forbidding stone along the southern horizon. The only break was the gorge of the Santa Catarina through which passed the road to Saltillo. Towering over the town to the west and east were a pair of sharp, detached peaks known from their configuration as the Bishop's Mitre and Saddle Mountain. In traditional Mexican fashion the city stretched out in a regular pattern from a main plaza and two or three smaller ones to form a rough rectangle slightly more than a mile from east to west and nine squares wide.

About 1,000 yards northward from the city, amid a level plain with well-tilled fields and orchards, stood the citadel, the ruins of an uncompleted cathedral now surrounded by bastioned walls. It mounted thirty guns and was garrisoned by 400 men under Colonel José López Uraga of the 4th Infantry. The fortification, which the Americans called the Black Fort, protected the junction of the roads running to the north and east. The Ojo de Agua Canal skirted the northern side of the town. The Marín road crossed it on a bridge called La Purísima which was guarded by a *tête-de-pont*. Here General Mejía had his headquarters. The position itself was held by Lieutenant Colonel Patricio Gutierrez with 300 infantry from the *Activos* of Aguascalientes (Lieutenant Colonel José Ferro) and Querétaro (Lieutenant Colonel José María Herrera) and batteries. Protecting the northeast corner of the city was a three-gun earthwork named La Tenería because of its proximity to a tanyard. The post was manned by 200 men of the 2d Light Infantry and the Querétaro Battalion under Colonel José María Carrasco. It mounted three guns. On a long low ridge some 500 yards to the southwest stood a smaller fortification, El Fortin del Rincon del Diablo, commanded by Colonel Ignacio Joaquín del Arenal.

West of the town the Saltillo road passed between two hills, Independencia and Federación. Atop the western point of the former, a gourd-shaped, 800-foot-high eminence, stood Fort Libertad. It was a small work manned by fifty or sixty men and contained a pair of light guns. About halfway down the slope toward the city lay the fortified ruins of the Obispado, an abandoned bishop's palace. Here were stationed 200 men and four guns under Lieutenant Colonel Francisco de Berra of the *Activo* of Mexico. Federación on the south side of the road thrust upward only about half as far but hosted two small works, a one-gun redan at its western end and Fort Soldado at its eastern.

The single-story stone houses of the city proper with their flat, parapeted roofs were themselves small fortresses and the straight streets were easily barricaded and offered open fields of fire to the defenders. The temporary magazines established in the cathedral fronting the Plaza Mayor held sufficient ammunition for a long fight. Ampudia had 7,303 men and some forty-two guns to defend the town. These defenders should have been ample to hold as well fortified a position as Monterrey against an army of only 6,000 men ill-equipped with siege guns. The large number of cavalry in Ampudia's force, however, reduced the odds considerably, since they were of little use in city fighting.

Mansfield's reconnaissance confirmed Taylor in his plan of attack. This called for sending Worth's division on a wide sweep to the north and west of the town which would cut Ampudia's supply line to Saltillo. With his opponent isolated, Taylor would execute a double envelopment, Worth from the west and the main body from the east. It was a bold, imaginative plan and so uncharacteristic of Taylor as to suggest it was authored by Bliss. The greatest difficulty, as experience would demonstrate, was the near impossibility of coordinating the two assaults.

About two o'clock on the afternoon of September 20, Worth started his move with his regulars and Colonel John C. Hays's regiment of Texans. Toward sundown, as a diversion, Taylor marched the rest of the army out onto the plain and held them there until after dark. Although the troops probably enjoyed the antics of some of the Texans who rode about dodging cannonballs, the move deceived the Mexicans little if at all. A bombardment opened from a nearby quarry by a pair of 24-pounder howitzers and a 10-inch mortar was no more effective. The Mexicans accurately divined the objective of Worth's column. Ampudia rushed reinforcements to Independencia and sent a large force of cavalry under Torrejón to keep open the supply line.

The soft ground of the cane and grain fields across which Worth's division marched permitted it to advance only the six miles to the Pasqueria road before dark. Since continuing the remaining three miles to the Saltillo road would expose the column to the fire of the Independencia works and a possible night attack from the Mexican cavalry, Worth had his men bivouac. They spent a bitterly cold and rainy night without shelter or fires.

Worth's men arose from the frosty sleep about 6:00 A.M. on the twenty-first and shuffled wearily forward with the Texans screening the advance. Before long they met the advance guard of General Manuel Romero's brigade, about 200 Mexican cavalry from the Jalisco (Lieutenant Colonel Juan Nájera) and Guanajauto (Lieutenant Colonel Mariano Moret) Regiments. The horsemen gallantly charged into the fire of the Texans, who had taken cover behind a fence, and that of Duncan's and Mackall's splendid batteries. Within twenty minutes the American fire had killed Nájera and perhaps thirty others to break up the attack and scatter the Mexican horsemen. Passing through an ineffectual fire from Independencia, the column by 8:15 A.M. had severed the Saltillo road. "The town is ours," Worth wrote to Taylor.

After some uncertainty, Worth decided to attack the redoubt atop the western summit of Federación. The assault force under the able and reliable Captain Charles F. Smith consisted of 300 red-legged infantry and dismounted Texans. They forded the waist-deep Santa Catarina amid a shower of shot about 12:30 P.M. and began working their way up the steep, rock-strewn hillside. Worth, concerned about the disparity in numbers between Smith and the defenders, sent Captain Miles with the 7th Infantry to his support. Scarcely had Miles's command departed than Worth directed Persifor Smith to join the attack with the remaining infantry of the 2d Brigade.

Miles found a direct path to the summit and arrived in time to support C. F. Smith's assault on the redoubt. It fell easily. The fleeing Mexicans abandoned a 9-pounder which was manned by Lieutenant George Deas and a scratch crew. The gunners turned it on Soldado toward which Persifor Smith had turned his attention. Deas's first shot dismantled the gun at Soldado and sent that garrison fleeing also. The dismounted gun was quickly righted by the Americans and with its sister began barking at the Independencia positions. While the assault troops seized Federación, the rest of Worth's force beat off a series of moves by Torrejón's cavalrymen to isolate them.

Before daybreak Taylor dispatched Henderson with May's squadron of dragoons and Colonel George T. Wood's Texas regiment to reinforce Worth but later recalled them. This kept them out of the day's fight. During the early morning Twiggs's and Butler's divisions formed on the plain while Major Mansfield and the engineers reconnoitered the eastern and northern sides of Monterrey. Taylor's intent was to stage a diversionary attack against the former. He told Lieutenant Colonel John Garland, temporarily in command of Twiggs's division:[34]

> Colonel lead the head of your column off to the left, keeping out of reach of the enemy's shot, and if you think (or if you find) you can take any of them little forts down there with the bay'net you better do it—but consult with Major Mansfield. You'll find him down there.

Since the 4th Infantry remained in reserve near the siege battery, Garland's command numbered about 800 men from the 1st and 3d Infantry and the Maryland and District of Columbia Battalion (Lieutenant Colonel William H. Watson).

Garland led the men across broken ground along a route only partially screened from the Mexicans. Even that protection vanished when the troops started cheering Worth's men, who could be seen on the heights to the southwest. This drew the fire of the citadel upon the American's right flank and rear and that of Tenería and the lower fortifications upon their front. Garland, not unreasonably, had interpreted Taylor's order as one for an assault rather than a demonstration. So, after a short conference with Mansfield, he continued the advance. When Mansfield, who had gone to take a closer look at the northeast angle of the town, waved the troops in that direction, Garland veered his line to the right which exposed his left to Tenería's fire. At this the Maryland and District of Columbia Battalion, closest to the Mexicans, broke. Only Colonel Watson and about seventy men remained on the field and continued the advance. Moving forward gallantly through the scathing fire, the division drove into the town but lost its cohesion in the welter of streets and the intense fire from Mexican infantry in and atop the houses. Even after Bragg got some guns implanted within the town, the Americans could make no progress. Garland therefore, on Mansfield's recommendation, withdrew his men.

Meanwhile, at about eight o'clock Captain Electus Backus's company of the 1st Infantry seized the tannery. The company was soon joined by the parts of two other companies. By ten o'clock they had cleared the Mexicans from positions in the rear of Tenería. The fort's open gorge now lay under American guns, but unfortunately Backus's success was unknown to Garland. The American designs on Tenería were clear to Mejía, however, who rushed 100 to 140 men of the 3d Light Infantry and one gun to assist Carrasco.

When Taylor realized that Garland had been stopped, he sent the 4th Infantry, 1st Ohio (Colonel Alexander M. Mitchell), and Brigadier General John A. Quitman's brigade to reinforce the assault. They arrived after Garland's withdrawal. The leading element, three companies of the 4th Infantry, came under such a murderous fire from Tenería that they lost nearly a third of their officers and men before recoiling.

Quitman's brigade, the 1st Tennessee (Colonel William B. Campbell), and the Mississippi Rifles advanced by a route far enough to the east of Garland's to avoid much of the Citadel's fire. They assaulted Tenería directly and carried it at about noon with the assistance of Backus's men. About thirty Mexicans were taken prisoner during the action. Even so, the American casualties were heavy. The Tennesseans took nearly a quarter of all the losses in the battle and ever thereafter referred to themselves as the "Bloody First." The ailing Twiggs shortly arrived to direct the organization of a defense of the newly won position. Under his arrangement, Quitman's and Backus's men held the fort while an improvised artillery detachment under Captain Randolph Ridgely plied its guns upon their former owners.

On learning of the fall of Tenería, the Buckeye regiment returned to the attack, crossed the stream below La Purísima and cut through the city to attack Fort Diablo. Exposed to a fire upon its left and rear by the Mexicans at Purísima and unable to breach Diablo without artillery, the regiment abandoned its attack but not before both General Butler and Colonel Mitchell were wounded. During their withdrawal the Buckeyes beat off an attack by two regiments of cavalry under Brigadier General José María García Conde.[35] Between one and two o'clock Garland's command launched an attack in the same area with no better success. It then withdrew to relieve the Tenería garrison. At dusk Mexican cavalry again appeared but were driven back into the city by American artillery.

Taylor's attack was as poorly executed as any action by American forces during the war outside California. He issued ambiguous orders; committed units piecemeal, without apparent plan or coordination; sent unsupported infantry against artillery; and exposed large masses to the fire of the Mexican forts. The only success was the capture of

Tenería. That resulted from the gallantry of the assault troops and Backus's savvy rather than a good battle plan. The price for Taylor's ineptitude was 394 men killed or wounded.

The night again was cold with a violent rain that intensified the discomfort of Worth's men lying unprotected on the hills above the town and the anguish of the wounded who awaited the creaking, jolting wagons which moved through the battlefield searching for the injured.

Worth's plan for the twenty-third called for a picked force from the Texas Rangers, artillerymen, and 4th and 8th Infantry under Lieutenant Colonel Childs to steal up the slopes of Independencia and carry its western point by a surprise attack. They set out in a cold rain at 3:00 A.M. and groped slowly and quietly through the darkness up the hill. They were within sixty feet of Fort Libertad before the Mexican sentinels discovered them in the predawn light. The Americans then charged and cleared the fifty to sixty defenders in a short hand-to-hand fight. The rays of the rising sun disclosed to the armies below a red-white-and-blue banner flapping on Libertad's flagpole. The Mexicans attempted one limited counterattack before the 5th and 7th Infantry worked into positions to enfilade any force moving from the Obispado. After Captain John Sanders of the Engineers found a practicable path, a 12-pounder howitzer was dismantled and dragged up to Libertad. Manned by gunners from Duncan's battery under Lieutenant John F. Rowland, it soon silenced the artillery at the Obispado. Lieutenant Colonel Berra's orders were to remain on the defensive, but by late afternoon his position had become too critical to permit that. He ordered an attack but it collapsed in the face of the American crossfire. The Mexicans streamed back to the Obispado with the Americans so close on their heels that the two forces cleared the walls together. This so disconcerted the defenders that they abandoned the fortifications without a fight. By late afternoon Worth held firm control of the western approaches to the city.

Taylor staged neither attack nor sortie during the twenty-second although Quitman's brigade replaced Garland's in Tenería. Neither did the Mexicans attempt to retake the lost fort, which perhaps as much as anything indicated Ampudia's state of mind. Toward midnight of September 22–23 the Mexican commander decided to abandon all his outer defenses, except the Citadel, and concentrate his forces in the Plaza Mayor. The troops who had so successfully beaten back the attacks during the twenty-first retired sullenly but quietly. Not until daylight did the Americans at Tenería discover that the

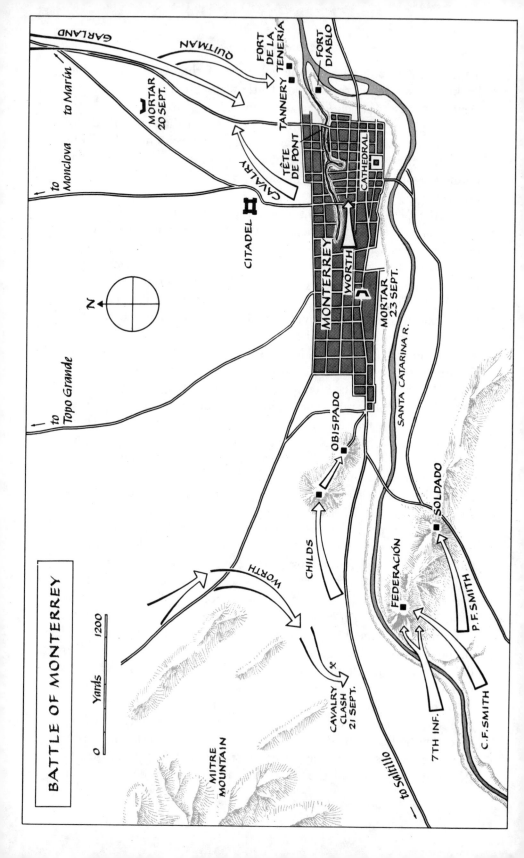

BATTLE OF MONTERREY

Yards

0   1200

MITRE
MOUNTAIN

to Saltillo

CAVALRY
CLASH
21 SEPT.

WORTH

CHILDS

7TH INF.

C.F. SMITH

P.F. SMITH

FEDERACIÓN

OBISPADO

SOLDADO

SANTA CATARINA R.

MONTERREY

WORTH

MORTAR
23 SEPT.

CATHEDRAL

TÊTE
DE PONT

CITADEL

N

to Topo Grande

to Monclova

to Marín

GARLAND

QUITMAN

MORTAR
20 SEPT.

CAVALRY

FORT DE LA
TANNERY TENERÍA

FORT
DIABLO

nearby works had been evacuated. Quitman then began a cautious reentry into the city and by eleven o'clock held the eastern outskirts.

Worth, who had no orders, assumed the firing arising from Quitman's advance to be the signal for a general attack and sent his men to join. At about 2:00 P.M. they started a house-to-house drive. Instead of attempting to sweep the Mexicans from the streets they burrowed from house to house. By eleven o'clock that night they were within one square of the plaza. Further assistance came late in the afternoon when the mortar, which Taylor had sent to Worth, began firing from the Plaza de la Capella (sometimes called the cemetery in American accounts). It threw a shell every twenty minutes toward the plaza.

General Taylor and his staff joined the assault by Quitman's men against the eastern part of the town "perfectly regardless of danger." At 2:00 P.M. Taylor inexplicably[36] directed the men to withdraw even though they were within two squares of their target. Apparently he wished not only to extricate the tired force from the rabbit warren of the town before nightfall brought the possibility of a night counterattack, but to remove them from possible danger from the exploding shells of the mortar as well.

Victory was now clearly within the American grasp. During the evening Governor Morales asked Taylor to permit the noncombatants to leave the city. Ampudia also opened discussions. In an attempt to salvage something he proposed to surrender the city and withdraw with his men and munitions. The proposition reached Taylor at 3:00 A.M. on the twenty-fourth and he countered four hours later with a demand for the surrender of both the city and the army.[37] Ampudia then requested a personal meeting which occurred about one o'clock that afternoon. The Mexican announced that peace commissioners had been received by the new government in Mexico City, but Taylor doubted this since it did not agree with his information. When someone suggested a mixed commission to settle the terms of the capitulation, he agreed. The American members were Generals Worth and Henderson and Colonel Jefferson Davis. Ampudia named Generals José María Ortega and Tomás Requena and Governor Manuel M. Llano.

The American commissioners demanded the surrender of the town, all arms, and public property. The Mexicans, however, insisted on keeping their personal arms, to which the Americans in a spirit of compromise agreed. They also permitted the Mexican force to retain one six-gun field battery. Other arrangements included the immediate surrender of the citadel and the total evacuation of the city within one week. The Mexican forces would retire behind the line Rinconada Pass–Linares–San Fernando de Parras. Taylor agreed not to advance beyond that line for eight weeks or until the armistice was disavowed by either government.

Taylor's motives for concluding the armistice have been widely discussed, as has the justification for it. Undoubtedly the American commander was influenced by the oft-communicated desire of the administration "to win a peace" on the battlefield and believed that an accommodation would further those aims. Indeed, this was essentially the response called for by his instructions. "These terms are liberal," he wrote his son-in-law, "but not considered too much so by all reflecting men . . . considering our situation: besides it was thought it would be judicious to act with magnanimity towards a prostrate foe . . . as their [sic] was a genl wish for peace on the part of the [Mexican] nation."[38] From a purely military standpoint, Taylor could not expect to complete the seizure of the town without heavy additional losses. His army was already much smaller than he believed necessary and clearly could not stand significant additional losses. Moreover, Twiggs's division was badly damaged and scarcely able to resume the fight; Worth's was tired but effective; and Butler's was badly demoralized although capable of limited use. The whole force was short of ammunition and Taylor had no arrangement to restock his units. Moreover, the American commander had no experience in city fighting and clearly lost his self-assurance when involved in it, as can be seen in his unfortunate withdrawal of Quitman's men on the twenty-third.

Nevertheless, the armistice was a mistake on Taylor's part. As badly mauled as his army had been, it was not in much worse shape than Ampudia's and had the psychological advantage which goes with the attacker. But Zachary Taylor was not an aggressive general though he was a very stubborn fighter. He clearly never fully recognized that the moment to attack was when your enemy was as tired as you were. Taylor had his artillery on the surrounding heights and the Mexicans huddled in a gradually shrinking domain. Had the attack continued, the pressure of the civilian authorities upon Ampudia for surrender would have mounted. He had lost the will to fight and would certainly have found his excuse to surrender in that pressure.

The action cost Taylor's force 120 men killed, 368 wounded, and forty-three missing, or about 8.5 percent of his 6,220 effectives. It was a very high price to pay for the Nuevo León capital. Ampudia lost 367 men killed and wounded, or 5.0 percent of his 7,303. He left twenty-three serviceable and two unserviceable pieces of artillery in American hands plus a few muskets, carbines, lances, and 60,000 musket cartridges.[39]

Ampudia's army evacuated Monterrey between September 26 and 28. Despite their bright, clean uniforms, the Mexicans did not impress many of the Americans. One noted that the cavalry was mounted on "miserable little half-starved horses that did not look as if they could carry their riders out of town." He reported that the riders looked little better. When the last of the Mexican soldiers had left, the Americans marched in and ran up the Stars and Stripes to the accompaniment of "Yankee Doodle" and a twenty-eight-gun salute from the Obispado battery.[40]

By September 30 Ampudia had moved his troops along the rough road through the Rinconada Pass and along the Sierra's ribs to Saltillo. There they rested until October 4. Ampudia's intention had been to make Saltillo his base, but its residents refused to permit their town to become another Monterrey, so Ampudia led his men southward to San Luis Potosí. The last unit departed on November 1.[41] The way was now open for Taylor's army to occupy the capital of Coahuila once the armistice was terminated.

The cessation of fighting did not bring with it an end to the killing. The problem of control of the occupation troops was a continuing one throughout the war. Taylor had trouble with the volunteers around Matamoros, as we have noted earlier. One difficulty in bringing the problem under control was the courts-martial's lack of authority to punish troops for offenses which in the United States would be handled by civilian courts. In May General Scott had proposed a law to close that loophole but Congress took no action. On October 8 he drafted a letter for Marcy's signature which established a code based on martial law that would allow military courts to deal with offenses involving civilians and soldiers in Mexico. Unfortunately, the Secretary took no action.

The need for such a court was emphasized in a chilling letter from Taylor. He reported the cold-blooded murder of a Mexican lancer by an American soldier in the streets of Monterrey. Taylor asked for instructions, since there was no court with jurisdiction. Marcy answered on November 25 with the scarcely helpful advice that there was no way to try the man, since the crime was not specifically embraced in the Articles of War and since any conviction would probably not be sustained by an appeals court in the United States. He recommended that the man be sent from the army.[42]

Taylor's problems with uncontrollable troops declined somewhat at the start of October when the two regiments of Texas Mounted Volunteers left. "With their departure we may look for a restoration of quiet and good order in Monterey," wrote Taylor, "for I regret to report that some disgraceful atrocities have been perpetrated by them. . . ." That the improvement was purely relative can be seen from the mid-November complaint of Juan Manuel Ramírez at Camargo that American soldiers were murdering Mexicans with impunity.[43]

Nor should it be concluded that the irritants to good relations between the Army of Occupation and the local inhabitants were solely on the American side. A priest was detected trying to entice Americans to desert; soldiers were assaulted by highwaymen and others, both in the countryside and in the cities. Many of the assaults and even murders which American troops committed were themselves in retaliation for attacks by Mexicans. It would have been difficult for any commander of a force including significant numbers of poorly disciplined volunteers to prevent these collisions, but other commanders, notably Wool and Scott, devised methods of holding incidents to a minimum.

NOTES

For key to abbreviations used in Notes, see page xi.

1. On May 17 it was renamed Fort Brown in honor of its late commander. The post at Point Isabel had become Fort Polk on May 12, 1846. AO, Orders #60, 62, *AOGO*, I.

2. Oficial de infantría, *Campaña contra los americanos*, 22–25; Ramsey, *Other Side*, 57; Roa Bárcena, *Recuerdos*, I, 85; Arista to Taylor, May 10, 1846, *AOLR*, Box 2; Castillo Negrete, *Invasión*, I, 193; Wilcox, *Mexican War*, 69–70; Henry, *Campaign Sketches*, 104.

3. Grant, *Memoirs*, 48; Hamilton, *Taylor*, 192; Capt. John Sanders to Taylor May 10, 1846, *AOLR*, Box 2.

4. AO, SO #64, May 14, 1846, *H. Ex. Doc. 60, 30th Cong., 1st Sess.*, 522; Conner to Aulick, May 18, 1846, *CLB*; Sanders to Bliss, May (15), 1846, *Conner (NY)*; Wilson to Bliss, May 17, 18, Smith to Taylor, May 18, Smith to Bliss, May 22, 1846, all in *AOLR*, Boxes 2-3; *Niles*, LXX (May 30, 1846), 203. Smith's rank was that of a Louisiana volunteer. He became the colonel of the regiment of Mounted Riflemen on May 27 and served throughout the war as a brigade commander.

5. AO, Orders #61, May 15, 1846, *H. Ex. Doc. 60, 30th Cong., 1st Sess.*, 488–89; Taylor to Dr. R. C. Wood, May 19, 1846, William H. Samson (ed.), *Letters of Zachary Taylor from the Battle-Fields of the Mexican War* (Rochester, 1908), 3–5; Doubleday, *Journal of Barbour*, 61–62, 64.

6. Arista to Taylor, May 17, 1846, *H. Ex. Doc. 56, 30th Cong., 1st Sess.*, 396–97; Taylor to AG, May 18, 1846, *H. Ex. Doc. 60, 30th Cong., 1st Sess.*, 297–98; Henry, *Campaign Sketches*, 107; Smith, *War with Mexico*, I, 177–78, Hamilton, *Taylor*, 192–93.

7. Roa Bárcena, *Recuerdos*, I, 89; Valades, *Breve Historia*, 120; Oficial de Infantría,

Campaña contra los Americanos, 29–36; Ramsey, *Other Side*, 58–61; Smith, *War with Mexico*, I, 178.

8. Roa Bárcena, *Recuerdos*, I, 90; Vigil and Robles, *Invasión*, 19; Ramsey, *Other Side*, 61.
9. Huston, *Sinews of War*, 139; Smith, *War with Mexico*, I, 178; Frost, *Mexican War and Its Warriors*, 56–63; Hamilton, *Taylor*, 193–4; Henry, *Campaign Sketches*, 108, 113.
10. *Autobiography of Joseph Jefferson* (New York, 1897), 67, quoted in Hamilton, *Taylor*, 194–95.
11. AO, Order #62, May 17, 1846, *H. Ex. Doc. 60, 30th Cong., 1st Sess.*, 489; *Niles*, LXX (July 25, 1846), 326.
12. Kenly, *Memoirs*, 47–48; *Niles*, LXXI (Sept. 12, Oct. 10, 1846), 21, 88; Wilbur G. Kurtz, Jr., "The First Regiment of Georgia Volunteers in the Mexican War," *The Georgia Historical Quarterly*, XXVII (Dec. 1943), 310, 316–17; Blair, *Baker*, 34–35. Captain John McMahon was later cashiered, probably unfairly, for his part in the riot. AO, Orders #132, Oct. 17, 1846, *AOGO*, I; Edwin P. Hoyt, *Zachary Taylor* (Chicago, 1966), 87.
13. Thomas to Bliss, June 1, 11, 1846, *AOLR*, Box 3; Jesup, Memorandum, n.d., *H. Ex. Doc. 60, 30th Cong., 1st Sess.*, 549–50; Quaife, *Diary of Polk*, II, 117–19; Risch, *Quartermaster Support*, 267–70; Huston, *Sinews of War*, 146; Smith, *War with Mexico*, I, 205–6. Perhaps the best indictment of the logistic support is in Taylor to AG, Sept. 9, 1846, *H. Ex. Doc. 60, 30th Cong., 1st Sess.*, 557–58, and the most effective defense is in Risch, 257–58.
14. For instance, see Vicente Fuentes Díaz, *La Intervención Norte-americana en México* (México, 1947), 216. Ted C. Hinckley "Anti-Catholicism During the Mexican War," *PHR*, XXXI (May 1962), 121–38, points out, however, that anti-Catholic friction in the United States as a whole was minimized.
15. Marcy to Taylor, May 20, to Vorhagen [*sic*], to McElroy and Rey, May 21, 1846, to Kendrick, May 29, 1846, all in *SWMA*, XXVI, 247–48, 260–61; Quaife, *Diary of Polk*, III, 104; Sister Blanche Marie McEniry, *American Catholics in the War with Mexico* (Washington, 1932), 34–35, 54–56, 64–66; Dom Aidan Henry Germain, *Catholic Military and Naval Chaplains 1776–1917* (Washington, 1929), 38–39. The latter, p. 36, also mentions a "mutiny" by Catholic troops who were forced to attend a Protestant service.
16. Marcy to Taylor, June 4, 1846 (with proclamation), in *H. Ex. Doc. 60, 30th Cong., 1st Sess.*, 284–87.
17. Taylor to AG, May 21, Marcy to Taylor, May 28, June 8, Scott to Taylor, June 12, 15, Jones to Taylor, June 16, 1846, all in *ibid.*, 281–82, 300, 323–27, 454–55, 1328–29.
18. Taylor to AG, July 2, Marcy to Taylor, July 9, 1846, *ibid.*, 155–58, 329–32; Quaife, *Diary of Polk*, III, 5, 16–17; Sellers, *Polk Continentalist*, 430.
19. Taylor to Polk, Aug. 1, 1846, *H. Ex. Doc. 60, 30th Cong., 1st Sess.*, 336–38.
20. Taylor to AG, June 18, 1846, *AGLR'46*, T-261; Taylor to AG, July 1, 16, AO, Orders #91, July 21, 1846, SO #126, Aug. 22, 1846, *H. Ex. Doc. 60, 30th Cong., 1st Sess.*, 315–18, 495–96, 524–25; Doubleday, *Journal of Barbour*, 99; Henry, *Campaign Sketches*, 152; Johnston, *Johnston*, 135–36.
21. AO, SO #78, June 4, 1846, *H. Ex. Doc. 60, 30th Cong., 1st Sess.*, 522–23; Wilson to Bliss, June 10, 1846, *AOLR*, Box 3; Brooks, *Complete History*, 163.
22. Taylor to AG, June 3, 1846, *H. Ex. Doc. 60, 30th Cong., 1st Sess.*, 305–6.
23. Walter Prescott Webb, *The Texas Rangers* (Boston, 1935), 95–99; Samuel C. Reid, Jr., *The Scouting Expeditions of McCulloch's Texas Rangers* (Philadelphia, 1860), 43–46; Victor M. Rose, *The Life and Service of Gen. Ben McCulloch* (Philadelphia, 1888), 70–75.

24. Henry, *Campaign Sketches*, 120; Niles to Bliss, July 8, 14, 1846, Smith Transcripts, XI, 42–4, 47–50; Brooks, *Complete History*, 163–64.

25. Taylor to AG, July 22, AO, Orders #93, July 30, *H. Ex. Doc. 60, 30th Cong., 1st Sess.*, 398–99, 401; Taylor to Wood, July 25, 1846, Samson, *Taylor's Letters*, 29–32; Bliss to Duncan, July 23, 1846, James Duncan Papers, USMA, #636, Taylor to Davis, Aug. 3, 1846, Hudson Strode (ed.), *Jefferson Davis, Private Letters 1823–1889* (New York, 1966), 41; Henry, *Campaign Sketches*, 124–25.

26. Reid, *McCulloch's Rangers*, 78–82, 96–102; Rose, *McCulloch*, 91–93; AO, SO #119, Aug. 11, 1846, *H. Ex. Doc. 60, 30th Cong., 1st Sess.*, 534; Brooks, *Complete History*, 165; Frost, *Mexican War and Its Warriors*, 65.

27. Henry, *Campaign Sketches*, 125, 152; Taylor to AG, Aug. 8, 1846, *H. Ex. Doc. 60, 30th Cong., 1st Sess.*, 408; Quitman's Diary, Claiborne, *Quitman*, I, 240; Blackwood, *To Mexico with Scott*, I, 211–12.

28. Taylor to AG, Sept. 3, 12, Whiting to Jesup, Sept. 3, AO, Orders #98, 102, 108, 109, 112, 113, Aug. 17, 22, 28, 29, Sept. 2, 4, SO #124, Aug. 19, 1846, all in *H. Ex. Doc. 60, 30th Cong., 1st. Sess.*, 417–19, 421, 500–4, 608–81; AO, Orders #111, Aug. 31, SO #132, Aug. 30, 1846, *AOGO*, I, II; Worth to Bliss, Aug. 25, 1846, *AOLR*, Box 4; Taylor to Wood, Aug. 19, 1846, Samson, *Taylor's Letters*, 41–42; Henry, *Campaign Sketches*, 152; Webb, *Texas Rangers*, 101–2.

29. Taylor to Wood, Aug. 23, Sept. 16, 1846, Samson, *Taylor's Letters*, 45–50, 57–59; Brooks, *Complete History*, 171.

30. Roa Bárcena, *Recuerdos*, I, 90–91; Ramsey, *Other Side*, 64; Balbontín, *Invasión*, 10–11, 24; *Niles*, LXX (Aug. 22, 1846), 401; Rives, *U.S. and Mexico*, II, 256; Smith, *War with Mexico*, I, 230; Santa Anna to Ministro de Guerra y Marina, Sept. 26, 1846, Justin H. Smith (ed.), "Letters of General Antonio López de Santa Anna Relating to the War Between the United States and Mexico, 1846–1848," *Annual Report of the American Historical Association . . . 1917* (Washington, 1920), 364–65.

31. Roa Bárcena, *Recuerdos*, I, 91–92; Ramsey, *Other Side*, 63; Smith, *War with Mexico*, I, 231; Ampudia, Proclamation, Aug. 4, 31. Addresses, Aug. 27, 28, Sept. 15, 1846, all in YWA. Those of Aug. 31 and Sept. 15 are reprinted in *H. Ex. Doc 60, 30th Cong., 1st Sess.*, 420–21, 424–26. Another proclamation dated Sept. 14 appears in Kenly, *Memoirs*, 104.

32. Capt. L. P. Vinton to Worth, Aug. 18, 1846, *AOLR*, Box 4: Brooks, *Complete History*, 169–70; AO, Orders #115, 119, 120, Sept. 11, 17, 18, 1846, *H. Ex. Doc. 60, 30th Cong., 1st Sess.*, 504–6; Ramsey, *Other Side*, 67, Valdes, *Breve Historia*, 131; Balbontín, *Invasión*, 25; Smith, *War with Mexico*, I, 235–37; Reid, *McCulloch's Rangers*, 177; Rose, *McCulloch*, 94–95; Webb, *Texas Rangers*, 102.

33. The account of the Battle of Monterrey is based upon: Taylor to AG, Sept. 25, 1846, with enclosures, *H. Ex. Doc. 60, 30th Cong., 1st Sess.*, 345–50; Taylor to AG, Oct. 9, 1846, with enclosures, *S. Doc. 1, 29th Cong., 2d Sess.*, 83–102; Worth's reports in *AOLR*, Box 4; the reports of the Texas regiments in the Smith Papers, UTA; Ampudia to Ministro de Guerra y Marina, Sept. 25, 1846, *Niles*, LXXI (Nov. 7, 1846), 166; Pedro de Ampudia, *Manifesto del General Ampudia a Sus Concuidadanos* (México, 1847); Electus Backus, "Details of the Controversy . . . Capture of Battery No. 1 . . . ," NYHS; Balbontín, *Invasión*, 25–45; Brooks, *Complete History*, 174–89; William C. Carpenter, *Travels and Adventures in Mexico* (New York, 1851), 24–27; Claiborne, *Quitman*, I, 243–55; Varina H. Davis, *Jefferson Davis* (2 vols., New York, 1890), I, 294–300; Dawson, *Battles of U.S.*, II, 464–78; Abner Doubleday, "Miscellaneous Accounts," NYHS; Duncan, "Medical History," 90–96; Dyer, *Taylor*, 206; John S. Ford, "John C. Hays in Texas," 28–44, John S. Ford Papers, UTA; French, *Two Wars*, 61–66; Frost, *Mexican War and Warriors*, 69–96; Luther Gidding, *Sketches of the Cam-*

paign in Northern Mexico (New York, 1853), 170–82; Grant, Memoirs, 51–55; Hamilton, Taylor, 204–16; Henry, Campaign Sketches, 189–216; Henry, Mexican War, 142–53; Howard, Taylor, 149–78; Jenkins, War Between U.S. and Mexico, 160–76; Kenly, Memoirs, 105–50; Lavender, Climax at Buena Vista, 102–20; McCall, Letters, 467; Grady and Sue McWhinney (eds.), To Mexico with Taylor and Scott (Waltham, 1969), 73; William W. Mackall, A Son's Recollections of His Father (New York, 1930), 95–99; Meade, Life and Letters, 130–36, 163–66; Niles, LXXI (Oct. 17, Nov. 7, 1846), 103–4, 151–57; Ramsey, Other Side, 65–66, 70–99; Reid, McCulloch's Texas Rangers, 149–99; Ripley, War with Mexico, I, 199–243; John B. Robertson, Reminiscences of a Campaign in Mexico (Nashville, 1849), 138–46; Rose, McCulloch, 103–5; Dunbar Rowland (ed.), Jefferson Davis Constitutionalist (10 vols., Jackson, 1923), I, 65–69, 106–34; Smith, War with Mexico, I, 237–60, 497–506; Smith and Judah, Chronicles of the Gringos, 80–89; Stevens, Campaigns of Rio Grande & Mexico, 22–29; Hudson Strode, Jefferson Davis, American Patriot (New York, 1955), 164–69; Barna Upton to Elias Upton, Dec. 12, 1846, Goetzmann, "Our First Foreign War," 95; Valdes, Breve Historia, 131–35; Vigil, Invasión, 21–22; Wallace, Worth, 87–103; Webb, Texas Rangers, 105–7; Wilcox, Mexican War, 91–100.

34. Twiggs was temporarily incapacitated by the medicine he had taken to "loosen the bowels, for a bullet striking the belly when the bowels were loose might pass through the intestines without cutting them," Kenly, Memoirs, 119.

35. There is some inconclusive evidence that they lanced some of the wounded. Giddings, Sketches, 180; Duncan, "Medical History," 93.

36. Various explanations have been given, none wholly satisfactory; Taylor in his Oct. 9, 1846, report merely averred to Quitman's men being tired. Henry, Campaign Sketches, 206, suggests it came from the expectation of the bombardment by the mortar. Ripley, War with Mexico, I, 232, attributes it to both the weariness of Quitman's troops and the "lack of concert with Worth." Stevens, Campaigns of the Rio Grande and Mexico, p. 25, suggests that Taylor, who as yet was unaware of Worth's impending assault, wished to organize a coordinated attack on the twenty-fourth.

37. The description of the armistice negotiations is based upon: the Ampudia-Taylor correspondence and Taylor to AG, Nov. 8, 1846, in H. Ex. Doc. 60, 30th Cong., 1st Sess., 348–49, 359–60; Davis, "Memoranda of the transactions in connection with the capitulation of Monterrey . . . ," Rowland, Davis, I, 65–69; Dyer, Taylor, 206; Hamilton, Taylor, 214–15; Howard, Taylor, 176–202; McCormac, Polk, 449–50; Rives, U.S. and Mexico, II 272–75; Strode, Davis, 166–69; The text of the capitulation is in H. Ex. Doc. 60, 30th Cong., 1st Sess., 349–50 and the official English-language copy is in USMA MS-1164.

38. Taylor to Wood, Sept. 8, 1846, Samson, Taylor's Letters, 61.

39. Niles, LXXI (Nov. 21, 1846), 182; Bliss, Return of killed . . . , n.d., AGLR'46, T-390; Smith, War with Mexico, I, 494, 496.

40. Grant, Memoir, 55; Smith, War with Mexico, I, 260; Hamilton, Taylor, 215; Balbontín, Invasión, 46–47.

41. Balbontín, Invasión, 48; Brooks, Complete History, 191; Vito Alessio Robles, Coahuila y Texas desde la Consumación de la Independencia Hasta el Tratado de Paz de Guadalupe Hidalgo (2 vols., México, 1845–46), I, 341.

42. H. L. Scott, Military Dictionary (New York, 1968), 659–60; Justin H. Smith, "American Rule in Mexico," AHR, XXIII (Jan. 1918), 293–94; Taylor to AG, Oct. 11, 1846, H. Ex. Doc. 60, 30th Cong., 1st Sess., 431.

43. AO, Orders #124, Oct. 1, Taylor to AG, Oct. 6, 1846, H. Ex. Doc. 60, 30th Cong., 1st Sess., 430, 508; Ramírez to Patterson, Nov. 15, 1846, AOLR, Box 4.

7: The Naval War in the Gulf of Mexico, 1846

W HILE ZACHARY TAYLOR'S MEN marched and fought in northern Mexico a different and far less colorful war absorbed the attention of the Navy on the Gulf of Mexico. The overriding responsibility of Commodore David Conner's Home Squadron was maintaining a tight blockade of the Mexican east coast. Mexico's only two significant warships, the steamers *Moctezuma* and *Guadalupe* had been transferred to British commercial owners at the start of fighting. The other vessels, mostly small craft, took refuge at Alvarado or at Tampico. Although the Mexican warships took part in the defense of both ports, they did not attempt to take the sea in the face of the overwhelming superiority of Conner's force.[1]

An effective blockade of Mexico's east-coast ports presented special problems. Eight major ports flew the red-white-and-green tricolor with the eagle and serpent. Of these, Matamoros fell into American hands at the start of the war. Carmen was neutralized by the Yucatán insurrection. Five of the remaining six—Tampico, Soto la Marina, Tuxpan, Alvarado, and San Juan Bautista (generally referred to as "Tabasco" in contemporary American accounts, a usage that will be followed here[2])—lay up shallow-mouthed rivers. Normally such a port was shut by placing a vessel either off the mouth of the river or inside it. This was not easily done, since the entrances of all of the rivers were so shallow that only very light draft could pass, while the open coast afforded blockaders no protection from storms. The sixth,

Veracruz, had no real harbor, although the port could be used with difficulty by taking advantage of the slight protection offered by Gallega Reef, upon which squatted the Castle of San Juan de Ulúa. Its normal peacetime anchorages, behind a series of low offshore islands and reefs stretching nearly twenty miles southward along the coast, were controlled by the American squadron. Even so, blockade runners occasionally slipped into Veracruz by running close to shore when storms forced blockading vessels to seek safety offshore.

Along the Mexican east coast there are really only two seasons. From April to October the weather is wet and miserable, and *vómito*, or yellow fever is rampant. That scourge could immobilize a vessel or a squadron, as it did during the summer of 1847, and since medical knowledge had yet to discover its cause or cure the only effective treatment was time or a change of climate. Veracruz was particularly noted as a yellow-fever area. The dry season stretches from October to April and brings the vicious northerly gales, called northers, which strike with minimal warning and are among the most vicious known to mariners. Vessels cannot ride them out in open roadsteads and even in protected anchorages frequently encounter problems.

The blockade was tiresome and irksome duty. As one of the participants said: "During the parching heats of summer, and the long boisterous nights of winter, our vigilance was expected to be, and was, unremitting."[3] It was a monotony of cruising back and forth or lying at anchor before a port, usually alone, with little interruption except an occasional sail on the horizon and less frequently a vessel trying to run into the port.

Conner issued precise orders to his subordinates. Neutral commerce was to be disturbed as little as possible and the stipulations of international law and usage were to be scrupulously respected. "In all cases," he ordered, "you are to act upon the doctrine that 'free ships make free goods,' and except in cases of contraband, with respect to France, the Netherlands, and Sweden, upon that of 'enemy's ships, enemy's goods.'"[4] These instructions followed the then current American doctrine that blockades must be effective to be legal and that a neutral flag protected all goods embarked except contraband. So carefully did the squadron follow the law that all of its captures were sustained by the courts and very few complaints arose from the blockade. This was a marked contrast to the extensive difficulties which arose from the blockades established by the Pacific Squadron.

In June Conner relaxed the blockade slightly. He permitted neutral mail packets to carry gold and silver bars outward and quicksilver inbound. As strange as this sounds to modern ears, it was in keeping with the nineteenth-century conception of a blockade. Since the gold and silver mines in Mexico were owned almost exclusively by foreigners, the reasoning ran, so was their product. As neutral property, therefore, the bullion was not subject to seizure. Quicksilver entered because it was indispensable for the refining of the foreign-owned metal.[5]

Immediately following the declaration of war, Secretary of the Navy George Bancroft instructed Conner to "exercise all the rights that belong to you as commander-in-chief of a belligerent squadron." After dwelling at some length on the opportunities for detaching some of the Mexican states from their allegiance to the central government, Bancroft advised, "Your own intimate acquaintance with the condition of Mexico, will instruct you what measures to pursue in the conduct of hostilities." The blockade should permit only neutral warships and the English mail steamers running to Veracruz and Tampico to pass. The blockaders should allow any neutral vessels caught in port twenty days to load and leave. The letter also informed Conner that reinforcements ordered to the Gulf would increase his squadron to a pair of frigates, three sloops-of-war, two steamers, five brigs, and a schooner. It was scarcely an opulent force with which to blockade the entire Mexican east coast. Yet Bancroft exhorted his commander:

> The country relies on you to make such a use of this force as will most effectually blockade the principal Mexican ports, protect our commerce from the depredations of privateers, assist the operations of our army, and lead to the earliest adjustment of our difficulties with Mexico.[6]

These were good instructions which clearly described the aims of the naval operations in the Gulf of Mexico and pointed out the navy's only possible contributions to victory. Since the negligible Mexican Navy could offer no contest for the control of the sea the principal objective of the American Navy, clearing the seas for the transportation of troops and supplies, was secured even before hostilities began. At no time during the war did the Mexican Navy send a vessel to sea in the Gulf of Mexico. The best Mexican hope of disrupting the American supply lines lay in privateers, but that threat never materialized. The main activity of Conner's squadron was the institution of a tight blockade which absorbed most of its energy. In practice, except for the support of General Scott's Veracruz expedition, there was little direct support that the navy could render the army. No one saw this more clearly than Conner, who wrote his wife:

The Navy in this war will I fear have few opportunities for distinction. Mexico presents scarcely any thing assailable but the castle of San Juan D'Ulloa, and that would be as little effected by our shot as Mount Ararat.[7]

The nature of the war which the squadron had to wage required a large number of vessels with a sufficiently shallow draft to enter the Mexican rivers and a smaller group of sloops-of-war capable of enforcing the blockade even during the stormy winter months. The squadron needed seagoing steamers to serve as dispatch vessels and tugs. The deep-draft frigates and big awkward ships-of-the-line were nearly useless on the blockade, although their crews could and did furnish manpower for landing parties. The larger vessels were necessary only for an attack on San Juan de Ulúa in Veracruz harbor, an order that never came. The Gulf Squadron, therefore, fought the war with small craft, sloops-of-war, steamers, and one or more frigates.

Since President Polk believed that if exiled General Antonio López de Santa Anna could be returned to power in Mexico he would help bring a quick end to the war, Conner was directed: "If Santa Anna endeavors to enter the Mexican ports, you will allow him to pass freely."[8]

Because most of his vessels were short of water, nearly all would have to visit Pensacola before assuming their blockading stations. Commodore Conner intended to hold the squadron at the Brazos Santiago only so long as their presence was urgent. Five days later he advised Bancroft that although his force was inadequate to attack San Juan de Ulúa, he would base his operations at Antón Lizardo, the chief anchorage of Veracruz. He requested that storeships be stationed there and stressed the need for a constant supply of water.[9]

On May 14 Conner issued a proclamation placing Veracruz, Alvarado, Tampico, and Matamoros under blockade and threatening its extension elsewhere. Commodore Conner initiated that blockade by sending the sloop-of-war *St. Mary's* to close Tampico and directing the *Mississippi* (Captain Andrew Fitzhugh) and the *Falmouth* to shut Veracruz and Alvarado. The other Mexican ports in the Gulf remained open until the necessary vessels to blockade them appeared. As the vessels which had replenished supplies and water at Pensacola arrived in Mexican waters, Conner extended the blockade.[10] Coincident to the start of the blockade, Commander Duncan N. Ingraham in the *Somers* headed southward on an intelligence mission to Campeche, Yucatán. His instructions were to "conciliate" Yucatán and to determine whether the secessionist state would continue to hold aloof from Mexican affairs. He quickly discovered that the Campeche authorities intended to continue their independent course.[11]

The *St. Mary's*, under energetic Commander John L. Saunders, reached Tampico on May 19. He proclaimed the blockade the following day but had to resort to threats before the local authorities would permit an American brig, caught in port by the outbreak of war, to sail. Also on the twentieth, Captain Andrew Fitzhugh of the *Mississippi* proclaimed the blockade of Veracruz and Alvarado. Four days later the first two prizes were taken, but they were released in recognition of the Mexicans' permitting four American vessels to sail from Veracruz.[12]

The dull, dreary monotony of the blockade quickly palled for Commander Saunders of the *St. Mary's*. He soon concluded that Tampico could be easily taken. Despite instructions to avoid hostilities if possible,[13] Saunders in early June decided that the strengthening of the defenses at the mouth of the river justified an attack. During the afternoon of June 8 the *St. Mary's* bombarded the fort there and three gunboats anchored nearby. Shoal water kept the Americans from working in close enough to inflict more than superficial damage on one of the gunboats. Saunders returned to the attack on the night of the fourteenth-fifteenth, sending an expedition in his ship's boats to cut out the gunboats. Discovered by Mexican sentinels as they crossed the bar the Americans had to return empty-handed.[14]

While the blockaders took their stations, Commodore Conner established his forward base at the anchorage of Antón Lizardo, about twelve miles south of Veracruz. There a chain of shoals, reefs, and small barren islands stretching about nine miles broke the sea sufficiently for vessels to ride at anchor safely through even the strongest of northers. Throughout their terms Conner and his successor, Matthew C. Perry, were plagued by shortages of vessels, good charts, and competent pilots. Additionally the logistic support of the squadron, notably water, fresh fruit, and coal, was haphazard. While Secretary Bancroft and the bureau chiefs recognized the problems, the combination of time, distance, and the difficulty of forecasting the future needs, however, limited their success. The squadron commanders must share part of the blame because none provided the supply bureaus with sufficient advance warning of operations to permit the necessary supplies to be forwarded in advance of need.[15]

During July Conner attempted to overcome his water shortage by drawing it from the Antigua River north of Veracruz. That solution was abandoned after the watering parties skirmished with Mexican defenders.[16] Thereafter the Americans limited their activities to streams under their own control.

While Commodore Conner's force settled into its routine, Secretary Bancroft raised the question of the practicality of seizing Ulúa and the force needed to do so. Commodore Charles Morris followed up the request in mid-June with more detailed queries. Conner's estimate was less than heartening: five ships-of-the-line, three frigates, four bomb vessels, and some sloops. He added to the gloom by observing that even with this force Ulúa would be difficult to overcome if resolutely defended. The Commodore made a further, more detailed report following his arrival at Veracruz. The garrison had such limited provisions and supplies that a landing and siege could force surrender before the arrival of help from the interior. Land operations around Veracruz, however, were complicated by the climate and yellow fever during the wet season. Conner also emphasized that the port was valuable only as a depot for an advance on Mexico City—and he believed that Tampico was better suited for that.[17] It is no wonder that the administration quickly abandoned all thought of seizing Ulúa and Veracruz.

In the same letter in which he raised the questions about Ulúa, Bancroft inquired if Conner wished a Marine field-grade officer. The question probed Conner's intended use of his Marines. If they were to be combined into a single unit for amphibious operations, he would need a field officer to command it. Conner limited himself to a request for another Marine Captain, thus confirming that he did not intend to use his Marines in a consolidated unit.[18]

Conner had frequently reminded the Navy Department of the need for light-draft vessels for his squadron. Once the May 13 appropriation made money available, Secretary Bancroft authorized the purchase of likely vessels. The first acquired were a pair of small sidewheel steamers lying at the famous New York shipbuilding firm of Brown and Bell. Since they had been designed for use by the Mexican Navy they were admirably suited for the duties assigned them. Some 188-feet long on deck and twenty-two and a half feet in beam, they carried three guns. Easily recognized by their large paddleboxes they quickly acquired the nickname of the "Pollies" in honor of some now forgotten buxom young lady. Officially their names were *Vixen* and *Spitfire*. A second purchase, on May 25, added three 59-foot schooners also building for the Mexicans at Brown and Bell's yard. The *Bonita*, *Petrel*, and *Reefer*, as they were named in American service, were handy vessels which mounted a single 32-pounder carronade. They saw more action than any other vessels in the squadron. Owing to various delays, the first of the schooners did not appear in the Gulf until mid-July, while the steamers were delayed until autumn. As a result Conner lacked the vessels necessary for successful attacks upon the Mexican ports during the period of good weather.[19]

Contributing to Conner's inability to attack was the appearance of scurvy during the early summer. It reached such proportions on some vessels, notably the big frigate *Raritan*, as to render them nearly useless. The disease resulted from the difficulties in securing fresh fruits upon the hostile coast. The solution came in the form of a shuttle of vessels to Pensacola and the opening of trade with Carmen in the rebellious Mexican state of Yucatán.[20]

Further complicating Conner's task, the Mexican Congress on June 15, 1846, authorized the issuance of privateer commissions. The Mexican invocation of the traditional method for weak nations to contest the power of stronger ones upon the sea came as no surprise to American authorities. Nor did the provision that foreigners who secured commissions were to be considered Mexican nationals. Mexico lacked more than a small handful of vessels adequate for conversion into privateers and was too short of experienced deep-water sailors to mount any significant campaign from her own resources. The threat of foreigners accepting the commissions which flooded the West Indies, Britain, France, and Spain in the fall of 1846, however, did pose a problem. Despite frequent rumors of privateers, only two Spanish vessels were actually outfitted. While the large American merchant marine was an inviting target, the arrangements made for its protection, the threat to treat all foreigners serving under the Mexican flag as pirates, and the difficulties almost certain to be met in disposing of the prizes discouraged others.[21]

On July 21 the Mexicans attempted to counter the blockade by designating Tecaluto, Tuxpan, and Soto la Marina as additional ports of entry. On September 11 blockade runners were exempted from port dues and a quarter of the import tax. How effective these measures were in inducing shippers to chance seizure by the blockaders is uncertain.[22]

Although he was still short of vessels capable of moving upstream to attack the Mexican warships collected in the Alvarado River, Conner decided in late July to make the effort. Alvarado, about twenty miles southeast of Antón Lizardo, had become an important place of entry for war supplies after Veracruz was closed. The broad bar that restricted entry into the river's mouth made blockade by the large, deep-water sloops and frigates of Conner's squadron extremely difficult. A successful attack on the town, therefore, would not only close a port difficult to blockade but might provide some of the shoal draft craft which the squadron lacked. "Northers" would start in October and any vessel cruising off the Alvarado bar would be in danger of being forced ashore by the wind and current.

The defenses of Alvarado were weak. The commander, Captain (*Capitán de Fragata*) Pédro Díaz Mirón of the Mexican Navy, had only one brig, three gunboats, and a single four-gun fort to protect the port. More important to the attackers was the shallow, eight to ten feet, depth of water on the bar. This permitted only the American shallow-draft gunboats to enter the river.[23]

Conner's first attempt on July 28 had to be abandoned when the flagship *Cumberland* (Captain French Forrest) ran aground exiting from Antón Lizardo. Although she was freed the following day with little damage, she went north in November to have her copper bottom-plates renewed.[24] In early August a few days of settled weather prompted Conner to try again. During the early afternoon of the seventh, the steamers *Mississippi*, *Princeton* (Commander Frederick Engle), frigates *Cumberland* and *Potomac* (Captain John H. Aulick), and gunboats *Reefer* (Lieutenant Isaac Sterrett), *Petrel* (Lieutenant T. Darrah Shaw), and *Bonita* (Lieutenant Timothy Benham) joined the sloop *Falmouth* off the mouth of the Alvarado. The strength of the current pouring across the bar proved to be so strong that even the big American steamers could not work in close enough to the fort to inflict damage. About seven o'clock that evening the American gunboats and the steamers exchanged fire with some Mexican gunboats, and the steamers also exchanged fire with some Mexican musketeers in the chapparal before moving out of range. During the night Conner organized a boat expedition, probably to seize the fort, since the strength of the current would have precluded cutting out the vessels lying behind it. Before it could be mounted, however, Conner had to call off the attack because of the threatened appearance of a norther.[25]

Following the attack the Mexicans strengthened Alvarado's defenses. Militia marched in from nearby villages and a new fort arose on the north point of the river's mouth. Conner's failure was more than just a repulse. It convinced him that he could not launch a successful attack on Alvarado until the high water on the river receded and the weather improved. By that time he could expect the arrival of the additional small craft which he had been promised. Undoubtedly the Commodore's continuing belief that the Mexicans would agree to peace negotiations also affected his planning at least into early September.[26]

As long as Conner lacked the small craft with which to stage assaults on the secondary Mexican ports, the operations of his squadron were limited to the shifting of vessels among the blockade stations and the tightening of the blockade. As part of that movement Conner on August 12 directed the newly arrived brig *Truxtun* (Commander Edward W. Carpender) to relieve the *John Adams* (Commander William J. McCluney) off Tampico.

Commander Carpender headed his vessel northward in boisterous weather. During the late afternoon of August 14 he arrived off Tuxpan, about halfway to his station. Despite the gale, Carpender headed the brig inshore, hoping to send a boat ashore in the morning to purchase some fresh provisions. The wind and current, however, carried the brig onto the reefs which paralleled the coast. There she stuck despite all her crew's efforts to free her. Carpender dispatched a ship's boat under command of Lieutenant Ortway H. Berryman to Antón Lizardo for assistance, but before aid could arrive he was forced to surrender.

The first news of the *Truxtun's* accident reached Antón Lizardo during the morning of August 19 when Barryman appeared, having fallen in with the *St. Mary's* earlier in the day. Conner immediately sent the steamer *Princeton* to the stricken brig's assistance. The *Princeton* reached Tuxpan during the early afternoon of the nineteenth only to learn that Carpender had surrendered two days before. High seas kept the Americans from inspecting the wreck until the twentieth. By then she was too badly damaged to be salvaged and the Mexicans had removed nearly everything worth salvaging. The *Princeton's* boarding party brought off some spars and then burned the hulk.[27]

The monotony of the blockade and the uninterrupted confinement on board ship raised problems of morale and discipline on many of Conner's vessels. Some captains resorted to increased use of the cat-o'-nine-tails, while others appear to have devised less drastic means of maintaining control. The problems were worst on the *St. Mary's* and Conner seized upon an incident on board her to warn his crews of the danger of a loss of discipline. Seaman Samuel Jackson had loosed a torrent of abuse and twice struck the officer of the deck in an altercation over Jackson's shoes being on deck after an inspection. He was court-martialed on a variety of charges including striking an officer, and sentenced to be hanged. The sentence was carried out during the morning of September 17. Many of the officers in the squadron thought that the sentence was unduly harsh, but Conner believed that it was very important to make an example of the sailor as a deterrent.[28] Whether or not he was correct, there were no further incidents of a comparable gravity.

Another problem was eased by the partial solution of the shortage of fresh food when the *Porpoise* (Lieutenant Willam E. Hunt) in early September returned to Antón Lizardo from a voyage to Carmen in Campeche. She brought back wood and some vegetables, although her commander reported that the amount available there was limited. Hunt also brought back intelligence on events in Yucatán where the revolutionary government appeared to be safely in control. Perhaps the most encouraging aspect of the expedition to Conner, however, was the *Porpoise*'s seizure of the Mexican merchant schooner *Nonata*. She was promptly given four guns and taken into service. Larger than the three schooners purchased in New York, she was therefore better able to keep the sea in poor weather.[29]

One of the causes of the Navy Department's difficulty in providing the vessels which the Gulf and Pacific Squadrons needed was a shortage of sailors. Despite the passage of an August 10, 1846 Act which authorized a wartime increase in enlisted strength from 7,500 to 10,000 men, the Navy had difficulty recruiting sufficient men to man its vessels. Wages were high in the merchant marine and jobs plentiful, with the result that the Navy never exceeded 8,100 men during the war.[30]

When Commodore Conner's normal term as commander of the Home Squadron approached its end in the fall of 1845, Secretary Bancroft selected Commodore Matthew C. Perry as his relief. The continuing crisis leading up to the outbreak of fighting rendered it so undesirable to change leaders that Conner remained in command. On August 12, 1846, for reasons that are unclear, the Secretary offered Perry command of the steam frigate *Mississippi* until he succeeded to the leadership of the squadron. Probably Bancroft was motivated by a desire to give Perry as long a period of transition to command as possible and a concern that Conner's delicate health might break down at any moment.[31]

Perry reached Antón Lizardo on September 23 on board the small steamer *Vixen* (Commander Joshua R. Sands). His arrival introduced a problem seldom encountered in the American Navy of the mid-nineteenth century: two flag officers serving in the same squadron. Some writers have suggested that the command of the squadron was somehow split, with Perry commanding the steamers and Conner retaining control of the sailing craft. This was not so. Perry, who hoisted the red pennant of a junior commodore on the *Mississippi*, served as second-in-command and as such was assigned command of several independent operations.[32]

In September an even more significant change in leadership also occurred in Washington. The general direction of the Navy's war effort changed hands. Secretary Bancroft desired assignment to a diplomatic post in Europe which would permit further research on his monumental *History of the United States*. When the retirement of Louis McLane opened the London mission, President Polk offered it to Bancroft. He quickly accepted. Polk asked Attorney General John Y. Mason to resume charge of the Navy Department, which he did on September 9.[33]

The new Secretary was a Virginian who had been a lawyer, politician, and jurist before joining President Tyler's cabinet in 1844 as Secretary of the Navy. He was a close friend of President Polk and the only man retained from Tyler's cabinet. While Mason lacked the intellectual brilliance of Bancroft, he was a better and less abrasive administrator. Under his leadership the Department sailed a smooth course although it produced few innovations.

The hobble of a shortage of small craft which had restricted covert operations began to break in October. The arrival of the Revenue Steamer *McLane* (Captain W. A. Howard, USRM) gave him two shallow-draft steamers. The Commodore therefore hastened to mount another attack on Alvarado. He recognized that success there would work wonders on the squadron's morale as well as fulfill the administration's desire that "the Navy should do something which will answer to make newspaper noise."[34]

The defenses of Alvarado had improved greatly since the earlier attack. Five batteries containing some thirty-six guns now guarded the entrance to the river, while the three largest Mexican warships were moored in a crescent between them and the town. This ingenious arrangement of Commodore Tomás Marín was an effort to catch the unsuspecting American small craft in a *cul de sac* beyond the range of the heavy guns of the larger United States vessels.[35]

Soon after midnight on October 15 Conner led the *Mississippi* and the small craft out of the Antón Lizardo anchorage toward the mouth of the Alvarado. They reached their destination shortly after daylight only to discover that the onshore breeze upon which the Commodore had counted to assist the small craft in crossing the bar at the mouth of the river did not appear. While awaiting the afternoon sea breeze, Conner contented himself with a short bombardment of the outer fortifications. Since the swell on the bar dropped during the morning, Conner, after conferring with his captains, decided to push ahead during the afternoon irrespective of the state of the winds.

At about 1:20 P.M. Conner in the *Vixen* led two columns of small craft toward the bar. As they approached it, the fast current slowed them to less than a mile and a half per hour. Nevertheless, the *Vixen*'s column safely crossed the bar and opened fire. The second column in tow of the *McLane*, delayed by her slower speed, reached the bar at 2:15, but almost immediately the revenue steamer grounded, throwing her tow into confusion. Since it was clear that the second column could not be brought into action, Conner abandoned the attack despite Commander Sand's advice to "Go ahead and fight like hell!" In retrospect, the decision seems very sensible. Without even considering whether Marín's trap would have worked, the force that crossed the bar was too small and weak either to put the Mexicans to rout or to seize the craft in the river. For Conner to have persisted in the attack with the forlorn hope which he headed was to run the risk of considerable damage and possible loss to his already under-strength forces.

Following the abortive Alvarado attack, Conner accepted a suggestion by Commodore Perry for an expedition to offset the impact of the defeat. This involved a sweep of the coast from the Coatzac-oalcos River to Carmen combined with, should circumstances permit, the seizure of the city of Tabasco and other towns along the Tabasco River.[36]

Perry's force, consisting of the steamers *Mississippi*, *Vixen*, and *McLane*, and the schooners *Reefer*, *Bonita*, *Nonata* (Lieutenant Samuel F. Hazard), and *Forward* (Captain H. B. Nones, USRM), along with a 253-man landing force under Captain French Forrest, exited from the Antón Lizardo anchorage during October 16.[37]

Despite a heavy storm the craft, except the *Reefer* which got separated, collected off the mouth of the Tabasco.

During the early afternoon of October 23 Perry shifted his flag to the *Vixen*, since the *Mississippi* drew too much water to pass the bar. The *Vixen* led the other small craft over the bar, but once again the *McLane* struck in passing. The other vessels pushed on, seized a pair of steamers[38] moored to the wharf at the village of Frontera, and secured the town as well as the other shipping there.

After landing a small garrison and manning the *Petrita* (one of the steamers seized), Perry and the expedition pushed upriver toward Tabasco. By nine o'clock the next morning they were within sight of the defenses below the town. Lieutenant Colonel Juan B. Traconis, the departmental commander, who had less than 300 men, chose not to fight. He withdrew beyond the town which the Americans occupied at about 5:00 P.M. The squadron seized five small vessels which were lying off the town. As night approached Perry recalled the landing party, fearing that it could be cut up by infiltrating Mexicans during darkness.

During the night Mexican soldiers returned to the town and took up positions in buildings from which they could be driven only by shelling. Thus the American commander faced the choice of either abandoning his assault on the town or risking injury to noncombatants. Since he did not have the men to hold the town even if he retook it, Perry decided "from motives of humanity, not to fire again but to pass down to Frontera with my prizes." That was not what happened.

At daylight on the twenty-sixth Mexican soldiers ashore started firing at the American vessels. The Americans replied. The foreign merchants, fearing damage to their property, asked for a cease-fire. Perry agreed. He had a white flag hoisted on the *Vixen* as an indication of his sincerity and ordered his vessels to begin moving downstream. When one of the prizes grounded in front of the town at ten o'clock, the Mexicans began shooting at her. She was freed, but only after one of the boats sent to her assistance was badly shot up and one officer mortally wounded. Perry ordered the squadron to return fire in retaliation for the apparent treachery of the Mexicans but directed that wherever possible the homes of consuls and other noncombatants be spared.

Having made his point, Perry resumed the trip to Frontera where the force arrived during the morning of the twenty-seventh. During the fighting the Americans lost one killed, one mortally wounded, two drowned, and two wounded. The Mexicans lost five soldiers and four civilians killed.

Perry returned to Antón Lizardo on the last day of the month, having left the *McLane* and the *Forward* to keep the river closed and protect the neutral merchants at Frontera from reprisals by the Mexicans. The success, coming as it did after the long succession of failures, was a tonic for the squadron and infused a new spirit into the men. It had broken the monotony for those who took part and helped make life more endurable for the others. The *Petrita* and the schooner *Laura Virginia* (renamed *U.S.S. Morris*) were added to the squadron's growing force of small craft. Several others undoubtedly would have also entered service had they not been sunk during a late November gale at Antón Lizardo.[39]

Those vessels would have been useful on the next operation. As early as September 2 Secretary Marcy had alerted General Taylor to the administration's interest in seizing Tampico as soon as weather permitted. Later in the month the cabinet agreed to specific orders to the Home Squadron to take it. Two days later, September 22, Taylor was directed to send a column under Major General Robert Patterson to occupy the state of Tamaulipas, including Tampico. The column could move to Tampico by water if its commander desired, since it was assumed that Commodore Conner's force would have taken the port before the Army column moved. When Conner was informed of the impending movement of Patterson's column, he was reminded that the seizure of the port "will be of the utmost importance."[40]

Santa Anna learned of the American designs on Tampico through the interception of Marcy's September 2 letter. Since the port was weakly defended, and the means to improve the defenses unavailable, he ordered it abandoned. The garrison completed its evacuation during October 27 and 28 after demolishing the defenses and shipping the guns upriver to Panuco. The news reached Conner almost immediately from two sources. One was Anna Chase, the English wife of the former American consul at Tampico, who had remained there following her husband's expulsion. The second source was Lieutenant Hunt of the *Porpoise*, which was blockading the port.[41]

Tampico was an attractive objective. It was the second most important port on Mexico's Gulf coast. Moreover, it was the most dangerous port to blockade because the very shallow bar, normally less than eight feet, forced the blockaders to anchor in unprotected waters. Another appeal to the Americans was the carriage road, which it was erroneously believed ran from there to San Luis Potosí. Even without the imaginary road, the port was a better base for future operations than the Rio Grande.

During November 11-12 the expedition departed Antón Lizardo

with Conner in personal command.[42] On reaching the rendezvous at Lobos, he found that the two big frigates *Raritan* (Captain Francis H. Gregory) and *Potomac* had not arrived. He decided, however, not to risk the weather turning bad and headed for the mouth of the Panuco rather than await the missing vessels. The *Mississippi, Princeton, Spitfire* (Commander Joshua Tattnall), *Vixen, Bonita, Petrel, Reefer,* and *Nonata* reached there at daybreak on November 14. The *Porpoise* and *St. Mary's* were already anchored off the bar. As soon as he had a report from Lieutenant Hunt, Conner organized his small craft into two divisions accompanied by about 300 men in ships' boats.

The Commodore himself boarded the *Spitfire*, and at about 11:00 A.M. led the force toward shore. By 11:30 they had entered the muddy Panuco River and in little over an hour could make out the American flag which had been hoisted over the former consulate by the indomitable Mrs. Chase. A truce party put out from shore shortly afterward to arrange the capitulation of the port, which had neither the means nor the will to resist. The Mexican negotiators haggled over the terms so long that Conner occupied the town and finally, in exasperation, had his negotiators terminate the discussions as no longer necessary.

Off the town the Americans found three ex-Mexican Navy gunboats and a pair of merchant schooners. The three gunboats were similar to the three former Mexican craft which had been purchased at the start of the war and were taken into service as U.S.S. *Union, Tampico,* and *Falcon*. The merchant schooner *Mahonese* was also outfitted as a warship.

Since Conner did not have the men to garrison Tampico permanently, he sent Commodore Perry in the *Mississippi* to request the garrison from the commander at Point Isabel. Perry delivered his message during the sixteenth and hurried on to carry the news to New Orleans. In his wake Lieutenant Colonel Francis Belton hastily embarked 450 men of the 2d Artillery on the steamer *Neptune* at the Brazos Santiago. They sailed during the twenty-first and arrived the following day. At New Orleans, Perry secured fifty men, an engineer officer, and the State of Louisiana's field battery. The *Mississippi* unloaded her reinforcements at Tampico during the thirtieth.[43]

Meanwhile, Conner had sent Commander Tattnall up the Panuco with a small detachment of seamen in ships' boats. They returned with a few small prizes but none of the munitions evacuated from the town. These were stored at the town of Panuco as Conner soon learned. On November 17 he ordered Tattnall there with the *Spitfire,*

Petrel, and a small landing party. The force returned on the twenty-first with the 24-pounder from one of the gunboats and forty large bales of "excellent imported tent pins" after destroying the munitions there.[44]

The capture of Tampico had been expected by the planners in Washington to yield great benefits to the American war effort. It appeared to them to be the potentially very valuable base for operations against central Mexico. That appearance was a mirage, but it did serve as a staging point for the bulk of the troops drawn from Zachary Taylor's army for the Veracruz operation. Moreover, the occupation gave a further taste of success to the victory-starved men of the Home Squadron and it yielded as many gunboats as Conner had been able to secure from the Navy Department in six months.

The prizes, however, would not offset losses which the squadron was about to suffer. The first came during the early hours of November 15 when the sloop-of-war *Boston* (Commander George F. Pearson) on her way to join the squadron was wrecked on Eleuthra Island in the Bahamas.[45] This left the deep-sea force off Mexico with only two frigates, two sloops of war, two brigs, and a pair of large steamers. Of these only the sloops and brigs made satisfactory blockaders. The others were either too large or too valuable for the duty.

A different but no less bothersome loss occurred on November 26 when a boat from the brig *Somers* silently rowed into Veracruz harbor and burned the blockade-running schooner *Criolla* as she lay tied to the walls of Ulúa. Unknown to the young American officers who planned and executed the assault, she had entered the port with Conner's blessing as a spy ship.[46]

The *Somers* figured in another escapade near Veracruz in early December. Two of her officers learned of the location of a Mexican powder magazine and attempted to destroy it. On their third try, during the night of December 5-6, Midshipman R. Clay Rogers was captured by a Mexican patrol. Despite his capture in full uniform, the Mexicans threatened to try the young American as a spy. This led to extensive efforts on the part of the American officers and political leaders to gain his release on parole and culminated in Lieutenant Raphael Semmes accompanying General Scott's army for the sole purpose of securing Rogers's release. Rogers ultimately contrived to escape from Mexico City and safely make his way to the American army.[47]

On December 8 the *Somers* was caught in a sudden squall while chasing a blockade runner. Before Lieutenant Semmes could take the necessary corrective action, she was thrown on her beam ends, quickly filled with water, and sank. Despite the rescue efforts of nearby British, French, and Spanish men-of-war, thirty-two of her crew were drowned.[48] Not only did the *Somers*'s loss reduce the squadron's blockading capacity; it came at a time when the impending Veracruz expedition would put increased demands on Conner's forces.

Conner dispatched Perry on another expedition in late December. It was an attempt to cut the clandestine, contraband trade which passed between Yucatán and the rest of Mexico by seizing Carmen and stationing a few small craft there. Perry, in the *Mississippi*, departed Antón Lizardo on December 17 in company with *Vixen*, *Bonita*, and *Petrel*. Three days later the four vessels anchored off the bar which limited entry into the Laguna del Carmen. Perry, with the three small craft, moved to the anchorage off the town and secured its surrender on the morning of December 21. After carrying off or destroying what munitions they found, Perry left Commander Joshua R. Sands in charge with the *Vixen* and *Petrel* to enforce the blockade. Reembarking on the *Mississippi*, Perry continued on to Frontera at the mouth of the Tabasco where he left the *Bonita* to assist in maintaining the blockade. After replenishing the *Mississippi*'s water tanks, Perry headed his ship back to Antón Lizardo, arriving two days after Christmas with two prizes seized off Alvarado.[49] Upon her return Conner concluded that the *Mississippi* could no longer safely delay repairs to her boilers. Despite the rapid approach of the Veracruz landings, he sent her to Norfolk for the necessary work.[50]

The approach of the Veracruz operation added such a host of new problems for Conner's squadron that supplies became one of the lesser concerns. In part, also, the supply bureaus were beginning to hit their stride and, after the start of the new year, storeships reached Antón Lizardo in greater numbers to ease the supply crisis.

NOTES

For key to abbreviations used in Notes, see page xi.

1. Conner to Bancroft, June 30, 1846, *HSL*; Roa Bárcena, *Recuerdos*, I, 249; *Memoria de Ministro de . . . Guerra y Marina, 9 de Diciembre 1846 . . .* (México, 1846), 41; Robert L. Scheina, "Seapower Misused: Mexico at War 1846-8," *The Mariner's Mirror*, LVII (July 1971), 204-5; Enrique Cardenas de la Peña, *Semblanza Marítima del México Independiente y Revolucionario* (2 vols., México, 1970), II, 27.
2. Its modern name is Villahermosa.

3. Semmes, *Service Afloat and Ashore*, 76.
4. Conner to Capt. W. A. Howard, USRM, Feb. 9, 1847, *CLB*. See also Conner, Blockade Instructions, May 14, 1846, *HSL*; Mason to T. apC. Jones, Oct. 28, 1847, *S. Ex. Doc. 1, 30th Cong., 1st Sess.*, 1304.
5. Conner, Orders, June 28, 1846, *CLB*.
6. Bancroft to Conner, May 13, 1846, *H. Ex. Doc. 60, 30th Cong., 1st Sess.*, 233-35.
7. Conner to wife, May 29, 1846, *Conner (FDR)*.
8. Bancroft to Conner, May 13, 1846, *H. Ex. Doc. 60, 30th Cong., 1st Sess.*, 774.
9. Conner to Bancroft, May 8, 13, 1846, *Niles*, LXX (May 30, 1846), 197-98. While the squadron was anchored at the Brazos Santiago the impetuous Commander Saunders apparently suggested a surprise descent on Veracruz. Amos Lawrence Mason (ed.), *Memoir and Correspondence of Charles Steedman* (Cambridge, 1912), 138.
10. Conner, Proclamation, and Conner to Fitzhugh, May 14, Conner to Saunders, and to Gregory, May 17, 1846, all in *CLB*.
11. Conner to Ingraham, May 20, 1846, *CLB*, Consul J. F. McGregor to Ingraham, June 11, Ingraham to Gov. Cardenas, June 12, Ingraham to Conner, June 18, 1846, all in *HSL*. The visit anticipated orders from Washington to support the secessionist movements in Yucatán and Tabasco. Bancroft to Conner, May 19, 1846, *RCL*, I, 181. The mission is discussed extensively in Francis Joseph Manno, "Yucatán en la Guerra entre México y Estados Unitos," *Revistade la Universidad de Yucatán*, V (July-Aug. 1963), 52-54.
12. Saunders to English and French Consuls, May 20, to Bancroft, June 5, to Conner, June 20, Gregory to Nicholas Bravo, May 27, 1846, all in *Conner (LC)*; Chase to Buchanan, June 28, 1846, *Tampico Cons.*, III; Gregory to Conner, May 30, Fitzhugh to Commanders of Foreign Warships, May 20, 1846, both in *Conner (NY)*; Bravo to Gregory, May 28, 1846, Manuel B. Trens, *Historia de Veracruz* (4 vols., México, 1950), IV, 334.
13. Conner apparently agreed with the hope then current in Washington that Tampico might revolt against the Mexican central government. Obviously any attack on the town would retard, if not eliminate, such a movement.
14. Saunders to Conner, June 5, 17, 20, 1846 all in *Conner (NY)*; Conner to Saunders, June 5, 1846, John Lloyal Saunders Papers, L.C.; [Anastasio Parrodi] *Memoria sobre la Evacuación Militar del Puerto de Tampico de Tamaulipas* (San Luis Potosí, 1848), 4; Ramsey, *The Other Side*, 100; [James D. Bruell], *Sea Memories* (Biddeford Pool, 1886), 34-38.
15. Extensive correspondence concerning the logistic support of the Home Squadron exists in *HSL*, *Conner, (LC)*, *Conner (NY)*, *Conner (FDR)*, and in *LB*.
16. Conner to Gregory, July 2, 1846, *CLB*; Gregory to Conner, July 10, 1846, *Conner (NY)*; Rivera, *Historia Antigua y Moderna de Jalapa*, III, 765-66; Trens, *Historia de Veracruz*, IV, 361-62; Parker, *Recollections*, 61-64. In December Conner contracted with a Texan for 50,000 gallons of water. Conner to Mason, Jan. 5, 1847, *HSL*.
17. Bancroft to Conner, May 30, 1846, *RCL*, I, 188; Morris to Conner, June 10, 24, 1846, *Conner (FDR)*; Conner to Bancroft, June 11, 22, 1846, *HSL*.
18. Henderson to Bancroft, May 29, 1846, *MCL*, Supplement 1838-47, #152; Conner to Bancroft, June 10, 1846, *HSL*.
19. Bancroft to Wetmore, May 19, 28, 30, July 16, 1846, all in *LNA*, VII, 96-98, 108; Wetmore to Bancroft, May 25, 1846, *NAL* Jan.-June 1846, #115; Morris to Bancroft, May 22, 1846, *BL* May-Aug. 1846, #14; Conner to Bancroft, July 28, 1846, *HSL*; Bauer, *Surfboats and Horse Marines*, 25-26, 253ff.
20. Conner to Bancroft June 5, 1846, *HSL*.
21. Paredes, Manifesto, July 26, 1846, *YWA*; Ministerio de Guerra y Marina,

Reglamento para el Corso de Particulares Contra los Enemigos de la Nación (México, 1846); Black to Buchanan, July 29, 1846, *M.C. Cons.*, IX; Buchanan to R. M. Saunders, July 13, 1847, Moore, *Works of Buchanan*, VII, 335.

22. Conner to Bancroft, July 28, 1846, *HSL*; Hubert Howe Bancroft, *History of Mexico* (6 vols., San Francisco, 1883–88), V, 490n; Scheina, "Seapower Misused," 212–14.

23. Roa Bárcena, *Recuerdos*, I, 249, 252; Alfonso Toro, *Compendia de la Historia de Mexico* (México, 1943), 449; Vicente Riva Palacio (ed.), *Mexico a Través de los Siglos* (6 vols., México, 1940), IV, 645; Cardenas, *Semblanza Maritima*, I 125–26; Parker, *Recollections*, 65.

24. Conner to Bancroft, July 30, 1846, *Niles*, LXXI (Sept. 5, 1846), 2.

25. Conner to Bancroft, Aug. 10, 1846, *HSL*; Parker, *Recollections*, 65–66; *Niles*, LXXI (Sept. 19, 1846), 34, 36, logs of the vessels involved; Ripley, *War with Mexico*, I, 307; Bauer, *Surfboats and Horse Marines*, 34–35.

26. Conner to wife, June 26, July 3, Sept. 4, 1846, *Conner (FDR)*.

27. Conner to Carpender, Aug. 12, to Engle, Aug. 19, to Jarvis, Aug. 19, 1846, *CLB*, Carpender to Conner, Aug. 18, 1846 enclosing copies of his exchange of letters with General Antonio Rosas in *Conner (FDR)*; Conner to Bancroft, Aug. 12, 24, Hunter to Conner, Aug. 23, Engle to Conner, Aug. 22, 1846, all in *HSL*; Lieutenant C. S. Boggs to Engle, Aug. 22, 1846, in *Conner (NY)*; Taylor, *Broad Pennant*, 256–60. Carpender's men were later exchanged for General la Vega and his staff. Mason to the President, Oct. 27, 1846, *ELB*, V, 309–10; *Niles*, LXXI (Feb. 27, 1847), 402.

28. Conner to Saunders, Sept. 14, 1846, *CLB*; Saunders to Conner, Aug. 15, 1846, *Conner (NY)*; letter of Winslow, Sept. 20, 1846, quoted in John M. Ellicott, *The Life of John Ancrum Winslow* (New York, 1905), 38–39; Taylor, *Broad Pennant*, 262–83.

29. Hunt to Conner, Sept. 7, Conner to Bancroft, Sept. 12, 1846, *HSL*; Robert W. Neeser, *Statistical and Chronological History of the United States Navy* (2 vols., New York, 1909), II, 66, 312.

30. *S. Ex. Doc. 1, 30th Cong., 1st Sess.*, 945; Charles Oscar Paullin, *Paullin's History of Naval Administration*, (Annapolis, 1968), 228.

31. Bancroft to Perry, Aug. 12, 1846, *LO*, XXXIX, 431; Bancroft to Conner, May 7, and Morris to Conner, Nov. 14, 1846, *Conner (NY)*; Samuel Eliot Morison, *"Old Bruin" Commodore Matthew Calbraith Perry* (Boston, 1967), 187.

32. Bauer, *Surfboats and Horse Marines*, 44–45.

33. Quaife, *Diary of Polk*, II, 60–61, 66, 125.

34. Morris to Conner, Sept. 21, 1846, *Conner (FDR)*.

35. The account of this second Alvarado attack is based upon: Conner to Mason, Oct. 17, 1846, *S. Doc. 1, 29th Cong., 2nd Sess.*, 630–31; Conner to Forrest, Nones, Howard, Sands, Shaw, and Benham, Oct. 13, 1846, *CLB*; logs of the vessels involved; Raphael Semmes, *Service Afloat and Ashore During the Mexican War* (Cincinnati, 1851), 88; Parker, *Recollections*, 71–72; Riva Palacio, *México a Través de los Siglos*, IV, 645; Roa Bárcena, *Recuerdos*, I 252–54; Trens, *Historia de Veracruz*, IV, 371–73; Enrique Hurtado y Nuño, "Ataque y Defensa del Puerto de Alvarado." *Revista General de la Armada de México*, III (Aug. 1963), 13–14; Cardenas, *Semblanza Maritima*, I, 127–29; Bauer, *Surfboats and Horse Marines*, 45–47.

36. Today the river is known as the Grijalva.

37. The account of the Tabasco expedition is based upon: Conner to Perry, Oct. 16, to Commanders of the *Vixen*, *McLane*, *Forward*, *Nonata*, *Bonita*, and *Reefer*, Oct. 16, to Forrest, Oct. 16, to Gregory, Oct. 16, 1846, all in *CLB*; Perry to Conner, Nov. 3, 5, 11, 1846, with enclosures, *S. Doc. 1, 29th Cong., 2nd Sess.*,

632–39; Perry to Conner, Oct. 22, 1846, with enclosures, *Conner (NY)*; logs of vessels involved: Semmes, *Service Afloat and Ashore*, 88–90; Parker, *Recollections*, 74; Ramsey, *Other Side*, 433–44; Roa Bárcena, *Recuerdos*, I, 149–50; Manuel Mestre Ghigliazza, *Invasión Norteamericana en Tabasco* (México, 1948), 23–146; Ellicott, *Winslow*, 41; Morison, *"Old Bruin,"* 194–98; Bauer, *Surfboats and Horse Marines*, 49–52; William Elliot Griffis, *Matthew Calbraith Perry* (Boston, 1890), 201–5; Juan de Dios Bonilla, *Historia Marítima de México* (México, 1962), 284–85.

38. Both vessels, the *Petrita* and the *Tabasqueño*, belonged to Luis S. Hargous, the American who held a monopoly of steam navigation on the Grijalva. Deposition of Hargous, Nov. 26, 1846, *M.C. Cons.*, IX.

39. Conner to Lockwood, Nov. 9, 1846, *CLB*; Lockwood to Forrest, Nov. 26, 1846, Samuel Lockwood Papers, YWA; Forrest to Conner, Nov. 26, 1846, *Conner (FDR)*; George Fox Emmons, *The Navy of the United States* (Washington, 1853), 82–83; Neeser, *Statistical and Chronological History*, II, 314–15.

40. Quaife, *Diary of Polk*, II, 147; Marcy to Taylor, Sept. 22, 1846, *H. Ex. Doc. 60, 30th Cong., 1st Sess.*, 341–43; Mason to Conner, Sept. 27, 1846, *RCL*.

41. Santa Anna to Parrodi, Oct. 12, 1846, in Smith, "Letters of Santa Anna," 371; Ramsey, *Other Side*, 100–4; Anna Chase to Conner, Oct. 20, 1846, Hunt to Conner, Oct. 24, 1846, both in *Conner (LC)*.

42. The description of the Tampico seizure is based upon: Conner to Mason, Nov. 5, 11, 24, Dec. 1, 1846, with enclosures, in *S. Doc. 1, 29th Cong., 1st Sess.*, 632–35, 639. *H. Ex. Doc. 1, 30th Cong., 2d Sess.*, 1171–73, and *HSL*; Conner's orders in *CLB*; logs of the vessels involved; Conner to wife, Nov. 17, 1846, *Conner (FDR)*; *Niles*, LXXI (Dec. 19, 1846) 240, 242; Ramsey, *Other Side*, 103–5; Parrodi, *Memoria Sobre la Evacuación* 4, 32–33; Wilcox, *Mexican War*, 177–78; Griffis, *Perry*, 205–8; Bauer, *Surfboats and Horse Marines*, 54–56; Smith, *War with Mexico*, I, 276–81; M. Almy Aldrich, *History of United States Marine Corps* (Boston, 1875), 96.

43. Conner to Mason, Nov. 24, Dec. 1, 1846, *HSL*; Perry to Commanding Military Officer at Point Isabel, Nov. 16, Gates to Bliss, Nov. 26, 1846, *AOLR*, Box 5; Perry to Conner, [Dec. 29, 1846], Patterson to Perry, Nov. 22, 1846, *Conner (NY)*; Smith, *War with Mexico*, I, 281; *Niles*, LXXI (Nov. 28, 1846), 209; Martha Clinton Collins (ed.), "Journal of Francis Collins," *Quarterly Publication of the Historical & Philosophical Society of Ohio*, X (April–July 1915), 42.

44. Conner to Tattnall, Nov. 17, 1846, *CLB*; Tattnall to Conner, Nov. 22, 1846, *H. Ex. Doc. 1, 30th Cong., 1st Sess.*, 1174–75; logs of *Spitfire*; Wilcox, *Mexican War*, 178–79; Ramsey, *Other Side*, 105.

45. Pearson to Mason, Nov. 26, 1846, *Niles*, LXXI (Dec. 19, 1846), 256; Pearson to Conner, Nov. 21, 1846, *AF*, Box 173.

46. James Parker to Semmes, Nov. 28, 1846, *Conner (NY)*; Semmes, *Service Afloat and Ashore*, 91; Parker, *Recollections*, 59–60; Colyer Meriwether, *Raphael Semmes* (Philadelphia, 1914), 35–38.

47. Semmes, *Service Afloat and Ashore*, 91–92, 158–456; Parker, *Recollections*, 60; Semmes to Conner, Dec. 6, 1846, *Conner (FDR)*. See Mason to Perry, March 27, 1847, *H. Ex. Doc. 60, 30th Cong., 1st Sess.*, 977–78 for an indication of Washington's concern about Rogers's fate.

48. Semmes to Perry, Dec. 10, Perry to Mason, Dec. 12, 1846, *S. Doc. 43, 29th Cong., 2nd Sess.*, 1–5; Conner to Mason, Feb. 7, 1847, *HSL*; Semmes, *Service Afloat and Ashore*, 94–95. Congress on March 3, 1847 authorized gold and silver medals for the foreign seamen involved in the rescues. *9 U.S. Stat.*, 208.

49. Conner to Perry, Dec. 16, 1846, *CLB*; Perry, Memorandum, Dec. 21, Perry to Sands, Dec. 21, to Benham, Dec. 23, to Howard, Dec. 23, 1846, all in *Conner*

(NY); Conner to Mason, Dec. 28, Perry to Conner, Dec. 27, 1846, *H. Ex. Doc. 1, 30th Cong., 2d Sess.*, 1176–77; Morison, *"Old Bruin,"* 202–3.

50. Conner to Perry, Dec. 29, 1846, *CLB*. Perry, who wished to be present for the landings, used his considerable political leverage within the navy to get the work done in a third the estimated time. While waiting for the repairs to be finished, he supervised the outfitting of the small craft destined for the Gulf of Mexico. When he left Washington he carried orders to relieve Conner in command of the Home Squadron.

8: The Army of the West

NEWS OF THE OUTBREAK of hostilities along the Rio Grande reached St. Louis in early May when General Gaines's call for volunteers arrived. The metropolis of the West was gripped by excitement as the St. Louis Legion formed and hastened to the assistance of Zachary Taylor's army.[1] In Washington, however, decisions were being made which would direct the attention of Missourians elsewhere.

When President James K. Polk conferred with Secretary William L. Marcy and General Winfield Scott during the afternoon of May 13 they decided as one of their first acts to direct Colonel Stephen W. Kearny, commanding the 1st Dragoons at Fort Leavenworth, to protect the caravans of traders then enroute to Santa Fe. They also agreed to dispatch a column to seize New Mexico. Simultaneously a call was made on Governor John C. Edwards of Missouri for 1,000 mounted volunteers to supplement Kearny's handful of regulars. As a stopgap measure the well-known Santa Fe trader George T. Howard was sent posthaste to overtake the traders and warn them of the hostilities. Howard was to continue on to Santa Fe spreading the alarm among the Americans. In part the warning to the caravans arose from a rumor that they carried munitions and in part from a fear that Governor Manuel Armijo would confiscate the million dollars' worth of American-owned goods in the wagons.[2]

Neither the President nor his advisers appear to have expected opposition to the seizure of New Mexico. The disillusionment of the New Mexicans with the Mexico City government was as well known as their close economic ties to St. Louis. Moreover, as quickly became clear, Polk considered New Mexico one of the priority areas for conquest.[3]

Howard left Washington immediately upon receiving his instructions and reached St. Louis on May 21 but failed to catch the leading caravan. Howard himself stopped at Bent's Fort on the Arkansas to halt the caravans which were plodding along behind him. He sent agents to warn the Americans in Taos and Santa Fe, but the news of war preceded them.[4]

Another factor in the New Mexico situation entered the equation on May 25 when James W. Magoffin received a letter from Senator Thomas Hart Benton requesting him to visit Washington. After a meeting with the President, Benton, and Marcy on June 15, Magoffin received orders to hasten to Santa Fe and Chihuahua ahead of the invasion force. In both towns he was to use his considerable influence to smooth the way for conquest and occupation. The significance of Magoffin's contributions to the conquest has never been satisfactorily established, but there is no uncertainty about Magoffin's view. He claimed credit for undermining the arrangements for the defense of Santa Fe and to have made possible the later entry into Chihuahua. Following the war he submitted an expense account of $37,780.96, of which the Secretary of War concluded $17,670 was legitimate and recommended that he be paid $30,000 to cover both expenses and salary.[5]

As soon as he received orders for the Santa Fe expedition, Colonel Kearny ordered the dragoons to Fort Leavenworth. He sent his aide to Jefferson City to expedite the call for volunteers: one regiment of mounted men, two companies of horse artillery, and a two-company battalion of infantry. Kearny asked Bishop Peter Kendrick of St. Louis for a Catholic priest to accompany the expedition. The latter anticipated a directive issued by Marcy. Like the similar addition of two Catholic chaplains to Taylor's command, this was an attempt to overcome the Mexican fear of militant American Protestantism and to offset some of the potentially most damaging aspects of Mexican propaganda.[6]

On the last day of the month Kearny was directed by General Scott to recruit as many men as possible from among the caravans halted at Bent's Fort and in New Mexico and was told that another thousand Missourians would join his force. Implementing an earlier cabinet decision, Scott also directed him, when New Mexico was safely garrisoned, to lead a force via "the most southern practicable route" to seize Monterey and San Francisco in California. Scott stressed speed. Celerity was important if the expedition was to avoid winter storms in the Sierras.[7]

The cabinet on June 2 approved additional steps aimed at the seizure of California. These included authorizing Kearny to recruit men in California and among the Mormon bands fleeing Illinois. The directive grew out of a series of meetings between the President and Elder Jesse C. Little, the eastern leader of the church. Little had been directed by Brigham Young to investigate the possibility of governmental assistance in emigration to the west coast. He arranged to see the President on May 21 and transmit the request. Polk seized upon it as a means of recruiting additional men for California service. After further discussions with Little, it was agreed that 500 to 1,000 Mormons would be organized under their own officers with a commander appointed by Kearny. The men would enlist with the understanding that they would be discharged in California following a year's service. This ingenious scheme permitted the administration to "placate" the Mormons and at the same time to raise the number of Americans in California. To the Mormons the arrangement represented a workable answer to their request for government assistance.[8]

To carry out the arrangement, Kearny on June 19 directed Captain James Allen to raise four or five companies of Mormons and take command of the battalion as a lieutenant colonel. A week later the Army officer issued his call and, after gaining Brigham Young's support, had no difficulty in securing the men. Four companies and part of a fifth were mustered in at Council Bluffs on July 16.[9]

Kearny's formal orders were issued on June 3 after consultation between the President and Secretary Marcy. The key section, drafted by Polk himself, called for establishing a temporary civil government in the conquered areas and retaining "all such of the existing officers as are known to be friendly to the United States, and will take the oath of allegiance." As guidance for his public statements, Kearny received a copy of the proclamation which had been prepared for Taylor's use. The message further confirmed Kearny's designation as commander of the expedition, and promised him a brigadier general's brevet upon leaving Santa Fe for California.[10]

Kearny was one of the ablest officers in the Army but a Whig who owed his appointment largely to the influence of his fellow St. Louisian, Senator Benton.[11] It is one of the ironies of the war that Benton would become Kearny's implacable enemy as a result of the latter's collision with Benton's son-in-law, John C. Frémont.

In early June reports, which later proved to be inaccurate, reached Fort Leavenworth that Governor Armijo had sent two companies of Mexican dragoons to escort the munitions to Santa Fe. Kearny promptly dispatched Captain Benjamin D. Moore with two companies of the 1st Dragoons to prevent it. Moore's command rode out on June 5, the advance element of nearly 2,000 men destined for New Mexico. Moore also had orders to seize about $10,000 worth of goods in the caravan belonging to Armijo. Kearny, who well understood his opponent, concluded that "if we can secure that property, we hold the governor as our friend & ally . . . ."[12]

The day following Moore's departure, the advance elements of Colonel Alexander Doniphan's 1st Missouri Mounted Volunteers began arriving at Fort Leavenworth. Over the next two weeks other Missouri volunteers marched into the base, were organized, mustered into service, and given the rudiments of military training. As soon as they were ready, Kearny sent Doniphan's men off on the dusty march to Santa Fe. The advance in small detachments served to conserve the scarce grass and water along the route as much as feasible.[13] Since the likelihood of meeting any Mexican troops north of the Arkansas River crossing at Bent's Fort was negligible, the division of the army presented no danger. The real obstacles to the expedition were distance and logistics.

Doniphan's companies marched between June 22 and 28, followed on the thirtieth by Kearny, his staff, and the artillery. The Army of the West, as Kearny called his command, consisted of 1,458 men, plus some 1,000 who would follow later. It had as artillery Major Meriwether Lewis Clark's Battalion of Missouri Volunteer Artillery with twelve 6-pounders and a quartet of 12-pounder howitzers. In its train the army had 1,556 wagons, 459 horses, 3,658 draft mules, and 14,904 cattle and oxen.[14] The mere acquisition of transport speaks highly of the efficiency of the Quartermaster office in St. Louis and of Kearny's capabilities, since he lacked a staff quartermaster throughout the buildup.

The 537-mile march from Fort Leavenworth to Bent's Fort was an exercise in human misery.[15] Most of the men were not yet acclimated to long marches and their discomfort was heightened by the heat, dust, and aridness of the plains. The army's route took it south across the Kansas River to Elm Grove where it picked up the Santa Fe Trail. It followed that well-marked road to the Arkansas River and then marched along that stream until the various elements moved into their camps which were scattered across the prairie about seven miles east of the famed adobe-walled trading post of Bent's Fort on July 29.

While Kearny's force plodded doggedly forward, a rumor reached Jefferson City and flew on to Washington that Armijo had a much larger force than originally anticipated. The rumor had little basis in fact, as Kearny learned on July 19 when Howard returned from his Paul Revere mission. The populace, he reported, was ready to accept occupation but not the leaders, who were attempting to collect 2,300 men to defend Santa Fe. This was confirmed by other information available at Bent's.[16]

During the final day of July Kearny issued a proclamation which played upon the divisions within New Mexico. It announced the impending arrival of the American force "for the purpose of seeking union with, and ameliorating the condition of the inhabitants" and promised protection of civil and religious rights.[17]

The same day Major Edwin V. Sumner reached camp with two additional companies of dragoons. Close on their heels came Magoffin, the Santa Fe agent. After conferring, Kearny and Magoffin agreed that the agent would continue on to Santa Fe with an escort of twelve dragoons under Captain Philip St. George Cooke. To give cover to his mission, Cooke carried a letter to Armijo. In it Kearny reiterated most of the arguments of his proclamation and closed by pointing out that resistance would only inflict suffering on the civilians.[18]

The Army of the West broke camp on August 2.[19] It crossed the Arkansas at Bent's and moved south generally following the present U. S. Routes 85 and 87 through the Raton Pass, which was traversed on August 7. The road proved to be nearly impassable in stretches. To add to their discomfort the troops ate half rations or less, so that one young officer reported Major Clark was "wholly cast down" although his artillery battalion "bear up tolerably well, but Col. Doniphan's Regiment to a man is sick and tired of the business."[20] Once through the pass the Americans met several groups of Mexicans whom they considered for the most part, undoubtedly correctly, to be spies. Along the way Kearny's men also learned that Armijo was fortifying Apache Canyon about twelve miles from Santa Fe.

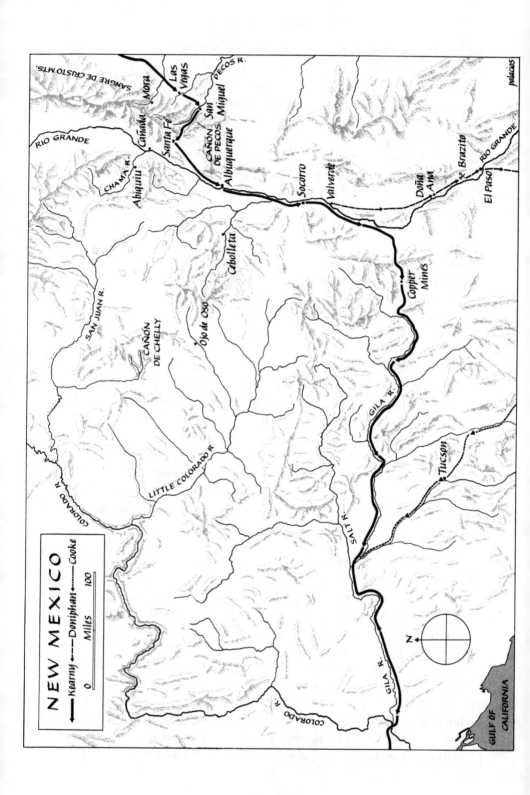

NEW MEXICO

Kearny ←→ Doniphan ·····→ Cooke

Miles
0   100

SANGRE DE CRISTO MTS.

Las Vegas

PECOS R.

Mora

Cañada

San Miguel

Santa Fe

CAÑON DE PECOS

RIO GRANDE

Albuquerque

CHAMA R.

Abiquiu

Socorro

Valverde

Doña Ana

Brazito

RIO GRANDE

El Paso

Cebolleta

Ojo de Oso

Copper Mines

CAÑON DE CHELLY

SAN JUAN R.

GILA R.

Tucson

LITTLE COLORADO R.

COLORADO R.

SALT R.

COLORADO R.

GILA R.

N

GULF OF CALIFORNIA

palacios

The New Mexico Governor is best described as a crafty adventurer whose generally affable exterior cloaked unexpected energy and cunning. He had ample warning of the impending invasion but was hampered by limited resources. His appeals to Colonel Mauricio Ugarte, the *commandante-general* of Chihuahua, produced reassuring words but no troops. Therefore, on August 8 Armijo summoned the New Mexicans to take up arms to repel the invader. About 4,000 Mexicans and Indians gathered at Canoncito in Apache Canyon under Colonel Manuel Pino. There the road ran between walls as close as forty feet apart and was obstructed by an abatis. A battery emplaced on a hill 300 yards beyond commanded the passage. Although the position could have been bypassed and the abatis was poorly placed, it would have entailed heavy fighting to carry the position.

Magoffin and Captain Cooke's escort reached Santa Fe on the twelfth and immediately delivered Kearny's letter. The Governor refused to recognize the Rio Grande boundary and announced that, since the people had risen en masse, he must lead them. Nevertheless, Armijo proposed negotiations to be carried out at the village of Las Vegas. All of this was contained in a letter delivered to Kearny on August 14. Kearny bade the messenger: "Say to General Armijo I shall soon meet him, and I hope it will be as friends."

Before the army broke camp on August 15 to resume its southward march, Major Thomas Swords arrived from Missouri with Kearny's commission as a permanent Brigadier General. When the force reached Las Vegas later that day, Kearny addressed about 150 uncertain citizens, promising them good government and protection of their freedoms, and administered oaths of allegiance to the local officials. Armijo failed to appear, despite his promise, although Cooke and his men rejoined at noon. At San Miguel, another small village, Kearny repeated the ceremony of an address followed by the swearing in. When the alcalde demurred at taking the oath, preferring to await the fall of Santa Fe, Kearny exploded: "It is enough for you to know, Sir, that I have captured your town." The point was not lost on the Mexican. Even more important in the long run was the General's insistence on paying for some corn which had been stolen by the troops.

If Armijo and Colonel Pino were ready and willing to fight for the New Mexico capital, few others had it in their hearts. That lack of will and unity of purpose had been strengthened by Magoffin's argument that American rule would benefit Santa Fe and increase its trade. The American agent also argued that resistance was impractical. To Lieutenant Governor Diego Archuleta he hinted that the United States would leave him unmolested and in control of the portion of the state west of the Rio Grande. Armijo felt so unsure of his own position that he kept the ninety regular dragoons who were the backbone of the defending army with him as a bodyguard. During the sixteenth he convened a council of war and found his officers so opposed to fighting that he disbanded the army. The New Mexicans drifted back to their homes while Armijo and his body-guard rode hard for Chihuahua.[21]

News of the welcome development reached Kearny in a letter from Acting Governor Juan Bautista Vigil y Alarid. It was carried by Secretary of State Nicholas Quintaro, who appeared astride a mule and with a roar of laughter cried: "Armijo and his troops have gone to Hell and the canyon is all clear." During the morning of the eighteenth the army traversed Apache Canyon with its silent cannon, breathed a collective sigh of relief at the departure of the cannoneers, and beheld the "irregular cluster of low, flat roofed, mud built, dirty houses" which from a distance resembled "more a prairie-dog village than a capital."[22] They had come 856 miles in less than two months.

About one o'clock that afternoon the advance guard under Lieu-tenant Thomas C. Hammond led the Army of the West into Santa Fe. Vigil welcomed the conquerors and Kearny replied with a short address. The army then paraded through the little town and honored the raising of the American flag over the one-story, adobe gover-nor's palace with a 13-gun salute. On the nineteenth Kearny made a second, more formal address in which a mixture of courtesy and firmness produced an excellent impression on the inhabitants. Vigil responded with a short talk accepting annexation, although clearly without enthusiasm. The following day the chiefs of the nearby Indian pueblos made their submissions. Kearny followed on August 22 with a proclamation which emphasized the protection of religion, persons, and property; freed all New Mexicans from their allegiance to Mexico; and announced annexation of the state to the United States.[23]

Kearny showed great tact and understanding in his dealings with the New Mexicans. He made a point of attending Mass in the cathe-dral on the twenty-third and on the following Thursday gave a ball which attracted 400 or 500 New Mexicans and Americans despite music which Kearny's adjutant reported as "'execrable."[24] Equally successful was Kearny's visit on September 2-11, with 700 dragoons and volunteers, to the downriver settlements as far as Tomé, below Albuquerque. Everywhere along the line of march the Americans were greeted warmly. The excursion served both to show the flag and to investigate rumors of an uprising supported by Ugarte's troops from Chihuahua. Actually Ugarte turned back after reaching El Paso because of semidesert ahead and Armijo's report that 6,000 Americans held Santa Fe.[25]

Nor did Kearny overlook his duties as military governor. On August 27 he established standard license fees for a wide variety of businesses including stores, taverns, pool halls, and gambling houses. Colonel Doniphan and Private Willard P. Hall, a lawyer in civilian life, undertook to prepare a law code for the territory. Drawing upon numerous sources including the existing New Mexico laws as well as those of Missouri and Texas, they prepared a code which Kearny published on September 22. The same day he appointed Charles Bent of Taos, one of the proprietors of Bent's Fort, Territorial Governor.[26]

In establishing a civilian government, Kearny introduced a complex legal issue. Since the area had not yet been transferred to American title and since the Constitution reserves to Congress the right to establish governments in territories and unorganized lands, he had no statutory authority for his actions. As Secretary Marcy later explained: "The temporary civil government in New Mexico results from the conquest of the country. It does not derive its existence directly from the laws of Congress, or the Constitution of the United States, and the President cannot in any character than that of Commander-in-chief exercise any control over it."[27]

Nevertheless, Kearny's government was severely attacked in Congress. Polk readily conceded the excess when pressed in order to prevent the issue from becoming a political football. But he took no steps to censure Kearny.[28]

Kearny set September 25 as the target date for his departure for California even though the Mormons and the second regiment of Missourians would not yet have arrived. The Mormons, he concluded, could follow in his trace. He spelled out his plans in detail in a September 16 letter to the Adjutant General which also suggested recruiting special units for service in California and forming military colonies there from among discharged soldiers. He also requested orders to send the dragoons back to their permanent station at Fort Leavenworth in the spring if the danger to California had then disappeared.[29]

Kearny concluded that two regiments were a larger force than needed to garrison a pacified New Mexico. Since he had earlier promised to dispatch any surplus troops to the Chihuahua column of General John E. Wool, he directed Doniphan to lead his regiment there upon relief by Price. This would leave Price his regiment, Captain William Z. Angney's battalion of Missouri infantry, and Clark's artillery. They would be sufficient, Kearny reasoned, to hold the Indians in check if wisely placed.[30] Another consideration had to be the difficulties of supplying the New Mexico troops. Very few supplies, except for meat, could be secured locally. The distances involved and the nature of the country offered nearly insurmountable obstacles to bringing supplies from Missouri.

Of immediate concern to Kearny was the security of the New Mexico settlements. They dotted the Rio Grande valley and the headwaters of the Great River. A few others, as we have seen, were strung along the Santa Fe Trail east of the Sangre de Cristo Range. A second group of villages and ranches in the Santa Cruz River valley near Tucson played no great role in our story. Along the northern and western fringes of the settled area ranged the Jicarilla Apaches who lived by raiding the herds and the Mexican and Indian ranches.

In mid-September Kearny threw garrisons into Abiquiu and Cebolleta on the northern frontier. He also sent mounted detachments into Apache country in search of stolen property. All of the detachments were directed to bring the "principal men among those Indians" to Santa Fe for a council. Most successful was Major William Gilpin, who induced fifty or sixty Ute leaders to meet with Doniphan at Santa Fe in mid-October. Kearny's efforts to contain the Indians through the use of scattered garrisons and active patrols failed. The depredations continued. On October 3 he postponed Doniphan's departure until the Indians had been brought to heel, and on the eighteenth resorted to the traditional local-police method of authorizing punitive expeditions by aggrieved settlers.[31]

Doniphan's response to the Indian problem was decisive. He sent three separate columns into Navajo country. Between them they scoured all parts of it and met with nearly 75 percent of the tribe. One force of about 200 men under Gilpin left Abiquiu on October 22 and struggled through deep snow and nearly impassable mountains into present-day southern Colorado. There they convinced a large group of Navajo to meet with Doniphan at Ojo del Oso (Bear Spring), present-day Gallup, New Mexico. Another column, thirty volunteers under Captain John Reid accompanied by the Navajo Chief Sandoval, left Cebolleta on October 20 on a twenty-day march through Navajo country. During this march they met the senior chief, Narbona, and encountered only friendly Navajo. Doniphan with 150 men marched through the heavy snow to the Ojo del Oso council point. There on November 22 he signed a peace treaty with about 500 Navajo. On the way back to the Rio Grande one American column visited the Zuñi and assisted in negotiating a treaty between them and the Navajo. All Doniphan's men had gathered at Valverde on the Rio Grande by mid-December.[32]

Meanwhile, Kearny's California column was making its way west. The General set out during the afternoon of September 25 with about 300 mule-mounted dragoons and a small group of topographical engineers accompanied by a small wagon train.[33] The force moved down the east bank of the Rio Grande until it reached Albuquerque where it crossed to follow the west bank. On October 3 the Americans had a touch of excitement as reports arrived of a Navajo raid on a small village about twelve miles to the south.

During the sixth, about ten miles below Socorro, the column met Kit Carson and his nineteen-man escort riding east with Commodore Robert F. Stockton's report of the seizure of California. The mountain man confirmed the truth of the reports. Since California had been pacified, the trail ahead was difficult, and forage and water were scarce, Kearny decided to send the bulk of his force back to Santa Fe under Major Sumner. Kearny kept only two companies, about 100 men, under Captain Moore and a pair of mountain howitzers as an escort. The General also prevailed upon Carson, who knew the route better than anyone else, to transfer his dispatches to Tom Fitzpatrick and guide the force westward.[34]

Shortly afterward Kearny, on Carson's advice, sent back for pack saddles. The road ahead was too rough for wagons. On October 14 the column, having replaced the wagons with pack mules, started again and during the following day swung inland from the river. By the eighteenth it had reached the Copper Mines near present-day Silver City, New Mexico. There Mangas Coloradas, the Chief of the Mimbros Apaches, promised to send men to point out a good wagon route for the Mormons to follow. Kearny's force struggled on through the rugged mountains of southern Arizona and crossed the continental divide the next day. On the twentieth they reached the southernmost branch of the Gila River. For nearly 450 miles the men and their weary animals trudged down its course, crossing deep gullies and passing through narrow canyons whose overhanging cliffs nearly shut out the sunlight. At other times they made wide detours to avoid impassable canyons.

In early November they secured a few fresh mules from the local Coyotero Apaches and on the tenth passed the remains of the Casa Grande pueblo. On the following afternoon they reached the main village of the Pina Indians, about ninety miles from the Mexican settlement at Tucson. Here the Americans rested for two days. By November 22 they had reached the junction of the Gila and the Colorado. Nearby they bought some mustangs from a party of Mexicans who also gave Kearny his first news of the revolt in southern California and the important information that Commodore Stockton was at San Diego. On the twenty-fifth Carson guided the force across the Colorado into what is today California. There the little army began the last but most difficult and destructive portion of its march. It quickly passed from well-watered bottomlands into desert. There the heat and scarcity of water soon told on the already jaded animals. They began to collapse in increasing numbers. Their riders were in scarcely better shape. It was a hungry and exhausted force that struggled into Warner's Ranch, the first habitation north of the desert, during the mid-afternoon of December 3. From there the force would move into the complicated politico-military maneuverings within California, as we shall see.

Kearny had left Santa Fe before the arrival of Colonel Price's regiment or the Mormon Battalion. Immediately after arriving on October 2, Price wrote that the President wished him to proceed to California immediately. On what this flight of fancy was based is not clear. Kearny, however, proved quite adept at handling the egocentric Missouri politician. You may lead 500 men to California, he replied, provided you can equip them.[35] Since that was a manifest impossibility, no more was heard of the project.

Price's letter also relayed the news of Colonel Allen's death. Kearny promptly named Captain Cooke as his replacement and ordered him to assume the lieutenant colonelcy of the battalion and lead it to California, cutting a wagon road as it went. The Mormons reached Santa Fe between October 9 and 13 and were elated that Colonel Doniphan greeted their arrival with a 100-gun salute. Their old adversary, Sterling Price, had received no such ovation.[36]

Cooke assumed command on the thirteenth. One of his earliest actions was to send the sick and most of the families which had accompanied the force into winter quarters near what is today Pueblo, Colorado. In the spring most of them rejoined the main body of the Mormons for the trek to Utah.[37] The rest of the battalion marched westward on October 19, accompanied by a dozen wagons and half that number of oxcarts.[38] It moved down the Rio Grande until November 13 and then swung west over the Old Spanish Trail. Following a route considerably to the south of Kearny's, the Mormons reached the vicinity of Tucson on December 14. The Mexican garrison there fled on their approach. Cooke replenished his supplies there from the government stores but assured Governor Manuel Gandara of Sonora that he had not come to make war on the civilians. He had, he explained, entered the state only on a scientific mission, exploring for the wagon road to California. The Mormon command then passed north along the Santa Cruz River and on December 21 struck the Gila. Like Kearny's force they followed that stream down to about the site of present-day Yuma, Arizona, where on January 11 they crossed to start the desert passage. During January 29-30, 1847 they straggled into San Diego, nearly naked and shoeless, but with most of their wagons. Their commander cheered them with the claim that "History may be searched in vain for an equal march of infantry."[39] While the dispassionate historian may eschew such verbal fireworks, the Mormon march was clearly one of the most notable accomplishments of a war in which American soldiers made some of military history's more illustrious marches. Cooke's accomplishment ranks with those of Kearny, Doniphan, and Wool.

While the California columns marched westward, the occupation forces in New Mexico faced a revolt. On December 15, 1846 Colonel Price learned that an uprising was being planned. Price arrested most of those implicated and, although the ringleaders escaped, concluded that the revolt had been scotched. Governor Bent felt so confident that he returned home to Taos on January 14 to spend time with his family. There, on the nineteenth, he and six others were killed by Indians. Whether this was part of a larger conspiracy as claimed by Colonel Price, Acting Governor Donaciano Vigil, and others or was an isolated incident is uncertain. It was followed by the murder of seven Americans at the Arroyo Hondo, four at Mora, and two others on the Rio Colorado. Although Pablo Montoya was later convicted of masterminding the revolt, the leader was undoubtedly former Lieutenant Governor Archuleta who felt aggrieved by Kearny's annexation of all of the state despite Magoffin's promise that he could rule the western portion. The following day Jesus Tafolla and Antonio María Trujillo called for a general revolt to take place on the twenty-second.[40]

Colonel Price learned of the insurrection of the twentieth and promptly organized his counterstroke. He ordered the troops stationed at Albuquerque to march north to form the bulk of his mobile force, and on the twenty-third led 353 men and four howitzers into the field. During the early afternoon of January 24 his advance party discovered a large body (perhaps as many as 1,500) of New Mexicans in a valley bordering the Rio Grande near present-day Santa Cruz. When Price and his men rushed them, the untrained insurgents fled. Meanwhile, other units had moved into the trouble area. Captain Israel R. Hendley occupied Las Vegas with his company to forestall any difficulties there. On the twenty-fourth he cornered a group of 150 to 200 insurgents at Mora but lost his own life along with those of four of his men in the assault. The survivors, however, claimed to have killed fifteen or twenty rebels as well as seizing another fifteen. The Las Vegas force then hastened back to Santa Fe, which was rumored to be in danger.

After his successful action at Santa Cruz, Price continued up the Rio Grande picking up scattered detachments as he marched. On the twenty-ninth he drove the insurgents from a strong position along the Embudo road through excellent use of flanking parties. The Americans pushed through deep snow toward Taos, which was the center of the resistance. On February 3 they made contact with the insurgents dug in at the Pueblo de Taos. Price's attempt that afternoon to force them out by shelling the town failed. During the fourth the Americans surrounded the town but discovered that their artillery was too light to breach the adobe walls. After over four hours of shelling and infantry attacks, the Americans finally broke through the wall of the church and fought their way into the town. The insurgents fled to houses on the east side of the town but were soon forced from them and fled toward the mountains. They were pursued by some of the mounted Americans, who killed fifty-one of them. The remainder surrendered on the fifth. In the action, Price lost seven men killed, including Captain John H. Burgwin of the dragoons, and forty-five wounded. Price claims to have killed 150 insurgents, but the number seems excessive.

Two of the alleged ringleaders in the insurrection were captured.

One, Tomás Baca, an Indian implicated in Bent's murder, was killed by one of his guards before being brought to trial. The other, Pablo Montoya, was tried and hanged for treason.[41]

Price's response to the uprising was decisive and effective. As soon as he was aware of the magnitude of the revolt he collected a strong force and moved without hesitation to destroy the centers of insurrection. The effect was salutary. Never again was the American hold on New Mexico threatened. Price had put the finishing touches on the conquest begun by Kearny's Army of the West.

NOTES

For key to abbreviations used in Notes, see page xi.

1. Thomas Fitzpatrick to Abert, May 12, 1846, J. W. Abert Papers, Missouri Historical Society.
2. Quaife, *Diary of Polk*, I, 396; Marcy to Edwards, and to Howard, both May 13, 1846, *SWMA*, XXVI, 252–55; Marcy to Kearny, May 14, 1846, *H. Ex. Doc. 17, 31st Cong., 1st Sess.*, 235; Jones to Kearny, May 13, 14, 1846, *AGLS*, XXII, 638, 640; Leo E. Oliva, *Soldiers on the Santa Fe Trail* (Norman, 1967), 57.
3. William H. Goetzmann, *Exploration and Empire* (New York, 1966), 52. As early as August 1845 the War Department had solicited detailed information and recommendations from Major Richard B. Lee, who had recently returned from the New Mexico capital. Jones to Lee, Aug. 31, 1845, *AGLS*, XXI, 845. Kearny in March had recommended establishing posts at Santa Fe and near present day Presidio, Texas, in order to control the road to Chihuahua. Kearny to Marcy, March 4, 1846, *AGLR'46*, K-36.
4. Ralph P. Bieber (ed.), *Journal of a Soldier under Kearny and Doniphan 1846–1847, George Rutledge Gibson* (Glendale, 1935), 28–29 (The original is in MoHS); Smith, *War with Mexico*, I, 289; Oliva, *Soldiers on Santa Fe Trail*, 58.
5. Bernard DeVoto, *The Year of Decision, 1846* (Boston, 1943), 250–51; Marcy to Kearny, and to CO Chihuahua Expedition, both June 18, 1846, *H. Ex. Doc. 17, 31st Cong., 1st Sess.*, 240–41; Magoffin to Sec. War G. W. Crawford, April 4, and Crawford to the President, April 1, 1849, in Ralph Emerson Twitchell, *The Conquest of Santa Fe 1846* (Truchas, 1967), 52–66; Oliva, *Soldiers on Santa Fe Trail*, 72–74; Benton, *30 Years View*, 683.
6. Kearny to Jones, May 28, and to Marcy June 15, 1846, *KLB*, 2–5, 23; Marcy to Kearny, May 27, 1846, *H. Ex. Doc. 17, 31st Cong., 1st Sess.*, 236; Marcy to Kendrick, May 29, 1846, *SWMA*, XXVI, 260–61. The project never materialized. McEniry, *American Catholics*, 49n.
7. Scott to Kearny, May 31, 1846, *H. Ex. Doc. 60, 30th Cong., 1st Sess.*, 241–42; Quaife, *Diary of Polk*, I, 429, 438–39. The additional Missourians were a regiment raised by Sterling Price which Polk directed to be taken into service. Marcy to Edwards, June 2, 3, and to Price, June 3, 1846, all in *S. Doc. 439, 29th Cong., 1st Sess.*, 2–4; Smith, *War with Mexico*, I, 290.
8. Quaife, *Diary of Polk*, I, 443, 445–46, 449, 473; Daniel Tyler, *A Concise History of the Mormon Battalion in the Mexican War 1846–1847* (n.p., 1881), 111–12; Frank Alfred Golder, *The March of the Mormon Battalion from Council Bluffs to California. Taken from the Journal of Henry Standage* (New York, 1928),

75–88; Brigham Henry Roberts, *The Mormon Battalion. Its History and Achievements* (Salt Lake City, 1919), 8–11. A rumor current among the Mormons at a later date held that the federal government had decided that if they did not provide the desired volunteers, Missourians would be recruited instead and turned loose on the Mormons. See "Extracts from the Journal of Henry W. Bigler," *UHQ*, V (April 1932), 36. A good example of the Missourians' antagonism toward the Mormons is Governor Edwards's protest to Marcy, Aug. 11, 1846, in Golder, *March of the Mormon Battalion*, 97–99.

9. Kearny to Allen, June 19, H. Ex. Doc. 17, 31st Cong., 1st Sess., 236; Hubert Howe Bancroft, *History of California* (7 vols., San Francisco, 1884–90), V, 474–77; Tyler, *Mormon Battalion*, 119–31; Golder, *March of the Mormon Battalion*, 109–38; Bigler, "Extracts," 35–36; Erwin G. Gudde, *Bigler's Chronicle of the West. The Conquest of California, Discovery of Gold, and Mormon Settlement as Reflected in Henry William Bigler's Diaries* (Berkeley, 1962), 16–17.

10. Marcy to Kearny, June 3, 5, 1846, H. Ex. Doc. 60, 30th Cong., 1st Sess., 153–55, 168; Polk to Marcy, June 2, 1846, William L. Marcy Papers, XI.

11. Thomas Kearny, "Kearny and 'Kit' Carson As Interpreted by Stanley Vestal," *NMHR*, V (Jan. 1930), 2.

12. Abraham R. Johnston, "Journal of the March of the Army of the West . . . to Santa Fe . . . 1846," in Ralph P. Bieber (ed.), *Marching with the Army of the West 1846–1848* (Glendale, 1936), 73 (The original is in *AGLR'46*, K-209); Kearny to G. T. Thomas, June 4, to Jones, June 5, to Moore June 5, 6, 1846, all in *KLB*, 12, 14, 16–17.

13. Army of the West, Orders #4, June 27, 1846, AGLR'46, K-209; Smith, *War with Mexico*, I, 286; Hubert Howe Bancroft, *History of Arizona and New Mexico* (San Francisco, 1889), 409; Jacob S. Robinson, *A Journal of the Santa Fe Expedition Under Colonel Doniphan* (Princeton, 1932), 1.

14. Kearny to Jones, June 29, 1846, AGLR'46, K-209; Dwight L. Clarke, *Stephen Watts Kearny Soldier of the West* (Norman, 1961), 108–9. John T. Hughes, *Doniphan's Expedition* (Cincinnati, 1848), 27, gives 1,658 men, which is probably a misprint.

15. The march to Bent's Fort is described in Dwight L. Clarke (ed.), *The Original Journals of Henry Smith Turner* (Norman, 1966), 58–66; Hughes, *Doniphan's Expedition*, 30–57; Johnston, "Journal," 73–90; Marcellus Ball Edwards, "Journal," in Bieber, *Marching with the Army of the West*, 115–60 (The original is in MoHS.); Kearny to Jones, Aug. 1, 1846, AGLR'46, K-209; Bieber, *Journal of Gibson*, 30–165; Frank S. Edwards, *A Campaign in New Mexico* (Philadelphia, 1847), 23–36.

16. Quaife, *Diary of Polk*, II, 31; Marcy to Edwards, July 18, 1846, *SWMA*, XXVI, 411; Jones to Shields, July 18, 1846, *AGLS*, XXII, 1062; Clarke, *Kearny*, 121; Johnston, "Journal," 91. As a result of the rumor, Brigadier General James Shields was ordered to join Kearny with an Illinois regiment but he departed for the Rio Grande before receiving the orders. A Missouri unit was substituted.

17. Kearny, Proclamation, July 31, 1846, H. Ex. Doc. 60, 30th Cong., 1st Sess., 168.

18. Kearny to Jones and to Armijo, both Aug. 1, 1846, AGLR'46, K-209; Smith, *War with Mexico*, I. 290.

19. The march from Bent's to Santa Fe is described in Clarke, *Journals of Turner*, 67–72; Johnston, "Journal," 92–103; Bieber, *Journal of Gibson*, 170–95; Hughes, *Doniphan's Expedition*, 58–79; William H. Emory, *Notes of a Military Reconnaissance from Fort Leavenworth . . . to San Francisco . . .* (Washington, 1848), 15–32; Edwards, *Campaign in New Mexico*, 36–45.

20. Turner to wife, Aug. 5, 1846, Clarke, *Journals of Turner*, 137.

21. Smith, *War with Mexico*, I, 289–90, 293–95; Bancroft, *History of Arizona and*

New Mexico, 413; Clarke, *Kearny*, 133; Ralph Emerson Twitchell, *The Military Occupation of New Mexico from 1846–1851* (Denver, 1909), 60–63; Philip St. George Cooke, *The Conquest of New Mexico and California* (New York, 1878), 7–34; William A. Keleher, *Turmoil in New Mexico, 1846–1868* (Santa Fe, 1952), 8–12, 18–20; Howard Roberts Lamar, *The Far Southwest 1846–1912* (New Haven, 1966), 60–62; *Niles*, LXXI (Oct. 10, 1846), 92; reports of "Citizens of New Mexico" and Armijo reprinted in *NMHR*, XXVI (Jan. 1951), 68–78. Armijo's problems in arranging for a defense of the state are detailed in Daniel Tyler, "Governor Armijo's Moment of Truth," *Journal of the West*, XI (April 1972), 307–16.

22. [Frederick] A. Wislizenus, *Memoir of a Tour to Northern Mexico, Connected with Col. Doniphan's Expedition, in 1846 and 1847* (Glorieta, N. M. 1969), 20; John Porter Bloom, "New Mexico as Viewed by Americans, 1846–1849," *NMHR*, XXXIV (July 1959), 165–98, is a good summary of the impressions which the area made on its conquerors.

23. Smith, *War with Mexico*, I, 295–96; *Niles*, LXXI (Oct. 3, 1846), 80; Johnston, "Journal," 103; Keleher, *Turmoil in Mexico*, 13; Kearny's speech and Vigil's written reply are in Twitchell, *Military Occupation of New Mexico*, 73–75; the proclamation is in *H. Ex. Doc. 60, 30th Cong., 1st Sess.*, 120–21.

24. Clarke, *Journals of Turner*, 74.

25. Army of the West, Orders #16, 20, Aug. 25, 30, 1846, *AGLR'46*, K-209; Kearny to Jones, Sept. 16, 1846, *H. Ex. Doc. 60, 30th Cong., 1st Sess.*, 175–76; Hughes, *Doniphan's Expedition*, 99–117; Edwards, "Journal," 165–71; Clarke, *Kearny*, 151, 153–54; Cooke, *Conquest*, 49; Smith, *War with Mexico*, I, 297.

26. Kearny, Proclamation, Aug. 27, 1846, Kearny to AG, Sept. 22, 1846, enclosing the "Organic Law of the Territory of New Mexico," and "Laws for the Government of the Territory of New Mexico," all in *H. Ex. Doc. 60, 30th Cong., 1st Sess.*, 172–73, 195–229; David Yancy Thomas, *A History of Military Government in Newly Acquired Territory of the United States* (New York, 1904), 101–5. Lamar, *Far Southwest*, p. 65, attacks the choice of officials as favoring Taos and ex-Missourians while overlooking men from Santa Fe and the downriver settlements.

27. Marcy to Price, June 11, 1846, *H. Ex. Doc. 70, 30th Cong., 1st Sess.*, 31–33.

28. *Cong. Globe, 29th Cong., 2d Sess.*, 1412; Polk to House, Dec. 22, 1846, Richardson, *Messages and Papers*, V, 2356–57; Quaife, *Diary of Polk*, II, 281–82; Thomas, *Military Government*, 106–8, 112.

29. Kearny to Jones, Sept. 16, 1846, *H. Ex. Doc. 60, 30th Cong., 1st Sess.*, 175–76, The Mormons left Fort Leavenworth on Aug. 12–13. Colonel Allen died of "congestive fever" on Aug. 23 and the unit completed its march under Lieutenant A. J. Smith. They reached Santa Fe October 9–13. The march is described in Tyler, *Mormon Battalion*, 138–44; "The Journal of Robert S. Bliss, with the Mormon Battalion," *UHQ*, IV (July 1931), 68–74; "Extracts from the Journal of John Steele," *ibid.*, VI (Jan. 1933), 8–10; Bigler, "Extracts," 37–41; Golder, *March of the Mormon Battalion*, 147–71; David B. Gracy II and Helen J. Rugeley (eds.), "From the Mississippi to the Pacific: An Englishman in the Mormon Battalion," *Arizona and the West*, VII (Summer, 1965), 135–43. Col. Sterling Price's 2d Missouri Mounted Riflemen left Fort Leavenworth about two weeks after the Mormons but, being mounted, reached Santa Fe between Sept. 28 and Oct. 10. Bieber, *Journal of Gibson*, 244–45; Richardson, *Journal*, 9–22.

30. Kearny to Jones, Aug. 24, 1846, *ibid.*, 169; Army of the West, Orders #30, Sept. 23, 1846, *AGLR'46*, K-209 (misdated Sept. 18 in Hughes, *Doniphan's Expedition*, 126).

31. Army of the West, Orders #23, SO#7, Aug. 16, Kearny, Proclamation, Oct.

18, 1846, *AGLR'46*, K-209; Turner to Waldemar Fischer, to C. F. Ruff, to Gilpin, all Aug. 16, 1846, *KLB*, 59–61; Hughes, *Doniphan's Expedition*, 128–30; Robinson, *Journal*, 37; Keleher, *Turmoil in New Mexico*, 23; Thomas L. Karnes, *William Gilpin Western Nationalist* (Austin, 1970), 157.

32. Bancroft, *Arizona and New Mexico*, 421–22; Hughes, *Doniphan's Expedition*, 143–90; Keleher, *Turmoil in New Mexico*, 24–26; Jenkins, *War Between U.S. and Mexico*, 306; Horatio O. Ladd, *The War with Mexico* (New York, 1883), 101–9; Karnes, *Gilpin*, 157–61; Edwards, "Journal," 177–212; William H. Richardson, *The Journal of William H. Richardson, A Private Soldier in the Campaign of New and Old Mexico* (Baltimore, 1848), 23–38; Doniphan to Jones, March 5, 1847, *S. Ex. Doc. 1, 30th Cong., 1st Sess.*, 498–502 (misdated April 4).

33. Kearny to Jones, Dec. 12, 1846, *ibid.*, 513–14. The march is described in Emory, *Notes of a Military Reconnaissance*, 45–113; Clarke, *Journals of Turner*, 76–124; Johnston, "Journal," 567–614; Clarke, *Kearny*, 163–94.

34. Army of the West, Order #34, Oct. 6, 1846, *S. Ex. Doc. 33, 30th Cong., 1st Sess.*, 331; Emory, *Notes of a Military Reconnaissance*, 30–31; Swords to Jesup, Oct. 8, 1847, *H. Ex. Doc. 1, 30th Cong., 2nd Sess.*, 227. See Clarke, *Kearny*, 166–75, for an extensive commentary upon the various questions which have arisen about the meeting, particularly whether Carson was forced to accompany the expedition against his will. George Ruhlen, "Kearny's Route from the Rio Grande to the Gila River," *NMHR*, XXXII (July 1957), 213–230, describes the route taken by the army using modern place names.

35. Turner to Price, Oct. 2, 1846, *AGLR'46*, K-209.

36. Army of the West, Orders #33, Oct. 2, 1846, in Hughes, *Doniphan's Expedition*, 143–34; Tyler, *Mormon Battalion*, 164; Golder, *March of the Mormon Battalion*, 171.

37. Bancroft, *Arizona and New Mexico*, 421; Cooke, *Conquest of New Mexico and California*, 90; Bigler, "Extracts," 41; Steele, "Journal," 13–14; Mormon Bn., Orders #7, 8, Oct. 13, 15, 1846, in Tyler, *Mormon Battalion*, 166–67.

38. The march is described in Cooke, *Conquest of New Mexico and California*, 92–110, 125–97; Philip St. George Cooke, "Journal of the March of the Mormon Battalion," in Ralph P. Bieber (ed.), *Exploring Southwestern Trails 1846–1854* (Glendale, 1938), 67–240 (the original is in *AGLR'46*, K-209 and was reprinted in *S. Doc. 2, 31st Cong., Special Sess.*, 1–85, but Bieber's edition is more accurate); Tyler, *Mormon Battalion*, 174–254; Golder, *March of the Mormon Battalion*, 179–206; Bigler, "Extracts," 41–56; Bliss, "Journal," 75–85; Rebecca M. Jones (ed.), "Extracts from the Life Sketch of Nathaniel V. Jones," *UHQ*, IV (Jan. 1931), 5–11; Gracy and Rugeley, "From the Mississippi to the Pacific," 144–56.

39. Mormon Battalion, Orders #1, Jan. 30, 1847, *AGLR'46*, K-209.

40. Price to AG, Feb. 15, 1847, *S. Ex. Doc. 1, 30th Cong., 1st Sess.*, 520–26; Bent to Buchanan, Dec. 26, 1846, *H. Ex. Doc. 70, 30th Cong., 1st Sess.*, 17–18; Ladd, *War with Mexico*, 266–67; Army in New Mexico, Orders #115, Feb. 6, 1847, *Niles*, LXXII (May 15, 1847), 173; Robert R. Rea, *Sterling Price, the Lee of the West* (Little Rock, 1959), 19.

41. Price to AG, Feb. 15, 1847, *loc. cit.*, and the enclosed reports of his subordinates; Vigil to Buchanan, Feb. 16, 1847, Smith Transcripts, XIII, 26–30; Bancroft, *Arizona and New Mexico*, 433–34; Albert G. Brackett, *History of U.S. Cavalry* (New York, 1968), 111. Secretary Marcy ruled that the *insurrectos* could not be guilty of treason, since they owed no allegiance to the U.S. Marcy to Price, June 26, 1847, *H. Ex. Doc. 17, 31st Cong., 1st Sess.*, 252–53.

9: The Chihuahua Expeditions

COINCIDENT WITH THE SEIZURE of Santa Fe, the Polk administration planned a second column against the western Mexican city
of Chihuahua. That outpost, 350 miles northwest of Monterrey and
200 miles south of El Paso, was the closest large Mexican settlement
to New Mexico and, like Santa Fe, had economic ties to St. Louis.
Not only did the Army have no troops in position for a Chihuahua
expedition, but the choice of a commander posed difficulties. Since
none of the about-to-be-appointed Democratic generals had sufficient
experience or desire to command the expedition, the natural choice
was Brigadier General John E. Wool, the third-ranking officer in
the Army.

Secretary Marcy called Wool to Washington at the outbreak of
war apparently as a step in assigning him an active command.[1] But
when Wool joined Scott in a strong protest against the plan to create
new generals it nearly ruined the chances for a command for Marcy
and Polk lumped him with the Whig generals to whom they ascribed
political motives for that opposition. This was ironic, since Wool
was himself a Democrat, although at the time not an active one. On
May 27 he received orders to oversee the raising of the volunteers
from Ohio, Indiana, Illinois, Kentucky, Tennessee, and Mississippi,
but no promise of an active command.[2] On June 11 he finally received orders to take charge of the Chihuahua expedition. His force,
a separate division of Taylor's Army of Occupation, consisted of

two Illinois infantry regiments, one of Arkansas horsemen, and a small contingent of regulars.[3]

In mid-July Wool and the Illinois regiments moved by river steamers to New Orleans for trans-shipment to Port Lavaca on the Texas coast. The cavalry rode cross-country to the rendezvous at San Antonio.[4] At Port Lavaca, Wool discovered that few of the arrangements for the expedition had been completed, so he hastened to San Antonio only to find matters no better there.

Wool had considerable difficulty in organizing his force. The causes were several. Troops did not arrive as early as expected; Lieutenant Colonel William S. Harney, who commanded the regulars at San Antonio,[5] had taken twenty badly needed wagons to the Rio Grande; and finally, twenty days of rain in late July and early August flooded the Lavaca–San Antonio road over which all of the supplies for the expedition had to move.

Another factor was the nature of the command, which was composed primarily of semitrained volunteers. Wool put them through a rough training period which earned him the intense hatred of many of the ebullient volunteers. Some units profited more than others. The Illinois units, for instance, showed a steadiness at Buena Vista which would have done credit to regulars, while the Arkansas horsemen were proof against all the efforts of the General. They were, he wrote near the end of the march through Mexico, "wholly without instruction, and Colonel [Archibald] Yell is determined to leave [them] in that condition." Yell, he continued, had a "total ignorance of his duties as Colonel."[6]

During August 24–29 most of Wool's force, officially called the Centre Division, reached San Antonio and moved into Camp Crockett some three miles from the spot where the immortal Davy fell. The last major unit, Captain John M. Washington's six-gun field battery from Carlisle Barracks, Pennsylvania, arrived September 4.[7]

The advance party rode out of San Antonio on September 23 to mark the route to the Rio Grande. The main body of 1,400 men and 118 wagons laden with provisions followed three days later under Harney's eagle eye. Wool, with a dragoon escort, set out on the twenty-ninth. Since wagons were few, Wool left the two Illinois regiments at San Antonio to follow later under the charge of Colonel Sylvester Churchill.[8]

On October 8 the leading elements caught sight of the Rio Grande, having marched 164 miles in two weeks. A small Mexican force of about 200 men, which had been watching the river around the Presidio del Rio Grande, retired to Monclova without tarrying to dispute the American passage.⁹ On the ninth Harney's dragoons and the "topos" waded the swift yellowish-gray river which was about three and a half feet deep and a sixth of a mile wide. The crossing was near present-day Eagle Pass, Texas. During the following day, Captain Robert E. Lee of the Engineers fashioned a "flying bridge," or pontoon barge, out of four specially built boats brought from San Antonio for the purpose. The force crossed, 200 at a time, during the twelfth.¹⁰

Before the crossing, Wool published an order reminding his command of the practical necessity as well as the moral imperative of good treatment of Mexican civilians. Wool strictly enforced the order despite the rough character of some of his men. This, together with Wool's insistence on scrupulous payment for goods taken, kept incidents to a minimum.¹¹ It was a sharp contrast to the experience of Taylor's army and demonstrated the value of having a strict disciplinarian at the head of volunteer forces.

Wool threw a party for his officers to mark the start of the campaign, but neither his champagne, port, nor Mexican whiskey could break down the antagonism between volunteers and regulars.¹² Indeed, the separation of the two groups at the party scarcely hinted at the gulf which would separate them throughout the campaign. Shortly after crossing, the Americans were visited by a Mexican officer carrying a letter from the Governor of Coahuila protesting the crossing, as a violation of the Monterrey convention. Wool ignored the complaint and prepared to move deeper into Mexico.¹³ Technically and ethically he was correct. The armistice did not apply to operations north of Monterrey.

Colonel John J. Hardin's 1st Illinois marched out of San Antonio on October 2 and reached the Rio Grande ten days later. Close behind came the 2d Illinois under Colonel William H. Bissell along with Colonel Churchill and the remaining stores. While awaiting their arrival the rest of the force endured a series of false alarms of Mexican attacks caused by the overanxiousness of green sentries. Their commander worried about the best route to Chihuahua. The limited information which he could secure indicated that the only practicable route ran through Parras, 200 miles south of Monclova.

On the thirteenth Brigadier General James Shields joined, having come upriver from Camargo with a small escort. The addition of the energetic and able Illini politician-soldier did much to ease the strain on Wool, for he served as a buffer between the stiff profes-

sional soldier and his fun-loving, ill-disciplined volunteers. As one of
the latter commented: "All the Illinoisians were glad to meet him
as it gave them the 2d officer in command, who was in a position
sufficient to represent their rights." Wool took advantage of the
opportunity which Shields's arrival afforded to reorganize the expedition, giving the latter command of the infantry, both regular and
volunteer.[14]

Wool set his army in motion on October 16. The land on the
immediate south bank of the Rio Grande had once been heavily
farmed by Indians who had developed a good irrigation system
under Jesuit guidance. The project, however, had collapsed after the
expulsion of the order from Mexico. As far south as San Juan de
Nava, about twenty-two miles, nearly three quarters of the farms
had been abandoned. A short march brought the army to the beautiful and friendly town of San Fernando de Rosas which perched
on the banks of the crystal-clear Rio Escandido. South of there the
road wound its way into the awesome and towering peaks of the
Sierra Nevadas. As it climbed, the countryside grew wilder with
"bold, treeless peaks cut sharp against the clouds beyond." The road
followed a canyon which broke through the mountains to the Llano
[Plain] de San José that stretched thirty miles to the Sierra de Santa
Rosa. On October 24 the Americans entered the neat, tastefully
laid-out town of Santa Rosa, 105 miles from the Rio Grande. The
2,500 strongly pro-Federalist inhabitants welcomed the Americans
warmly.[15]

During the march to Santa Rosa, Wool became embroiled in
another dispute with the irascible Harney. The 2nd Dragoon's commander found his assignment to a subordinate command irksome:
one suspects he also despaired of making disciplined troops out of
the untrained Arkansas frontiersmen who made up most of the
cavalry. He therefore asked to rejoin his regiment. Wool initially
granted the request and then decided to await word from Taylor,
which did not come until mid-November.[16]

The most direct route to Chihuahua ran west from Santa Rosa.
It proved to be little more than a pair of mule tracks impassable for
either artillery or wagons. Wool decided to follow his original plan
of marching through Monclova to the Saltillo–Chihuahua road at
Parras. The army remained a week in Santa Rosa, leaving on October
26. From there the column wound its way through the valley which
separated the Santa Rosa and San José mountain chains, a bleak and
barren country devoid of inhabitants. At the Paso de las Hermanas

the Americans reached the hacienda of Don Miguel Blanco, one of the principal citizens of Coahuila, who welcomed them profusely. From the Paso the column descended into the Monclova valley and on the twenty-ninth encamped before the well-laid-out, clean town of 8,000.[17]

Although the Monclova authorities were not openly hostile, Wool formally occupied the town on November 3 and established his headquarters in the governor's palace. He established a supply depot and had the quartermaster store there the five tons of flour which had been collected locally for the Mexican army. At Monclova, Wool received orders from Taylor to halt until the expiration of the Monterrey armistice. On November 5, while awaiting the lifting of the restrictions on its operations, the army was joined by Colonel Churchill, 660 men, and wagon loads of supplies.

The twenty-seven-day stay at Monclova was a trying one for Wool's force. The enforced halt irritated the volunteers, who had joined to fight Mexicans not to suffer strict discipline and constant training. As one of the volunteers commented: "Wool is very unpopular with the command; he has quarreled with every field officer in it . . . . the management of an army in the field is 'above his head' . . . ." During the march to Monclova the General had a major contretemps with Colonel Hardin, during which he castigated the entire volunteer officer corps. The Illinois colonel complained that Wool told him to "go tell my men that he had confidence in them & a damned sight more than he had in me or any of my officers."

Many of the men became sick and the rations grew monotonous and sometimes scarce. When Wool attempted to conserve flour by substituting corn and having the troops grind their own meal, the volunteers adamantly refused and forced a rescinding of the directive. All of this added to the friction between the volunteers and the regulars and led to a series of intrigues against the commander.[18]

Intelligence confirmed that a scarcity of water made a march directly from Monclova to Chihuahua impracticable. Wool's informants also reported that the troops stationed at Chihuahua had marched south to reinforce Santa Anna's force gathering at San Luis Potosí. Wool therefore querried Taylor: "What is to be gained by going to Chihuahua? For aught I can learn, all that we shall find to conquer is distance. . . . Under these circumstances I should be glad to join your forces." He also asked for permission to shift his supply base from San Antonio to Camargo because of the distances involved.[19]

If Wool was prevented from marching to Parras because of the armistice, that document did not prevent him from sending out patrols. Shortly after the column reached Monclova, a fifteen-man dragoon patrol caught a Mexican supply train in the Arroyo de los Palmos. The Americans seized seventy prisoners along with 360 pack mules carrying food and powder. Another patrol took a company of Arkansas horsemen on a reconnaissance of the Chihuahua road.[20]

Wool grew increasingly impatient with his inactivity at Monclova. On November 16 he exploded in an exasperated note to the Adjutant General, pointing out that despite three requests for permission to advance, Taylor had failed to issue any new orders. The column would move to Parras, "the key to Chihuahua," on the twentieth, Wool reported, unless he heard from Taylor. The plan was to send a detachment[21] to Chihuahua while leading the rest of his force either to Durango or to reinforce Taylor.[22]

Two nights later the long-awaited orders arrived, but they merely directed the Centre Division to remain at Monclova although abandoning the Chihuahua operation. Wool responded with a plea to Major Bliss: "I hope the general will not permit me to remain in my present position one moment longer than it is absolutely necessary. Inaction is exceedingly injurious to volunteers." To add stress Wool sent the letter in care of his aide, Lieutenant Irwin McDowell. McDowell returned on November 26 with Taylor's instructions to proceed to Parras.[23]

A good example of what concerned Wool has survived in the Hardin Papers at the Chicago Historical Society. It is a letter, addressed to the General and signed by Colonels Hardin and Bissell as well as forty-seven other officers of the two Illinois regiments, complaining that Wool had insulted them by saying that the officers of the two units were "not worth a damn" and that if they continued their infractions of army regulations he would cashier them from the force. Another example is Wool's November 23 order prohibiting gambling in camp.[24]

During November 23 Wool assigned Major William B. Warren's battalion of the 1st Illinois as garrison for Monclova and its supply depot. At the same time he directed the remainder of the force to march the following morning. What followed was a long, wearying, circuitous march across deserts and mountains which even today no highways traverse. On December 5 Wool's men reached Parras, having covered 181 miles in twelve days.[25]

Parras was a town of about 5,000 inhabitants surrounded by gardens and vineyards which were watered by clear rushing streams. It produced Mexico's finest wines, although very few Americans commented on them. The inhabitants treated the occupiers with kindness, once they were convinced of Wool's peaceful intentions and willingness to pay for any supplies they needed.

At Parras, Wool received orders from Taylor to gather all available flour, bread, grain, and other foodstuff. Scarcely had the purchasing begun when Wool, on December 17, received a note from Brigadier General William J. Worth at Saltillo reporting the imminent appearance of Santa Anna's army from San Luis Potosí and asking for assistance. Wool had his force in motion within two hours, which illustrates the success of their strict training. It reached Agua Nueva on the twenty-first and from there was directed to Encantada, by which time the alarm had proven false.[26]

While Wool's column happily abandoned its march to Chihuahua, the second force destined for that isolated city gathered in New Mexico. By mid-December Colonel Alexander Doniphan's 1st Missouri Mounted Volunteers had returned to Valverde from its incursion into Navajo country, "much worse by the arduous Campaign" as one of its members reported.[27] Doniphan had 856 well-mounted and hardened riflemen under his command. The tall, red-haired Doniphan was equal to his men. A lawyer without military experience, he was a born leader and a competent military commander. On learning that Governor Angel Trías Álvarez of Chihuahua had sent 480 troops to reinforce El Paso, Doniphan ordered Major Meriwether Lewis Clark to join the expedition with a six-gun battery and 100 men. Without waiting for these reinforcements, Doniphan sent his vanguard southward on December 14.

The regiment moved in three echelons, two days apart, between December 14 and 18. Included in the last contingent was a colorful detachment of ninety-five men, under Captain Thomas B. Hudson, calling itself the Chihuahua Rangers. They were volunteers from Colonel Sterling Price's regiment serving as escort for Lieutenant Colonel David D. Mitchell who had orders to open communications with General Wool at Chihuahua. Instead of following the Rio Grande, Doniphan sent his command on a ninety-five-mile ride across the arid Jornada del Muerto, a trackless desert valley which had once been the bed of the Rio Grande. While this saved considerable distance because the river swings far westward before looping back to

El Paso, the trail offered no settlements, scarce water, and little vegetation except sagebrush. Doniphan's plan was for the elements to rendezvous at Doña Ana about sixty-five miles from Valverde, but the troops moved largely as they wished and the concentration was nominal at best. At Doña Ana the force was joined by a caravan of traders bound for Chihuahua.[28]

On the twenty-third the force left Doña Ana more or less as an organized unit. Meanwhile, at El Paso indecision reigned. The townspeople seem to have been pro-American and the military split between those who wished to fight and those who did not. Colonel Gauno Cuylti, the commander, was among the latter. During the evening of the twenty-third he contracted a malady which his surgeon diagnosed as brain fever and forthwith departed for Chihuahua in the company of the physician. Command passed to Lieutenant Colonel Luis Vidal, who assigned the duty of stopping the Americans to *Commandante de Escuadrón* [Major] Antonio Ponce de León.

On Christmas Day Doniphan called an early halt, about 1:00 P.M., at Temascalitos, at Brazito, on the Rio Grande some thirty miles from El Paso.[29] As the advance party let its horses out to graze and began to make camp in the river bottom, a dust cloud appeared to the south. It was preceded by the American advance picket which dashed into camp with news of an approaching force. Doniphan interrupted his game of three-trick loo and had rally sounded. He formed his men, most of them on foot, in a crescent-shaped line with the points resting on the river. The Mexicans soon appeared and formed on a hill about a quarter of a mile away. The regular Veracruz lancers in their scarlet coats, white belts, and brass helmets on the right made up in color what they lacked in numbers; the El Paso militia supported by a howitzer formed the center; and a battalion of Chihuahua infantry formed the left. All told, Major Ponce had about 500 men.

Instead of the conventional white flag, the Mexicans sent forward a black one and a demand that the American commander go with them or no quarter would be given. It was not a threat to frighten Doniphan. "Charge and be damned," he replied. The Mexicans did just that and at 400 yards opened an ineffective fire. Doniphan waited until the attackers got within good rifle range before ordering his men to fire. The cascade of lead checked the assault and threw the Mexicans into confusion. On the American left, Lieutenant John Reid with about eighteen men from his company who were still mounted charged the Mexican lancers and drove them off the field. In the center Lieutenant Nicholas B. Wright's company advanced to seize the Mexican gun while the teamsters drove off a squadron of lancers. After some more desultory firing, the Mexicans withdrew under Captain Rafael Carabajal, who replaced the wounded Ponce. In all, the fight lasted less than half an hour. Only seven Americans needed medical attention, while the Mexicans admitted having eleven men killed and seventeen wounded. Although the Americans claimed to have inflicted much higher casualties, the official Mexican figures appear reasonable.[30]

After the battle the Mexican forces dispersed, leaving the road open to Doniphan's men. They appeared before El Paso on the twenty-seventh and gazed with relief upon the town of 10,000 to 12,000 people set amid well-irrigated fields. A deputation of its citizens met them outside the town and escorted them to the plaza. Upon searching the town the conquerors seized five tons of powder, 500 stands of arms, 400 lances, four small artillery pieces, and other munitions.[31]

At the Rio Grande metropolis, Doniphan learned that Wool had abandoned his march to Chihuahua and that the Mexicans were prepared to fight for it. Nevertheless, he decided to push ahead as soon as the artillery arrived. Its arrival was delayed by Colonel Price's reluctance to release the unit until the northern revolt had been squelched. The guns reached El Paso on February 1, and four days later Major Clark himself arrived with ammunition and supplies. Doniphan led his command column southward again on February 8. It included 924 soldiers, about 300 civilian traders and teamsters formed into an impromptu battalion under "Major" Samuel Owens, Clark's six guns, and about 312 military and merchants' wagons.[32]

The route followed by Doniphan's men was nearly as desolate as the dreaded *jornada* they had crossed to reach El Paso. On February 25, after crossing about 200 miles of sandy deserts and arid prairies, they reached the Laguna de Encinillas, a shallow, brackish, twenty-mile-long lake. There a prairie fire, started earlier by their own carelessness, confronted them with a wall of roaring, snapping, raging flames ten to twenty feet high. Only by driving some of the wagons into the water and building backfires could the Americans save themselves and their supplies. Two days later Doniphan learned that the Mexicans had decided to make their stand at the Rio Sacramento crossing some fifteen miles north of Chihuahua. "Cheer up, Boys," the Missourian told his men. "Tomorrow evening I intend to have supper with the Mexicans on the banks of a beautiful spring."

Doniphan's advance came as no surprise to the authorities in

Chihuahua. While such an expedition had been expected since the start of the war, the defensive preparations had been limited. Although both lethargy and the pro-American feelings of many Chihuahuans contributed to the failure, more damaging was the concentration of the central government on the buildup of Santa Anna's force. Nevertheless, Governor Trías, a wealthy and sophisticated hacendado who hated Americans with nearly the intensity he loved the area,[33] had built up a respectable defending force overcoming nearly insurmountable obstacles. The defenders, led by Brigadier General José A. Heredia, numbered about 1,200 indifferent cavalry, 1,500 infantry of varying reliability, and 119 artillerymen with twelve 4- to 9-pounders and nine lighter pieces. An additional 1,000 rancheros armed with machetes and crude lances added to Mexican numbers if not military capacity.

The Mexican position, chosen by Brigadier General Pedro García Conde, the cavalry commander, guarded the passage of the Rio Sacramento by the El Paso road. About two miles before that ford, the road dropped into the deep declivity of an old stream bed, the Arroyo Seco, and climbed its sharp southern bank onto a two-mile-wide plateau before dipping sharply again to the Sacramento. Dominating the crossing on the southern bank was the thick-walled hacienda of Sacramento which nestled against a steep hill upon which stood a redoubt. The twenty-three separate works that the Mexicans had constructed in the days before the battle formed an inverted L along the east side of the El Paso road and the south bank of the arroyo. In addition to the redoubt near the Hacienda Sacramento, another covered a secondary crossing about two miles to the west at the Hacienda El Torreón. The Mexicans considered the position impregnable, and so it might have been had they faced a conventional army.

The Americans arose early on the morning of February 28 to prepare their equipment, mounts, and weapons for the day's battle. Doniphan realized that he must keep his force together for mutual protection, since the wagon train could not defend itself and his horsemen might need the wagons as a mobile fort. His solution was unorthodox. He formed the wagons into four well-separated columns between which marched the artillery and the bulk of the mounted men. Three companies screened his front. The force moved steadily down a four-mile-wide valley until it came in sight of the Mexican positions at about 1:30 in the afternoon. Doniphan and a handful of advisers then rode ahead and carefully surveyed the defenses through their glasses.

Doniphan settled upon a brilliant but highly dangerous tactic. While the cavalry screened the move, he turned his force 90° to the right. They marched parallel to the Arroyo Seco for approximately two miles before crossing the gully and climbing onto the plateau. The shift kept the Americans out of range of the Mexican artillery and bypassed the main enemy positions but exposed the column to attack as it struggled to haul the wagons and artillery up the steep forty- to fifty-foot-high bank of the arroyo.

As soon as he realized Doniphan's plan, Heredia sent General García Conde with about 1,000 cavalry, to check the invaders until the slower-moving artillery and infantry could join in the slaughter. But he failed to anticipate the incredible drive, tenacity, and ingenuity of the American teamsters and soldiers who pushed, tugged, and cursed the teams, wagons, and pack mules onto the plateau before the Mexican horsemen could interfere. Undoubtedly many of the Americans displayed the strength of desperation, since they expected the Mexicans to show no quarter. When they realized that the American axis of movement pointed to the Sacramento rather than the El Torreón crossing, the Mexican cavalry halted to allow the infantry and artillery to join.

Doniphan used the time to prepare his position. He had the wagons form a fort and Major Clark moved his guns forward. Their fire caused the lancers twice to break and finally to flee to their camp. Nor did the Mexican artillery long continue its exchange with the American guns. Nevertheless, it was sufficient to illustrate an interesting phenomenon: the Mexican cannonballs left behind them a blue streak as they sped to their targets through the clear mountain air. This, several of the Americans commented later, allowed the combatants to dodge oncoming missiles.

After the flight of his cavalry, Heredia withdrew his remaining troops into the fortifications, but his plan of battle and the esprit of his men had been shattered. He sent a pair of guns to occupy the redoubt overlooking the Sacramento crossing, and several other pieces, without orders, joined in the move. That further weakened the Mexican line.

As Doniphan's men chased the retreating Mexicans, their oblique direction, intended to keep them as far from the Mexican artillery for as long as possible, carried them toward the southernmost pair of earthworks on a finger of land overlooking the Sacramento crossing. Heredia countered the move by sending his best troops to hold the threatened points. Doniphan directed Captain Richard H. Weightman with the two howitzers to rush the works in conjunction with three cavalry companies. Only Captain Reid received the orders, although some other horsemen joined on their own authority. When the assault was frustrated by an unexpected gully which ran in front of the positions, a few intrepid souls (including Major Owens) dashed across. Owens was killed as he emptied his pistols on the defenders. Other Americans formed a skirmish line and worked their way down the ravine while the howitzers passed around the head of the declivity and opened fire within fifty yards of the works. Some of the American horsemen followed but failed in their efforts to storm the northernmost of the two posts.

The Mexicans mistook Owens for the American leader, which caused Trías, now exercising command, and García Conde to attempt a counterattack with such lancers as they had rallied. The charge was halted by canister fired from the American guns. Meanwhile a large, disorganized body of American horsemen arrived to join in the assault on the upper fort. This time the Missourians, supported by the howitzer fire, took the fort after a short, vicious, hand-to-hand fight.

A final Mexican cavalry thrust against the wagons collapsed before Clark's guns and by five o'clock the fighting on the plateau was over. The Americans, however, were still under fire from the guns on the Sacramento hill around which many of the Mexicans had rallied. While Clark's battery threw roundshot into the position from a range of 1,225 yards, Weightman took his howitzers across the river. Their fire, combined with the appearance of some horsemen who had worked their way to the rear of the position, caused the Mexicans to abandon it. Although a few of the Americans attempted to pursue the retreating defenders the fighting was over, and as the moon rose Doniphan's command reassembled to celebrate its victory.

It was a lopsided fight. Only Owens among Doniphan's men had died, while but eight others were wounded. The precise Mexican losses are not known although Doniphan claimed to have killed 300 and wounded as many more. At least forty others were captured along with large numbers of horses, mules, cattle, provisions, and ammunition.[34]

Unable to defend his capital further, Trías fled to Parras, and on March 2 the Americans marched into Chihuahua with the band playing "Yankee Doodle." Although they were well received, the antics of the Missourians must have quickly cooled much of the friendliness. Susan Magoffin, who arrived a month later, complained strongly about the damage they caused: homes turned into stables; roofs converted to kitchens; the public drinking fountain used as a bath; and the wanton spoliation of the beautiful *alameda*, or public walk.[35] On the other hand, the troops resorted to an activity common to troops stationed near a town for any length of time. On March 18 appeared the first issue of a newspaper, *The Anglo Saxon*, published by John S. Webb and edited by Lieutenant Christian Kribben.[36]

Doniphan had accomplished his objective but now faced a dilemma. His command, less than 1,000 men, found itself isolated in a Mexican city of 14,000 at the end of a very long and difficult supply line with no prospect of early reinforcement. Moreover, the enlistments of his men would expire on June 1. Yet he could not abandon the traders and their merchandise, since the local authorities would not guarantee them protection.

Doniphan outlined his problems in a March 20 letter to General Wool, from whom he requested orders. His men, he added, lacked pay, horses, and clothing, but they had "arms and a disposition to use them" which was not satisfied by playing wagon guards for the merchants.[37] An express party led by a Chihuahua trader, John L. Collins, carried the letter and made the 1,000-mile round trip to Saltillo in thirty-two days.

On April 5, since he had no orders from Wool, Doniphan and 600 men set out for Durango, but on the eighth, after riding about fifty miles, Doniphan turned back to defend Chihuahua against what turned out to be a phantom force.

On April 23 Collins returned with the long-awaited orders which directed Doniphan to bring his men to Saltillo.[38] Two days later the regiment started the long, 524-mile march through Chihuahua, Durango, and Coahuila states to Encantada. Once again the force struggled through mountainous and arid land, but for a change along reasonably good roads. Outside of Parras, Captain Reid and the advance guard helped Mexican ranchers beat off an attack on Rancho El Paso by sixty or seventy Lipan warriors. In the process the Americans freed thirteen women and children held by the Indians.[39] The action, naturally, contributed to the continued friendship of the local inhabitants, who had earlier warmly welcomed Wool's column.

Doniphan led his force into Encantada on May 21, and on the following day the elated but ragged force passed in review before General Wool at Buena Vista. Although the artillery which they had brought with them the whole way from Fort Leavenworth had to be turned in, Wool allowed them to keep as trophies the guns taken at Sacramento. On the twenty-third the 1st Missouri Mounted

Volunteers started its homeward journey. Marching via Monterrey, it boarded river steamers at Reynosa on June 1 for the trip to the mouth of the Rio Grande. There the men boarded oceangoing craft on June 10 which carried them to New Orleans where they were discharged. The Missourians had marched over 2,100 miles and fought two battles in what was probably the most difficult trek in a war which saw several American units make long, arduous marches.

While Doniphan's men made their way across Old Mexico, the troops remaining in New Mexico once again confronted hostile Indians. Punitive expeditions had little effect. Colonel Sterling Price's problem was his lack of sufficient troops to patrol his Indian frontier effectively. Moreover, like Taylor and Scott, he faced the loss of his twelve-months' men and could do little until replacements arrived.[40]

The experience of Lieutenant John Love was indicative of the problems faced by the small detachments of dragoons who attempted to protect the supply line to Santa Fe from marauding Indians. With eighty men of the 1st Dragoons he escorted a paymaster with $300,000 in specie to Santa Fe. On June 26 at Pawnee Ford on the Arkansas River a nearby provision train was attacked, with loss of some cattle. When some of Love's men went to the train's assistance, five were killed and six wounded. A second nearby train on the south bank of the river had two men killed and lost eighty yoke of oxen. This led to two decisions in the War Department. The first assigned Brevet Brigadier General Matthew Arbuckle to command of the 3d Military District, in which the Santa Fe Trail fell, so as to place an experienced general officer in charge. He was directed to punish the tribes raiding the Santa Fe trains and, if necessary, to call for additional troops from Missouri. Since Arbuckle was physically incapable of active service in the field, that duty went to Lieutenant Colonel Clifton Wharton of the 1st Dragoons. In a second action Secretary Marcy requisitioned a mixed force of five companies to serve as the protection from the Santa Fe route. Informally called the "Indian Battalion" it formed at Fort Leavenworth in September and October and wintered on the plains in an effort to dissuade the Indians from resuming their attacks in the spring of 1848.[41]

While these steps to protect the supply line to Santa Fe got under way, Price, who received the Brigadier General's stars refused by Jefferson Davis, planned a new campaign unbeknown to Washington. He started by proposing to take a force into "the lower provinces of New Mexico," but received only reluctant approval to strike into Chihuahua if an invasion force gathered there.[42] For Price, who wished the glory of seizing the Mexican city, that prohibition had little strength. As early as November 8 elements of the 3d Missouri Mounted Volunteers moved into El Paso to block any invasion. A month later Price ordered the remainder of the regiment to the border. By early February Price had all of his forces except Colonel Edward B. Newby's Illinois regiment and a few Missourians concentrated between Socorro and El Paso. Price himself reached El Paso on February 23 and immediately ordered a reconnaissance of the initial segment of the Chihuahua route. The patrol captured a Mexican courier carrying letters which indicated that General José Urrea with 3,000 men was advancing toward El Paso.[43]

On March 1 Price left El Paso with three companies of the 1st Dragoons, four companies of the 3d Missouri, and a pair of howitzers. Governor Angel Trías met the Americans at the Sacramento battlefield with reports of the signing of the peace treaty. Price, who did not trust the Mexican and had no independent confirmation of the news, refused to fall into what he suspected was a trap. On March 7 the Americans rode into Chihuahua while Trías retired to Santa Cruz de Rosales. On March 8 Price and 200 men set out in pursuit. Trías, with 804 men and eight pieces of artillery, occupied the fortifications at Santa Cruz which had been started the year before to halt Doniphan. Price lacked sufficient artillery to challenge the Mexicans so he called Lieutenant John Love's battery from El Paso. Love covered the 200 miles in four days and nights, sixty-five miles in the final twenty hours. Meanwhile, on the tenth, Trías again attempted to get a suspension of hostilities on the basis of reports of the signing of the peace treaty, but Price refused. The Americans launched their assault at midmorning of the sixteenth and took the town in a house-to-house fight. The action cost the lives of four Americans, while nineteen others were injured. Price's claim to have killed some 328 Mexicans is undoubtedly inflated.[44]

Not until April 15 did Price finally receive instructions from General William O. Butler in Mexico City to withdraw from Santa Cruz and restore captured property. On May 16 Marcy ordered Price back to El Paso with a strong slap on the wrist for violating orders against just such an expedition. Price led his men back into Santa Fe on August 4, and on October 8 they returned in triumph to Brunswick, Missouri,[45] the last volunteer units to return home.

NOTES

For key to abbreviations used in Notes, see page xi.

1. Marcy to Wool, May 13, 1846, Gunther Collection, CHS; Francis Baylies, *A Narrative of Major General Wool's Campaign in Mexico* (Albany, 1851), 7; Scott to Marcy, May 27, 1846, *S. Doc. 378, 29th Cong., 1st Sess.*, 14-17; Wool to wife, May 18, 1846, John E. Wool Papers, New York State Library, Box 1, folder 11.

2. Wool to wife, May 21, 26, 27, 1846, Wool Papers, Box 1, folder 11; Quaife, *Diary of Polk*, I, 417-18, 435; Jones to Wool, May 28, 1846, *AGLS*, XXII, 741.

3. Jones to Wool, June 11, Bliss to Wool, Aug. 4, 1846, *H. Ex. Doc. 60, 30th Cong., 1st Sess.*, 328, 410-11. Initially a regiment of Texas horsemen and a battalion of Lone Star infantry were also included. Lt. W. G. Freeman to Wool, June 20, 1846, *AGLS*, XXII, 890. The regulars were Captain John M. Washington's artillery battery, five companies of dragoons under Lieutenant Colonel William S. Harney, and a battalion of infantry under Major Benjamin L. E. Bonneville. Because of the large number of Illini, Wool asked that Brigadier General James Shields be assigned as his second-in-command. Wool to Marcy, July 16, 1846, *WLB*, XII, 37. Shields, however, joined Taylor's army before the orders attaching him to Wool's command reached him. With a small escort he rode up the Rio Grande to join the Chihuahua column at the Presidio on Oct. 13. George W. Hughes, *Memoir Descriptive of the March of a Division of the United States Army, under the Command of Brigadier General John E. Wool, from San Antonio de Bexar, in Texas, to Saltillo, in Mexico* (*S. Ex. Doc. 32, 31st Cong., 1st Sess.*).

4. Wool to Bliss, July 25, 1846, *AOLR*, Box 4; Wool to Hunt, July 26, 1846, *WLB*, XI, 6; John J. Hardin, "Memorandum of Travel in Texas & Mexico. . . ." Hardin Papers, 1; Walter Lee Brown, "The Mexican War Experience of Albert Pike and the 'Mounted Devils' of Arkansas," *Arkansas Historical Quarterly*, XII (Winter 1953), 303; Samuel E. Chamberlain, *My Confession* (New York, 1956), 35; Isabel Wallace, *Life and Letters of General W. H. L. Wallace* (Chicago, 1909), 14-15, 18-19.

5. Harney had exhausted most of the few supplies already gathered in a fruitless dash to the Rio Grande during July and August. Taylor to AG, July 29, 1846, *AGLR'46*, T-302; Harney to Bliss, July 27, Aug. 12, 15, 1846, Wool to Taylor, Sept. 15, 1846, all in *AOLR*, Box 4; L. U. Reavis, *The Life and Military Services of Gen. William Selby Harney* (St. Louis, 1878), 154-55. Because Harney so delayed his return, Wool placed him under arrest and sent a special courier with an explicit recall order. He released Harney from arrest on his return to San Antonio.

6. Wool to Taylor, Aug. 18, 1846, *AOLR*, Box 4; Wool to Hardin, Aug. 9, 1846, Hardin Papers; Wool to Worth, Dec. 10, 1846, *WLB*, XI, 212-13; Chamberlain, *My Confession*, 38; Brown, "Pike and the 'Mounted Devils,'" 305; Hughes, *Memoir*, 6; Hardin, "Memorandum," 6.

7. Wool to Jones, Sept. 2, 3, 1846, *WLB*, XI, 72-74; 79-80; Wool to Taylor, Sept. 15, 1846, *H. Ex. Doc. 60, 30th Cong., 1st Sess.*, 426; Hardin, "Memorandum," 5; Jay Langdon, "Diary," NYHS.

8. Langdon, "Diary"; Jonathan W. Buhoup, *Narrative of the Central Division* (Pittsburgh, 1847), 17-19; Baylies, *Campaign in Mexico*, 12; Centre Div., Orders #81, Sept. 27, 1846, *WOB*, XXXIV, 57; Wool to Churchill, Sept. 28, 1846, *WLB*,

XI, 120–21; Smith, *War with Mexico*, I, 270. Wool, who appears to have intercepted some of the wagons intended for Taylor, had more wagons than the
main army. Risch, *Quartermaster Support*, 273–77.

9. Hughes, *Memoir*, 12–16; Baylies, *Campaign in Mexico*, 12. The route is described
in Capt. B. M. Prentiss, Memoranda, n.d., *WOB*, XXXIV, 65–67; Lt. C. P. Kings-
bury to Wool, Oct. 13, 1846, *Niles*, LXXI (Dec. 6, 1846), 210; Maurice Garland
Fulton (ed.), *Diary and Letters of Josiah Gregg* (2 vols., Norman, 1941–44),
I, 251–56. Chamberlain, *My Confession*, pp. 48–49, has a highly colored account
of Wool's encounter with a Comanche band under Santana.

10. Wool to Jones, Sept. 28, 1846, *AGLR'46*, W-583; Douglas Southall Freeman,
R. E. Lee (4 vols., New York, 1934), I, 208; James Henry Carleton, *The Battle
of Buena Vista* (New York, 1848), 162.

11. Wool, Orders #89, Oct. 9, 1846, *Niles*, LXXI (Dec. 5, 1846), 208. The require-
ment for payment caused considerable problems for Wool's supply officers. The
army had no specie and the Mexicans were unwilling to accept American
treasury notes. Wool to Jones, Oct. 14, 1846, *ibid.*

12. Adolph Engelmann to parents, Oct. 13, 1846, typescript copy in MoHS. This
and other Engelmann letters in the Illinois State Historical Society are printed
in Otto B. Engelmann (trans., ed.), "The Second Illinois in the Mexican War,"
Journal of the Illinois State Historical Society, XXVI (Jan. 1934), 357–452.

13. Wool to Col. Francisco de Castañeda, Oct. 12, 1846, *WLB*, XII, 182.

14. Jenkins, *War Between U.S. and Mexico*, 186; Wallace, *Life and Letters*, 21;
Chamberlain, *My Confession*, 51; Buhoup, *Narrative*, 22–23, 31–32; Hardin,
"Memorandum," 17–19; Hughes, *Memoir*, 6–7; Shields to Jones, Oct. 19, 1846,
AGLR'46, S-508; Wool, Orders #99, Oct. 15, 1846, *WOB*, XXXIV, 77–78;
1st. Brig., Centre Div., Orders #1, Oct. 14, 1846, 1st Illinois Order Book, 4,
Hardin Papers; George T. M. Davis, *Autobiography* (New York, 1891), 101–5.
On Nov. 19 Shields was detached and sent to Patterson's Tampico force. Centre
Div., SO #136, Nov. 19, 1846, *WOB*, XXXVIII, 65. The quote is from Hardin,
"Memorandum," 15.

15. Hardin, "Memorandum," 37; Carleton, *Buena Vista*, 166, 169; Wallace, *Life and
Letters*, 22; Smith, *War with Mexico*, I, 272.

16. Lt. I. McDowell to Harney, Oct. 18, Lt. D. H. Rucker to Harney, Oct. 21, and
Prentiss to Harney, Nov. 6, 1846, *WLB*, XI, 147–48, 153, 167–68; AO, SO #174,
Nov. 10, 1846, *AOSO*, II, 68.

17. The march to Monclova is described in Hughes, *Memoir*, 18–26; Buhoup, *Narrative*, 30–102; Fulton, *Diary and Letters of Gregg*, I, 256–60, 264–71; Carleton,
Buena Vista, 164; and Baylies, *Campaign in Mexico*, 13–16.

18. Wallace, *Life and Letters*, 25; Engelmann to parents, Nov. 7, 1846, Engelmann,
"2d Illinois," 407–8; Hardin, "Memorandum," n.p. (Oct. 29, 1846); Buhoup, *Narrative*, 67–72.

19. Baylies, *Campaign in Mexico*, 16–17; Smith, *War with Mexico*, I, 272–75; *Niles*,
LXXI (Dec. 26, 1846), 262; Wool to Taylor, Nov. 12, 1846, *WLB*, XII, 215–16.
The quotation is from Wool to Taylor, Nov. 1, 1846, Baylies, 17.

20. Chamberlain, *My Confession*, 61–63; Buhoup, *Narrative*, 60.

21. Apparently Yell's Arkansas Mounted Regiment. Hardin to D. A. Smith, Nov. 7,
1846, J. J. Hardin Correspondence, Hardin Papers.

22. Wool to Jones, Nov. 16, 1846, *AGLR'46*, W-651.

23. Wool to Bliss, Nov. 19, 1846, Baylies, *Campaign in Mexico*, 18–19; Wool to
AG, Jan. 17, 1847, *AGLR'47*, W-116.

24. Hardin, *et al.*, to Wool, Nov. 22, 1846, Hardin Correspondence; Centre Div.
Orders #144, Nov. 23, 1846, *WOB*, XXXIV, 142.

25. Wool to Warren, Nov. 23, 1846, *WLB*, XI 199–202; Centre Div. Orders #143,

WOB, XXXIV, 141; Hughes, *Memoir*, 27–33; Wool to Taylor, Dec. 7, 1846, *AGLR'47*, W-116; Wallace, *Life and Letters*, 29; Baylies, *Campaign in Mexico*, 19; Fulton, *Diary and Letters of Gregg*, I, 278–99.

26. Harvey Neville, Diary, 17, CHS; Corydon Donnavan, *Adventures in Mexico* (Boston, 1848), 43; Wool to People of Parras and its vicinity, Dec. 5, 1846, Wool Papers, Box 1, folder 63; Wool to Taylor, Dec. 16, 1846, to AG, Jan. 3, 17, 1847, all in *AGLR'47*, W-116; *Niles*, LXXII (May 8, 1847), 156; Smith, *War with Mexico*, I, 275.

27. J. T. Hughes to R. H. Miller, Jan. 4, 1847, Robert H. Miller Papers, MoHS. That collection also has a copy of Trías's florid exhortation to "The Van Guard who march to the Northern Frontier," Nov. 19, 1846.

28. Doniphan to Jones, March 4, 1847, *S. Ex. Doc. 1, 30th Cong., 1st Sess.*, 497–98; *Niles*, LXXI (Jan. 16, 1847), 320; Hughes, *Doniphan's Expedition*, 255–59; Richardson, *Journal*, 39–43; Jenkins, *War Between U.S. and Mexico*, 307; Smith, *War with Mexico*, I, 299–300.

29. Its present-day location is uncertain because of shifts in the river's course. It is probably near Vado, New Mexico, off U.S. Route 80. Andrew Armstrong, "The Brazito Battlefield," *NMHR*, XXXV (Jan. 1960), 74.

30. Doniphan to Jones, March 4, 1847, *S. Ex. Doc. 1, 30th Cong., 1st Sess.*, 497–98; Hughes to Miller, Jan. 4, 1847, Miller Papers; Richardson, *Journal*, 46–48; Robinson, *Journal*, 65–67; Gibson, "Journal," 300–9; Edwards, "Journal," 229–35; Edwards, *Campaign in New Mexico*, 83–87; Hughes, *Doniphan's Expedition*, 259–69; Lt. C. H. Kribben letter, Dec. 25, 1846, in James Madison Cutts, *The Conquest of California and New Mexico by the Forces of the United States in the Years 1846 and 1847* (Philadelphia, 1847), 77–78; Jenkins, *War Between U.S. and Mexico*, 309–10; Smith, *War with Mexico*, I, 300–2; Armstrong, "Brazito Battlefield," 64–65; Vidal to Ponce, Dec. 25, 1846, Ponce to Vidal, Dec. 26, 1846, F. M. Gallaher (ed.), "Official Report of the Battle of Temascalitos (Brazito), *NMHR*, III (Oct. 1928), 385–88; Ramsey, *Other Side*, 169–71.

31. Hughes to Miller, Jan. 4, 1847, *loc. cit.*; Richardson, *Journal*, 48; Gibson, "Journal," 310, Edwards, "Journal," 238; Smith, *War with Mexico*, I, 302.

32. Richardson, *Journal*, 53; Smith, *War with Mexico*, I, 303. The march to the Sacramento is best described in Hughes, *Doniphan's Expedition*, 286–301; Edwards, *Campaign in New Mexico*, 102–11; Richardson, *Journal*, 54–61.

33. Florence C. and Robert H. Lister, *Chihuahua. Storehouse of Storms* (Albuquerque, 1966), 117.

34. Doniphan to Jones, March 4, 1847 (with enclosures), *S. Ex. Doc. 1, 30th Cong., 1st Sess.*, 497–513; Hughes to Miller, March 4, 1847, Miller Papers; Edwards, *Campaign in New Mexico*, 111–20; James Hobbs, *Wild Life in the Far West* (Hartford, 1872), 158; Richardson, *Journal*, 61–64; Robinson, *Journal*, 74–76; Gibson, "Journal," 344–51; Edwards, "Journal," 260–70; Hughes, *Doniphan's Expedition*, 301–24; Brooks, *Complete History*, 274–79; Smith, *War with Mexico*, I, 304–13; Wilcox, *Mexican War*, 156–59; Ramsey, *Other Side*, 173–78; Carlos María de Bustamante, *El Nuevo Bernal Díaz de Castillo* (2 vols., México, 1949), I, 224–25.

35. Richardson, *Journal*, 63; Stella M. Drumm (ed.), *Down the Santa Fe Trail and Into Mexico* (New Haven, 1926), 228–29.

36. Photocopy in UTA.

37. Doniphan to Wool, March 20, 1847, *S. Ex. Doc. 1, 30th Cong., 1st Sess.*, 247–49.

38. Wislizenus, *Memoir of a Tour*, 62; Hughes to Miller, May 25, 1847, Miller Papers; Bliss to Doniphan, April 5, 1847, *AOLB'47*.

39. Reid to Wool, May 21, 1847, *H. Ex. Doc. 56, 30th Cong., 1st Sess.*, 334–35.

40. Maj. B. B. Edmundson to Price, June 14, Price to AG, July 20, 1847, *S. Ex. Doc.*

1, 30th Cong., 1st Sess., 534–37; Price to AG, July 26, 1847, *AGLR'47*, P-186; Jones to Price, May 22, 1847, *AGLS*, XXIV, #772; Brackett, *Cavalry*, 111; Frank McNitt, "Navajo Campaigns and the Occupation of New Mexico, 1847–1848," *NMHR*, XLIII (July 1968), 174.

41. Unsigned letter, June 17, 1847, Miller Papers; Bieber, *Marching with the Army of the West*, 295n; Theodore F. Rodenbough and William L. Haskin (eds.), *The Army of the United States* (New York, 1896), 158; Olivia, *Soldiers on the Santa Fe Trail*, 82–85; Marcy to Edwards, July 24, 1847, *SWMA*, XXVII, 479–80; Jones to Arbuckle, July 7, 26, to Wharton, Aug. 16, Nov. 21, 1847, *AGLS*, XXIV, #982, 1108, 1238, 1809; Elvid Hunt, *History of Fort Leavenworth 1827–1927* (Fort Leavenworth, 1926), 79.

42. Jones to Price, July 23, Oct. 1, Nov. 20, 1847, *AGLS*, XXIV, 1019, 1531, 1796; Rea, *Price*, 23.

43. Diary of Philip Gooch Ferguson, Bieber, *Marching with the Army of the West*, 339, 353; Jones to Price, Nov. 20, 1847, *AGLS*, XXIV, #1796; Price to Jones, Dec. 17, 1847, *AGLR'47*, P-466; Price's orders to his subordinates to gather at El Paso are in *ibid.*, '48, P-170. See also Price to Jones, Feb. 6, R. W. Lane to W. E. Prince, Jan. 26, 1848, Smith Transcripts, XIII, 68–69, 72–73; J. V. Masten to C. Masten, Feb. 7, 1848, John Vosburg Masten Papers, MoHS; Price to Walker, Feb. 24, 1847, *H. Ex. Doc. 1, 30th Cong., 1st Sess.*, 113.

44. Ferguson, "Diary," 353–58; A. B. Dyer to J. A. Early, April 5, 1848, Smith and Judah, *Chronicles of the Gringos*, 143; Roa Bárcena, *Recuerdos*, III, 535–37; Smith, *War with Mexico*, II, 419; Price to Jones, April 5, 1848, with enclosures, Trías, Report, April 1848, *AGLR'48*, P-170, 269; Lister, *Chihuahua*, 132.

45. Thomas to Price, April 1, 1848, *AMLB*; Price to Laurecano Muñoz, April 15, 1848, UTA; Marcy to Price, May 22, 1848, *H. Ex. Doc. 17, 31st Cong., 1st Sess.*, 256–57; McNitt, "Navajo Campaign," 192; Rea, *Price*, 24.

10: California Conquest

IN THE SPRING OF 1845 Mexican reaction to the annexation of Texas caused Secretary of the Navy George Bancroft to alert his commander in the Pacific Ocean. On March 21 he warned Commodore John D. Sloat of the possible imminence of war and directed a concentration in Mexican waters; and on June 24 he told him: "Should you ascertain beyond a doubt that the Mexican government has declared war against us, you will at once . . . possess yourself of the port of San Francisco, and blockade or occupy . . . other ports. . . ."[1] The orders were clear, but Sloat's overly cautious nature and the still-fresh memory of Thomas apCatesby Jones's seizure of Monterey served to paralyze the naval commander when war finally came.

Not until mid-November did Sloat in his flagship, the frigate *Savannah*, reach Mazatlán, Mexico. The rest of his squadron followed shortly. Mazatlán was an excellent base for the squadron. Not only was it the chief Mexican west-coast port but it had fast and reliable communications with Mexico City. Upon learning of the Slidell mission and the withdrawal of the Home Squadron from Veracruz, Sloat sent some of his vessels to lesser ports.[2]

While the Commodore awaited the outcome of the diplomatic moves, events were taking shape in California which would profoundly influence his future actions. On December 9 the famed explorer and son-in-law of Thomas Hart Benton, Brevet Captain John

C. Frémont, and a few men rode into Sutter's Fort at the junction of the Sacramento and American rivers. Why they were in California has never been satisfactorily explained. Frémont's orders were to survey the Arkansas and Red rivers with special attention to the headwaters of the former.[3] Frémont ignored them to make another transcontinental trek. The explanation appears to lie in what Josiah Royce called "a Benton Family plot."[4] It was in keeping with Frémont's need for ego-satisfaction to ignore the directive for a mundane survey of the Arkansas and attempt instead to locate a usable wagon route to California. For what greater glory could the western explorer hope? In overriding the orders of his immediate superior, Frémont knew he could count on the support of a father-in-law who was probably the most powerful single individual in the Senate. If the explorer succeeded in finding the magic route to California, it would become the highway for that host of American settlers upon whom Benton counted to convert the Pacific commonwealth into another Texas. Even if Frémont missed the passage through the Rockies, his presence in California might upset the British plans for annexation, which most American statesmen accepted as an article of faith.

From Sutter's, Frémont went to Monterey in late January to request permission to reoutfit his whole party in California. That permission was certainly granted, but whether he also was told he could continue his surveys in California cannot be determined.[5] However uncertain we may be about the details of the agreement, the actions which followed are clear. Frémont, joined by the rest of his men, crossed the Santa Cruz Mountains, reached the sea near Santa Cruz, and moved south. On March 5, near present-day Salinas, the American received from the local authorities preemptory orders to leave California. Frémont, taking offense at both the tenor of the letters and the manner of their delivery, refused to comply and entrenched his force atop Gavilan Peak (modern San Juan Mountain) about thirty miles from Monterey. To emphasize his annoyance he hoisted the American flag. Commandante General José María Castro laid siege to the camp with a force that outnumbered the Americans six to one. After much bombast on both sides and desperate attempts by Consul Thomas O. Larkin to avoid bloodshed, Frémont retired toward Oregon on March 9.[6]

Frémont's highhanded dealing with the California authorities confirmed their suspicions that he was there to aid in the conquest of the state. There is no solid evidence, however, to support those suspicions.

Larkin naturally saw in Frémont's difficulties the strong possibility of bloodshed and reprisals which would defeat his efforts to cultivate the inhabitants. On the very day that Frémont began his withdrawal toward Oregon, Larkin asked that a warship be dispatched to Monterey in case her presence became necessary to protect American lives and property. Commodore Sloat sent the *Portsmouth* (Commander John B. Montgomery),[7] which reached Monterey on April 23. Once there, Commander Montgomery decided to remain in California waters to await Commodore Robert F. Stockton in the *Congress*, who was expected daily.[8]

Sloat's problems at Mazatlán were complicated by the presence of a strong British squadron. He realized that the two countries might be plunged into war over Oregon at any moment and he distrusted the British designs on California. Into this tense situation on February 9 rode Lieutenant Archibald H. Gillespie, USMC, enroute to his station as assistant secret agent in California. Gillespie told Sloat little of his mission but stressed the importance of his speedy arrival in California. The Marine sailed on February 22 in the sloop-of-war *Cyane* (Captain William Mervine).[9]

Sloat was not alone in his concern about the British. Several orders issued to him at the turn of the year stressed the seriousness of the Oregon situation and played down the difficulties with Mexico.[10] These orders had such a great impact on Sloat's thinking that even after hostilities began, his actions were motivated more by a fear of the British than by the necessity of waging war against Mexico.

Lieutenant Gillespie landed at Monterey on April 17. He immediately called on Larkin and repeated the instructions which required the two men to counter foreign attempts to secure California and to support native independence moves. Since Gillespie carried family mail for Frémont, and the explorer was believed to be near Sutter's, the Marine hastened after him.[11]

Gillespie did not find Frémont at Sutter's but followed him to the shores of Klamath Lake in Oregon before making contact on May 9. Beyond the fact that Gillespie delivered his packet of letters very little is known of what transpired between the two men.[12] It is clear from Frémont's later statements that the most significant information came from Benton and stressed countering the supposed designs of the British. This was natural, since the letter had been written in the midst of the October–November scare induced by Larkin's report of British meddling in California. The timing of the letter, coming as it did at the outset of the pre-Slidell mission thaw in Mexican–American relations as well as the cool relations between Polk and Benton, precludes its being a vehicle for ordering a revolt against Mexican rule in California. Moreover, such action runs counter to everything we know about Polk's methods and his California strategy. Gillespie, however, did know that a Mexican–American war had probably broken out, since Larkin had relayed Commander Montgomery's report of a March 28-29 flight from Mazatlán by Mexican authorities reacting to rumors of an impending attack and had observed "that our Flag may fly here in thirty days."[13]

Apparently, also, the exploring party had found late snow clogging the passes into Oregon and was about to return to California. Whatever the reason may have been, it was after his meeting with Gillespie that Frémont began retracing his steps.[14]

Meanwhile, far to the south, Squadron Surgeon Dr. William Maxwell Wood and Consul John Parrott left Mazatlán on May 1 on the *Warren* (Commander Joseph B. Hull), landed at San Blas, and made their way across Mexico enroute home. At Guadalajara on May 10 they learned of the ambush of Captain Thornton's command on the Rio Grande and promptly sent a messenger to Sloat. The rider delivered their letter a week later. On the following day Sloat notified Larkin that "it appears certain that hostilities have commenced on the North bank of the Rio Grande. . . . It is my intention to visit your place immediately." The Commodore entrusted the warning to Captain Mervine in the *Cyane*, cautioning him to allow no news of war to leak but to seize any Mexican vessels suitable for conversion into vessels of war. The *Cyane* sailed on May 19. The following day the sloop *Levant* (Commander Hugh N. Page) and the storeship *Erie* (Lieutenant James M. Watson) left for Hawaii to take on supplies.[15]

Although he had promised to follow the *Cyane*, Sloat procrastinated. He was still at Mazatlán on May 20 when the British flagship *Collingwood* left for an unannounced destination which most Americans assumed correctly to be California. Sloat was still there six days later when he learned of the Battles of Palo Alto and Resaca de la Palma. He promptly dispatched a code message to Secretary Bancroft announcing his immediate departure for California. "Upon more mature reflection," however, Sloat changed his mind. He concluded that he should not take any hostile action until he learned definitely of a declaration of war or of offensive actions by Commodore Conner's squadron. Thus he followed the letter, if not the spirit, of the June 24, 1845 instructions which cautioned against any aggressive ac-

tions before a declaration of war. Most military leaders would have
concluded that they had sufficient indication of war, but Sloat (with
the example of Jones before him) insisted upon an unequivocal
situation before acting.

Sloat received confirmation of the earlier reports on June 7 from
Surgeon Wood in Mexico City. This news, he concluded, "would
justify my commencing offensive operations on the west coast" although "upon my own responsibility," i.e., before the receipt of
official notification of war. Leaving the *Warren* to await that news,
Sloat sailed in the *Savannah* on June 8, twenty-two days after first
learning of the fighting.[16]

Following the declaration of war, Secretary Bancroft sent new
orders to the Pacific. These directed the implementation of the June
1845 orders; spelled out the blockade instructions; and ordered
the seizure, if the forces available permitted, of Mazatlán and Monterey. Otherwise, the Secretary left the selection of ports to be seized
or to be blockaded to the commander on the scene, which was highly
sensible considering the problems of communication. With only
slight modification, these orders controlled the Pacific operations
throughout the war. In mid-July Bancroft directed the establishment
of a civil government in the newly won territory but failed to indicate whether that government should function under Army or
Navy direction. This oversight created unnecessary complications
and an unseemly interservice struggle.[17]

In the American settlements in the Napa and Sacramento river
valleys profound events also transpired. Most of the Americans had
entered the state without permission from the local authorities and had
never become Mexican citizens. They grew increasingly fearful that
the California authorities would enforce the laws excluding unauthorized immigrants and carry out their threats to expel those
already there. The alarm grew as rumors of preparations for the
eviction flew, and with them arose thoughts of resistance. Frémont's
return acted as a catalyst to solidify this resistance.[18]

On June 6 Frémont threw in with the settlers.[19] General José
María Castro, as part of his preparations for possible trouble, gathered
a force at Santa Clara. Outside Sonoma on June 10, Ezekiel Merritt
and ten or eleven other American settlers surprised a small detachment of Californians who were bringing horses south to Santa Clara.
Four days later Merritt led another group to the Sonoma home of
General Mariano Guadalupe Vallejo, the pro-American titular com-

mander of northern California. They seized Vallejo, some others, and the few arms stored there. The degree of Frémont's involvement in these raids is not clear, but the relationship is unimportant since the revolt would not have broken out at all without his presence and cooperation. On the other hand, it must have been abundantly clear by mid-June to the explorer and Gillespie that war probably did exist.[20]

Castro responded swiftly to the uprising. He called for the crushing of the uprising and imposed a *levée en masse*. His advance party of some fifty or sixty men under Joaquín de la Torre crossed over to the Marin Peninsula, where it clashed on June 23 with a small body of Americans, losing one man killed and some injured. This brought Frémont into open support of the rebels, whereupon Torre retired across San Francisco Bay. On July 1 Frémont and a few men followed the Californians across San Francisco Bay to spike the guns in the abandoned Castillo de San Joaquín overlooking the Golden Gate.

Elated by their success at beating off Torre, the rebels, called Bear Flaggers after their flag, held a gala celebration at Sonoma on July 4 and under Frémont's pressure declared California independent. The next day they established a military organization headed by Frémont. The California Battalion, as it was called, numbered 224 men. Leaving a garrison at Sonoma, Frémont led the remainder to Sutter's.[21]

While the caldron of rebellion bubbled in California and the naval force in the Pacific prepared to seize the state's ports, President Polk and his advisers decided to contribute an overland invasion force. On May 30 the cabinet agreed to the President's proposal for such an expedition and to its assignment to Colonel Stephen W. Kearny. Kearny, once he had pacified New Mexico, would press on to California and establish a temporary civil government. Three days later the cabinet also concurred in the dispatching by water of a coast artillery company with its weapons. On June 26 the cabinet further agreed to the shipment of a full regiment of New York volunteers. That unit, raised by John D. Stevenson, a political ally of Secretary Marcy, consisted of men who wished to be discharged in California. It belatedly sailed from New York on September 26, rounded Cape Horn, and reached its destination in March 1847.[22]

During the afternoon of June 19 the *Cyane* reached Monterey. She carried Commodore Sloat's May 18 letter reporting the outbreak of fighting on the Rio Grande. During the evening of June 30 the *Levant* arrived, but since she had left Mazatlán only a day behind the *Cyane* she had no later news. Commodore Sloat in the *Savannah* finally appeared during the afternoon of July 1. In addition to conferring with Larkin, Sloat did many things—but securing the port was not one of them. He granted shore leave to the frigate's crew during the third and went ashore himself to ride with Larkin. Why is not clear. Apparently Sloat was troubled by the lack of official notice of hostilities and Larkin did nothing to precipitate action, since he hoped for a peaceful conquest.[23]

The indecision changed during the evening of July 5 when the *Portsmouth*'s launch arrived from San Francisco with Commander Montgomery's report of Frémont's open support of the rebels. Sloat seems to have reasoned that Frémont must have information that war had begun or have newly received orders to conduct such open operations. And if the explorer's activities were premature? Then a large part of Sloat's responsibility for his actions could be shifted to Frémont. The fear of British intervention was an additional motive.[24]

Sloat decided, therefore, to seize Monterey and San Francisco. On July 6 he wrote Montgomery that he would seize Monterey the next day and directed the *Portsmouth*'s commander to take possession of San Francisco and its bay area. Sloat added, "I am very anxious to know if Captain Frémont will cooperate with us." The Commodore had finally committed himself to a course of action.[25]

The seizure of Monterey began at about 7:30 on the morning of July 7 when Captain William Mervine of the *Cyane* and a small party rowed ashore from the *Savannah* to demand the surrender of the port. Captain Mariano Silva, the commandant, responded that he was "not authorized to surrender the place, having no orders to that effect; the said matter may be arranged by the Señor Commodore with the Commandant General. . . ."

The objective was a scattered collection of single-story houses meandering down a gently sloping hillside toward the shoreline. There the two-story, frame Customs House and its wharf dominated the scene. Forming the backdrop for the village was a high, pine-topped line of hills on whose slopes grazed herds of horses and cattle. Atop a hill to the southward of this pastoral scene stood the yellow-stone presidio whose nonexistent garrison formed Silva's command.

While awaiting Mervine's return, Sloat had a general order read to his sailors. That carefully phrased document announced the impending landing, spelled out the rules of conduct to be obeyed while ashore, and impressed upon the sailors the necessity for cultivating the good will of the Californians.

Shortly before ten o'clock the flagship broke the signal for the landing. Within twenty minutes boats from the three American warships set ashore somewhat over 225 sailors and marines. They formed before the Customs House where Purser Rodman M. Price read a proclamation from Sloat announcing the existence of war and the annexation of California. It extolled the advantages which would come from annexation and guaranteed the freedom of return to Mexico after the war for those who wished to do so. It formally recognized Mexican real estate titles as well as church lands and guaranteed fair payment for goods furnished to the occupiers. Sloat had no authority to annex California, but he and Larkin both knew that the American government desired its ultimate attachment. Otherwise, the proclamation was a sound, calm document which promised nothing that could not be delivered. When Price finished, Midshipmen William P. Toler and Eugene Higgins hoisted the American flag over the Customs House to the accompaniment of three cheers and a salute from the squadron.[26]

Since the alcaldes refused to continue in office, Sloat appointed Purser Price and Surgeon Edward Gilchrist justices of the peace. Beyond this Sloat made little effort to organize a government. He named Captain Mervine commander of the garrison of Marines who took up quarters in the Customs House. To prevent trouble between the sailors and the local population, Mervine closed all stores and shops for two days and strictly forbade the sale of liquor. During the eighth, Purser Daingerfield Fauntleroy organized a company of horsemen to patrol the nearby countryside. They discovered and seized several caches of arms.[27]

Sloat's July 7 message ordering the seizure of San Francisco arrived early the following evening. Montgomery hastily made his preparations and asked Vice Consul William B. Leidesdorff to translate Sloat's proclamation into Spanish. At four o'clock on the morning of July 9, Lieutenant Joseph W. Revere left the *Portsmouth* for Sonoma to forward news of the seizure of Monterey to Frémont and to deliver American flags to Sonoma and Sutter's Fort.

Only a handful of curious inhabitants greeted Montgomery and his seventy men when they landed shortly before 8:00 A.M. and marched to the Customs House on what is now Portsmouth Square. Montgomery read an address announcing the conquest and the replacement of the Bear Flag with the American; promised fair and safe treatment for the inhabitants; and called for the formation of a local militia company. After Lieutenant John S. Missroon read Commodore Sloat's proclamation, the American flag was run up on the flagpole to the accompaniment of a 21-gun salute from the *Portsmouth*.

Montgomery sent Purser James H. Watmough to notify Frémont personally of the occupation and to relay Sloat's request for an early meeting. Meanwhile, Revere had hoisted the American flag at Sonoma, bringing the Bear Flag Republic to an end.[28] That step appeared highly significant to many on board the *Portsmouth* when she was joined on July 11 by the British sloop *Juno*. The Americans assumed that she had come to interfere with the conquest and Montgomery took emergency steps to defend the village. Such was not the case. She had come simply to observe events. Neither Captain P. J. Blake nor his superior, Rear Admiral Sir George F. Seymour, had instructions to intervene. A similar reaction greeted Seymour's arrival at Monterey on July 23 in the ship-of-the-line *Collingwood*.[29]

While the Americans strengthened their hold on northern California, the local leaders tried to organize a defense in the south. General Castro and Governor Pico agreed to cooperate in the face of the foreign invasion and to concentrate their forces in the Los Angeles area. Pico with face-saving bravado directed the conscription of all men between fifteen and sixty years, but the order produced few recruits.[30]

During the morning of July 15 the *Congress* bearing Commodore Robert F. Stockton anchored in Monterey Bay. Sloat greeted the arrival of his junior commodore with relief. As he informed Stockton at their first meeting he intended to transfer command in the near future. Sloat's already precarious health had deteriorated under the pressure of recent days.[31]

Frémont learned of the seizure of Monterey on July 10 and with his men headed there from his camp near Sutter's two days later. They reached San Juan Bautista on July 16 about thirty minutes before Fauntleroy and a detachment of his mounted troop arrived from Monterey. The two detachments reached Monterey during the nineteenth. Their entry into the coastal village created quite a stir, since the rifles, pistols, long knives, dusky buckskins, flowing hair, and beards of Frémont's men gave them the appearance of savages.[32]

Frémont hastened to call upon Sloat. Each looked forward to the meeting as the source of justification for his actions. Sloat hoped to learn of the instructions which led Frémont to join the rebels, thereby finding justification for the seizure of the California ports. Frémont wished approval of his actions and an agreement to continue operations on land. Both men were disappointed. Sloat learned to his horror that the army officer had acted without orders or knowledge of war; while Frémont learned that he could expect no support from the Commodore, who did not propose active operations ashore. The explorer was surprised, since Larkin had led him to believe otherwise. Sloat was so unnerved by Frémont's lack of authority that he abruptly ended the meeting and fled from the cabin.[33] Sloat's reaction was not surprising considering his state of health, his cautious nature, and his thirty years of stultifying peacetime service since the War of 1812.

The interview hastened Sloat's decision to return home. Such a course would allow him to escape the consequences of further decisions about operations in California with their inherent possibility for a misstep. It would also allow him to escape from an abrasive and politically powerful second-in-command whose strategic ideas were clearly different. Therefore, on July 23 Sloat transferred command of operations ashore to Stockton, ostensibly because his health prevented him from handling them. Actually it was a preliminary to the transfer of the whole command on July 29, although it is unclear why Sloat moved in two stages.[34]

Despite his overcautiousness Sloat left behind a considerable accomplishment. He had occupied the two most important ports in California; had built the framework for securing the rest of the state; and had laid claim to the area for the United States. Had Stockton followed the quiet and careful path of his predecessor many, if not all, of the problems which he was to face would have been avoided. This, however, does not excuse Sloat's vacillation at Mazatlán or at Monterey. They caused no damage only because Mexico could not exploit the delay, although a Britain truly interested in California might have done so. Sloat's unwillingness to act without express orders, while perhaps understandable, was less than a nation was entitled to expect from her distant commanders in those days of poor communications.

On the twenty-third Stockton accepted the ex-Bear Flaggers as "the California battalion of United States troops," with Frémont as major and Gillespie as a captain and second-in-command. The battalion conformed to no law governing volunteer organizations and ultimately required a special act of Congress to pay for its expenses. In addition to a field force, Stockton arranged for volunteer garrisons to be established at Sonoma, San Juan Bautista, Santa Clara, and Sutter's Fort.[35]

The new commodore was a small, rather underjawed officer, fifty-one years old, who was also one of the leading politicians of New Jersey. A close personal and political friend of President John Tyler, he had arranged for the construction of the *Princeton* to test John Ericsson's revolutionary screw propulsion. Although a competent seaman and an energetic officer, he was also vain, tactless, zenophobic, and glory-thirsty. Few officers in the Navy would have been a worse choice as ruler of the proud and mercurial Californians.[36]

Stockton celebrated his ascension to command with a proclamation which was the antithesis of Sloat's. It covered much the same ground but bitterly attacked Castro and threatened to drive him from the country. Despite Larkin's efforts to get the document softened, it included an imperious demand that the local officials recognize American authority. The tone and the demands ended any hope of a peaceful conquest.[37]

As the first step in his campaign to drive out Castro, Stockton ordered the *Cyane* (Commander S. F. DuPont) to carry Frémont's men to San Diego. After they acquired horses and cattle, they would ride inland to block any southward move by Castro's force at Los Angeles; and Stockton would land an army of sailors and marines at San Pedro and move overland against Castro. Thus the Californian force would be crushed between the two strong American units and any possibility of continued active resistance eliminated. Frémont's men landed about four o'clock in the afternoon of July 29 after a naval landing party determined that there would be no resistance. Frémont remained at San Diego until August 8 but had little success finding horses.[38]

Stockton in the *Congress* (Lieutenant J. W. Livingston) dropped off a small garrison at Santa Barbara and reached San Pedro on August 6. There he landed about 360 men armed with a motley collection of muskets, carbines, pistols, cutlasses, and boarding-pikes. They were ill-prepared to fight the skillful lance-wielding California horsemen. The Americans seized three 6-pounders from a Hawaiian merchantman and added a gun from the *Congress* to form a small artillery train.

While Stockton drilled his makeshift army, Larkin had some political success on August 7 when Castro proposed a truce to be followed by a conference between the two commanders. Unfortunately, Stockton's response that he would agree only if California declared her independence under American protection killed any hope of negotiations. Stockton's demands were ill-conceived. Their

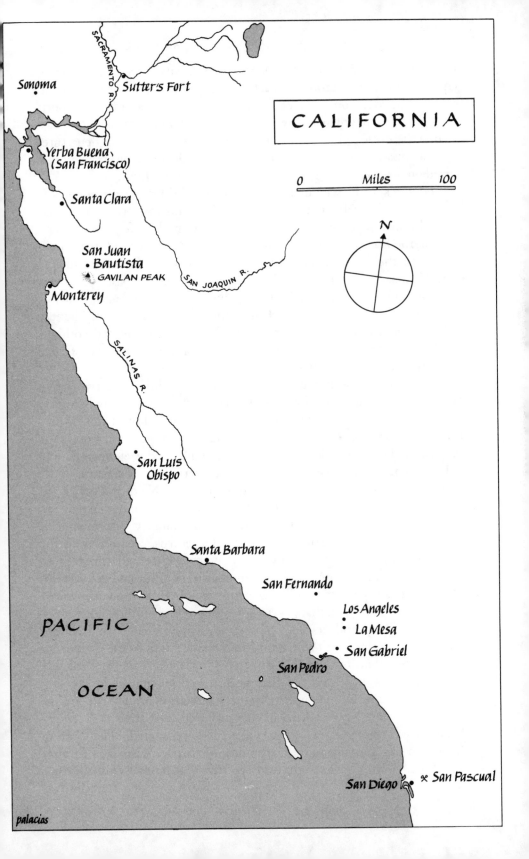

CALIFORNIA

0   Miles   100

N

Sonoma

Sutter's Fort

SACRAMENTO R.

Yerba Buena
(San Francisco)

Santa Clara

San Juan
Bautista
GAVILAN PEAK

SAN JOAQUIN R.

Monterey

SALINAS R.

San Luis
Obispo

Santa Barbara

San Fernando

Los Angeles
La Mesa
San Gabriel

PACIFIC

San Pedro

OCEAN

San Diego   San Pascual

palacias

acceptance would have left Castro without any bargaining points. Upon receiving Stockton's terms, Castro called a council of war which hastened his decision to leave California. Lacking money or support among his countrymen and with only 100 men still in arms, there was no other realistic option available to him. Castro covered his departure with a missive to Stockton on August 10 denouncing the latter's "insidious" letter and announcing his intention to fight.

Stockton's army set out for Los Angeles during the afternoon of August 11. Upon learning of the American advance, the California army broke up. Castro and Governor Pico with a few supporters set out for Sonora that day while the largest segment of the force retired to the Rancho San Pasqual in modern-day South Pasadena. The Mexican government in California had ceased to exist.

Not until August 13, however, did Stockton's column, led by the *Congress'* brass band, march into the town of 1,500 inhabitants. A half hour later Frémont's force arrived, having contributed nothing to the campaign. During the fourteenth various remnants of the California army surrendered and were released on parole.[39]

On August 15 Stockton established customs duties and two days later promised early elections and the establishment of a civilian territorial government. The plan for the government followed closely the traditional organization of American territorial governments. On August 22 the Commodore established September 15 as election day.[40]

Like Kearny in New Mexico, Stockton clearly exceeded his authority in establishing a civil government. Neither American statutes nor international law and usage sanctioned the formation of a civil government by the fiat of the senior military officer in the area. Indeed, the Constitution specifically entrusts that power to Congress. Stockton argued, however, that tranquility had returned to California; a functioning civil government would be undeniable evidence of possession; it would make opposition to the occupation a civil rather than a military crime; civil government could better protect property and civil rights; and finally, he wished to free his forces for an attack on Acapulco. In a private letter to the President he indicated that fear of a Mormon influx influenced his timing. Stockton apparently assumed that he had a right under the law of nations to establish any kind of government he wanted.[41]

Stockton feared attacks on American commerce in the Pacific from Mexican privateers based at Acapulco. This prompted him to alert American ship captains to the availability of San Francisco as a harbor of refuge. It also led him to decide to seize Acapulco. This, he reasoned, would not only deprive the Mexicans of their privateer base but would give him a point from which to attack Mexico City from the rear. Since the projected expedition would require his whole naval force, Stockton authorized Frémont to enlarge the California Battalion to 300 men. This would provide both a mobile field force and garrisons for the major California settlements. At the same time Stockton assured Frémont that he would become Governor and Gillespie Secretary of the territory when the Commodore left. For the interim Stockton named the explorer Military Commandant.[42]

Stockton reembarked his sailors at San Pedro in September and ordered the *Congress* to shape a course for Monterey. There Stockton learned of rumors of an impending attack on the settlements around Sutter's Fort by 1,000 Walla Walla Indians. It posed a grave threat to the Acapulco operation because, if the Indian attack actually materialized, it would require all of Stockton's force to defeat it. Stockton sent the *Savannah* (Captain William Mervine) to San Francisco on September 21 and followed in the *Congress* himself. There the Commodore learned that the threat was imaginary; that the Indians had come to trade and seek justice for the murder of one of their chiefs by an American a year earlier.[43]

Stockton then resumed his preparations for the Acapulco expedition, but they soon hit a snag. An advance inland from Acapulco required a larger and more efficient force than he could form from the squadron. When he asked Frémont to raise 700 men for the expedition, the California Battalion leader found it nearly impossible to recruit them. Stockton may have decided in late September to postpone the expedition because of the shortage of men but the evidence is conflicting. In any event, developments in Los Angeles would put a stop to any further consideration of the Acapulco operation.[44]

NOTES

For key to abbreviations used in Notes, see page xi.

1. Bancroft to Sloat, March 21, May 5, 1845, *RCL*, I, 109, 118–19; same to same, June 24, 1845, *H. Ex. Doc. 60, 30th Cong., 1st Sess.*, 231. The originals of most of Sloat's orders are preserved in "Manuscripts, Documents, Letters, &c. Relating to the Conquest of California. Sloat Documents," Library of the California Historical Society.
2. Sloat to Bancroft, Nov. 19, Dec 3, 25, 1845, *PSL*. The *Constitution*, enroute home from the Far East, was technically not a part of Sloat's command.
3. J. J. Abert to Frémont, Feb. 12, 1845, William H. Goetzmann, *Army Exploration in the American West 1803–1863* (New Haven, 1959), 117.

4. Royce to H. L. Oaks, Aug. 8, 1885, H. H. Bancroft Collection, BLUC.

5. The best summary is in Larkin to Secretary of State, March 27, April 2, 1846, Manning, *Diplo. Corres.*, VIII, 834–36, 839–41. Frémont's account is in his "Conquest of California," *The Century Magazine*, XLI (April 1891), 920–21; his testimony in *S. Ex. Doc. 33, 30th Cong., 1st Sess.*, 372; his *Memoirs of My Life* (2 vols., Chicago, 1887), I, 451, 454, 459; and Josiah Royce, "Notes of an Interview with General Fremont," 24–25, H. H. Bancroft Collection. The correspondence between Larkin and the California authorities is reprinted in Hammond, *The Larkin Papers*, IV, 156–57, 185–86. The California viewpoint appears in Juan Bautista Alvarado, "Historica de California," BLUC.

6. The events leading to Frémont's expulsion are described from various viewpoints in his *Memoirs*, I, 439, 451, 454, 458–59, 462–64, 491; Royce, "Notes of an Interview," 1, 24–25; Bancroft, *History of California*, V, 3–18; Allan Nevins, *Fremont. Pathmarker of the West* (New York, 1955), 226–30; J. M. Castro to Ministro de Guerra y Marina, March 6, April 1, 1846, CHSQ, IV (1925), 83–85, 375. The extensive correspondence concerning the incident in the Thomas Oliver Larkin Papers and the "Official Correspondence of Thos. O. Larkin . . . 1844–1848," BLUC are reprinted in Hammond, *The Larkin Papers*, IV, 227–50, 270–73.

7. Larkin to Commander of Any American ship of war in San Blas or Mazatlán, to Consul John Parrott, both March 9, 1846, Hammond, *The Larkin Papers*, IV, 243–45; Sloat to Montgomery, April 1, 1846, Fred B. Rogers, *Montgomery and the Portsmouth* (San Francisco, 1958), 19–20.

8. Montgomery to Sloat, May 29, 31, 1846, MLB; Josiah Royce, "Montgomery and Fremont: New Documents on the Bear Flag Affair" *The Century Magazine*, XLI (March 1891), 782.

9. Gillespie to SecNav, Feb. 11, 18, April 15, 1846, all in George Walcott Ames, Jr. (ed.), "Gillespie and the Conquest of California," CHSQ, XVII (June–Dec. 1938), 125, 130–35; Alonzo C. Jackson, "Journal of a Cruise in the U.S. Frigate Savannah. . . ." L.C.; "Log of U.S.S. Cyane, Wm. Mervine Comdg." (hereafter cited as Mervine's Journal), RG 45, NA. The sailing was delayed because several of the *Cyane's* officers were serving on a court-martial. She sailed via Honolulu in order to keep her destination secret.

10. Bancroft to Sloat, Dec. 5, 1845, RCL, 163–64; same to same, Feb. 23, 1846, LO, XXXIX, 130. See also Bancroft to Commo. James Biddle, Jan. 6, 1846, RCL, 164–67; Mervine's Journal; Gillespie to Larkin, April 17, 1846, Hammond, *The Larkin Papers*, IV, 290; Raynor Wickersham Kelsey, "The United States Consulate in California," *Publications of the Academy of Pacific Coast History*, I, no. 5, 218–19. In order to preserve their secrecy Gillespie before entering Mexico had destroyed his official correspondence after memorizing it.

11. Extensive debate has arisen over the possibility that Gillespie carried secret orders to Frémont to instigate an uprising. Such a possibility flies in the face of Polk's clear statement (Quaife, *Diary of Polk*, I, 83–84) that Gillespie's "secret instructions & the letter to Mr. Larkin . . . will explain the object of his mission." Those instructions called for countering British and French designs and cultivating conditions conducive to peaceful American annexation. It is not even clear that the administration, as distinct from the Benton family, knew for certain that Frémont was enroute to California in early November when the instructions were issued, Buchanan's letter of introduction to the contrary not withstanding.

12. Good discussions of the meeting from various standpoints are in Gillespie's and Frémont's depositions in *S. Rpt. 75, 30th Cong., 1st Sess.*, 12, 33–34; Royce, "Notes of an Interview," 7–9; Frémont, "Conquest of California," 920–24; Frémont, *Memoirs*, I, 488–90; Nevins, *Fremont*, 239–50; DeVoto, *Year of Decision*, 193–94; Roa Bárcena, *Recuerdos*, I, 240; Josiah Royce, *California* (New York,

1948), 91–118; George Tays, "Fremont Had No Secret Instructions," *PHR*, IX (May 1940), 157–71; Gillespie to SecNav, July 25, 1846, Ames, "Gillespie & Conquest of California," 272–78; William N. Chambers, *Old Bullion Benton* (Boston, 1956), 295, 306, 310; Benton, *30 Years View*, II, 689–90; Cardinal Goodwin, *John Charles Frémont* (Stanford, 1930), 97–99. It is ironic that by June 1 Larkin could assure Washington on the basis of conversations with Alexander Forbes, the resident British agent, that Britain had no designs on California. Larkin to Buchanan, June, 1, 1846, *Mont. Cons.*

13. Larkin to Gillespie, April 23, 1846, Gillespie to Larkin, April 25, 1846, Hammond, *The Larkin Papers*, IV, 340–41, 346–47.

14. That night Frémont's sleeping camp was attacked by Indians who killed three of the party. Benton, *30 Years View*, II, 690; Bancroft, *History of California*, V, 24–25; Stanley Vestal, *Kit Carson. The Happy Warrior of the Old West* (Boston, 1928), 220–22.

15. "Extracts from the Log of the U.S. Frigate *Savannah* Kept by Robert Carson Duvall," *CHSQ*, III (July 1924), 108; William Maxwell Wood, *Wandering Sketches of People and Things in South America, Polynesia, California, and Other Places Visited during a Cruise on Board of the U.S. Ships Levant, Portsmouth, and Savannah* (Philadelphia, 1849), 362–69; Wood to Bancroft, June 4, 1846, *PSL*; Parrott to Buchanan, June 4, 1846, Dispatches from United States Consuls in Mazatlán, I, RG-59, N.A.; Sloat to Larkin, May 18, 1846, Hammond, *The Larkin Papers*, IV, 378; Sloat to Mervine, May 18, 1846, *AF*, Box 250; Mervine's Journal.

16. Sloat to Bancroft, May 31, June 6, 1846, *S. Rpt. 75, 30th Cong., 1st Sess.*, 70; Sloat to Bancroft, July 31, 1846, *H. Ex. Doc. 60, 30th Cong., 1st Sess.*, 258–60; Sloat to Wood, May 20, 1855, Edwin A. Sherman, *The Life of the Late Rear Admiral John Drake Sloat* (Oakland, 1902), 65–66; Bancroft, *History of California*, V, 204; Smith, *War with Mexico*, I, 333. The *Warren*, with official notice of war, reached Monterey on August 12. Mervine to Montgomery, Aug. 13, 1846, *AF*, Box 250; Walter Colton, *Three Years in California* (New York, 1850), 28.

17. Bancroft to Sloat, May 13, 15, July 12, 1846, *H. Ex. Doc. 60, 30th Cong., 1st Sess.*, 233, 235–36, 238–39; Bancroft to Commo. Lawrence Rousseau, May 13, 1846, to Biddle, May 16, 1846, *RCL*, I, 176, 178. Among the reinforcements ordered to the Pacific during the middle of 1846, the frigate *Potomac's* orders were canceled; the sloop of war *Saratoga* was damaged in a storm and forced to return home; the sloop of war *Dale* (Commander William W. McKean) sailed from New York June 3; the razee *Independence* (Captain Elie A. F. La Vallette) carrying Commodore W. Branford Shubrick as Sloat's relief departed Boston August 22; and the sloop-of-war *Preble* (Commander William F. Shields) left New York on September 26 as convoy for the transports carrying Stevenson's regiment. The ship-of-the-line *Columbus* (Captain Thomas W. Wyman) carrying Commodore James Biddle was in the Far East and would not reach California for ten months. In addition the storeship *Lexington* (Lieutenant Theodorus Bailey) carrying a company of artillery men and their guns for the coastal defenses of California departed New York on July 14.

18. Frémont, *Memoirs*, I, 503, 509; Gillespie to SecNav, July 25, 1846, Ames, "Gillespie & Conquest of California," 273; Montgomery to Frémont, June 3, 1846, *CHSQ*, VI (Sept. 1927), 265; John Adam Hussey, "Commander John B. Montgomery and the Bear Flag Revolt," *USNIP*, LXXV (July 1939), 975; Montgomery to J. M. Castro, June 24, 1846, Sloat Documents; Gillespie to Larkin, June 8, 1846, Hammond, *The Larkin Papers*, V, 6–7. Much of the military prepa-

rations stemmed from a struggle for power between General Castro and Governor Pio Pico which erupted in April.

19. Frémont to Benton, July 25, 1846, Frémont, *Memoirs*, I, 546.

20. Edwin Bryant, *What I Saw in California* (New York, 1848), 287–88; William Heath Davis, *Seventy-Five Years in California* (San Francisco, 1929), 142–43; Frémont, *Memoirs*, I, 509; W. B. Ide to Montgomery, June 15, 1846, *CHSQ*, I (April 1920), 82–83; Larkin to Gillespie, June 11, 1846, William A. Liedesdorff Papers, Henry E. Huntington Library and Art Gallery; Bancroft, *History of California*, V, 85, 105–11; Irving Berdine Richman, *California Under Spain and Mexico* (Boston, 1911), 307–9.

21. Castro, Proclamations, June 16–17, 1846, *CHSQ*, I (April 1922), 93–94, and Hammond, *The Larkin Papers*, V, 39–40; Frémont to Benton, July 25, 1846, *loc. cit.*; Montgomery to Larkin, July 2, 1846, Hammond, *The Larkin Papers*, V, 94–95; Gillespie, Narrative, n.d., Gillespie Papers; Frémont, *Memoirs*, I, 515–16; Fred B. Rogers, "Bear Flag Lieutenant," *CHSQ*, XXIX (Oct. 1950), 169–70; Bancroft, *History of California*, V, 134–36, 165–66, 171, 176–79; Royce, *California*, 63; Richman, *California Under Spain and Mexico*, 31; Werner H. Marti, *Messenger of Destiny* (San Francisco, 1955), 61.

22. Quaife, *Diary of Polk*, III, 439, 443, 473; Smith, *War with Mexico*, I, 341; Stevenson to Marcy, June 10, 1846, Jonathan D. Stevenson, Letter Book, NYHS; Marcy to Kearny, June 3, 1846, *H. Ex. Doc. 17, 31st Cong., 1st Sess.*, 236–39; Marcy to Mason, June 8, 1846, *SWMA*, XXVI, 320–21; Bancroft to Bailey, July 11, 1846, *RCL*, I, 201; Scott to C. Q. Tompkins, June 20, 1846, *H. Ex. Doc. 60, 30th Cong., 1st Sess.*, 245–6; A. DeWolfe Howe (ed.), *Home Letters of General Sherman* (New York, 1909), 36–84.

23. Larkin to Montgomery, June 19, 20, 1846, Hammond, *The Larkin Papers*, V, 58–59; Sloat to Larkin, June 2, 1846, L. W. Sloat to Larkin, July 2, 1846, all in Hammond, *The Larkin Papers*, V, 58–59, 96, 98; Robert Carson Duvall, "Cruise of the U.S. Frigate *Savannah*," photostat copy in Los Angeles Public Library; logs of *Cyane*, *Levant*, and *Savannah*; Reuben L. Underhill, *From Cowhides to Golden Fleece* (Palo Alto, 1946), 120–21.

24. Montgomery to Mervine, July 2, 1846, *MLB*; Jackson, "Journal of a Cruise;" William Baldridge, "The Days of 1846," BLUC; William Heath Davis, *75 Years in California* (San Francisco, 1929), 267 attributes the reversal to pressure from Mervine at a council of war held on July 6. This story is not elsewhere supported.

25. Sloat to Montgomery, July 6, 7, 1846, *H. Ex. Doc. 1, 30th Cong., 1st Sess.*, 1014–15.

26. Sloat to Bancroft, July 31, 1846, with enclosures *H. Ex. Doc. 60, 30th Cong., 1st Sess.*, 258–63; Duvall, "Cruise of the Savannah;" Jackson, "Journal of a Cruise;" "Mervine's Journal;" Colton, *Three Years in California*, 63; Larkin to Buchanan, July 10, 1846, *CHSQ*, VII (April 1928), 84; logs of the vessels involved; Aubrey Neasham, "The Raising of the Flag at Monterey, California, July 7, 1846," *CHSQ*, XXV (June 1946), 202; George Walcott Ames, Jr., "Horse Marines: California, 1846," *CHSQ*, XVIII (March 1939), 72–84; Sherman, *Sloat*, 74–78; Bancroft, *History of California*, V 230–35; Bauer, *Surfboats and Horse Marines*, 149–54.

27. Mervine, Proclamation, July 7, 1846, *MLB*; Colton, *Three Years in California*, 63; Mervine's Journal; Sloat to Fauntleroy, July 8, 1846, PSL; Bancroft, *History of California*, V, 231, 233n–5n; Theodore Grivas, *Military Governments in California, 1846–1850* (Glendale, 1963), 83; Ames, "Horse Marines," 72–84.

28. Montgomery to Sloat, July 9, 11, 1846, with enclosures *H. Ex. Doc. 1, 30th Cong., 1st Sess.*, 1015–22; Cutts, *Conquest of California and New Mexico*, 118; J. M. Ellicott, "Comedy and Tragedy in Our Occupation of California," *Marine*

Corps Gazette, XXXV (March 1951), 50. Sloat's directive and most contemporary American references are to Yerba Buena, the settlement around what is today Portsmouth Square. San Francisco at that time referred to a second group of houses near the Mission. In 1846 Yerba Buena settlement changed its name to San Francisco.

29. Montgomery to Sloat, July 11, 20, 1846, *H. Ex. Doc. 1, 30th Cong., 1st Sess.,* 1019–20, 1030; Adams, "English Interest in Annexation of California," 758; Sherman, *Sloat,* 81; Cutts, *Conquest of California and New Mexico,* 119.

30. Bancroft, *History of California,* V, 262–63; Pico, Proclamation, July 16, 1846, "Documentos para la Historia de California . . . al Archivo de Don Antonio F. Coronel," BLUC. Sloat made strong efforts to induce Castro to surrender. Sloat to Castro, July 7, 1846, *H. Ex. Doc. 60, 30th Cong., 1st Sess.,* 1012; Castro to Sloat, July 9, 1846, Hammond, *The Larkin Papers,* V, 121–22; which also reprints, on pp. 110–23, Larkin's extensive correspondence.

31. Mervine's Journal; Duvall, "Extracts from Log," 111–12; Walter Colton, *Deck and Port* (New York, 1850), 367, 379, 385; Samuel Francis DuPont, "The War with Mexico: Cruise of the *Cyane,*" *USNIP,* VIII (Sept. 1882), 420; Henry A. DuPont, *Rear Admiral Samuel Francis DuPont* (New York, 1926), 45; Samuel John Bayard, *A Sketch of the Life of Com. Robert F. Stockton* (New York, 1856), 101; Bancroft, *History of California,* V, 252–53.

32. Frémont, *Memoirs,* I, 530–32; Frémont, "Conquest of California," 935; Gillespie to SecNav, July 25, 1846, to Bancroft, Feb. 16, 1847, Ames, "Gillespie and Conquest of California," 277, 281; Larkin to Sloat, July 16, 1846, Sloat Documents; Bryant, *What I Saw in California,* 297; Mervine's Journal; Rogers, "Bear Flag Lieutenant," 273; Colton, *Deck and Port,* 390–91; Bancroft, *History of California,* V, 247–48.

33. William Baldridge, "The Days of 1846," 29–30, BLUC; Stockton's testimony, *S. Ex. Doc. 33, 30th Cong., 1st Sess.,* 178–80, and deposition, *S. Rpt. 75, 30th Cong., 1st Sess.,* 13; Frémont, *Memoirs,* I, 534–35; Frémont, "Conquest of California," 926–28; Marti, *Messenger of Destiny,* 69–70; Bayard, *Sketch of Stockton,* 110–21; Bancroft, *History of California,* V, 249–51. Gillespie's account in his July 25, 1846 letter to SecNav cannot be trusted.

34. Sloat to Bancroft, July 31, 1846, *H. Ex. Doc. 60, 30th Cong., 1st Sess.,* 258–60; Stockton to Mason, Feb. 18, 1848, *H. Ex. Doc. 1, 30th Cong., 2nd Sess.,* 1037–54; Bauer, *Surfboats and Horse Marines,* 160–61; Sherman, *Sloat,* 85; Bancroft, exasperated at the delay in carrying out the June 1845 orders, directed their execution "at once" on Aug. 13 and on the same day relieved Sloat. *RCL,* I, 21. News of the conquest reached Washington on Aug. 31 through British diplomats in Mexico City. Quaife, *Diary of Polk,* II, 108.

35. Stockton, Memorandum for Captain Frémont, July 22, 1846, *SLB,* 75; Stockton to Frémont, July 23, 1846, *S. Ex. Doc. 33, 30th Cong., 1st Sess.,* 175; Sloat to Montgomery, July 23, 1846, *H. Ex. Doc. 1, 30th Cong., 2nd Sess.,* 1033. The battalion's commissions are in *SLB,* 103–14. Various documents bearing on the raising and status of the northern California garrisons are in the Fort Sutter Papers, Henry E. Huntington Library and Art Gallery and in the Leidesdorff Papers.

36. Harold and Margaret Sprout, *The Rise of American Naval Power 1775–1918* (Princeton, 1942), 125; Bayard, *Sketch of Stockton,* Charles J. Peterson, *The American Navy* (Philadelphia, 1858), 535. Stockton broke his command pennant in the *Congress* at daybreak of July 30. Log of *Congress.*

37. Various surviving copies of the proclamation bear dates between July 23 and 30. It was probably written prior to July 28 but not issued until July 31. It is reprinted in *H. Ex. Doc. 1, 31st Cong., 1 Sess.,* 31–33, and Hammond, *The*

Larkin Papers, V, 175-77. See also Bauer, *Surfboats and Horse Marines*, 277; Bancroft, *History of California*, V, 257, 259; Larkin to Buchanan, July [29], 1846, Hammond, *The Larkin Papers*, V, 180-82.

38. Stockton to DuPont, July 23, 1846, *SLB*, 99; Stockton to Frémont, July 23, 1846, *loc. cit.*; DuPont to Stockton, July 29, 31, 1846, Samuel Francis DuPont, *Official Despatches and Letters of Rear Admiral DuPont* (Wilmington, 1883), 2-3, 507; DuPont, "Cruise of the *Cyane*," 420; Frémont, *Memoirs*, I, 563; Log of *Cyane*.

39. Duvall, "Extracts from Log," 113; log of *Congress*; Bayard, *Sketch of Stockton*, 118-21; Duncan Gleason, "The Lost Islands of San Pedro," *Sea*, XV (May 1951), 18-19; Jenkins, *History of the War*, 132; Stockton to Mason, Feb. 18, 1848, *loc. cit.*; Larkin to Buchanan, July [29], Aug. 23, 1846, Hammond, *The Larkin Papers*, V, 180-82, 211-14; the exchange of letters concerning Castro's proposal for an armistice are in *S. Ex. Doc. 31, 30th Cong., 2nd Sess.*, 3-6; Bancroft, *History of California*, V, 272-73; Smith, *War with Mexico*, I, 337; Richman, *California Under Spain and Mexico*, 319; James M. Guinn, "Siege and Capture of Los Angeles," *HSSCP*, III (1893), 47-48; James M. Guinn, *A History of California and an Extended History of Los Angeles* (3 vols., Los Angeles, 1915), I, 124; Corrine King Wright, "The Conquest of Los Angeles," *HSSCP*, XI (1918), 18-21; Frémont, *Memoirs*, I, 566. Gillespie Papers, #23A is a blank copy of the parole form.

40. Stockton, Proclamations, Aug. 15-22, 1846, *H. Ex. Doc. 19, 29th Cong., 2nd Sess.*, 107-10.

41. Stockton to Mason, Feb. 18, 1848, *loc. cit.*, Stockton to Polk, Aug. 26, 1846, *SLB*, 241-43; same to same, Nov. 30, 1846, Polk Papers; Stockton's testimony, *S. Ex. Doc. 33, 30th Cong., 1st Sess.*, 197-98.

42. Stockton, Circular, ca. Sept. 1, 1846, General Order, Sept. 2, 1846, Stockton to Gillespie, Aug. 31, 1846, all in *S. Ex. Doc. 31, 30th Cong., 2nd Sess.*, 7-8; Stockton to Frémont, Aug. 24, 1846, Stockton, Commission to Frémont, Sept. 2, 1846, *S. Ex. Doc. 33, 30th Cong., 1st Sess.*, 109-10; Stockton to Maddox, Aug. 31, 1846, *SLB*, 254; Smith, *War with Mexico*, I, 338; Bancroft, *History of California*, V, 290.

43. Stockton to Mason, Feb. 18, 1848, *loc. cit.*; Stockton to Bancroft, Sept. 18, Oct. 1, 1846, *S. Ex. Doc. 31, 30th Cong., 2nd Sess.*, 1-2, 13; Colton, *Three Years in California*, 59; Stockton to Montgomery, Sept. 20, 1846, *AF*, Box 251; Montgomery to Mervine, Sept. 10, 1846, *MLB*; Bancroft, *History of California*, V, 301.

44. Stockton to Bancroft, Oct. 1, 1846, to Mervine, Sept. 30, 1846, *S. Ex. Doc. 31, 30th Cong., 2nd Sess.*, 12-13; Stockton to Frémont, Sept. 28, 1846, Frémont, *Memoirs*, I, 572-73.

II: California Lost and Regained

W<small>HILE COMMODORE STOCKTON</small> pushed the preparations for his projected attack on Acapulco, Captain Gillespie at Los Angeles found the task of keeping his area quiet very difficult. The City of the Angels boasted a large and turbulent Mexican population and was the center of pro-Mexican feeling in California.

Gillespie's forty-eight-man garrison scarcely earned respect from the local populace. Many were undisciplined and discontented over being stationed in the south. They contributed to their own difficulties by appearing so unmanageable as to invite harassment and an uprising. If the garrison earned the natives' scorn, their commander was not one to inspire the confidence of those over whom he ruled. He was a tall, red-haired officer of thirty-three who sported a stiff, pointed beard. Although he spoke fluent Spanish his intense dislike of the Californians combined with his quick temper to produce the overriding tactlessness that marked his dealings with the Angelinos. Adding further to the complications, the garrison was too small to overawe the turbulent southern town and therefore served more as a provocation than a quieting influence.[1]

Upon hearing rumors of an uprising, Gillespie sent ten of his most undisciplined men to an outpost near present-day Chino on the road to Sonora where they were captured by the Californians on September 27. He also sent a handful under Ezekiel Merritt to San Diego. The Marine requested reinforcements on September 20 but the message fell into the hands of the Californians.

At 3:00 A.M. on Wednesday morning, September 23, about twenty men led by Cérbulo Varela exchanged shots with the Americans in their quarters at the Government House. The attack struck a spark to the latent hostility against the garrison and by nightfall Los Angeles was in arms. During the twenty-fourth about 150 Californians met near Castro's old camp at La Mesa, about a mile and a quarter from the American barracks. Varela quickly lost the leadership to Captain José María Flores, an intelligent and able Mexican who, like most of the leaders of the revolt, broke his parole by joining the rebels. The rules of war made them subject to execution if again captured.

Gillespie seized what powder and lead he could and set his men to work repairing four old spiked cannon. During the night of September 24-25 Juan "Flaco" Brown slipped past the Californians to make a fabled five-day ride to San Francisco where he delivered the report of the rising to Commodore Stockton.

At Los Angeles the two forces watched each other like a pair of wary tomcats until the evening of September 28 when Gillespie's men slipped out of the Government House to a more defensible position about a quarter of a mile away atop Fort Hill. Unfortunately, Gillespie had not first determined whether the position had water, which it did not, so a very thirsty group of Americans had to surrender the next day. Under the surrender terms they evacuated Los Angeles but kept their small arms. Gillespie also was permitted to keep his cannon until he reached San Pedro. The Americans trudged down to the sea on September 30 and, four days later, boarded the American merchantman *Vandalia* (Captain T. Everett), having first spiked their cannon in violation of the surrender agreement.[2]

Flores sent detachments to clean out the other American forces in southern California.[3] On October 1 Stockton held no more of California than he had when he took command of the squadron. The responsibility for the debacle was his. His insistence on crushing Castro doomed any chance of a negotiated settlement, just as his overbearing manner and obvious contempt for the inhabitants prevented a smooth transition from one government to another. Nor did he display military sense of any high quality. The use of small garrisons in the midst of the highly inflammable and disgruntled southern Californians was like presenting a two-year-old with matches and kerosene.

Flaco Brown reached San Francisco with the news of the uprising on October 1. Stockton hastily drew up plans for the relief of Gillespie. As later modified, these called for Frémont to move his men by water to Santa Barbara while Captain William Mervine in the *Savannah* sailed to San Pedro to assist Gillespie. After securing mounts for his men, Frémont would march down the coast. At the same time Stockton would join Mervine with the *Congress* and their combined landing parties would move against the rebels. The strategy was a slight modification of that employed in August.[4]

Fog delayed the *Savannah*'s departure until October 4. She reached San Pedro two days later to find the *Vandalia* swinging at anchor with Gillespie's men still embarked. After conferring with the Marine, Mervine decided to march immediately to Los Angeles. He set out in the morning of October 7 with about 285 sailors, Marines, and Bear Flaggers but without a supply train, ambulances, or artillery. Why Mervine, a normally competent officer, assumed his untrained sailor-infantrymen could fight their way through the Californian cavalry to the city is unclear. Probably he was influenced by Gillespie's ill-concealed disdain for the Californians.

In midafternoon the Americans camped at the Rancho Domínguez in present-day North Long Beach. During the night the Californians started sniping at the American bivouac. At 2:00 A.M. they brought up their lone artillery piece, a 4-pounder which had been hidden from the Americans in a Los Angeles garden, to shell the American position.

At daylight Mervine's force set out again. When he sighted the Californians astride the road with the gun, Mervine formed his men in a square in order to beat off any cavalry charge and resumed the march. As the Americans came within range of the gun, the Californians fired at them.. When the Americans in their compact square charged, the Californians hauled the piece out of danger with *reatas*. Since the Californians were mounted and the Americans were not, the race was no contest. After repeating the act three times, Mervine halted his men and called a council of war. It concluded that it was impossible to capture the gun and that as long as the Californians had artillery it would be foolhardy to attempt to take Los Angeles. At 9:00 A.M., therefore, the force began its slow, dreary march back to San Pedro. Five hours later they safely reembarked on their ships. Ten of the Americans had been wounded by cannonballs. Four of them later died and were buried on Isla de Muertos, or Deadmen's Island, in San Pedro harbor.[5]

While Mervine made his abortive effort to retake Los Angeles, Frémont rushed the preparations for his move to the south. His men embarked on the chartered merchantman *Sterling* (Captain G. W. Vincent) at San Francisco and departed October 12 in company with the *Congress*. They separated after receiving a call for assistance from the Monterey garrison who feared an attack. The flagship went there to shore up the defenses while Frémont and his men continued on to Santa Barbara. Before reaching that destination, Frémont learned of Mervine's debacle and had the *Sterling* shape her course to Monterey.

After landing reinforcements at Monterey, the *Congress* resumed her voyage to San Pedro but missed Frémont. The flagship joined the *Savannah* at San Pedro on October 25. The following morning the two frigates landed their Marines, a detachment of sailors, and Gillespie's men. Although the Californians neither contested the landing nor harassed the American encampment, Stockton shifted his base to San Diego at the end of the month.

The change grew out of the Commodore's fear of the open roadstead at San Pedro and his discovery that Frémont had gone to Monterey. At San Diego, Stockton began preparing an army to reconquer Los Angeles. He sent an expedition into Baja California to secure horses, cattle and sheep, and had shoes, saddles, and other equipment manufactured. The sailors spent the time learning basic drill.[6]

Coincidentally, Frémont, by use of strong pressure on newly arrived immigrants to enlist and by reducing the northern garrisons, collected 428 men. On November 17 he led about 300 of them out of Monterey.[7]

Stockton's shift of base to San Diego handed Flores badly needed time to organize his forces. The California leader had so little to work with that he needed all the assistance his opponent was unwittingly giving him. The Californians in the field numbered but 400 with only forty rounds of artillery and a thousand rounds of musket ammunition between them. More damaging to his position was the clearly evident lack of enthusiasm for resistance on the part of many of the southern Californians. Flores's strategy called for guerrilla operations to pin the Americans in their ports. To accomplish this he sent about 100 men to San Luis Obispo to harass Frémont's force. A similar-sized force watched San Diego, while the main body remained at Los Angeles ready to move against whichever American force became the most threatening.[8]

While Flores's attention focused on the two groups of Americans facing him, a third one rode toward his rear. Brigadier General

Stephen W. Kearny had left Santa Fe September 25 to carry out the second part of his orders to secure New Mexico and California. Accompanied by a small and very travel-weary escort he reached Warner's Ranch on December 2. Kearny learned little beyond the fact of Stockton's continued presence at San Diego. Therefore, the General apprised Stockton of his arrival and asked for news and an escort to San Diego. Kearny's letter reached Stockton at about 6:30 on the evening of December 3. An hour and a half later Gillespie with thirty-nine men and a brass 4-pounder left to make contact with the army detachment. With him Gillespie brought Stockton's suggestion that Kearny attempt to surprise Californians outside San Diego.[9]

Kearny remained at Warner's through the third while his men rested and the Quartermaster purchased about 100 wild and almost useless horses. The soldiers set out again on the fourth, meeting Gillespie's force during the afternoon of the following day. When the combined force camped that night, they learned that Captain Andrés Pico with a body of Californians watched the road at the nearby village of San Pascual. Pico knew nothing of Kearny's arrival but was aware of Gillespie's move. Since the Californian assumed that the Americans were on a foraging expedition and would not return for several days, he allowed his men to let their horses out to graze.

A dragoon patrol under Lieutenant Thomas C. Hammond successfully reconnoitered Pico's position, and Rafael Machado, Gillespie's guide, actually entered the Californian camp without being detected. As the party rode off, however, the clanking of the dragoons' heavy swords destroyed all hope of surprise. Pico immediately had his horses collected. They reached the camp just in time to permit the Californians to mount before the American attack struck.

Kearny set the time of attack at daylight on December 6 although his force was in no condition for a fight. The men had yet to recover from the long and arduous march and their mounts were either jaded or scarcely broken to the saddle. To complicate the issue further, the dragoons were neither trained nor equipped to fight lancers like the Californians. Undoubtedly the Americans could have forced their way through to San Diego without attacking Pico, for their force was large, well supplied with artillery, and able to withstand any Californian attack. Why then did Kearny, one of the most competent officers in the army, choose to attack? He was undoubtedly influenced by Stockton's request that he surprise Pico and by Kit Carson's and Gillespie's misleading advice that even his bedraggled force could risk the attack. A successful attack, the reasoning would have run, would eliminate one of the larger Californian forces in the field and probably hasten an end to insurrection. Moreover, such an attack would clear the route to San Diego.

Kearny's force arose at 2:00 A.M. and mounted its motley assortment of horses and mules. The cold numbed minds and limbs while the dampness wet down the powder in the dragoons' carbines. When Captain Abraham R. Johnston's twelve-man advance guard came within about three-quarters of a mile of the enemy camp, Kearny ordered an advance at a trot. Johnston apparently misunderstood the order and sent his men forward in a gallop. This increased the distance between them and the main body so that Johnston's men reached the Californian mass before the rest of the Americans were in supporting position. The charge caught the Californians still forming and threw them into confusion. They quickly recovered, however, and forced the outnumbered dragoons to withdraw.

Kearny's main body straggled on the scene in ragged order because of the differing qualities of their mounts. At this, Pico withdrew to more even ground about a half mile to his rear. Captain Benjamin D. Moore, commanding the main body of dragoons, ordered a charge which separated the Americans even more widely. The Californians met them with a countercharge. In the ensuing melée the sabre-wielding Americans were no match for the Californian lancers. After about ten or fifteen minutes the American artillery and Gillespie's men arrived. Unwilling to face the artillery, Pico ordered a withdrawal. As they left the battlefield the Californians took with them one of the dragoon's howitzers whose mule team had bolted into the Californian lines.

The fight had been a disaster for the Americans. Of approximately 150 men engaged, eighteen, including Captains Moore and Johnston, and Lieutenant Hammond, were dead and thirteen others, including Kearny and Gillespie, wounded. Pico had approximately seventy-five men, of whom about twelve suffered wounds and one fell into American hands. The Americans were in no condition to pursue the Californians. Their provisions had been exhausted, their mounts worn out or unusable, and the men tired. Without vehicles to carry the wounded they could not even continue their advance. Captain Henry S. Turner, the acting commander while Kearny was incapacitated, sent Stockton an appeal for help. Until relief arrived or the wounded were able to travel there was nothing for the stranded men to do but to make camp, bury the dead, and treat the injured.[10]

The first news of the fight reached Stockton during the evening of December 6 but it lacked details. The following morning Turner's letter arrived. The Commodore decided to send all of his available men. Preparations for such a large party took time and before it could leave a second letter arrived. It made clear that the Californians were few in number but that speed was essential. Stockton then changed the force to a small but highly mobile one. During the evening of December 7 a third messenger arrived. On the basis of his report Stockton enlarged the relief force and ordered its commander, Lieutenant Andrew V. F. Gray, to move by night marches. Gray's force marched on the eighth.

During the seventh Kearny's column, still encumbered by the injured, resumed its march. At a small hill near Rancho San Bernardo the Americans clashed again with Pico's men, took the hill, but lost their few remaining cattle. The Californians besieged the hungry troops there until the tenth, but during the night of the tenth-eleventh Gray's force arrived. The combined force reached San Diego without incident during the late afternoon of December 12.[11]

With the dragoons' arrival all of the forces available for the decisive Los Angeles campaign were in position. Kearny promptly conferred with Stockton, but what transpired is nearly as unclear as the exact relationship of the two men in the campaign which followed. Although both later claimed the command, just as each would claim to be governor of California, Stockton exercised it. Whether as governor of California and commander in chief of the expedition as Stockton claimed, or simply as the supplier of the bulk of the troops as Kearny claimed, is not important. The cause of the conflict was the distance from Washington. Stockton, who arrived on the scene first and had seized most of the area, claimed supremacy, while Kearny relied on his explicit orders to take command and serve as governor. Stockton did not question Kearny's orders but held that they had been rendered inoperative by events.

Stockton planned to move his force to San Luis Rey from whence his operations would be guided by the movements of Frémont and Flores. His strategy was to use the main body as a diversion while Frémont and the northern column seized Los Angeles. The Commodore seems to have been obsessed by a fear that if he advanced further the Californians would cut his supply line to San Diego. Kearny apparently finally convinced the naval officer that the main body had little to fear from attacks on its supply line and should fight its way through to Los Angeles.

Stockton set his force in motion on December 28 and 29. When the last units departed San Diego, the force numbered 607 men variously armed with muskets, carbines, boarding pikes, and six pieces of artillery. The draft animals were so feeble that the men had to help drag the artillery and the few store wagons. The only fresh provisions were a few cattle kept penned within a hollow square of men to prevent their straying during the march. The route, which roughly followed modern U. S. Highway 101, covered approximately 140 miles.

Shortly after the start of the year Stockton refused to discuss Flores's proposal of a truce and informed the Californian that he would shoot him as a parole violator. Stockton did, however, offer amnesty to all other Californians who would surrender.

Flores had expected that Frémont would constitute the worst threat and had planned to intercept his force before dealing with Stockton's. By January 5 or 6 he concluded that the reverse was true and prepared to ambush Stockton's men at La Jaboneria Ford on the San Gabriel River. During the night of January 7-8 Stockton's scouts discovered the Californians and he ordered his men to cross at a higher ford, Bartolo. Flores followed suit and his well-mounted men were able to take up their positions before the slower-moving Americans reached the crossing.[12]

The ford was about fifty yards wide with knee-deep water. The bottom, while generally solid, had some patches of quicksand. The approach from the south, or American, side was level, but on the opposite bank a range of low hills, about fifty feet high, thrust up about 600 yards beyond the stream. There the Californians took their stand. Flores placed 200 men and two small artillery pieces to cover the ford itself, while about 300 yards distant on either wing he positioned another 100 to 150 horsemen.

When the Americans reached the plain south of the river, Stockton formed his force into a square enclosing the baggage and cattle. When they were about two miles from the river they first made out the flashing lances of the enemy horsemen. At about two o'clock, when a quarter of a mile from the river, Stockton halted the American formation to strengthen its left flank and to send some mounted riflemen ahead as skirmishers. When the advance resumed, Flores attempted to break up the square by having horses driven into it. That failed. The Californian artillery fired repeatedly at the advancing Americans, but poor powder and makeshift projectiles ensured inaccuracy.

As the American formation reached the riverbank, the artillerymen, apparently on Kearny's order, began to unlimber their pieces. Stockton countermanded the directive and sent the whole force across the stream without any covering fire. Because of the soft bottom and the quicksand, it required much hard pushing by both officers and men to get the heavy guns across. While the artillerymen prepared their pieces, the infantry at the head and flanks of the square took cover under the four-foot-high riverbank. The rear, burdened with the baggage carts, and the livestock, advanced more slowly. While the infantry took up their positions, Stockton personally directed the firing of the American artillery. He disabled one of the Californian guns and silenced the other. The mounted riflemen then drove Flores's left wing from its hilltop but had to be recalled to reinforce the American right. Flores tried to counterattack, but a mixup in orders caused the Californian left to retire in confusion. Flores then sent in his right wing, but it was driven back by the fire of the Americans on the left and the artillery.

Having beaten off the attacks, Stockton ordered his men forward. They charged, crying "New Orleans" in honor of Jackson's victory thirty-one years earlier, and easily seized the Californian position as the locals fell back in good order. To cover his withdrawal, Flores sent the horsemen of his right wing to attack the American rear but they were again beaten off by a curtain of fire. Flores fell back about a half mile but the accurate fire of the American field pieces drove his artillerymen from their guns and caused a further withdrawal toward Los Angeles. Stockton, who had only a handful of mounted men, did not pursue. Although many of Flores's men deserted during the retreat, the remainder halted at the Cañada de los Alisos[13] near the road to Los Angeles. Some later returned to the battlefield and about midnight exchanged fire with the American pickets.[14]

The Battle of San Gabriel, as the action came to be called, lasted about ninety minutes and cost each side about two killed and nine wounded. Stockton's sailors had not flinched under artillery fire or cavalry charge. If the Commodore's tactics, particularly forcing the ford without artillery support, were open to question, his personal courage was not. He had personally contributed greatly to the victory by his sighting and firing of the American artillery. Following the battle, Stockton's men camped near the hill which had been the original position of the Californian right wing.

At daylight on January 9 American scouts visited Pio Pico's nearby ranch but failed to find any Californians. When the Americans resumed their march they crossed a wide, dry plain between the San

Gabriel and Los Angeles rivers which was called simply La Mesa. After marching about six miles the Americans sighted about 300 Californians, deployed in a long line from the cañada, or ravine, nearly to Stockton's line of march. Flores had stationed his artillery on the left in front of the ravine. The Americans advanced in their usual square and turned slightly to the left to open the range. When they came within range of the Californian guns, the latter opened an ineffective fire. The Americans responded from the field pieces at the front corners of the square and continued advancing. Flores then extended his line to interdict the American axis of advance and brought up two additional guns. Stockton in turn halted his force and formed the guns at the leading corners of his square into a single battery. After about fifteen minutes of shelling, these pieces and a 6-pounder at the rear of the right flank drove the Californian artillery out of range.

Since Flores's artillery wasted nearly all of its powder in the futile exchange, Flores sent his horsemen against the American left. The attack met such a concentrated fire that the horsemen fell back. At this most of the Californians deserted the field. The Americans continued toward Los Angeles. Stockton halted them about three miles outside the town, since he had decided to postpone entry until daylight when visibility would be better and liquor less plentiful. Neither side suffered extensively in the clash. The Americans reported one killed and five wounded, while Flores lost one killed and some additional men injured. Nevertheless, Stockton had destroyed the Californian resistance.

About noon on January 10 the Americans entered the town with their band playing. Although some of the diehard Californians could be seen in the offing, no incidents marred the entry and Gillespie raised the flag which he had hauled down in surrender over the Government House.[15]

While the main body successfully completed the recapture of Los Angeles, Frémont's force slowly made its way south. Frémont anticipated the first resistance would come at San Luis Obispo and laid elaborate plans to catch the defenders. His men surrounded the town and during the dark, rainy night of December 14-15 successfully rushed the nonexistent defenses. Outside the town, however, the Americans did seize Jesus Pico, the local California commander, and thirty-five of his men. Since Pico had broken his parole by taking up arms, Frémont had him brought to trial. The court-martial sentenced the Californian to death, but Frémont bowed to the entreaties of Señora Pico at well as several American officers and pardoned the prisoner. It was a sagacious act. Pico, feeling that he owed his life to Frémont, volunteered to accompany the expedition.

The column left San Luis Obispo during December 17, crossed the San Rafael Mountains in a bad storm, and reached Santa Barbara ten days later. Assisted by the prize schooner *Julia*, the Americans safely passed the critical Rincon Pass just below Santa Barbara where the road ran between high hills and the sea. On January 5, 1847 the force had a short skirmish with a few Californian horsemen near the Mission of San Buenaventura.

Four days later the explorer received a letter dated January 3 from Stockton which informed him of the advance of the southern force and counseled against battle if possible. Kearny passed on word of the fall of Los Angeles on the tenth and instructed the explorer to join the main body. Frémont received the letter on the eleventh. Late that day he discovered about 100 of Flores's men, including their commander, encamped nearby. Frémont sent Jesus Pico into their camp to convince them to surrender. That Pico did. Flores, either because he feared for his life or because he did not wish to complicate the negotiations with his presence, transferred command to Andrés Pico and left for Sonora.

Upon learning of the decision, Frémont granted a truce. The articles of capitulation were drawn up during December 12 and signed the following morning at the Rancho Cahuenga. The generous and statesmanlike terms allowed the Californians to return home on parole; promised protection to those surrendering and absolved them from having to take an oath of allegiance during the war; guaranteed equal rights for all Californians; and granted to all who so wished the right to leave the country.[16]

The terms were exceptionally generous and nearly duplicated ones which Stockton had refused earlier. That Frémont offered very statesmanlike terms cannot be denied although his motivation may be questioned. It may well be that since he expected to become governor he hoped in this way to reduce the problems he was likely to face. But he erred in signing the surrender while within communicating distance of his superior and he lacked authority to make such a far-reaching arrangement. Stockton, however, could scarcely repudiate the document and had to accept the *fait accompli*. The Cahuenga document was yet another instance of Frémont's insubordination. He made no effort to communicate with either Stockton or Kearny, despite direct orders to do so, and the first word they received of his operations was the arrival of the surrender document. Frémont himself arrived at the head of his men during a heavy rainstorm on January 14. This completed the active campaigning in southern California.[17]

The Navy's Pacific Squadron, aided by the California Battalion and two weak companies of dragoons, in slightly more than six months had seized and pacified the whole of California. Commodore Stockton deserves most of the credit for planning and executing the conquest. Whether the campaign was unavoidable is another question, since the October revolt primarily resulted from Stockton's poor judgment and high-handed actions. Despite his good strategy, the Commodore's execution of it was poor. He exercised little control over Frémont or his other detached subordinates and made little effort to coordinate operations with them. Similarly his tactics, notably the crossing of the San Gabriel without artillery support, involved unnecessary risks and seem to have been derived from a disdain of the natives.

During the Los Angeles campaign, a separate and unconnected revolt occurred in the north. It grew out of the harsh and arbitrary treatment of the native Californians near San Francisco by some of the newly arrived American settlers. On December 8 the rebels seized the acting alcalde of Yerba Buena, along with a small party of sailors. The Californians then attempted unsuccessfully to exchange the alcalde for the chief perpetrator of the harassment. Captain Ward Marston, USMC, pursued the Californians with 100 Marines and mounted volunteers. He had a short skirmish with them near Mission Santa Clara on January 2, 1847. After some negotiations the Californians surrendered in return for a promise that the depredations would stop.[18]

After the fall of Los Angeles the long-brewing confrontation between Kearny and Stockton over the political control of California finally developed. Stockton claimed exclusive control of the area because of his prior possession and the existence of a functioning government. Kearny relied upon his orders from Washington. The clash came into the open on January 16 when Stockton issued Frémont a commission as Governor of California. Kearny immediately demanded that Stockton cease the formation of a civil government. The Commodore responded with a caustic letter refusing to recognize the General's authority and his intention to ask for Kearny's recall. On the following day, January 17, Frémont notified Kearny that he would obey only Stockton's orders.[19]

Faced with Stockton's refusal to surrender control of the government and lacking sufficient force to enforce his demands, Kearny had no alternative but to withdraw and bide his time. Nevertheless, he aimed a strong blast at the Commodore: in order to avoid the possibility of a civil war I "remain silent for the present, leaving with you the great responsibility of doing that for which you have no authority & preventing me from complying with the President's orders."[20] Kearny and the dragoons returned to San Diego on the twenty-third. There they were joined by Lieutenant Colonel Philip St. George Cooke and the Mormon Battalion. Although the addition of the Mormons made his position stronger, the army commander still refused to make an issue of the command. As the next few weeks would demonstrate, that reticence would take on the characteristics of statesmanship.[21]

On the day before Kearny reached San Diego, Commodore W. Branford Shubrick arrived at Monterey in the razee *Independence.* As the senior officer on the coast, Shubrick immediately assumed command.[22] Kearny hurried north to meet him, leaving San Diego on the *Cyane*, January 31. The two men quickly arrived at a mutually satisfactory division of authority and settled upon Monterey as the temporary capital of the territory. Kearny continued north to San Francisco, where he met Colonel Richard B. Mason who had just arrived from Washington. Although he brought new orders reiterating the Army's responsibility for the government of California, the chief reason for Mason's dispatch was to ensure that a senior Army officer reach California ahead of Colonel John D. Stevenson and his New Yorkers.[23]

Kearny returned to Monterey in late February. There he and Shubrick issued a series of proclamations dated March 1 but actually issued three days later. The reasons for the delay are unclear but probably involve the March 2 arrival of Commodore Biddle. The first of these pronouncements defined the responsibilities of the two services, placing the Army in control ashore and limiting the naval responsibilities to customs and port regulations. The second announced Kearny's ascension to control of the civil government.[24] Thus the problem of control of the government of California was finally settled.

With the question of control of California settled, Kearny proceeded to carry out that part of his orders which called for regularizing the California Battalion. Shubrick had begun the move earlier when he directed all the naval officers serving with it to return to the squadron. Kearny followed this on March 1 with a series of directives:

1. ordering Cooke to relieve Gillespie as commander of the Southern Military District;

2. ordering Gillespie to return to Washington;

3. directing Frémont to bring the battalion's archives to headquarters;

4. instructing Cooke to have the battalion mustered out and reenlisted according to law.[25]

Ordering Frémont and company to do something was a great deal easier than ensuring that the order would be obeyed. The matter came to a head during mid-March. When Frémont refused to muster the battalion for discharge, Kearny sent Colonel Mason with peremptory orders to inspect the troops and give them any necessary orders. Mason also carried instructions for Frémont to report to Monterey preparatory to returning to Washington. When Mason reached Los Angeles he had such hot words with Frémont that the latter challenged him to a duel. It was never fought, probably because Kearny forbade it. Frémont now had no choice but to comply with the orders, which grudgingly he did. In April the battalion was finally mustered out and offered the opportunity of reenlisting under the volunteer laws. Few men were willing to take the cut in pay which that entailed.[26]

On May 13 Kearny advised the War Department that he was returning overland in company with Frémont and would prefer charges once the party reached St. Louis. Lieutenant Colonel Cooke also returned with the General's party. The travelers left on May 31 when Colonel Mason assumed command of the 10th Military District, the official name for the California command.[27] The other actors in our drama were not much longer on stage. Gillespie left Monterey during the next day, having been delayed for three days by Commodore Biddle in order to answer charges levied by Kearny. He joined Stockton and the two began their return on June 20, reaching St. Louis on November 4.[28]

California would have very little time for rest, however, for on January 24, 1848 James W. Marshall, a former member of the California Battalion and Gillespie's ill-fated Los Angeles command discovered gold in the trace of John Sutter's new mill. It would set in motion an even more significant race for California.

NOTES

For key to abbreviations used in Notes, see page xi.

1. Gillespie to Bancroft, Feb. 16, 1847, Ames, "Gillespie and Conquest of California," 281–84; William D. Lanier, "The Halls of Montezuma," *USNIP*, LXVII (Oct. 1941), 1386; Charles Lee Lewis, *Famous American Marines* (Boston, 1950), 92; Bancroft, *History of California*, V, 306; Smith, *War with Mexico*, I, 338–39. See also "List of names of volunteers . . . Guilty of Insubordination and exciting the troops to Mutiny," Sept. 19, 1846, Gillespie Papers, #78. *Ibid.*, #59, is a Sept. 11 list of eight Mexican officers then at large in the town.

2. The account of the siege of Gillespie's command is based upon: Gillespie to Bancroft, Feb. 16, 1847, *loc. cit.*; Mervine to Stockton, Oct. 25, 1846, *PSL*; S. E. Arguillo to Gillespie, H. D. Fitch to Gillespie [both Sept. 19, 1846], Jhon Broney [*sic*], Receipt for $30.00, Sept. 24, 1846, Articles of Surrender, Sept. 29, 1846, all in Gillespie Papers, #61, 75, 88, 90; Varela, Proclamation [Sept. 24, 1846], *H. Ex. Doc. 1, 30th Cong., 2nd Sess.*, 15–16; José del Carmen Lugo, "Life of a Rancher," *HSSCP*, XXXII (Sept. 1950), 199–200; Bancroft, *History of California*, V, 308–9, 311–13, 315–17, 331; Marti, *Messenger of Destiny*, 77–83; Arthur Woodward, "Juan Flaco's Ride," *HSSCQ*, XIX (Jan. 1937), 23; Margaret Romer "'Lean John' Rides for Help," *Journal of the West*, V (April 1966), 203–6; Guinn, *California and Los Angeles*, I, 127; Dawson, *Battles of U.S.*, II., 456–57.

3. That at Warner's Ranch on the Sonora road surrendered; the Santa Barbara garrison escaped to Monterey; and the San Diego force took refuge on a vessel in the harbor. Bayard, *Sketch of Stockton*, 128; Frémont, *Memoirs*, I, 570, 596–97; Colton, *Three Years in California*, 89–91; Letter of Lt. T. Talbot, Jan. 15, 1847, A Captain of Volunteers, *Alta California* (Philadelphia, 1847), 45–46; Merritt to Pedrorena, Oct. 11, 1846, "Documentos para la Historia de California . . . Thomas Savage," BLUC, 73.

4. Stockton to Gillespie, Oct. 1, 1846, Gillespie Papers, #104; Stockton to Larkin, Oct. 1, 1846, Hammond, *The Larkin Papers*, V, 256; Joseph T. Downey, *The Cruise of the Portsmouth* (New Haven, 1958), 149; Bryant, *What I Saw in California*, 327; Stockton to Bancroft, Nov. 23, 1846, *S. Ex. Doc. 31, 30th Cong., 2nd Sess.*, 10; Stockton to Mervine, Oct. 2, 1846, Oscar Lewis, *California in 1846* (San Francisco, 1934), 54.

5. The account of Mervine's defeat is based upon Mervine's Journal; Mervine to Stockton, Oct. 9, 25, 1846, *PSL*; "Adjutant's Report of Marine and Small arms-men of the U.S. Ship Savannah and Captain Gillespie's Riflemen on shore in California, October 7th and 8th, 1846," *AF*, Box 251; Duvall, "Cruise of the Savannah;" Duvall, "Extracts from the Log," 115–18; Gillespie to Bancroft, Feb. 16, 1846, *loc. cit.*; [Helen Hunt Jackson], "Echoes in the City of the Angels," *The Century Magazine*, XXVII (Dec. 1883), 208; Flores to Varela, Oct. 26, 1846, "Documentos para la Historia de California . . . Augustin Olvera," BLUC; Bancroft, *History of California*, V, 304–5, 318–20; Marti, *Messenger of Destiny*, 87–90; Leo Driver, "Carrillo's Flying Artillery: The Battle of San Pedro," *CHSQ*, XLVIII (Dec. 1969), 335–349. The gun later was used at The Battles of San Gabriel and La Mesa, after which it passed into American hands. It served in the seizure of Mazatlán and the siege of San José del Cabo. It is now in the U.S. Naval Academy Museum.

6. Stockton to Mason, Feb. 18, 1848, *loc. cit.*; to Bancroft, Nov. 23, 1846, *loc. cit.*; to Vincent, Oct. 12, 1846, to Mervine, Nov. 9, 1846, *SLB*, 386, 404; Stockton

to [Montgomery], Oct. 10, 1846, *AF*, Box 251; Stockton, General Order, Oct. 26, 1846, *S. Ex. Doc. 31, 30th Cong., 2nd Sess.*, 16–17; Bryant, *What I Saw in California*, 332–33; Colton, *Three Years in California*, 73–74, 79–83; Bancroft, *History of California*, V, 304–5, 322, 367; Duvall, "Cruise of the Savannah;" Downey, *Cruise of the Portsmouth*, 169. The Baja California expedition returned in mid-December with a few horses, cattle, and sheep. The horses were so poor that the dragoons rejected them. Capt. H. S. Turner to Stockton, Dec. 23, 1846, *S. Ex. Doc. 33, 30th Cong., 1st Sess.*, 190.

7. Revere to Kern, Oct. 17, and Montgomery to Kern, Oct. 15, Nov. 8, 1846, all in Fort Sutter Papers, 42, 70, 74; Nevins, *Fremont*, 295; Colton, *Three Years in California*, 98; Bancroft, *History of California*, V, 358n, 373.

8. Flores to Cota, Nov. 22, 1846, "Documentos . . . Olvera," 63–65; Bancroft, *History of California*, V, 320–21; Guinn, *History of California and Los Angeles*, I, 133; Richmond, *California under Spain and Mexico*, 329; Roa Bárcena *Recuerdos*, I, 231; Smith, *War with Mexico*, I, 340–41. Castro's force captured Consul Larkin near Salinas on Nov. 15 and on the following day inflicted severe losses on some volunteers enroute to join Frémont. Henry L. Ford, "The Battle Salinas," Library of the Society of California Pioneers.

9. Kearny to Stockton, Dec. 2, 1846, Stockton to Kearny, Dec. 3, 1846, *S. Ex. Doc. 31, 30th Cong., 2nd Sess.*, 26–27; Stockton, Testimony, *S. Ex. Doc. 33, 30th Cong., 1st Sess.*, 187; Bayard, *Sketch of Stockton*, 133; Clarke, *Kearny*, 190–92; Arthur Woodward, "Lances at San Pascual," *CHSQ*, XXVI (March 1947), 24; George Walcott Ames, Jr. (ed.), "A Doctor Comes to California," *CHSQ*, XXI (Sept. 1942), 220.

10. The account of the Battle of San Pascual is based upon: Kearny to Jones, Dec. 12, 13, 1846, *S. Ex. Doc. 1, 30th Cong., 1st Sess.*, 513–16; Gillespie to Bancroft, Feb. 16, 1847, *loc. cit.*; Emory, *Notes of Military Reconnaissance*, 105–9; Gillespie to Stockton, Dec. 25, 1846, Gillespie Papers, #140; Marti, *Messenger of Destiny*, 95–100; Clarke, *Kearny*, 195–220; Ames, "A Doctor Comes to California," 333; Kearny's Testimony, *S. Ex. Doc. 33, 30th Cong., 1st Sess.*, 47; Woodward, "Lances at San Pascual," 25–44; Bancroft, *History of California*, V, 343–45; Turner to wife, Dec. 21, 1846, Clarke, *Journal of Turner*, 145–46; Turner to Stockton, Dec. 6, 1846, *S. Ex. Doc. 31, 30th Cong., 2nd Sess.*, 27–28; Bernard DeVoto, *Year of Decision, 1846* (Boston, 1943) 357. Clark, *Kearny*, p. 219, suggests that the eleven men reported killed by Indians at Pauma were actually San Pascual casualties.

11. Stockton to Mason, Feb. 18, 1846, *H. Ex. Doc. 1, 30th Cong., 2nd Sess.*, 1049; Stockton, Testimony, *S. Ex. Doc. 33, 30th Cong., 1st Sess.*, 188–89; Gillespie to Bancroft, Feb. 16, 1847, *loc. cit.*; Kearny to Jones, Dec. 13, 1846, *loc. cit.*; Stockton to Turner, Dec. 7, 1846 (2 letters), Stockton to Gary, Dec. 9, 1846, *SLB*, 446, 448, 451–52; Edwin Legrand Sabin, *Kit Carson Days 1809–1868* (2 vols., New York, 1933), II, 536–38; DeVoto, *Year of Decision*, 358; Stephen Bonsal, *Edward Fitzgerald Beale* (New York, 1912), 14–22; Bayard, *Sketch of Stockton*, 134; Emory, *Notes of a Military Reconnaissance*, 109–12; Downey, *Cruise of the Portsmouth*, 173–75; Kearny, "Kearny and Carson," 7.

12. Kearny to Stockton, Dec. 22, 23, 24, 1846, Stockton to Kearny, Dec. 23, 24, 1846, all in *AGLR'46*, K-209; Stockton to Mason, Feb. 18, 1848, *loc. cit.*, Hensley, Statement, *S. Rpt. 75, 30th Cong., 1st Sess.*, 190; Hensley, "Notes of the cattle & provisions . . . ," Gillespie Papers, #136; Stockton, GO, Dec. 23, 1846, *S. Ex. Doc. 33, 30th Cong., 1st Sess.*, 113; Stockton to Bancroft, Jan. 11, 15, 1847, Flores to Stockton, Jan. 1, 1847, all in *S. Ex. Doc. 31, 30th Cong., 2nd Sess.*, 19–21, 30–36; Stockton, Proclamation, Jan. 5, 1847, "Documentos . . . Olvera"; Emory, *Notes of a Military Reconnoissance*, 115–19; Downey, *Cruise of the Portsmouth*, 181–99; Duvall, "Cruise of the Savannah;" Clarke, *Kearny*, 233–45;

Bayard, *Sketch of Stockton*, 42–44; Bancroft, *History of California*, V, 288, 290, 356, 385–86. The ford was approximately where Whittier Boulevard crosses the Rio Hondo today.

13. Approximately a mile north of the Union Stockyards.

14. The account of the Battle of San Gabriel is based upon: Stockton to Bancroft, Feb. 5, 1847, *S. Ex. Doc. 31, 30th Cong., 2nd Sess.*, 30–36; Emory, *Notes of a Military Reconnaissance*, 119; Bayard, *Sketch of Stockton*, 144–46; Bancroft, *History of California*, V, 391–95; Downey, *Cruise of the Portsmouth*, 202–6; Clarke, *Kearny*, 245–48; Smith, *War with Mexico*, I, 343–44; Asst. Surgeon Charles Eversfield to Surgeon J.S. Griffin, Feb. 10, 1847, Vida Lockwood Warren, (ed.), "Dr. John S. Griffin's Mail, 1846–53," *CHSQ*, XXXIII (June 1954), 105; Griffin to Emory, Jan. 11, 1846, *AGLR'46*, K-209; Marti, *Messenger of Destiny*, 103–6; Bauer, *Surfboats and Horse Marines*, 193–96; John Douglas Tanner, "Campaigns for Los Angeles-December 29, 1846 to January 10, 1847," *CHSQ*, XLVIII (Sept. 1969), 230–32.

15. The account of the Battle of La Mesa and the occupation of Los Angeles are derived from: Stockton to Bancroft, Feb. 5, and Griffin to Emory, Jan. 11, 1847, *loc. cit.*; Kearny to Jones, Jan. 12, 1847, *S. Ex. Doc. 1, 30th Cong., 1st Sess.*, 516–17; Emory, *Notes of a Military Reconnaissance*, 120–21; Downey, *Cruise of the Portsmouth*, 212–13; Joseph Warren Revere, *Keel and Saddle* (Boston, 1871), 146–47; Duvall, "Cruise of the Savannah;" Bancroft, *History of California*, V, 369, 395, 407; Smith, *War with Mexico*, I, 344; Bayard, *Sketch of Stockton*, 147–48; Clarke, *Kearny*, 249–53; Bauer, *Surfboats and Horse Marines*, 196–99; Tanner, "Campaigns," 233.

16. Frémont, *Memoirs*, I, 598–601; Bryant, *What I Saw in California*, 375–91; Enoch G. Parrott Letter, Feb. 11, 1847, E. G. Parrott Papers, YWA; Colton, *Three Years in California*, 125; Frémont to Stockton, Jan. 2, 1847, *AGLR'46*, K-209; Stockton to Frémont, Jan. 3, 1847, Bayard, *Sketch of Stockton*, 143–44; Kearny to Frémont, Jan. 10, Fremont, Proclamation, Jan. 12, 1847, *S. Ex. Doc. 33, 30th Cong., 1st Sess.*, 2173; Flores to Pico, Jan. 11, 1847, "Documentos . . . Olvera;" Articles of Capitulation . . . Corvenga [*sic*], Jan. 13, 1847, *H. Ex. Doc. 1, 30th Cong., 2nd Sess.*, 1067–68; Bancroft, *History of California*, V, 375–404; William H. Ellison, "San Juan to Cahuenga," *PHR*, XXVII (Aug. 1958), 245–61; Rogers, "Bear Flag Lieutenant," 51.

17. Stockton to Bancroft, Jan. 15, 1847, *S. Ex. Doc. 31, 30th Cong., 2nd Sess.*, 20–21; Kearny to Frémont, Jan. 12, 13, to Stockton, Jan. 13, to Jones, Jan. 14, Frémont to Kearny, Jan. 13, 1847, all in *S. Ex. Doc. 33, 30th Cong., 1st Sess.*, 6–7, 73–74, 80, 109.

18. Letter of Forbes, Jan. 15, 1847, Ernest A. Wiltsee, "The British Vice Consul and the Events of 1846," *CHSQ*, X (June 1931), 125–26; Hull to Marston, Dec. 29, 1846, Marston to Mervine, Jan. 7, March 4, Marston to Hull, Jan. 2, 3, Marston to Shubrick, March 4, Mervine to Marston, Jan. 5, 1847, all in *MCL*, Supplement 1838–47, #194; Clyde H. Metcalf, *History of the U.S. Marine Corps* (New York, 1939), 150–51; Aldrich, *History of the U.S. Marine Corps*, 95–96; Fred Blackburn Rogers (ed.), *A Navy Surgeon in California 1846–1847* (San Francisco, 1957), 73–83.

19. Stockton, Frémont's Commission, Jan. 16, 1847, Frémont to Kearny, Jan. 17, 1847, *S. Ex. Doc. 33, 30th Cong., 1st Sess.*, 6, 190; Kearny to Stockton, Dec. 28, 1846, *AGLR'46*, K-209; same to same, Jan. 16, Stockton to Kearny, Jan. 16, 1847, *S. Ex. Doc. 31, 30th Cong., 2nd Sess.*, 28–29. Stockton to Bancroft, Feb. 4, 1847, in *ibid.*, p. 20, did request the General's recall. Gillespie Papers, #208, is an April 1, 1847 letter from Stockton asking the marine to secure statements from "important men" stating that the Californians were heartened by Kearny's "defeat."

20. Kearny to Stockton, Jan. 17, 1847, *KLB*, 90–91.

21. Excellent detailed discussions of the dispute are in Grivas, *Military Governments in California*, 63–78, and Thomas Kearny, "The Mexican War and the Conquest of California," *CHSQ*, VIII (Sept. 1929), 251–61. Both support Kearny's position. See also Clarke, *Kearny*, 256–87, and the comments in Quaife, *Diary of Polk*, III, 10–11. Stevenson's regiment arrived March 6–26 to strengthen further Kearny's position. H. C. Matsell to Stevenson, March 6, 1847, Stevenson to Kearny, March 7, 1847, Stevenson Letter Book, 144, 146; 10th Mil. Dist., Orders #4, March 12, 1847, *AGLR'47*, S-561.

22. At Valparaiso, Chile, Shubrick had met Commodore James Biddle who was also under orders to the California coast. Since his flagship, the ship-of-the-line *Columbus*, had to replenish supplies after her voyage from the Orient, Biddle sent Shubrick northward to exercise temporary command. Shubrick to Bancroft, Dec. 2, 12, 1846, *AF*, Box 251; Susan F. Cooper, "Rear Admiral William Branford Shubrick," *Harpers New Monthly Magazine*, LIII (Aug. 1878), 404.

23. Kearny to Jones, March 15, 1847, *H. Ex. Doc. 17, 31st Cong., 1st Sess.*, 283–84; Bancroft, *History of California*, V, 428–29; Colton, *Three Years in California*, 172–75; Clarke, *Kearny*, 246; Quaife, *Diary of Polk*, II, 215; Turner to wife, Feb. 21, 1846, Clarke, *Journal of Turner*, 153.

24. Shubrick and Kearny, Circular, and Kearny, Proclamation, March 1, 1847, *H. Ex. Doc. 17, 31st Cong., 1st Sess.*, 288–89.

25. Shubrick to Frémont, Feb. 23, 1847, *AGLR'46*, K-209; 10th Mil. Dist., Orders #2, Kearny to Frémont, March 1, 1847, *S. Ex. Doc. 33, 30th Cong., 1st Sess.*, 33; Kearny to Cooke, March 1, 1847, *KLB*, 101–4.

26. Turner to Kearny, March 25, 1847, W. H. Russell to Cooke, March 16, 1847, Kearny to Mason, March 27, 1847, Kearny to Frémont, March 28, 1847, Mason to Turner, April 10, 1847, *AGLR'46*, K-209; Turner to wife, March 16, 31, 1847, Clarke, *Journal of Turner*, 159–62; Grivas, *Military Governments*, 77–78; Clarke, *Kearny*, 309.

27. Kearny to Marcy, May 13, 1847, *AGLR'47*, K-237; Kearny to AG, May 13, 30, 1847, *H. Ex. Doc. 17, 31st Cong., 1st Sess.*, 303–4, 306; 10th Mil. Dist., Order #20, May 31, 1847, 7th NY Order Book, NYHS. For Kearny's activities as governor see Clarke, *Kearny*, 288–326, and Grivas, *Military Governments*, 105–9. Mason's civil activities are covered in Grivas, 109–20.

28. Stockton to Gillespie, March 11, 1847, undated draft narrative, Gillespie Papers, #191, 243; Bayard, *Sketch of Stockton*, 159; Niles, LXXIII (Nov. 13, 1847), 178.

12: The War in the North after Monterrey

❧

A S HAD BEEN PROJECTED in his conversations with Commander Mackenzie, Santa Anna returned to Mexico in mid-August 1846. He quickly abandoned any intention he may have had in seeking a settlement with the United States and within a month assumed command of the Mexican Army. Immediately he began efforts to reinforce General Ampudia's Army of the North. Men and money were too scarce for Santa Anna or any of the reinforcements to leave Mexico City before the fall of Monterrey, and not until October 8 did Santa Anna reach San Luis Potosí with the first troops.[1]

San Luis Potosí, about 300 miles south of Monterrey on the southern edge of the arid highlands which stretched nearly to Saltillo, became the focal point of the efforts to create a new army capable of crushing Taylor's invaders. The town welcomed Santa Anna warmly, but the reality behind the façade was far different. The army had no money and the traditionally anti-Santanista state governments in Durango, Jalisco, and Zacatecas refused assistance.

Yet Santa Anna wrought wonders. He wheedled money from the state and federal governments, forced loans from the church, seized property where necessary, and pledged his personal fortune to support a buildup of the force to 25,000 men. This exposed him to sniping from his political enemies, who claimed that he intended using the army to establish his dictatorship.

On November 2 Major James Graham reached Monterrey with

Secretary Marcy's directive to abrogate the armistice. Taylor informed Santa Anna of the disallowance and set November 13 for the resumption of active operations.[2] The Mexican's response was to rush the completion of the San Luis Potosí defenses and to have the water tanks along the Saltillo road destroyed. He sent two strong cavalry detachments to watch for any approaching Americans.

The precautions were reasonable but unnecessary, since Taylor was "decidedly opposed to carrying the war beyond Saltillo in this direction. . . . If we are (in the language of Mr. Polk and General Scott) under the necessity of 'conquering a peace,'—we must go to Vera Cruz. . . ," he wrote to General Gaines. An advance to San Luis, he argued, would require 10,000 to 15,000 additional men. Equally compelling in Taylor's view was the 300-mile march, nearly half of it through land with little water and no supplies.[3]

Saltillo, on the other hand, was both an obtainable objective and an important one. It covered the southern approaches to Monterrey, commanded the road to the rich farming center of Parras, and was undefended. Despite Major Robert M. McLane's arrival on November 12 with instructions to halt the movement southward, Taylor chose to regard the order as merely advisory and went ahead with his plans to occupy Saltillo.[4]

General Worth with about 1,000 men and a battery of field artillery, accompanied by Taylor, left Walnut Springs on the twelfth, passed through spectacularly beautiful and rugged country; and marched through Rinconada Pass out into the plain beyond. There fields of wheat and oats interspersed with cherry and apple orchards reminded many a homesick soldier of his distance from hearth and loved ones. The Americans entered Saltillo on November 16, ignoring the *pro forma* protest from the newly elected Governor of Coahuila, José María de Aguirre. From the new position, American patrols reconnoitered the roads toward San Luis Potosí and Parras. It was to the latter that Taylor directed General Wool to move his division from Monclova. There the erstwhile Chihuahua force would control a rich agricultural area, protect an alternative route to San Luis, and be in position to move toward Zacatecas or Durango if desired.[5]

Taylor had reached the farthest point to which he wished to advance. His army now settled down into garrison duty which had little appeal for the Americans, particularly the volunteers who had joined to fight not to drill and police camps. There was little recreation available to the troops and the occupation was marked by many

Regular soldiers of the Mexican War. In the foreground are a mounted dragoon and an infantry officer in campaign dress uniforms. Behind them pass a column of infantry also in campaign dress.

President James K. Polk.

Secretary of State
James Buchanan.

John Slidell.

Secretary of War William L. Marcy.

Secretary of the Navy
George Bancroft.

Official U.S. Navy
photograph.

Secretary of the Navy
John Y. Mason.

Painting by Robert Hinckley.
Official U.S. Navy
photograph.

Major General Zachary
Taylor.

Brevet Major General
David E. Twiggs.

Brevet Major General
William J. Worth.

Brevet Major General
John E. Wool.

Photograph by Matthew B.
Brady, courtesy the
National Archives.

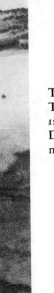

The camp at Corpus Christi looking south.
The tents in the foreground are those of the
1st Brigade; beyond the creek are the 2d
Dragoons; and in the distance the encamp-
ments of the 2d and 3d Brigades.

Battle of Palo Alto, showing Lieutenant William H. Churchill's heavy battery in action. General Taylor, astride "Old Whitey," and some of his staff are just to the right of the road.

Lithograph by F. Swinton, courtesy the
Library of Congress.

The Battle of Buena Vista during the morning of
February 23, 1847. Brevet Major John M. Washington's battery can be seen firing on the right,
while American units rush to confront the Mexican
flanking column.

Lithograph by H. R. Robinson, courtesy the Library of Congress.

Monterrey as viewed from the Obispado. Appearing from behind the hill are the extensive gardens of General Mariano Arista's mansion. The city of Monterrey extends eastward from the gardens toward the towering heights of Sierra Silla (Saddle Mountain).

Brevet Major General Stephen W. Kearney.

Senator Thomas H. Benton.

Commodore Robert F. Stockton.

Lieutenant Colonel John C. Frémont.

The landing at Veracruz.

Commodore David Conner.

Commodore Matthew
C. Perry.

Major General Winfield Scott.

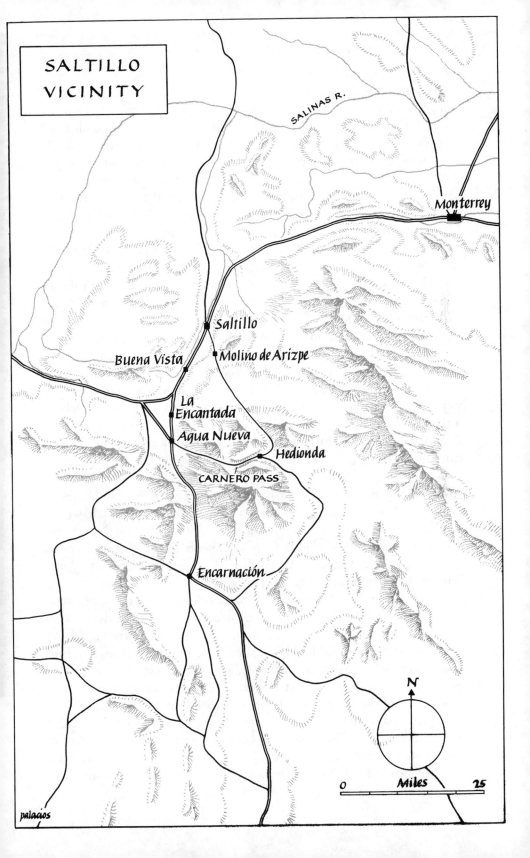

SALTILLO
VICINITY

SALINAS R.

Monterrey

Saltillo

Buena Vista

Molino de Arizpe

La
Encantada

Agua Nueva

Hedionda

CARNERO PASS

Encarnación

N

0   Miles   25

palacios

incidents. In an effort to cut disorder, Taylor directed enlisted men to dispose of their horses, mules, and donkeys. But incidents continued. In late November some men from the Kentucky regiment shot a Mexican boy as he worked in a field. Taylor responded by ordering the regiment to the rear but later canceled the directive when the regiment's officers promised to find the culprits and prevent further outrages. On December 2 Taylor issued a strong reminder of the importance of respecting the rights of the Mexicans. The value of this would become clear in February when General José Urrea's guerrillas infested the Monterrey–Camargo road. The center of their activities were between Marín and Ramos where the depredations by American troops had been extensive. In the somewhat prejudiced view of the professional soldiers, most of the volunteer officers were incompetent. They could not control their men, who did not take care of themselves, consumed twice as many provisions as the regulars, plundered civilians, and killed innocents.[6] Even the volunteers themselves complained. One wrote, "Plundering is getting pretty common and often with bad results, recently an old gray headed sheep herder was shot because he objected to the shooting of his sheep." On January 4, 1847 Wool had his adjutant write Colonel Archibald Yell a strong letter concerning depredations committed by the Arkansas regiment, which was the worst offender among the American units.[7]

While the Army of Occupation struggled with the problems of inactivity, Santa Anna set in motion a new campaign which would give the Americans all the action they could wish. By mid-November Mexican intelligence deduced from comments in the American press that an attack on Veracruz was probable. A month later Santa Anna learned of Taylor's projected thrust 150 miles southeast toward Victoria. Since he expected that Wool's force would move westward against Chihuahua once it reached Parras, the Mexican commander concluded that the propitious moment had arrived for an attack on Worth at Saltillo. He planned to march north from San Luis Potosí just before Christmas with 9,000 of his best infantry, 4,000 cavalry, and twelve guns. At the same time a second cavalry force would harass the Victoria column before rejoining the main force.

Worth heard rumors of the impending attack and on December 16 in near panic called for help, believing that the Mexicans were only two or three days away. Taylor, enroute to Victoria with General David E. Twiggs's division and General John A. Quitman's brigade, received the message on the seventeenth at Montemorales. He ordered Quitman to continue but turned back with Twiggs's regulars. Major General William O. Butler, commanding at Monterrey, hastened a regiment from Camargo and ordered up others from further down stream. He himself hurried to Saltillo with all the troops he could gather, arriving on the nineteenth to take command. Wool received Worth's invitation "to put your troops in rapid motion for this place" at 2:00 P.M. on the seventeenth and had his command on the road by 4:30 P.M. In an amazing forced march of 120 miles it reached Agua Nueva on the twenty-first accompanied by 350 wagons carrying fifty-five days' provisions, 400,000 musket cartridges, and 400 rounds of artillery ammunition. Santa Anna heard of Wool's move about Christmas Eve, concluded that the likelihood of a successful campaign was nil, and canceled the operation. Similarly Taylor, after passing Monterrey, learned that Wool was marching to Worth's assistance, decided that the alarm was false and on the twenty-third began retracing his steps with Twiggs's men.[8]

This was not the end of the alarms, or "stampedes" as some of the volunteers called them. On Christmas Wool heard that the Mexicans were two days away on both the San Luis Potosí and Parras roads. Wool, who as early as December 23 had noted the defensive possibilities of Angostura Pass, wished to make the stand there, but Butler considered it too close to Saltillo and ordered the unhappy regular to move his men from Agua Nueva back to Encantada.[9] Quartermaster General Thomas S. Jesup, undoubtedly suffering frustrations from being restricted to a supporting role, deprecated the alarm. "The panic," he wrote the Secretary, "was produced by a small party that approached Saltillo, perhaps composed of marauders, or more probably of rancheros who had deserted the standard of Santa Anna and were on their return to their homes." Butler did not take such a sanguine view of matters. He strengthened his screen of cavalry patrols early in the new year.[10]

Even if the immediate threat had evaporated by early January, a graver one developed as a result of the difficulties which General Scott faced on the Gulf coast. His expected troops did not appear as rapidly as he believed necessary to permit them to take their initial objectives and move out of the coastal fever belt before the return of yellow fever in March or April. Therefore, he instructed General Butler to add Worth's regulars to the Veracruz force. They left Saltillo on January 9.[11]

A copy of Scott's order to Butler, listing the troops to be withdrawn, fell into Mexican hands when a courier, Lieutenant John A. Richey, was ambushed and killed on January 13. Its information caused Santa Anna to revive his plans to attack Saltillo, for now its defenders were so weakened as to be a safe target for his motley force.[12] Santa Anna's ambitious plan of campaign held promise of great rewards if successful, and the odds against its success were not prohibitive. Any lesser strategy would not have gained sufficient advantage to have been worth the risks involved. The plan called for General Urrea with about 6,700 cavalry and guerrillas to retake Victoria and cut the American communications between Monterrey and Matamoros. Simultaneously, General José Vicente Miñón with another cavalry force would threaten Taylor's army and keep it in place until the main Mexican force arrived. Santa Anna hoped to draw Taylor into battle under conditions in which the Mexican preponderance in numbers would offset the better training of the Americans. Since Urrea would be astride Taylor's route of retreat, this would eliminate the northern American force, drive the Americans back to the Rio Grande, and permit the victorious Mexican troops to turn their attention to Scott's column wherever it chose to attack.[13]

The Mexican vanguard, the sappers and the artillery, departed San Luis Potosí on January 27. The brigades of Generals Francisco Pacheco, José García Conde, and Francisco Pérez followed on January 28–30, while the final two brigades marched on the last day of the month under Major General Luis Guzman. Nearly all were green troops. Santa Anna himself rode out of town in a mule-drawn carriage on February 2 with his personal escort, the crack Regiment of Hussars. All told the army numbered 21,553 men. The twenty-one pieces of artillery were a mixed collection of indifferent quality and less than half as numerous as Mexican practice required. Because of the immense difficulties facing the army during its march across the near desert between San Luis and Saltillo, the Mexican commander took extreme steps to prevent desertions. On one hand, he promised the troops the riches of the American camp, while on the other he threatened to shoot as a deserter any man found more than a half league from camp.[14]

While the Mexican soldiers trudged forward in their exhausting march across arid wastelands, the Americans nervously threw out patrols in unsuccessful attempts to find them. One patrol, a detachment of Texas Rangers, skirmished with some Mexicans at the isolated and fortified hacienda of Encarnación. Wool then sent a second scouting party toward Encarnación, a fifty-man detachment of Arkansans under Major Solon Borland. Prophetically, Wool cautioned: "The Major must be careful not to let the enemy get the advantage of him. . . ." The patrol reached its destination on the nineteenth but found no trace of the Mexicans. Instead of returning to Saltillo as he should have done, Borland remained at Encarnación and called for reinforcements. Butler, wisely as it turned out, refused permission.[15]

Meanwhile, General Butler sent Major John P. Gaines on a similar patrol. Gaines and his escort of Kentucky horsemen under Captain Cassius Marcellus Clay made a circuitous three-day trip east and south of Agua Nueva without finding any signs of the enemy. They then swung west to Encarnación where they unexpectedly discovered Borland. The united forces under Borland tentatively probed southward but concluded the reports of Mexicans were erroneous and returned to Encarnación late on the evening of January 22. Borland threw out no pickets and hence was surprised when the rays of the morning sun disclosed 500 Mexican lancers under Colonel Miguel Andrade from General Miñón's force surrounding the hacienda. The Americans, who numbered only five officers and sixty-six men, had little choice but to surrender.[16]

Upon learning of the capture, Wool ordered an investigation by five companies from Yell's regiment. Yell violated his instructions to exercise caution by riding hell-for-leather all the way to Encarnación. Only warnings that Miñón with 3,000 lancers was nearby caused the Arkansans to beat a hasty retreat to Saltillo rather than riding further south. Another patrol, under Captain William J. Heady of the Kentucky cavalry, was captured on the morning of the twenty-seventh about thirty miles from Encarnación without firing a shot.[17] These clashes proved to Wool that the Mexicans were advancing in strength. But more important, the incidents convinced Taylor that he had to settle the violent dispute raging between his two senior commanders. He did so by assigning Wool command of the forces around Saltillo and giving responsibility for Monterrey and the supply line to Butler.[18]

Responding to Wool's suggestion that his presence at Saltillo was desirable, Taylor rode out of Monterrey on the last day of January at the head of his reserves: a squadron of dragoons, two batteries of artillery, and the Mississippi Rifles. While awaiting his superior, Wool continued active patrolling and collected the 2nd Illinois and the eight artillery pieces of Captain John M. Washington's battery at Saltillo.[19]

Taylor doubted the reports of Santa Anna's advance, since he believed that a large army could not move beyond San Luis Potosí in the wintertime because of the scarcity of water. Nevertheless, as a move to buoy the confidence of his men, Taylor ordered them from Buena Vista[20] to Agua Nueva, about seventeen miles south of Saltillo. By February 14 he had 4,650 men encamped there. The camp was a pleasant one spread out on a wide, well-watered plain surrounded by towering mountains. The engineers soon discovered, however, that roads through the highlands allowed the position to be bypassed on either side.[21]

While the Americans at Agua Nueva awaited the appearance of Santa Anna's army, the Arkansans committed one of the most bloody of the atrocities which plagued Taylor's command. Like so many incidents it grew out of a long history of ill-feeling between the Americans and the local populace. On Christmas some of the volunteers had insulted women at the Rancho Agua Nueva. Apparently in retaliation, one of the best-liked privates in Yell's regiment was brutally murdered outside the camp on February 9. The next day about a hundred men from two Arkansas companies went in search of the culprits. At a settlement called Catana they met some Mexican refugees fleeing the expected battle. Upon finding a carbine sling which they identified as belonging to the dead man, the Arkansans opened fire. The Mexicans fled into a nearby cave where they were besieged by the Americans until other men sent by Wool and drawn by the sound of firing were able to stop the massacre. How many Mexicans were actually killed is uncertain. The investigatory commission reported four men killed, but most of the eyewitness accounts speak of 20 or 30.

When Yell failed to produce the murderers, Wool appointed a military commission under Brigadier General Joseph Lane to investigate. It identified the two companies involved but not the actual individuals. When Yell still could not, or would not, produce those responsible, Taylor ordered the two companies involved, B and G, to the mouth of the Rio Grande as a mark of stigmata. "Such deeds," Taylor reminded his troops, "cast indelible disgrace upon our arms and reputation of our country," but it is doubtful that his words had much effect upon the wild frontier types in Yell's regiment, nor caused them to revise their belief that Mexicans were scarcely human.[22] The best method to prevent both the incidents and their antecedents was to maintain a tight discipline over the troops and to insist on the proper treatment of the local population by the soldiers. Taylor was simply not disciplinarian enough to do that.[23]

During February 16 one of the patrols from Agua Nueva clashed with some Mexican cavalry near Encarnación.[24] Although the Americans did not yet know it, those horsemen were the advance screen of the long-awaited army. The bulk of the Mexican force reached Encarnación during February 18 and 19. Despite the loss of several thousand men during the indescribably wearing and difficult march, the army numbered 15,142 men when Santa Anna reviewed it during the twentieth. He was highly impressed by the self-confidence and enthusiasm of his men. Although he had come this far without detection, the Mexican's luck now deserted him.[25]

Brevet Lieutenant Colonel Charles A. May, with a 400-man cavalry detachment, on February 20 searched the possible bypass route through Rancho Hedionda, about sixteen miles east of Agua Nueva. They sighted Mexican signals and captured a Mexican soldier who confirmed Santa Anna's proximity. At the same time Captain Ben McCulloch and some of his Texas Rangers returned to Encarnación, carefully reconnoitered the Mexican encampment, and accurately estimated its numbers.[26] Upon receiving reports from both scouting parties, Taylor ordered a withdrawal to the Angostura position.[27] He left Colonel Yell's Arkansas horsemen to cover the evacuation of the supplies and screen the withdrawal. About midnight Yell's pickets were driven in, whereupon the Arkansans panicked and burned the remaining stores. Their flight, however, had an unexpected benefit. Santa Anna mistook them for the entire army.

At Angostura, Taylor told Wool: "General, as you have reconnoitered the ground, and I have not, you will select the field of battle and make such dispositions of the troops on the arrival of the enemy as you may deem necessary." He then led Davis's regiment, May's dragoons, and two artillery batteries the additional five miles to Saltillo in order to assist Major William B. Warren's garrison counter any raids by Miñón's cavalry.

The Angostura position, about a mile and a quarter south of Hacienda San Juan de la Buena Vista, had caught Wool's attention as an excellent defensive site as early as December 23. Here the road passed through a narrow valley. In so doing it hugged the steep sides of a two- to three-mile-wide plateau scarred by a series of deep ravines running roughly at right angles to the road. Some of the ravines ran nearly a mile and a half toward the precipitous slopes of the Sierra Madre chain. To the west of the road an impenetrable tangle of arroyos protected the flank of the defenders. Wool stationed five guns from Captain Washington's battery on the road at a point where the gap between the plateau and the arroyos narrowed to forty feet. Two wagons loaded with stones waited to be pushed across the road to block it. Eight companies of the 1st Illinois under Colonel John J. Hardin supported the gunners from breastworks on two nearby heights. The 2d Kentucky (Colonel William R. McKee) held a hill immediately behind the guns. On the Kentuckians' left and about a half mile behind, Wool placed Colonel William H. Bissell's 2d Illinois. General Joseph Lane's Indiana Brigade (2d and 3d Indiana) formed a second line along a ridge immediately to the rear of the first. The Kentucky and Arkansas horsemen took station to the left of the Hoosiers, covering the space between them and the mountains. Wool held two squadrons of regular dragoons and a company of Texans in reserve.

While the Americans moved into position to await him, Santa Anna issued orders for his men to draw three days' food and be ready to march at 11:00 A.M. on the twenty-first. In an effort to surprise the Americans, the Mexican commander pushed his men to the extreme, making a forced march across the dry country between Encarnación and Carnero Pass just below Agua Nueva. There the soldiers spent a cold and sleepless night.

About nine o'clock on the following morning, February 22, the advance screen of Mexican cavalry appeared before Wool's position, which had gone to a state of readiness an hour earlier as regimental bands played "Hail Columbia." It was a beautiful, clear, sunny mountain morning with a soft breeze moving across the field. On the appearance of the horsemen, Wool notified Taylor, who hastened back from Saltillo with his escort. They arrived before the Mexican infantry had moved into position. At about 11:00 A.M. Mexican Surgeon General Pedro Vanderlinden rode forward under a white flag to deliver a surrender demand. Taylor's reply, shorn of its expletives and moderated by Major Bliss, was short and simple: "I beg leave to say that I decline acceding to your request."

While these formalities were being observed and his last units arrived, Santa Anna arranged his forces. Two divisions of infantry under Major Generals Manuel María Lombardini and Francisco Pacheco, supported by fourteen pieces of artillery, formed the Mexican center. On their left, overlooking the road, were the three heavy 16-pounders and Colonel Santiago Blanco's elite Regiment of Engineers. Since Mexican artillery had such limited capability for movement upon the battlefield, the sites for the batteries were very carefully chosen. Santa Anna himself selected the locations for two batteries behind the center of his line; Chief Engineer General Ignacio Mora y Villamil and Chief of Artillery General Antonio Carona, those for the three heavy guns manned by the *Legión de Estrangeros*.[28] The third infantry division, commanded by Major General José María Ortega, formed a reserve behind the other two infantry forces. Major General Pedro de Ampudia's light infantry, Brigadier General Julián Juvera's strong cavalry brigade and two batteries formed the Mexican right. The artillery, placed on high ground, enfiladed much of the American line.

Santa Anna began his attack by having Brigadier General Francisco Mejía's brigade feint a turning movement against the American right beyond the arroyos where Taylor had sent the 2d Kentucky, a section of artillery, and some cavalry. Since the ground before the Mexicans was impassable, the step was unnecessary and demonstrated Taylor's limited acquaintance with the battlefield. It quickly became apparent, however, that the main Mexican thrust would be against the American left. Shortly before 3:00 P.M. Wool ordered Colonel Humphrey Marshall with three companies of Kentucky cavalry, Lieutenant Colonel John S. Roane with four dismounted rifle companies from the Arkansas regiment, and Major Willis A. Gorman with four companies of Hoosiers into the mountainside to prevent any movement there to turn the American left. General Lane with the 2nd Indiana (Colonel William A. Bowles) and a section of guns under Brevet Captain John P. J. O'Brien advanced into the gap between Marshall and the main American position.

At about 3:30 P.M. Marshall's riflemen began skirmishing with General Ampudia's light infantry along the slopes of the mountains. The fighting there continued all afternoon although neither side suffered appreciably. Marshall kept his men in hand and prevented the Mexicans from turning his flank by extending his line uphill as rapidly as Ampudia extended his. Darkness finally brought the race to an end and both forces rested in place.

Taylor continued to worry about the ability of Major Warren's garrison at Saltillo to fend off Miñón. Therefore, after dark he hastened there with Davis's regiment and May's dragoons. Finally convinced that the defenses[29] were adequate to protect his rear, Taylor and his escort turned their faces southward again early on the morning of the twenty-third.

During the night Santa Anna sent reinforcements to Ampudia and had his chief of staff, Brigadier General Manuel Micheltorena, superintend the movement of five 8-pounders to high ground about 800 yards from the American lines on the plateau. The Mexican plan was to mass in overwhelming strength on the right and, under the supporting fire of the newly emplaced battery, sweep the Americans from their positions on the plateau. Santa Anna had his weary men aroused at 2:00 A.M. and marched into position to begin their attack by daylight. Although the American position was too large for the 3,000 men he had available, General Wool had organized his defenses as effectively as possible. He reinforced Marshall's force with two companies of Illini under Major Xerxes F. Trail and a detachment of Texans. The 1st Illinois remained in its original position near the road as the support for Washington's battery. The 2d Illinois, with Captain Thomas W. Sherman's battery, took the post about a mile away at the head of a deep ravine. Slightly to the south and left of the 2d Illinois was Colonel Bowles's 2d Indiana, supported by O'Brien's three guns. Captain Enoch Steen, with two troops of the 1st Dragoons and McCulloch's Texas Rangers, waited somewhat to the rear while covering the gaps between the infantry formations. The 3d Indiana (Colonel James H. Lane) served as reserve.

The initial Mexican assault, by Ampudia's brigade, hit the Americans on the mountainside. Despite stiff resistance the pressure slowly forced them back. On the opposite end of the front, at about eight o'clock, General Mora with the Engineer Regiment and some other units demonstrated against the American right but were greeted by such a concentrated and accurate fire from Washington's battery that they broke. At almost the same time the black-helmeted, blue-coated infantry of Lombardini's division burst out of a broad ravine onto the plain, faced by the left flank, and in a brilliantly executed maneuver formed a column of brigades to start the main assault. Pacheco's division followed and took a similar formation on Lombardini's right. Ortega's division and Juvera's cavalry brigade moved into position to join the attack. The point of contact between this mass of 7,000 Mexicans and the American line was the ground held by the 2d Indiana and O'Brien's three guns. When the Mexican plan became clear, Wool sent Colonel Sylvester Churchill to warn General Lane and order the Hoosiers to hold at all costs. Lane, probably prematurely, responded by ordering O'Brien forward with Bowles's regiment in support. The combined fire of the Hoosiers and O'Brien's guns from the front and that of the 2d Illinois and Sherman's battery

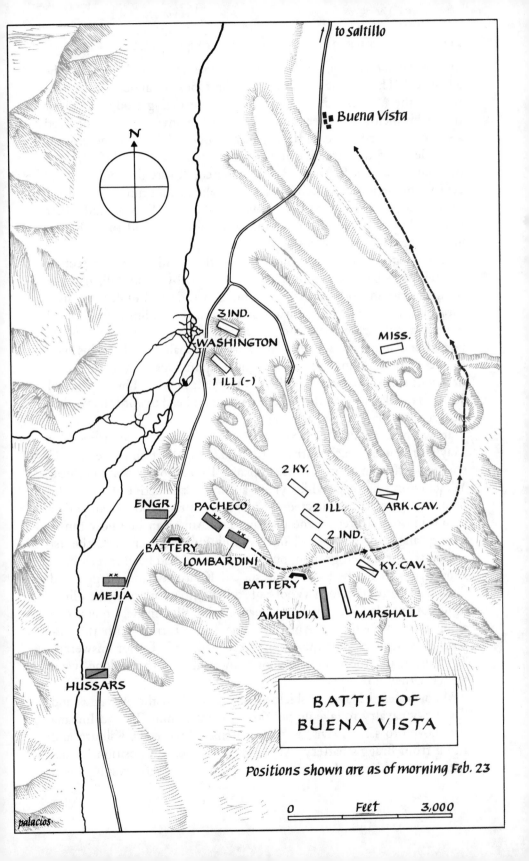

to Saltillo

Buena Vista

N

3 IND.

WASHINGTON

1 ILL (−)

MISS.

2 KY.

ENGR.

PACHECO

2 ILL.

ARK. CAV.

BATTERY

LOMBARDINI

2 IND.

MEJÍA

BATTERY

KY. CAV.

AMPUDIA

MARSHALL

HUSSARS

BATTLE OF
BUENA VISTA

Positions shown are as of morning Feb. 23

0   Feet   3,000

palacios

on the flank tore gaps in the Mexican lines but could not stop the advance.[30] The advance had brought the Hoosiers under the fire not only of the Mexican batteries but of the advancing troops. In order to put his men in a better position to halt the advance, Lane ordered a second forward move. O'Brien gallantly obeyed, but Colonel Bowles misunderstood the directive and misconstrued O'Brien's shift. Instead of sending his men forward, Bowles ordered, "Cease fire and retreat." At this the regiment, which had already taken about ninety casualties, broke and fled. Some 200 men were rallied by Bowles and other officers, but O'Brien was left without support. He had to withdraw also, losing a 4-pounder in the process.

The weight of the attack now fell on the 2d Illinois and a section of Sherman's battery. Colonel Bissell, assisted by Churchill, handled his men magnificently in a slow, fighting withdrawal under the pressure of nearly all of Lombardini's division. The Illini's withdrawal opened a gap which left the Americans on the mountains unsupported and under very strong pressure. Marshall withdrew his men to the plateau. Many of the horsemen upon regaining their steeds fled northward toward the Buena Vista hacienda. This permitted Juvera's cavalry to turn the American left and head toward the weakly held supply point at the hacienda.

It was now about 9:00 A.M. and General Taylor, accompanied by May's dragoons, reached the battlefield.[31] A short distance behind trudged Jefferson Davis's Mississippians. Taylor took his station near Washington's battery, while Wool assumed "the active duty of the field" and personally collected the remnants of the Hoosiers and other troops in order to regain the plateau. The American line now ran at a sharp angle to the original one. Washington's battery and the 1st Illinois still held their ground, but the 2d Illinois had been forced back almost parallel to the road while the 2d Kentucky and Bragg's and Sherman's batteries which Wool had rushed into position on the Illini's right commanded little of the plateau. Major Bliss made a quick trip along the length of the American line and returned with the dispiriting conclusion that the troops were whipped. Taylor answered: "I know it, but the volunteers don't know it. Let them alone, we'll see what they do."

Wool ordered Davis to shield Buena Vista, and the Arkansas and Kentucky cavalry to take up position in front of him. The 3d Indiana also moved to assist Davis, as did Lieutenant Charles L. Kilburn and a gun from Bragg's battery. Although the American position looked critical, it was in reality still a strong one. The left, resting upon

Buena Vista, had been strengthened with fresh troops; the center, although short in numbers, still held some of the high ground; and the right was solidly anchored in the tangled arroyos of the gorge.

When it became clear that the Mexican cavalry had as their target the train camped at Buena Vista, Wool dispatched the dragoons there. Upon arrival they found Yell and Marshall arguing over seniority. Steen ignored the volunteer officers, but his command was thrown into confusion by Marshall's order to fire and Yell's to check fire until the Mexicans had come closer. As Juvera's horsemen rode closer most of the volunteers fled, but a handful, including Yell, held. In the ensuing melée the Arkansan was killed while Steen and the dragoons made a highly effective flank attack which split Juvera's column in two. The advance segment continued past the hacienda into a valley where they came under fire from some of Sherman's guns. The rest, pursued by the dragoons, were forced back upon those following, which threw the Mexicans into confusion. This was compounded by the shelling of the American artillery. Bissell's 2d Illinois, along with portions of Bragg's and Sherman's batteries, tried to cut off retreat while Davis fell upon those near his position. The Mississippians' fire and a charge, in which Davis received a painful wound in his heel, sent some Mexicans fleeing in disorder toward the security of the mountains.

Meanwhile, the survivors of the fight in the mountains, some of the 2d Indiana, and other defenders hastily organized by the redoubtable Major John Munroe made excellent use of the thick walls of the hacienda twice to beat off Juvera's attacks. The horsemen then turned their attention to the Mississippians and the 3d Indiana who had linked up on the plateau to form a large V with the open end facing the Mexicans. The Mexican horsemen rode to within a hundred yards of the American lines before halting. They were well inside the lethal range for the Mississippians' rifles, which opened a withering fire upon the brightly clad horsemen. The survivors retired into a ravine where 2,000 men huddled unable to break out and rejoin the main body. A clever young Mexican, Lieutenant José María Montoya, used a ruse to free them from the trap. With three other officers he galloped to the American lines carrying a white flag. The Americans ceased firing, although they were suspicious, while Montoya was conducted to Taylor. There the Mexican demanded, in Santa Anna's name, to know "what General Taylor wanted." Perplexed, Taylor sent Wool to meet with the Mexican commander, but since the Mexican heavy batteries continued firing the Americans quickly concluded they had been duped. The trapped men, however, used the lull to work their way back to the main body.[32]

Meanwhile, Miñón appeared before Saltillo but wisely refrained from attacking the fortifications. He retired to the southwest, pursued as far as the Molino de Arispa by Captain William H. Shover and a mixed detachment of Illini and artillerymen. They brought the Mexicans under fire for a short time but did not close.[33]

On the main battlefield, Santa Anna moved his artillery forward, brought up his reserves, shifted the Engineer Regiment to his right wing, and combined the remnants of Lombardini's, Pacheco's, Ampudia's, and Ortega's commands under General Francisco Pérez for a new attack. At about five o'clock in the afternoon the head of Pérez's column reached the plateau but was quickly pushed off by the fire of O'Brien's guns and a second section under Lieutenant George H. Thomas. Colonel Hardin, assuming that the Mexicans were in retreat, probably without orders,[34] led a mixed group of men from the two Illinois and the Kentucky regiments in a counterattack. They ran headlong into the main body of Pérez's men as it appeared on the plateau. In hand-to-hand fighting Hardin personally seized the flag of the Hidalgo Battalion before receiving a mortal wound. Lieutenant Colonel Henry Clay, Jr., of the Kentucky regiment, fell nearby along with many other Americans. Although the fire of the American artillery tore horrible gaps in the Mexican line—the engineers, for instance, lost half their men—the attackers kept coming. O'Brien had to abandon two guns when he no longer had cannoneers to work them or horses to pull them.

At this critical moment, Bragg arrived with his battery, having been told by Taylor to "Maintain the position at every hazard." When Bragg asked who would support him, the General responded: "Major Bliss and I will support you," and moved off with the battery. As the Mexicans bore down upon the guns, Taylor had one final discussion with the artilleryman:

"What are you using, Captain, grape or canister?"

"Canister, General."

"Single or double?"

"Single."

"Well, double-shot your guns and give 'em hell, Bragg." Bragg's first salvo staggered the Mexican line, while the second and third drove it back. To all intents and purposes this ended the fighting.

A final Mexican thrust by Brigadier General Anastasio Torrejón's cavalry against the remnants of Hardin's force was shattered by the accurate shooting of Washington's cannoneers. An unseasonable rain squall then swept the field, putting an end to the firing on both sides. When it lifted, the valley was spanned by a rainbow as if in celebration of the American victory. For the men in their wet uniforms, however, that conclusion was not yet so clear. The American infantry had suffered such losses that it scarcely could give the artillerymen the support they needed. Even though the latter had once again won the battle, it is doubtful if Taylor's troops could have held had the Mexicans retained the will to stage another heavy assault. That is precisely what worried the Americans as they spent a second cold, damp night on the battlefield. But Santa Anna's army, although not as badly mauled as the American, had lost its belief in itself. During the night the Mexicans retired to Agua Nueva.

When the rolls were called, Taylor's army reported 272 killed, 387 wounded, and six missing, or about 14 percent of the 4,594 men engaged. Mexican losses were over twice that. Santa Anna reported 591 killed, 1,048 wounded, and 1,894 missing. During the night of February 23-24 all possible wounded men were sent to Saltillo along with many of the Mexican injured who were abandoned on the field by their compatriots. By the same road hastened fresh companies from Saltillo as well as Brigadier General Thomas Marshall with the garrison from Rinconada Pass.

The battle had been a series of small actions, frequently with little relationship to either general's overall plans. While Santa Anna as the assailant had a general plan of action to which he adhered closely, Taylor as the defender did little beyond countering the Mexican initiatives. He did not attempt to organize any counterstroke, being content simply to preserve his own position. Since the American army was composed nearly 90 percent of volunteers, of whom only Davis's regiment had been in battle before, it was a sensible strategy. In the view of many if not all of the regular officers, had the force contained a leavening of regular infantry it would have turned a narrow defensive victory into a brilliant destruction of Santa Anna's force.[35]

During February 25 Santa Anna held a council of war at Agua Nueva which advised retreat. That day Bliss visited the Mexican camp to arrange for an exchange of prisoners and for the care of the wounded. The following day Wool dispatched Captain Albert Pike with a mixed command of dragoons and Arkansas cavalry to scout Agua Nueva. Although Taylor led the army back to the Agua Nueva campsite on the twenty-seventh, he made no serious attempt to catch the retreating Mexicans. Colonel William G. Belknap, with a reconnaissance party, did reach Encarnación on March 1 where he discovered 222 wounded Mexicans crowded into the chapel under atrocious conditions. The air in the chapel, reported one of the Americans, "was so foul and pestiferous that it seemed impossible to breathe it and live." The Americans did what they could for the unfortunates and returned to Agua Nueva. The army did not remain there long, however; the spring winds swirled dust about the camp in such unpleasant quantities that Wool on March 9 sent the men back to Buena Vista.[36]

The Buena Vista campaign represented Santa Anna's sole offensive of the war. It showed a better grasp of the strategic realities and more sophisticated conception than execution. Santa Anna was not a good battlefield general. Neither he nor his troops were capable of responding rapidly to changing tactical situations. Taylor, conversely, was a successful battlefield commander because he seldom intervened to distract his subordinates from the tasks before them and let them design their own responses to battlefield conditions.

As Santa Anna undoubtedly anticipated, the shifting of units before the Battle of Buena Vista weakened the garrisons along the American supply route. About February 22 Urrea, with a detachment of cavalry, reached the Monterrey–Camargo road to unite with the irregulars operating nearby under General Canales. The first train to run the gauntlet contained 110 wagons and 300 pack mules under escort of thirty-four men. On February 22, about five miles from Ramos, Urrea struck. The guards isolated at the head of the column could not protect their charges and the train could neither move forward to safety at Marín nor retreat. After the attackers seized the train and slaughtered forty or fifty of the teamsters, the guards surrendered.[37]

Urrea continued on to Marín. The garrison there, three companies of the 2d Ohio under Lieutenant Colonel William Irvin, held off the attackers until a relief force from Monterrey arrived on the twenty-fifth. Meanwhile, Colonel George W. Morgan collected the remainder of the 2d Ohio at Cerralvo preparatory to moving to Monterrey. The Buckeyes were joined enroute by about twenty-five survivors of the Ramos massacre. They reached Marín late on the afternoon of February 25, shortly after Irvin's garrison had departed. Resuming their march at midnight, Morgan's men soon had the first of a series of small skirmishes with Urrea's gray-clad lancers. Morgan promptly called for reinforcements. In response, Irvin hastened back with about 150 men. Shortly after they joined, the reinforced column had one final skirmish and then proceeded unimpeded. Morgan claimed to have inflicted forty to fifty casualties while losing but five men wounded, one fatally.[38] Urrea's attacks halted passage of any supply trains in either direction although, as Morgan demonstrated, a strong unit could fight its way through.

On March 2 Taylor took the initial steps to reopen his communications with the Rio Grande. He ordered Major Luther Giddings with a mixed command of 260 men, chiefly from the 2d Ohio, and a pair of field pieces to escort 150 wagons to Camargo. Thomas L. Crittenden, a civilian volunteer aide to Taylor, accompanied them as the courier bearing the General's report on Buena Vista. The force left Monterrey on the fifth and all went well until Sunday afternoon, March 7. About a mile outside Cerralvo, the Americans learned of an impending attack. Giddings promptly parked his wagons and got his men into a defensive position. They held off the attackers until dark but lost forty wagons when their unattended teams bolted. Giddings waited at Cerralvo, however, until a relief expedition reached him from Camargo on the twelfth. The action cost the Americans at least two soldiers and fifteen teamsters killed, while they claimed to have inflicted sixty-five casualties on the attackers.[39]

Following up on Giddings's successful march, Taylor ordered Colonel Marshall's Kentucky cavalry to Camargo. No sooner had they left than Taylor learned that Urrea was near Marín. Assembling a mixed force of dragoons, Bragg's battery, and Davis's regiment, Taylor hastened after the Kentuckians. Early in the morning of March 16 the two forces linked up near Marín. The cavalry commander reported that the enemy were nearby waiting for the opportunity to attack a train moving up from Camargo. Taylor rushed reinforcements to the train and set out after the Mexicans but could not catch them. Shortly afterward Urrea retired to Montemorelos and later in the month left the area entirely, since strengthened American train guards made further attacks too dangerous.[40]

On March 2 Colonel Samuel D. Curtis at Camargo became so concerned about the break in communications and the uncertainty over the results of the clash with Santa Anna that he requested Governor J. Pinckney Henderson of Texas call out 2,000 mounted men for four months' service to reopen the road to Monterrey. This coincided with the publication in the March 3 Matamoros *Flag* of a report of Taylor's defeat. The New Orleans papers promptly picked up that report and added another from Galveston that the Americans had lost 2,000 men and six guns and were in danger of being cut off in Monterrey.

The reports reached Washington on March 24. Secretary of War

Marcy, with presidential approval, promptly ordered General George M. Brooke at New Orleans to reopen the communications. One or two thousand new recruits, he was informed, would be rushed to the Rio Grande as quickly as they could be located. Brooke also received authority to call on the Governors of Alabama, Mississippi, and Louisiana for twelve-month volunteers. Marcy sent Brigadier General George Cadwalader to Brazos Santiago to command the relief force and warned Scott that it might be necessary to divert part of the Veracruz force to a new campaign on the Rio Grande.[41] Actually, Taylor was not in danger as long as his army remained on the defensive. He had enough men to protect his supply line and maintain a field force around Saltillo to deal with any Mexicans who might venture north from San Luis Potosí. Adjutant General Roger Jones on March 23 estimated Taylor's force at 9,374 men, of whom 1,150 were regulars.[42]

By late March the scare was over and the trains between Camargo and Monterrey could operate with reduced escorts. One of the reasons for the decrease in incidents was a reshuffling of troops, which increased those garrisoning the route. Among these new troops was a detachment of Texas Rangers who quickly meted out rough justice to those suspected of complicity in attacks. On March 28, for instance, they massacred twenty-four Mexicans at the Rancho Guadalupe near Ramos in retaliation for the February 22 ambush. More politic and certainly more beneficial in the long run was Taylor's proclamation on the last day of March which required indemnification from the governments in the occupied areas for the value of any goods lost in attacks on wagon trains.[43]

Taylor's antiguerrilla campaign continued throughout the spring. In mid-April he personally led a mixed command in an unsuccessful attempt to trap a band operating near Ramos. Later in the month Major Michael H. Chevallie and a detachment of Texas Rangers searched Urrea's old base area around China and Montemoralos but found that most of the regulars had retired to Victoria, although numerous small bands remained in the field.[44]

The guerrilla activities often brought rapid, if unauthorized, retaliation by groups of Americans. When a former member of the 1st Missouri Mounted Riflemen was killed by guerrillas near Camargo, several Mexican suspects were apprehended by the local authorities. They were released when their complicity could not be proven, only to be ambushed on their way home by some Americans who killed four or five. The problems caused by the discharged volunteers were constant, since some went on a veritable frenzy of robberies, murders, and rapes as they returned home. Most of those responsible were men who took their discharge in Mexico in hopes of finding employment there rather than those who marched to the Rio Grande embarkation points in military formations. As had been true earlier, the worst offenders were the Texans. The atrocities on both sides involved Taylor in a flurry of correspondence with General Ignacio Mora y Villamil at San Luis Potosí. When the Mexicans complained of American atrocities, Taylor responded that he did not condone them and then attacked Mexican excesses, particularly the Ramos massacre, as "an atrocious barbarism unprecedented in the existing war." In reporting the exchange, Taylor laid his difficulties almost entirely to the volunteer regiments.[45]

Although General Wool at Buena Vista contended with many of the same problems, he had more success in combating them. One of his methods involved warnings to his troops of the possibility of an imminent forward movement. This came in the face of Taylor's refusal to advance. Despite the obvious benefits to the main column which the distraction of some of the Mexican forces would bring, Taylor adamantly refused to move forward without a nucleus of 2,000 or 3,000 regulars. Had Taylor been willing to gamble on an advance across the miserable region between Saltillo and San Luis Potosí, he would undoubtedly have discovered that the Mexicans lacked the capacity for a serious resistance. Once established in San Luis he would draw from an area well stocked with supplies, and open communications with Tampico. An American Army in San Luis at the same time Scott's men pounded up the National Road toward the Mexican capital would have represented a strategic situation in which Santa Anna could not have planned a successful defense of his capital. Indeed, he might well have been then convinced of the necessity of a capitulation and have had the psychological impetus to carry the politicians with him. On May 6 Marcy agreed to let Taylor decide whether to advance or not, although he clearly indicated the administration's desire for a forward movement. The truth was that Taylor was now so disenchanted with the administration that he lost all interest in the war and would have left the army except for the bad publicity that would cause.[46]

As a result of the inactivity the troops became increasingly restless. In mid-May two lieutenants of the Virginia Regiment lost their lives in a duel.[47] Wool had to resort to a curfew and roadblocks in an effort to keep incidents at Buena Vista to a minimum. When brawls between drunken soldiers and teamsters continued at Saltillo, he ordered the garrison out of the town. The benefit was short lived, however, for Wool complained in August to General Cushing of the tendency of the men to visit Saltillo "after night" and attributed much sickness to "too great an intercourse with Mexican women." Wool also attempted to halt the indiscriminate slaughter of cattle and sheep as well as the theft of fruit, vegetables, and other items at gunpoint. If acts "perfectly disgraceful to the American arms" continued, he threatened, the offending individuals or companies would be discharged.[48]

Wool's efforts to reduce depredations by his soldiers produced only limited results. In late August he complained of individual soldiers visiting ranches, stealing, and "insulting the families and particularly the women." In mid-October he pointed out that troops leaving camp without permission in order to drink and gamble were enticing the Mexicans to murder them. He was so aggravated by the deportment of Major Walter P. Lane's battalion of Texas horsemen that in December he directed that it be stationed only at posts where its behavior could be closely watched.[49]

Another aspect of the problems induced by the inactivity of the volunteers surfaced at Buena Vista in mid-August. Colonel Robert Treat Paine of the North Carolina Regiment was a strict disciplinarian who earned the dislike of many of his men and some of his officers. Several of the enlisted men, egged on by troublemakers from the Virginia and 2d Mississippi Regiments, mutinied during the night of August 15. Paine personally put down the uprising but without support from his officers. In the process he shot two men, killing one. Wool, promptly and summarily, dishonorably discharged Lieutenants Josiah S. Pender and George E. B. Singletary along with two enlisted men who, he believed, were particularly culpable. The two officers appealed their discharges to the President, who ruled that they must be convicted by a court-martial before discharge.[50]

Although some Mexicans welcomed the invaders either because they brought business or because they brought an unfamiliar feeling of security to person and property, others for patriotic and various reasons continued active opposition. One of the latter was Governor Aguirre of Coahuila. In July he attempted to call the state's legislature into session at Monclova. Wool, suspecting that the object was to authorize steps to oppose the invaders, prohibited it and sent a company of dragoons to enforce the edict.[51]

Armed opposition also continued. In late August Colonel John W. Tibbatts with six companies of the 16th Infantry clashed with some guerrillas near Mier. Less than two weeks later, in the early hours of September 8, a band raided Mier itself and seized $25,000 to $30,000 worth of goods belonging to the French consul at Matamoros. A detachment of the 3d Dragoons and some civilians later recovered the merchandise. Although open clashes between American detachments and guerrillas were rare along the Rio Grande front during the fall of 1847, on the morning of November 2 a twenty-five-man patrol under Lieutenant Reuben C. Campbell of the 2d Dragoons was attacked at Agua Fria, near Marín by an estimated 124 men. The Americans cut their way out of the ambush but lost one man killed, nine wounded, and one missing. They killed several guerrillas including their leader, Mucho Martinos. Taylor believed that a firefight near Ramos five days later finally cleared the Camargo–Monterrey road. He may have been correct about that stretch of the road, but on December 2 Lieutenant Colonel Thomas B. Randolph and a small escort were attacked by some thirty-five irregulars between Saltillo and Monterrey.[52]

The fall of 1847 saw the start of a program which finally brought the guerrilla war under control. In late September Taylor granted Wool authority to try by military commission any Mexicans in his area accused of murder or other grave crimes against Americans. Adding to the impact of the occupation were the contributions which Secretary Marcy ordered imposed. Their implementing instructions appeared on December 17. These spelled out the methods for levying contributions and served as a vehicle for Wool to attack local Mexicans who supported guerrilla warfare. He required the local authorities to ferret out offenders in their area and turn them over to the American authorities. If this were not done, the whole of a village would be held responsible for depredations in their area. Persons paying tribute to the guerrillas, he warned, would be treated as such and have their goods confiscated. That he meant to enforce the provisions, as well as earlier ones requiring the formation of local police, Wool brought home with a $500 fine against the alcalde of Salinas when it was shown that he cooperated with the guerrillas. Another town paid $80 to compensate a Mexican who had been robbed nearby.[53]

Wool was convinced that this system worked. By the end of the year he reported that it had cut into guerrilla operations and had shown an $8,000 profit. In part this resulted from his refusal to accept excuses for not fulfilling assessments. As one alcalde learned, his reasons for not providing some requisitioned mules were "frivolous and unsatisfactory and cannot be received." If the mules did not appear without delay, Wool warned, troops would take them without payment and in addition levy a fine on the town. The mules did not appear but the dragoons did. They returned to camp with both the mules and $1,000 in fines.[54]

Despite his insistence that he would remain with the Army of Occupation, Taylor, by the fall of 1847, had decided to return home and await political developments. In late October he called Wool to Monterrey preparatory to transferring command. The two traveled together to Mier. From there Taylor continued on to Matamoros while Wool returned to Walnut Springs. Taylor, whose October 4 request for leave had been approved on November 6, took passage for New Orleans, arriving November 30. After the Crescent City honored him with the hero's welcome which he so richly deserved, he hastened to his plantation outside Baton Rouge.[55]

Wool formally announced his ascension to command on November 25, but it did not bring him the chance for the glory for which he thirsted. As Marcy warned in a private letter, Scott's column had swallowed nearly all the troops which the War Department had raised. Undaunted, Wool called upon his men to prepare for unspecified "coming events."[56]

He proposed a campaign against either San Luis Potosí, Zacatecas, Durango, or Querétaro. Any of those towns he believed he could occupy if 2,000 or 3,000 men were added to his command. Such a move, he argued, would prevent the Mexicans from recruiting a new army in the north and keep the restive American volunteers employed. Marcy directed Wool in mid-January to link up with Scott's projected moves against Zacatecas and San Luis Potosí. He cautioned, however, against expecting additional troops, since "I begin to entertain doubts as to the favorable action of Congress upon the war measures."[57]

Even if the offensive operations stalled, the police operations continued. The North Carolina Regiment caught a pair of robbers in mid-January, and on the nineteenth five other highwaymen were hanged for the murder of three discharged American soldiers. By January 24, however, the roads were free enough to permit the train guards to be reduced further. That success, Wool argued, came as a result of his use of police parties; the holding of local officials personally responsible; and subjecting localities to fines for losses. In a related action he ordered Colonel John F. Hamtramck at Saltillo to send to Monterrey all Americans and other foreigners without "pursuit or occupation or who cannot satisfactorily account for themselves, as well as all gamblers." The value of the move is debatable. It probably served mostly to increase the number of American deserters and discharged soldiers who plundered, murdered, and raped their way from the front to the Rio Grande.[58]

Despite his discipline problems, Wool decided to garrison Victoria and Parras. The reoccupation of the former was in part a response to renewed efforts by General Antonio Canales to establish an independent Tamaulipas. Wool refused to be drawn into Canales's scheme, but promised to protect all who declared their neutrality, although he would continue to collect assessments and conduct antiguerrilla operations. Wool concluded that Canales's moves resulted from the success of the antiguerrilla campaign and that several of the northern Mexican states could be induced into forming a separate nation if the United States would guarantee their independence. As evidence he cited the neutrality of most of the populace of Coahuila, which defeated the efforts of Governor Aguirre to raise guerrillas.[59]

In larger part the dispatch of the garrisons grew out of Wool's January 10 directive for the collection of internal taxes and the transfer to the occupation forces of all revenues beyond local requirements. To offset the bad taste of the forced tax collection, to reduce the power of the guerrillas, and to stabilize the area, Wool in late February granted a general amnesty to former guerrillas.[60] How sagacious that move would have been we do not know, since the fighting stopped shortly after its promulgation.

News of the armistice following the signing of the Treaty of Guadalupe–Hidalgo reached the northern army on March 23. It is perhaps fitting that one of General Wool's first acts after directing the cessation of hostilities was to order Colonel Hamtramck to assist a mother in recovering her daughter who was the mistress of one of the Texans.[61]

In mid-April Wool began preparations to evacuate his force. He directed the Quartermaster to sell all unserviceable goods and began calling in his advanced detachments. He issued his general instructions for the withdrawal on June 12 and reached Matamoros himself on July 2. By July 6 Wool could report that all the volunteers had embarked for New Orleans and that five companies of dragoons, as well as the 10th and 16th Infantry, would follow within two weeks. Two days later he asked for relief from his duties because of sickness and on the twenty-third transferred command of the Army of Occupation to Colonel William Davenport, directing him to withdraw his forces to Fort Brown on the American side of the river.[62]

NOTES

For key to abbreviations used in Notes, see page xi.

1. Santa Anna to Ministro de Guerra y Marina, Sept. 26, 1846, Smith, "Letters of Santa Anna," 366; Callcott, *Santa Anna*, 243; Jones, *Santa Anna*, 109.

2. Taylor to AG, Nov. 3, to Santa Anna, Nov. 5, Santa Anna to Taylor, Nov. 10, 1846, *H. Ex. Doc. 60, 30th Cong., 1st Sess.*, 358-59, 437-38.

3. Taylor to AG, Nov. 9, 1846, *ibid.*, 361; Taylor to Gaines, Nov. 5, 1846, *Niles*, LXXI (Jan. 23, 1847), 342-43; Jenkins, *War Between U.S. and Mexico*, 189-90.

4. Taylor to Wood, Nov. 10, 1846, Samson, *Taylor's Letters*, 67; Taylor to AG, Nov. 12, 1846, *H. Ex. Doc. 60, 30th Cong., 1st Sess.*, 374-76. Marcy attempted to soften the blow in a long soothing letter on November 25 which detailed the reasons for it and the removal of troops from Taylor's command. Marcy to Taylor, Nov. 25, 1846, *ibid.*, 369-71.

5. AO, Orders #139, Nov. 8, Taylor to AG, Nov. 16, 24, Aguirre to Taylor, Nov. [16], 1846, all in *ibid.*, 377-78, 436, 511.

6. AO, Orders #146, 149, Nov. 27, Dec. 2, 1846, *ibid.*, 512-13; Henry, *Campaign Sketches*, 254; Meade, *Life and Letters*, I, 161-62; Dyer, *Taylor*, 211.

7. Englemann to parents, Jan. 2, 1847, Englemann, "Letters," 423-24; McDowell to Yell, Jan. 4, 1846 [*sic*], Archibald Yell, Letter Book, RG-94, N.A.

8. Worth to Bliss, to Wool, to Butler, Dec. 16, 1846, *AOLR*, Box 5; Butler to Bliss, Dec. 16, Lorenzo Thomas to Humphrey Marshall, Dec. 17, 1846, *1 VolDivLB*, 34-35, Wool to Worth, Dec. 21, 1846, *WLB*, XII, loose sheet; AO Orders #160, Taylor to AG, Dec. 22, 1846, *H. Ex. Doc. 60, 30th Cong., 1st Sess.*, 385-86, 515; Baylies, *Campaign in Mexico*, 20-21; Wallace, *Life and Letters*, 29; Smith, *War with Mexico*, I, 275-76, 357-58. Despite his panic, Worth wrote: "The desert in front, without water, absolutely forbids a forward movement until the rainy season, which they say is not till June." Worth to Crittenden, Dec. 28, 1846, Coleman, *Crittenden*, 263-64.

9. Wool to Butler, Dec. 25, 1846, *AOLR*, Box 5; Thomas to Wool, Dec. 28, 1846, *1 VolDivLB*, 43-44; Wool to AG, Jan. 17, 1847, *AGLR'47*, W-116; Baylies, *Campaign in Mexico*, 23-24.

10. Jesup to Marcy, Jan. 2, 1847, *JMLB*, 23; Gaines to Worth, Jan. 3, 1847, in Gaines, "March of the First Regiment of Kentucky Volunteer Cavalry, from Memphis, Tennessee, to Mexico, During the War with Mexico in 1846" (typescript), UTA.

11. Scott to Butler, Jan. 3, Butler, Orders #23, Jan. 8, Worth to Scott, Jan. 9, 1847, *H. Ex. Doc. 60, 30th Cong., 1st Sess.*, 851-53, 859-61. Taylor later charged that the withdrawal was (*a*) an attempt to drive him from his command and (*b*) the result of fear of his presidential ambitions. Taylor to Wood, Feb. 9, 1847, Samson, *Letters of Taylor*, 85-87; to R. F. Allen, Feb. 12, 1847, YWA.

12. Antonio López de Santa Anna, *Guerra . . . con Tejas y los Estados Unidos* (México, 1910), 220; Santa Anna, to Ministro del Guerra y Marina, Oct. 10, 1846, Smith, "Letters of Santa Anna," 369; Callcott, *Santa Anna*, 244-49; Smith, *War with Mexico*, I, 375-79.

13. There is an interesting discussion of this plan in J. P. Taylor to Scott, Feb. 12, 1847, Taylor Papers.

14. Army of the North, General Order, [Jan. 26, 1847], Proclamation, Jan. 28, 1847, *S. Ex. Doc. 1, 30th Cong., 1st Sess.*, 153–56; Santa Anna to Ministro del Guerra y Marina, Feb. 2, 1847, Smith, "Letters of Santa Anna," 411; Alessio Robles, *Coahuila y Texas*, II, 353; Balbontín, *Invasión*, 60–62; Lavender, *Buena Vista*, 164; Ramsey, *Other Side*, 94–96. The march is described in *ibid.*, 115–22.

15. Thomas to H. Marshall, Jan. 14, 1847, *1VolDivLB*, 55; Wool to Yell, Jan. 15, 17, 1847, Yell, Letters Received Book; McDowell to Gaines, to Yell or Officer in Command at Encantada, Jan. 15, Wool to Butler, Jan. 17, 20, 1847, *WLB*, XI, 260–61, 268, 296–97; Wool to Bliss, Jan. 27, 1847, *H. Ex. Doc. 60, 30th Cong., 1st Sess.*, 1106–108; Rose, *McCulloch*, 112–13.

16. Gaines letter Feb. 10, 1847, *Niles*, LXXII (March 27, 1847), 61; Gaines to Scott, May 3, 1847, *AGLR'47*, T-67; John A. Scott, *Encarnacion Prisoners* (Louisville, 1848), 35–36; Chamberlain, *My Confession*, 94–96; Lavender, *Buena Vista*, 155–57; Cassius Marcellus Clay, *The Life of Cassius Marcellus Clay* (New York, 1969), 143–46; David L. Smiley, *Lion of White Hall* (Madison, 1962), 123–24. During the evening of Jan. 21 Daniel D. Henrie, an old Texas scout who feared retribution from the Mexicans, made a break and found his way back to the American lines.

17. McDowell to Yell, Wool to Yell, Jan. 25, 1847, *WLB*, XI, 273, 300; Wool to Bliss, Jan. 27, 1847, *loc. cit.*; Wool to Jones, Sept. 12, Heady to H. Marshall, Aug. 30, 1848, *AGLR'47*, T-67; Chamberlain, *My Confession*, 93. Wool charged the Kentuckians with drunkenness which they stoutly denied.

18. McDowell to Yell, Wool to BGen Joseph Lane, Jan. 26, to Bliss, Jan. 22, to Taylor, Jan. 20, 1847, *WLB*, XI, 277, 302, XII, 287–92, 295–305; AO, Orders #6, Jan. 28, 1847, *AOGO*, III. On Feb. 9 Butler received leave to return home because of the poor healing of the wounds he received at Monterrey. AO, Orders #8, Feb. 9, 1847, *ibid.*

19. Wool to Taylor, Jan. 29, 31, McDowell to Yell, Jan. 29, 1847, *WLB*, XI, 281, 304–7; Wool, SO #220, Jan. 31, 1847, *WOB*, XXXVI, 80; Taylor to AG, Jan. 30, 1847, *H. Ex. Doc. 60, 30th Cong., 1st Sess.*, 1106.

20. Buena Vista was the name of the ranch whose buildings stood about a mile north of the narrowest point of the Pass of Angostura. The battle fought there is known as Buena Vista to Americans and Angostura to Mexicans.

21. Taylor to AG, Feb. 4, 7, 1847, *ibid.*, 1109–11; Wool, Orders #211, 212, 214, 215, SO #237, Feb. 4–9, 1847, *WOB*, XXXIV, 204–6, XXXVIII, 106; Smith, *War with Mexico*, I, 373–74.

22. Taylor to AG, June 4, 1847, with enclosures, *AGLR'47*, T-352; Chamberlain, *My Confession*, 86–88; Englemann, "Letters," 439–40; Buhoup, *Narrative*, 106–8; Neville, Diary; G. N. Allen, *Mexican Treacheries and Cruelties* (Boston, 1847), n.p.; AO, Orders #9, 24, 30, Feb. 11, April 2, 11, 1847, *AOGO*, III. Because of the Arkansas's service in the Battle of Buena Vista the orders to the coast were canceled.

23. Another problem occurred on Feb. 20 when General Lane and Col. J. H. Lane of the 3d Indiana had a fist fight in front of the entire regiment. Although he took no action against the two officers, Taylor kept the 3d Indiana away from Lane's direct command. Lavender, *Buena Vista*, 168–69.

24. Webb, *Texas Rangers*, 112.

25. Ann Fears Crawford (ed.), *The Eagle* (Austin, 1967), 92; Balbontín, *Invasión*, 68; Smith, *War with Mexico*, I, 381.

26. Bliss to May, Feb. 19, 1847, *AOLB'47*, 29–30; Webb, *Texas Rangers*, 112; Rose, *McCulloch*, 113–15; Carleton, *Buena Vista*, 12–19.

27. The account of the Battle of Buena Vista is based upon: AO, Order #15, March 6, 1847, *AOGO*, III; Proceedings of Courts of Inquiry . . . O'Brien, March 4, 1847, . . . Bowles, April 12, 1847, EE-381, FF-123; Joseph Lane to AG, March 24, 1847, *AGLR'47*, T-169; Santa Anna to Ministro de Guerra y Marina, Feb. 23, 27, 1847, *Niles*, LXXII (April 3, 1847), 69, 80, (April 24, 1847), 112-19; Taylor to Marcy, March 3, to AG, Feb. 24, March 8, 1847, with enclosures, *S. Ex. Doc. 1, 30th Cong., 1st Sess.*, 97-98, 132-210; Wool, Orders #279, 281, April 26, 27, 1847, *WOB*, XXXIV, 55-61; to H. B. Dawson, May 18, 21, 24, 1860, John Ellis Wool Papers, CHS; to J. A. Spencer, *et al.*, March 30, 1847, *WLB*, XIV, 16; to Col. J. J. Abert, March 1848, YWA; Lyman Gunnig, "Account of death of Col. John J. Hardin at Battle of Buena Vista, Feb. 23, 1847," Hardin Papers; Neville, *Diary*, 47-54; R. S. Garnett to "L," March 2, 1847, YWA; W. A. H. Wallace to George, March 1, 1847, William H. L. Wallace Collection, CHS; "An Engineer Officer" [Henry W. Benham], *Recollections of Mexico and the Battle of Buena Vista, Feb. 22 and 23, 1847* (Boston, 1871); Buhoup, *Narrative*, 111-27; Carleton, *Buena Vista*, 11-186; Chamberlain, *My Confession*, 111-31; Dawson, *Battles of U.S.*, II, 489-98; Duncan, "Medical History," 98-102; French, *Two Wars*, 77-83; Gregg, *Diary and Letters*, II, 46-54; Henry, *Campaign Sketches*, 307-27; Hobbs, *Wild Life*, 159; *Rough and Ready Annual*, 100-11, 250-58; Santa Anna, *Las Guerras . . . con Tejas y EE.UU.*, 237-50; Isaac Smith, *Reminiscences of a Campaign in Mexico* (Indianapolis, 1848), 37-50; S. Compton Smith, *Chile con Carne* (New York, 1857), 218-54; Lew Wallace, *An Autobiography* (2 vols., New York, 1906), I, 170-75; Alessio Robles, *Coahuila y Texas*, II, 357-70; Balbontín, *Invasión*, 53-101; Baylies, *Campaign in Mexico*, 27-41; Federico Berruto Ramón, *En Defensa de Un Soldado Mexicano* (Saltillo, n.d.), 41-42; Brooks, *Complete History*, 205-23; Brown, "Pike," 309-10; R. C. Buley, "Indiana in the Mexican War," *Indiana Magazine of History*, XV (Dec. 1919), 295-305, XVI (March 1920), 46-68; Frost, *Mexican War and Warriors*, 104-20; Hamilton, *Taylor*, 232-41; Henry, *Mexican War*, 244-54; Howard, *Taylor*, 240-90; Jenkins, *War Between U.S. and Mexico*, 217-39; Kelly, *Lane*, 43-45; Lavender, *Climax at Buena Vista*, 174-212; Oran Perry, *Indiana in the Mexican War* (Indianapolis, 1908), 186-91, 308-11; Ramsey, *Other Side*, 121-28; Rea, *Apuntes Históricos*, 18; Ripley, *War with Mexico*, I, 393-423; Rives, *U.S. and Mexico*, II, 360-61; Roa Bárcena, *Recuerdos*, I, 158-209; Smith, *War with Mexico*, I, 381-400, 555-62; Strode, *Davis*, 179-83; David Urquhart, "Bragg's Advance and Retreat," Robert Underwood Johnson and Clarence Clough Buel (eds.), *Battles and Leaders of the Civil War* (4 vols., New York, 1888), II, 604n-605n; Vigil, *Invasión*, 23; Herman J. Viola, "Zachary Taylor and the Indiana Volunteers," *Southwest Historical Quarterly*, LXXII (Jan. 1969), 335-42; Wilcox, *Mexican War*, 211-41.

28. A group of foreigners who were enlisted or impressed into Mexican service. They included some American deserters and would be reorganized before the fighting around Mexico City as the San Patricio Battalion.

29. Warren garrisoned the town with two companies of the 1st Illinois. A two-gun field work manned by Brevet Major Lucien B. Webster's company of the 1st Artillery commanded the approaches while the American camp outside of the town was held by two companies of Mississippians under Capt. William P. Rogers and a field piece manned by a detachment from the 3d Artillery under Captain William H. Shover.

30. Pacheco's division suffered heavily. The Guanajuato battalions were "dispersed," to use the phrase of one Mexican officer. Indeed, he concluded that a strong American counterattack would have cleared the Mexicans from the field. "Extract from Report of a Mexican Engineer on Santa Anna's Staff," *WLB*, XIV, 84-85.

31. Whether Wool was preparing to retreat and so advised Taylor is a moot question. Apparently he merely advised that preparations be made to do so if it became necessary.

32. Wool to Dawson, May 21, 1860, *loc. cit.*, gives an entirely different version, not elsewhere supported: Taylor ordered the cease-fire while his aide took a surrender demand to the trapped men.

33. Chamberlain, *My Confession*, 132–33, tells the probably apocryphal story of Miñón being delayed at Arispa by a dalliance with Miss Caroline Porter, an American teacher at the mill.

34. Wool to Dawson, May 21, 1860, *loc. cit.*, claims Taylor ordered Hardin to attack the Mexican battery on the plateau. No other account mentions the order.

35. See Taylor to Wool, March 20, 1847, Samson, *Taylor's Letters*, 91; Wool to J. A. Spencer, April 6, 1847, *WLB*, XIV, 19; Bragg to W. T. Sherman, March 1, 1848, McWhinney, *To Mexico with Taylor and Scott*, 95.

36. Santa Anna, *Las Guerras Con . . . Tejas y EE. UU.*, 243–47; Taylor to AG, Feb. 25, March 1, 1847, *locs. cit.*; Wool, Orders #229, Feb. 26, 1847, *WOB*, XXXIV, 217; Taylor to AG, March 14, 1847, *H. Ex. Doc. 60, 30th Cong., 1st Sess.*, 1118–19; Chamberlain, *My Confession*, 126–29, 136; Baylies, *Campaign in Mexico*, 43, 47; Carleton, *Buena Vista*, 146–47; Buley, "Indiana in the Mexican War," 307.

37. AO, Orders #11, Feb. 21, 1847, *AOGO*, III; Carpenter, *Travels and Adventures*, 48–54; Furber, *12 Months Volunteer*, 485–87; Chamberlain, *My Confession*, 175–76; Smith, *Chile Con Carne*, 161–62; Giddings, *Sketches*, 303–5. Among those in the train were a merchant and his daughter, who was returning home after fifteen year's schooling in Ireland. The father was killed but Urrea sent the daughter to Monterrey with a gift of $20 in compensation. Chamberlain's lurid story of her being made to sit naked at Urrea's dinner table is undoubtedly one of the inventions which adds color to his book.

38. Col. S. Ormsby to Taylor, Feb. 26, 1847, *Niles*, LXXII (April 17, 1847), 101; Shepherd to Ormsby, Morgan to Bliss, Feb. 26, 1846, *S. Ex. Doc. 1, 30th Cong., 1st Sess.*, 210–13; Furber, *12 Months Volunteer*, 487–88; George W. Morgan, *Manuscript Left by Major General George W. Morgan*, UTA, 27–28; Giddings, *Sketches*, 293–94; Smith, *Chile Con Carne*, 152–59.

39. Giddings to Mitchell, March 16, 1847, *S. Ex. Doc. 1, 30th Cong., 1st Sess.*, 213–14; Giddings, *Sketch*, 307–20; Smith, *Chile Con Carne*, 256–64.

40. Taylor to AG, March 20, 28, 1847, *H. Ex. Doc. 60, 30th Cong., 1st Sess.*, 1119–20, 1125; AO, Orders #18–19, March 19, 20, SO #19, March 14, 1847, *AOGO*, III; Henry, *Campaign Sketches*, 329.

41. Curtis to Henderson, March 2, 1847, Henderson Family Papers; Ford, "Hays," 53; McMaster, *History of the People of the U.S.*, VII, 460–61; Quaife, *Diary of Polk*, II, 428, 435; Marcy to Brooke, March 22, 23, April 2, to Govs. Johnson, Morton, and Brown, March 23, to Scott, March 22, 1847, all in *SWMA*, XXVII, 214, 240–42, 259; Jones to Cadwalader, March 20, 26, 1847, *AGLS*, XXIII, #396½, 426; Graham A. Barringer (ed.), "The Mexican War Journal of Henry S. Lane," *Indiana Magazine of History*, LIII (Dec. 1957), 418. Instructions to individual units to hasten to their ports of embarkation for Brazos Santiago are in *ibid.*, #375–77, 383–84, 386, 393–95. Polk pointedly did not accede to General Gaines's request for authority to raise a division of volunteers for service under his orders in Mexico. Gaines to Polk, March 25, 1847, Polk Papers.

42. Jones, Memorandum, March 23, 1847, Polk Papers.

43. Giddings, *Sketches*, 325; Smith, *Chile Con Carne*, 294–95; Taylor, Proclamation, March 31, 1847, *Niles*, LXXII (May 8, 1847), 152. The Rancho Guadalupe massacre caused Gen. Canales to order a *levée en masse* and direct that no quarter be given. *Ibid.*, (May 29, 1847), 199.

44. Taylor to AG, April 21, 1847, *Niles*, LXXII (May 29, 1847), 202, *AGLR'47*, T-260; Cushing to Taylor, May 11, 12, 1847, Caleb Cushing Papers, L. C., Box 53.

45. Wislizenus, *Memoir of a Tour*, 80; Taylor to AG, June 16, 1847, *H. Ex. Doc. 60, 30th Cong., 1st Sess.*, 1178; Mora to Taylor, May 10, Taylor to Mora, May 19, to AG, May 23, 1847, *H. Ex. Doc. 56, 30th Cong., 1st Sess.*, 328–31.

46. Taylor to H. L. Scott, April 16, Marcy to Taylor, May 6, 1847, *ibid.*, 360–61, 311–12. Wool believed an advance was possible and put the volunteers through intensive drilling. Wool to Bliss, April 17, 1847, *WLB*, XIV, 41. Taylor even spoke of an offensive before the enlistments of the 12-month regiments expired. Taylor to Wool, April 28, 1847, Taylor Papers. See also Taylor to J. P. Taylor, June 4, 1847, *ibid.*

47. Lee A. Wallace, "First Regiment of Virginia Volunteers," *Virginia Magazine of History and Biography*, LXXVII (Jan. 1969), 52.

48. Buena Vista, Orders #245, 293, 394, 405, March 1, 15, Aug. 10, 16, 1847, *WOB*, XXXIV, 228, 275, Cushing Papers, Box 53; Wool to Cushing, Aug. 6, 1847, *ibid.*

49. Buena Vista, Orders #275, Aug. 23, 1847, 1st Illinois Letter Book, Hardin Papers; Wallace, "First Regiment of Virginia Volunteers," 69; McDowell to Hamtramck, Dec. 10, 1847, *AGLR'47*, W-1037.

50. Paine to wife, Aug. 13, 30, 1847, Smith and Judah, *Chronicles of the Gringos*, 424–26; Buena Vista, Orders #404, Aug. 16, 1847, Cushing Papers, Box 53; Proceedings of Court of Inquiry, Jan. 26–April 12, 1848, *S. Ex. Doc. 62, 30th Cong., 1st Sess.*, Wool to Taylor, Aug. 18, 1847, *WLB* XIV, 203–4; Marcy to Taylor, Oct. 18, 25, 1847, *H. Ex. Doc. 56, 30th Cong., 1st Sess.*, 378, 398–400; Marcy to Wool, Jan. 17, 1848, *SWLG*, 12–16. A good description is in Wallace, "First Regiment of Virginia Volunteers," 65–68.

51. Buena Vista, Orders #394, 405, Aug. 10, 16, 1847, Cushing Papers, Box 53; AO, GO #109, Sept. 29, 1847, *AOGO*, III.

52. Tibbatts to Bliss, Sept. 1, 1847, *AGLR'47*, T-650; John Butler to E. G. W. Butler, Aug. [*sic*.] 9, 1847, *AOLR*, Box 5; Belknap to Bliss, Sept. 9, Campbell to Bliss, Nov. 3, Taylor to AG, Nov. 14, 1847, *H. Ex. Doc. 56, 30th Cong., 1st Sess.*, 488–89, 401–3; *Niles*, LXXIII (Oct. 9, 1847), 88; George Berry to J. A. Hendricks, Nov. 9, 1847, John Abram Hendricks Papers, UTA, Wallace, "First Regiment of Virginia Volunteers," 70.

53. AO, Orders #109, 11 (new series), SO #147, Sept. 29, Dec. 11, 17, 1847, *AOGO*, III; Marcy to Taylor, Oct. 11, 1847, *H. Ex. Doc. 56, 30th Cong., 1st Sess.*, 377–78; Wool to Capt. J. F. Hunter, Dec. 14, 1847, *WLB*, XV, 8–9; Baylies, *Campaign in Mexico*, 54.

54. Wool to Jones, Dec. 26, 1847, to Bragg, Jan. 1, 1848. McDowell to Alcalde of Montemorelos, Dec. 30, 1847, *AGLR'47*, W-1028, '48, W-413; Fulton, *Diary and Letters of Gregg*, II 206.

55. Taylor to AG, Nov. 2, 23, Jones to Taylor, Nov. 6, 1847, *H. Ex. Doc. 56, 30th Cong., 1st Sess.*, 397, 400–1, 403–4; Baylies, *Campaign in Mexico*, 52; Hamilton, *Taylor*, 248–49; *Niles*, LXXIII (Dec. 25, 1847), 257.

56. AO, Orders #132, #1, Nov. 25, Dec. 9, 1847, *AOGO*, III; Marcy to Wool, Nov. 18, 1847, William L. Marcy Letters, YWA, folder 4.

57. Wool to SW, Oct. 11, 1847, Baylies, *Campaign in Mexico*, 51–52; Marcy to Wool, Jan. 17, 1848, *SWLG*, 12–16.

58. Paine to G. A. Porterfield, Jan. 17, Hamtramck to McDowell, Jan. 20, McDowell to H. C. Webb, Jan. 24, to Hamtramck, Feb. 22, 1848, *AGLR'48*, W-99, 413; Wool to Marcy, Feb. 26, 1848, *WLB*, XVI, 30–31.

59. Wool to E. G. W. Butler, Jan. 20, to Jones, Feb. 4, 1848, *WLB*, XIV, 356–57, XVI, 2–3; Wool to Canales, Feb. 3, 1848, Baylies, *Campaign in Mexico*, 55.

60. AO, GO #11, 66, Jan. 10, Feb. 26, 1848, *AGGO*, XLII.

61. McDowell to Davenport, Butler, and Webb, March 24, 1848, *AGLR'48*, W-435; Wool to Hamtramck, March 27, 1848, *WLB*, XVI, 90. A week later he issued a similar one relating to the mistress of one of the Topographical Engineers. *Ibid.*, 99.

62. Wool to D. H. Vinton, April 17, 1848, *WLB*, XVI, 123–25, to Jones, May 9, July 6, to Marcy, July 8, to Davenport, July 23, 1848, *AGLR'48*, W-379, 514, 550, 612; AO, Orders #156, June 12, 1848, *AGGO*, XLI. Wool complained that Col. Hamtramck had abandoned his regiment to hasten to New Orleans. Maj. Jubal Early, the senior remaining officer, attempted to bring charges against his commander for that and other actions. Early to AG, July 4, 1848, *AGLR'48*, W-517.

13: The Veracruz Expedition

I

N LATE AUGUST 1846, while awaiting the reply to their peace feelers, President Polk and his advisers rethought their strategy. If the Mexican response to the peace overtures continued to be negative, new operations would have to be launched to force Mexico to sue for peace. Polk suggested the seizure of Veracruz, Mexico's chief port, and a possible thrust from there to Mexico City. The proposal drew an immediate and favorable response. During the discussions, Secretary of the Navy Bancroft sent for Commodore Conner's reports on the port's defenses. After reviewing those the President asked for additional details about the road from Tampico to San Luis Potosí; the force necessary to take and hold Tampico and the best time for landings there; the force necessary to take and hold Veracruz; possible landing places near the port; the availability of provisions locally; and the condition of the road to Mexico City.[1]

Conner replied in October that there was no Tampico–San Luis Potosí road; Tampico could be taken by naval forces alone; the winter months were the best for campaigning along the coast; there were two good landing places near Veracruz but he refused to estimate the force necessary to take the port; supplies, except for beef, were not available nearby.[2]

The uncertainty over Mexican intentions came to an end on September 19 when Foreign Minister Manuel Crescencio Rejon's August 31 note arrived. Polk brought the cabinet together in an unusual Sunday meeting on the following day to decide on the response to this further rebuff to his peace efforts. By evening, orders directing Conner and General Taylor to seize Tampico were ready. On the twenty-first Polk, because of his growing disenchantment with Taylor, directed Marcy to assign the mission to Major General Robert Patterson.[3]

Since it was not intended to draw the Tampico force from the troops at Monterrey, the problem of providing a regular contingent to stiffen the volunteers taxed the War Department's ingenuity. They came in the form of seven artillery companies stolen from the eastern seacoast fortifications and a newly recruited company of dragoons.[4]

The next and more significant step came at an October 10 cabinet meeting which considered again the possibility of an expedition against Veracruz, since the President had "recently received" information that a landing could be made south of the city, near the island of Sacrificios, which would permit Veracruz to be invested from the rear. Action was delayed, however, until the former consul, Francis M. Dimond, could reach Washington from his home in Rhode Island.[5]

It was into this climate that word of the Monterrey armistice came on October 11. Polk was understandably upset. The Mexicans had rebuffed his peace overtures and the administration had set itself on a course of increased military pressure, with the result that even a temporary suspension of hostilities was most unwelcome. Since Taylor had never been explicitly directed to execute such an armistice, Polk directed its suspension. The President also concluded that the military conditions had not warranted the suspension of hostilities and this further confirmed his belief in Taylor's incompetence. On October 13 one of Marcy's best letters ordered the cancellation of the armistice. The Secretary phrased the instructions softly to avoid an open repudiation and referred to circumstances which to Taylor might have justified the arrangements.[6]

Since Patterson's expedition was controlled by the Monterrey armistice, Marcy apprised him of the termination order and added the hope that Tampico could be occupied before the Mexican Congress met in December. The administration hoped thereby to increase the pressure on the reluctant Mexicans to agree to negotiations. Polk followed this with a confidential message to Patterson which detailed the administrations's strategy.[7]

To assist in the discussions of a Veracruz operation, General Winfield Scott on October 7 presented a masterful planning paper which he called "Vera Cruz and Its Castle." It set forth in clear terms the tactics and resources necessary to seize a foothold at the Mexican port. It argued cogently that a capture of the port without an advance inland would be meaningless and not worth the cost. Scott estimated the forces necessary to accomplish the seizure at 10,000 men, including 2,000 cavalrymen and 600 artillerymen; sufficient landing craft to put ashore 2,500 men and two field batteries at once; and the reinforcement of the naval forces by bomb ketches. Such a force, he calculated, could reach the target area by the start of the new year and therefore have sufficient time to complete the operation before yellow fever arrived. Scott's proposals received backing when Dimond briefed the President, the Secretaries of State, War, and Navy, along with General Nathan Towson and Commodore Lewis Warrington on October 17. Further buttressing reached Washington on November 2 when Conner's already discussed October 7 report arrived.[8]

A week after Conner's extensive report, Taylor responded to Marcy's September 22 query about suggestions for future strategy. The seizure of San Luis Potosí, the most obvious move from Saltillo, would require 20,000 men, half regulars, plus another 5,000 regulars to protect the supply lines. Since he could not undertake the San Luis and Tampico operations simultaneously, "It will be well for the Government to determine whether the war shall be prosecuted by directing an active campaign against San Luis and the capital or whether the country already gained shall be held and a defensive attitude assumed." He favored holding the line of the Sierra Madres because of the difficulties in moving south from Saltillo and the unsettled state of the Mexican government. If the administration decided upon active operations, Taylor recommended an amphibious assault on Veracruz. Such an operation, he estimated, would require 25,000 men, including at least 10,000 regulars. He concluded with the first of what was to become a steady stream of complaints about the Department's directing detachments from his army, i.e., Patterson's force, without consulting him.[9]

Since Santa Anna's declaration in favor of the Constitution of 1824 had eliminated nearly all hope of independence movements in the northern states, the main purposes in Polk's eyes for Taylor's and John E. Wool's expeditions had vanished. Therefore, when the cabinet again reviewed strategy on October 22 he proposed holding Taylor at Monterrey but giving him discretionary authority to call in Wool. The President decided to concentrate on the Veracruz operation while Marcy's prudently written letter informing Taylor

Major General John
A. Quitman.

Brevet Brigadier General Persifor F. Smith.

Major General William O. Butler

Monterey, California, looking south past the customshouse and wharf
where the landing party came ashore on July 7, 1846.

The sloop-of-war *Dale* off San José del Cabo. The *cuartel* which Lieutenant Charles S. Heywood's garrison manned can be seen at the left end of the village.

Commodore W. Branford Shubrick, the most successful naval commander in the Pacific.

The bombardment of Veracruz, showing a
Mexican shell bursting in the naval battery.

Engraving by D. G. Thompson. Official
U.S. Navy photograph.

The Battle of Sacramento, showing the charge of the Mexican lancers. Major Meriwether Lewis Clark's battery can be seen firing in the right foreground.

The Battle of Contreras, depicting the assault on the Mexican camp on the morning of August 20, 1847.

The Battle of Cerro Gordo, showing
the storming of El Telégrafo.

Storming the *tête de pont* at Churubusco.

Washing day in camp, a much more common experience than battle.

General Antonio López de Santa Anna.

View of Chapultepec from the ruins of the Casa de Mata. Part of the Molino del Rey can be seen in the middle ground.

Lithograph by N. Currier, courtesy
The New-York Historical Society,
New York City.

Mexican troops defending the
Garita de Belén.

Major General Winfield Scott's formal entry into Mexico City. The cathedral is in the center of the picture, while the national palace flies the American flag.

Guerrilla attacks on supply trains, in this case consisting of pack mules, were a constant problem to the occupation forces even after the seizure of Mexico City.

of the new strategy was considered paragraph by paragraph at the cabinet meeting. In addition, with a vain hope of softening the blow to Taylor's vanity, Major Robert M. McLane, was carefully briefed on the change in the administration's plans and sent to deliver the letter in person.[10]

The decision for Veracruz had been made but the selection of a commander still remained. It was a ticklish political problem. Since the man named presumably would become a war hero and probably the next president, it behooved Polk to choose a Democrat if possible. The only Democratic major generals were Patterson and Butler, but the former was foreign born and the latter an unknown quantity as an army commander. Taylor, in Polk's view, was both unfit for command and politically unreliable. This left Gaines who was unthinkable and Scott who was an anathema to the President. John Wool, the third-ranking officer in the prewar Army and a Democrat, seems never to have been considered.

On November 10 Senator Thomas Hart Benton, who had earlier supported a Veracruz landing followed by an advance inland, suggested he be given the command with the rank of lieutenant general. While the proposal offered a novel solution, Benton could not be appointed until Congress created the post—and Congress was not in session. As a result the command inched toward the capable hands of Winfield Scott whose impressive staff work during the fall had won over Secretary Marcy.[11]

While these discussions of potential commanders were under way, Scott prepared a second planning paper, "Vera Cruz and Its Castle —New Line of Operations, Thence Upon the Capital." It retained the 10,000-man force and an early January date but proposed drawing 4,000 regulars and 5,000 volunteers from Taylor's force and adding up to 1,200 men from Conner's squadron. This would allow launching the expedition earlier than one composed entirely of newly raised units. Scott followed this on November 16 with a revised estimate of the forces needed: 4,000 regulars, 10,000 volunteers, 1,000 Marines and sailors, fifty 500- to 750-ton transports, and 140 flat boats sufficient to land 5,000 men and eight guns simultaneously.[12] After considering Scott's memoranda and Benton's recommendations, the cabinet gave final approval to the Veracruz assault. Two days later (November 19) Polk, with the approval of the majority of the cabinet, appointed Scott to command the expedition.[13] Winfield Scott was the leading American general of his generation and one of the handful of truly great combat leaders in American history. Yet Polk appointed him with grave misgivings, for he was a Whig and had a volcanic personality which proved particularly abrasive to the dour Tennessean.

Polk discussed the forthcoming expedition with Scott during the morning of November 19. The two men parted cordially after agreeing on the need for mutual confidence. Scott, who was capable of spurts of prodigious activity, outdid himself in the next four days. He drew up and submitted to Marcy a memorandum detailing his requirements for men and supplies, including $30,000 in secret-service funds. He even prepared a cover story to be published in the administration's paper, the Washington *Union*, asserting that he was bound for the war front as an observer, not to relieve Taylor, although he might be sent on an expedition to Tampico. The four days were sufficient for him to outline his requirements but not enough for him to oversee their implementation. Later when he wished to demonstrate the lack of support which he received from the War Department, Scott would complain that he had been allowed only four days "when twenty might have been most advantageously spent in the great bureaux."[14]

The surfboats which Scott requested for his landing were the first specially built American amphibious craft. They were designed by the Navy's Lieutenant George M. Totten and built at Philadelphia for the Army's Quartermaster Department. The contracts for 141 craft negotiated by the Army's agent, Captain Robert F. Loper, stipulated a price of $795 apiece and delivery within one month. They came in three sizes, 35 feet 9 inches to 40 feet in length, to permit nesting for shipment in specially prepared transports. Each carried approximately forty men and was manned by a crew of eight. They were double-ended, broad-beamed, and flat-bottomed, which made them admirably suited for their purpose although the relatively light planking limited their life and use as cargo carriers.[15]

In order to reinforce Conner's squadron for the landings, Secretary of the Navy Mason temporarily diverted the ship-of-the-line *Ohio* (Captain Silas H. Stringham) intended for the Pacific and ordered three additional sloops-of-war to the Gulf. Four coastal brigs or schooners were purchased and outfitted as bomb vessels, mounting a ten-inch columbiad amidships. The latter were intended to cooperate in the bombardment of Veracruz's San Juan de Ulúa fortress. None of the naval reinforcements, however, reached the squadron until after the landings. Those responsible in the Navy Department blamed "the inclemency of the weather and other causes," but bureaucratic inefficiency appears to be the chief reason. President Polk noted a lack of coordination between the services, such as Secretary Mason's ignorance of the date of the projected landings.[16]

Scott left Washington on November 23 for New York where a week later he boarded the steamer *Union* for New Orleans. With him the General carried Secretary Marcy's formal orders:

> The President several days since communicated in person to you his orders to repair to Mexico, to take command of the forces there assembled, and particularly to organize and set on foot an expedition to operate on the gulf coast, if on arriving at the theater of action you shall deem it to be practicable. It is not proposed to control your operations by definite and positive instructions, but you are left to prosecute them as your judgment, under a full view of all the circumstances, shall dictate. The work is before you and the means provided, or to be provided, for accomplishing it, are committed to you, in the full confidence that you will use them to the best advantage.[17]

The instructions were about as broad as any could be and they ensured that if grief came to the expedition the blame would rest on Scott's Whig shoulders.

On November 28 word of the seizure of Tampico reached Washington. In what is one of the earliest, if not the earliest, military use of the new communications medium, Adjutant General Jones attempted to telegraph the information to Scott in New York.[18] More immediately important, Scott sent Dimond to Havana to recruit a pair of agents to operate inside Mexico.[19] Scott also wrote Taylor from New York. In hopes of breaking the unwelcome news without unduly ruffling Taylor's sensitive vanity, Scott warned him that the expedition would probably absorb most of the seasoned troops in the Army of Occupation. Later Scott asked Taylor to meet him at Camargo or somewhere else on the Rio Grande for an exchange of views. He further requested that General Worth, with 4,000 regulars, 500 dragoons, 500 volunteer cavalry, and as many volunteer infantry as could be spared, be sent to the mouth of the Rio Grande by mid-January.[20]

Scott tarried only four days in New Orleans where he designated the Island of Lobos, about sixty-five miles southeast of Tampico, as the rendezvous point for his transports. The anchorage there was commodious and safe; the island large enough for the troops to get some exercise.[21]

From New Orleans, Scott moved to the Rio Grande and his expected meeting with Taylor. The latter never occurred. Taylor had built up a king-sized tantrum over what he considered to be the slights which he had suffered from Washington in the cancellation of the Monterrey armistice and the orders for General Patterson's Tampico force. Taylor delayed the latter's march until late December, and when Patterson's men reached Victoria, the first stage of their march, they were surprised to find it already in the hands of Taylor's troops.[22] After a week's delay Twiggs's and Patterson's divisions continued the march to Tampico, the leading elements arriving on January 23. Taylor returned to Monterrey with an escort of the Mississippi Rifles and two batteries.[23]

Coming as it did at the same moment that Scott was making a special effort to meet with him, Taylor's personal participation in the seizure of Victoria was pure spite. Although he assured Scott that "at all times and places I shall be happy to receive your orders and to hold myself and troops at your disposition," in reality at Victoria Taylor was effectively out of Scott's reach. More indicative of his feelings was his complaint that he had lost the confidence of the administration and felt outraged and mortified at being stripped of most of his regulars and half of his veteran volunteers. He had less than a thousand regulars and "such raw recruits as might be sent" to hold the whole northern front. To his brother he explained that Scott, Marcy, and Worth were conspiring "to break me down" and driving him from his command. Finally on January 27 he wrote an ill-tempered letter to Secretary Marcy complaining that the "President did not . . . relieve me from a position where I can no longer serve the country with that assurance of confidence and support so indispensable to success."[24] The open break so long building had finally happened, but Polk and Marcy were too politically astute to remove the greatest hero of the war thus far. They left him at Monterrey in charge of what was now a secondary theater.

When Taylor failed to appear at Camargo, Scott directed General Butler to order Worth's regulars at Saltillo to the coast. Scott's letter of explanation and a copy of the orders fell into Mexican hands when the courier, Lieutenant John A. Richey, was waylaid and killed.[25]

The movement of the troops to their ports of embarkation proceeded with few hitches. Worth reached the Brazos Santiago on January 18, followed by his men, while Patterson's and Twiggs's divisions reached Tampico a week later. The first of the new volunteer regiments put to sea on the twenty-eighth.[26] Now problems began to develop. The War Department had planned to secure forty-one transports for the expedition, but a series of misunderstandings and other unforeseen developments completely upset the program. Some were canceled by mistake and others delayed because the material which they were to carry was not ready. Most lost nearly a month to a combination of particularly bad weather and scarcity of crews. In the end fifty-three vessels came from Atlantic ports and 163 from Gulf ones.[27]

Scott did not yet know the depth of his logistic difficulties and expected to meet a mid-February target date when he reported to Marcy on January 26 that he expected to start embarking Worth's command in three or four days and anticipated that sufficient ordnance, ammunition, and surfboats to make the landing would reach Lobos by February 10. Now Scott began to feel the pinch of the transport shortage. On February 2 the Quartermaster at Brazos Santiago reported twelve craft due from New Orleans had not arrived. Scott directed him to charter enough vessels at the Brazos to get the troops there afloat by February 10 and those at Tampico by the fifteenth. The problems at New Orleans, Quartermaster General Thomas S. Jesup reported from first-hand observation, were enough to try the patience of mere men. The Quartermaster there had to charter vessels with their incoming cargoes still on board, only to have bad weather slow the unloading.[28]

On February 5 the sloop-of-war *St. Mary's* moved to Lobos to protect and assist the transports gathering there. That necessity occurred on the morning following her arrival when she sailed hastily to aid about 300 Louisiana volunteers under Colonel Lewis G. DeRussey whose transport had gone ashore on February 1 about forty miles south of Tampico. The Americans were closely watched by Brigadier General Martín Perfecto de Cos and 800 men. Before either the *St. Mary's* or the assistance sent from Tampico could reach them, however, DeRussey's men made their escape by the classic ruse of marching off into the night, leaving behind burning campfires.[29]

Few transports had arrived at the Brazos when Scott broke his red-and-blue pennant on the Army steamer *Massachusetts* during the fifteenth and headed south, reaching Tampico three days later. Worth could not complete the embarkation of his division until the twenty-fifth and even then had to leave behind six companies of dragoons. Meanwhile, the regiments of new volunteers collected at

Lobos. Scott joined them on the twenty-first. Behind him at Tampico Patterson's men began embarking when Twiggs's completed out-loading on the twenty-ninth.[30]

When Winfield Scott reached Lobos, he found only three regiments of new volunteers and parts of three other units. Until other troops and more of the vessels carrying his siege train and supplies arrived, he could do little but wait and fret. Fretting was not an occupation congenial to the General in Chief and brought forth another hot letter to abrade his relations with the administration.[31] On the other hand, he used the time to drill his green regiments—except for the smallpox-infected 2d Pennsylvania.[32]

Although Scott sent some supply craft ahead to Antón Lizardo, he grew increasingly impatient over the failure of others to appear and fearful of the approach of the yellow-fever season. Finally, on the last day of February, he concluded: "I cannot wait more than forty-eight hours for anybody, except Brevet Brigadier General Worth, and Duncan's and Taylor's horse artillery companies . . . [although] two thirds of the ordnance and ordnance stores, and half the surfboats, are yet unheard of . . . ."[33]

The missing troops finally appeared during the first two days of March. Shortly after breakfast on the second the *Massachusetts* signaled each transport to send an officer. On boarding the flagship they received sailing orders for Antón Lizardo. During the afternoon the *Massachusetts* tripped her anchors, passed through the assembled transports, and headed south. The troops saluted Scott with cheers, while on board one transport the crew and passengers took up the refrain:

With a stout vessel and a bully crew,
we'll carry the Ship *Statesman* through the storm,
hi oh, hi oh.
We are now bound for the shores of Mexico
and there Uncle Sam's soldiers we will land,
hi oh, hi oh.[34]

The vanguard of the transports reached Antón Lizardo during March 4. Well into the next day the vessels continued to arrive, picked up pilots or directions, and stood in for the anchorage. At times the whole eastern horizon appeared to be a solid wall of white canvas. The *Massachusetts* arrived during the fifth and Scott immediately conferred with Commodore Conner. They decided on an early landing lest a norther hit the mass of shipping in its restricted anchorage.[35]

During the morning of March 6 Conner, Scott, Worth, Twiggs, Patterson, and several members of Scott's staff, including such future military leaders as Captains Robert E. Lee and Joseph E. Johnston, and Lieutenants Pierre G. T. Beauregard, and George G. Meade, boarded the *Petrita*. First they visited Conner's suggestion for a landing site, Collado Beach, about two and a half miles southeast of Veracruz. Lieutenant Samuel Lockwood then turned his steamer northward toward the city on a course normally used without incident. When she was about a mile and a half from Ulúa, one of the big guns boomed. The shell splashed harmlessly beyond the *Petrita* but Lockwood quickly headed his small steamer out of range before a following round found its mark.[36]

Since the reconnaissance showed no defenses at Collado, Scott concurred in Conner's proposal that the landings be made there. While the waters of Collado were well protected by Isla de Sacrificios, about three quarters of a mile offshore, that island's very proximity limited the size of the anchorage. Scott therefore adopted Conner's suggestion that the troops be ferried to the landing area by the larger warships and transport steamers. Since empty transports would surrender their places to supply vessels, the buildup could proceed uninterrupted and the number of vessels in the crowded Sacrificios anchorage be kept within manageable numbers. Because of the need to maintain control within the anchorage, the transports were placed under naval supervision, a radical departure from Scott's initial landing plans.[37]

Scott organized his forces into three divisions, two of regulars under Worth and Twiggs, and the third of volunteers under Patterson.[38] Scott intended to send Worth's division ashore first, followed by the volunteers. Twiggs's regulars would be committed last. During the seventh the troops were apportioned among the assault vessels and the final arrangements completed. The actual ship-to-shore movement was superintended by Captain French Forrest of the frigate *Raritan*. The plan was simple and effective. The Navy's mosquito flotilla of light-draft steamers and gunboats would form a line close to the shore ready to shell any Mexicans who might appear. If needed they could be assisted by the larger vessels although the latter's effectiveness was limited by the crowded anchorage. Once the shelling had cleared the beach, the surfboats carrying the assault troops would form a single line parallel to the beach, sweep in, and deposit their passengers. The assault troops would seize the beach, regroup, and push inland, supported where possible by the guns of the squadron.

Conner set the landing for March 8 but postponed it when a norther threatened. The storm not appearing, he rescheduled the operation for the ninth. He could scarcely have chosen a better day. A brilliant sun sparkled in the cloudless blue sky and illuminated the snowcapped grandeur of distant Mount Orizaba once again looking upon a conqueror landing at Veracruz. A gentle, soothing breeze blew from the southeast, rippling but not breaking the surface of the sea, yet sufficient to permit the beaching craft to retract with ease. To add to the occasion, it was the thirty-third anniversary of Scott's elevation to flag rank.[39]

At daylight the sailors began to prepare the surfboats for service and the soldiers cleaned their arms once more, drew their ammunition and rations, filled their canteens, and formed on deck. Soon they tumbled into the surfboats which ferried them to the vessels that would carry them to the anchorage behind Sacrificios. At 9:45 A.M. the inshore covering force hoisted anchor and stood for the landing area. At eleven o'clock Conner's flagship broke the signal to get under way, and within half an hour the force began issuing in single file through the narrow exit from the anchorage. Scott, clearly visible in his dress uniform on board the *Massachusetts*, drew cheers from the soldiers and sailors.

The force made its leisurely way toward the target. The sailing craft moved quietly under masses of white canvas, the steamers snorted and puffed, and tugged at their tows of surfboats. Every deck was thronged by masses of blue- and gray-clad troops while here and there the brilliant sun flashed off a burnished bayonet or button. Snatches of music could be heard above the hum of conversation, the creak of rigging, and the slap of wave on bow.

At about 12:15 P.M. the inshore covering force hove to off Collado beach. Over the next three hours the larger vessels appeared and took their assigned posts. Once safely anchored the steamers cast loose the surfboats whose oarsmen propelled them to the troopships to embark their passengers. At 3:30 the two steamers and four schooner-gunboats of the inshore force closed to within about ninety yards of shore. At about five o'clock the *Tampico* (Lieutenant William P. Griffin) hurled a 24-pound shell at some cavalry who could be seen in the dunes behind the beach. Since the shot had no visible effect, the anxious American observers concluded that the landing would be opposed.

Although the *Massachusetts* broke the preparatory signal for the landing of Worth's division at 3:30, the strong current swirling

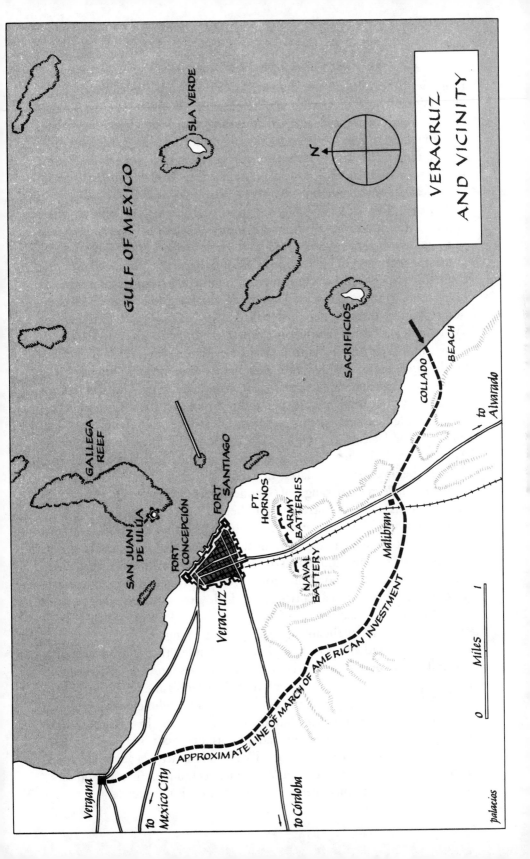

VERACRUZ AND VICINITY

GULF OF MEXICO

ISLA VERDE

N

SACRIFICIOS

GALLEGA REEF

SAN JUAN DE ULÚA

FORT CONCEPCIÓN

FORT SANTIAGO

PT. HORNOS

ARMY BATTERIES

NAVAL BATTERY

Veracruz

Malibran

COLLADO BEACH

to Alvarado

APPROXIMATE LINE OF MARCH OF AMERICAN INVESTMENT

Vergana

to Mexico City

to Córdoba

0   Miles   1

palacios

around Sacrificios threw the surfboats into such a confusion that it took two hours to restore any semblance of order. Finally Forrest and Worth were reduced to arranging the boats with regimental colors along a pair of hawsers thrown out from the *Princeton*. The remaining craft they ordered to shift as necessary once they headed for shore. Finally at 5:30 the *Massachusetts* fired a gun and ran up the signal for the landing.

A deathlike stillness fell over the onlookers as the line of boats closed the 450 yards between them and the beach. The sinking sun etched sand dunes which rose 150 yards behind the beach, picked out the silhouettes of the walls and towers of Veracruz and the warships anchored off Sacrificios. To nearly everyone's surprise, as the small craft swept within range of the beach no pop of musket-fire greeted them. Then just before the landing craft touched the beach, a gig dashed ahead on the left flank, grounded, and General Worth, followed by his staff, leaped ashore.

In a matter of moments the rest of the first wave followed, 2,595 in all, without a single casualty. It was 5:40 when the first troops rushed up the sand hills to plant the American flag. The observers still afloat responded with a shout and a dozen bands struck up "The Star-Spangled Banner." From atop the hills the troops answered the riddle of the lack of opposition. The horsemen seen earlier had fled. Apparently Brigadier General Juan Morales, the Mexican commander, believed that he dared not risk any of his small garrison in an open battle within range of Conner's heavy guns. Undoubtedly he overestimated Scott's strength and believed that the losses he could inflict would not be commensurate with those his forces would suffer. It is difficult to accept that argument, since a small force of lancers bursting out of the sand dunes to ride down the Americans at the critical moment of disorganization as they scrambled ashore could have inflicted heavy casualties with little loss and possibly even turned back the assault.

As each of the surfboats discharged its passengers, it returned to the transports and embarked another load, landed those, and returned for still more. After the initial wave there was no attempt to land the troops in a fixed order except that Patterson's men followed the first wave, and Twiggs's came ashore last. The whole force, something more than 8,600 men, landed by 11:00 P.M. In slightly over four hours Conner's squadron had put ashore Scott's assault force without the loss of a single man. Even today, after a century and a quarter of development of amphibious technique, that would be an impressive accomplishment. In 1847 it was an unprecedented one.

Even though the army was safely ashore, it faced an extremely difficult task in subduing Veracruz and particularly San Juan de Ulúa. Many, if not most, knowledgeable military experts considered the fortifications to be the strongest in North America. Few believed that Ulúa could be taken without a long, costly siege even if the city itself fell. Veracruz contained about 15,000 people crowded into the irregular hexagon slightly over a quarter by a half mile formed by the city walls. At each end stood strong forts, while between were nine smaller posts connected by a musket-proof wall about fifteen feet high. Unfortunately, from Morales point of view, he had but 3,360 men to man the defenses which in several places had badly deteriorated. In addition a considerable number of his artillery pieces were either unserviceable or mounted on inadequate carriages. Indeed, Morales privately considered the city indefensible, particularly when the Mexico City authorities could not answer his calls for assistance.

Veracruz perched on the seaward side of a level sandy plain that stretched inland for as much as two miles before giving way to a series of sand hills. Those rose in height until they reached as much as 300 feet some two or three miles inland. Southeast of the city a complex of ponds and marshes drained into the small stream which served, along with cisterns, as the inhabitants' water supply. To the south of the city the track of a yet locomotiveless railway stretched a tentative tendril toward Orizaba.

The massive works of the Fortress of San Juan de Ulúa about 1,000 yards offshore on the western edge of Gallega Reef dominated the port side of Veracruz. Basically a large bastioned quadrangle covered on the east by a demi-lune, redoubts, and a water battery, it mounted 135 guns, thirty-six of which were modern shell guns, and had a garrison of 1,030 men. Like those on the mainland, its defenders suffered from shortages of powder and provisions.[40]

The first clash was an inconclusive skirmish at about 2:00 A.M. on the tenth and only cost the Americans some sleep.[41] General Morales, holding to his strategy of avoiding a fight in the open, made little effort to resist either the American advance to the sea north of his city or to the establishment of the siege lines. After dawn broke on the tenth Commodore Conner sent the *Spitfire* to attract the Mexicans' attention by bombarding Ulúa. The little steamer ineffectively exchanged fire with the fortress for about twenty minutes before Conner ordered her out of range. Patterson, as planned, used the diversion to start the encirclement. After passing through Worth's division, Patterson sent Brigadier General

Gideon J. Pillow's brigade to clear some Mexican horsemen from the heights around the settlement of Malibran. This cut the Alvarado road and gave the Americans control of the city's water supply.

During the morning Scott and some additional troops landed. This effectively completed the force available to Scott to reduce the Mexican fortress. Only a handful of volunteers and cavalry would join before the city's fall. The landing of supplies, however, went on constantly from four o'clock in the morning to nine or ten at night whenever the sea conditions permitted. Surfboats ferried most of the supplies ashore but horses had to swim to the beach. By modern standards the amount of material landed was small, but one observer reported supplies piled along the beach for a mile. One critical problem was a shortage of wagons and draft animals. As late as March 12 there were only fifteen carts and 100 horses ashore. As a result all goods had to be slowly moved by hand across the rough, sandy, pond-laced ground with its patches of thorny mimosa, prickly pear, and other nearly impenetrable thickets.

Despite the difficulties the investment continued. During the eleventh Quitman's brigade relieved Pillow's and skirmished with some Mexican horsemen searching for soft points in the American lines in order to break through to the besieged city. At about the same time another force from General James Shields's brigade drove back about 1,000 Mexicans under General Morales himself, who had issued from the city on a reconnaissance in force. Once the volunteers consolidated their positions to the southwest of the city, Twiggs's division passed through to form the final links in the fence which confined the Veracruz defenders. A norther which set in during the morning of the twelfth so delayed Twiggs's men that they did not reach the sea near Vergara until about noon on the following day and then only after a short but sharp clash.

While the infantry completed the encirclement, Scott and his "little cabinet" of Colonel Joseph G. Totten, Lieutenant Colonel Ethan Allen Hitchcock, Captain Robert E. Lee, and Captain Henry L. Scott considered how best to take the city and Ulúa. General Scott's position is best told in his own florid Victorian prose:

We, of course, gentlemen, must take the city and castle [Ulúa] before the return of the *vomito*—if not by head-work, the slow, scientific process, by storming—and then escape, by pushing the conquest into the healthy interior. I am strongly inclined to attempt the former unless you can convince me that the other is preferable. . . . I think the suggestion practicable with a very moderate loss on our part. The second method would no doubt be equally successful, but at the cost of an immense slaughter on both sides, including non-combatants . . . because assaults must be made in the dark. . . . Besides these objections, it is necessary to take into account the probable loss of some two thousand, perhaps three thousand of our best men in an assault, and I have received but half the numbers promised me. . . . For these reasons, although I know our countrymen will hardly acknowledge a victory unaccompanied by a long butcher's bill I am strongly inclined—policy concurring with humanity—to "forego their loud applause and aves vehement" and take the city with the least possible loss of life.[42]

His staff concurred and the construction of siege lines was ordered.

The weather finally cleared early on the seventeenth. The surf-boat crews quickly resumed landing supplies, and the troops dug the first segments of the siege lines. During the afternoon the engineers also started laying out the positions for the batteries which would bombard the city's defenses. Ground for their construction was broken during the eighteenth. Although Scott had only a fifth of the siege artillery he had requisitioned, nearly all that had arrived was now ashore. Those guns, he concluded, were sufficient to take the city but not Ulúa.

The batteries stood on sand ridges to the southeast of the city and about a half mile from its walls. The difficulties in moving the heavy guns into place had as much to do with the choice of emplacement as did the terrain. The batteries were built by working parties of 200 or 300 men directed by one or more of the engineer officers. Scott hoped to have them ready to fire by noon on March 21, but that proved impossible. More successful was his arrangement with Commodore Conner for a naval bombardment to coincide with the opening of the land batteries.

Pickets and patrols covering the inland, or back, side of the American lines frequently clashed with groups of poorly coordinated Mexican troops, largely ill-trained or irregular cavalry. The Mexicans were trying to find holes in the American line around Veracruz in order to bring in supplies or reinforcements. Some, like Colonel Juan Aquayo who took advantage of the norther on the twelfth to lead the Alvarado garrison into the city, were successful. More usual, however, was the experience of Colonel Mariano Cenobio, later the chief guerrilla leader in Veracruz state, who lost two men killed, seven wounded, and 157 "dispersed" in an unsuccessful effort on the nineteenth.

The frequent clashes with Mexican horsemen made many of the American sentries overly nervous, as two future Confederate generals discovered. While returning from a scouting foray, Pierre G. T.

Beauregard and Robert E. Lee were shot at by an overanxious sentry. Both escaped injury although the bullet passed between Lee's arm and body, singeing his uniform. Nor were trigger-happy sentinels the only threat which the besiegers faced. More troublesome than even the Mexicans were the sand fleas which seemed to pervade all space. Lee and Gustavus Smith tried greasing themselves with salt pork which, while it may have reduced their attractiveness to humans, had no effect on the fleas. The more common expedient of a canvas sleeping bag with a drawstring around the neck proved no more effective.

Commodore Matthew Calbraith Perry, Conner's second-in-command, had missed the landing because of the imperative need to take the *Mississippi* to Norfolk for repairs. While there he received his long-promised orders to succeed Conner. "The uncertain duration of the war with Mexico," Secretary of the Navy John Y. Mason wrote Conner, "has induced the President to direct me no longer to suspend the rule which limits the terms of command in our squadrons in its application to your command of the Home Squadron."[43] The *Mississippi* carrying Perry and the relief orders reached the Sacrificios anchorage during the twentieth.

Those orders arrived at a very unfortunate time. His relief in the midst of the Veracruz operation has cost Conner much of the recognition that he deserves. He selected the landing site, devised the method of transporting the troops to the debarkation point, and superintended the details of the landing. Like his counterparts a century later, he was responsible for putting the troops ashore. The success of the landing was basically Conner's; that of the campaign, Scott's.

If at times Conner was overly cautious it must be remembered that his operations were conducted with an undersize squadron so critically short of small craft that he could not afford losses. Moreover, he was plagued with ill-luck, particularly in the two Alvarado attacks, which cost him the hero's role and the opportunity to become the Navy's first admiral.

Perry more than any other officer bridged the gap between the generation of naval officers who received their training during the War of 1812 and those who grew to command after it. He had more experience than any other line officer in the service with steam men-of-war yet was an accomplished sailing master.

The new commodore took command during a furious norther on

the morning of March 21. Ambitious and unscrupulous, yet highly regarded by most of his contemporaries, he brought to the squadron the spirit of offensive which it lacked as well as better luck. After taking the *Mississippi* out to Isla Verde to rescue the survivors of two vessels wrecked there, Perry joined Conner in a call on Scott. They discussed the Navy's role in the siege, particularly an earlier offer by Conner to land some of the squadron's heavy guns. Since it was clear that the guns available to the Army were not heavy enough to batter down the Veracruz walls as rapidly as Scott desired, he accepted the proposal. The three agreed that the squadron would provide a battery of six guns and the gun crews. Perry personally took the news to each vessel of the squadron, where it was met by wild cheering by the sailors who looked forward to the novelty of fighting ashore.

Scott issued the formal call for the surrender of Veracruz on March 22 which General Morales rejected. Commodore Perry at the same time halted communication between the town and the neutral men-of-war anchored at Sacrificios and Antón Lizardo. At 4:15 P.M. the seven 10-inch mortars in the three completed batteries opened fire. The first shell exploded in the Plaza de Armas at the center of the city but the chief target was the powder magazine at Fort San Agustín. As soon as the army guns began firing, Perry sent Commander Josiah Tattnall with the Mosquito Flotilla to join in the bombardment. Two steamers and four schooner-gunboats at 5:45 anchored about a mile from the city near Point Hornos and promptly opened fire on the city. Ulúa answered ineffectively, and after about an hour and a half the small craft retired, having exhausted their ammunition. The excursion boosted the morale of both services as well as disclosing some hitherto undiscovered guns on Ulúa.

The flotilla returned to action at daylight the next morning. This time Tattnall led them to within grapeshot range of Fort Santiago before opening fire. The responding Mexican shells churned the water around them into foam. Tattnall either failed to see or ignored Perry's recall signal and remained on station until Captain Isaac Mayo arrived in an open boat with peremptory orders to withdraw. Despite, or perhaps because of, their close proximity to the Mexican batteries Tattnall's vessels suffered only minor damage.

Ashore, the construction of batteries continued. Three additional mortars were in place by noon on the twenty-third but a return of high seas limited the amount of ammunition landed. As a result

American fire slackened during the afternoon. The high winds of the norther wrought havoc along the siege lines, filling trenches and mortar batteries with sand as fast as it could be cleared. Even so, a new battery was completed during the night. When the norther continued into the twenty-fourth, the ammunition supply became so short that the mortars were reduced to firing a shell every five minutes. Luckily, the storm died down during the night and at daylight on March 25 the landing of ammunition was resumed. That moderation allowed the ship-of-the-line *Ohio* to slip into Antón Lizardo. Her eighty guns were a vital addition to the squadron if it became necessary to assail Ulúa.

The six guns for the Navy Battery, three 32-pounders and three 8-inch shell guns, came ashore during the twenty-second. While gangs of soldiers dragged the pieces toward it, the battery was built under the direction of Robert E. Lee upon a sand ridge some 700 yards from Fort Santa Barbara. Despite the storm, the work was completed and the guns emplaced during the night of March 23-24. At ten o'clock the next morning it opened fire. Its effectiveness could be seen almost at once. The heavy cannonballs easily shattered the brittle coral walls, while shell fragments raked casemates and barracks. One lucky shot cut the flagpole at Santa Barbara, a fort manned by Mexican sailors and Marines. When the flag fell Lieutenants Sebastián Holzinger of the Marines and Francisco A. Velez of the National Guard leaped atop the wall, seized the fallen ensign, and nailed it to the stump of the staff. A second cannonball struck nearby and nearly buried them under an avalanche of debris but miraculously they escaped.

The attack took on a more frightening aspect for the Veracruzanos during the twenty-fourth when Lieutenant George H. Talcott's rocketeers loosed forty Cosgreve rockets on the city. They followed this the next day with ten of the more modern Hale design. The bombardment reached its peak on the twenty-fifth, despite some accurate counterbattery fire by the Mexicans. That day a final battery joined in raining devastation upon the city. During the afternoon the fire drove the gunners at Fort Santiago from their posts. They were not alone in losing the will to fight. To others it was clear that the damage and carnage within the city were so great that it would have to surrender to save the noncombatants. Only one bakery remained whole; priests no longer dared leave shelter to visit the injured and dying. In sum, the morale of both inhabitants and defenders was on the verge of shattering.

Nevertheless, the clashes along the inland front of the American lines continued. On the twenty-fourth a patrol from Colonel Persifor F. Smith's brigade encountered strong opposition near Vergana and had to be rescued by a relief force. The following day information from a prisoner that Santa Anna and 6,000 men were moving toward the sea to relieve the siege caused Scott to shuffle his troops. That report drew credibility from the obvious buildup of Mexicans in the American rear. Scott sent Colonel William S. Harney with about 100 dragoons to check on one large group reported near the center of the American line. Harney reported 2,000 men and two guns entrenched at a stone bridge, called for reinforcements, and contrary to his orders prepared to attack. General Patterson hastened to his assistance with a mixed force from the two Tennessee regiments, a pair of field guns, and a handful of freshly disembarked dragoons. The reinforced command had no difficulty in clearing the 140 or 150 Mexicans from their works, and chasing them about six miles to the village of Madellin. The skirmish cost the Americans two killed and nine wounded and the Mexicans an unknown number but certainly not the fifty claimed by Harney. Harney later complained that the importance of the fight was not sufficiently recognized,[44] but in reality it was no more significant than most of the other skirmishes with the Mexicans who hung about outside the American lines.

Scott, naturally, could not guess the state of morale within the city and had to go ahead with his plans for an assault should it become necessary. He projected a three-column assault to which Commodore Perry added a boat expedition against the water battery of Ulúa.

Much of the preparations for the assault had been completed when the firing ceased at 5:00 P.M. on the twenty-fifth while a Mexican officer delivered a proposal from the foreign consuls for the evacuation of women and children which Scott refused. During the night Morales held a council of war which advised surrender. Since Morales could not bring himself to do so, he resigned the command to Brigadier General José Juan Landero. That night was one of horror for the besieged. The wind and rain of a particularly vicious norther[45] lashed the ruins of the city without appreciably diminishing the American bombardment.

The bombardment ceased at 8:00 A.M. on the twenty-sixth when Landero opened negotiations for surrender. He did so by forwarding a renewed request from the consuls for a truce to allow the evacuation of civilians and by naming Colonels José Guiterrez Villa-nueva, Pedro Miguel Herrera, and Manuel Robles to work out the arrangements. Scott again refused to permit evacuation but appointed Generals Worth and Pillow and Colonel Totten to arrange for the city's surrender. The Americans offered to release the officers and irregular troops on parole while sending the men to imprisonment in the United States; demanded the surrender of all materials of war; and the inclusion of Ulúa in the surrender. The Mexicans countered with demands that the garrison be allowed to withdraw to Orizaba or Jalapa; the Mexican flag continue flying until the garrison had marched out of sight; and the Veracruz National Guard be permitted to return home.

Worth, who assumed that the Mexicans were merely temporizing, recommended breaking off the talks and launching the assault. Scott, however, understood that the Mexicans were trying to save face and on the morning of March 27 moderated his demands. He agreed to parole the whole garrison and to allow the civilians freedom of movement. In order to keep Landero from dragging out the talks further, he demanded an answer by nine o'clock that evening. Scott's assessment was correct. Landero accepted the modified terms which were signed later in the day at Point Hornos. They provided that the garrisons of both the city and Ulúa would march out with full honors of war and be placed on parole. Mexican officers were permitted to keep their arms and personal property, including horses and their trappings.[46] The inclusion of Ulúa was especially welcome as it eliminated a potentially long, difficult, and bloody siege.

During the four days of bombardment the American artillery fired 6,700 shot and shell, weighing about 463,000 pounds, into the city. Nearly a third of the number, and half the weight, were shells from the massive ten-inch mortars, while another 1,800 rounds were fired by the heavy guns of the Navy Battery. We do not know how many casualties, military or civilian, the city suffered. Mexican estimates run as high as 400 or 500 civilians and 600 soldiers killed but the number was probably closer to British Captain Henry J. Matson's 100 civilians and eighty soldiers killed. The Americans, on the other hand, lost but thirteen killed and fifty-five wounded despite the often heavy and accurate Mexican counterbattery fire.

The formal surrender occurred on Monday, March 29. It was another brilliant, cloudless day with a gentle southeast breeze. At 8:00 A.M. Ulúa fired a 21-gun salute as the Mexican colors dropped. As the reverberations ceased, the Mosquito Flotilla sailed into the harbor and anchored behind Point Hornos to await the conclusion of the ceremonies. At 9:30 the guns in the Veracruz forts fired a 21-gun salute as the city's flag came down. A half hour later combined garrisons marched out through the south gate to the railroad yard where they stacked arms, colors, musical instruments, and similar property. The admiring Americans, however, made no effort to interfere when one Mexican soldier stripped his nations's colors from their staff and hid them in his clothes before surrendering the naked staff. The victors then marched into the city to be reviewed by Scott from a balcony facing the plaza. At 11:10 the American flag rose over the fortifications to a 29-gun salute by both the Army and the Navy. Fifty minutes later the process was repeated as the Stars and Stripes ascended the flagpole at San Juan de Ulúa.[47]

Immediately after the surrender ceremony, the *Princeton* put to sea. She carried Commodore Conner and Colonel Totten. The latter had in his baggage Scott's official announcement of the seizure of the port. The steamer touched at Pensacola on April 3 from whence an express rider carried the news of the victory to Charleston, South Carolina, and from there a steamer took it to Baltimore. There it rode the telegraph wires to Washington, arriving on the tenth, two days before Totten.[48]

Worth assumed charge of Veracruz as military governor. His rule seems to have been even handed and well received. He closed the liquor stores until they could be licensed, while in order to prevent hoarding and profiteering he established price ceilings on bread, meat, and milk. Before leaving Tampico, Scott had issued a stringent code of conduct to his troops, General Order 20. It pointed out that there were crimes not covered by the Articles of War when the troops were outside the United States, such as assassination, murder, malicious robbery, assault and battery, rape, robbery, theft, desecration of churches and private property. Yet were they committed within the United States the crimes would be severely punished. Therefore, Scott declared the unwritten code of "Military Law" in effect and directed that transgressors be tried before military commissions. Scott reiterated the rules on April 1 along with a call on "all who honor their country or respect themselves" to assist in maintaining law and order. The hanging of a camp follower on April 10 for the rape and robbery of a Mexican woman had a salutary effect on those in the army who might have been tempted to follow suit.[49]

NOTES

For key to abbreviations used in Notes, see page xi.

1. Quaife, *Diary of Polk*, II, 104–5; Bancroft to Conner, Aug. 29, 1846, *Conner (NY)*.
2. Conner to Bancroft, Oct. 7, 1846, HSL.
3. Quaife, *Diary of Polk*, II, 147–49, 156–58; Marcy to Taylor, to Patterson, Sept. 22, 1846, *H. Ex. Doc. 60, 30th Cong., 1st Sess.*, 341–43, 373; Mason to Conner, Sept. 22, 1846, RCL. Buchanan's original draft of the reply to the Mexicans included an explicit statement that the United States expected indemnity for additional war costs, but Polk deleted it, although the final letter clearly implied so. Buchanan to Minister of Foreign Relations, Sept. 26, 1846, Moore, *Works of Buchanan*, VII, 127.
4. Jones to Patterson, Sept. 28, 1846, *H. Ex. Doc. 60, 30th Cong., 1st Sess.*, 472–73.
5. Quaife, *Diary of Polk*, II, 179–80, 195–97; Marcy to Dimond, Oct. 27, 1846, *SWMA*, XXVII, 20. Polk's source of the "recently received" information is unknown.
6. Quaife, *Diary of Polk*, II, 181; Marcy to Taylor, Oct. 13, 1846, *H. Ex. Doc. 60, 30th Cong., 1st Sess.*, 355–57.
7. Marcy to Patterson, Oct. 13, 1846, *ibid.*, 358; Polk to Patterson, Oct. 22, 1846, *PLPB*, II, 14–15.
8. Scott, "Vera Cruz and Its Castle," Oct. 27 [*sic*], 1846, *H. Ex. Doc. 60, 30th Cong., 1st Sess.*, 1268–69; Quaife, *Diary of Polk*, II, 195–96.
9. Taylor to AG, Oct. 15, 1846, *H. Ex. Doc. 60, 30th Cong., 1st Sess.*, 351–54. For an even more violent complaint about the detachment of the Tampico force see same to same, Dec. 14, 1846, *ibid.*, 381–82.
10. Quaife, *Diary of Polk*, II, 198–200, 204; Marcy to Taylor, Oct. 22, 1846 (2 letters), *H. Ex. Doc. 60, 30th Cong., 1st Sess.*, 362–67; McCormac, *Polk*, 451–52.
11. Quaife, *Diary of Polk*, II, 204, 221–23, 227–28, 236–37; Marcy to Patterson, Oct. 28, 1846, *H. Ex. Doc. 60, 30th Cong., 1st Sess.*, 367–69; Ivor Debenham Spencer, *The Victor and the Spoils* (Providence, 1959), 160–61; Chambers, *Old Bullion Benton*, 308–9; William M. Meigs, *The Life of Thomas Hart Benton* (Philadelphia, 1904), 363–65; Joseph M. Rogers, *Thomas Hart Benton* (Philadelphia, 1905), 238–40. John D. MacPherson, a War Department clerk, claimed in "A Controversy of the Mexican War," *The Century Magazine*, LVI (July 1898), 477, that Taylor could have had the command if he wished, but this is not elsewhere supported.
12. Scott, Vera Cruz and Its Castle . . . , Nov. 12, Memorandum, Nov. 16, 1846, *H. Ex. Doc. 60, 30th Cong., 1st Sess.*, 1271–74; Quaife, *Diary of Polk*, II, 232.
13. Quaife, *Diary of Polk*, II, 239–45. Because of Scott's rank Polk, for a while, considered sending the Navy's senior officer, Commodore Charles Stewart, to assume temporary command of the naval forces for the landing. Mason to Conner, Nov. 29, 1846, *Conner (FDR)*.
14. Quaife, *Diary of Polk*, II, 243–46; Scott, *Memoirs*, 399; Wright, *Scott*, 159; Scott to Marcy, Nov. [19], 1846, *H. Ex. Doc. 60, 30th Cong., 1st Sess.*, 836; Scott, draft of story for the *Union*, Nov. 1846, Marcy Papers, XII; Scott to SW, Feb. 24, 1848, *H. Ex. Doc. 59, 30th Cong., 1st Sess.*, 3.
15. Marcy to Mason, Dec. 12, 1846, *SWMA*, XXVII, 97; Risch, *Quartermaster Support*, 287–88; William Granville Temple, "Memoir of the Landing of the United States Troops at Vera Cruz in 1847," in Conner, *Home Squadron*, 60–62.

16. Extensive correspondence concerning the acquisition and outfitting of the bomb brigs exists in *RCL*, *ELB*, *NAL*, *LB*, and *LNA*. The quotation is from Morris to Conner, March 4, 1847, *Conner (NY)*. See also Quaife, *Diary of Polk*, II, 146–47, 388; Alfred Hoyt Bill, *Rehearsal for Conflict* (New York, 1947), 186.

17. Marcy to Scott, Nov. 23, 1846, *H. Ex. Doc. 60, 30th Cong., 1st Sess.*, 372; Charles Wilson Elliott, *Winfield Scott* (New York, 1937), 445.

18. Quaife, *Diary of Polk*, II, 257; Jones to Scott (telegram), Nov. 28, 1846, *AGLS*, XXIII, 1734½. It is an interesting commentary on the reliability of the new medium that the line was out of order and Jones could not send the message until the morning of the thirtieth.

19. Scott to R. B. Campbell, Nov. 28, 1846, Marcy Papers, XII.

20. Scott to Taylor, Nov. 25, Dec. 20, 1846, *H. Ex. Doc. 60, 30th Cong., 1st Sess.*, 373–74, 839–40.

21. Scott to Brooke, to Marcy, to Conner, all Dec. 23, 1846, *H. Ex. Doc. 60, 30th Cong., 1st Sess.*, 840–43. Although neither Scott nor any of his staff were responsible for the leak, one of the New Orleans newspapers published the plan of the campaign during his stay. This destroyed a cover story which Scott floated that his objective was San Luis Potosí. Scott to Conner, Dec. 26, 1846, *ibid.*, 846–47; Elliott, *Scott*, 445.

22. Bliss to Patterson, Nov. 28, 1846, *H. Ex. Doc. 60, 30th Cong., 1st Sess.*, 383–84; George C. Furber, *The Twelve Months Volunteer* (Cincinnati, 1857), 275–318; Gustavus W. Smith, "Company A Engineers in Mexico, 1846–1847" *The Military Engineer*, LVI (Sept.–Oct. 1964), 337; D. E. Livingston-Little (ed.), *The Mexican War Diary of Thomas D. Tennery* (Norman, 1970), 46–53. Taylor's troops were there as a result of his deciding to establish a chain of posts from Tampico to Parras. Taylor, with General John A. Quitman's brigade of volunteers and General David E. Twiggs's division of regulars, departed Monterrey on December 13 but Taylor and the regulars turned back on learning of a rumored advance by Santa Anna's San Luis Potosí force. Quitman occupied Victoria on Dec. 29 where Taylor, Twiggs, and Patterson all arrived on Jan. 4, 1847. Taylor to AG, Dec. 8, 1846, *H. Ex. Doc. 60, 30th Cong., 1st Sess.*, 1379–81; Quitman to Bliss, Dec. 30, 1846, *AOLR*, Box 5; Henry, *Campaign Sketches*, 262; Claiborne, *Quitman*, I, 276; Smith, *War with Mexico*, I, 357. For Lt. Col. May's ambush, Dec. 29, while on a scouting expedition to Labradores, see May to Bliss, Jan. 2, 1847, *H. Ex. Doc. 60, 30th Cong., 1st Sess.*, 1095–97, and Dabney Herndon Maury, *Recollections of a Virginian in the Mexican, Indian, and Civil Wars* (New York, 1894), 31.

23. AO, Orders #3, 5, Jan. 13, 14, 1847, *AOGO*, III; 1st Brig., 2d Div., Order #63, Jan. 14, 1847, *POB*; Patterson to H. L. Scott, Jan. 24, 1847, *H. Ex. Doc. 60, 30th Cong., 1st Sess.*, 879–80; Furber, *12 Months Volunteer*, 383; Livingston-Little, *Diary of Tennery*, 54–60; Hamilton, *Taylor*, 229.

24. Taylor to Winfield Scott, Dec. 26, 1846, Jan. 15, 1847, to H. L. Scott, Jan. 15, to AG, Jan. 26, 1847, *H. Ex. Doc. 60, 30th Cong., 1st Sess.*, 848, 861–63, 1100–2; Taylor to J. P. Taylor, Jan. 14, 1847, McWhinney, *To Mexico with Taylor and Scott*, 77; Scott to Conner, Dec. 26, 1846, *Conner (NY)*; Smith, *War with Mexico*, I, 362. See also Hamilton, *Taylor*, 228.

25. Scott to Taylor, to Butler, Jan. 3, 1847, Butler, GO, #23, Jan. 8, 1847, Taylor to AG, Jan. 26, 1847, all in *H. Ex. Doc. 60, 30th Cong., 1st Sess.*, 851–60, 1097–98; Thomas Kearny, *General Philip Kearny* (New York, 1937), 77. Scott later in the month again explained the necessity for the summary removal of Worth's troops and ordered Taylor to fall back on Monterrey but Taylor ignored the directive. Scott to Taylor, Jan. 26, 1847. *H. Ex. Doc. 60, 30th Cong., 1st Sess.*, 864–65.

26. Scott to Marcy, Jan. 26, 1847, *ibid.*, 865–66; George W. Hartman, *A Private's*

Own Journal (Greencastle, 1849), 6; H. Judge Moore, *Scott's Campaign in Mexico* (Charleston, 1849), 1.

27. Scott to SW, Feb. 24, 1848, Jesup to Marcy, April 17, 1848, *H. Ex. Doc. 59, 30th Cong., 1st Sess.*, 3, 38–39; Marcy, Memo for Quartermaster General, Dec. 15, 1846, *SWMA*, XXVII, 117–18; Marcy to Scott, Dec. 22, 1846, *Marcy Letters*, folder 7; Jones to Scott, Jan. 23, 1847, *AGLS*, XXIII, 97; Risch, *Quartermaster Support*, 287–90. Scott to Marcy, Jan. 26, 1847, *H. Ex. Doc. 60, 30th Cong., 1st Sess.*, 845–46.

28. Scott to Marcy, Jan. 26, to Hetzel, or Senior Officer . . . Brazos, Feb. 2, Hetzel, Memorandum for Scott, Feb. 9, 1847, *H. Ex. Doc. 60, 30th Cong., 1st Sess.*, 882–86, 894–96; Jesup to Scott, Feb. 25, 1847, *JMLB'46–7*, 196–97. Jesup had been at New Orleans since November supervising the shipment of troops from there and from Mobile. He accompanied Scott to Veracruz. Risch, *Quartermaster Support*, 284–85, 287. Another problem holding up the sailing of the vessels intended as transports was a shortage of water casks.

29. Scott to Saunders, Feb. 1, 1847, *H. Ex. Doc. 60, 30th Cong., 1st Sess.*, 882; Saunders to Conner, Feb. 4, 22, 1847. *Conner (NY)*; Saunders to CO Tampico, Feb. 8, 1847, Saunders Papers; Eba Anderson Lawton (ed.), *An Artillery Officer in the Mexican War 1846–7* (New York, 1911), 32–35; Moore, *Scott's Campaign*, 3; Bruell, *Sea Memories*, 46–47; "Memoranda of Campaigns in Mexico," 7, YWA; Furber, *12 Months Volunteer*, 432.

30. Scott to Marcy, Feb. 12, 28, to Patterson, Feb. 19, Memorandum for Worth, Feb. 14, 1847, *H. Ex. Doc. 60, 30th Cong., 1st Sess.*, 891–92, 896–901; Scott, *Memoirs*, 413; Smith, *War with Mexico*, I, 358, II, 17. Only four regiments of new volunteers, 1st and 2d Pennsylvania, Louisiana, and New York, were assigned to the expedition but the South Carolina regiment by error sailed to Lobos. Scott incorporated it in his force but left the Louisianians to garrison Tampico. HQ Army, GO #6, Jan. 30, 1847, *AGGO*, XLI½, 111.

31. Scott to Marcy, Feb. 28, 1847, *H. Ex. Doc. 60, 30th Cong., 1st Sess.*, 896–98. Earlier Scott had overreacted to an attack by Senator Benton, complaining of "a fire upon my rear, even before I have been able to draw the fire of the enemy upon my front." As Scott should have anticipated, Polk and Marcy chose to read the complaint as one directed at them. Scott to Marcy, Jan. 12, 1847, *H. Ex. Doc. 60, 30th Cong., 1st Sess.*, 844–46; same to same, Jan. 16, 27, 1847, Marcy Papers, XII.

32. Henry Marlin Tinkcom, *John White Geary, Soldier-Statesman, 1819–1873* (Philadelphia, 1940), 12–13.

33. Scott to Marcy, Feb. 28, 1847, *loc. cit.*; Scott to Conner, Feb. 22, 1847, *Conner (LC)*.

34. Oswandel, *Notes*, 63; E. Parker Scammon, "A Chapter in the Mexican War," *Magazine of American History*, XIV (December 1885), 567; Lawton, *Artillery Officer*, 65; Scott to Marcy, March 1, 1847, *H. Ex. Doc. 56, 30th Cong., 1st Sess.*, 92; Blackwood, *To Mexico with Scott*, 109; HQ Army, GO #40, March 2, 1847, Conner, *Home Squadron*, 75, Collins, "Journal," 46.

35. Parker, *Recollections*, 82; An Eyewitness, "The Capture of Vera Cruz," *The Knickerbocker*, XXX (July 1847), 6; Conner to wife, March 2, 1847, *Conner (FDR)*; Conner to Mason, March 10, 1847, *H. Ex. Doc. 1, 30th Cong., 2d Sess.*, 1177–79. In a humanitarian gesture Conner allowed foreign subjects in Veracruz to seek refuge on HBMS *Hermes*. H. J. Matson to F. Gifford, March 5, to C. G. Fischer, March 8, to H. d'Oliere, March 9, 1847, all in Smith Transcripts, VIII.

36. McCall, *Letters from the Frontier*, 475–76; Hitchcock, *50 Years*, 237; Blackwood, *To Mexico with Scott*, 112; Collins, "Journal," 49; Scammon, "Chapter in the War," 567.

37. Semmes, *Service Afloat and Ashore*, 125; W. S. Lott, "The Landing of the

Expedition Against Vera Cruz in 1847," *Military Service Institution of the United States*, XXIV (May 1899), 424; Conner to Mason, March 10, 1847, *H. Ex. Doc. 1, 30th Cong., 2d Sess.*, 1177–79. For Scott's general instructions for the landings see HQ Army, GOs #26, 34, 42, Feb. 23, 26, March 3, 1847, *AGGO*, XLI½, 148, 163–65, 177.

38. HQ Army, GO #26, 45, Feb. 23, March 7, 1847, *ibid.*, 148, 181–83. Worth's 1st Division consisted of the 2d and 3d Artillery, 4th, 5th, 6th, and 8th Infantry, the Engineer company, 180 Marines, and Taylor's and Talcott's batteries; Twiggs's 3d Division contained the 1st and 4th Artillery, 1st, 2d, 3d, and 7th Infantry, and Duncan's battery; while Patterson's 2d Division consisted of the 1st and 2d Pennsylvania, 1st and 2d Tennessee, South Carolina regiments, and Steptoe's battery. Scott retained control of the few mounted men.

39. Unless otherwise indicated, the account of the Veracruz landing is based upon: Scott to Marcy, March 12, 1847, *S. Ex. Doc. 1, 30th Cong., 1st Sess.*, 216–17; Conner to Mason, March 10, 1847, *loc. cit.*; Conner to Forrest, to COs *Potomac*, *Albany*, etc., March 7, 1847, CLB; HQ Army, GOs #42, 45, 47, March 3, 7, 1847, *AGGO*, XLI½, 177, 181–83, 185–86; "List of transports, showing the number & class of troops in each," and "Distribution of troops of 2nd Brigade," *Conner (NY)*; logs of vessels involved; Alexander to Beth, March 24, 1847, Edmund Brooke Alexander Papers, USMA; Benjamin Huger to Baker, March 10, 1847, Rufus Lathrop Baker Papers, USMA; "Memorandum of Campaign in Mexico," 20–21; George Ballentine, *Autobiography of an English Soldier in the United States Army* (New York, 1853), 143–50; Bauer, *Surfboats and Horse Marines*, 79–82; K. Jack Bauer, "The Veracruz Expedition of 1847," *Military Affairs*, XX (Fall 1956), 165–68; Blackwood, *To Mexico with Scott*, 113–15; Collins, "Journal," 48–50; Conner, *Home Squadron*, 18–20; Davis, *Autobiography*, 125; Eyewitness, "Capture of Vera Cruz," 2; Hartman, *Private's Own Journal*, 6; Lawton, *Artillery Officer*, 74–79; Lott, "Landing," 423–27; McCall, *Letters from the Frontier*, 475; Maury, *Recollections*, 34; Moore, *Scott's Campaign in Mexico*, 5–7; William Starr Myers (ed.), *The Mexican War Diary of George B. Mc-Clellan* (Princeton, 1917), 53; J. Jacob Oswandel, *Notes of the Mexican War* (Philadelphia, 1885), 67–71; Parker, *Recollections*, 83–86; Ripley, *War with Mexico*, II, 23–26; Robertson, *Reminiscences*, 216–20; Scott, *Memoirs*, 413–21; Sedgwick to father, March 27, 1847, John Sedgwick, *Correspondence of John Sedgwick* (2 vols., New York, 1903), I, 71; Semmes, *Service Afloat and Ashore*, 125–28; Smith, "Company A Engineers," 340; Smith, *War with Mexico*, II, 25–27, 336–37; Taylor, *Broad Pennant*, 125; Temple, "Memoir of the Landing," 66–68; Wilcox, *Mexican War*, 242–46; T. Harry Williams (ed.), *With Beauregard in Mexico* (New York, 1969), 25–26.

40. *Memoria del Ministerio de Guerra y Marina, 1846*, carta 11; Roa Bárcena, *Recuerdos*, I, 268–70; Riva Palacio, *México a Través de los Siglos*, IV, 647; Miguel M. Lerdo de Tejada, *Apuntes Históricos, de la Heróica Ciudad de Veracruz* (3 vols., México, 1850–58), II, 508–10; Rivera, *Historia de Jalapa*, III, 864–66; Ramsey, *Other Side*, 182–83; Bancroft, *History of Mexico*, V, 440–41; Ripley, *War with Mexico*, II, 19–20, 27–29; Smith, *War with Mexico*, II, 18–22, 333–34; John Bonner, "Scott's Battles in Mexico," *Harpers New Monthly Magazine*, XI (Aug. 1855), 311. Scott to Marcy, March 29, 1847, *S. Ex. Doc. 1, 30th Cong., 1st Sess.*, 229–30, inventories 113 guns surrendered at Veracruz and 136 at Ulúa. The powder shortage had been somewhat offset by the unloading of fifty tons in early January from the French blockade runner *Anax*. More came in during the siege on the *Jeune Nelly*.

41. Unless otherwise indicated, the account of the siege of Veracruz is based upon: Scott's reports, with enclosures, *S. Ex. Doc. 1, 30th Cong., 1st Sess.*, 216–52;

Conner's and Perry's reports, with enclosures, *H. Ex. Doc. 1, 30th Cong., 2d Sess.*, 1177–89; HQ Army, GOs #52–74, *AGGO*, XLI½, 191–222; *H. Ex. Doc. 24, 31st Cong., 1st Sess.*, 13, 29; logs of vessels involved; "Memorandum of a Campaign," 22–61; Ballentine, *English Soldier*, 151–64; Bauer, *Surfboats and Horse Marines*, 83–96; Bonilla, *Historia Maritima*, 286–88; Bustamante, *El Nuevo Bernal Díaz*, 265; Cardenas, *Semblanza Maritima*, I, 131–36; Claiborne, *Quitman*, I, 293–95; Collins, "Journal," 50–54; Davis, *Autobiography*, 126–27; Freeman, *R. E. Lee*, I, 228–32; Frost, *Mexican War and Its Warriors*, 134–39; Furber, *12 Months Volunteers*, 501–48; Griffis, *Perry*, 216–39; Hartman, *Private's Own Journal*, 7–10; Hitchcock, *50 Years*, 233–48; Jenkins, *Mexican War*, 254–62; Lawton, *Artillery Officer*, 73–104; Lerdo, *Apuntes Históricos*, II, 540–66; McCall, *Letters from the Frontier*, 477–84; Edward D. Mansfield, *The Mexican War* (New York, 1898), 168; Maury, *Recollections*, 34; Morison, *"Old Bruin,"* 215–20; Paul D. Olejar, "Rockets in Early American Wars," *Military Affairs*, X (Winter 1946), 27; Oswandel, *Notes*, 71–95; Parrott to mother, March 25, 1847, Parrott Papers; Francis Effingham Pinto, Diary, 23–27, NYPL; Ramsey, *Other Side*, 183–84; Reavis, *Harney*, 185–86; Ripley, *War with Mexico*, II, 27–30; Risch, *Quartermaster Support*, 290–91; Rivera, *Historia de Jalapa*, III, 860–73; Roa Bárcena, *Recuerdos*, I, 267–325; Robertson, *Reminiscences*, 220–32; Scott, *Memoirs*, 423–30; Semmes, *Service Afloat and Ashore*, 127–42; Smith, *War with Mexico*, II, 27–33, 339–43; Trens, *Historia de Veracruz*, IV, 417–33, 441–43; Wilcox, *Mexican War*, 246–62; Williams, *Beauregard in Mexico*, 27–30.

42. Scott, *Memoirs*, 423–24.

43. Mason to Conner, March 3, 1847, Griffis, *Perry*, 221. Many of his contemporaries believed that Perry had intrigued to have Conner removed, but it appears improbable in this case. In any event Conner on March 5 requested relief. Conner to wife, March 2, 1847 (postscript of March 5), *Conner (FDR)*.

44. Harney to H. L. Scott, Aug. 6, 1847, *S. Ex. Doc. 1, 30th Cong., 1st Sess.*, A2–3. Harney was an old and open enemy of Scott, who first banned Harney from the expedition and then relented. The correspondence relating to Harney's joining the Veracruz force is reprinted in *H. Ex. Doc. 60, 30th Cong., 1st Sess.*, 853–54, 567–71. For Polk's comments see Quaife, *Diary of Polk*, II, 314–16.

45. The storm, which Commodore Perry considered one of the worst he had ever experienced, blew ashore twenty-three transports and supply vessels.

46. The norther prevented Commodore Perry from having an article inserted to secure the release of Midshipman R. Clay Rogers.

47. P. V. Hagner to M. M. Hagner, March 30, 1847, Smith and Judah, *Chronicles of the Gringos*, 195–96; Oswandel, *Notes*, 98; Semmes, *Service Afloat and Ashore*, 145–46; Livingston–Little, *Diary of Tennery*, 75; Lerdo, *Apuntes Históricos*, II, 566–68.

48. Scott to Marcy, March 27, 29, 1847, *S. Ex. Doc. 1, 30th Cong., 1st Sess.*, 229–30, 235–36; Quaife, *Diary of Polk*, II, 465; A. N. Procter to brother, April 11, 1847, Arthur W. Thompson (ed.), "A Massachusetts Mechanic in Florida and Mexico, 1847," *The Florida Historical Quarterly*, XXXIII (Oct. 1954), 132.

49. Scott to Marcy, April 5, HQ Army, GOs #75, 87, 101, March 28, April 1, 9, Veracruz, Orders #1, 3, 6, 6 [*sic*], March 29, April 1, 3, 4, 1847, all in *H. Ex. Doc. 60, 30th Cong., 1st Sess.*, 908–12, 914, 930, 932, 934–36; HQ Army GO #20, Feb. 19, 1847, *AGGO*, XLI½, 139–40.

14: Into the Valley of Mexico

ALTHOUGH THE GREATEST single obstacle to the advance on Mexico City, the establishment of a base of operations, was removed with the seizure of Veracruz, the move inland had to await the solution of the logistics problems. They were enormous! Quartermaster General Thomas S. Jesup calculated that a 25,000-man force moving from Veracruz to Mexico City would require 2,893,950 pounds of supplies carried in 9,303 wagons and on the backs of 17,413 mules. Among the supplies were 300,000 bushels of oats and 200,000 of corn, 200,000 muleshoes, and 100,000 horseshoes, 100 pounds of blister ointment, 5,000 quills, 300 bottles of ink, and 1,000 pounds of office tape. Scott projected more limited needs and anticipated that two thirds of the draft animals could be secured in Mexico along with some of the forage and food.[1] As events proved, the quartermaster rather than the commander best estimated the army's needs.

Even before Scott's recommendations reached Washington, Polk had become exasperated at the quantity of animals purchased by the Quartermaster Department. He was "much vexed at the extravagance & stupidity of purchasing these animals in the U. S.," since he believed they could be acquired in Mexico for a quarter of the price. This was but another indication to Polk of the incompetence of the War Department's supply bureaus. Secretary of War Marcy finally admitted in July that he could not exercise any control over them. Polk himself then called in Jesup and Commissary General George Gibson, upbraided them for their poor cost control, and informed them in no uncertain terms that he wished their operations better managed.[2]

Scott's concern over the transport shortage grew rapidly as each day lost reduced the margin between the departure of the army for higher, yellow-fever-free country and the arrival of the scourge. In an effort to secure horses, mules, and beef cattle, Scott sent General Quitman's brigade to Alvarado, the center of a large ranching area. Commodore Perry planned to lead a large segment of his squadron, including the Mosquito Flotilla, in a coordinated assault on Alvarado's seaward defenses. Perry hoped, as had Conner in his two abortive attacks on the port, to seize the remnants of the Mexican Navy, which still swung at anchor there. While Perry and most of his vessels prepared to assist Quitman's force in crossing the Madellin River, Lieutenant Charles G. Hunter in the steamer *Scourge* took up station to keep a watch on Alvarado. On the evening of March 30 in a thoughtless act of bravado, Hunter fired a few rounds at the fort guarding the river mouth. That sufficed to warn the defenders, who spent the night destroying their military stores, scuttling and burning the warships, and evacuating the town.

To compound the problem, the *Scourge* steamed into the river, seized Alvarado, and followed the retreating garrison upstream as far as Tlacotalpán. Not only did Perry and Quitman find the warships destroyed but most of the livestock out of their reach. Perry was so incensed at Hunter's actions that he banished him from the squadron. A second expedition on April 8 to 11 located some additional horses but, overall, Scott's hope of locating a source of draft animals around Alvarado proved as ephemeral as a similar one he held for Jalapa.[3] Nor was transport Scott's only concern. Since hard money was scarce at Veracruz, most of the transactions were handled with quartermaster's drafts. When the merchants there insisted on a 6 percent discount to cash the drafts, Scott threatened to suspend all export of specie. Thereafter the drafts passed at par.[4]

While Scott struggled to organize his advance inland, Santa Anna returned to Mexico City to seize control of the government and organize the defense of his nation's capital. As troops became available he sent them to Jalapa to form the Army of the East under Major General Valentín Canalizo.[5]

After Santa Anna had organized his government and secured a 2-million-peso loan from the church, he arranged for an interim chief of state, Pedro María Anaya, to serve while he was in the field. On April 2 Santa Anna left to take command of the capital's defenders at the head of a caravan of 200 carts carrying 7,000 fresh but largely untrained troops.[6]

While the Mexicans prepared to fight for Jalapa, Scott set it as the target of his initial advance. About seventy-four miles inland, it was above the yellow-fever belt, offered a plentiful supply of subsistence and forage, and lay in an area reputedly friendly to the Americans. American intelligence erroneously reported that the Mexicans would not defend it.[7]

The great highway which wound its way up the Sierra Madres 4,680 feet to Jalapa and 7,091 to Puebla offered a number of strong defensive positions. The strongest was in La Hoya Pass above Jalapa. Before reaching that stronghold, however, an invading army had to cross the Rio Antigua on the famed and picturesque Puente Nacional and traverse the easily defended passes at the Plan del Rio, Cerro Gordo, and Corral Falso. Santa Anna organized a defense in depth with General Canalizo in overall charge.

Santa Anna reached his hacienda at Encero between Jalapa and Cerro Gordo on April 5. Two days later he selected Cerro Gordo for his stand, since this would keep the Americans in the yellow-fever belt below Plan del Rio. He also mistakenly believed the position could not be turned.[8]

The American advance began on April 2 when Harney with a mixed command opened the way inland by forcing a crossing of the Rio Antigua near its mouth. The leading division, Twiggs's, marched on the eighth, followed the next day by Patterson's division less Quitman's brigade. Worth's division had to remain at Veracruz until additional transport appeared.[9]

Scott accompanied the advance with assurances to the Mexican civilians that the Americans came as friends. The Yankees would free them from misgovernment, he promised, as well as protect both the church and peaceful inhabitants. Although it won few active supporters, the pronouncement helped offset the Mexican propaganda and the natives' natural zenophobia and also eased the acquisition of supplies. The need for such a statement was documented in a complaint from an inhabitant who was furnishing the Americans with beef. When some volunteers passed his ranch, they broke into his house, beat him, robbed him despite the presence of some officers, destroyed his well, and stole six mules.[10] Scott's proclamation demonstrated to both the Mexicans and the army that such activities were not acceptable.

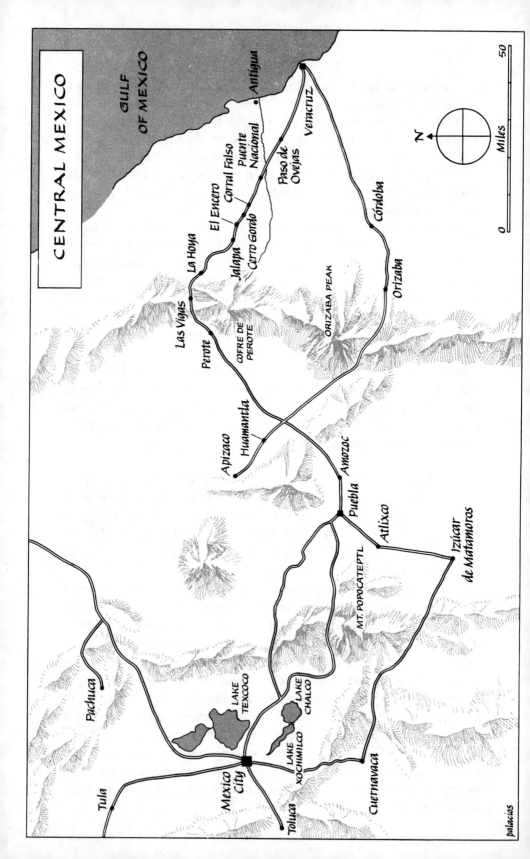

CENTRAL MEXICO

GULF OF MEXICO

Antigua
Puente Nacional
Corral Falso
El Encero
Paso de Ovejas
Veracruz
Cerro Gordo
Jalapa
La Hoya
Córdoba
Las Vigas
Orizaba
ORIZABA PEAK
Perote
COFRE DE PEROTE
Apizaco
Huamantla
Amozoc
Puebla
Atlixco
Izúcar de Matamoros
MT. POPOCATEPTL
Pachuca
LAKE TEXCOCO
LAKE CHALCO
Mexico City
LAKE XOCHIMILCO
Cuernavaca
Toluca
Tula

N

Miles
0   50

palacios

The advance screen of dragoons reached Plan del Rio during April 11, followed by the rest of Twiggs's division. The next morning reconnaissance disclosed the Cerro Gordo Pass defenses but Lieutenant Pierre G. T. Beauregard, one of the engineer officers scouting the Mexican position, discovered a hill which thrust up about a quarter mile behind it. Beauregard concluded that possession of the hill, called Atalaya, would allow the whole Mexican position to be turned, but Twiggs evinced little interest in the information.

Before Patterson marched, Scott had assured the volunteer general that if the Mexicans chose to fight he would quickly join the army. Late on the eleventh Scott received Twiggs's estimate of 4,000 Mexicans before him. Scott immediately rushed forward himself with an escort of dragoons after ordering Worth, Quitman, and the siege train to follow.[11]

"Old Davy" Twiggs, a physically impressive figure with powerful shoulders and a bull-neck, stood nearly six feet tall. He was not one of the army's intellectuals and held to a simple tactical concept— attack. On the morning of April 12, despite the clear evidence that the Mexicans were in the pass in force, he set his column in motion in marching order. His advance guard soon drew fire which permitted the rest of the division to withdraw without bringing on a disastrous general action. Following more scouting during the afternoon which further developed the strength of the Mexican position, Twiggs ordered a frontal attack to start at four the next morning. However, at the request of Generals Pillow and Shields, whose tired brigades had just arrived, he postponed the attack twenty-four hours. Before it could be launched, General Patterson rose from a sickbed to assume command of the two divisions and canceled the potentially suicidal attack.[12]

The fortifications at Cerro Gordo had been laid out by the very competent Lieutenant Colonel Manuel M. Robles Pezuala and built in part by peons from Santa Anna's Encero estate. About a half mile below the village of Cerro Gordo the National Road entered a mile-long ravine. To the north of the road rose the steep face of El Telégrafo, some 500 to 600 feet high.[13] Forming the opposing side of the ravine was a hill from whose three points batteries swept the road nearly as far as the Plan del Rio crossing. The three batteries contained nineteen guns between them and were supported by 1,800 men under Brigadier Generals Luis Pinzón and José María Jararo, and a Colonel Badillo. At the head of the ravine General Rómulo

Díaz de la Vega commanded a six- or seven-gun battery supported by the 900 men and the reserve of 500 men from the crack Regiment of Grenadiers.

Dominating the whole was the strongpoint embracing El Telégrafo and a spur to the left, rear, and slightly below the tower which gave the hill its name. A hundred men of the 3d Infantry and a quartet of 4-pounders defended the summit. Beyond El Telégrafo, close to the village of Cerro Gordo, was the main Mexican camp containing the remaining reserves. The position Santa Anna reported to Mexico City was manned by 12,000 men who would throw back the invaders and forever crush the weak-willed in the capital who counseled peace.

Santa Anna's roseate report bore little resemblance to reality. The leader's self-evident overconfidence and his refusal to accept advice kindled talk of impending disaster among his officers. The troops were insect-plagued, short of water, and suffering from bronchial and digestive ailments. Most of the men lacked training and many were infected with the notion of Yankee invincibility. Indeed, the Mexican army, if not its commander, was psychologically ready for a rout with one foot already turned toward the rear.

Scott arrived during the afternoon of the fourteenth and ordered additional reconnaissance. The following day Captain Robert E. Lee discovered a path which led around the Mexican left to Beauregard's hill of Atalaya. His report settled any questions about the plan of attack. It called for the envelopment of the Mexican positions by Twiggs's division moving down Lee's trail after it had been made passable for infantry and, after a fashion, for artillery.

Twiggs's men, after surprising the Mexican flank, would break through to block the Jalapa road. This involved a considerable gamble. The Americans were not certain that the Jalapa road ran close enough to the Cerro Gordo position to permit them to cut the Mexican escape route.

The engineers improved the path during the sixteenth, and the next morning Twiggs's division moved out. Although the initial portions of its route were screened from Mexican eyes by the rough terrain, sharp-eyed lookouts on the summit of Atalaya discovered the movement during the late morning. Twiggs responded with an assault on that key feature, led by Colonel Harney, which swept the few defenders from its top. Some of the Americans, either carried along by their momentum or by Twiggs's admonition to "Charge 'em to hell," chased the Mexicans up the slopes of El Telégrafo but were pinned down before reaching its top. They withdrew under cover of fire from Lieutenant Jesse L. Reno's mountain howitzers which had been rushed to the top of Atalaya.

The clash on El Telégrafo frustrated Scott's plans, since the Mexicans had been alerted without Twiggs cutting the road. The damage, however, was less than Scott imagined, for the Mexicans assumed that El Telégrafo had been Twiggs's objective and concluded that they had beaten back the American move. Nevertheless, Santa Anna strengthened the defenses there. He had a breastwork containing a pair of 12-pounders thrown up near the base of the hill and sent Brigadier General Ciriaco Vásquez with the 2d Light and 4th Regular Infantry to reinforce the summit. Near the camp he had a five-gun battery emplanted with the 11th Infantry and some cavalry in support.

Scott reinforced Twiggs with Shields's newly arrived brigade, but it arrived too late in the day to see action. The volunteers did, however, assist in moving three heavy 24-pounders from Captain Edward J. Steptoe's battery to the top of Atalaya. Simultaneously Major James C. Burnham with a battalion of the New York regiment dragged an eight-inch howitzer into an enfilading position across the river from the Mexican lines.

Scott's plan for the eighteenth, spelled out in his General Orders Number 111, called for Twiggs's division, reinforced by Shields's brigade, to seize El Telégrafo and cut the road. Upon hearing the firing which signaled the attack, Pillow's brigade was to attack the batteries on the three fingers at the eastern end of the Mexican line; break through; and attack the Mexican rear. Worth's division, as it arrived, would follow Twiggs's route and join in the pursuit.

Twiggs directed the brigades of Shields and Colonel Bennet Riley to bypass El Telégrafo on the west and cut the Jalapa road near the Mexican camp. At the same time Harney, temporarily in command of Persifor Smith's brigade, was to move directly against the El Telégrafo positions under a covering fire from the guns on Atalaya. As Riley's and Shields's columns set out, the batteries on the two hilltops began a duel.

At about seven o'clock Harney's men attacked. The hillside was so steep that officers had to use their swords and many men their muskets for support in working their way up the slope. Despite the nearly impossible ascent they struggled to within seventy-five yards of the summit before stopping to catch their breath. Harney, roaring like a bull, got them going again and they easily overran the Mexican

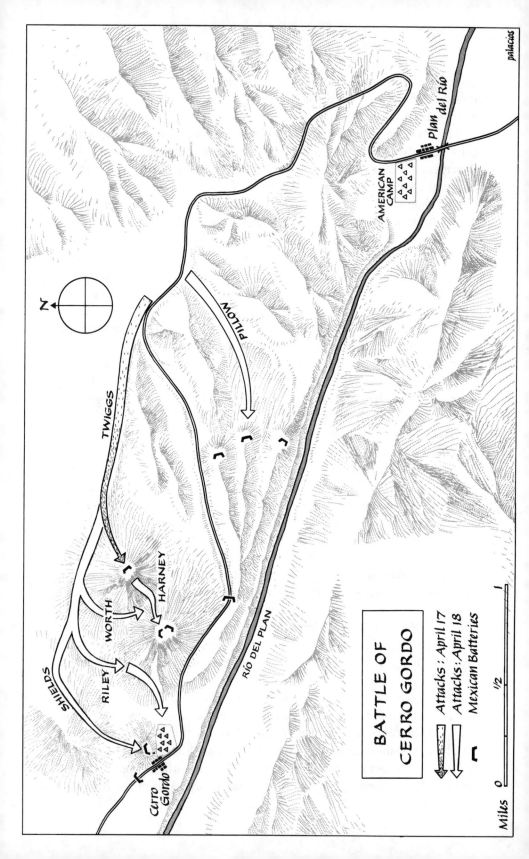

BATTLE OF
CERRO GORDO

Attacks: April 17
Attacks: April 18
Mexican Batteries

Miles
0   ½   1

palacios

Plan del Río

AMERICAN CAMP

PILLOW

TWIGGS

N

HARNEY

WORTH

RILEY

SHIELDS

RÍO DEL PLAN

Cerro Gordo

breastworks. In the melée General Vásquez was killed. Sergeant Thomas Henry of the 7th Infantry ran up the American flag over the tower while Captain John B. Magruder took charge of the Mexican guns and had them turned on the fleeing defenders. Meanwhile, Twiggs diverted a part of Riley's brigade to assist the assault by attacking along the reverse slope of the hill. The rest assailed a battery behind the hill. This combination of attack from front, rear, and above caused the Mexicans on El Telégrafo to flee.[14]

At about the same time the defenders of El Telégrafo began their headlong dash for the rear, Shields's men appeared out of the thickets flanking the Mexican camp. The gunners at the five-man battery there greeted them with a blast of grapeshot which momentarily checked the advance. Shields himself was struck by a missile which passed through his right lung and should have been, but was not, fatal.[15] Colonel Edward D. Baker of the 4th Illinois assumed command and led a charge through the Mexican camp which put the Americans in possession of the Jalapa road. Scott's objective had been achieved.

Pillow's supporting attack against the batteries commanding the road was mishandled from the start. He failed to reconnoiter the ground traversed by his approach march. Not only did his men have a three-mile march to reach their jump-off position, but they had to approach it along a single narrow trail. This so delayed them that they were not in position when the battle started, and when they did arrive they were in the wrong order.[16] Moreover, as the regiments moved along the trail they came under heavy fire, especially the leading unit, Colonel William Haskell's 2d Tennessee. The Tennesseans attempted to break through the thickets and tangled brush which separated them from the Mexicans only to be driven back by the heaviest losses, nearly eighty men, suffered by any American regiment that day. Their support, the 1st Pennsylvania (Colonel Francis M. Wynkoop), could not get into position before the fight was over, while Pillow, who had been wounded, never issued the attack order to the other assault regiment, Colonel William Roberts's 2d Pennsylvania. That oversight did little damage, however, since the Mexican commanders on the three prongs of the hill, once they realized they were isolated by the cutting of the road behind them, surrendered.

The Battle of Cerro Gordo lasted only slightly more than three hours. By ten o'clock those Mexicans who could, including their commander, began a headlong flight. The Mexican Army, for the moment at least, had ceased to exist. Because of the nearly total destruction of Mexican organization, there are no reliable figures on losses beyond the American count of 199 officers and 2,837 men taken prisoner. Lieutenant Colonel Ethan Allen Hitchcock, the army's inspector general, estimated that an additional thousand prisoners slipped away from their captors before being processed. Perhaps half the Mexican force escaped, but very few units preserved any integrity. The Americans came through the battle with relatively light casualties considering the intensity of the fighting: sixty-three killed and 368 wounded out of approximately 8,500 men engaged.

The pursuit of the fleeing defenders by the dragoons and two batteries netted few prisoners, although the chase reached Encero before the Americans' horses gave out. Among the booty seized was Santa Anna's personal carriage and baggage wagon with a chest containing $20,000 in coin. The 4th Illinois reveled in its seizure of Santa Anna's wooden leg, which for years afterward was kept on display in the Illinois state capitol. A story retold with glee in Mexico City circles concerned Brigadier General Joaquín Rangel. With seven other escaping officers, he was seized by three bandits "who paid them the insulting compliment of returning their swords."

The American army rested from the fight, ministered to the wounded, rounded up prisoners, and collected booty during the remainder of the eighteenth. The next morning the Americans occupied Jalapa, a pretty, friendly city surrounded by hills aflame with white, purple, green, and scarlet plants.[17]

While the main body paused at Jalapa, Worth's division continued on to Perote. On April 22 the advance guard occupied the famed, dusty-brown Fort San Carlos de Perote outside the city. Inside they discovered a large munitions dump, a number of American prisoners, and Generals José Juan Landero and Juan Morales imprisoned for the surrender of Veracruz. The area, as Worth happily discovered, offered corn and flour at fair prices.[18]

Meanwhile, at Jalapa Scott quickly established a good working relationship with the local authorities. Nevertheless, the area continued to be plagued by the pillaging and plundering of stragglers from the Cerro Gordo force. Nor were Mexican troops the only malefactors. Americans, particularly the volunteers, so commonly trespassed on Mexican property that General Patterson had to issue an order imploring his men to cease, since the acts "lessen the confidence of the general in the efficiency of the Division."[19]

The weather, the need to garrison points along the supply route to the coast, the danger to the supply trains from ambushes and other guerrilla activities, and the persistent shortage of transport hampered Scott's operations. Without the necessity of protecting his supply line, Scott claimed he could seize the Mexican capital with the loss of less than 100 men. The shortage of men grew out of the temporary diversion of troops to the Rio Grande when it was feared that Taylor had been cut off in Monterrey.

In late April Scott advised Colonel Henry Wilson at Veracruz that within a month he might be cut off from the seaport. At the same time but less explicitly Scott also alerted Marcy to the same prospect. The cause of these warnings was the General's intention to withdraw the garrisons in the yellow-fever belt during the fever season. Scott believed that he could secure sufficient food locally to maintain his army and anticipated that within a fortnight his depots would hold enough clothing, ammunition, and medicine to permit the army to survive in the midst of a hostile country.[20]

Complicating the logistics was the growth of guerrilla bands. They ambushed trains and individuals, caring little whether their nationality was American or Mexican. The creation of the guerrilla bands stemmed from the formation of a "light corps of the National Guard," and calls for guerrillas in late April by the Governor of Veracruz and the legislature of the state of Mexico.[21]

Unconventional warfare is the method normally resorted to by a group so inferior in traditional military power as to be unable to take the field, as was the case with Mexico immediately following Cerro Gordo. Moreover, guerrilla activities were a form of unconventional warfare which fitted well the traditional Mexican pattern.

Scott responded to the appearance of the new menace with a tough antidote. He held the alcalde nearest the scene responsible for the apprehension and delivery to the occupation forces of all persons guilty of murder or robbery of an American on the highways. In the event that the guilty parties were not delivered, a fine of $300 was levied on the personal property of the alcalde.[22]

As April began to turn toward May, the twelve-month men, who made up the bulk of Scott's volunteers, took an ever larger place in the thoughts of both their commander and the War Department. Polk, after consulting with Secretaries Marcy and Mason, decided to replace the twelve-month regiments with six or eight new ones enlisted for the war's duration. The cabinet approved this on April 17 and Marcy issued the calls two days later.[23] In addition some 4,077 other men already had orders to Mexico, of whom 1,500 were expected to reach Point Isabel by the end of the month.[24]

During the last day of April, Scott issued orders to start the army on its next stride toward the Mexican capital. But at the last minute the General in Chief abandoned his forward move, deciding instead to send home before the onset of the yellow-fever season those twelve-month men who would not reenlist for the duration. It is an interesting commentary on late Jacksonian ethics and patriotism that less than one man in ten extended his enlistment for the duration. The common man saw no immorality in abandoning his fellow man to whatever lay in store for him in the midst of a hostile land. The volunteer had served his twelve months and that was as much as he was obligated to give his country! Undoubtedly, Scott also realized that the men would become increasingly difficult to control as the time for their discharge approached and that the unrest would coincide with a critical period in his advance. Moreover, discontented troops would scarcely enhance his reception by the Mexican populace upon whom he must rely for the supplies to sustain his force. The sagacity of that decision was amply illustrated by the complaints about damage inflicted by those units on their march to the sea. The seven regiments departed on June 6 and 7, leaving behind their tents and camp equipage. Their departure left Scott with only 7,113 men.[25]

Having divested himself of the short-term regiments, Scott resumed his interrupted march. He directed Worth to seize Puebla, and wait there for Scott's appearance with Twiggs's division. Scott considered the risk in sending the relatively small force to Puebla minimal because of the strong anti-Santanista and pro-clerical sentiments in Mexico's second city.[26]

In support of his move to win over the clerical and other peace forces, Scott on May 11 issued another proclamation "a la Nación Méjicana." The carefully prepared paper, drawn up in consultation with a representative of the clerical party, declared the war had been forced upon the United States despite her desire for peace and friendship. After vividly describing conditions in Mexico, it insisted that the Americans were true friends and brothers of the Mexicans. The American army came to assist in the fight for republican institutions and the welfare of the continent. The statement concluded by promising protection for all who would remain neutral. In Puebla, at least, the message undercut whatever disposition to resist still remained.[27]

It did not, however, have that effect on Santa Anna. Following the battle of Cerro Gordo, he had fled to Orizaba, hurried along by reports that American patrols were close on his heels. There he collected some 2,500 men from an Oaxaca brigade, a few National Guard detachments, and stragglers from the Cerro Gordo force. Although Santa Anna initially intended to attack the American army in the mountains beyond Jalapa, he abandoned that in favor of concentrating his forces at Puebla. There he could secure supplies as well as influence the May 15 presidential elections.[28]

On May 10, the day before Santa Anna reached Puebla, Worth's force began its advance. When his scouts reported that Quitman's small brigade, laden with a large wagon train, marched well to the rear of Worth, Santa Anna concluded that he had a chance to destroy the Americans in detail. He dispatched 3,000 cavalry to overwhelm Quitman before the two American forces could combine. Worth, who feared just such a move, halted his men at Amozoc, about ten miles from Puebla, to await Quitman. During the morning of the fourteenth, while Worth's men polished their equipment and brushed up their uniforms for the triumphal entry into Puebla, they suddenly sighted the Mexican cavalry. A few shells from Steptoe's battery chased the horsemen into the nearby woods. Worth correctly assumed that their objective was Quitman, now only three miles away, and quickly sent reinforcements. The Mexicans upon discovering that Quitman's force was aroused and reinforced wisely retired to Puebla without attacking. The following morning they joined the rest of Santa Anna's force in the march to Mexico City.[29]

During the fifteenth Worth met with commissioners from Puebla to work out the details of the occupation, and shortly before 10:00 A.M. 4,200 American troops marched into Puebla.[30] A city of 80,000 people, it was laid out in a rectangular grid and was noted for comely women, large cotton mills, and a beautiful twin-towered cathedral. Nearly as far above sea level as Mexico City, the new American position offered the occupation forces bracing climate and a rich agricultural hinterland.[31]

The rest of the army followed about a week behind Worth, with the headquarters group arriving on May 29. On considering his position from the viewpoint of Puebla, Scott concluded that it was imperative to reinforce his command even at the cost of abandoning Jalapa and Perote. Therefore he ordered Brevet Colonel Thomas

Childs at Jalapa and Colonel Wynkoop at Perote to rejoin the main body.[32] To all intents and purposes the army now lived off the country and had cut all connections with the coast. But until the reinforcements which were enroute arrived, the American force was still too small to push on to the Mexican capital.

Washington had foreseen the need for more troops. At the end of April, Marcy promised Scott 20,000 additional men by the end of June.[33] The letter coincided with the arrival of the first indications of Scott's decision to abandon communications with Veracruz. Marcy concluded that "this appears to me to be a very strange order" and the President that it was "a great military error." Nevertheless, he directed that all troops not needed by Taylor to police his occupation zone be sent to Scott. Polk also ordered Colonel John C. Hays's regiment of Texas horsemen be shifted to Veracruz to clear the road of guerrillas. It was more than one regiment could do, even if they were the feared Texas Rangers, but they did help dampen the spirits of the guerrillas around the areas in which they were stationed.[34]

In early August Polk conferred with his service secretaries. They decided to postpone calling out additional volunteers until the situation cleared, but agreed to send Major General William O. Butler to join the main force. This was a precaution in case Scott became incapacitated or otherwise abandoned the command. Polk foresaw a struggle, in that instance, between Pillow and Worth. "I have great confidence in Pillow," the President wrote, "but he is young in the service & the country do[es] not know his merits as well as I do." In a letter to Butler, Polk prophetically commented that "contingencies may happen which would in a short time devolve upon you the chief command."[35]

Polk decided in mid-August to call out the remaining 6,000 men authorized in the war act if the War Department had sufficient money to pay and equip them. The attempts to determine how much money was available unearthed both shoddy record-keeping by the Quartermaster and Commissary offices and some shady maneuvering by the department's bankers. It developed that in mid-June McClintock Young, the Chief Clerk of the Treasury, and the Washington banker, William W. Corcoran, had talked Quartermaster General Thomas S. Jesup into transferring $2 million to New Orleans and naming the firm as transfer agent. Jesup did not need that much money in New Orleans. Indeed, by late July only $400,000 had been spent. The rest had been used by Corcoran's firm for stock speculation.[36]

While the top-level discussions and planning progressed toward an uncertain conclusion, the reinforcements which Scott awaited were enroute. Brigadier General George Cadwalader, with the leading elements of the troops who had been diverted to the Rio Grande, reached Veracruz on June 1. While he awaited additional troops, Colonel James S. McIntosh, still somewhat handicapped by wounds received at Resaca de la Palma, led a mixed force of 700 men, largely raw recruits, as guards for a wagon train carrying ammunition and $350,000 to replenish Scott's coffers. They left Veracruz on June 4, but the reports of specie in the train drew so many guerrillas that McIntosh had to halt at Paso de Ovejas, since his inept teamsters could not keep the column sufficiently compact to defend effectively. He appealed to Cadwalader for reinforcements. The Pennsylvanian rushed forward with about 500 men, linking up on the eighth. Five days later the combined force drove the guerrillas from the beautiful, big-arched, stone Puente Nacional. The column reached Jalapa on the sixteenth and incorporated Childs's garrison.

The guerrillas in the area, about 700 men under Padre Caledonio Domeco Jarauta, prepared an ambush for the five-mile-long column in La Hoya Pass, about ten miles beyond Jalapa. Unfortunately for the Mexicans, Colonel Wynkoop, who commanded the garrison at Perote, learned of the ambush. He warned Cadwalader and sent Captain Samuel Walker with about thirty men to break up the guerrilla base at Las Vigas. Walker surprised the defenders and laid waste to the town on the twentieth. Later that day Walker's men and a battalion from Perote scattered the rest of the Mexicans who had been forced from their positions by the alerted column. Cadwalader halted his force at Perote to allow a second column under Pillow to join.[37]

The Tennessean departed Veracruz on June 8 with 2,000 men. They had no opposition, probably because of the damage wrought by Walker and Cadwalader and the guerrillas' unwillingness to attack such a strong column. After adding Cadwalader's men to his column, Pillow had an easy march to Puebla where he arrived on August 8. The new men raised Scott's total force to 8,061 effectives plus 2,235 on the sick list.[38]

On the heels of Pillow's force came a smaller one under Brigadier General Franklin Pierce. Although he reached Veracruz on June 19, he did not get his leading elements on the road until July 14. Like most of the reinforcement columns, it was a composite of new recruits and new regiments. It also included the Marine Battalion under Lieutenant Colonel Samuel E. Watson. All told, Pierce had approximately 2,500 men to guard a train of about fifty wagons and $85,000 in drafts. At the partially destroyed Puente Nacional the Americans dispersed about 150 Mexicans in a sharp ten-minute skirmish, and by the time the column entered Puebla on August 6, it had fought five other small actions.[39] Part of the reason for the scarcity of resistance was a well-executed raid during July 30 by Captain Charles F. Ruff from Puebla, with two mounted companies, on the guerrillas at San Juan de Los Llanos about twenty-five miles to the northeast.[40]

Another step toward improving the security of the army's communications was Colonel Hitchcock's hiring of Manuel Dominquez, one of Mexico's most noted robbers, as a courier. So successful was the experiment that Hitchcock hired both Dominquez and his band, about 200 men, to serve as guides, couriers, and spies. They served faithfully and became an excellent antiguerrilla unit.[41]

Scott issued the order for the advance to Mexico City on August 5. Two days later General Twiggs formed his division, faced his men, and bellowed: "Now my lads, give them a Cerro Gordo shout!" He got one. The head of the column then began moving, the first of 10,738 officers and men who would force open the gates of the Mexican capital. The divisions of Worth, Quitman, and Pillow followed at one-day intervals. By the tenth only a small garrison under Brevet Colonel Thomas Childs remained to guard the supplies and the sick.[42]

Although he commanded about 30,000 troops in and around Mexico City, Santa Anna offered no resistance to the American advance. Whether this resulted from his efforts to set the stage for an armistice or merely reflected a lack of trust in his ill-trained troops is uncertain. Twiggs's division occupied Ayotla, some fifteen miles from the capital, on August 11. Scott himself arrived later that day. The other divisions moved into supporting positions at Chalco and Chimalpa during the next thirty-six hours.[43] The stage was now set for the critical struggle for the control of the Mexican capital.

NOTES

For key to abbreviations used in Notes, see page xi.

1. Jesup to Col. Henry Stanton, Feb. 12, 1847, *JMLB'46-7*, 149-53; Scott to Jesup, March 19, 1847, *H. Ex. Doc. 60, 30th Cong., 1st Sess.*, 913. Scott's estimates were 800-1,000 wagons, 2,000-3,000 mules, and 300-500 draft animals for the siege train.
2. Quaife, *Diary of Polk*, II, 430-31, III, 79-82.

3. Scott to Marcy, April 5, 1847, Quitman to H. L. Scott, April 7, 1847, *H. Ex. Doc. 60, 30th Cong., 1st Sess.*, 909–11, 917–18; Perry to Mason, April 4, 1847, *H. Ex. Doc. 1, 30th Cong., 2nd Sess.*, 1200–2; Hunter to Perry, April 2, 1847 (with enclosures), *Niles* LXXII (May 1, 1847), 131–32; Morison, *"Old Bruin,"* 222–23; Bauer, *Surfboats and Horse Marines*, 100–2; Risch, *Quartermaster Support*, 292.

4. Worth and McCluney, Proclamation, March 31, E. Pleammon to Marcy, April 23, 1847, *AGLR'47*, S-249, -877; Scott to Marcy, April 11, HQ Army, GOs #103, 108, April 10, 12, 1847, *H. Ex. Doc. 60, 30th Cong., 1st Sess.*, 928–29, 939.

5. Santa Anna to Canalizo, March 21, 1846, Smith, "Letters of Santa Anna," 415; Ramsey, *Other Side*, 155.

6. Roa Bárcena, *Recuerdos*, II, 10–12; Smith, *War with Mexico*, II, 15, 41; Callcott, *Santa Anna*, 256; Ramsey, *Other Side*, 147; Scholes, *Mexico During the War*, 112; José C. Valadez, *Historia del Pueblo de México* (2 vols., México, 1967), II, 395.

7. Scott to Marcy, April 8, 1847, *H. Ex. Doc. 56, 30th Cong., 1st Sess.*, 126; Scott, *Autobiography*, 430–31; Smith, *War with Mexico*, II, 39.

8. Smith, *War with Mexico*, II, 39–42; Callcott, *Santa Anna*, 257–59; Jones, *Santa Anna*, 113.

9. Harney to H. L. Scott, April 4, HQ Army, GO #91, 94, April 6, 1847, *H. Ex. Doc. 60, 30th Cong., 1st Sess.*, 914–16, 921–22.

10. Scott, Proclamation, April 11, 1847, *H. Ex. Doc. 60, 30th Cong., 1st Sess.*, 937; Nicholas Dorich, Statement, April 1847, *AGLR'47*, S-877, encl. 10.

11. Jenkins, *War Between U.S. and Mexico*, 273; Williams, *With Beauregard in Mexico*, 12–13; Scott to Patterson, April 9, Twiggs to H. L. Scott, Pillow to Scott, April 11, 1847, *H. Ex. Doc. 60, 30th Cong., 1st Sess.*, 936, 939–40; HQ Army, GO #105, April 11, 1847, *AGGO*, XLI½, 270. Command of Veracruz passed to Brevet Col. Henry Wilson.

12. The account of the Battle of Cerro Gordo is based on: Scott to Marcy, April 19, 23, 1847, with enclosures, *S. Ex. Doc. 1, 30th Cong., 1st Sess.*, 255–300; Hitchcock to H. L. Scott, April 24, 1847, *H. Ex. Doc. 56, 30th Cong., 1st Sess.*, 279–80; Beauregard to Patterson, April 20, 1847, Pierre G. T. Beauregard Papers, MoHS; HQ Army, GO #249, Aug. 6, 1847, *AGGO*, XLI½, 463–66; 2d Div., GO #46, April 13, 1847, *1VolBrig G & SO*; Jarero to Ministro Guerra y Marina, April 22, Wynkoop to W. L. Hodge, July 6, 1847, *Niles*, LXXII (June 5, 1847), 219, LXXIII (Oct. 2, 1847), 75; Twiggs to G. E. Twiggs, April 20, 26, 1847, Levi Twiggs Papers, MCM; Pinto, Diary, 33–34; Joseph Rowe Smith, Diary, YWA; Ballentine, *English Soldier*, 174–89; Brooks, *Complete History*, 323–39; Callcott, *Santa Anna*, 259–60; Dawson, *Battles of U. S.*, II, 503–8; Ralph W. Donnelly, "Rocket Batteries of the Civil War" *Military Affairs* XXV (Summer 1961) 74–75; Elliott, *Scott*, 464–68; Freeman, *Lee*, I, 238–41; Furber, *12 Months Volunteer*, 600–1; Grant, *Memoirs*, 63–64; Henry, *Mexican War*, 280–87; Max L. Heyman, *Prudent Soldier* (Glendale, 1959), 63–64; Hitchcock, *50 Years*, 250–53; Jenkins, *War Between U.S. and Mexico*, 273–87; Livingston–Little, *Diary of Tennery*, 80–82; Myers, *Diary of McClellan*, 79–90; Olejar, "Rockets," 28–29; Oswandel, *Notes*, 122–27; Ramírez, *Mexico During the War*, 128; Ramsey, *Other Side*, 205–14; Ripley, *War with Mexico*, II, 63–77; Rivera, *Historia de Jalapa*, III, 880–93; Roa Bárcena, *Recuerdos*, II, 9–150; Robertson, *Reminiscences*, 240–48; Scott, *Memoirs*, 431–32; Crawford, *The Eagle*, 96; Santa Anna, *Las Guerras . . . con Tejas y los EE. UU.*, 250–57; Semmes, *Service Afloat and Ashore*, 175–83; Smith, *War with Mexico*, II, 44–45, 52–58, 350–55; Smith and Judah, *Chronicles of the Gringos*, 207–8, 211–12; Wilcox, *Mexican War*, 278–97; Williams, *With Beauregard in Mexico*, 12–13, 32–38.

13. Generally called Cerro Gordo in American reports.

14. Riley later concluded that the actions of his brigade had been slighted in Twiggs's reports of the battle and asked for a court of inquiry. Scott initially refused but later relented. The findings, which have been followed here, did not support Riley's claim that his men seized El Telégrafo. H. L. Scott to Riley, May 21, 1847, Statement made by Brevet Colonel Riley . . . in Renewing His Application for a Board of Inquiry, n.d., both in Bennet Riley Papers, USMA; HQ Army GO #249, Aug. 6, 1847, *loc. cit.* The court-martial record was published in *H. Ex. Doc. 85, 30th Cong., 1st Sess.*

15. Shields's life was saved by an Irish surgeon in the Mexican army who cleansed the wound by drawing a silk handkerchief through it. Condon, *Shields,* 69–70.

16. Pillow's plan called for an assault by the 2d Tennessee and the 2d Pennsylvania, supported by the 1st Pennsylvania and 1st Tennessee respectively. But the order of march was 2d Tennessee, 1st Tennessee, 2d Pennsylvania, 1st Pennsylvania. Myers, *Diary of McClellan,* 83, claims that Pillow himself drew the fire by bellowing at the top of his voice: "Why in Hell don't Colonel Wynkoop file to the right?"

17. Smith, *War with Mexico,* II, 59; Semmes, *Service Afloat and Ashore,* 189–93.

18. Worth to H. L. Scott, April 22, 1847, *S. Ex. Doc. 1, 30th Cong., 1st Sess.,* 300–1; Inventory of Artillery in Fort San Carlos de Perote, n.d., *AGLR'47,* W-1048; Anderson to wife, April 26, 1847, Lawton, *Artillery Officer,* 143–44; untitled paper, Caleb Cushing Papers, LC, Box 170; Donnavan, *Adventures in Mexico,* 100.

19. HQ Army, GO #115, April 23, 1847, *AGGO,* XLI½, 285; Vol. Div., Orders #7, April 24, 1847, *1VolBrig G & SO.* There is a large body of material dealing with the problems of governing Jalapa in the "Official Correspondence and Papers of the Ayuntamiento de Jalapa," ·YWA.

20. Scott to Wilson, April 23, 1847, Henry Wilson Papers, YWA; same to same, April 28, 1847, *AGLR'47,* S-279; Scott to Marcy, April 28, 1847, *H. Ex. Doc. 60, 30th Cong., 1st Sess.,* 944–46.

21. Mariano Salas, Proclamation, April 21, 1847, *H. Ex. Doc. 60, 30th Cong., 1st Sess.,* 951–52; *La Legislatura del Estado Libre y Soberano de México a los Habitantes del Mismo* (Toluca, 1847).

22. HQ Army, GO #127, April 29, 1847, *AGGO,* XLI½, 295; Oswandel, *Notes,* 152–53.

23. Quaife, *Diary of Polk,* II, 475, 480; Marcy to govs., April 19, 1847, *SWMA,* XXVII, 82–87; Marcy, Circular Letter April 19, 1847, *SWML,* Jones, Circular, April 21, 1847, *AGLS,* XXXIII, #556. The call was for a regiment each from Indiana, Ohio, and Illinois; a battalion each from Missouri, New Jersey, Louisiana, Alabama, and Georgia. Pennsylvania, Virginia, Maryland, the District of Columbia, Illinois, Arkansas, and Florida would each contribute one or two companies, seven of which would be mounted. In December the administration had asked for ten regiments of regulars and a lieutenant general to assume field command. The latter, a transparent sop to Thomas Hart Benton, was eliminated in the Senate before the bill became law on Feb. 11, 1847. Polk to Senate and House, Dec. 26, 1846, Richardson, *Messages and Papers,* V, 2358; 9 *U.S. Stat.,* 123–26. The new regiments were: 3d Dragoons, 9th through 16th Infantry, and the Regiment of Voltigeurs and Foot Riflemen. The law added a second major to each regiment and authorized some needed additional surgeons. It also created land bounties for the veterans of the war. Additional generals were created by a March 3, 1847 law. One major generalcy was refused by Sam Houston, Senator Thomas J. Rusk, and Benton, the latter because he could not be commander of the Mexico City force. It passed to Pillow. The other went to Quitman after William Cummings refused it. The new brigadier generals were Franklin Pierce,

George Cadwalader, and Enos D. Hopping. Caleb Cushing and Sterling Price filled the vacancies caused by the promotion of Pillow and Quitman. 9 *U.S. Stat.*, 184–86; Quaife, *Diary of Polk*, II, 406–7, 409–10, 412, 414, III, 28–29; Polk to Benton, March 9, to Pillow, April 18, 1847, *PLPB*, II, 247–48, 357–66; Benton to Polk, March 9, 1847, Polk Papers.

24. Jones to Scott, April 20, 1847, *AGLS*, XXIII, 555.

25. HQ Army, GOs #128, 135, 136, April 30, May 4, 5, 1847, *AGGO*, XLI½, 297–98, 304–6; F. deP. Castro to Alcalde de [Jalapa], May 8, 1847, Jalapa Correspondence, #34; H. L. Scott to Wilson, May 3, 1847, *H. Ex. Doc. 60, 30th Cong., 1st Sess.*, 955; Vol. Div., Orders #17, May 5, 1847, Furber, *12 Months Volunteer*, 613; Smith, *War with Mexico*, II, 64.

26. Scott to Quitman, to Worth, May 6, 1847, *H. Ex. Doc. 60, 30th Cong., 1st Sess.*, 957–58; Smith, *War with Mexico*, II, 65–66.

27. Scott, Proclamation, May 11, 1847, *H. Ex. Doc. 60, 30th Cong., 1st Sess.*, 986–74; Roa Bárcena, *Recuerdos*, II, 240–41; Smith, *War with Mexico*, II, 66–67, 337–38, 357.

28. Crawford, *The Eagle*, 97; Callcott, *Santa Anna*, 260; Ramsey, *Other Side*, 214–19; Vargas Rea (ed.), *Apuntes Históricos Sobre los Acontecimientos Notables de la Guerra entre México y los Estados Unidos del Norte* (México, 1945), 25.

29. Anderson to wife, May 8, 1847, Lawton, *Artillery Officer*, 162; Worth (signed by J. C. Pemberton) to H. L. Scott, May 15, 1847, *H. Ex. Doc. 60, 30th Cong., 1st Sess.*, 994–95; Claiborne, *Quitman*, I, 301; Smith, *War with Mexico*, II, 69–70; Wilcox, *Mexican War*, 308–9.

30. Worth to H. L. Scott, May 15, 1847, *loc. cit.* See Santa Anna's bitter attack on the Puebla authorities for surrendering without a fight in his *Mi Historia Militar y Política 1810-1847* (México, 1905), 69–70. Because of Scott's disappropriation of the conditions of the surrender, Worth demanded a court of inquiry. It found the terms "improvident and detrimental to the public service" as well as chiding Worth for a later order accusing the Mexicans of attempting to poison his troops.

31. Good descriptions of Puebla can be found in Fanny Calderón de la Barca, *Life in Mexico* (Garden City, 1970), 404–13; Anderson to wife, May 15, 1847, *loc. cit.*; Semmes, *Service Afloat and Ashore*, 237–79.

32. Jenkins, *War Between U.S. and Mexico*, 295; HQ Army, GO #162, May 30, 1847, *AGGO*, XLI½, 337–38; Scott to Quitman, May 31, to Childs, June 3, 1847, *H. Ex. Doc. 60, 30th Cong., 1st Sess.*, 997–98, 1002–3; Collins, "Journal," 67–68. The forces at Jalapa and Puebla, especially, were subjected to a concerted effort to induce desertions. As many as 200–300 men may have deserted at the former. Ramírez, *Mexico During the War*, 127; Ballentine, *English Soldier*, 144.

33. Marcy to Scott, April 30, July 19, 1847, *H. Ex. Doc. 60, 30th Cong., 1st Sess.*, 922–23, 1002–4. Among those reinforcements were six companies of marines scraped up from navy yard and other guard detachments. Mason to President, May 13, 1847, *ELB*, V, 376; Mason to Henderson, May 14, 1847, *MCO*, V, 460–61; Henderson to Watson, *CMCLB*, 207–8; HQMC, Orders, May 21, 28, 1847, *HQMCO*, 491–92, G. D. to A. C. Twiggs, June 2, 1847, Twiggs Papers.

34. Marcy to Polk, June 26, 1847, Polk Papers; Quaife, *Diary of Polk*, III, 84, 89; Marcy to Taylor, July 15, to Scott, July 19, 1847, *H. Ex. Doc. 56, 30th Cong., 1st Sess.*, 192–94, 383–84; Marcy to Hays, July 16, 1847, *SWMA*, XXVII, 456.

35. Quaife, *Diary of Polk*, III, 113; Polk to Butler, Aug. 7, 1847, *PLPB*, IV, 73–83.

36. Quaife, *Diary of Polk*, III, 123–29, 131–35, 137, 140–141; A. K. Parris to Mason, Aug. 19, Walker to Young (telegram), Aug. 23, Young to President, Aug. 26, 27, 1847, all in Polk Papers; Leonard D. White, *Jacksonians* (New York, 1954), 61–62.

37. Cadwalader to AG, June 1, 1847, *AGLR'47*, C–529; McIntosh to H. L. Scott, July 9, 1847, with enclosures, Cadwalader to H. L. Scott, July 12, 1847, with enclosures, all in *S. Ex. Doc. 1, 30th Cong., 1st Sess.*, A4-24; Oswandel, *Notes*, 189–92; Collins, "Journal," 68–69; Jenkins, *War Between U.S. and Mexico*, 299–302; Smith, *War with Mexico*, II, 76–77.

38. Pillow's Div., SO #2, June 16, 1847, Wilson Papers; Hitchcock, *50 Years*, 265; Jenkins, *War Between U.S. and Mexico*, 302; Smith, *War with Mexico*, II, 77.

39. Franklin Pierce, Diary, 3–60 (photostat), M. L. Bonham to A. Wood, July 27, 1847, all in Franklin Pierce Papers, L.C.; Pierce to brother, Aug. 24, 1847, McWhinney, *To Mexico with Scott and Taylor*, 184; Pierce to Scott, Aug. 1, 1847, *S. Ex. Doc. 1, 30th Cong., 1st Sess.*, A25; Pierce's Brig., GO #5, 12, July 7, 12, 1847, Brig. Gen. Franklin Pierce, Order Book, RG-94, N.A.; Roy Franklin Nichols, *Franklin Pierce: Young Hickory of the Granite Hills* (Philadelphia, 1931), 152–59; Nathaniel Hawthorne, *Life of Franklin Pierce* (Boston, 1852), 73–92.

40. P. F. Smith to H. L. Scott, Aug. 2, 1847, *S. Ex. Doc. 1, 30th Cong., 1st Sess.*, A25-6. Brackett, *Cavalry*, 90; Smith, *War with Mexico*, II, 427. In Sept. 1848 Ruff complained that his report of the action had not been published and that his name had been kept off the list of brevets by Col Harney. This he attributed to his having denounced Harney's keeping of "that vicious & notoriously abandoned prostitute Mrs. Shepard [and] using the public ambulances & wagons for the transportation of her body & baggage." Ruff to Smith, Sept. 11, 12, 1848, C. F. Ruff Papers, MoHS. Similar but less successful efforts to break up nearby guerrilla bands were tried at Tampico. Guerrilla attacks also threatened the naval-controlled ports. Somewhat different was Col. Louis De Russey's expedition in July from Tampico in an effort to gain the release of American prisoners held at Huajutla. The American force was ambushed at the Rio Calabasa and badly mauled, escaping to Panuco only with difficulty. Tampico, SO #27, 32, 41, 45, June 11, 17, July 5, 15, 1847, Tampico Dept., Order 1847–48, 83–84, 90–91, RG 94, N.A.; De Russey to Gates, July 18, Gates to H. L. Scott, July 21, 1847, *AGLR'47*, G-297; Perry to Mason, July 15, Aug. 16, 1847, *HSL*; Scott, *Encarnación Prisoners*, 70; *Rough and Ready Annual*, 239–44.

41. John Hammond Moore (ed.), "Private Johnson Fights the Mexicans, 1847–1848," *South Carolina Historical Magazine*, LXVII (Oct. 1966), 217. HQ Army, COs #198, 206, July 2, 9, 1847, *AGGO*, XLI½, 407, 413; Hitchcock, *50 Years*, 259, 263–65. Before approving the arrangement, Scott secured the concurrence of Generals Quitman, Twiggs, and Smith.

42. HQ Army, GOs #211, 246, July 12, Aug. 5, 1847, *AGGO*, XLI½, 417–18, 457–58.

43. Smith, *War with Mexico*, II, 92–95.

15: On to Mexico City

WHILE WINFIELD SCOTT's soldiers marched and fought their way from the sea to the environs of Mexico City, diplomats sought to end the hostilities. The efforts to arrange negotiations faced nearly insurmountable obstacles because Mexico lacked sufficient political stability to enter into serious and realistic negotiations. That flaw had negated Polk's efforts to force talks before the war. The hope that Santa Anna might provide such a stable and reasonable government likewise lay behind the clandestine discussions with him in July and the midsummer attempt to reopen discussions.

Mexico scarcely had a national government during the summer of 1846. President Paredes neither developed an extensive following nor succeeded in eliminating his enemies. By early August he had lost all support and forfeited the titular leadership of the nation to General Mariano Salas, the commander of the Mexico City garrison.[1]

Santa Anna returned from Cuba on August 14.[2] He quickly discovered, if he had really entertained any doubts, that the temper of the Mexican populace precluded any attempt to reach a settlement with the United States. On August 31, although not yet formally a member of the government, he rejected American proposals for reopening negotiations, thus indicating a shift to support of the war.[3] In early September he assumed command of the Mexican Army although he had insufficient political support to take full control of the government. When later in the month he left to take command of the army gathering at San Luis Potosí, his agents intrigued in vain to complete the takeover of the government.

The unstable political situation was further complicated by the results of the congressional elections. The new legislature contained a large number of poorly educated but highly motivated radicals ill-equipped to deal with the problems facing the country. The radicals were not even able to select one candidate for president. Under the prodding of Gómez Farías's *puros* they supported Santa Anna for president because the Constitution prevented him from serving as both the chief of state and chief military officer. They assumed correctly that given the choice he would take the field and leave the government to Gómez Farías as vice president. Although strongly opposed, the two men were elected on December 6.

While Santa Anna prepared the San Luis Potosí force for the Buena Vista campaign, Gómez Farías attempted to levy forced loans on the Church. He not only failed in this attempt, but the effort led to a church-supported uprising in Mexico City during March. To some extent that revolt was fomented by an American agent, Moses Y. Beach, editor and proprietor of the New York *Sun* and a man with close contacts with the American Catholic leadership. He came to Mexico City in January 1847 on a private business trip and as an agent of Secretary of State James Buchanan to investigate the possibilities of a settlement.[4] The revolt provided the excuse Santa Anna needed to return to Mexico City, overturn Gómez Farías, and resume the mantle of the chief of state. After arranging for a two-million-peso loan from the church and the election of an interim president, Pedro María Anaya, to head the government while he was in the field, Santa Anna left Mexico City April 2 to engage Scott.

After Cerro Gordo, the Mexican Congress complicated the political situation even more. It enacted legislation which guaranteed that nothing would be done to end the fighting by forbidding any cession of territory or peace talks without prior consent of Congress. Moreover, the law declared that anyone who dealt with the Americans was a traitor and any agreement reached with them automatically void.[5]

In mid-May Anaya declared Mexico City in a state of siege and named Santa Anna as the commanding general of the Federal District, which most people, including Anaya, thought would prevent his assuming political control of the government. Santa Anna considered resigning the presidency while retaining command of the army but was convinced by some of his advisers to change his mind. On May

18 he occupied the capital and two days later announced his return as chief of state. Although he issued a rather halfhearted manifesto calling for unity,[6] the assumption of the presidency cost him both popular support and the devotion of the army. Yet, for a variety of reasons, he successfully banished most of his opponents from the city, and certainly in his own heart believed that he alone could prevent the utter humiliation of his country. There was more reality than one might expect in that conclusion, for he was in truth the government of Mexico.

Polk paralleled Santa Anna's return to power with new peace moves. At the turn of the year, while considering Senator Thomas Hart Benton for commander of the newly authorized Veracruz expedition, Polk discussed the advisability of having a three-man peace commission accompany the army. When Benton refused to accept John Slidell as a commissioner, the plan came to naught. Buchanan added a further complication when he told the President that he would like to be a commissioner.[7]

In mid-January Colonel Alexander J. Atocha approached Buchanan and Benton with information that he claimed proved Santa Anna still desired peace. Atocha indicated that Santa Anna would accept the Rio Grande boundary if the area north to the Nueces remained an unsettled buffer zone and he would also sell California for fifteen to twenty million dollars. After consulting with the cabinet and with Benton, Polk made a counterproposal: cession of New Mexico and California; the Rio Grande boundary without a buffer zone; and a continuation of the blockade until a treaty was reached. Atocha personally carried the offer to Mexico.[8]

Foreign Minister J. M. Ortiz Monasterio rejected the offer on February 22. No commissioners could meet, he wrote, until the Americans promised to evacuate all Mexican territory and lift their blockade. A more devastating response to the administration's peace moves is hard to imagine.[9] After Atocha returned to Washington on March 20 with the letter, Polk finally concluded that nothing short of a smashing military victory could bring the Mexicans to the negotiation table. He was to learn, as others before and since have done, that battlefield success does not always ensure serious negotiations.

In his first response Polk ordered duties applied to goods entering the American-held portions of Mexico.[10] The taxes, imposed by Polk unilaterally as Commander in Chief of the occupying army, largely reflected his hope that the Mexican civilian populace would find them so onerous that they would force the Mexican government to seek peace. Since the greatest weight of the impost fell on those under American rather than Mexican control, it is difficult to follow his logic.

When the news of the fall of Veracruz reached Washington on April 10, Polk concluded that conditions now warranted sending a commissioner to accompany Scott's army. That arrangement would place a negotiator on the scene when the Mexicans decided to talk. The cabinet agreed in principle but stumbled over the choice of the diplomat. Buchanan solved the dilemma by suggesting the Chief Clerk of the State Department, Nicholas P. Trist, an experienced diplomat who spoke fluent Spanish. Since the glory of negotiating the treaty had to be reserved for a major Democratic politician, Trist would carry a draft treaty which he could sign only if the Mexicans accepted it virtually unchanged. If extended negotiations became necessary, Buchanan would take over the discussions.

Although a visit by Tom Thumb interrupted the cabinet discussions of the draft treaty on April 13, it was ready late that day. The principal provisions called for a Rio Grande boundary, the acquisition of New Mexico and the two Californias, and the securing of the right of transit across the isthmus of Tehuantepec. For that settlement Trist was authorized to pay up to $30 million. Polk considered the price too high but was willing to pay it if necessary to acquire the territory. Since the Rio Grande boundary was considered already settled the only mandatory territorial provisions were the securing of Upper California and New Mexico. The discussions, however, did indicate the continuing divergence of opinion in the cabinet.[11]

During the fifteenth Trist received that host of papers which a diplomat in his situation needed: letters to the Mexican Foreign Minister announcing his appointment and presence with Scott's army; the draft treaty; a formal commission from the President and a letter of credence from the Secretary of State; and authority to draw on the Treasury for $3 million on the ratification of the treaty.[12]

Marcy notified Scott that "Mr. Trist is clothed with such diplomatic power as will authorize him to enter into agreements with the government of Mexico for the suspension of hostilities." Moreover, if Trist asked for a suspension of hostilities in writing, Scott should "regard such notice as a direction from the President to suspend them until further notice from this department." The army, however, was not to withdraw from any position under such an agreement unless necessary for the health of the troops. Marcy also directed him to send notice of Trist's arrival and an open copy of the dispatch to the Mexican government and to the Mexican military commander. Secretary of the Navy John Y. Mason sent similar instructions to Commodore Matthew C. Perry.[13]

Trist left Washington April 16 and reached Veracruz on May 6. He promptly forwarded Buchanan's message to the Mexican Foreign Minister and Marcy's instructions to Scott. Two days later Trist departed for Jalapa. With his usual suicidal ability to discover a slight whether intended or not, Scott interpreted the authority for Trist to arrange a cessation of hostilities as a plot by Marcy "to degrade me, by requiring that the commander of this army shall defer to . . . the chief clerk of the Department of State [on] the question of continuing or discontinuing hostilities." That, Scott exploded, was a military decision which belonged to him unless Trist was "clothed with military rank over me."[14] Marcy's instructions were poorly written and misconstrued. The message he meant to convey was that if Trist negotiated an armistice with the Mexicans which was acceptable militarily to Scott, the General should implement it at once without referral to Washington. Under the circumstances most commanders would have so interpreted the directive, but Scott's distrust of the administration and its motives was now so great that he automatically assumed evil intent. Trist's response to Scott's outburst was restrained. He denied that Marcy's orders contained any extraordinary provisions, noting Commodore Perry concurred in Trist's interpretation.

After Trist reached Jalapa on May 14 the relations between the General and the diplomat worsened, if that was possible. Neither would take the first step to arrange a meeting, while Scott trumpeted that if Trist sent him a letter, "It is not probable that I shall find leisure to read [it], much less give a rejoinder." On May 20 Trist did ask for the return of Buchanan's letter to the Mexican Foreign Minister and added a stinging rebuke to Scott for his failure to forward it. Scott ignored Trist's May 9 and 20 letters until the evening of the twenty-second. Then he had a member of his staff open and read them: "My first impulse was to return the farrago of insolence and arrogance to the author; but on reflection I have determined to preserve the letters as a choice specimen of diplomatic literature and manners." Scott then threatened the diplomat: "If you dare to use the style of orders or instructions again, or indulge yourself in a single discourteous phrase, I shall throw back the communication with the contempt & scorn which you merit at my hands."[15]

Trist accompanied the army to Puebla, staying with Persifor Smith.

Scott, meanwhile, brooded about what he viewed as a series of studied insults culminating in the sending of a second-rank bureaucrat with powers to supercede him. Adding to his black mood was the apparent diversion of his reinforcements and the clash with his long-time friend General Worth over the terms of surrender at Puebla. On June 4 Scott again proved that he was his own worst enemy by writing to Marcy:

> Considering the many cruel disappointments and mortifications I have been made to feel since I left Washington, or the total want of support and sympathy on the part of the War Department which I have so long experienced, I beg to be recalled.[16]

On June 6 Trist decided to go outside his officially prescribed channels and asked British Minister Charles Bankhead to forward his letters to the Mexican government. Bankhead, who ardently desired a settlement immediately, dispatched Secretary of the Legation Edward Thornton to fetch the communications. Thornton reached Puebla on June 10. He reported that Foreign Minister Manuel Baranda, who favored negotiations, had resigned because of the pressure from the war party. Others, Thornton appears to have hinted, would not be so weak-willed, particularly if the $3 million was distributed among the proper persons. Many Mexicans, he reported, assumed that to be the purpose of the money.[17]

Bankhead passed the messages to new Foreign Minister Domingo Ibarra, who insisted that any decision to negotiate had to originate in Congress. This bargaining move was recognized for what it was, since Santa Anna called Congress into special session to consider the proposal. Thornton, British Consul Edward Mackintosh, and Turnbull, an English friend of Santa Anna, visited Puebla on June 24. Turnbull confided that Santa Anna was willing to negotiate but needed time to win support. Therefore he proposed the Americans remain at Puebla but transfer $10,000 at once and $1 million on the conclusion of the treaty. Trist, who had been scandalized at the earlier bribery hint, thought the proposal worth considering. He discussed it with Pillow and Persifor Smith, both of whom favored it. The question of bribes was a delicate one. It ran counter to the traditional American practice but was a normal one in Mexico. The British merchants and diplomats in the capital believed unshakably that peace could come no other way. It is scarcely surprising, therefore, that the idea loomed large and attractive to Trist and other Americans.

After his meeting with the British agents, Trist informed Scott that he was ready to open negotiations, and for the first time sent the General a copy of his commission. Scott responded by forwarding a letter which had reached him from Thornton, also suggesting bribery. Trist readily accepted the proposal.[18]

At this point Trist became ill. On the sixth of July, Scott sent him a box of guava marmalade. From that kind gesture a very close working relationship developed between the two men.[19] On the fifteenth Scott and Trist discussed the bribery scheme and the General offered to make the initial payment from his secret-service funds. The diplomat then formally asked for the money, since it was "the only way in which the indefinite protraction of this war can possibly be prevented." Scott, apparently less impressed with the probability of success or perhaps more concerned about the repercussions when the payments became known, called an informal council of his generals to secure their approval.

The council met on July 17 with Generals Quitman, Pillow, Shields, Twiggs, and Cadwalader present. Scott posed two questions. The first was the purely military one of whether to await the reinforcements enroute under General Franklin Pierce before advancing. All agreed to wait. The second was whether to pay the bribe. Pillow, who spoke first, strongly supported the scheme. Twiggs considered the act to be a political one and refused to comment. Shields, Quitman, and Cadwalader all demurred mildly. Scott therefore advanced $10,000 from his secret-service funds later that day and agreed to provide $1 million upon the signing of the peace treaty. Who the recipients, primary or secondary, were is not certain. Pillow later implied that the funds were transmitted through Thornton and Mackintosh, which appears reasonable, although Justin Smith believes it was Miguel Arroyo, later secretary to the Mexican peace commission. Whether the money went to Santa Anna, as was commonly believed, or eased other consciences is clouded in obscurity.[20]

When the Mexican Congress met on July 13 it refused to authorize discussions, which may well have been what Santa Anna intended. This put an end to the bribery project. Indeed the whole bribery scheme may have been just an effort on Santa Anna's part to bilk the gullible Americans of money. Even Thornton believed that the Americans must now resume their advance, although he still insisted that Santa Anna's desire for peace was genuine. There is apparently irrefutable evidence that the Mexican leader was in clandestine communication with the Americans through one or more intermediaries. His position after Congress scattered in mid-July, insofar as it can be deduced, was that he should negotiate a peace and use the money it produced to smooth any ruffled feelings. On the other hand, he evidently believed that he could not make such a peace without at least appearing to defend the nation's capital.

Trist forwarded to Washington on July 23 the comments of one of his sources within Mexico City, possibly Thornton, that "Santa Anna is afraid to make peace now and cannot. M[ackintosh] can do nothing with him, even with the aid he possesses from you [Trist]. S. A. now says secretly, that he shall allow your army to approach this city, even as far as the Peñon, and then endeavour to make peace." Trist later assured Buchanan on the basis of reports from his British contacts that the Army would not have to enter Mexico City in order to secure a peace. An armistice would come, he predicted, after the first action before the Mexican capital. As late as August 14, after Scott's forces had reached the Mexico City defenses, Trist reported "the business is rapidly maturing."[21] However, such was not to be the case.

Santa Anna's conception of any situation seldom remained stable. That included his peace negotiations. On July 27 he called a council of his generals, apparently to induce them to join in his decision to send Baranda and ex-President Manuel Gómez Pedraza to negotiate peace. Unfortunately for the cause of peace the unscrupulous opportunist and dedicated enemy of Santa Anna, Major General Gabriel Valencia, arrived that day at Guadalupe Hidalgo with the 4,000 soldiers of the Army of the North. He took an unyielding and vocal stand against negotiations while waiting like a jackal for Santa Anna's first misstep. Valencia's opposition and Scott's prolonged halt at Puebla allowed the council to procrastinate. As the time passed, Santa Anna reacted to the pressures from the war party and to his own returning self-confidence by exiling the thought of negotiations further and further from his mind.[22]

As one might expect, Washington's reaction to the Trist-Scott squabble was one of mystification. The President considered Scott's letters "highly exceptionable" and "not only insubordinate, but insulting to Mr. Trist and the Government." He considered, but rejected, removing Scott as having "not only no sympathies with the Government, but [being] hostile to my administration." Both Buchanan's and Marcy's responses were carefully considered by the President and the other cabinet members. The former was much the milder, merely chiding Trist for the tone of his letters. Marcy, in a series of good papers, gently took the General to task and attempted to correct his warped thinking. When the cabinet reconsidered the problem on July 9 it decided not to recall either man, although the President, returning to his initial unhappiness, favored so doing.[23]

During July 13 Buchanan sent Trist a significant modification of his instructions. The boundary line could run along the 32d parallel west from the Rio Grande to a point due south of the southwest corner of New Mexico. From there if he could not secure Baja California, Trist could draw the line either due west from the southwest corner of New Mexico or along the 32d parallel to the Pacific. El Paso was added to the list of highly desirable acquisitions but not made a *sine qua non*. The directive stressed the importance of the Gila River valley as a potential railroad route foreshadowing the later railway-induced border changes. These instructions had an unusual subsequent history. They, along with a letter from Marcy insisting that Scott cooperate with Trist, were entrusted to Colonel Lewis D. Wilson of the 12th Infantry. He unfortunately died of fever at Veracruz on August 12 and the dispatches were among some mail subsequently seized by guerrillas. It was sent to Mexico City where Foreign Minister Francisco Pacheco forwarded it to Trist on September 9. It was this Mexican knowledge that Baja California was not a *sine qua non* which ensured that the peninsula remain Mexican.[24]

An interesting commentary on the administration's view of the likelihood of peace appears in Secretary of the Navy John Y. Mason's August 4 order for Commodore Matthew C. Perry to delay any further occupation of Mexican ports.[25] If nothing else, it demonstrated how little information the administration had of events in Mexico and its consequent lack of understanding of the problems faced by its agents on the scene.

In April 1847, after Santa Anna departed for the front, Mexico City's military and political leaders conferred over the defense of Mexico City. The discussions discovered unity only in opposition to any serious resistance to an American attack, since the conferees feared the damage of the accompanying bombardment. Except for a few posts capable only of turning a cavalry raid, few defenses were constructed.[26] When he took control of the city in mid-May, Santa Anna faced not only the chronic shortage of money but one also in troops and artillery. Moreover, many of his subordinates were ineffectual and the troops green.

Mexico City sits in the center of a shallow basin about thirty-two by forty-six miles. The best places to construct defensive positions, therefore, were along the rim of the basin and the roads leading into it. Fortifications there would protect the city from any stray American shells and render unnecessary any flooding of the low-lying meadows which surrounded the city. Unfortunately, this strategy called for more men than Santa Anna had. Since the basin was a slowly drying lake bed, its floor contained not only six lakes but extensive marshes and low-lying fields which were crossed by elevated roads and causeways.[27] Santa Anna counted on the wetlands to limit the American routes of advance to those he could defend. While the invaders were bogged down in the mud and ooze, he intended that Major General Juan Álvarez with the cavalry would cut Scott's communications with Puebla and harass the American rear. Since most of the Mexican military experts expected the main American effort would be directed against El Peñon, Santa Anna established his headquarters there. Valencia's 7,000-man Army of the North took a position to the south of El Peñon where it would be on the American flank. General Nicholas Bravo commanded the defenses at the second most likely target, Mexicalzingo.[28]

Even if the troops available were too few and too green, even if the artillery was too infrequent and too poorly served, and even if the Mexican leadership was divided and too often inept, the natural strength of the defenses of the city, rising as it did out of the lush greenery of the surrounding wetlands, was great. The only approaches were along the raised roadways commanded by well-placed defenses. No army could hope to seize Mexico City without a hard fight so long as the defenders retained the will to resist.

The topography restricted the Americans to four possible routes of advance from their position at Ayotla, twenty-five miles east of the capital:

1. through Texcoco toward the north and northwest parts of the city;

2. the road along the north shore of Lake Chalco and the south shore of Lake Texcoco via El Peñon;

3. the difficult road through Mexicalzingo;

4. along the south shores of Lakes Chalco and Zochimilco to the village of San Agustín.

Scott had his engineers check the routes. Captains Robert E. Lee, James L. Mason, and Lieutenant Isaac I. Stevens examined the El Peñon route. Lee reported: "I saw nothing that would render an assault impracticable." Nevertheless, his report confirmed that seizing the position would be extremely costly, since the only approach to

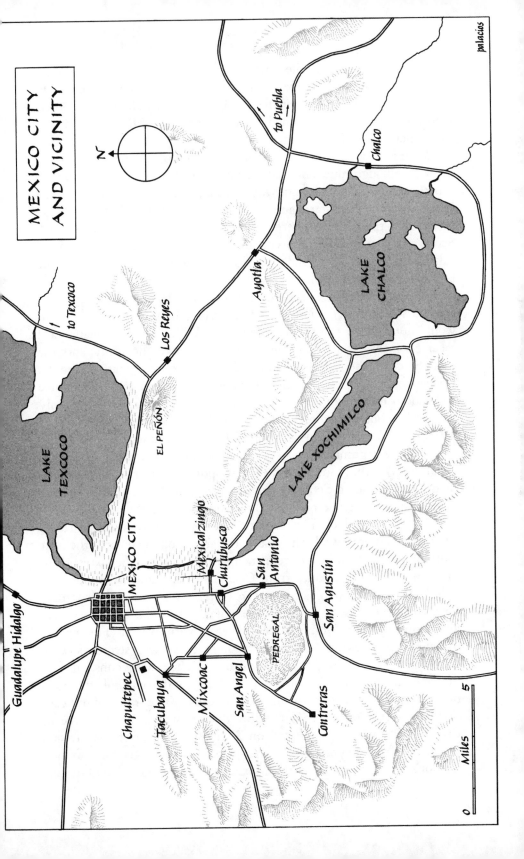

MEXICO CITY
AND VICINITY

N

to Texcoco

LAKE
TEXCOCO

Guadalupe Hidalgo

MEXICO CITY

Chapultepec

Tacubaya

Mixcoac

San Angel

PEDREGAL

Contreras

San Agustín

San
Antonio

Churubusco

Mexicalzingo

EL PEÑÓN

Los Reyes

Ayotla

LAKE XOCHIMILCO

LAKE
CHALCO

Chalco

to Puebla

palacios

Miles

0   5

the fortress was over a mile-long causeway which carried the Puebla road across a wet marsh along the south shore of Lake Texcoco. El Peñon itself was a 450-foot-high hill, 1,000 yards long at its base, whose fortifications contained thirty pieces of artillery and nearly 7,000 men under Santa Anna himself.

The engineers also reported that the guns atop Peñon commanded the Mexicalzingo route and that the village itself was heavily defended. More careful reconnaissances by Mason, Stevens, and Lieutenants Pierre G. T. Beauregard and George B. McClellan, however, suggested that the defenses were actually weaker than at first believed. Scott, therefore, ordered preparations for an assault against Mexicalzingo, covered by a feint toward El Peñon if the road south of the lakes proved impractical.

Scott's initial choice, the route south of Chalco, had been sidetracked when information gained at Ayotla indicated that the road would not support the artillery and train. When Lee and Beauregard received information that the road would take the army and the train, Scott on the thirteenth directed Worth to investigate the route. Brevet Colonel James Duncan volunteered to make the reconnaissance and did so the following day. He reported: "The road is not only practicable, but as a whole, excellent, and . . . not easily obstructed or defended." Worth quickly submitted Duncan's findings to Scott with an elaborate argument for its adoption. This led to later erroneous claims by Worth, Duncan, and their supporters that it was the latter's report which caused Scott to shift the direction of his attack.[29]

Scott on August 15 ordered the army to move toward the south side of Lake Chalco. The cavalry and Worth's division marched late that afternoon, while the rest of the army followed early the next morning. Twiggs's division remained at Ayotla until the sixteenth to mask the move. The route from Chalco to San Agustín, about nine miles south of Mexico City on the Cuernavaca or Acapulco road, covered approximately twenty-five miles. The road was very wet and muddy and in some places covered with water. The efforts expended in working the trains through these wet stretches were incalculable. Moreover, the Americans marched with constant fear of harassment, since the bold and broken land south of the road offered excellent cover for lurking cavalry. The only significant skirmish occurred on the sixteenth. Álvarez, with a mixed force of cavalry and infantry, appeared on Twiggs's flank after his division withdrew from Ayotla, but a few rounds from Captain Francis Taylor's battery drove off the Mexicans. Álvarez concluded at that point that the difficulties in pursuing the Americans were too great, and he rode off to Mexico City.[30]

At San Agustín the main road ran generally northward through San Antonio and Churubusco to the San Antonio Garita, or gate of the capital. At San Antonio, however, a secondary road ran westward to Coyoacán and Tacubaya. The latter was Scott's next objective. On the eighteenth the engineers were out as usual. Mason, Stevens, and Lieutenant Zealous B. Tower investigated the San Antonio defenses with an escort from Worth's division. Despite Mexican shelling, the first round of which killed Captain Seth Thornton of the escort, the engineers completed their reconnaissance. They found the defenses extremely strong and impossible to turn except by moving across the Pedregal, a lava field described by one soldier as "a heap of Rocks allmost [*sic*] impassable for infantry and totally so for Artillery and Cavalry."[31] Meanwhile, Captain Lee and Lieutenant Beauregard searched the western portion of the lava field for crossing. From the hill of Zacatepec they could see Mexican defenses along the western edge of the Pedregal near the farm of Padierna.[32] Then their escort clashed with Mexican pickets to prove that a path across the lava field existed. The Mexicans were members of Valencia's Army of the North, which had moved to San Angel[33] on the northwest corner of the Pedregal during the preceding day.[34]

Valencia's initial reaction to the appearance of the Americans was to propose a retreat into the city. Santa Anna forbade this but agreed the troops could withdraw to Tacubaya if the Americans advanced. By the morning of the eighteenth, when the American engineers began their study of the Pedregal, Valencia had changed his mind. Instead of retiring he decided to advance about four miles along the road that skirted the lava field from San Angel to the village of Contreras. About two thirds of the way to Contreras a commanding promontory overlooked the road and the Padierna farm. It was a strong position but not an impregnable one as Valencia believed. The road ran along the eastern face of the hill, below which a small stream had cut a nearly impassable ravine that extended almost to the Pedregal. The Padierna buildings huddled together on the far slope.

During the evening of August 18 Santa Anna ordered Valencia to fall back to the main position between San Angel and San Antonio. That location, astride either of the possible American routes of advance, was well chosen. Valencia viewed matters differently, for if he fought a successful battle there Santa Anna would receive the credit. Moreover, the withdrawal of the American scouts seemed the preview of a victory which would enhance him, not Santa Anna. Valencia retorted to Santa Anna's order that neither patriotism nor his "conscience as a military man" permitted withdrawal. Santa Anna, who wished to avoid a showdown on the eve of battle, merely noted his lack of approval and placed responsibility for the consequences on Valencia.

Scott planned to open a road across the Pedregal which would allow the siege train to move into positions from which to enfilade the San Antonio defenses. The actual construction would be by men from Pillow's division, who would be supported in turn by Twiggs's units. Worth's division would continue to threaten San Antonio, while Quitman's drew the assignment of protecting the train and depot at San Agustín.

Captain Lee superintended some 500 men during the morning of the nineteenth as they carved a passage through the lava. About noon they met the first Mexican pickets. Pillow sent Major William W. Loring with a pair of companies of the Rifle Regiment to clear the ground. They did so with ease and occupied Padierna. Within an hour, however, the work on the road ceased as the men came under fire from some of Valencia's twenty-two pieces of artillery. Pillow, the senior officer on the field, concluded that further work would have to wait the silencing of the guns.

Pillow called up his artillery, Captain John B. Magruder's field battery, Lieutenant Franklin D. Callender's mountain howitzers, and Lieutenant Jesse L. Reno's rockets. He placed them near the western edge of the lava, about 1,000 yards from Valencia's position. The Mexican, when told that the American artillerymen were moving their pieces across the Pedregal, roared with laughter and disbelief: "No! No! You're dreaming, man. The birds couldn't cross that Pedregal." He soon learned the contrary as shells began exploding nearby, but the American pieces were both too light and too few to inflict much damage. The Mexican counterbattery fire soon forced the American gunners to pull back their guns. The artillery, however, did hold the Mexicans' attention while the infantry worked forward on the American right. On the American left Colonel Trueman B. Ransom, with the 9th Infantry and a battalion of the 12th under Lieutenant Colonel Milledge L. Bonham, worked across the ravine to within 200 yards of Valencia's camp and remained there until after nightfall. Their success went unnoticed by the American commanders and was not exploited.

Early in the afternoon Pillow sent Brevet Brigadier General Bennet Riley's brigade from Twiggs's division to seize the hamlet of San Gerónimo and cut Valencia's retreat route. Pillow seems to have envisioned a plan which called for Persifor Smith's brigade to strike at Valencia's front while Riley turned his left. General Cadwalader's regiments would support Riley while those of General Pierce's brigade assisted Smith. Upon sighting some Mexicans marching toward Padierna, Pillow committed his reserves, the 15th Infantry (Colonel G. W. Morgan) to strengthen Cadwalader. Riley's men struggled through the lava field, dropped down the sides of the ravine, forded the stream, crossed the road, and marched up a small valley north and west of Valencia's camp to San Gerónimo. Enroute they beat off a weak attack by some cavalry under General Anastasio Torrejón. Cadwalader's men followed a generally similar route shortly afterward. As they came out on the road they were approached by part of Santa Anna's force which was driven back by a volley from three companies of the 11th infantry. When he learned of the start of the action, Scott sent General Shields's brigade from San Agustín to Pillow who in turn sent it to follow Cadwalader.

Meanwhile, Persifor Smith concluded that his men could not cross the ravine near Valencia's camp. Smith informed Pillow that unless otherwise directed he would move to his right in hopes of finding a crossing which would permit turning the Mexican position. Leaving his artillery and a few infantry to maintain the demonstration before Valencia's camp, Smith moved the bulk of his brigade to the right. Like Riley's and Cadwalader's, this force came down from the Pedregal near the Rancho Ansaldo. There they linked up with the others. Although not by design, the Americans had turned Valencia's position and had three brigades at his rear, and a fourth on the way.

Scott, who had neither planned nor expected a battle that day, left his headquarters at San Agustín as soon as he learned of the fighting and reached the battlefield shortly before 4:00 P.M. After a briefing by Pillow, he approved the dispositions already made. The fighting was a magnet which also attracted the Mexican commander in chief. Valencia had exultantly informed Santa Anna that the battle which he had planned had begun. Santa Anna immediately hurried Brigadier General Francisco Pérez's 3,000-man brigade from Coyoacán as reinforcements and then followed with two additional regiments and five guns. Overtaking Pérez, Santa Anna reincorporated that brigade. These were the troops which Pillow had sighted. Sometime before 5:00 P.M. Santa Anna posted his men on the heights before San Angel, having decided not to reinforce Valencia because a move down the road would expose his men to Smith's flanking fire. Even if Santa Anna feared to advance to his subordinate's aid, his mere presence served to cut off the three American brigades around San Gerónimo. Had he wished to exploit the situation, Santa Anna could have crushed a major portion of Scott's army between two appreciably larger forces. But the Mexican Army lacked both the unity of command and the will to achieve such a success.

Smith well understood the precarious position in which he found himself and planned to attack Santa Anna's force, but darkness fell before he could complete his preparations. Night brought a heavy, cold rain. Santa Anna pulled his men back into the shelter of the houses at San Angel and ordered Valencia to spike his cannon and take advantage of the darkness to slip past the Americans. Valencia "scorned and disobeyed" the order because he had convinced himself that the Americans were beaten. All that was needed, he haughtily informed Santa Anna, was to mop up the remnants in the morning.

While Valencia congratulated himself on his imagined victory, Lieutenant Tower explored a ravine which ran southwest from San Gerónimo. He discovered that it offered a very difficult but usable route to the rear of Valencia's camp. Smith, who had assumed command of the three brigades, recognized that it permitted precisely the quick and decisive attack which was imperative if he was to salvage his position. Therefore he ordered an attack at daylight. Lee volunteered to carry word of the decision to Scott so that a diversion might be made by the troops remaining on the Pedregal. With only lightning flashes to illuminate the ground, the engineer picked his way among the dark boulders, unseen fissures and chasms, and featureless terrain of the lava field. It was as Scott afterward wrote: "the greatest feat of physical and moral courage performed by any individual" during the campaign.

At about eight o'clock in the evening Lee reached the foot of the Pedregal where he discovered General Shields's brigade. He directed the reinforcements to Smith's location and continued on to Zacatepec but found it deserted. At about 11:00 P.M. he reached Scott's headquarters at San Agustín. There he reported that Smith would begin his move at 3:00 A.M. and relayed the request for a diversion. Shortly afterward Pillow and Twiggs arrived, having failed to negotiate the Pedregal themselves. Scott ordered Twiggs to make a diversion at five o'clock with what troops he could collect. Lee, making his third crossing of the Pedregal that day, accompanied Twiggs. Scott ordered

Worth to send one of his brigades to support the attack while Harney's cavalry relieved Quitman's brigade at San Agustín to permit it to join the fight.

Shields's reinforcements brought Smith's strength up to about 4,000 men. Although he ranked Persifor Smith, Shields had the good sense not to complicate further a complex situation by claiming command. He left Smith free to execute his plan and remained at San Gerónimo with his brigade to cover the rear. The assault forces began their march at 3:00 A.M. Each man held onto the one in front so as not to get lost in the pitch blackness of that miserable night. Lieutenant Tower guided Riley's men, who were followed by Cadwalader's brigade, which Smith accompanied. The latter's brigade, temporarily under the orders of Major Justin Dimick, brought up the rear. The route was so rugged and slippery because of the rain that the column was not in position for its attack until well after daylight.

Twiggs and Lee found the troops, chiefly from Pierce's brigade,[35] which Smith had left behind bivouacked near Zacatepec hill. They roused the men shortly after 1:00 A.M. and had them in position before five o'clock. They began their demonstration on schedule. The men scampered down the steep incline into the stream and up the far side ignoring the Mexican fire. As intended, this attracted the defenders' attention. Scarcely had the Mexicans awakened to the threat to their front than they were hit in the rear by Smith's force which fired one volley and then charged with fixed bayonets. Within seventeen minutes the Mexicans broke and ran, with Valencia among the foremost. His second-in-command, ex-President Brigadier General José Mariano Salas, tried to rally the cavalry which refused his entreaties and dashed down the road to safety, trampling many of the infantry under hoof in the process. The fugitives had scarcely started their retreat before they had to run the gauntlet of fire from Shields's men.

As a result, Valencia's force ceased to exist as an organized unit. About 700 men died, 843 surrendered, including four generals, and the remainder scattered. Seven hundred pack mules, twenty-two pieces of artillery, and great quantities of small arms and ammunition fell into American hands. Among the artillery were the two 6-pounders lost by O'Brien's battery so heroically at Buena Vista. They were taken by Captain Simon Drum of the 4th Artillery, the parent organization of O'Brien's unit. The American losses of only sixty men killed and wounded illustrates the unequal nature of the fight.

During the night Santa Anna had called up Brigadier General Joaquín Rangel's reserve brigade preparatory to an attack to reopen communications with Valencia. At daylight the enlarged command set out for the positions which had been abandoned when the rains came. Even before reaching the heights beyond San Angel, they met the first panic-stricken residue of Valencia's force. Santa Anna vented his exasperation at his disobedient subordinate by striking about with his riding crop at the fleeing soldiers. He retired to San Angel but soon regained his composure and began taking steps to minimize the damage. He directed Rangel to guard the southwestern approaches to Mexico City with his brigade. He ordered Major General Nicolás Bravo at San Antonio and Brigadier General Antonio Gaona at Mexicalzingo to evacuate their positions, and Santa Anna led his immediate command back toward Churubusco where the San Antonio and Mexicalzingo roads joined.

In order to protect the withdrawal route of the San Antonio force, Santa Anna ordered Major General Manuel Rincón to hold the Franciscan Convent of San Mateo at Churubusco as long as possible and placed a regiment from General Pérez's brigade in the very strong *tête de pont*, or fortified bridgehead, on the south bank of the Churubusco River about 300 yards from the convent. Two other regiments took up positions along the riverbank, while the rest of Santa Anna's force formed a reserve along the highway north of the river. The convent had been partially fortified with earthworks containing seven guns. It was manned by a garrison of some 1,500 to 1,800 men from the Independencia and Bravo Battalions of the Mexico City National Guard, the San Patricio Battalion of foreigners, and a few other units.[36]

Scott left San Agustín before Smith's attack, crossed the Pedregal, and near San Angel met the victorious troops. He promptly took charge of Pillow's and Twiggs's divisions and turned them toward Coyoacán in order to flank the San Antonio position. Scott dared not send a force down the Tacubaya road even though that was now open, because to do so would leave Worth, Quitman, the artillery park, the supply train, and the hospital exposed to the 25,000 men reportedly at San Antonio.

Worth's orders were to turn the San Antonio position once he learned of Valencia's defeat. To assist, Scott sent Lee with an escort to reconnoiter the defenses. Later he sent Pillow with Cadwalader's brigade, but Worth did not wait for the assistance. At about eleven o'clock he sent Colonel Newman S. Clarke's brigade and Brevet Lieutenant Colonel Charles F. Smith's light battalion along a tortuous path across the Pedregal to cut the retreat route of the San Antonio defenders. While they picked their way across the lava field, Brevet Colonel John Garland's brigade, with Duncan's battery, took a safe position near San Antonio. The Mexicans could see Clarke's column but were powerless to halt it. After receiving the withdrawal order, the defenders spiked some of their guns and attempted to escape with the rest. Most of the troops were poorly trained militia unequal to the task of a fighting retreat, so when two companies of the 5th Infantry struck the column the Mexicans could not prevent a split. The advance portion, led by General Bravo, reached the Churubusco bridgehead safely but the rest scattered. When Garland realized that the troops before him were withdrawing, he quickly threw his troops forward to take the fortifications, seizing four guns and a general before linking up with Clarke.

Bravo's column was a mass of cavalry, infantry, artillery, wagons, mules, families, servants, refugees, and campfollowers bunched together with little order or organization. It churned the road, still wet from the evening's rain, into a quagmire which held tight to a pair of artillery pieces and some wagons. These fell into American hands. As the mass swept toward the Churubusco bridge it merged with the hard-pressed units covering the retreat from San Angel. To the Americans who surveyed the scene from the vantage point of the Coyoacán church tower it seemed that Santa Anna was leading a rabble back to Mexico City which could be dispersed if attacked while in flight. This caused Scott to order an assault against the Churubusco convent in order to open the way for an attack on the mass caught at the bridge.

High cornfields surrounding the convent combined with a hasty, superficial investigation by engineers obscured the strength of the position. Moreover, in order to conserve ammunition, General Rincón's artillery held its fire until the Americans were within musket range. Twiggs haphazardly threw his troops into the assault as they arrived on the field. But their rush failed. Riley's brigade joined the attack on the American right but lost its momentum when the men became scattered in the cornfields.

For the first time in the experience of some of the American troops, a Mexican force put up a truly inspired defense. Rincón's gallant leadership, the good defensive position, and the presence of the San Patricio companies all combined to bring out the tenacity and courage of the Mexican soldiers at the convent. They beat off every rush of the success-drunk American troops. Moreover, the Mexican gunners dueled with Taylor's battery for an hour and a half so successfully that the American had to withdraw his guns after losing twenty-four men and fourteen horses.

About half an hour before Taylor's withdrawal, Worth's division reached the *tête de pont*, having come as fast as its legs and wind permitted. Worth placed Clarke's brigade in front of the work, with the 6th Infantry (Major Benjamin L. E. Bonneville) athwart the road and the 5th (Brevet Colonel J. S. McIntosh) and 8th Infantry (Major C. A. Waite) on its right. Garland's brigade, deployed in a column of battalions, and Smith's light troops formed beyond Clarke to assail the left of the Mexican line. Worth was so sure of himself and his troops that he neglected to have the engineers check out his objective. This was the only time during the war in which such a study was not made before a major attack. Worth simply ordered the 6th Infantry, perhaps the best unit in the army, to charge. Twice it had to retire "butt-end first" from the Mexican fire. These checks so shook the troops that they began to show signs of panic. The troops on the right of the highway even after reinforcement by the 11th (Lieutenant Colonel W. M. Graham) and 14th Infantry (Colonel William Trousdale) accomplished nothing because the tall corn, ditches, and dikes broke the unity of their assaults. To further complicate Worth's problem, the ground alongside the road was too soft and the road itself so dangerous that Duncan's battery could not be brought into action.

Neither of the direct assaults had been in Scott's original plan, but he initiated them because he misjudged both Mexican positions and intentions as the result of poor intelligence. A third move, however, was planned. Shortly after committing Twiggs against the convent, Scott ordered Pierce, followed by Shields, to cross the river via the Coyoacán–Mixcoac road and then swing northeast to cut the Mexican retreat. The American troops pushed through about a mile and a half of cornfields and marshes toward the highway, some three quarters of a mile north of the river. Santa Anna countered by rushing about 2,200 men to the threatened point. He also sent some 1,500 to 2,000 cavalry to threaten the American left.

The Mexicans took cover in a pair of ditches and opened a devastating fire on the advancing Americans. Shields's men, poorly handled, broke and sought shelter among some buildings. Pierce's brigade led by Colonel Ransom, hung back. The attack came to nothing.

Meanwhile Worth's persistent attacks began to make headway. The bridgehead defenses had been reduced by the detachment of

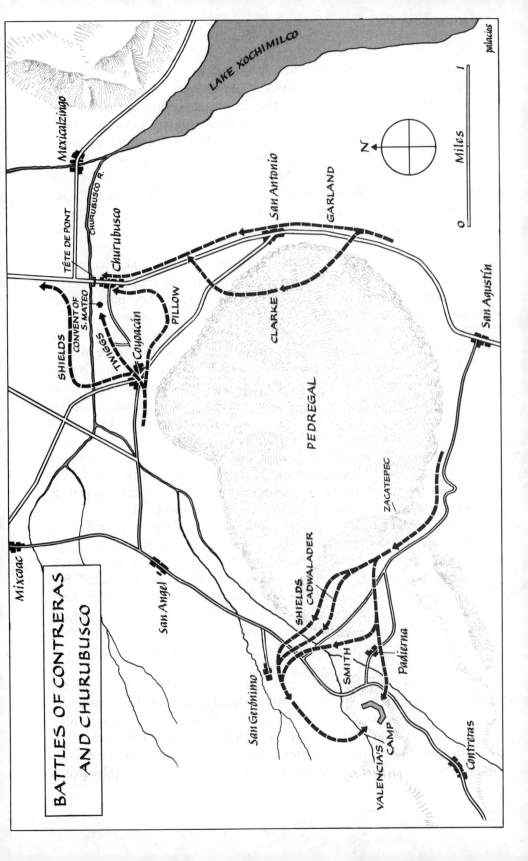

BATTLES OF CONTRERAS
AND CHURUBUSCO

LAKE XOCHIMILCO

Mexicalzingo

CHURUBUSCO R.

Churubusco

TÉTE DE PONT

SHIELDS

CONVENT OF
S. MATEO

TWIGGS

Coyoacán

PILLOW

San Antonio

GARLAND

CLARKE

PEDREGAL

ZACATEPEC

San Agustín

Míxcoac

San Angel

SHIELDS

CADWALADER

SMITH

Padierna

San Gerónimo

VALENCIA'S
CAMP

Contreras

N

0   Miles   1

palacios

troops to counter Shields's attack. Undoubtedly Shields's enveloping move, so similar to Scott's tactics at Cerro Gordo and Contreras, also weakened the will of some of the defenders. Gradually, portions of Worth's command worked their way eastward, outflanked the shortened Mexican left, crossed the river, and moved toward the road. At about the same time some of the 8th Infantry, followed by parts of the 5th Infantry, forced the twenty-foot-wide ditch, climbed the parapet, and took the *tête de pont* in a hand-to-hand fight. Their booty included 192 prisoners, three pieces of artillery, and ammunition. One of the guns, a 4-pounder, they immediately turned on the convent.

With the fire from the bridgehead silenced, Captain Duncan placed a pair of his guns on the highway from where they could safely bombard the convent. For ten or fifteen minutes they pounded out a stream of shot and shell. The Mexicans moved a cannon to reply. Its shifting so weakened the defenses at the southern end of the convent that the 3d Infantry (Captain E. B. Alexander) was able to scale the parapet there. The defenders, including the San Patricios, retired into the convent building. Resistance was hopeless but three times the deserters prevented the raising of a white flag. Finally Captain James M. Smith of the 3d Infantry stopped the slaughter by putting up a white handkerchief himself. The Mexicans, given the opportunity, quickly laid down their arms. Seven pieces of artillery and 1,259 prisoners, including three generals, fell into American hands. Among the prisoners were eighty-five San Patricios,[37] including their commander, Lieutenant Colonel Francisco Rosenda Moreno.

After the fall of the bridgehead, Shields reestablished control of his troops and, followed by his men and Pierce's, mounted another charge against the Mexicans defending the road. It was a bloody assault which saw a third of Shields's brigade fall. The South Carolina Regiment lost both their colonel and lieutenant colonel and the New Yorkers their commander. Gaining confidence as they advanced, even so the Americans cleared the Mexican infantry from their ditches, took 380 prisoners, and linked up on the road with Worth's van.

The pursuit was as haphazard as much of the fighting. Worth halted his troops after about a two-mile chase but the dragoons under Harney continued nearly to the walls of Mexico City. Captain Philip Kearny brought that sweep to a colorful end with a foolhardy but successful dash against a battery just outside the San Antonio Garita.

Santa Anna had lost almost a third of his forces or roughly 10,000 men in the two actions on the twentieth.[38] Scott's losses were heavy, 133 killed (1.5 percent) and 865 wounded (10.5 percent) of his 8,497 men engaged. Churubusco is not one of Scott's best battles. He lost control of the fight for some time although he ultimately regained it and ordered a well-conceived, if not well-executed, envelopment. More than in any other battle of the war, the American success resulted from the élan of the individual soldier who simply refused to believe that he could be beaten. If Contreras was an outstanding example of a subordinate seizing the opportunity for a decisive stroke, Churubusco was an equally fine example of one in which the direction and directives from headquarters failed to produce victory.

Without doubt Scott could have continued the pursuit into Mexico City and probably could have occupied it. He did not because his troops were hungry and he feared that discipline might give way to pillage. More important, however, as he reported to Secretary Marcy:

[Both Trist and I] had been admonished by the best friends of peace —intelligent neutrals and some American residents—against precipitation—lest by wantonly driving away the government and others—dishonoured—we might scatter the elements of peace, excite a spirit of national desperation, and thus indefinitely postpone the hope of accommodation. . . . Willing to leave something to this republic—of no immediate value to us—on which to rest her pride, and to recover temper—I halted our victorious corps at the gates of the city.[39]

NOTES

For key to abbreviations used in Notes, see page xi.

1. The Mexican political situation is covered in detail in Smith, *War with Mexico*, I, 213–19, 222–23, II, 3–14; Callcott, *Santa Anna*, 237, 243, 246–47; Wilfrid Hardy Callcott, *Church and State in Mexico 1822–1857* (Durham, 1926), 182–91; Vigil y Robles, *Invasión*, 19; *Niles*, LXX (July 4, 1846), 273, LXXI (Oct. 24, 1846), 113–14; Hutchinson, "Gómez Farías and the Return of Santa Anna," 189.

2. For the return of Santa Anna see Santa Anna, *Las Guerras de México con Tejas y los EE. UU.*, 218; Saunders to Conner, Aug. 16, 1846, *Conner (NY)*; Semmes, *Service Afloat and Ashore*, 117–20; George Frederick Augustus Ruxton, *Adventures in Mexico and the Rocky Mountains* (New York, 1848), 17–18; Rivera, *Historia de Jalapa*, III, 781; Rives, *U.S. and Mexico*, II, 242–46.

3. Manuel Crecencio Rejón to Secretary of State, Aug. 31, 1846, *H. Ex. Doc. 4, 29th Cong., 2d Sess.*, 43.

4. For the Beach mission see: Buchanan to Beach, Nov. 21, 1846, Beach to Buchanan, June 4, 1847, Manning, *Diplo. Corres.*, VIII, 195–96, 906–7; Quaife, *Diary of Polk*, II, 467–77, III, 22, 25; Moses S. Beach, "A Secret Mission to Mexico," *Scribner's Monthly Magazine*, XVIII (May, 1879), 136–40; Smith, *War with*

Mexico, II, 11–14, 330–31; Edward S. Wallace, *Destiny and Glory* (New York, 1957), 245–50. Beach and his assistant, Jane McManus Stormes, fled Mexico City on the collapse of the revolt. Mrs. Stormes made her way to Veracruz where she delivered a detailed report to Scott.

5. Law of April 20, 1847, *H. Ex. Doc. 60, 30th Cong., 1st Sess.*, 951–52; Riva Palacio, *México a Través*, IV, 656; Rives, *U.S. and Mexico*, II, 434; Smith, *War with Mexico*, II, 367.

6 Anaya, Decreto, May 6, 1847, Smith Papers; Santa Anna to Ministro de Guerra y Marina, May 18, 1847, Manifesto, May 22, 1847, *Niles*, LXXII (July 3, 1847), 277–78; Smith, *War with Mexico*, II, 83.

7. Quaife, *Diary of Polk*, II, 261–62, 338. The three commissioners proposed by Benton were John J. Crittenden, Silas Wright, and himself. Buchanan to Sen. George Evans, Feb. 25, 1847, Moore, *Works of Buchanan*, VII, 227, requested an appropriation to send the commissioners to Mexico.

8. Quaife, *Diary of Polk*, II, 323, 325–27, 331–33; Buchanan to Minister of Foreign Relations, Jan. 18, 1847, Manning, *Diplo. Corres.*, VIII, 197–98.

9. Monasterio to Buchanan, Feb. 22, 1847, Manning, *Diplo. Corres.*, VIII, 896–97.

10. Polk to Secretary of the Treasury, March 23, to Secretaries of War and Navy, March 31, Walker to President, March 30, 1847, Richardson, *Messages and Papers*, V, 2373–80. The tariff and regulations are reprinted in *S. Ex. Doc. 1, 30th Cong., 1st Sess.*, 567–75. Military or naval officers at each port served as collectors.

11. Quaife, *Diary of Polk*, II, 466–67, 471–75; Buchanan to Trist, and Draft Treaty, April 15, 1847, Manning, *Diplo. Corres.*, VIII, 201–7. For New Mexico and the two Californias the price was $25 million; for New Mexico and Upper California alone, $20 million.

12. Copies of the originals of all these are preserved in Nicholas P. Trist Papers, L.C. XXIII. Printed copies of the more important ones are in Manning as noted above and in *S. Ex. Doc. 52, 30th Cong., 1st Sess.*, 38–40, 81–86, 108.

13. Marcy to Scott, April 14, 1847, *H. Ex. Doc. 60, 30th Cong., 1st Sess.*, 940; Mason to Perry, April 15, 1847, *RCL.*

14. Trist to Buchanan, May 6, 7, 1847, *H. Ex. Doc. 56, 30th Cong., 1st Sess.*, 3, 153; Trist to wife, May 8, 1847, Trist Papers, XXIII; Scott to Trist, May 7, 1847, Manning, *Diplo. Corres.*, VIII, 902*n*-3*n*.

15. Trist to Scott, May 9, 20, to Buchanan, May 21, Scott to Marcy, May 20, to Trist, May 29, all in *S. Ex. Doc. 52, 30th Cong., 1st Sess.*, 153–57, 159–68, 172–73. One reason for Scott's evil temper was the appearance in Jalapa of the navy's Lieutenant Raphael Semmes with a letter to the Mexican authorities protesting the treatment of Passed Midshipman R. Clay Rogers. Scott initially refused even to receive the naval officer and complained bitterly, as he did also on Trist's appearance, about the wasting of escorts on useless messengers. Although Semmes continued with the army to Mexico City he could not deliver the letter before Rogers escaped in July. The rift between Scott and Semmes never healed and the latter became one of the most vocal of the General's critics. Perry to Semmes, to Scott, April 28, Semmes to Scott, May 8, Scott to Semmes, May 9, 1847, all in Semmes, *Service Afloat and Ashore*, 159–61, 198–99, 201–2.

16. Scott to Marcy, June 4, 1847, *H. Ex. Doc. 60, 30th Cong., 1st Sess.*, 993–94. See also Scammon, "Chapter in the Mexican War," 575, and Elliott, *Scott*, 471. Marcy forwarded the request to Polk, with the observation that Scott was "in very bad humor." Marcy to Polk, June 26, 1847, Polk Papers.

17. Trist to Bankhead, June 6, to Buchanan, June 13, 1847, Manning, *Diplo. Corres.*, VIII, 908–14.

18. Ibarra to Secretary of State, June 22, 1847, Manning, *Diplo. Corres.*, VIII, 914;

Trist to Scott, June 25, Thornton to Louis Hargous, Trist to Thornton, July 3, 1847, Trist Papers, XXIV.

19. Scott went so far as to suggest to Marcy on July 25 that all of his previous comments on Trist be suppressed. *H. Ex. Doc. 60, 30th Cong., 1st Sess.*, 1011–14.

20. Trist to Scott, July 16, Scott to Trist, July 17, 1847, Trist Papers, XXIV; Quitman to Marcy, March 9, 1848, Pillow Testimony, Court of Inquiry, FF300; Smith, *War with Mexico*, 391; Baltimore *Sun*, Dec. 6, 1847. The disbursements from Scott's secret-service funds are detailed in *S. Ex. Doc. 34, 34th Cong., 3d Sess.*, 21–22, 25. The bribe project is discussed from different points of view in McCormac, *Polk*, 507–12; Carlos E. Castañeda, "Relations of General Scott with Santa Anna," *HAHR*, XXIV (Nov. 1949), 460–68; Rives, *U.S. and Mexico*, II, 443–44; Roa Bárcena, *Recuerdos*, II, 156–62; Elliott, *Scott*, 495–99; Hitchcock, *50 Years*, 266–68; Claiborne, *Quitman*, I, 316–17, 326–29; Jones, *Santa Anna*, 165; Mariano Cuevas, *Historia de la Nación Méxicana* (México, 1967), 663–67; Smith, *War with Mexico*, II, 130–32.

21. Trist to Buchanan, July 23, 31, Aug. 14, 1847, Manning, *Diplo. Corres.*, VIII, 915–21. See also Thornton to Trist, July 29, 1847, *ibid.*, 918n.

22. Smith, *War with Mexico*, II, 88, 132. See also Thornton to Trist, July 29, 1847, *loc. cit.*

23. Quaife, *Diary of Polk*, III, 57–59, 62–63, 77–78; Buchanan to Trist, June 14, 1847, Manning, *Diplo. Corres.*, VIII, 208–9; Marcy to Scott, May 31, June 15, July 12, 1847, *S. Ex. Doc. 60, 30th Cong., 1st Sess.*, 860–63, 975–76, 998–1002.

24. Buchanan to Trist, July 13, 1847, Manning, *Diplo. Corres.*, VIII, 209–13. Eugene Keith Chamberlain, "Nicholas Trist and Baja California," *PHR*, XXXII (Feb. 1963), 62. The instructions of July 19, 1847, Manning, pp. 915–17, altered the boundary to the 32° line from the Rio Grande to middle of the Gulf of California and thence to the Pacific. See also Kenneth M. Johnson, "Baja California and the Treaty of Guadalupe Hidalgo," *Journal of the West*, XI (April 1972), 328–47.

25. Mason to Perry, Aug. 4, 1847, *RCL*.

26. Vigil, *Invasión*, 41–42; Jenkins, *War Between U.S. and Mexico*, 289; Smith, *War with Mexico*, II, 79–80, 421.

27. The best contemporary description of the geography of Mexico City is in M. L. Smith to J. J. Abert, November 30, 1848, *S. Ex. Doc. 19, 30th Cong., 2d Sess.*, 2–4.

28. Smith, *War with Mexico*, II, 89–90, 95; Ramírez to D. F. Elorriaga, Aug. 11, 1847, Ramírez, *Mexico During the War*, 150. The defenses are described in Bravo Ugarte, *Historia de México*, III, t. 2, 221. J. O'Reiley, "To my friends and country-men in the Army of the United States of America," n.d., George W. Kendall Papers, UTA; Santa Anna, Proclamation, Aug. 15, 1847, Smith and Judah, *Chronicles of the Gringos*, 236, represent a final effort to induce desertion.

29. Lee to J. L. Smith, Aug. 12, 1847, Smith and Judah, *Chronicles of the Gringos*, 236; Scott to Marcy, Aug. 19, 1847, *S. Ex. Doc. 1, 30th Cong., 1st Sess.*, 303–15; H. L. Scott to Worth, Aug. 13, 1847, Trist Papers, XXIV; Worth to Duncan, March 31, 1848, Duncan to Worth, Worth to Scott, Aug. 14, 1847, all in Duncan Papers; Hitchcock, *50 Years*, 274; Lee to Mrs. J. G. Totten, Aug. 22, 1847, Freeman, *Lee*, I, 252–53; Semmes, *Service Afloat and Ashore*, 351–55; Williams, *Beauregard in Mexico*, 41–44; Stevens, *Life of I. I. Stevens*, I, 166–67; Claiborne, *Quitman*, I, 333–35. The defenses of Peñon are described in Ramsey, *Other Side*, 246–54.

30. Scott to Marcy, Aug. 19, 1847, *loc. cit.*; HQ Army, GO #257, Aug. 15, 1847, *AGGO*, XLI½, 476; Twiggs to H. L. Scott, Aug. 16, 1847, *S. Ex. Doc. 1, 30th Cong., 1st Sess.*, A28; Smith, *War with Mexico*, II, 96–98.

31. George S. May (ed.), "An Iowan in the Mexican War," *Iowa Journal of History*, LIII (April 1955), 172.

32. Lee and most other Americans confused the buildings at Padierna and those at the nearby hamlet of San Gerónimo with the village of Contreras which lay well to the south of the battlefield. As a result the American name for the battle is Contreras rather than the more appropriate Mexican title of Padierna.

33. Modern Villa Obregon.

34. Unless otherwise indicated, the account of the Battle of Contreras is based upon Scott's reports to Marcy Aug. 19, 28, 1847, with those of his subordinates contained in *AGLR'47*, S-726 and largely reprinted in *S. Ex. Doc. 1, 30th Cong., 1st Sess.*, 303–46, A38–134, *passim*, *H. Ex. Doc. 60, 30th Cong., 1st Sess.*, 10–18; Lee to J. L. Smith, Aug. 21, 1847, Smith Transcripts, IX; HQ Army, GO #258, Aug. 19, 1847, *AGGO*, XLI½, 476–77; testimony in *S. Ex. Doc. 65, 30th Cong., 1st Sess.*; J. H. Smith, interview with Ignacio Molina, Smith Papers; Balbontín, *Invasión*, 110–23; Ballantine, *English Soldier*, 207–33; Brooks, *Complete History*, 366–85; Callcott, *Santa Anna*, 267; Claiborne, *Quitman*, I, 337–44; Crawford, *The Eagle*, 99; Davis, *Autobiography*, 196–302; Dawson, *Battles of U.S.*, II, 511–17; Elliott, *Scott*, 506–18; Freeman, *Lee*, I, 258–64; George H. Gordon, "The Battles of Contreras and Churubusco," Military Historical Society of Massachusetts *Papers*, XIII (1913), 574–92; Grant, *Memoirs*, 71; Percy Gatling Hamlin (ed.), *The Making of a Soldier* (Richmond, 1935), 68–69, 72; Henry, *Mexican War*, 329–42; Hitchcock, *50 Years*, 275–82; An Officer of the Staff, *A Series of Intercepted Mexican Letters* (Mexico, 1847), 14, 17, 22–23, 25–26, 28; Jenkins, *War Between U.S. and Mexico*, 356–73; Richard McSherry, *El Punchero* (Philadelphia, 1850), 73–76; Ramsey, *Other Side*, 268–99; Ripley, *War with Mexico*, II, 216–80; Rives; *U.S. and Mexico*, II, 462–74; Roa Bárcena, *Recuerdos*, II, 213–305; Antonio López de Santa Anna, *Detall de las Operaciones Ocurridas en la Defensa de la Capital de la República, Atacada por el Ejército de los Estados-Unidos del Norte en el Año de 1847* (México, 1848), 12–16; Santa Anna, *Las Guerras . . . Tejas y los EE. UU.*, 273–86; Santa Anna, *Mi Historia*, 72–74; Scott, *Autobiography*, 477–502; Semmes, *Service Afloat and Ashore*, 379–402; Smith, *War with Mexico*, II, 100–19, 374–80; Smith and Judah, *Chronicles of the Gringos*, 239–44; Stevens, *Stevens*, I, 170–83, 192–200; Gabriel Valencia, *Detall de los Acciones de los Dias 19 y 20 en los Camps de Padierna* (Morelia, 1847), 558; Vigil, *Invasión*, 43–51; Wilcox, *Mexican War*, 358–404; Williams, *Beauregard in Mexico*, 48–55.

35. Pierce having been injured earlier in the day when his horse threw and then fell on him after tripping on a hole in the lava, the brigade was now commanded by Colonel Ransom.

36. The sources for the account of the Battle of Churubusco are the same reports as those for the preceding plus *Churubusco en la Acción Militar del 20 de Agosto de 1847* (México, 1947); Hawthorne, *Pierce*, 100; S. G. Hopkins to J. H. Smith, June 8, 1917, Smith Papers; Charles S. Hamilton, "Memoirs of the Mexican War," *Wisconsin Magazine of History*, XIV (Sept. 1930), 72–75; Lawton, *Artillery Officer*, 294–98; Nicholas, *Pierce*, 163; Ramírez, *Mexico During the War*, 151–52; Blackwood, *To Mexico with Scott*, 197–204; Stevens, *Campaigns*, 67–74; Moore, "Private Johnson Fights the Mexicans," 221–22.

37. The San Patricio deserters were tried by two courts-martial on August 28; one at San Angel headed by Brevet Colonel Bennet Riley and a second at Tacubaya headed by Brevet Colonel John Garland. The case which attracted the most attention was that of Private John Reilly formerly of Company K, 5th Infantry. Reilly was the ranking turncoat and popularly considered by the Americans to have been the chief organizer of the battalion. However, the surviving evi-

dence indicates that he had little, if anything, to do with the formation of the unit. Only twenty-seven of the deserters, all regulars, were Irish. The myth that the San Patricios were Irish deserters seems to stem from the importance given Reilly and the fact that their unit flag had an Irish harp on it. Garland's court sentenced thirty-six men to hang, two to be shot for desertion, and three to be given fifty lashes and be branded with a D. All those brought before Riley's court were sentenced to hanging. Scott reduced the sentences of seven to fifty lashes and remitted those of two entirely. The remainder were hanged, seventeen at San Angel on September 10; four there on the eleventh; and the remaining thirty at Micoac on the thirteenth. Tradition claims that Colonel William S. Harney delayed the execution of the last group until the American flag rose over Chapultepec. The men, it is said, died with a cheer for American success on their lips. Proceedings of General Court-Martial Convened at San Angel . . . , Office of Judge Advocate General, Courts-Martial, EE-531; Proceedings of General Court-Martial Convened at Tacubaya . . . , *ibid.*, EE-525; HQ Army, GOs, #281, 282, 283, Sept. 8, 10, 1847, *AGGO*, XLI½, 497–504; Davis, *Autobiography*, 226–29; Edward S. Wallace, "Deserters in the Mexican War," *HAHR*, XV (Aug. 1935), 381–82; Wallace, "Battalion of St. Patrick," 89; Hopkins, "San Patricio Battalion," 280–84; McCornack, "San Patricio Deserters," 136–42.

38. Scott estimated the Mexican losses at 4,297 killed and wounded. He had 2,637 men, including eight generals, in his prisoner-of-war stockade. In late August an incomplete count of the Mexican forces at Mexico City listed 13,828 privates.

39. Scott to Marcy, Aug. 19, 1847, *S. Ex. Doc. 1, 30th Cong., 1st Sess.*, 303–15.

16: The Fall of Mexico City

W INFIELD SCOTT believed that the devastating defeats handed
Santa Anna's army during August 20 would bring immediate negotiations. Many Mexicans also recognized that nothing short of an
armistice could keep the strutting, insulting *gringos* from the city's
streets.

At about midnight on August 20 Foreign Minister Francisco
Pacheco asked British Minister Charles Bankhead to use his influence
to save the city from sack. Bankhead, whose efforts to arrange peace
had been consistently rejected out of hand by the Mexican leaders,
refused to take any action beyond forwarding a letter. That letter
took the form of an answer to Buchanan's April offer of negotiations.
Bankhead covered the message with one of his own to Nicholas
Trist expressing hope that peace might soon come.[1]

Unaware of what was transpiring within the city, Scott prepared
to move his siege guns into positions which would allow him to
demand its surrender. Early on the morning of August 21 as he and
Trist rode toward Tacubaya they met a highly polished and beauti-
fully accoutered carriage. It carried Brigadier General Ignacio Mora
y Villamil who had entered the American lines under a flag of truce
as bearer of the letters from Pacheco and Bankhead and verbal assurance that Santa Anna wished an armistice. Although the formal
request for an armistice should have come from the defeated com-

mander, Scott allowed his desire for an end to the shooting to over-come his sense of propriety and made the proposal himself:

Too much blood has already been shed in this unnatural war between the two great Republics of this Continent. It is time that the differences between them should be amicably and honorably settled; and it is known to your Excellency, that a Commissioner on the part of the United States, clothed with full powers to that end is with this army. To enable the two Republics to enter on negotiation, I am willing to sign, on reasonable terms, a short armistice.

Scott offered to wait until the twenty-second for an answer, although reserving the right to occupy new positions outside the capital.[2]

Brigadier General Lino José Alcorta, Santa Anna's Minister of War, accepted the proposal. He assigned Mora and Brigadier General Benito Quijana to arrange the details with Scott's commissioners, Quitman, Pierce, and Persifor Smith. The terms, signed on the twenty-third, provided for a cessation of hostilities within seventy-eight miles of the capital for as long as negotiations continued, but they could be terminated by either of the commanders on forty-eight hours' notice. During the armistice neither side would be reinforced or strengthen its positions. The Americans agreed that supplies could enter the city, while the Mexicans permitted Scott's quartermasters to purchase provisions there. Since the large number of prisoners who had to be fed and guarded were a liability, Scott agreed to their release.[3]

Scott and Trist rather naïvely assumed that the signing of the armistice presaged serious negotiations. They were wrong. Santa Anna's position was too insecure to permit serious discussions, if indeed that was his intention at all, and countervailing pressures forced him into extravagant demands. As a result, Trist's meetings with the Mexican negotiators between August 27 and September 6 accomplished nothing. The respite from the fighting restored Santa Anna's confidence and allowed the war faction to gain his ear. Moreover, he had misinterpreted statements made by Trist at Puebla and felt duped by the American's insistence on a Rio Grande boundary.

On September 3 Santa Anna began to prepare for a resumption of fighting. He banned further sale of provisions to Scott's force; called in all soldiers within thirty leagues of the capital; had the governors of the states warned that the American terms were un-acceptable; and on the fourth or fifth began strengthening the Mexico City fortifications.[4] After Trist's September 6 meeting with the Mexicans produced only unreasonable demands, Scott denounced the armistice on the basis of the halting of the provisions purchases and the strengthening of the fortifications.[5]

The American Army lay encamped in a rough arc south of Mexico City. General Worth's division and Scott's headquarters were at Tacubaya; General Pillow's division at Mixcoac, about two miles further south; General Twiggs's at San Angel; and General Quitman's at San Agustín. During the evening of September 6 Scott informally discussed his strategy with some of his subordinates. They expressed a common preference for the southern approach, via the Niño Perdido and San Antonio Garitas,[6] since an attack from the southwest involved storming the fortress of Chapultepec.[7]

The initial reconnaissance reports supported the southern approach, but during the evening of September 7 two developments changed the picture. Santa Anna shifted the bulk of his forces from the southwest to the south. Of more immediate concern to Scott, however, was the presence of a large body of horsemen near a range of massive stone buildings just west of Chapultepec called El Molino del Rey, for during the evening of the seventh he received reports that the Mexicans were melting down church bells there and casting them into cannon. Although a moment's thought should have convinced him that an undertaking of that kind could not have been put into effect at such short notice, Scott decided to stage a night raid to destroy the works. Worth, however, convinced him to allow a conventional daylight assault even though that would require a larger force.

The Molino del Rey buildings formed the western end of the walled park of Chapultepec, about 1,000 yards from the castle itself. They were manned by the Oaxaco Brigade of Brigadier General Antonio León and supported by another under General Rangel. Five hundred yards west of the supposed cannon factory stood another massive stone building, the Casa Mata, around which Mexican engineers had constructed bastioned earthworks. Some 1,500 regulars under Brigadier General Francisco Pérez manned it. Connecting the two was a dry drainage ditch backed by a cactus hedge where Brigadier General Simeon Ramírez's brigade with seven guns took station. Beyond the Casa Mata the ground broke sharply into a ravine, while beyond it and about a mile west at the Hacienda Morales, General Juan Álvarez and 4,000 cavalry waited to ride down the flank of any attacker. How many troops manned the complex position is uncertain, although certainly considerably less than the contemporary American estimates of 12,000 to 14,000 men. The defenses were extremely strong, with interlocking fields of fire. Even the lay of the land aided the defenders. A gentle downward slope extended from a ridge west of Tacubaya all the way to the Mexican positions and helped to offset the tendency of Mexican soldiers to shoot high.

Scott's orders called for Worth to make the assault with his whole division, 3,250 men, at dawn on September 8 while Twiggs's division reinforced by one of Pillow's brigades made a feint toward the southern gates. Worth's three assault columns began moving into position at 3:00 A.M. Garland's brigade on the right had the south and east sides of the mill as its objective. Firing in direct support were two 24-pounder siege guns under Captain Benjamin Huger and the two "Buena Vista" 6-pounders under Captain Simon H. Drum. A picked command of 500 men under Major George Wright drew the mission of assailing the western front of the buildings; while Clarke's brigade on the left, temporarily commanded by Brevet Colonel James S. McIntosh and supported by Duncan's battery, attacked the Casa Mata. In reserve was Cadwalader's brigade of Pillow's division, while Major Edwin V. Sumner with three squadrons of dragoons, 270 men, screened the left flank.

Worth began the assault after only skimpy bombardment at 5:45 when the preliminary reconnaissance by Captain James L. Mason and Lieutenant John G. Foster of the Engineers indicated that the mill had been abandoned. They were wrong. Ramírez had merely moved his artillery into positions closer to the buildings. When the American assault columns came within range, the Mexican gunners opened such a devastating fire that it drove them back. The carnage was horrible. Wright's column lost eleven of its fourteen officers. When Lieutenant Colonel Miguel María Echeagaray, the able leader of the 3d Light Infantry, without orders launched a counterattack from Chapultepec, it shattered the remnants of Wright's command. In that fight the Mexicans slit the throats of some of the American wounded, or so the Americans believed. This caused some Yankees to refuse to take prisoners during the attack on Chapultepec. When the assault staggered, Worth sent the light battalion, temporarily under the command of Captain Ephraim Kirby Smith, and part of the 14th Infantry to assist.

On the American left McIntosh's men advanced with Duncan's guns firing over their heads until they masked his fire. Shortly a hail of fire from the Casa Mata and a strong counterattack stopped them about thirty yards short of their objective. They beat back the counterattack but in the process took heavy casualties. McIntosh fell, his second-in-command Major Martin Scott was killed, and Major Carlos A. Waite upon whom the command descended was himself wounded. Finally the survivors could withstand no more and sought safety out of range of the Mexican muskets. As the fleeing troops moved back they unmasked Duncan's guns, which opened a rapid and effective fire on Casa Mata. That forced Pérez at 6:15 to withdraw, since his men lacked artillery with which to respond and he could see that the Molino defenses were crumbling.

When Álvarez's cavalry threatened to strike McIntosh's flank, Cadwalader sent the Voltigeur Regiment (Colonel T. P. Andrews) to the brink of the ravine while Sumner led his dragoons across it. Duncan, whose guns were then masked by the advancing infantry, swung his pieces to support and after a few rounds convinced the Mexican horsemen to retire. Why Álvarez failed to push the attack as Santa Anna expected and ordered has never been satisfactorily explained. Probably it was a result of his fear of the American artillery.

It was on the right of the field that the fight was decided. There the action degenerated into a disorganized series of rushes, withdrawals, and rallies by small groups of men—the classic, confused small-unit action. Worth recalled the Voltigeurs from their blocking position and sent them, as well as the 11th Infantry, into the assault. Most of the Americans worked close to the walls of the Molino searching for some means of entering the buildings. Finally a gate at the southern end yielded to persistent battering and at almost the same moment another at the northwest corner was forced. Even after entering the buildings the Americans had to fight their way from room to room. Meanwhile the 11th Infantry beat off an attempt to retake the guns in which both General León and Colonel Lucas Balderas of the *Batallón de Mina* were killed. The persistence of the American attacks finally drove the defenders from the Molino buildings, and the 9th Infantry, rushed to the battlefield by Scott when he realized that the battle was developing into a major one, joined Garland's men in turning back the reinforcements moving down from Chapultepec.

The Mexicans withdrew fighting and twice Brigadier General Matías Peña y Barragán led the troops along the northern face of the Chapultepec hill in unsuccessful counterattacks. After two hours of fighting and the loss of 116 men killed, 665 wounded, and eighteen missing—one quarter of his command—Worth held the mill. Clarke's brigade, which took the heaviest casualties, lost half of its officers and nearly a third of its men. The irony of the attack became clear when a search of the buildings produced only a few gun molds but no pieces. Scott ordered the buildings destroyed and abandoned. Casa Mata, which had caught fire during or immediately after the battle, blew up shortly before noon, killing several Americans. By one o'clock in the afternoon the American troops were back in their old positions. All that Scott had to show for the casualties was 685 prisoners, fifty-three of them officers, and three additional trophy guns for the artillery park. Perhaps 2,000 Mexican soldiers had been killed or wounded. Colonel Hitchcock spoke the truth when he called it a pyrrhic victory.

The destruction of the Molino del Rey position did not solve Scott's major problem, the selection of the best route to assail the Mexican capital. Three causeways, each about 1,000 yards long, connected the American positions with the southern gates of the city. One carried the Acapulco road from Churubusco to the San Antonio Garita; a second brought the San Angel road to the Niño Perdido Garita; while the third ran north from Piedad to the Garita de Belén at the southwest corner of the city. Two additional causeways approached the town from the west, both connected it to the hill and castle of Chapultepec. The northernmost of these was a dog-legged route which ran generally north-northeast from the castle along the Verónica causeway for about two miles to a junction at Santo Tomás with the San Cosmé Garita. The more direct route ran directly eastward from Chapultepec to the Belén gate.

The engineers resumed their surveys. During the afternoon of September 8 Captain Lee and Lieutenants Beauregard and Tower checked the Piedad, Niño Perdido, and San Antonio roads to determine if they were practical for artillery and if the land surrounding them could be traversed by infantry. Mexican fire prevented their actually inspecting other than the Piedad approach, but the engineers could see Mexican troops strengthening the defenses at San Antonio and discovered entrenchments running from there to Niño Perdido. During the ninth Beauregard, Tower, and Lieutenant Isaac I. Stevens, after another study, concluded that it was feasible to turn the right flank of the San Antonio Garita position.[8]

During the morning of September 11 Scott called a conference of his generals to discuss the point of attack. Once the discussion began, it became clear that Scott favored an approach via Chapultepec against San Cosmé and Belén. Pillow followed with a long harangue which supported the southern approach. Quitman announced he reserved his opinion until he had heard the engineers' report. Scott then asked for it and Major John L. Smith, the senior engineer, indicated support for a move against San Antonio. This convinced Quitman, Shields, Pierce, and Cadwalader. Twiggs, however, sided with Scott. Riley inquired which approach would require the least time and labor in building batteries. Major Smith responded, "The western." "Then," said the old soldier, "I go in for more fighting and less work." Finally at Hitchcock's and Trist's urging Beauregard took issue with the other engineers, arguing that San Antonio was being strengthened hourly as the Mexicans expected an assault there. The argument caused Pierce to shift his position and Scott, who undoubtedly intended to do so in any event, quietly announced that the attack would be against the western gates.[9]

During the twelfth, as a cover for the forthcoming operation, Quitman's division demonstrated near Piedad and after dark along with Pillow's moved to Tacubaya. This was Scott's gamble. He left Twiggs with only Riley's brigade and two batteries to protect the right side of the American lines. While the assault troops moved into position, Huger in cooperation with the engineers chose sites for four batteries to bombard Chapultepec. The first, mounting a captured eight-inch howitzer, stood along the Tacubaya–Chapultepec road; the second, built on a ridge south of the Molino del Rey, had a 24-pounder and an eight-inch howitzer; the third, 300 yards north and east of the second, contained a Mexican 16-pounder and an eight-inch howitzer; while the fourth built near the Molino contained a single ten-inch mortar. A 16-pounder intended for the first battery could not be moved into place because of Mexican fire, so it was emplaced along with an additional eight-inch howitzer north of the Molino. The first two batteries opened fire during the morning of the twelfth and the others in the course of the day.[10]

Santa Anna made indifferent use of the time consumed by the American preparations. He set 2,000 men to work strengthening the southern defenses but broke them up into such small detachments that they accomplished little. Quitman's demonstration drew troops and cannon from Chapultepec and Belén, while intelligence of an impending attack on the San Lazaro Garita in the southeast corner of the city caused Santa Anna to send Brigadier General Antonio Vizcaino there and to follow himself. In the morning when the American target became clear he hastened troops to the threatened point, but it was too late—too late to move the troops into position through the American shells and too late to complete the defenses. By evening American shells had disabled two of Chapultepec's best guns and shorn the garrison of much of its morale. Yet within the American lines there was little joy. Scott had hoped that the bombardment would drive the Mexicans from the works, but it had not and now he must face an assault.

During the night Scott met with his commanders and engineers to refine the final plans. Quitman's division, reinforced by a storming party of 265 from Twiggs's division under Captain Silas Casey, would attack along the Tacubaya road toward the battery and cross-roads southeast of the castle. Pillow's division, with a similar group from Worth's force led by Captain Samuel Mackenzie, would advance through the ruins of the Molino toward Chapultepec.[11]

Although Santa Anna recognized the importance of Chapultepec to the defense of the capital, the persistent shortages of materials and time prevented its full development. It lacked the necessary supporting works, particularly in the grove. The buildings housing the Military College crowning the summit of the 200-foot-high hill appeared stronger than they actually were. The buildings were not artillery-proof, nor had their parapets and other defensive measures been finished. Moreover, the extensive works needed at least 2,000 men to defend them properly but Major General Nicolás Bravo had only 832 infantry plus some artillerymen and engineers. Nevertheless, the position represented a major obstacle to the Americans. The castle and its grounds were bounded by a high stone wall along the eastern and southern sides. The ruins of El Molino del Rey closed the western end, while the northern reaches were protected by the Anzures aqueduct whose arches had been filled in with masonry. Some well-drained fields extended from the Molino to a ditch and a cyprus swamp, which gave way as the ground rose to a grove of ancient trees. The south wall had a single opening covered by a redan of sandbags. Southeast of the castle, near the junction of the Tacubaya road with the aqueduct and road to Belén, two batteries and a ditch across the road guarded the back of the fortress. Astride the long winding approach to the Colegio Militar were two redoubts, one containing a 4-pounder. A fosse and a minefield protected the western wall of the castle itself. About halfway down the slope, near the northern wall, stood another redan and an infantry breast-work.

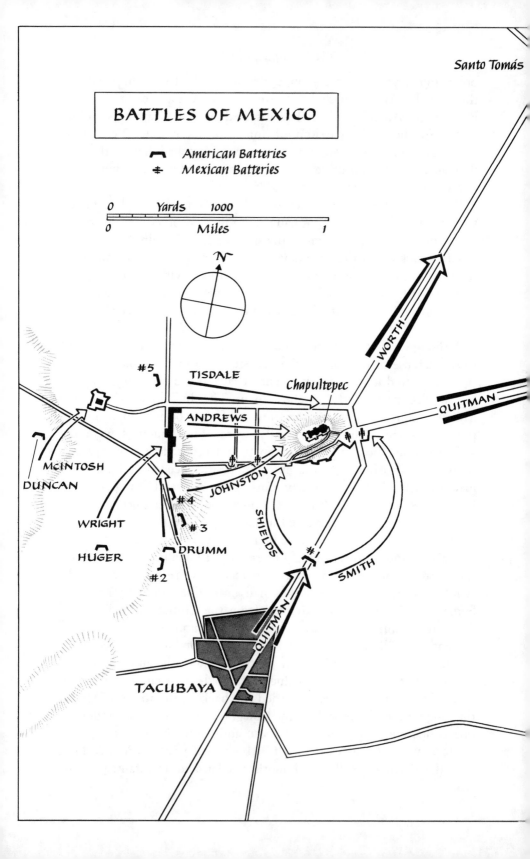

BATTLES OF MEXICO

⌒ American Batteries
‡ Mexican Batteries

0   Yards   1000
0   Miles   1

Santo Tomás

#5
TISDALE
Chapultepec
WORTH
QUITMAN
ANDREWS
McINTOSH
DUNCAN
JOHNSTON
#4
WRIGHT
#3
SHIELDS
HUGER
DRUMM
#1
SMITH
#2
QUITMAN
TACUBAYA

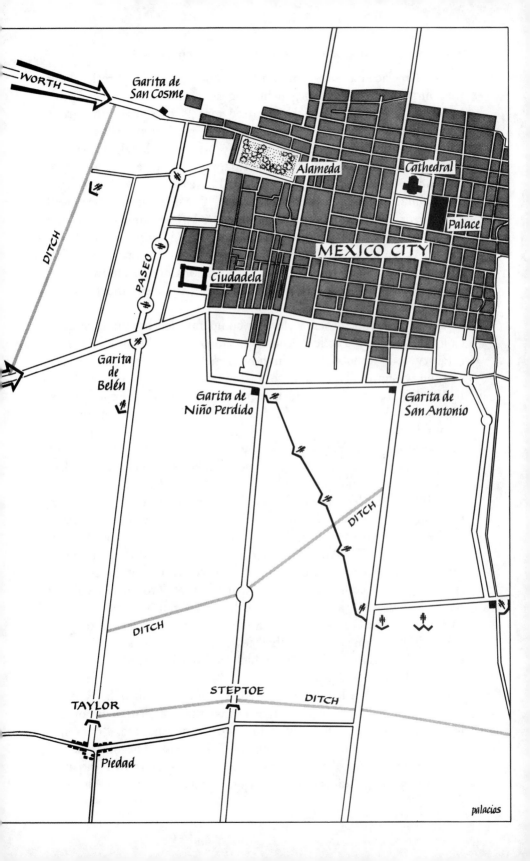

WORTH

Garita de
San Cosme

Alameda

Cathedral

Palace

MEXICO CITY

DITCH

PASEO

Ciudadela

Garita
de
Belén

Garita de
Niño Perdido

Garita de
San Antonio

DITCH

DITCH

DITCH

TAYLOR

STEPTOE

DITCH

Piedad

palacias

The American assault came on September 13. At daybreak, about five-thirty, the batteries began hurling shot and shell at the fortifications. Two hours later they shifted targets to shower the grove with grape, canister, and shells. At eight a momentary pause in the firing signaled the start of the infantry attack. Colonel William B. Trousdale with the 11th and 14th Infantry, supported by a section of artillery under Lieutenant Thomas J. Jackson, moved east from the Molino along the Anzures aqueduct. Outside the southern wall Lieutenant Colonel Joseph E. Johnston led four companies of the Voltigeurs in a parallel move. That column easily cleared the defenders from the sandbag redan, broke through the opening behind it, and swept up the hill to seize the positions at the elbow of the approach road. From there they took the castle itself under musket fire.

Meanwhile, four other Voltigeur companies led by the Irish-born Colonel Timothy Patrick Andrews, along with the 9th and 15th Infantry and Reno's mountain howitzers,[12] thrust into the swamp and the western edge of the grove. The action there was a confused fight from tree to tree, or so it seemed to many of the combatants. Finally the Mexicans were cleared from the grove and Andrews's men able to link with Johnston's. The defenders were in a precarious position, their morale shaken by the bombardment, the lack of reinforcements, and the loss of some of their most able leaders like General Pérez. Among the defenders were a handful of cadets from the Military College who had not left with their classmates when the institution was evacuated. Six of them would die in the defense of the castle, to become the venerated *Niños Heroicos* of Mexican patriotic lore. Santa Anna, unsure of whether the assault represented the main American thrust or merely served as a feint to cover an attack up the Tacubaya road and worried that Trousdale's column might bypass the castle on the north, dared not send many reinforcements. The San Blas Battalion which he did send was so roughly handled by Johnston's men that few of its members reached the castle. The 3d Light Infantry which followed arrived too late to assist in the defense.

Once the grove had been cleared, Colonel Trueman B. Ransom led the 9th Infantry in a charge against the western point of the hill. No sooner had he waved his sword and shouted, "Forward, the 9th!" than he fell from a bullet in the head. The 9th charged but got no further than the fosse. For reasons unknown the men with the scaling ladders were not with them. Therefore the 9th, like the 15th Infantry on its left and the Voltigeurs on its right, took shelter and began sniping at the parapets. They were soon swept of defenders. The storming party, without ladders to climb, waited and gradually lost their élan. However, the delay did give them time to find and cut many of the canvas hoses which carried powder trains to the mines.[13]

Pillow, who was at the foot of the hill suffering from a painful wound, panicked at the pause in the assault and called for reinforcement by the whole of Worth's division. His assistance, however, came from Quitman. The volunteer division's attack was spearheaded by a party of forty pioneers under Captain John G. Reynolds, USMC, Casey's storming party, and a second picked force of 120 men commanded by Major Levi Twiggs, USMC. Four pieces of artillery trailed the infantry, firing at targets of opportunity. Quitman's attack soon faltered. The Marines in the van did not press their advance aggressively; Major Twiggs became separated from his command and had some difficulty locating it.[14] The attackers, confined to the road by wide ditches on either side and confronted by a five-gun battery supported by part of the crack Morelia Battalion, were stopped about 200 yards short of the battery. After a renewed rush failed, with both Twiggs and Casey among the fallen, the men retired around a bend in the causeway about fifty yards to the rear.

Meanwhile, in an effort to assist that attack, protect his own right, and turn the Mexican defenses, Quitman had sent Persifor Smith's brigade through the meadows on the right. Following the withdrawal of the troops on the road, Quitman ordered General Shields with the New York (Colonel W. B. Burnett) and 2d Pennsylvania (Lieutenant Colonel J. W. Geary) Regiments to join in the Chapultepec assault. That move offered an opportunity to flank the defenses and open the road for the rest of the division. In the process, Shields's force came under a very heavy fire which wounded Shields and both regimental commanders. Clarke's brigade, the first of Worth's reinforcements, arrived on the western slope of the Chapultepec hill at about the same time as Shields's men. The fresh units had the momentum necessary to carry the attack forward. They crossed the minefield safely and reached the walls at about the same time that the long-delayed ladders arrived.

Up went the ladders. Some stayed, some did not, and up the former scrambled a handful of men and after them a growing stream; Captain Moses Barnard planted the bullet-riddled Voltigeur flag on the parapet; and an unstoppable tide of blue- and gray-clad Americans swept through the buildings. The ground was strewn with the shattered bodies of the defenders, some of whom received the same inhuman treatment that American wounded had suffered outside the Molino. Private William A. Gray from the Voltigeurs found and cut the powder train to the mines. Shortly before 9:30 A.M. General Bravo surrendered to Lieutenant Charles B. Brower of the New York Regiment and the Stars and Stripes supplanted the tricolor over the castle. Along with a gaggle of prisoners the Americans seized sixteen cannon.

As the American flag broke over the castle, Santa Anna exclaimed, "I believe if we were to plant our batteries in Hell the damned Yankees would take them from us."[15] Another officer simply shook his head and sighed, "God is a Yankee."

The men in the castle quickly turned their fire on the Mexicans at the gateway below. Captain Benjamin S. Roberts led Quitman's troops on the causeway in an unstoppable rush which carried the batteries at the gateway. Scott, who had observed the attack from Tacubaya, hastened to the castle and was mobbed by the ecstatic soldiers. But there was much fighting yet to be done that day.

Quitman gathered what men he could and quickly pushed down the Belén causeway. Behind him came nearly all the troops who had taken Chapultepec, except the 15th Infantry which remained to guard the castle and the prisoners. A two-gun battery about a mile down the causeway held up the advance for about an hour, but after Drum brought up his guns, the battery was seized by the Rifle Regiment. Thereafter nothing stopped the American flood short of the garita.[16]

The defenses of Belén Garita were manned by about 180 infantrymen, chiefly from the Morelia Battalion, commanded by Brigadier General Andrés Terrés. It was a critical point because both the Belén and Piedad roads entered the city through the garita. Running north from the customs post was a wide *paseo*, or promenade. About 300 yards to the northeast of the gate stood the Ciudadela, a converted tobacco factory which served as the barracks and strong point for the permanent garrison of the city. After the fall of Chapultepec, Santa Anna sent three small cannon and some additional troops to Belén and ordered General Ramírez to occupy the Paseo.

Although the defenders loosed a withering stream of musket and cannon shot at the advancing Americans, the attackers kept coming. Drum and Lieutenant Calvin Benjamin brought up an 18-pounder and a 24-pounder howitzer on either side of the causeway. Their fire caused extensive damage, showering the Mexican gunners with shell fragments and masonry splinters. At about one o'clock in the afternoon rumors that the Americans were turning the position caused the newly arrived troops to withdraw without warning. Terrés, who at about the same time ran out of ammunition for his artillery, withdrew into the Ciudadela with about seventy men. Despite the gallant defense of Belén, Santa Anna made Terrés the scapegoat for the loss of the capital and branded him a traitor in his memoirs.

The Rifles chased the Mexicans over the parapet and at 1:20 Quitman himself entered the garita waving a red handkerchief from the muzzle of a rifle. As the American artillerymen learned when they tried to turn the captured guns on their former owners the garita was exposed to heavy fire from the Ciudadela. Drum was killed and his successor, Lieutenant Fitz John Porter, had twenty-seven of his thirty men injured. That fire, plus the exhaustion of its ammunition by Quitman's artillery, stopped any further American advance. Indeed, the Americans had to beat back several Mexican counterattacks from the troops in the Ciudadela. An indication of the ferocity of the fighting involving Quitman's forces can be seen from its losses. Nearly every member of Quitman's staff and all his artillery officers had been struck. Scott, following the battle, was rightly critical of Quitman's insistence on pushing home the attack, since it was designed only as a feint. He considered, as most historians have since, that the division suffered unnecessary casualties largely as a result of Quitman's thirst for glory. But Scott saluted the Rifles later for their part with a phrase that became the regimental motto: "Brave Rifles, you have gone through fire and come out steel."

Meanwhile, Trousdale's column pushed along the road bordering the northern side of the Chapultepec park. Jackson's guns eliminated a one-gun redoubt which blocked the way. After the fall of the castle, Scott sent Worth with Garland's brigade, C. F. Smith's light battalion, Duncan's and Magruder's batteries, and Sumner's dragoons to reinforce the column. They reached the northeast corner of the Chapultepec quadrangle just in time to hurl a few rounds at the retiring brigade of General Rangel. The American column moved left on the Verónica causeway and followed it without opposition to its junction with the San Cosmé road. Since Scott intended that the main weight of his attack should follow the San Cosmé route, he added Clarke's and Cadwalader's brigades as well as Huger's siege guns to Worth's force. It took Worth some time to organize his troops and refill their cartridge pouches. His men had to clear some minor fortifications near the junction and beat off an attack by Torrejón and about 1,500 cavalry, so that it was nearly 4:00 P.M. before they began their advance down the San Cosmé causeway.[17]

Because of its distance from the probable points of attack, the San Cosmé Garita had held a low priority in the allotment of resources and men. Except for a small parapet which did not even block the entire road, it was defenseless when Chapultepec fell. General Rangel hastily extended the defenses when he arrived. Santa Anna contributed three cannon and three additional battalions. Using these men, General Peña threw up a redoubt, manned the roofs of the nearby houses, and had the nearer arches of the aqueduct filled in with sandbags.

Worth's men found it impossible to advance down the roadway in the face of the Mexican fire, but Garland's brigade worked forward on the right, using the arches of the aqueduct for protection. On the left sappers tunneled through a line of buildings fronting the northern side of the road to open a passage for Clarke's men. Lieutenant U. S. Grant with a party of the 4th Infantry dragged a mountain howitzer across some ditches on the right and hauled the gun into the tower of San Cosmé church. Lieutenant Raphael Semmes of the Navy accomplished a similar mission on the other side of the road. The fire of the American artillery soon forced the Mexicans to abandon the redoubt in the garita. The position was promptly occupied by Lieutenant Henry J. Hunt with a gun from Duncan's battery. By five o'clock Rangel had been badly wounded and his 24-pounder howitzer knocked out. As if this were not enough, Lieutenant George H. Terrett and some Marines suddenly appeared atop a three-story house behind the Mexican position and in a single volley eliminated nearly every gunner and the artillery's mules. When the Americans charged out of the house to finish the work with the bayonet, they met other blue-clad troops advancing down the highway.

At this the Mexicans fled in panic, sweeping Santa Anna and a body of reinforcements ahead of them. Some of the fugitives collected at the Ciudadela, but most scattered. By six o'clock Worth's men were inside the city. Rather than push farther into the city as darkness fell, Worth bedded down his force in houses near the garita. As a goodnight message, Worth had Huger's gunners drop five 10-inch mortar shells near the National Palace.

The cost to the Americans for the days successes had been considerable but less than that of Contreras and Churubusco: 130 killed, 703 wounded, and twenty-nine missing. The Mexican losses are unknown but approximated 3,000, including 823 men taken prisoner. The latter included six generals. The Mexico City defenses had been breached but the city had yet to be taken. As his exhausted American troops fell asleep, they could look forward to another day of bloody fighting to clear the city of its defenders. Santa Anna had about 5,000 troops and eighteen cannon at the Ciudadela and perhaps 7,000 others in the city.

But that fight was not to be. The city's leaders had always resisted the idea of a fight to the death within its streets because of the damage and civilian casualties which would result. They urged Santa Anna to abandon it. He concluded that honor had been satisfied, and by 1:00 A.M. the Mexican Army had made an orderly withdrawal to Guadalupe Hidalgo.

The city authorities hastened to communicate the changed state of affairs to the Americans. A delegation from the *ayuntamiento* appeared at Scott's headquarters near Chapultepec at 4:00 A.M. "to demand terms of capitulation in favor of the church, the citizens, and the municipal authorities." Since the city was at his mercy, Scott refused to grant any concessions.[18]

In preparation for the occupation of the center of the city, Worth occupied the Alameda, that great park just to the east of San Cosmé, but halted at six o'clock to await the official entry. At about the same time, Quitman sent Beauregard and Lieutenant Mansfield Lovell to arrange for the surrender of the Ciudadela. They were confronted with the unusual request from the officer left in charge that they sign a receipt for it. They assured him that the American forces "gave our receipts with the points of our swords!" He did not argue further. At seven o'clock the American flag rose over the barracks. As the sun rose higher over the gray peaks of the surrounding mountains, Quitman, wearing only one shoe, and Persifor Smith led the former's division into the Grand Plaza. The troops in their battle-stained uniforms, some with bandages, struck a startling contrast to the cleanly clothed populace who thronged the streets waving white handkerchiefs, and with the sparkling foreign flags flapping from the houses of the neutrals.

Lieutenant A. S. Nicholson, USMC, hoisted an American flag over the National Palace to the cheers of the waiting troops. A growing clatter of hooves then announced the approach of Harney's dragoons, who escorted General Scott and his staff into the plaza, the General in Chief in full uniform mounted on a bay charger. Scott slowly rode along the line of troops to the accompaniment of patriotic music. The troops presented arms and cheered and hurrahed. After naming Quitman governor of the city, Scott entered the palace. Soon Marines moved into it to chase out the escaped convicts and others who had taken up temporary residence there. Then the Marines began regular patrols of the Halls of the Montezumas.[19]

Scott issued a general order congratulating his troops and reminding them that their safety lay in continued discipline. Before the day had well begun that discipline was put to the test. As Worth's command marched toward the plaza it was fired upon from some housetops, the first shot badly wounding Colonel Garland. This was the signal for rather widespread shooting, some of it from stragglers but much of it from some of the 30,000 convicts which the retreating army had freed from the prisons. Worth responded by having Lieutenant Peter V. Hagner of Huger's battery shell the offending houses with an eight-inch howitzer. Santa Anna may have contributed to the fighting with a call for an uprising to coincide with a counterattack by his army which never occurred. The sniping and the counterfire continued into the seventeenth before all the nests of resistance were rooted out.[20]

Scott's campaign drew unlimited praise from the Duke of Wellington, Europe's most distinguished soldier: "His campaign was unsurpassed in military annals. He is the greatest living soldier."[21] Indeed, the campaign deserved the accolade. With an army of less than 11,000 troops, Scott had overcome one exceeding 30,000 well dug in and defending its own capital. The Americans inflicted casualties of more than 7,000, took an additional 3,730 prisoners, and seized seventy-five cannon and 20,000 small arms along with large quantities of munitions. Few military leaders in American history would have attempted such an undertaking and fewer yet would have done so with an army cut off from its supply bases and reinforcements. Like Douglas MacArthur a century later, Scott's transcendent ability was not his strategic sense (which was acute), nor his tactical sense (which was not), but his strength of will, egotism if you like, which allowed him to plunge into operations that lesser commanders would have avoided as too risky. He simply refused to accept the possibility that he could be wrong. Nothing like the Mexico City campaign exists in American military history for sheer audacity of concept except for MacArthur's Inchon–Seoul campaign of 1950.

NOTES

For key to abbreviations used in Notes, see page xi.

1. Pacheco to Buchanan, Aug. 20, Bankhead to Trist, Aug. 21, 1847, Manning, *Diplo. Corres.*, VIII, 921–22, 926n; McCormac, *Polk*, 514; Rives, *U.S. and Mexico*, II, 500–7; Smith, *War with Mexico*, II, 133.

2. Scott to [Santa Anna], Aug. 21, 1847, Manning, *Diplo. Corres.*, VIII, 922–23; Hitchcock, *50 Years*, 279–80.

3. Hitchcock, *50 Years*, 285; Alcorta to Scott, Aug. 21, Armistice, Aug. 23, HQ Army, GO #262, Aug. 24, 1847, all in *S. Ex. Doc. 52, 30th Cong., 1st Sess.*, 308–13, 350, 356–58. An attempt to call Congress into session to consider the American proposals failed when only twenty-six members appeared. Pacheco to President of Congress, A. M. Salonio to [Pacheco], Aug. 21, 1847, *ibid.*, 309–10.

4. Smith, *War with Mexico*, II, 395–96; Pacheco, Circular, Sept. 4, 1847, YWA; Frost, *Mexican War and Warriors*, 185.

5. Scott to Santa Anna, Sept. 6, 1847, *S. Ex. Doc. 52, 30th Cong., 1st Sess.*, 346. Santa Anna denied the occupations, *ibid.*, 360–61.

6. A garita was more than a mere gate. It was the point at which the transit taxes were collected on all goods entering the city and therefore was a relatively large paved space with strong buildings for the customs officials.

7. The account of the attack on El Molino del Rey is based upon Scott to Marcy, Sept. 11, 1847 with the reports of his subordinates, *S. Ex. Doc. 1, 30th Cong., 1st Sess.*, 354–56, 361–75, 425–31, A 134–67, 192–98; HQ Army, GO #279, Sept. 7, 1847, *AGGO*, XLI½, 495–96; Balbontín, *Invasión*, 125–29; Ballentine, *English Soldier*, 238–40; Blackwood, *To Mexico with Scott*, 216–17; Brooks, *Complete History*, 405–9; Francisco Castillo Nájera, *Invasión Norte-Americana* (México, 1947), 20–27; Dawson, *Battles of U.S.*, II, 518–19; Crawford, *The Eagle*, 104; Davis, *Autobiography*, 271; Elliott, *Scott*, 531–35; George H. Gordon, "The Battles of Molina del Rey and Chapultepec," Military Historical Society of Massachusetts *Papers*, XIII (1913), 603–14; Grant, *Memoirs*, 74–75; Hamilton, "Memoirs," 79–81; Henry, *Mexican War*, 351–56; Hitchcock, *50 Years*, 293–99; Jenkins, *War Between U.S. and Mexico*, 385–97; William B. Lane, "What Our Cavalry in Mexico Did and Did Not Do and Other Things," *United Service*, XVI (July 1896), 14–21; Lawton, *Artillery Officer*, 311–14, 323–26; Moore, *Scott's Campaign*, 155–63; Pinto, Diary, 54; *Niles*, LXXIII (Oct. 9, 23, 1847), 88–89, 119–20; Ramírez, *Mexico During the War*, 155–56; Ramsey, *Other Side*, 337–46; Rea, *Apuntes Históricos*, 39; Ripley, *War with Mexico*, II, 367–86; Roa Bárcena, *Recuerdos*, III, 9–55; Santa Anna, *Detall*, 23–25; Santa Anna, *Mi Historia*, 75–78; Semmes, *Service Afloat and Ashore*, 431–49; Smith, *War with Mexico*, II, 140–47; Stevens, *Stevens*, I, 204–7; Vigil, *Invasión*, 53–55; Wilcox, *Mexican War*, 429–42.

8. J. L. Smith to H. L. Scott, Sept. 26, 1847, *S. Ex. Doc. 1, 30th Cong., 1st Sess.*, 425-30.

9. Claiborne, *Quitman*, I, 353-55; Williams, *Beauregard in Mexico*, 68-72; Elliott, *Scott*, 536-39.

10. The main sources for the description of the assault on Chapultepec are Scott to Mason, Sept. 18, 1847, and the reports of his subordinates in *AGLR'47*, S-726, which are largely reprinted in *S. Ex. Doc. 1, 30th Cong., 1st Sess.*, 375-425, A169-231. Other sources include: the Testimony in *S. Ex. Doc. 65, 30th Cong., 1st Sess.*; Carlos Alvear Acevedo, *La Guerra del 47* (México, 1957), 59-62; Balbontín, *Invasión*, 130-31; Ballentine, *English Soldier*, 242-49; Bravo to Santa Anna, Sept. 14, 1847, YWA; Claiborne, *Quitman*, I, 355-86; Crawford, *The Eagle*, 102-4; Davis, *Autobiography*, 231-35; Dawson, *Battles of U.S.*, II, 521-28; John S. Devlin, *The Marine Corps in Mexico* (Washington, 1852), 17, 24; Elliott, *Scott*, 539-47; Gordon, "Molina del Rey and Chapultepec," 616-32; Robert Hagan, Diary, 58-59, UTA; Hamlin, *Making of a Soldier*, 69; Robert Debs Heinl, Jr., *Soldiers of the Sea* (Annapolis, 1962), 51-52; Henry, *Mexican War*, 359-62; Hitchcock, *50 Years*, 302-3; Huger, List of Cannon . . . , Oct. 1, 1847, *AGLR'47*, H-830; Joseph E. Johnston, Storming of the Castle of Chapultepec, Joseph Eggleston Johnston Collection, CHS; Lane, "Regiment of Mounted Riflemen in Mexico," 306-13; Metcalf, *History of USMC*, 131-32; Ignacio Molina, "El Assalto al Castillo de Chapultepec el Día 13 de Septiembre de 1847," *Revista Positiva*, II (Oct. 1, 1902), 449; May, "Brydolf's Reminiscences," 173; Pinto, Diary, 59-69; Ramsey, *Other Side*, 353-65; J. G. Reynolds to Mrs. P. D. Twiggs, Feb. 29, 1848, Twiggs Papers; John G. Reynolds, *Conclusive Exculpation of the Marine Corps in Mexico* (New York, 1853); Ripley, *War with Mexico*, II, 396-402; Riva Palacios, *México á Través*, IV, 690-95; Roa Bárcena, *Recuerdos*, III, 57-112; Miguel A. Sanchez Lamego, *El Colegio Militar y la Defensa de Chapultepec en Septiembre de 1847* (México, 1947); Santa Anna, *Detall*, 26-29, 38-42; Santa Anna, *Mi Historia*, 81-82; Semmes, *Service Afloat and Ashore*, 453-61; Smith, *War with Mexico*, II, 152-58, 405-11; Stevens, *Campaigns*, 88-94; Stevens, *Stevens*, I, 208-10; Wilcox, *Mexican War*, 443-68; Williams, *Beauregard in Mexico*, 79-83.

11. J. L. Smith to H. L. Scott, *loc. cit.*; Williams, *Beauregard in Mexico*, 76-77. In order to secure the volunteers for the storming parties "Strong incentives were held out . . . to the officers were promised an additional grade by brevet, to Sergeants, commissions as second Lieutenants, to corporals, promotion to sergeancies, to privates that their names should be borne on the regimental books forever and to receive pecuniary rewards also." D. H. Hill Diary, Sept. 14, 1847, Smith and Judah, *Chronicles of the Gringos*, 262.

12. Pierce, to whose brigade these troops belonged, was sick with diarrhea and unable to exercise command. The brigade's third regiment, the 12th Infantry, defended the supply depot at Mixcoac.

13. The mines were never exploded because Lieutenant Manuel Alemán, the young engineer charged with the duty, could not reach the firing station before it was overrun.

14. This was a problem too often overlooked in the creation of composite forces. The officers often could not recognize their men by sight.

15. Undated note in John W. Geary Papers, YWA.

16. The sources for the account of the attack on the Belén Garita are those in note 10 plus: William L. Wessels, *Born to Be a Soldier* (Fort Worth, 1971), 18-20.

17. The sources for the account of the assault on the San Cosmé Garita were the same as those in note 10 plus: Lloyd Lewis, *Captain Sam Grant* (Boston, 1950),

249–54; Rea, *Apuntes Históricos*, 46–47; Smith and Judah, *Chronicles of the Gringos*, 264–66; Frank E. Vandiver, *Mighty Stonewall* (New York, 1957), 37–39.

18. Scott to Marcy, Sept. 18, 1847, *loc. cit.*; Manuel R. Veramendi *et al.* to Scott, Sept. 13, 1847, *Niles*, LXXIII (Nov. 6, 1847), 151.

19. Beauregard to Quitman, Sept. 17, 1847, Beauregard Papers; Williams, *Beauregard in Mexico*, 97–98; Quitman to H. L. Scott, Sept. 29, 1847, *S. Ex. Doc. 1, 30th Cong, 1st Sess.*, 409–20; Metcalf, *History of USMC*, Scott, *Memoirs*, II, 535; Elliott, *Scott*, 551–52; Smith, *War with Mexico*, II, 167. Captain Benjamin S. Roberts, who is credited in most accounts with raising the flag, was the officer of the day who oversaw the raising. Lieutenant Nicholson did the actual work. T. Y. Field to R. R. Beale, Aug. 15, 1848, Thomas Y. Field Papers, MCM.

20. H.Q. Army, GO #284, Sept. 14, 1847, Worth to H. L. Scott, Sept. 16, Huger to H. L. Scott, Sept. 20, 1847, *S. Ex. Doc. 1, 30th Cong., 1st Sess.*, 386, 381–85, 421–25; Collins, "Journal," 86; Santa Anna to Veramendi, Sept. 15, 1847, *HAHR*, XXIV (Nov. 1944), 616–17.

21. Arthur D. Howden Smith, *Old Fuss and Feathers* (New York, 1937), 250n.

17: Mexico Occupied

ONCE SCOTT'S MEN had occupied Mexico City they faced the difficult task of governing the enemy capital and the other territory in their possession with occupation government which would win them the most friends and create the fewest enemies. General Quitman, who served as the first governor of Mexico City, kept the principal local officials in office. This reduced the irritation to the city's inhabitants and lessened the friction between them and the occupying soldiers. In another effort to limit incidents between the population and his army, Scott republished his General Order 20 with some important additions. These included military commissions to try Americans charged with crimes which, if committed in the United States, would have been "tried and severely punished by the ordinary or civil courts of the land," including murder, rape, robbery, theft, desecration of churches, and destruction of private property. The military commissions had jurisdiction over cases involving both Americans and Mexicans. Those involving Mexicans only, except for collaborators, continued to be handled by Mexican courts. The order established a Mexican police force to assist the occupation authorities in maintaining peace. "This splendid capital—its churches and religious worship"; the order continued, "its convents and monasteries; its inhabitants and property, are, moreover, placed under the special safeguard of faith and honor of the American army."

The order levied a contribution of $150,000 on the city, to be paid in two installments. Twenty thousand dollars, Scott announced, would be devoted to easing the suffering of the sick and wounded; $90,000 for blankets and shoes for the troops; and $40,000 for other military purposes.[1]

The provision for military commissions was unique in American military law but was forced on Scott by the lack of any statutory authority to deal with serious crimes once the troops left American soil. He had tried without success to fill this void in American law but could arouse little interest in either the War Department or Congress. Therefore, he relied upon unwritten "Martial Law," i.e., natural law as applied within the military sphere, for his authority. In practice the combination of a reliance on local officials to deal with purely Mexican matters and the military commissions to handle those involving Americans or American interests worked well. It gave a degree of stability and competence of administration which had not been seen in some areas within the memory of living man. It is not surprising, therefore, that there grew up in Mexico a movement for the incorporation of the nation within the United States or, if that failed, to offer the control of the nation to Scott.

The announcement of the military commission and the notice of the assessment appeared in the first issue of the Mexico City *American Star*, that ubiquitous newspaper which had followed the Army on its march from the coast. It was edited by John H. Warland, a Harvard graduate serving as a quartermaster sergeant in the 9th Infantry. The paper became the mouthpiece for the American command as well as the most professional of the journals published by the army.[2] On October 13 the opening of an officers' club, the Aztec Club of 1847, was another indication of a return to normalcy. General Quitman became the first president and the club numbered 160 members before closing its rolls on the evacuation of the city. It numbered among its members most of the major figures in the Mexican War army and a large group whose fame would come a decade and a half later.[3]

Naturally, American presence in the Mexican capital was not welcomed by all the natives. As Scott warned the army on September 22, a conspiracy was afoot for an uprising and a renewal of efforts to entice men to desert. He reminded any soldier so tempted of the fate of the San Patricio turncoats. A word to the wise was sufficient as neither the uprising nor widespread desertions occurred. Nevertheless, at the end of the month another order spelled out the duties of the guards who were stationed throughout the city as a step to prevent such occurrences. Another step toward preventing incidents was a directive for Americans to avoid interrupting Roman Catholic processions, services, priests' visits, and other religious activities. Although some incidents merely reflected the normal strutting of the conqueror, the basic religious antipathy shown by many American soldiers was a continuing problem.[4]

The Quartermaster soon had a thousand women at work sewing new uniforms to replace those which had seen too much of marching and battle. Since the limited supplies of clothing which had been sent to Veracruz were appropriated by troops passing through from the states, the veterans of Scott's army had received little if any new clothing since entering Mexico. Almost as interesting to some of the men was the news that the National Theater would reopen on September 26 with a troop of Italian opera singers. They faced competition from a specially scheduled bullfight.[5]

For the Americans the question of future operations was a vexing one. Scott feared launching a campaign which might destroy the feeble Mexican government and with it all hopes of a negotiated peace. Yet he needed to keep his troops occupied, the countryside pacified, and sufficient pressure on the Peña government to bring it to the bargaining table. With this in mind he explained to Marcy on October 27 that after clearing the road to Veracruz he would probably occupy Atlisco, eighteen miles south of Puebla; Toluca, sixty-five miles west of Mexico City; and perhaps Orizaba. To assist in implementing the administration's desire "to conquer a peace" Brigadier Generals Joseph Lane's and Caleb Cushing's brigades totaling 2,957 men were transferred from Taylor's force. In early October Adjutant General Jones estimated 15,250 troops had been dispatched or were under orders to Scott's army. These reinforcements, Marcy advised, would enable Scott to "carry on further aggressive operations; to achieve new conquests; to disperse the remaining army of the enemy in your vicinity, and prevent the organization of another." Future operations, however, should be designed to make the Mexicans sue for peace. As part of that effort, the army was to levy military contributions upon the Mexicans.[6]

Shortly after his withdrawal from Mexico City, Santa Anna split his army. He led one section in a desperate attempt to retake Puebla while the remainder retired to Querétaro under ex-President Herrera. The garrison of Puebla had a foretaste of what was to come on

August 25 when some Mexican cavalry seized 700 animals at a muleyard outside the city. Thirty-two men, chiefly teamsters, gave chase. They were surrounded and nearly annihilated, losing ten men killed. A more permanent group of Mexican visitors appeared before the town on September 7, much to the annoyance of the Americans who mistook the cloud of dust for that being raised by a relief column.

During the night of September 13-14 about 4,000 Mexicans under Brigadier General Joaquín Rea, the commander of the surrounding guerrillas, infiltrated the city. It was the start of a twenty-eight-day siege. The Americans, led by Brevet Colonel Thomas Childs, held three separate positions, the citadel of San José, Fort Loretto, and a convent. Although the Mexicans drove off most of the garrison's cattle and sheep, enough were rescued to prevent a food shortage developing.

Rea summoned Childs to surrender on the sixteenth, and on his refusal the Mexican horsemen unsuccessfully attacked San José. Two days later the American artillery broke up a second attack. Although they kept the Americans inside their works, the Mexicans avoided further confrontations with the artillery until Santa Anna arrived from Mexico City on September 22. The next day 500 men attempted to storm unsuccessfully the American strongpoint at the convent. Although he did not launch another assault, Santa Anna formally demanded the garrison's surrender. Once again Childs refused. The attacks resumed on the twenty-seventh and continued until October 1.

During the last night of September, Santa Anna withdrew most of the besiegers in an effort to intercept an approaching column under General Joseph Lane. Rea, with the remaining troops, kept up a close siege, although the Americans made a pair of sorties to remove annoying Mexican strongpoints. On October 2 Captain William F. Small and a detachment from San José killed seventeen Mexicans defending a barricade of cotton bales and blew up a nearby building. Three days later Captain John Herron with a company of Pennsylvanians drove the Mexicans from another building which enfiladed the plaza before San José. After Rea made a demonstration on the eighth, both sides accepted a three-day truce because of the death of the Archbishop of Puebla.[7]

The occupation forces at Mexico City could not move to Childs's assistance because fall rains had made the roads too soft to support heavy wagons. The relief had to come from the troops who were collecting at Veracruz. The first to leave was a mixed force of about 1,000 men initially assigned to Colonel Lewis D. Wilson. After his death from fever, the post passed to Major Folliot T. Lally. The column set out on August 6, but since its sixty-four wagons were erroneously rumored to contain $1 million in specie about 1,200 to 1,500 guerrillas collected under Padre Jarauta and Juan Aburto. The initial attacks near the Paso de Ovejas during the afternoon of the tenth caused Lally to ask for reinforcements. The two companies which responded lost their ammunition, money, and baggage, as well as Colonel Wilson's dispatches, and failed to break through to the column. Their fight, however, reduced the pressure on Lally's column, which continued its advance and seized the Puente Nacional after a hard fight on the twelfth. There it waited in vain two days for the reinforcements before resuming the advance. The column cleared the Mexicans from Cerro Gordo in another stiff fight and brushed aside a smaller force just outside Jalapa before entering that friendly town on the twentieth. Lally had lost twenty-four men killed and sixty-eight wounded but no wagons.[8]

The action was the last for Aburto. Shortly after the Paso de Ovejas fight, in which he commanded the Mexicans, he came down with a fever from which he subsequently died.[9] Since after Padre Jarauta he was the most active partisan leader along the Veracruz–Jalapa route, his death was a great blow to the Mexicans. Another came with the arrival of Colonel John C. Hays's regiment of Texas horsemen. One of its first missions was a raid on Colonel Mariano Cenobio's home and base at the Hacienda de San Juan, about thirty miles from Veracruz. Hays's men killed two or three guerrillas, scattered the remainder, and burned Cenobio's house.[10]

How much effect the death of Aburto or the stepped-up anti-guerrilla operations had are difficult to determine. Whatever the cause, the next columns passed with relatively little trouble. The first of these was General Lane's reinforced brigade. About 1,700 strong, it marched out of Veracruz on September 19 and fought several small skirmishes before reaching Plan del Rio on the twenty-seventh. There Lane learned that Lally's force had been ordered to push on rapidly to relieve Puebla. Lane and his force promptly set out to assist. Enroute he overtook Lally and at Perote he added Colonel Wynkoop's garrison.[11]

When Santa Anna learned of the approach of Lane's column, he pulled the bulk of his forces from the siege, intending to ambush the

Americans at the Paso del Pintal where the road ran along the side of a steep slope. While waiting for the Americans to advance into his trap, Santa Anna held his men at Huamantla. When about twelve miles away, Lane learned of Santa Anna's presence. Leaving his train under a strong guard, he marched in overpowering heat toward Huamantla. The advance guard consisted of Major Samuel H. Walker and four companies of cavalry. Three miles from their objective they sighted about 2,000 green-clad Mexican lancers. Without waiting for the main body to catch up, Walker ordered a charge. The attack drove the Mexicans through the town. Walker concluded that the fight was finished and collected his men in the town to secure some artillery that the Mexicans had abandoned. There his men were caught by a counterattack and cut to pieces. Walker himself fell, apparently shot by a civilian from the window of a nearby house. The survivors took shelter in a church until the infantry arrived. The Mexicans then withdrew toward Querétaro. In the fight the Americans had lost thirteen killed and eleven wounded. In retaliation for the death of Walker, Lane turned his men loose on the town. They ransacked churches, stores, and private houses in a drunken spree of pillage, murder, rape, and wanton destruction. One observer reported that 200 men were so drunk they could not march back to camp. The sack of Huamantla was the only one staged by a large body of Americans. Other atrocities which occurred were all limited to a small handful of men. Lane's column, now able to walk even if suffering a massive hangover, reached Puebla on October 12. It had to fight its way into the town through the remaining elements of Rea's force before linking with the garrison early in the afternoon.[12]

Coincident to his launching the abortive attack on Puebla, Santa Anna renounced his presidency. The resignation left the government in an ambiguous legal state. Santa Anna proposed to transfer power to a triumvirate composed of the President of the Supreme Court, General Herrera, and Brigadier General Lino José Alcorta. However, the Council of Government, whose approval was needed for the Herrera and Alcorta appointments, was not functioning and the President of the Supreme Court had died. Manuel Peña y Peña, the senior justice of the court, was acceptable to most factions but he was old and feeble. Under pressure from a group of leading Mexicans, Peña agreed to serve as acting president until an interim one could be chosen.[13]

On the last day of September in a strong move toward governmental stability, Peña named Herrera to replace Santa Anna as commander of the Mexican Army. A week later the acting president directed Santa Anna to surrender his command and prepare for a court-martial. Such a step was necessary if the new government were to establish its control over the country. As long as Santa Anna commanded the Army he could reclaim the right to the presidency by the simple act of resigning his command. Santa Anna, who realized that he could gain nothing by continuing to hold power, surrendered the post with only a mild protest against the injustice of the act. Mexico's helplessness was evident in any dispassionate view of her situation. The main army numbered about 3,000 men; Herrera at Querétaro with the remnants of the Mexico City command, had about the same number; while at best another thousand reinforcements were enroute from Jalisco. Moreover, discipline had virtually evaporated to leave the troops still in the field nearly valueless.[14]

Not until November 1 did the road to El Piñon dry sufficiently to permit the first train for Veracruz to pass. It numbered 400 wagons with a 350-man escort commanded by Colonel William S. Harney. It was the first eastbound train since before the army had departed Puebla over two months earlier and carried many of the wounded from the fighting before the city. For many of the injured the departure was a life-saver. One of the army's surgeons noted on the day of departure that the mortality of troops from diarrhea and typhus was high because their quarters were poor and sanitation in the city was generally lacking.[15] Other trains followed with increasing regularity as the road to the coast became safer. This was Scott's top priority, but that operation was as complex and difficult as any faced by modern American soldiers who think the problem unique to mainland Asia.

Scott in mid-October directed Colonel Henry Wilson at Veracruz to establish two or three posts between there and Jalapa, each manned by 500 to 750 men, including cavalry. He set the size of garrisons for Jalapa at 750 to 1,200 and for Puebla at 1,200 to 2,000 men. Meanwhile, the authorities at the War Department grew increasingly unhappy with the situation at Veracruz as the autumn progressed. They concluded that Colonel Wilson showed insufficient energy and activity either in pushing supplies and men through to Mexico City or in eliminating the guerrillas. Colonel James Bankhead received orders to relieve him, but Scott had anticipated the need and in mid-December sent Brigadier General David E. Twiggs to take charge there.[16]

Modern military thought holds that guerrillas are successful only when they have the support of a large portion of the local populace. For that reason modern antiguerrilla doctrine calls for winning the allegiance of the local populace away from the guerrilla as well as harrying him in his bases, fragmenting his organization, and eliminating his leadership. These tactics were employed successfully by the American commanders along the supply line between Veracruz and Puebla, particularly around Jalapa.

The adverse reaction from the more established segments of the Mexican population to the excesses of the guerrillas appears in a series of letters written by the *ayuntamiento* of Jalapa to the "Gefe Politico de Este Departmento." One, for example, warned of an impending attack on a wagon train. The town authorities hoped, correctly, that the warning would prevent the attack and eliminate any possibility of retaliation by the Americans. In another the Jalapa authorities worried about the safety of the American wounded entrusted to their care, since they appeared to be an enticing target, but the men were not disturbed. Another aspect of the guerrilla war struck each of the good men of the *ayuntamiento* in November. Colonel Wynkoop, the commander of the American garrison, assessed each man 22.02 pesos to pay for a stolen trunk.[17]

The Navy applied similar pressure in the ports which it ruled. At Alvarado some Mexicans broke into the public warehouse, stole fourteen bales of cotton and two canoes which had been impounded for blockade violations, and ambushed a Marine search party. Commodore Perry promptly had the alcalde and three other men seized as hostages for the delivery of the culprits, seized two vessels in the harbor, and fined the town a thousand dollars.[18]

General Lane, by far the best American antiguerrilla leader, quickly took the offensive against those in the Puebla area. On learning that General Rea had withdrawn to Atlisco, thirty miles to the southwest, Lane with 1,500 men drove the Mexicans from the town after a running fight and artillery bombardment on October 19. Lane claimed to have inflicted an unlikely 519 casualties, at the cost of two Americans. Later in the month Lane led his men in a raid on a guerrilla base at Tlaxcala, about thirty miles north of Puebla, where he took twenty prisoners and killed others.[19]

More disastrous to the guerrillas than Lane's raids, however, was the growing dissension in their ranks. As early as November 2 Commodore Perry reported a quarrel between Jarauta and Cenobio. Indeed, at that time Colonel George W. Hughes, commanding the Puente Nacional garrison, discussed Jarauta's possible surrender with his agents. Why the discussions failed is not clear.[20]

During the night of November 9-10 Lane and 500 men returned to Tlaxcala. This time they sought General Rea and the loot from a captured merchant's train. The Americans recovered twenty-one wagons but found seven others already burned. Thirteen prisoners and a large number of horses and cattle accompanied the Americans back to Puebla. On November 23 Lane led about 135 Texas and Louisiana cavalry against Izucar de Matamoros, inflicted sixty to eighty casualties, and drove out the defenders. In the town Lane's men liberated twenty-three American prisoners and seized two cannon, much ammunition, and other stores. While passing through Galaxra Pass on their return to Puebla, the Americans withstood an attack by Rea and some 500 lancers, largely due to the effective work of Hays and his Texans. The column lost only two men killed in the skirmish but claimed to have inflicted fifty casualties on the Mexicans.[21]

Earlier in November Colonel Wynkoop with a company of Texas Rangers swooped down upon Colonel Rebolledo's base at Halcomola in one of the best-executed of all the antiguerrilla operations. They seized every man there except one. Included in the haul were Rebolledo himself and a pair of young Mexican officers who had broken their paroles by joining the band. The latter were tried by a military commission, sentenced to death, and executed by a firing squad at Jalapa on November 24. Rebolledo escaped a similar fate because of an eloquent defense by one of the American residents of Jalapa.[22]

Just as a well-conducted antiguerrilla program requires quick and decisive action against the guerrillas, it must inflict rapid and effective punishment on members of its own forces who are guilty of crimes. General Patterson did that when he had two teamsters hanged at Jalapa after they were found guilty of murdering a Mexican boy. At the end of December a soldier in the 8th Infantry was hanged for murdering some Mexican women.[23] Such actions went far in keeping the friendship of the local inhabitants and weakening the position of the guerrillas.

During the middle of December Scott issued the toughest antiguerrilla order yet promulgated. Every American post, he directed, would patrol its neighborhood and show no quarter to known killers. When captured they were to be put to death with "due solemnity" following trial by a court of three or more officers.[24]

Not all actions were successful. Lieutenant Colonel Dixon S. Miles left Veracruz on January 3 with a 1,200-man force escorting a nine-mile-long train carrying government and merchants' goods. It was too extended to protect adequately and its richness drew guerrillas like ants to a picnic. Near Santa Fe, guerrillas drove off 250 to 300 mules carrying civilian goods, but the train was able to proceed without further difficulties.[25]

General Lane, with a mixed command of 350 Mounted Riflemen, dragoons, and Texas Rangers, left Mexico City on January 18 to attempt to capture Santa Anna, then at Tehuacán about seventy miles southeast of Puebla. Passing through Puebla on the twentieth, they moved at night for secrecy, but on the twenty-second they met a coach proceeding under a safeguard from General Smith at Mexico City which they allowed to pass. Its occupants quickly sent a warning to Santa Anna who escaped, although forced to leave behind much of his personal baggage. From Tehuacán the force continued on to Orizaba, which they seized on the twenty-fifth, and Cordova, which they reached three days later. The Americans were back in Mexico City by February 10 after a skirmish with a guerrilla band under Colonel Manuel Falcón on the eighth. Colonel Bankhead and a column from Veracruz occupied Orizaba and Cordova in mid-February.[26]

Lane's force departed Mexico City again on February 17 to attack the guerrillas under Padre Jarauta operating north and northeast of the city. The American column attacked a large body of Mexicans, probably commanded by the priest himself at Sequalteplán east of Pachuca on the twenty-fifth. Although they seized or killed over fifty of the guerrillas, Jarauta was not among them. This was the last significant clash in central Mexico.[27]

Although both had been instructed to do so, neither Taylor nor Scott had complied with the administration's directives to levy contributions upon the Mexicans in the occupied areas. Both believed that to apply the taxes would drastically reduce if not eliminate their ability to secure supplies and destroy their efforts to win the friendship of the inhabitants. The President, as he informed his cabinet, wanted the weight of the war to fall on the "wealthy inhabitants" so as to increase their pressure for peace. The argument was logical but not particularly realistic, since the pressure exerted on the Mexican government by persons living in the regions affected by contributions was quite limited. Nevertheless, Acting Secretary of War John Y. Mason in early September reiterated the President's hope that they would be imposed. A further tightening of the economic squeeze on Mexico occurred in early November when Secretary Walker increased the tariff on goods entering Mexico. To this was soon added an export duty on gold and silver.[28]

Scott complied with the instructions to impose assessments in a November 25 General Order. It halted the shipment of uncoined bullion; stopped payment of rent by the American forces; but permitted payment to continue for subsistence, forage, and other necessities. On December 15 Scott ordered that local taxes be collected on schedule and the share normally allotted to the central government be paid to the occupation forces. While he abolished the national lottery and the interstate duties, Scott issued a call for bids to collect the tobacco, playing-card, and stamped-paper taxes. On the last day of the year, the tax assessments to the states were announced. In general they were four times the direct taxes paid to the federal government in 1843 or 1844.[29]

In order to prevent the fraudulent shipment of bullion, Scott had it sent to the nearest assay office under a system of permits from the local American commanders. In this way the taxes could be collected before the metal moved to the mints for coinage and the attempts to smuggle untaxed metals from the country further inhibited. In mid-January 1848 Brevet Colonel John L. Gardner assumed responsibility for the collection of the taxes on bullion as Superintendent of Assessment for the Federal District. In practice, the bullion decrees were unenforceable. The mines were foreign-owned and the mining areas so widespread that the Americans could not occupy all of them, nor interdict all the routes by which bullion moved. For administrative reasons the monopolies were not enforced, while the nonpayment of rents was not always feasible nor wise, since many of the buildings occupied were owned by friendly Mexicans or neutrals. In all only $3,935,676 was collected, including $106,928 in customs duties imposed in ports under naval control.[30]

The sting of the assessments was reduced for some Mexicans at least by arrangements worked out by Archbishop Juan Manuel of Mexico City for the release of the prisoners which the Americans had held since the battles before the city. Under the agreement the Bishop visited the prisoners in person, explained to them the meaning of a parole, and administered the oath by which they agreed not to take up arms against the Americans.[31]

On the purely military front Scott decided to await General Butler and additional reinforcements before occupying more territory. Nevertheless, in preparation for establishing brigade-sized occupation forces in various parts of central Mexico, Scott in mid-December organized the regulars into three brigades under Brigadier Generals Persifor Smith, George Cadwalader, and Bennet Riley.[32] The day after Christmas the orders for the first of those moves appeared. It established a Department of Pachuca in the silver-mining region northeast of Mexico City. Others at Toluca and Cuernavaca soon followed.[33]

While the army pushed its occupation of central Mexico, Commander Matthew C. Perry's Home Squadron extended its control over Mexico's lesser east coast ports. After the seizure of Veracruz only two ports of consequence remained in Mexican hands, Tuxpán and Tabasco.

Perry first turned his attention to Tuxpán. It was a difficult target. Five batteries mounting eight guns protected the six-mile-long approach up the winding Tuxpán River. They were manned by 300 or 400 men under Brigadier General Martín Perfecto de Cos.[34]

The fortifications made a direct waterborne approach upriver so hazardous that Perry decided to employ both the Mosquito Flotilla and a landing party of 1,519 men with four pieces of artillery. The assault force reached Tuxpán Bar early on April 17. During the afternoon of April 18 the small craft and the thirty barges carrying the landing party slowly moved upriver. After landing detachments to secure two downriver fortifications, the flotilla seized the positions on the edge of the town at about 3:00 P.M. In another hour they had occupied the town without difficulty. Mexican resistance had been so light that Perry's force lost only two killed and nine wounded.

The night passed quietly except for some of the sailors who sampled General Cos's champagne. An expedition further upriver the next day visited some spectacularly beautiful country but garnered few prizes. Meanwhile, the rest of the force removed the guns and usable equipment and destroyed the fortifications and unwanted supplies. The Americans evacuated the town on April 22 and returned on board their vessels, which sailed for Antón Lizardo except for a pair of craft which remained on blockade off the bar.

Despite the success of the Tuxpán expedition, the squadron continued to face great difficulties. It needed engineers, medical officers, and repairs to the machinery of several of the small steamers. Other vessels, including the ship-of-the-line *Ohio* and the frigate *Raritan*, were due to return home and the loss of their large contributions to the landing force threatened to halt operations ashore. In part to offset the loss as well as to garrison the already occupied ports, and to combat the growing guerrilla menace, Perry requested additional Marines. His appeal crossed orders to add his Marines to the six-company force being sent to reinforce Scott.[35]

Moreover, Perry had to send five of his scarce vessels to watch the coast east of Veracruz when it appeared that Santa Anna might flee into exile after his defeat at Cerro Gordo.[36] The Mexican authorities in Tabasco and the eastern part of Veracruz state suspected that the concentration presaged an invasion and hastily improved the defenses of Tabasco. Since so many troops could be pinned without active operations on his part, Perry postponed any attack.

Tabasco's clandestine trade with Carmen, however, worried him. In order to investigate the situation and establish control over that Campeche port, he sailed from Veracruz on May 10. The Commodore with four vessels rendezvoused with the blockaders off the entrance to the Laguna del Carmen on May 16. The following day Perry took formal possession of the town and surrounding area. He established a military government there in hopes of controlling the flow of supplies which slipped through the myriad of interlocking waterways to Tabasco.[37]

Perry seized the opportunity to investigate affairs in Yucatán. The treatment to be accorded her was one of the most ticklish nonmilitary questions faced by American naval commanders in the Gulf of Mexico. Yucatán had broken with Mexico and declared her neutrality in the war with the United States. Perry's predecessor, Commodore David Conner, initially treated Yucatán vessels as neutrals but dropped the concession in the late summer of 1846 when it appeared that the pro-Mexican faction had gained control. At the end of the year the independence faction launched a diplomatic offensive aimed at convincing the Americans to restore the earlier treatment. This included the dispatch of an agent, José Rovira, to consult with Secretary of State James Buchanan in Washington. Although the policy was not changed, Secretary of the Navy John Y. Mason did direct his commander in the Gulf of Mexico to investigate the state of affairs in Yucatán. Commander Alexander Slidell Mackenzie and Captain Samuel L. Breese in the *Albany* made the investigation. They were assured by the local officials of the state's continued independence and neutrality. Without waiting for their report, Perry officially recognized Yucatán's neutrality on May 24. Commander Henry Adams in the *John Adams* repeated the visit in early September and received assurances of Yucatán's continued neutrality and of her mortification over negligible support from the United States and the occupation of Carmen. Coincident with Adams's voyage, Justo Sierra O'Reilly, the Yucatán agent-designate in the United States, left for his post. In November he met Secretary of State Buchanan and requested the lifting of the occupation of Carmen, the voiding of the tariff there, and a guarantee against Mexican reprisals.

Perry himself visited Campeche in early December and again after the turn of the year. He reported a growing need for active American support to counter a large Indian uprising. Sierra in mid-February formally asked for both a recognition of neutrality and a lifting of the embargo on arms shipments. Later in the month he filed a strong protest over the failure of the Treaty of Guadalupe Hidalgo to contain any protection for Yucatán. Finally, after much hesitation, Polk, in March, decided to allow Perry to supply arms to the whites in Yucatán; authorized the export of five tons of powder from New York; and exempted Yucatán vessels from duty at Carmen.

Perry, with an impressive force consisting of the *Mississippi*, three other steamers, and a bomb brig, returned to Campeche in early March. He conferred with Governor Santiago Mendez who reiterated Yucatán's need for foreign support for the hard-pressed whites, but that assistance was more than he could provide. He did, however, send the steamer *Iris* (Lieutenant Commander W. L. Herndon) to assist the refugees after the Indians overran Valladolid. Polk and the cabinet discussed the Yucatán request for intervention on April 22. They decided to forward the request to Congress along with the Yucatán proposal for annexation. Polk did so without recommendation, although he pointed out that the United States did not have the troops to assist the Yucatecos. He noted that similar annexation proposals had also been made to Britain and Spain. The acceptance by either of those states Polk announced, in what came to be known as the Polk Corollary, was contrary to the Monroe Doctrine.[38]

Soon after his return from Carmen, Perry decided to seize Tabasco. Undoubtedly the decision grew out of the difficulty in cutting illicit trade as well as the impending loss of the crews from the departing vessels. In addition, Perry had an accurate report on the town's strengthened defenses from Captain W. A. Howard, who had taken the *McLane* upstream on a reconnaissance during April 22. Perry therefore collected all available vessels off Frontera during June 12 and 13.[39]

As Howard reported, the defenses had grown since Perry's first visit. A new commander, Colonel Domingo Echagaray, arrived during April. He had piles driven in the river upstream from the aptly named Devil's Bend, some four miles below the town, to prevent passage by American warships. Three breastworks, extending from the river to the chaparral on the left, and a fort provided a defense in depth against any force advancing along the left bank of the river. The defenses, however, were too extensive for the available 900 men. Moreover, all except one were exposed to attack from the rear should a naval force break through the obstructions. Since none of the breastworks mounted cannon bearing on the river, nothing could stop such a force short of Fort Itúrbide, a mile from the town, and if it could be passed Tabasco was at the mercy of the invaders.

Perry's attack force gathered at Frontera during the early morning of June 14. It consisted of the four steamers of the Mosquito Flotilla (*Scourge, Scorpion, Spitfire, Vixen*), the brigs *Washington, Stromboli,* and *Vesuvius,* the merchant schooner *Spitfire* carrying Captain George W. Taylor's "patent India rubber camels," inflatable rubber bags which Perry hoped to use to remove the obstructions, forty ships' boats carrying 1,050 men, and seven surfboats with a field piece each. After the steamers completed coaling, the force got under way at about 5:30 in the afternoon. The expedition moved upstream slowly, with the steamers towing the other craft. Early in the morning it intercepted a canoe whose occupants warned of ambushes ahead. Perry, therefore, halted until daylight.

The squadron resumed the advance at about 7:00 A.M. At 4:15 P.M. near Santa Teresa, about twelve miles below Tabasco, it ran through an ambush without difficulty. About ninety minutes later the American vessels entered Devil's Bend and came under fire from some Mexicans in the chaparral. Even so, the greatest danger came from the indiscriminately aimed answering fusilade of the excited Americans. Shortly afterward the great cannon on the *Vesuvius* threw a ten-inch shell at some cavalry who quickly dispersed. Since they could not pass the obstructions a hundred yards ahead, and needed daylight to land the shore force, Perry had his vessels anchor in the Devil's Bend for the night. At dusk a lone Mexican came down to the riverbank, shot a man on the *Vesuvius*'s forecastle, and escaped. Beyond this the Mexicans avoided attacks on the American vessels, probably out of respect for their heavy guns.

At daybreak on July 16 Perry sent a party to study the obstructions. That effort came to an abrupt end when the defenders opened fire, severely wounding Lieutenant William May. Perry then decided to disembark his landing force at a point marked by seven palm trees. After a short bombardment, Perry led ashore 1,173 men and ten pieces of artillery. The sailors and Marines struggled forward in oppressive heat through tall grass and chaparral, following a trail marked and prepared for them by an advance party who doubled as pioneers.

Their route bypassed the first Mexican defenses and brought the Americans, instead, against the main work, Acachapán. Its 600 defenders, half cavalry, under Colonel Claro Hidalgo, had two pieces of artillery. Perry halted his men, brought forward his artillery, and began shelling the position. When the defenders appeared to waiver, Perry ordered a charge. The Americans sprinted forward with little organization but such great spirit that the Mexicans fled. They abandoned clothes, bedding, and uneaten breakfasts.

Meanwhile, the men on the vessels anchored in Devil's Bend busied themselves removing the obstacles. They loosened the piles with powder charges, and the *Spitfire*, temporarily commanded by her executive officer, Lieutenant David D. Porter, pulled them clear. At about ten o'clock in the morning the four steamers squeezed through the opening and headed upstream. Just beyond Acachapán they fired on the landing force, whom they mistook for Mexicans but luckily without damage. On passing the third breastwork the steamers came under the fire of Fort Itúrbide. The Mexican gunners hit both the *Scorpion* and the *Spitfire* but failed to check the Americans who ran past the fort and opened a rapid fire on it from the rear. Lieutenant Porter and a landing party of sixty-eight men took advantage of the confusion caused by that bombardment to swarm ashore and drive the Mexicans from the work. The steamers continued up the river and dropped anchor off the town, which surrendered unconditionally. At 11:50 Passed Midshipman Isaac N. Briceland planted a flagstaff and flag in a hole in the roof of the governor's house. Somewhat later the steamers ineffectually exchanged fire with Mexicans in the chaparral outside of the town.

The hot and tired land force, disappointed not to be able to share the action, glimpsed the American flag flying over Fort Itúrbide at about two o'clock in the afternoon and entered the town an hour and a half later. The Americans had inflicted some thirty casualties upon the Mexicans at a cost of six men wounded and three missing. Echagaray retired four miles upstream to Tamulté with approximately 111 soldiers and 115 civilians. The last significant port remaining in Mexican hands had fallen. Mexico was cut off from all outside aid except that which could be transported in dugouts and other small coastal craft from Campeche.

Pending instructions from Washington, Perry temporarily garrisoned the town. He placed Commander Gershom J. Van Brunt in charge with a detachment of Marines and three small craft. This force proved too small to disperse the guerrilla bands who hung about the town and made occasional forays into it. Although Perry reinforced the garrison, neither Van Brunt nor his successor Commander Abraham Bigelow could break up the Mexican bands. Since the garrison suffered badly from yellow fever, Perry on July 19 ordered evacuation. Three days later the Americans were gone.[40]

Perry attempted to soften the loss by stationing blockaders at Frontera to interdict trade bound for Tabasco. As part of that effort, Lieutenant Samuel Lockwood in the *Scorpion* periodically patrolled up the Tabasco and Usumacenta rivers. The American presence strengthened a movement in Chiapas and Tabasco states to secede from Mexico and join Guatemala. Quite understandably, the leaders of that movement wished Perry's approval before acting and, since he withheld it, the separation never occurred.[41]

Any further operations were crippled by a yellow-fever epidemic which hit the squadron in July and August. While the scourge killed few, it effectively immobilized most of the vessels during the summer.

The inactivity received official sanction on August 4, 1847 in Secretary Mason's directive to seize no additional points. Mason also suggested that the bomb brigs, whose reason for being there vanished with the capitulation of Ulúa, be sent to New Orleans for disposal. Perry refused because he was so short of vessels that he had to use them on the blockade.[42]

Despite the shortages, Perry submitted proposals for new operations in mid-October. By removing the garrisons from Tuxpán, Alvarado, Coatzacoalcos, Frontera, and Carmen, he could free enough men for a joint Army–Navy expedition across the Isthmus of Tehuantepec. This, he argued, would cut Tabasco and Chiapas states off from the rest of Mexico and permit their conquest by a 2,000-man force. To facilitate such an expedition, Perry requested reinforcement by small, flat-bottomed river schooners drawing not over eighteen inches of water; three river steamers; and Marines with light field equipment, engineering tools, and a few mountain howitzers.[43] The plan meshed with the administration's desire to secure control of the Isthmus and received its blessing. Mason ordered the Pacific Squadron to cooperate and dispatched additional Marines to the Gulf, but the approach of peace prevented any operations.

The prospect of a Tehuantepec expedition notwithstanding, Perry on January 10, 1848 requested relief. Secretary Mason turned down the request. Apparently he believed it undesirable to change commanders before Perry had served his full term, although he may well have concluded that Perry's request reflected the decrease in chances for distinction as the war passed into a passive phase. The Secretary issued instructions to govern the evacuation of the naval forces on May 19. They directed the sale of all goods not easily returned to the United States and gave Perry discretionary powers over the timing of departure and the destination of the Mosquito Flotilla. The latter were generally sold upon their return home.[44]

Perry learned of the Mexican ratification of the peace treaty on May 28. Two days later he authorized the start of restoration of the customs houses to the local officials. On June 11 Veracruz reverted to Mexican control and four days later Perry, in his flagship *Cumberland*, left for New York. Before the end of the month all of his squadron, except those vessels being sent north for sale, had orders to gather at Pensacola.[45] The problems facing the Navy in its withdrawal from Mexico were negligible compared to those facing the Army. Perry's squadron had maintained only limited depots on shore, and except for customs had had only limited financial dealings with the local inhabitants.

Operations along Mexico's western shore during the last year of the war were considerably more active than those in the Gulf of Mexico. Those activities aimed at throttling Mexican trade on the Pacific and seizing the long peninsula of Baja California. Except for sporadic attempts to impose a blockade on the Mexican ports along the Gulf of California, the southern operations had to await the completion of the seizure of Alta California.

As early as August 19, 1846 Commodore Stockton proclaimed a blockade of the whole of the Mexican west coast. Such an unenforceable blockade ran counter to both the laws of war and United

States policy. When it reached the attention of Secretary Mason he directed it be rescinded and replaced by an enforceable one.[46] In the interim Stockton began his blockade. In August the sloops-of-war *Warren* and *Cyane* departed California for Mazatlán and San Blas respectively. During September the *Cyane* landed a party who spiked thirty-four cannon at San Blas and then sailed north to the pearl-fishing village of La Paz, the capital of Baja California. After seizing nine small Mexican craft in the harbor, Commander DuPont of the *Cyane* arranged with Governor Francisco Palacio Mirranda for the neutralization of the peninsula. DuPont then hastened to the Sonora port of Guaymas in hopes of intercepting a Mexican gunboat reported headed there. Reaching Guaymas on October 6, DuPont demanded the surrender of the shipping in the port, including two small gunboats. The commandant, Colonel Antonio Campuzano, refused, but on the following day a boarding party seized the brig *Condor*, the largest vessel in port, and forced the burning of the gunboats. The Americans themselves destroyed the *Condor* when she proved to be unusable.[47]

Meanwhile the *Warren* had appeared off Mazatlán on September 6, and on the following morning her boats cut the Mexican privateer brig *Malek Adhel* out of the harbor. She quickly embarked an American crew and broke the Stars and Stripes as a United States warship. On the ninth Commander Hull declared the port closed.[48] When their supplies gave out in October and November, the two sloops returned to California, leaving no American vessels to enforce the blockade. In early October Stockton directed the *Portsmouth* to fill the void, but the Los Angeles campaign delayed her sailing as well as that of the *Cyane* bound for Acapulco.[49]

After the reconquest of southern California in January 1847, Commodore Stockton revived his plans for operations against the Mexican west coast, but he was relieved before putting them into effect. Meanwhile, new instructions from Washington called for occupation of at least one position in Baja California as a step toward ensuring American acquisition of the peninsula in the peace settlement.[50]

The first of a new wave of blockaders, and the first American vessel to be stationed in the area since November, was the *Portsmouth* which reestablished the blockade at Mazatlán on February 17, 1847. The reinstitution elicited a strong protest from the local British naval commander on the reasonable grounds that the blockade was paper and had been interrupted.[51]

The *Portsmouth* subsequently shifted to San José del Cabo, a small farming center which nestled in the southern end of Baja California. She seized the town on March 30 and four days later repeated the performance at San Lucas. In neither instance did the *Portsmouth* leave a garrison behind. Continuing along the coast she anchored off La Paz on April 13. Governor Mirranda agreed to a formal surrender, but the arrangement included some unusual provisions. Not only did it continue the civil officials in office but it granted the Bajacalifornians the rights and privileges of United States citizens. If Mirranda was willing to collaborate with the Americans, a sizable group of Bajacalifornians were not. In mid-February a group of loyalists, chiefly from Mulejé and Comondú, met at Santa Anita and declared that Mauricio Castro had replaced Mirranda. The loyalists, under the military leadership of Captain Manuel Pineda, prepared a guerrilla war against the invaders.[52]

In late April the *Cyane* returned to the Gulf of California. During the twenty-ninth she was joined off Mazatlán by the *Independence* with Commodore W. Branford Shubrick embarked. He carried a new notice formally reinstating the blockade. The sight of the two warships off the port threw the residents into panic. They believed that the Americans were about to land and wreak havoc on the town and its inhabitants. After the *Independence* and *Portsmouth* returned to California, the *Cyane* attempted to maintain the blockade alone by shuttling between Mazatlán and San José.[53] As a result she technically lifted the Mazatlán blockade although the summer hurricanes effectively closed the port after May.

On April 23 General Kearny received the order to seize a post in Baja California. He arranged for Commodore Biddle to ferry two companies to the peninsula but delayed their departure until he could verify rumors of a Mexican counterstroke against Alta California. As matters developed that expedition never advanced beyond Guanajuato because of the uncertainties of Mexican domestic politics.[54] On May 30, just prior to his departure from California, Kearny ordered Lieutenant Colonel Henry S. Burton and two companies of New Yorkers to the peninsula. The men sailed on the storeship *Lexington* (Lieutenant Theodorus Bailey) on July 4 and waded ashore at La Paz on the twenty-first. Burton quickly established a strong post on a rise overlooking the town and harbor.[55]

In July Commodore Shubrick replaced Commodore Biddle as commander of the Pacific Squadron and shortly ordered additional craft into the Gulf. They were the advance guard of the main body of the Pacific Squadron which, after clamping a blockade on Guaymas, would proceed to seize Mazatlán, San Blas, and Acapulco. One of the earliest vessels to reach the Gulf, the small sloop-of-war *Dale* (Commander T. A. Selfridge) at Burton's request visited Loreto and Mulejé in an effort to dampen the resistance of the Castro–Pineda supporters. At Mulejé on October 1 Pineda's band repulsed the *Dale*'s landing party in a sharp engagement lasting about six hours and prevented the Americans from cutting the supply line to Guaymas.[56]

More effective was the effort to shut Guaymas. On October 17 the *Portsmouth* anchored near the frigate *Congress* in the outer roads of the mainland port. Captain Elie A. F. La Vallette, the commander of the *Congress*, made an informal proposal for the port's surrender on the next day and followed it on the nineteenth with a formal one. Colonel Campuzano refused but hastily withdrew his men. Because Campuzano's reply arrived late in the afternoon, La Vallette postponed the landing until the morning of the twentieth. After a bombardment of over an hour which raised so much dust that the Americans thought the Mexicans were returning the fire, the civil authorities reported the evacuation. At two that afternoon the American vessels landed their Marines and fifteen minutes later hoisted the Stars and Stripes. Since he lacked the men to garrison the town and its shipping could be controlled by a single man-of-war anchored in the road stead, La Vallette contented himself with proclaiming the conquest and establishing a set of duties to be paid to an American-appointed collector of the port.[57]

Although La Vallette and his successors in charge of the port had to contend with occasional forays into the town, they denied its use to the Mexicans until the end of the war. The largest of those clashes took place on November 17 when Commander Selfridge and a landing party from the *Dale* were pinned down by about 250 Mexicans until they could get fire support from the sloop. As a result of the American blockade from the sea and Campuzano's denial of food and water, most of the port's inhabitants fled. Landing parties from the *Dale* launched a series of assaults near Guaymas between November 1847 and April 1848 which forced abandonment of the Mexican bases near the port and hastened the disintegration of Campuzano's force.[58]

Shubrick, with the main body of the American naval force, sortied from Monterey on October 16 and sailed independently for a rendezvous off Cape San Lucas. The *Independence* and the *Cyane* arrived off the white-granite bluff of the cape eleven days later. On October 29 they fell in with the *Congress* shortly before anchoring off San José del Cabo. There Shubrick learned that the Baja California guerrillas had gathered near Todos Santos, and dispatched a raiding party. The Americans made a night march on November 1-2 but were discovered in time for the Mexicans to flee.[59]

As a further step in solidifying the American hold on the peninsula, Shubrick on November 4 announced the start of active operations and the intention of the United States to keep possession after the war.[60] The proclamation drew a number of collaborators to the American side. Because of their active support of the occupation, a large number had to leave Baja California at the end of the war with the American forces in order to escape the wrath of their more patriotic neighbors.

Before leaving for Mazatlán, his next target, Shubrick placed a small garrison of Marines under Lieutenant Charles Heywood in San José del Cabo. They took station in a dilapidated old mission building on a rise overlooking the collection of rude cane and mud-built huts with straw-thatched roofs that made up the village.[61]

The Commodore, with the *Independence*, *Congress*, and *Cyane*, reached the target area on November 10. Mazatlán filled the triangular space between three hills, the apex of which thrust into the sea to form the north side of a well-protected harbor. On the seaward side of the triangle were two smaller but less used anchorages. The three American warships took positions, one in each anchorage, from which their guns dominated the city. Lieutenant Colonel Rafael Telles, the strutting insurgent who commanded the garrison, could muster about 560 men. Despite clear indications of the impending attack, he did nothing to prepare the defenses, and upon the Americans' arrival he hastily withdrew the garrison. From his safe camp at Palos Prietos, Telles haughtily refused Shubrick's surrender demand on the eleventh.

Captain La Vallette and a 730-man landing party came ashore during the early afternoon without difficulty, and shortly before 2:00 P.M. raised the American flag. Shubrick immediately issued military government regulations which shifted control of the customs-house to the conquerors, but otherwise interfered as little as possible with the lives of the townspeople. Four hundred American sailors and Marines garrisoned the town and manned the fortifications laid out by Lieutenant Henry W. Halleck of the Army engineers.[62] They and the guns of the warships lying in the harbor discouraged any Mexican thoughts of a counterstroke.

Telles hovered in the neighborhood of the port, throwing out cavalry patrols in an effort to prevent supplies reaching the garrison. On November 13 a raiding party entered the town to burn three small craft in the harbor. Two nights later other Mexicans pushed a sentry box off one of the wharfs. These attacks as well as a desire to return the sailors to their ships prompted Shubrick to request a garrison of 500 to 1,000 men from General Scott. The army commander agreed to provide them once he received sufficient reinforcements, but they never arrived.

Almost immediately the Americans mounted amphibious expeditions in an effort to subdue the hinterland. On November 18 a patrol attempted but failed to surprise the Mexican advance post at Urias. Two days later a larger force attacked Urias but the defenders escaped. A pair of skirmishes on the nights of December 12-13 and 13-14 and one during Christmas, which were more successful, completed actions around Mazatlán.[63]

While Shubrick consolidated his control of Mazatlán, the revolt in Baja California simmered. By early November Captain Pineda had organized his force sufficiently to start the long-expected offensive. Dividing his forces, he attacked both La Paz and San José del Cabo. He hit La Paz first. About 180 men attempted to force their way into the town during November 18 but were driven out by American fire. Pineda then withdrew about six miles to await the arrival of the forces which had been infesting San José. The combined force, now outnumbering the defenders nearly two to one, attacked during the afternoon of November 27 only to be badly mauled by the New Yorkers. Pineda remained in the area until after the arrival of the *Cyane* on December 8 but kept well away from American guns. The siege cost Burton's force one man killed and three wounded, while the Bajacalifornians lost nine or ten killed and six or seven injured.

The other prong of Pineda's offensive struck San José del Cabo on November 19. Heywood's small garrison held the well-placed but dilapidated old mission and a nearby house. The Bajacalifornians attempted to rush the American works during the next two nights without success. During November 21 the Mexicans withdrew when two vessels hove into sight. The attackers assumed that they were warships, but in fact they were a pair of American whalers. Nevertheless, the merchantmen agreed to lend some powder and reinforce the garrison until relief arrived. That appeared on November 26 with the arrival of the storeship *Southampton*.[64]

The Baja California attacks upset Shubrick's plans for operations south of Mazatlán by drawing off several of his scarce war craft. In order to maintain a blockade of San Blas he employed a small tender and the storeship *Lexington*. Although they destroyed the guns in the harbor fortifications and cut out two small schooners, the arrangement was makeshift at best. Nevertheless, the spiking of three guns at Manzanillo later in January eliminated all the seaward defenses along Mexico's Pacific coast except for the crumbling fortifications at Acapulco.[65]

Meanwhile in Baja California, Captain Pineda regrouped his forces and awaited an opportunity to renew his attack. He recognized that he could not retake the American posts in the face of naval support. The comparatively large forces represented by the naval landing parties and the heavy guns of the vessels gave too great superiority to the defenders. His only chance for success, Pineda realized, lay in attacking a post while its naval support was absent. If he concentrated his entire force for that attack, he believed it would give him sufficient superiority for a quick victory.

Finding San José del Cabo without support in early January, Pineda quickly shifted his forces there. Heywood's garrison had numbered seventy-two men, about a third of them Bajacalifornia volunteers, but the presence of almost fifty women and children strained the limited food supplies. Pineda seized a foraging party on January 22 but did not attack the American positions in the village. On February 4, however, the Mexicans worked their way into town and pinned the garrison into the mission, despite counterattacks on the sixth and seventh. The Mexicans drove off a schooner bringing supplies, and on the night of February 11-12 took control of the American water supply. Luckily for the garrison, relief arrived late on the fourteenth when the *Cyane* anchored off the town. The following morning Commander DuPont led ashore a large landing party and easily broke through the Mexican lines. Pineda withdrew about 15 miles inland to Santa Anita. An American surprise attack there on March 24 failed as Pineda's men escaped but ended any threat at San José.[66]

Coincident to the last attack on San José del Cabo, Colonel Burton began planning a campaign to wipe out resistance in Baja California. A newly arrived company of New Yorkers and some recruits provided Burton for the first time with sufficient men for a field force. Their first attack broke up the Baja California camp at San Antonio on March 25 and freed five prisoners. During the fight Pineda was badly wounded and forced to give up command. On the last day of the month Burton himself, with three companies, attacked the Todos Santos camp overlooking the Pacific Ocean, killed ten men, and scattered the remainder. The remnants of that force, including Mauricio Castro, surrendered soon afterward to a joint expedition from San José and the *Cyane*. By early April the resistance in Baja California had disappeared.[67]

On March 30 Commodore Shubrick received Major General William O. Butler's order promulgating the armistice in the Valley of Mexico and ordered offensive operations stopped. The armistice also ended any possibility of the Pacific forces striking the Isthmus of Tehuantepec in order to link up the projected expedition from the Gulf of Mexico.[68]

During the spring of 1847 Shubrick, disgusted 'at having a senior officer ordered to temporary command over him, had requested relief. Secretary John Y. Mason designated Commodore Thomas apCatesby Jones, the perpetrator of the premature 1842 seizure of Monterrey, as his successor. He reached Mazatlán on May 6, 1848 in the ship-of-the-line *Ohio*.[69]

To Jones, therefore, fell the responsibility of the withdrawal of American forces. On June 13, the day he learned of the ratification of the peace treaty, Jones directed Captain La Vallette to return Mazatlán to Mexican hands on the seventeenth. On schedule the American flag came down and La Vallette transferred the town to General Manuel de la Canal y Castillo amid a 21-gun salute.

Guaymas returned to Mexican control on June 24, but six weeks were spent in preparing for the evacuation of La Paz. The delay, in large part, stemmed from the failure of the peace treaty to protect the Baja California collaborators who, as Captain Halleck claimed, included "all the most respectable people." When La Paz returned to Mexican control on September 1, about 300 collaborators joined the exodus. Among them was Señorita Amparo Ruiz, who in January 1849 would become the bride of Colonel Burton. Stopping at San José del Cabo to embark the New Yorkers there on September 6, the *Ohio* set course for Monterey. The New Yorkers were the last Americans to leave Mexican soil.[70]

Commodore Shubrick's campaign along the Mexican west coast was both well conceived and well executed. Despite shortages of men and vessels he seized or neutralized Baja California and the entire Mexican coast north of Acapulco. His steady professionalism stands in sharp contrast to the flamboyant egocentricity of Stockton and Sloat's haunting fear of a misstep. He ranks with David Conner and Matthew Calbraith Perry as one of the outstanding naval figures of the war.

NOTES

For key to abbreviations used in Notes, see page xi.

1. Quitman, Proclamation, Sept. 16, 1847, YWA; HQ Army, GO #287, Sept. 17, 1847, *S. Ex. Doc. 1, 30th Cong., 1st Sess.*, 386–87. Quitman transferred control of the city to Persifor Smith and returned home with the November 1 train. His position was a difficult one, since he was a major general without a commensurate command. He had been complaining about this since May but after the abandonment of communications with the coast it had become impossible to send him to his command on the Rio Grande. He had stayed with the Army as commander of the small 2d Division of Volunteers. His relations with Scott had not been cordial and Quitman felt he had been deprived of the opportunity for glory at Contreras and Churubusco, while in the drive for the Belén Garita he exceeded his orders and in the view of many officers caused his men to suffer unnecessary losses. Quitman to H. L. Scott, May 29, 30, June 3, Oct. 25, 1847, *H. Ex. Doc. 56, 30th Cong., 1st Sess.*, 211–17; HQ Army, GO #325, Oct. 26, 1847, *H. Ex. Doc. 60, 30th Cong., 1st Sess.*, 56; HQ Army, SO #146, Oct. 26, 1847, Claiborne, *Quitman*, I, 395n. On his return to the States, Quitman received a promise of command of the Army of Occupation if it received another brigade. It did not, and Quitman remained unemployed. *Ibid.*, II, 9–10.
2. Mexico City *American Star*, Sept. 20, 1847; Edward S. Wallace, "The United States Army in Mexico City," *Military Affairs*, XIII (Fall 1949), 160; Thomas M. Davies, Jr., "Assessments During the Mexican War," *NMHR*, XLI (July 1966), 198. See also Ralph H. Gabriel, "American Experience with Military Government," *AHR*, XLIX (July 1944), 633–36.
3. Aztec Club of 1847, *Constitution of the Aztec Club of 1847 and List of Members* (n.p., 1909).
4. HQ Army, GOs #296–98, Sept. 22–24, 1847, *AGGO*, XLI½, 519–21.
5. Wallace, "U.S. Army in Mexico City," 161–62; Risch, *Quartermaster Support*, 295–96; Henry, *Mexican War*, 369.
6. Scott to Marcy, Oct. 27, Marcy to Scott, Oct. 6, 1847, *H. Ex. Doc. 60, 30th Cong., 1st Sess.*, 1006–9, 1027–28; Jones to Scott, Sept. 25, Oct. 6, 1847, *AGLS*, XXIV, #1485, 1629.
7. Childs to H. L. Scott, Black to Childs, Oct. 13, Gwynne to Childs, Oct. 15, 1847, *S. Ex. Doc. 1, 30th Cong., 1st Sess.*, 471–75, A28–31, 33–35; Oswandel, *Notes*, 255–334; Brackett, *Lane's Brigade*, 113–16; Jenkins, *War Between U.S. and Mexico*, 456–65; Wilcox, *Mexican War*, 493–96; Brooks, *Complete History*, 489–97; Smith, *War with Mexico*, II, 174–78. Santa Anna's surrender demand and Childs's reply are reprinted in the Oct. 2, 1847 Puebla *Flag of Freedom*.
8. Lally to AG, Aug. 27, H. B. Sears to B. Alvord, Aug. 13, H. Ridgely to Alvord, Aug. 23, 1847, *S. Ex. Doc. 1, 30th Cong., 1st Sess.*, 482–91; G. D. Twiggs to Miss A. C. Twiggs, July 30, to Mrs. Levi Twiggs, Aug. 10, 12, 1847, Twiggs Papers; Lally to Wilson, Aug. 25, 1847, Wilson Papers; Jenkins, *War Between U.S. and Mexico*, 349–52; Wilcox, *Mexican War*, 410–14.

9. *Niles*, LXXIII (Sept. 18, 1847), 34.

10. Ford, Hays, 62–65.

11. Kenly, *Memoirs*, 300–8, 320; Wilson to Jones, Sept. 19, 1847, AGLR'47, W-757; Brackett, *Lane's Brigade*, 45–78; Jenkins, *War Between U.S. and Mexico*, 462–65.

12. Lane to H. L. Scott, Oct. 18, 1847, *H. Ex. Doc. 60, 30th Cong., 1st Sess.*, 1030–31; Lane to AG, Oct. 18, 1847, *S. Ex. Doc. 1, 30th Cong., 1st Sess.*, 477–79; W. D. Wilkins to R. Wilkins, Oct. 22, 1847, Smith and Judah, *Chronicles of the Gringos*, 270–71; Brackett, *Lane's Brigade*, 88–89; Brackett, *History of the Cavalry*, 113–15; Ramsey, *Other Side*, 399–403; Frost, *Mexican War and Warriors*, 205; Oswandel, *Notes*, 345. Three large detachments followed Lane: Gen. Patterson with 550 men and a small train; Cushing's brigade; and Gen. Butler with 1,200 men. All reached Mexico City in December. Col. D. L. Miles to AG, Oct. 3, 1847, AGLR'47, M-1010; Vol.-Div. Orders #22, 25, Oct. 10, 15, 1847, Cushing, Orders #39, Oct. 29, 1847, Cushing Papers, Box 54; Jenkins, *War Between U.S. and Mexico*, 474; Butler, GO #4, Dec. 3, 1847, BOB, 11; Brackett, *Lane's Brigade*, 217; *Niles*, LXXIII (Dec. 4, 1847), 213. In his hurry to get his men to Veracruz, Cushing commandeered "some unused public steamers" on the Rio Grande, to the horror of the Quartermaster Department. Claude M. Fuess, *The Life of Caleb Cushing* (2 vols., New York, 1923), II, 55.

13. Santa Anna, Address, Sept. 16, 1847, Brooks, *Complete History*, 477–79; Peña, Address, Oct. 13, 1847, *Niles*, LXXIII (Dec. 4, 1847), 215; Smith, *War with Mexico*, II, 179–81; Cotner, *Herrera*, 163. Further complicating the political situation was the return from exile in late September of ex-President Paredes who became a focal point for the anti-Americans.

14. Luis de la Rosa to Santa Anna, Oct. 7, Santa Anna to Companions in Arms, Oct. 16, 1847, *Niles*, LXXIII (Dec. 12, 1847), 216; Cotner, *Herrera*, 163–64; Smith, *War with Mexico*, II, 182.

15. Scott to Patterson or Lane, Oct. 28, 1847, AGLR'47, S-738; Stevens, *Stevens*, I, 220; Collins, "Journal," 89; Hagan, Diary, 69. Among the officers invalided home were General Shields, Colonels Garland, Morgan, Burnet, and Lieutenant Colonels Watson and Loring.

16. Scott to Wilson, Oct. 13, 1847, *H. Ex. Doc. 60, 30th Cong., 1st Sess.*, 1028–29; Jones to Bankhead, Nov. 8, to Scott, Nov. 9, 1847, AGLS, XXIV, #1731–32; *Niles*, LXXIII (Jan. 8, 1848), 304; Hagan, Diary.

17. Ayuntamiento to Gefe Politico, Oct. 12, 13, Angel to Ayuntamiento, Oct. 14, 24, 27, Military Governor to Ayuntamiento, Nov. 11, Ayuntamiento to Military Governor, Nov. 11, 1847, all in Jalapa Correspondence, II, #1, 2, 4, 5, 12, 19, 32, 35.

18. Perry to Mason, Oct. 22, 1847, HSL.

19. Lane to Marcy, Oct. 22, 1847, *S. Ex. Doc. 1, 30th Cong., 1st Sess.*, 479–82; Brackett, *Lane's Brigade*, 146–51, 167; Brooks, *Complete History*, 508–10; Smith, *War with Mexico*, II, 178–79.

20. Perry to Mason, Nov. 2, 1847, HSL; Kenly, *Memoirs*, 329–30.

21. Col. E. Dumont to Lane, Nov. 14, 1847, AGLR'47, D-409; Lane to AG, Dec. 12, 1847, *H. Ex. Doc. 1, 30th Cong., 2nd Sess.*, 87–88; Bracket, *Lane's Brigade*, 167–70, 188–93; Ford, Hays, 80–90.

22. Wynkoop to Patterson, Nov. 22, 1847, AGLR'47, W-1047; Kenly, *Memoirs*, 365; Roa Bárcena, *Recuerdos*, II, 118–20; Livermore, *War with Mexico*, 158–59; Smith, *War with Mexico*, II, 423.

23. Kenly, *Memoirs*, 365; Livermore, *War with Mexico*, 159.

24. HQ Army, GO #372, Dec. 12, 1847, *Niles*, LXXIII (Jan. 1, 1848), 286.

25. Collins, "Journal," 93; Childs to H. L. Scott, Jan. 8, 1848, SWML; Miles to T. Marshall, Jan. 5, Marshall to H. L. Scott, Jan. 6, 1848, *H. Ex. Doc. 60, 30th Cong.*,

1st Sess., 1068–69; HQ Army, GO #45, Feb. 4, 1848, *AGGO*, XLI½, 739, Twiggs to Jones, Jan. 5, 1848, *AGLR'48*, T-37.

26. Lane to Scott, Feb. 10, 1848, *H. Ex. Doc. 1, 30th Cong., 2d Sess.*, 93–95; Brackett, *Lane's Brigade*, 234–47; Kelly, *Lane*, 56–57; Ford, Hays, 104–19; Callcott, *Santa Anna*, 273–74; Brooks, *Complete History*, 517–19; Dept. Veracruz, Orders #44, Jan. 31, 1848, *AGLR'48*, T-80; Orizaba Brig., Orders #6, 11, 12, Feb. 5, 16, 1848, Smith Transcripts, IX. Lane returned Santa Anna's personal possessions.

27. Lane to Thomas, A. M. Truett to J. S. Ford, W. H. Polk to J. C. Hays, March 2, Hays to Lane, March 1, 1848, all in *H. Ex. Doc. 1, 30th Cong., 2d Sess.*, 95–103; Ford, Hays, 119–50.

28. Quaife, *Diary of Polk*, III, 156; Mason to Scott, Sept. 1, 1847, *H. Ex. Doc. 56, 30th Cong., 1st Sess.*, 195–96; Walker to President, Nov. 5, 16, 1847, Richardson, *Messages and Papers*, V, 2381–82; Marcy to Scott, Nov. 8, 1847, *H. Ex. Doc. 60, 30th Cong., 1st Sess.*, 1014; same to same, Nov. 17, 1847, *S. Ex. Doc. 1, 30th Cong., 1st Sess.*, 588.

29. HQ Army, GOs #358, 376, 395, Nov. 25, Dec. 15, 31, 1847, *S. Ex. Doc. 56, 30th Cong., 1st Sess.*, 142–43, 240–41, 253–56. The prohibition on the shipment of bullion was later modified to allow its movement to a mint. This was a device to ensure that the army benefited from the processing tax which was collected there. GO #362, Dec. 2, 1847, *AGGO*, XLI½, 618. The assessments to the states were Chiapas $21,692; Chihuahua $49,118; Coahuila $5,657; Durango $85,556; Guanajuato $255,576; Jalisco $236,338; Mexico and Federal District $668,332; Michoacán $278,712; Nuevo León $50,437; Oaxaca $84,160; Puebla $424,276; Querétaro $85,944; San Luis Potosí $111,260; Sinaloa $33,524; Sonora $500; Tabasco $59,060; Tamaulipas $71,332; Veracruz $271,548; Zacatecas and Aguascalientes $249,076.

30. HQ Army, GO #8, Jan. 5, 1848, *H. Ex. Doc. 56, 30th Cong., 1st Sess.*, 256–57; Davies, "Assessments," 206, 208–12.

31. [Archbishop] to Scott, Nov. 5, Dec. 16, 23, Scott to Archbishop, Dec. 16, 23, 1847, all in *H. Ex. Doc. 60, 30th Cong., 1st Sess.*, 1054–57.

32. Scott to Marcy, Nov. 27, Dec. 14, 17, 1847, Jan. 8, 1848, GO #373, Dec. 13, 1847, all in *H. Ex. Doc. 60, 30th Cong., 1st Sess.*, 1031–39, 1046–47, 1050–51, 1061–63.

33. HQ Army, GOs #389, 7, 40, Dec. 27, 1847, Jan. 5, Feb. 1, 1848, *AGGO*, XLI½, 651, 673, 736; Scott to Twiggs, Dec. 26, 1847, *AGLR'47*, S-547; Clarke to H. L. Scott, Feb. 7, 1848, Department of Cuernavaca Letterbook, RG-94, NA; Collins, "Journal," 97.

34. The account of the Tuxpán attack is based upon: Perry to Mason, April 24, 1847, with enclosures, *H. Ex. Doc. 1, 30th Cong., 2d Sess.*, 1192–96, 1202–4; Perry to Mason, April 8, 1847, *HSL*; Perry, Order, April 21, 1847, Lockwood Papers; logs of the vessels involved; Semmes, *Service Afloat and Ashore*, 130, 150–56; Bauer, *Surfboats and Horse Marines*, 103–5; Morison, "Old Bruin," 224–27; Jenkins, *War Between U.S. and Mexico*, 445–46. The force consisted of the frigate *Raritan*, sloops-of-war *Albany*, *John Adams*, *Germantown*, and *Decatur*, steamers *Mississippi*, *Spitfire*, *Vixen*, and *Scourge*, gunboats *Bonita*, *Petrel*, and *Reefer*, and the bomb brigs *Vesuvius*, *Hecla*, and *Etna*.

35. Quaife, *Diary of Polk*, III, 23–24; Mason to Polk, May 13, 22, 1847, *ELB*, V, 376, 381; Perry to Mason, May 29, July 1, 1847, *HSL*. Because of Perry's obstinate resistance to the loss of his marines, few from the squadron joined Scott. Perry to Mason, July 4, 1847, with enclosures, "Transcript of Perry–Pierce Conversation, July 2, 1847," *H. Ex. Doc. 1, 30th Cong., 2d Sess.*, 1224–26; Mason to Perry, July 23, 1847, *RCL*; Metcalf, *History of USMC*, 127.

36. Perry to Mason, May 1, 10, 11, 1847, *HSL*.

37. Perry to Mason, May 13, to G. A. Magruder, May 17, 19, 1847, *HSL*; Perry to

Mason, May 24, 1847, *H. Ex. Doc. 1, 30th Cong., 2d Sess.*, 1204-6; logs of the vessels involved; Benjamin F. Sands, *From Reefer to Rear Admiral* (New York, 1899), 182.

38. Mary Wilhelmine Williams, "Secessionist Diplomacy of Yucatán," *HAHR*, IX (May 1929), 135-38; Louis De Armond, "Justo Sierra O'Reilly and Yucatán–United States Relations, 1847-1848," *ibid.*, XXXI (Aug. 1951), 421-26; Quaife, *Diary of Polk*, II, 394-95, 425, III, 374, 765; Mason to Conner, Feb. 25, 1847, to Perry, March 8, 1848, *RCL*; Perry to Breese and Mackenzie, May 19, Breese and Mackenzie to J. G. Rejón, May 27, Rejón to Breese and Mackenzie, May 28, Adams to Perry, Sept. 17, Perry to Mason, Sept. 21, Nov. 22, Dec. 11, 16, 1847, Jan. 30, Feb. 15, March 13, April 15, 1848, Bigelow to Mason, March 24, 1848, all in *HSL*; Manno, "Yucatán en la Guerra," 58-60; McCormac, *Polk*, 697; Polk to Senate and House, April 29, 1848, Richardson, *Messages and Papers*, V, 2431-32. During the summer of 1848 a number of men being discharged from the 13th Infantry at Mobile enlisted in the Yucatán service. Nelson Reed, *The Caste War of Yucatán* (Stanford, 1964), 111. Their activities are discussed in detail in Wallace, *Destiny and Glory*, 35-52.

39. The account of the Tabasco expedition is based upon: Perry to Mason, May 24, June 8, 24, 26, 1847, with enclosures, *H. Ex. Doc. 1, 30th Cong., 2d Sess.*, 1204-21; Howard to Perry, May 16, 1847, *HSL*; logs of the vessels involved; Aldrich, *History of USMC*, 99-100; Bauer, *Surfboats and Horse Marines*, 111-20; Griffis, *Perry*, 242-48; Jenkins, *War Between U.S. and Mexico*, 448-51; Charles Lee Lewis, *Admiral Franklin Buchanan* (Baltimore, 1929), 118-22; Mestre Ghigliazza, *Invasión Norte-americana en Tabasco*, 229-47; Morison, "Old Bruin," 230-37; Officer of the Navy, "Capture of Tabasco," *The Rough and Ready Annual*, 229-35; Parker, *Recollections*, 108-12; *Relacción Historica de la Segunda Invasión . . . en Tabasco* (Veracruz, 1847), 3-10; Roa Bárcena, *Recuerdos*, III, 171; Arthur Winslow, *Francis Winslow* (Norwood, Mass., 1935), 171-73.

40. Perry to Mason, June 28, with enclosures, D. D. Porter to Van Brunt, June 26, S. Lockwood to Bigelow, July 1, 1847, *H. Ex. Doc. 1, 30th Cong., 2d Sess.*, 1221-23, 1230, 1232; Perry to Bigelow, July 17, 19, Surgeons to Perry, July 19, Bigelow to Perry, July 23, 1847, *HSL*; logs of vessels involved; Porter, Journal, D. D. Porter Papers, L.C.

41. Perry to Mason, July 26, Van Brunt to Perry, Aug. 13, 1847, *HSL*; Van Brunt to Lockwood, July 27, Aug. 18, Nov. 12, 1847, Lockwood Papers.

42. Perry to Mason, July 14, Aug. 4, 7, 29, Sept. 25, 30, 1847, *HSL*; Lucius W. Johnson, "Yellow Jack, Master of Strategy," *USNIP*, LXXVI (July 1950), 1077; Griffis, *Perry*, 252-53; Mason to Perry, Aug. 4, 1847, *RCL*.

43. Perry to Mason, Oct. 17, 1847, *HSL*.

44. Perry to Mason, Jan. 10, 1848, *HSL*; Mason to Perry, Feb. 24, Aug. 19, 1848, *RCL*. Mason reiterated the department's position on July 3, 1848, *ibid.*

45. Perry to Mason, May 29, 1848, *HSL*; Perry to Engle, to Bigelow, May 30, to N. W. Duke, to J. F. Miller, June 7, to J. H. Ward, June 9, 1848, all in Letter Book of M. C. Perry, Comdg. U.S. Frigate *Cumberland*, RG-45, NA; Griffis, *Perry*, 258.

46. Stockton, Proclamation, Aug. 19, 1846, *H. Ex. Doc. 4, 29th Cong., 2d Sess.*, 670-71; Mason to CO Pacific, Dec. 24, 1846, *S. Ex. Doc. 1, 30th Cong., 1st Sess.*, 1304.

47. Stockton to Hull, to DuPont, Aug. 20, 1846, *S. Ex. Doc. 1, 29th Cong., 2d Sess.*, 673-74; log of *Cyane*; DuPont to Gov. and CinC of Lower California, Sept. 17, to Stockton, Sept. 23, 1846, DuPont, *Official Despatches*, 8-11; DuPont, *DuPont*, 47; Peter Gerhard, "Baja California in the Mexican War, 1846-1847," *PHR*, XIV (Nov. 1945), 413; DuPont, "Cruise of the Cyane," 421; Colton, *Three Years in California*, 125; DuPont to CO Guaymas, Oct. 6, Campuzano to CO *Cyane*,

Oct. 6, DuPont to Stockton, Oct. 12, 1846, *PSL*; Hubert Howe Bancroft, *History of the North Mexican States and Texas* (2 vols., San Francisco, 1884–89), II, 665.

48. Hull to Stockton, Sept. 12, Nov. 10, 1846, W. Radford *et al.* to Hull, Sept. 11, 1846, *PSL*; Colton, *Three Years in California*, 81–82; Sophie Radford de Meissner, *Old Naval Days* (New York, 1920), 131–32; *Niles*, LXXI (Dec. 12, 1846), 226–27, 233.

49. DuPont to Stockton, Dec. 1, 1846, *PSL*; Stockton to Montgomery, to DuPont, Oct. 7, 1846, *SLB*, 380–81, 384; Meissner, *Old Naval Days*, 138.

50. Stockton to Bancroft, Jan. 22, 1847, *S. Ex. Doc. 31, 30th Cong., 2d Sess.*, 23; Marcy to Kearny, Jan. 11, 1847, *H. Ex. Doc. 17, 30th Cong., 1st Sess.*, 244–45.

51. Stockton to Montgomery, Feb. 2, Cdr. Sir B. Walker to Montgomery, Feb. 27, 1847, *AF*, Box 251; Montgomery to CO Pacific, Feb. 15, to Biddle, Feb. 27, to Shubrick, April 6, to Gov. and Comdt. of Mazatlán, Feb. 17, 1847, all in *MLB*. In an effort to overcome the lack of a prize court, Kearny established an Admiralty Court in March, but it was later ruled illegal. Kearny, Notice, March 24, 1847, *H. Ex. Doc. 17, 31st Cong., 1st Sess.*, 291–92; James Brown Scott (ed.), *Prize Cases Decided in the United States Supreme Court 1789–1918* (3 vols., Oxford, 1923), II, 1393.

52. Montgomery to Alcalde of San José, March 29, Proclamation, March 30, Missroon to Montgomery, March 30, April 13, Council of San José to Montgomery, March 30, Mirranda to Montgomery, April 13, 1847, all in *H. Ex. Doc. 1, 30th Cong., 2d Sess.*, 1057–62; Montgomery, Proclamation, April 3, 1847, *AF*, Box 251; Montgomery to Gov. La Paz, to Missroon, April 13, 1847, *MLB*; Martinez, *Historia de Baja California*, 365, 372–73; Cardenas, *Semblanza Maritima*, I, 146; Chamberlain, "Trist and Baja California," 51.

53. Shubrick to Mason, June 1, 1847, *AF*, Box 251; Henry A. Wise, *Los Gringos* (New York, 1849), 85–86; DuPont to Shubrick, Sept. 26, 1847, DuPont, *Official Despatches*, 19–20.

54. Kearny to Marcy, April 28, 1847, *H. Ex. Doc. 17, 31st Cong., 1st Sess.*, 286–87; Parrott to mother, March 25, 1847, Parrott Papers; Stockton to Gillespie, April 26, 1847, Gillespie Papers, 225; William A. T. Maddox, "Abstract of a Cruise," W. A. T. Maddox Papers, MCM.

55. Kearny to Burton, May 30, 1847, *H. Ex. Doc. 17, 31st Cong., 1st Sess.*, 310; Francis D. Clark, *The First Regiment of New York Volunteers* (New York, 1882), 24; Memorandum of Captain H. W. Halleck, Concerning His Expedition in Lower California, 1846–1848, 11, BLUC.

56. Shubrick to E. A. F. La Vallette, Aug. 10, Craven to Selfridge, Oct. 3, 1847, *AF*, Boxes 251, 252; Shubrick to Mason, June 15, Selfridge to Shubrick, Oct. 10, 1847, with enclosures, *H. Ex. Doc. 1, 30th Cong., 2d Sess.*, 1073, 1096–1101; log of *Dale*; John Haskell Kemble (ed.), "Amphibious Operations in the Gulf of California," *The American Neptune*, V (April 1945), 122–25; Charles Belknap (ed.), "Notes from the Journal of Lieutenant T. A. M. Craven, U.S.N., *U.S.S. Dale* Pacific Squadron, 1846–49," *USNIP*, XIV (June 1888), 304–7; Cardenas, *Semblanza Maritima*, I, 148; Martinez, *Historia de Baja California*, 368–71; Bauer, *Surfboats and Horse Marines*, 211–13.

57. La Vallette to Shubrick, Oct. 28, 1847, with enclosures, *H. Ex. Doc. 1, 30th Cong., 2d Sess.*, 1076–83; logs of the *Congress* and *Portsmouth*; Joseph Warren Revere, *A Tour of Duty in California* (New York, 1849), 287; Parrott to mother, Nov. 14, 1847, Parrott Papers; *Niles*, LXXIII (Jan. 8, 1848), 295; Bauer, *Surfboats and Horse Marines*, 214–17; Cardenas, *Semblanza Maritima*, I, 148–49; Ripley, *War with Mexico*, II 603–4.

58. Selfridge to Shubrick, Nov. 21, 1847, F. Stanly to E. M. Yard, Feb. 13, 22, J.

Rudd to Shubrick, April 10, 1848, with enclosures, *H. Ex. Doc. 1, 30th Cong.,
2d Sess.,* 1102-4, 1135-36; 1158, 1160-61; log of *Dale*; Bancroft, *North Mexican
States and Texas,* II, 667; William L. Carshaw, "Journal of a Cruise in the Years
1846-1849," *AF* (A-9), Box 252; Kemble, "Amphibious Operations in Gulf of
California," 132-34; Belknap, "Notes from the Journal of Craven," 316; Bauer,
Surfboats and Horse Marines, 218-19.

59. Shubrick to Mason, Nov. 1, 4, 1847, *H. Ex. Doc. 1, 30th Cong., 2d Sess.,* 1074-75,
1083; Wise, *Los Gringos,* 136-37; DuPont, "Cruise of the Cyane," 426; Gerhard,
"Baja California in the War," 420; Halleck, Memorandum, 14-15, 38-39; Don
Meadows, *The American Occupation of La Paz* (Los Angeles, 1955), 20.

60. Shubrick, Proclamation, Nov. 4, 1847, *H. Ex. Doc. 1, 30th Cong., 2d Sess.,* 1058.

61. Shubrick to Mason, Nov. 5, Dec. 7, 1847, Shubrick to Haywood, Nov. 7, 1847,
ibid., 1083-85, 1088, 1111; Wise, *Los Gringos,* 140; J. Ross Browne, "Explorations
in Lower California," *Harpers New Monthly Magazine,* XXXVII (Oct. 1868),
582.

62. Shubrick to Mason, Nov. 12, 27, Orders, Nov. 15, 1847, with enclosures, "Memoranda of American Defenses at Mazatlán (Sinaloa)," *H. Ex. Doc. 1, 30th Cong.,
2d Sess.,* 1089-93, 1109-11, 1120; logs of the vessels involved; S. V. Wooldridge to
Secretary of the Admiralty, Nov. 18, 1847, Smith Transcripts, VII; Wise, *Los
Gringos,* 142-45; DuPont, "Cruise of the Cyane," 429; Ramsey, *Other Side,* 425,
428; F. Javier Gaxiola, *La Invasión Norte-Americana en Sinaloa* (2 vols., México,
1891), II, 149, 161-84; Bauer, *Surfboats and Horse Marines,* 224-25; Shubrick to
La Vallette, Nov. 15, Mazatlán, GO #1, Nov. 15, 1847, Elie Augustus Frederick
La Vallette Papers, YWA.

63. Shubrick to Mason, Nov. 26, Dec. 13, La Vallette to Shubrick, Nov. 20, Dec.
14, 1847, with enclosures, *H. Ex. Doc. 1, 30th Cong., 2d Sess.,* 1104-9, 1117-18,
1121-22; Shubrick to Scott, Nov. 16, Scott to Shubrick, Dec. 2, 1847, *H. Ex. Doc.
60, 30th Cong., 1st Sess.,* 1035-36; Wooldridge to Sec. Adm., Nov. 18, 1847, Smith
Transcripts, VII; Ramsey, *Other Side,* 431; Gaxiola, *La Invasión en Sinaloa,* II,
186-88; Wise, *Los Gringos,* 150, 155-56.

64. Shubrick to Mason, Dec. 17, 1847, *H. Ex. Doc. 60, 30th Cong., 1st Sess.,* 1083-84;
Shubrick to Mason, Nov. 25, Heywood to R. B. Mason, Nov. 25, to Shubrick,
Nov. 25, Dec. 15, 1847, with enclosures, DuPont to Shubrick, April 29, Burton
to Sherman, Jan. 16, 1848, all in *H. Ex. Doc. 1, 30th Cong., 2d Sess.,* 103-12,
1095-96, 1112-16, 1122-26; Halleck, Memorandum, 18-27; Gerhard, "Baja California in the War," 419-22; Martinez, *Historia de Baja California,* 374-80; Meadows, *Occupation of La Paz,* 21-22.

65. Shubrick to Mason, Jan. 24, 31, 1848, with enclosures, *H. Ex. Doc. 1, 30th Cong.,
2d Sess.,* 1127-29; Smith, *War with Mexico,* II, 448.

66. Heywood to Shubrick, Feb. 21, 22, DuPont to Shubrick, Feb. 16, March 25,
April 29, 1848, *H. Ex. Doc. 1, 30th Cong., 2d Sess.,* 1138-41, 1143-47, 1149-50,
1155-57; Heywood to Burton, Feb. 20, 1848, *H. Ex. Doc. 17, 31st Cong., 1st Sess.,*
513-15; Moreno *et al.* to Commandante en Gefe de los Americanos, Feb. 15,
letter Feb. 6, 1848, Documentos para la historia de California. Colección de Don
José Matias Moreno . . . , BLUC; Halleck, Memorandum, 26-27; log of *Cyane.*

67. Burton to Sherman, March 10, 20, April 13, Steele to Sherman, March 20; Burton
to H. M. Naglee, March 31, 1848, *H. Ex. Doc. 17, 31st Cong., 1st Sess.,* 516, 518-
20, 524; Burton to Shubrick, March 20, Shubrick to Mason, April 8, 15, DuPont
to Shubrick, April 6, 1848, *H. Ex. Doc. 1, 30th Cong., 2d Sess.,* 1149, 1151-52;
DuPont to Selden, March 30, 1848, DuPont, *Despatches,* 33; Halleck, Memorandum, 31, 55-66; Clark, *First New York Volunteers,* 32; Gerhard, "Baja California
in the War," 422-23.

68. Shubrick to Mason, April 25, 1848, *AF,* Box 252; Butler to Shubrick, March 19,

1848, *BLB*; Burton to Sherman, April 17, 1848, *H. Ex. Doc. 17, 31st Cong., 1st Sess.*, 528; Mason to CO Pacific, April 26, 1848, *RCL*.

69. Shubrick to Mason, June 1, 1847, *AF*, Box 251; Mason to Shubrick, May 7, 1847, *RCL*; Jones to Mason, May 8, 1848, *PSL*. Shubrick remained on the coast until mid-July when he left in the *Independence* for a cruise to South Seas.

70. Jones to Mason, June 19, July 11, Sept. 2, to La Vallette, June 13, 1848, Halleck to Shubrick, May 6, Jones to Sevier and Clifford, May 9, *PSL*; Jones to J. P. Anaya, June 13, 1848, Desp. Mex. XIII; Gaxiola, *La Invasión Norte-Americana*, 215–17; Meadows, *Occupation of La Paz*, 28–29; Clark, *First New York Volunteers*, 24, 32; Gerhard, "Baja California in the War," 424.

18: Politics and Mr. Polk's War

T HE PRESIDENT'S ASTUTE management of the declaration of war not
only obscured the size of the opposition to that act but, by making
the Whigs a party to the decision, quieted loud dissent until the very
end of the congressional session. It erupted in the Wilmot Proviso
and the strong antislavery reaction which that engendered. As the
summer dragged on without any smashing successes by Zachary
Taylor's army of semitrained farmboys and townsmen, many Americans became restive. In part the reaction stemmed from the increasingly shrill opposition of the radicals, who viewed the conflict as a
war unconstitutionally begun by Polk without congressional approval
for the purposes of enlarging the slave-holding part of the country.

The spectrum of opposition ran from moderate Whigs and antiadministration Democrats who considered the war either improperly
begun or who feared the effect on the country of the addition of the
Mexican territory to a radical clutch of abolitionists, pacifists, and re-
formers. The radicals were largely concentrated in New England,
the section which could see the least benefit from the conflict. The
Whigs split into conservative and radical camps. The conservatives,
who numbered most of the southern members of the party and a number of northerners like Daniel Webster and ex-Speaker Robert C.
Winthrop, attacked the fraud and aggressiveness of the war. They
avoided the charge commonly hurled by the radicals that the primary
aim of the war was the extension of slavery. Not only did such

charges offend the southern faction of the party but many of the conservatives doubted its validity. This reluctance earned them the epithet of Cotton Whigs.

The radical Whigs, like ex-President John Quincy Adams and the Ohio Representative Joshua R. Giddings, were mostly abolitionists. They came to be known as Conscience Whigs because their consciences were repelled, they said, by both the iniquity of the aggression against Mexico and the spread of slavery which was its purpose. The Democrats too had their radical, antislavery faction personified by John P. Hale of New Hampshire, David Wilmot, and the venerable Albert Gallatin. The administration party also contained Calhoun supporters who opposed the war for both constitutional and practical reasons. Far more numerous in the Democratic party and probably representing the majority view in the country were the expansionist "doughfaces" to whom the slavery issue was secondary to Manifest Destiny and a problem to be settled at some future date.

One of the problems with which the moderate Whigs struggled was the fear that opposition to the war would appear traitorous. That had been the rock upon which the Federalist bark had foundered after 1815. Moreover, the Whigs having voted for the war were effectively committed to furnishing the supplies needed to wage it.[1] Nevertheless, that policy of expediency proved effective. During the long 1846 congressional elections, the Whigs gained control of the House 115 to 108 but lost five Senate seats. Much of the shift reflected issues unrelated to the war, like the low rates of the Walker Tariff and the death of the independent Treasury proposal, but some of it represented a vote against the war.

The radicals had strong representation among the literary fraternity. Although Ralph Waldo Emerson, whose private opposition was caustic, avoided open attachment to the antiwar group and Nathaniel Hawthorne gave his allegiance to the administration, most of the New England intellectuals did not. Henry David Thoreau has.become the most famed for his "Essay on Civil Disobedience," but its call for a refusal to pay taxes earned scant support for the position espoused and added little to the stature of its author. More effective was the satirical *Bigelow Papers* of James Russell Lowell. They represented the peak of the antiwar propaganda.[2]

A more immediate and more visible reaction to the war was the rise of Zachary Taylor as a presidential candidate. Although others, notably Henry Clay, desired the Whig nomination, the battles along the Rio Grande made Taylor a national hero. Since those actions appeared to most contemporaries to have been thrust upon his army, Taylor avoided the onus of supporting an unpopular and aggressive war. Moreover, his other attributes appealed to an American not yet over her love affair with Jacksonian democracy. He radiated the homespun characteristics of simplicity, humility, and common sense. He was the man who was offered fifty cents by a newly arrived young lieutenant to polish his sword, and more important, had accepted it. "Old Rough and Ready" was the new "Old Hickory."

Within three weeks of Resaca de la Palma, Thurlow Weed, the astute editor of the Albany, New York, *Journal*, started a campaign to gain Taylor the 1848 Whig nomination. It both surprised and flattered the planter-soldier. Taylor's mid-August disclaimer of political aspirations[3] was undoubtedly genuine, although he would soon shift his ground. The news of the Monterrey victory and armistice hastened the transformation of the unassuming hero into a prime political personality. It convinced the President that Taylor was a Whig and caused Polk to grow increasingly critical and suspicious of his field commander.[4] The displeasure of the administration over the Monterrey armistice confirmed Taylor's growing belief of its hostility to him personally. Thereafter he became more receptive to political flattery and the suggestions that he was the political man of the hour.[5]

By the end of the summer other political straws portended trouble for the administration. Opposition to the war grew as many people concluded the return was too small for the expenditures in money and lives. The explanation for the rapid reversal of such a large block of public opinion is simple. Most Americans, like the President himself, had assumed in May that a few thousand men thrown into northern Mexico would bring a quick and successful peace. Like many of their countrymen in 1966–68, they were not ready for a major war. An increasing number of editors and writers of public letters began to doubt that the troops and money needed for a successful war could be raised. To that group Taylor's proposal expressed in the widely publicized November 5 letter to General Edmund P. Gaines had appeal: the United States, he said, should fix and hold a boundary, thereby forcing the Mexicans either to acquiesce or to attack. Since it appeared unlikely that Mexico could develop a stable government capable of arranging an effective peace settlement, the proposal had the attraction of establishing a definitive end to the struggle. Actually of course, such a plan was militarily impractical since it would have required more troops than an active campaign and ran counter to

American temperament. Moreover, to those who viewed with anticipation the prospects of enlarging America's share of the lucrative Mexican trade, the proposal had the major defect of leaving that trade in European hands.[6]

During the late fall of 1846 the cabinet considered not only the question of launching a new campaign but the best method of providing the men required. Out of those discussions came a decision to raise nine new regiments of volunteers to serve for the duration of the war. Secretary Marcy issued the call for them in mid-November. They were slow in forming, in part because of the general disenchantment with the war but probably more because of the unwillingness of many men to enlist for a long period. The New York Regiment was reduced to accepting jailbirds, bums, and men already rejected in order to fill its rolls. The regiment called from North Carolina never filled all of its companies and straggled into Mexico between mid-February and midsummer.[7]

The growing war-weariness which slowed recruiting also strengthened the support for the antiwar faction. In a passage in his December 8, 1846 annual message which could have been written by two of his more recent successors, Polk complained of the antiwar propaganda: "A more effectual means could not have been devised to encourage the enemy and protract the war than to advocate and adhere to their cause, and thus give them 'aid and comfort.' " He followed the charge with a long discussion of the antecedents of the war and the reasons for his sending troops into the disputed area. In the process the President handed fuel to his opponents by speaking of the "maintenance of our possession and authority" over California and New Mexico. He concluded by renewing the request for the $2 million to be available if Mexico agreed to a settlement.[8]

The message received harsh treatment from the antiadministration forces in Congress. Whig Representatives Joshua R. Giddings of Ohio, Garrett Davis of Kentucky, Luther Severence of Maine, and Milton Brown of Tennessee assailed Polk's claim that the Rio Grande represented a historic boundary line. They argued that it had never been a boundary in either Spanish or Mexican times and had not even been accepted by the Mexicans as a *de facto* line after San Jacinto. Indeed, they pointed out, the Mexicans had occupied both banks of the river before the spring of 1846. Few, however, went as far as the Tennessee Whig Meredith P. Gentry, who branded the President's claims "an artful perversion of the truth . . . to make the people 'believe a lie.' " Others, like the Ohio Whig Robert C. Schenk and Vermont Senator

William Upham, introduced resolutions calling for a withdrawal from Mexico or a speedy end to the war. Some of Polk's opponents seized upon his suggestion that they were giving aid and comfort to the enemy to proclaim their higher patriotism. In the tradition of the times, the rhetoric of the debates was violent and culminated often in the accusation that the President had assumed unconstitutional powers in the course of his fraudulent war.

In the House of Representatives, Garrett Davis attacked the Kearny and Stockton governments in New Mexico and California as being beyond the powers of the executive. Despite the best efforts of the Democrats, the House agreed to call for a statement of explanation from Polk. After some discussion in the cabinet, Polk complied, shrewdly admitting that the establishment of civil government went beyond the powers of the executive. No disciplinary actions were taken against either the General or the Commodore, however. It was a politically masterful act which took the wind from the sails of an antiadministration House sailing down a heading which would have led it into a violent confrontation with the White House.

From the President's standpoint the congressional attacks not only prevented necessary steps "strengthening the Executive arm," but they coincided with his loss of faith in his two senior field commanders. He concluded that both were disloyal. The evidence in Scott's case was the publication of his plan of campaign in a New Orleans newspaper coincident with his arrival there. We now know that the paper merely reprinted rumors then current and that neither Scott nor any of his subordinates were the source. Indeed, in retrospect it is clear that Scott had tried hard to gain the administration's approbation. The evidence against Taylor was stronger, since it involved the November 5 letter to General Gaines.

After the publication of the Gaines letter, Polk concluded that his position would be strengthened by the printing of all the correspondence between Taylor and the War Department. He arranged for the House of Representatives to call for them. Charles Ashmun of Massachusetts tried unsuccessfully to embarrass Polk by adding a call for the Mackenzie–Santa Anna correspondence. The difficulties in beating off such efforts led the President to complain of the inability of the Democrats to support the administration. On another occasion the apostasy of a group of Calhoun supporters temporarily blocked in the Senate a bill for ten new regular regiments. As a result it did not pass the Senate until February 10, despite the clear need for the men in the field.

The strongest attacks were reserved for the effort to create the grade of lieutenant general, a title heretofore reserved for the sainted Washington, and to confer the rank on Thomas Hart Benton in an open effort to supplant the Whig generals with a Democrat. In their opposition the Whigs had the subrosa support of other would-be 1848 Democratic candidates like James Buchanan. When combined with those in the Senate who opposed either the creation of the rank or Benton, they were sufficient to defeat the proposal.

In early February both houses turned their attention to the request for funds, now increased to $3 million, to be used as the down-payment on any financial settlement with Mexico. Both chambers rang with rhetoric but made little forward motion as the discussion bogged down in a fruitless argument over the extent of the territory to be secured. In the House some administration supporters like Representatives John W. Tibbatts (soon to be appointed Colonel of the 16th Infantry) called for a settlement following the line of the Sierra Madre Mountains. Their efforts accomplished little and the chamber voted 115 to 106, along sectional lines, to adopt the Wilmot Proviso once again.

In the Senate, Lewis Cass argued that the aim of the administration was not "deplorable amalgamation" with large numbers of Mexicans but the acquisition of uninhabited areas or those with people similar to Americans. The land, he argued, was needed for future growth. This brought a sharp retort on February 11 from Senator Thomas Corwin of Ohio, who cried:

> Sir, look at this pretense of want of room. With twenty millions of people, you have about one thousand millions of acres of land. . . . But the Senator from Michigan says we will be two hundred millions in a few years, and we want room. If I were a Mexican, I would tell you, "Have you not room in your country to bury your dead men? If you come into mine we will greet you with bloody hands, and welcome you to hospitable graves."

On February 15 Senator Daniel Webster heightened the tension by introducing a pair of resolutions calling for the nonacquisition of territory as a result of the war. John C. Calhoun responded with an ingenious argument that went to the heart of the sectional struggle. The slave-holding states, he pointed out, were in a minority everywhere in the government except in the Senate. Therefore, he demanded that new states be admitted with a free choice of being slave or free.[9] This, of course, was an open call for the repeal of the Missouri

Compromise. Neither of the great legislators forced a vote upon their resolutions, and on March 1 the Senate finally passed the long-delayed measure after beating back all efforts to attach the Wilmot Proviso. Since the House did not insist on the Proviso, the appropriation then became law.[10]

March 3 was the last day of the 29th Congress. As so commonly happens, the concluding days of the session saw a flurry of bills pass the two chambers. One was the Army Appropriation Bill which provided nearly $13.3 million in new funds and an additional deficiency appropriation of $5.3 million for fiscal 1847. Over $9 million was earmarked for transportation, attesting to the cost of fighting a war beyond the country's borders. Pay consumed nearly $7.5 million. As far as the men in Mexico were concerned the most important piece of legislation may well have been that which permitted letters, newspapers, and packets up to one ounce to be sent free to officers either in Mexico or guarding the southern frontier.[11]

Despite the antiwar tenor of much of the rhetoric of the Congress, the President had gained his key legislation. It demonstrated again the truism that the shrillest voice is generally not the majority one and that under normal conditions the legislature will seek the moderate or apparently most responsible route when offered a choice.

In New England, where the opposition to the war was strongest, bitter words and stringent actions decorated the public record. The Boston *Whig* scathingly attacked the President's message for claiming that the war was supported by a majority of the people. Why then, the paper asked, did Polk devote two thirds of his annual message to the war's justification? Yet even in Massachusetts, the center of the antiwar faction, its successes were limited. While it influenced the legislature to vote 4 to 1 against outfitting the volunteer regiment headed for Mexico under the distinguished Caleb Cushing, the antiwar faction could not gain a ruling from the state supreme court to prevent enlistments. A great antiwar rally at Faneuil Hall in Boston in February 1847 featured ringing speeches by Charles Sumner, a rising young politician, the abolitionist clergyman James Freeman Clarke, and the noted cleric Theodore Parker, but drew only a small crowd, many of them hecklers from Cushing's regiment. Despite the poor response, the antiwar forces pressured the Massachusetts legislature in April into declaring the conflict "a war of conquest, so hateful in its objects, so wanton, unjust and unconstitutional in its origin and character, [that it] must be regarded as a war against humanity, against justice, against the Union . . . and against the free states. . . ."

Even so, the legislature refused to follow the suggestions of Sumner and recommend Congress withhold supplies. The antiwar faction could be extremely petty in its actions. When Cushing advanced to brigadier general, Governor George N. Briggs refused to issue commissions to the new officers of the regiment because some of the technical regulations had not been fully met.[12]

As part of the pacifist drive against the war, the venerable American Peace Society in February 1847 offered a $500 prize for the best "review of the Mexican War on the principles of Christianity and on enlightened statesmanship." The prize fell to a Keene, New Hampshire, Unitarian cleric and biblical commentator, Abiel Abbot Livermore.[13] His *The War with Mexico Reviewed* was a closely argued attack on the war as an attempt to enlarge slave-holding territory.

One of the shrewder comments on the state of the public view of the war came shortly after the end of the congressional session from one of Calhoun's correspondents who insisted: "The Mexican war cannot last long. The people are tired of it." John Sherman from Mansfield, Ohio, wrote his brother in California that politics were in a state of "hotch potch" because of the slavery question, the sectional struggle, and the heroics of the war. "Nothing," he reported, "but a series of victories has sustained the administration in prosecuting the war; for there is no doubt that a large majority of the people consider it an unjust aggression upon a weak republic, excused by false reasons, and continued solely for the acquisition of slave territory." Similar sentiments were voiced by Robert Toombs, the Georgia congressman:

> It seems our successes in Mexico have greatly raised the pretensions of Polk and his cabinet and the weaknesses and division of Mexico will in all probability induce her to acceed [sic] to terms which we ought not demand and which will be disgraceful to her and ruinous to us.[14]

While these comments can and must be discounted as partisan comments by the President's opponents, they do show opposition existing in all parts of the country.

The war-weariness increased the support for Zachary Taylor's presidential candidacy. By late April he had inched closer to an open declaration of candidacy by agreeing to accept the nomination if offered "by the spontaneous wishes of his fellow citizens." At the same time Secretary of War Marcy, one of the more able political observers in the nation, concluded that Taylor was the likely Whig candidate and the probable winner in 1848. Much the same indications reached Calhoun from his correspondents.[15]

Actually all of the commentators were ahead of Taylor. It took his politically untutored mind some time longer to reach their conclusions. In May he noted that he would accept a draft but believed the timing wrong. In June Taylor freely admitted doubts about his qualification for the position, although willing to serve if elected. These self-doubts did not prevent his supporters from promoting his candidacy in various ways, such as a July 8 mass meeting in Detroit which called for his nomination. Taylor's response to a request for a statement from the Democratic convention in Clarksville, Tennessee, mirrored his continued ambivalence. He was, he replied, no politician and had little time to study political matters, so he could not state his views. He did not aspire to the presidency and if he did become a candidate it would be because others thought him deserving. In August he cast his lot with the Whigs by saying that while he had never voted, he would have supported Henry Clay in 1844. By mid-September he admitted a willingness to run for the presidency in order to keep it out of the hands of Scott or Lewis Cass.[16]

While all the statements could be construed as a cleverly contrived campaign to build a draft, such deviousness was foreign to Taylor's character. Clearly the attraction of the office and the intense hostility which he felt toward the administration combined to wear down his reticence. In mid-August he wrote a strongly political letter to an unidentified correspondent, probably Jefferson Davis, in which he conceded that he would win the election if it were held then.[17]

Rather illuminating is a letter which Taylor penned in mid-September to Jefferson Davis. The Wilmot Proviso, he wrote, is "at best a trifling affair for . . . no country will be attached to the union south of the Missouri Compromise [line]. The free states will not agree to it without the said proviso or an equivalent; nor can two thirds of the Senate be brought to vote for the acquisition of territory without any such restriction. . . ." Reflecting his steady drift toward an outright campaign for the nomination, he promised to return home as soon as negotiations started or Scott took Mexico City. Nevertheless, he refused to make any political deals to ensure the nomination. He confided in Davis that he had always considered himself a Whig, since it was the more Jeffersonian of the two parties. More precise was his letter on September 27 to John Danforth affirming his intention to act according to undefined "feeling and principle" if elected. The next step came on October 4 when he formally requested six months' leave.[18]

Adding greatly to the growing Taylor bandwagon was his attractiveness to the southern Whigs. They saw in his Virginia birth,

Kentucky boyhood, and Louisiana plantation a guarantee of a more favorable response to the section's interests than any other potential Whig candidates.

While the Taylor boom grew, the country elected members of the 30th Congress. The results are extremely difficult to assess, since the voting spanned a period of fifteen months from June 1846 to November 1847. Slightly over 60 percent of the seats were elected in 1846. The twenty House seats lost in those elections were insufficient to upset Democratic controls, but the 1847 elections, held largely in slave states, cost them more. The final results gave control of the House to the Whigs 115 to 108, but increased the Democratic dominance in the Senate by five seats. No single issue or even set of issues explains the results. Certainly the time-span of the elections and the muddled Whig position on the war eliminate the conflict as a significant factor.[19]

Nevertheless, it would be wrong to discount altogether the disillusionment with the war. This increased when the volunteers began returning home during the summer of 1847. They reported the realities of a soldier's life, giving vent to their disenchantment with what appeared to them the "inefficient manner" of conducting the war and the political nature of the senior appointments. As one opponent of the administration chortled, they "complain most bitterly of the discomforts and risks to which they have been subjected in the consequence of insufficient supplies, the paucity of men, and . . . impute it to a want of decision and energy on the part of the Administration."[20]

The summer of 1847 was a trying one for Polk. His field commanders produced little positive news. Taylor would not undertake any operations and Scott, for reasons which were difficult to comprehend in Washington, had cut himself off from his base at Veracruz and all contact with the outside world. Moreover, Marcy broke down under the strain of trying to control the headstrong horses of his War Department team and had to take a month's vacation in late August and early September. Although Secretary of the Navy John Y. Mason assumed some of the duties, the President had to take on others, which led him to complain that "much of my time is occupied with the details" of day-to-day operations.[21]

A further problem, potentially more politically damaging, arose from the clash between Kearny and Frémont in California. In mid-August Senator Benton discussed the clash with the President. Polk, who still lacked the facts of the case, limited himself to expressing the hope that a court-martial would be unnecessary. Benton concurred but quickly changed his mind and on August 22 asked for a trial, apparently in the belief that it was the best way to clear the explorer's name.[22]

The court-martial met at Fort Monroe in early November under the presidency of Brevet Brigadier General George M. Brooke. To the undoubted relief of the Benton group, the War Department ruled that Frémont would not be tried on matters occurring before the war, which precluded any embarrassing questions about Frémont's reasons for being in California at all. The court found the explorer guilty of mutiny and disobeying a lawful command as well as conduct prejudicial of good order. It sentenced him to dismissal from the service but recommended leniency. Polk concluded that Frémont was technically not guilty of mutiny but approved the findings on disobedience and misconduct. He ordered the explorer restored to duty and directed him to assume his duties as second-in-command of the Regiment of Mounted Riflemen. That was insufficient for the hot-headed explorer, who in a huff resigned his commission. It apparently surprised the Benton faction when Polk accepted the resignation on March 15, 1848.[23] During the court-martial Benton viciously attacked Kearny, deprecating the General's role in California. He carried the vendetta further in 1848 when he spoke for thirteen days in a vain attempt to prevent the confirmation of Kearny's brevet as a major general.[24] In the long run, however, Benton succeeded, and even today Kearny suffers from a greater obscurity than he deserves.

While the Frémont court-martial held the limelight, a new set of pressures began to build upon and within the administration—the movement to acquire all of Mexico. The idea of annexation was not a new one. Even before the war, John L. O'Sullivan's *Democratic Review* had proposed it and while a few of the more radical expansionists from the very beginning of the war had favored it that position had only limited support. It did not gain partisans until the frustrations of the Mexican refusal to negotiate began to build the conviction that she should be forced to surrender additional territory. The rather widespread fear of the divisiveness of the slavery issue as evidenced by the Wilmot Proviso fight, also tended to keep public support limited at least until the spring of 1847. The support for annexation came chiefly from persons in the North and West who held moderate or ambivalent views about slavery and for whom the riches of Mexico overshadowed all else. Among the strongest supporters were the newly immigrated urban Democrats of the North-east whose appetites for Mexico were whetted by a steady stream of expansionist propaganda from the penny press.[25]

The concept received its most prominent semiofficial support in a December 17, 1847 letter from Secretary of State James Buchanan to a Philadelphia meeting. He suggested that annexation might be necessary if a government could not be found in Mexico to negotiate peace. This was a good stance for a potential candidate, as Lewis Cass showed shortly afterward by also embracing it. Even if large numbers of Democratic politicians found it a useful badge to wear, it is doubtful that the all-Mexico sentiment commanded a strong following.[26] Nevertheless, the following month the New York State Democratic Convention as well as a party mass meeting at Tammany Hall called for the annexation of all Mexico "not for our use but for the use of man." Vice President George M. Dallas summarized the extreme position in a toast: "A more perfect Union; embracing the entire North American continent." Increasingly in the early weeks of 1848 the idea of redemption crept into discussions. The most outspoken speech was one delivered by Commodore Robert F. Stockton in Philadelphia which called for annexation in order to force the Mexicans to accept civil and religious liberty as well as republicanism. Cass suggested America's mission to be one of sweeping away "the abuses of generations."[27]

It was against this background of frustration, so akin to that engulfing the United States during the Vietnam War, that the 30th Congress began its first session on December 6, 1847. An indication of the intensity of feeling was Robert C. Winthrop's failure to win election as Speaker of the House on the first ballot because of the votes withheld from him by three of the radical Whigs. The following day the clerk read the President's annual message. It recited the unsuccessful efforts to negotiate peace and outlined Trist's terms: the Rio Grande to 32°N. latitude; New Mexico and the Californias; plus the transit rights across the Isthmus of Tehuantepec. As might be expected, this brought a counterblast on the floors of both chambers. In the Senate Calhoun offered a resolution denouncing the annexation of Mexico as inconsistent with the avowed objectives of the war, a radical departure from American practice, and a threat to American institutions. When Lewis Cass countered that "there is no man in this nation in favor of the extinction of . . . Mexico," Calhoun reminded him that scarcely a newspaper had failed to discuss it.

In the Whig-controlled House, Representative William A. Richardson of Illinois offered a resolution supporting the war as just and necessary and arguing that the rejection of American peace offers left no alternative but vigorous prosecution of the war. Two days later, December 22, the Whig response came from his fellow Illini freshman representative Abraham Lincoln who proposed that the administration demonstrate that Thornton's ambush had actually occurred on American soil. The outcome of the House debate was the passage on January 3, 1848 by a vote of 85 to 81 on a resolution introduced by John Quincy Adams and forty other northern Whigs declaring the war to be unnecessary and unconstitutionally begun. It called for the immediate withdrawal of American forces from Mexico; peace without any indemnity; a boundary somewhere between the Nueces and the Rio Grande; and Mexican payment of just American claims.[28] By mid-January the all-Mexico forces had a counteroffensive underway. Senator Edward A. Hannegan of Indiana introduced a resolution declaring "that it may be necessary and proper, as it is within the constitutional capacity of this Government, for the United States to hold Mexico as a territorial appendage." Two days later Senator Daniel S. Dickinson of New York called for the annexation of Mexico. It remained for Lewis Cass, however, to express the thoughts closest to those of the administration when he commented that the United States would not have to devour all of Mexico, but he was sure that if they did they would digest the meal.[29]

The situation remained unsettled throughout most of January and February of 1848 with neither side yet convinced that the time had come for compromise. Actually, the pressure for all-Mexico declined as the weeks passed. The reason for this is not entirely clear, but undoubtedly reflected in part the growing recognition of the validity of warnings which ex-Minister Joel R. Poinsett had been circulating since December that all-Mexico would require a large occupation force and hasten the development of Mexican nationalism.[30]

The arrival of the Treaty of Guadalupe-Hidalgo and the considerations of alternatives which it called forth dealt a death-blow to all-Mexico. The all-Mexico forces, like the antiwar forces, had proven unable to move the administration in directions which it did not wish to move. The opposition, shrill though its cries might be, proved once again that, lacking nationwide support among voters and party officials, it could not force a strong, self-confident administration convinced of the propriety of its own policies from its programs. The intensity of the attacks of the abolitionists and other radical antiwar factions too often appeared as childish tantrums which repelled rather than attracted support.

If the domestic opposition to the war often displayed petty opportunism rather than statemanship, its level was significantly higher than that shown by some of the officers in Mexico City. Scott considered himself the target of dark intrigues by a national administration in which he had little if any confidence. He had scarcely greater regard for many of his subordinates, who were political appointees of varying degrees of competence. On the other hand, Scott's acid pen had long before eroded the thin layer of confidence which the President had in him. The lack of confidence between the administration and its field commander need not have been fatal to their relationship had the army been in the midst of an active campaign, for the dynamics of the situation might have prevented it. But in an inactive force with politically oriented generals, infighting was bound to occur.

The key figure was Gideon Pillow. Not only was he the President's law partner, but he considered himself to be a masterful military and political figure and Polk's eyes and ears within the army. Pillow's reports of his operations before Mexico City, especially at Contreras, bore scant resemblance to the events. What had prompted this is uncertain, but Pillow suffered from an inflated ego and appears to have calculated that the inflating of his image would help secure him command of the army and the possibility of the glory which went with it. Undoubtedly, also, the presidential bug had nibbled. Nor was Pillow the only general with presidential ambitions. Worth had similar interests, although it is difficult to understand how he could have taken them seriously. Those interests undoubtedly reflected Worth's intense and growing animosity toward Scott. The third figure involved was Brevet Colonel James Duncan. The artilleryman was a confidant of Worth, who was also being cultivated by Pillow. Duncan, incensed by what he considered Scott's failure to recognize suitably his role in the decision to use the Chalco route, became a willing accomplice in the effort to overthrow him.

Scott on October 2 mildly requested that Pillow correct his reports. Pillow refused in an insulting letter which bred further correspondence. Scott's humor was not improved by the publication in Tampico and New Orleans newspapers of other slanted accounts of the operations before Mexico City. They were so blatant that the General in Chief could not ignore them. Scott assumed correctly that the letters were written either by or at the behest of Pillow, and as a pointed reminder to his subordinates issued a General Order republishing the President's January 28, 1847 proscription against writ-

ing private accounts of military operations for publication until a
month after the completion of a campaign.

Worth rose first to the bait of the General Order, complaining
that it was directed at him. After a bitter exchange with Scott, he
appealed to the President, charging his superior with conduct un-
becoming an officer. In the midst of this, Duncan admitted the authorship of one of the letters, although it had been considerably altered
before publication by the friend to whom he sent it. On November
18 Duncan was ordered to stand trial for the indiscretion. Then
Pillow waded in with an insulting letter to Scott's adjutant, which
brought a countercharge of authorship of the "Leonidas" letter in
the New Orleans *Delta*, which had extravagantly praised Pillow for
his actions at Contreras. Pillow responded with a request to Marcy for
a hearing. Since the letter bypassed him in violation of Army Regulations, Scott now had the opening he wished and brought charges.
Pillow exploded in a long and vitriolic letter to Polk, complaining of a
violation of his rights. By mid-December he had devised his defense
and reported to the President that Paymaster Archibald W. Burns
had admitted authorship of the letter. The whole uproar, Polk concluded, stemmed from "the vanity and tyrannical temper of Gen'l
Scott."[31]

Simultaneously with the outbreak of political warfare in Mexico,
Polk learned of the July bribery scheme. "I cannot express to you,"
he wrote to Pillow, "in terms too strong, my unqualified condemna-
tion of the secret negotiations or correspondence, which from your
statements I suppose took place at Puebla, between *Genl Scott* and
Mr. Trist on the one part and *Genl Santa Anna* through his agents
on the other by which it was contemplated that a million of dollars
was to be paid to the latter in consideration that he would make
peace." The following day Polk exploded in a denunciation at the
cabinet meeting. This led to discussion of the possibility of recall,
but the decision was postponed to await first-hand accounts from
Generals Shields and Quitman. At almost the same time, the Baltimore
Sun published an account of the Council of War. Both Buchanan and
Marcy wrote to the principals in Mexico City asking for details or a
denial. Nevertheless, the event gave Polk the excuse for which he
had been searching to sack Scott.

The responses of the participants are interesting. Shields and Quitman refused to discuss the meeting and the former even went so far
as to deny to the President that the bribery scheme was discussed.
They held to those positions until March. Twiggs expressed no

opinion; Cadwalader simply denied knowledge of a bribe; and Scott argued that the meeting was confidential and to disclose its details would be a breach of public faith. He did point out that the discussion did not propose the use of any of the $3 million for a bribe, which was correct. Pillow submitted a fourteen-page letter on January 18 claiming that he had opposed the proposal, which was not correct.[32]

The President discussed recalling Scott with the cabinet and others, notably Senators Lewis Cass and Jefferson Davis. Everyone concurred on the recall, but a split developed within the cabinet over his successor. On January 8 Polk chose Butler. Actually he had little choice. Taylor was patently politically unacceptable, while Butler outranked all other officers and was with the army. Everyone also agreed upon a court of inquiry to investigate the Scott–Pillow–Worth–Duncan controversies. In order to achieve some degree of objectivity, the court had to consist of officers not with the army although it would have to meet in Mexico.

During January 13 Marcy issued the orders for the change of command and the Court of Inquiry. At the same time he released Pillow, Worth, and Duncan from arrest. The court, consisting of Generals Nathan Towson and Caleb Cushing and Colonel Edward G. W. Butler, was directed to meet at Perote on February 18. Scott's notice gave as the reasons for his dismissal "the present state of things in the Army" and his June 4 request for relief. The same day the Secretary sent Scott a second, much longer letter attacking him for his handling of the Worth controversy and arguing that the complexity of the Pillow and Duncan cases required a court of inquiry.[33]

The transfer of command occurred on February 19. If Butler had any delusions about receiving the massive reinforcements which he needed to conduct extensive operations, they were crushed by Marcy's warning that congressional approval of additional forces was highly uncertain. If Congress declined to act, no reinforcements beyond those enroute were possible.[34]

The Court of Inquiry met in Mexico City on April 13-22 and at Frederick, Maryland, June 5–July 6. It was specifically instructed to investigate:

1. payment of money to anyone and the purpose therefore;
2. agreements for the payment of money;
3. any influence such arrangements had on Scott's operations;
4. any understandings between any American officers and any Mexicans concerning the discontinuance of offensive operations;

5. the influence of such arrangements on the subsequent movements of the American army;

6. any communications concerning payments or operations;

7. any propositions to or from Santa Anna or other Mexican agents and whether any money was paid to them on the basis of those propositions.

Although the hearings partook more of an inquisition than of an inquiry, Scott handled himself well despite difficulty in contending with the practiced courtroom tactics of Pillow. After taking testimony from Pillow, Persifor Smith, and Worth as well as written statements from Quitman, Shields, Twiggs, and Cadwalader, the court concluded that operations had not been influenced by any bribe. Since Scott and Trist refused to testify, the Court held that the payment of money could not be proven.

Polk decided to drop the matter at that point as it served him no useful purpose. Since the Court had cleared him of writing the "Leonidas" letter but had otherwise found against him, Pillow withdrew his charges against Scott. Marcy ordered the Court of Inquiry disbanded but notified Scott that the charges against Worth could be tried on the latter's return to the country. Scott left the decision to the War Department, whereupon Polk had the matter dropped.[35]

Pillow's court-martial on a charge of appropriating a pair of small howitzers captured at Chapultepec as personal souvenirs was largely a farce. It became clear that the General knew nothing about them although they had been taken by some of his entourage and stored with his baggage. The court therefore found him innocent.[36]

As soon as his presence at the Court of Inquiry was no longer required, Scott returned home. He left Mexico City on April 23 and embarked at Veracruz on May 2 on the brig *Petersburg* bound for New York.[37] No tumultuous welcome awaited him. Despite being the transcendent military figure of the war, his facility for the inept phrase had provided the opportunity for lesser men to reduce him, temporarily, to their stature.

NOTES

For key to abbreviations used in Notes, see page xi.

1. Frederick Merk has incisively discussed the Whig dilemma in *Manifest Destiny and Mission*, pp. 94–96, and "Dissent in the Mexican War," Samuel Eliot Morison, Frederick Merk, and Frank Freidel, *Dissent in Three American Wars* (Cam-

bridge, 1970), 45–47. Cheryl Haun, "The Whig Abolitionists' Attitude," *Journal of the West*, XI (April 1972) 260–72, is a recent study of the radical Whigs.

2. Merk, "Dissent in the Mexican War," 55; Louis Filler, *The Crusade Against Slavery 1830–1860* (New York, 1960), 183–84; Arthur A. Ekirch, Jr., *The Civilian and the Military* (New York, 1956), 84. Charles J. DeWitt, "Crusading for Peace in Syracuse During the War with Mexico," *New York History*, XIV (April 1933), 100–12, studies the failure of the pacifist movement in one area.

3. Harriet A. Weed (ed.), *Autobiography of Thurlow Weed* (Boston, 1883), 571–73; Taylor to George Folsom, Aug. 14, 1846, *Niles*, LXXI (Sept. 12, 1846), 20–1; Hamilton, *Taylor*, 198–99.

4. See the changes in Quaife, *Diary of Polk*, II, 119, 181, 250.

5. By mid-December, Taylor was willing to accept the nomination if tendered. Taylor to Wood, Dec. 10, 1846, Sansom, *Taylor's Letters*, 76.

6. Quaife, *Diary of Polk*, II, 393–94; Smith, *War with Mexico*, I, 347–48.

7. Spencer, *Victors and Spoils*, 159–60; Marcy to Govs. La., Mass., Miss., N.Y., N.C., Pa., Va., Tex., Nov. 16, to Gov. Fla., Nov. 27, to Gov. Pa., Dec. 14, 1846, *AGLS*, XXIII, 1666, 1800½, 1824. Louisiana, Massachusetts, Mississippi, New York, North Carolina, and Virginia each supplied a regiment of infantry; Pennsylvania, a pair; Texas, a regiment of mounted men; and Florida, a single company. For recruiting problems and the resultant delays see Corporal of the Guard [Albert Lombard], *The "High Private"* (New York, 1848), 8–9; Lee A. Wallace, Jr., "Raising a Volunteer Regiment for Mexico, 1846–1847," *North Carolina Historical Review*, XXXV (January 1958), 32–33; Wallace, "The First Regiment of Virginia Volunteers," 51–52; Jones to Scott, Dec. 30, 1846, *AGLG*.

8. Richardson, *Messages and Papers*, V, 2321–56; Benton, *Thirty Years View*, II, 693, claims that the original draft of the message called for an end to active campaigning. McCormac, *Polk*, 456, demolishes the claim.

9. *Cong., Globe, 29th Cong., 2d Sess.*, 12–33, 47–455 *passim*, A91, A217; Quaife, *Diary of Polk*, II, 169–70, 362, 371–72; *Niles*, LXXI (Feb. 27, 1847), 406–8; McCormac, *Polk*, 462–63, 468. The southern counterattack is the subject of John D. P. Fuller, "Slavery Propaganda During the Mexican War," *SWHQ*, XXXVIII (April 1935), 235–45.

10. *Cong. Globe, 29th Cong., 1st Sess.*, 572–73; 9 *U.S. Stat.*, 174. The Wilmot Proviso failed 102 to 97 largely because of the shift of Democratic congressmen from the Middle Atlantic states.

11. 9 *U.S. Stat.*, 149–52, 169–75, 188.

12. Fuess, *Cushing*, II, 38–39, 51; Merk, "Dissent in the Mexican War," 48–49; Charles Sumner, "Report on the War with Mexico," *Old South Leaflets*, VI, No. 132.

13. *Niles*, LXXII (April 3, 1847), 67; Francis A. Christie, "Abiel Abbot Livermore," *DAB*, XI, 303–4.

14. Wilson Lumpkin to Calhoun, March 11, 1847, Toombs to Calhoun, April 30, 1847, Boucher and Brooks, "Correspondence Addressed to Calhoun," 370, 373–74; John Sherman to W. T. Sherman, May 2, 1847, Rachel Sherman Thorndike (ed.), *The Sherman Letters* (New York, 1894), 38–39.

15. Joseph Davis to Jefferson Davis, April 16, 1847, Jefferson Davis Papers, USMA; J. T. Taylor to Weed, April 24, 1847, Weed, *Autobiography*, 573–74; Marcy to P. M. Wetmore, April 25, 1847, Marcy Papers; H. W. Conner, May 7, F. H. Elmore, May 16, and R. B. Rhett, May 20, 1847, all to Calhoun, in Boucher and Brooks, "Correspondence Addressed to Calhoun," 375–77.

16. Taylor to Wood, May 9, July 13, 20, Sept. 14, 1847, all in Samson, *Taylor's Letters*, 99, 113–14, 118, 128–31; to A. P. Merrill, June 20, 1847, *New York Times*, Feb. 1, 1931; to J. P. Taylor, June 24, 1847, Taylor Papers; to C. L. Wilcox,

et al., July 20, to F. S. Bronson, Aug. 19, 1847, *Niles*, LXXIII (Sept. 25, Oct. 9, 1847), 63, 83; John Norvell to Polk, July 19, 1847, Polk Papers.

17. Taylor to [Davis?], Aug. 16, 1847, Taylor Papers.
18. Taylor to Davis, Sept. 18, 1847, Princeton University Library; to Danforth, Sept. 27, 1847, YWA; to AG, Oct. 4, 1847, *AGLR'47*, T-548.
19. The elections are incisively discussed in Brian G. Walton, "The Elections for the Thirtieth Congress and the Presidential Candidacy of Zachary Taylor," *Journal of Southern History*, XXV (May 1969), 186–202. See also William E. Dodd, "The West and the War with Mexico," *Illinois State Historical Society Journal*, V (July 1912), 165.
20. Eustis Prescott to Calhoun, Aug. 20, 1847, Boucher and Brooks, "Correspondence Addressed to Calhoun," 390–91.
21. Quaife, *Diary of Polk*, III, 139, 158–59; Spencer, *Victor and Spoils*, 166. Particularly unfortunate was Marcy's absence during the discussions over calling out five additional volunteer regiments. Mason to Govs. Ind., Tenn., Ky., Aug. 26, 1847, *SWMA*, XXVIII, 8–9. The Indiana Regiment was planned to contain men from the 12-month units under Col. James K. Lane.
22. Quaife, *Diary of Polk*, III, 120–21; Benton to AG, Aug. 22, 1847, *AGLR'47*, B-766. Kearny placed Frémont under arrest and ordered him to Washington on August 22 when the two men reached Fort Leavenworth. The General submitted his formal charges, specifications, and evidence on Sept. 11. Benton and Mrs. Frémont both asked the President for a trial. Kearny to AG, Aug. 22, Sept. 11, 1847, *ibid.*, K-205, 217; Benton to Polk, Sept. 10, Jessie B. Frémont to Polk, Sept. 21, 1847, Polk Papers. See also Frémont to AG, Sept. 17, 1847, *Niles*, LXXIII (Sept. 25, 1847), 50–51.
23. The proceedings of the court were published as *S. Ex. Doc. 33, 30th Cong., 1st Sess.* The best summaries from the opposing viewpoints are in Nevins, *Fremont*, 327–39, and Clarke, *Kearny*, 347–73. The other members of the court were Colonels Sylvester Churchill and Icabod B. Crane, Brevet Colonel Matthew W. Payne, Lieutenant Colonels Joseph P. Taylor, René E. De Russy, and Thomas F. Hunt, Brevet Lieutenant Colonels Stephen H. Long and Henry K. Craig, Majors Rufus L. Baker, James D. Graham, Richard Delafield, Edwin W. Morgan, and George A. McCall. Captain John F. Lee acted as the judge advocate.
24. *Cong. Globe, 30th Cong., 1st Sess.*, A977–1040; McCormac, *Polk*, 477.
25. See John D. P. Fuller, *The Movement for the Acquisition of All Mexico 1846–1848* (New York, 1969), 40–63, and "The Slavery Question and the Movement to Acquire Mexico, 1846–1848," *MVHR*, XXI (June 1934), 48; Merk, *Manifest Destiny and Mission*, 107–43; Weinberg, *Manifest Destiny*, 165; and Paul F. Lambert, "The Movement for the Acquisition of All Mexico," *Journal of the West*, XI (April 1972), 317–27.
26. Merk, *Manifest Destiny and Mission*, 119–20, 149–50; *Cong. Globe, 30th Cong., 1st Sess.*, 79; Ray Allen Billington, *The Far Western Frontier 1830–1860* (New York, 1956), 191–92.
27. *Cong. Globe, 30th Cong., 1st Sess.*, 87; *Niles*, LXXIII (Jan. 22, 1848), 334–36; Weinberg, *Manifest Destiny*, 174, 177.
28. Polk, Annual Message, Dec. 7, 1847, Richardson, *Messages and Papers*, V, 2382–2414; *Cong. Globe, 30th Cong., 1st Sess.*, 2–3, 26, 54, 64, 93–95, 155; Roy P. Basler (ed.), *The Collected Works of Abraham Lincoln* (8 vols., New Brunswick, 1953), I, 421–22.
29. *Cong. Globe, 30th Cong., 1st Sess.*, 136, 215; *Niles*, LXXIII (Jan. 22, 1848), 336.
30. J. Fred Rippy, *Joel R. Poinsett, Versatile American* (New York, 1968), 229.
31. Scott to Pillow, Oct. 2, 3, Pillow to Scott, Oct. 3 (2 letters), 1847, *H. Ex. Doc. 56, 30th Cong., 1st Sess.*, 205–10; Worth to Scott, Nov. 13, 14, to Marcy Nov. 16,

Duncan to Editor of *North American*, Nov. 13, H. L. Scott to Worth, Nov. 14, 1847, all in Semmes, *Service Afloat and Ashore*, 361–62, 364–66; H. L. Scott to Duncan, Nov. 18, 1847, Duncan Papers; Pillow to H. L. Scott, Nov. 14, 23, to Marcy, Nov. 15, to Polk, Nov. 24, Dec. 12, H. L. Scott to Pillow, Nov. 15, 22, 1847, all in Polk Papers; Quaife, *Diary of Polk*, III, 266; Smith, *War with Mexico*, II, 434–35, contains a good discussion of Worth's fancied slights. His conduct is defended in Wallace, *Worth*, 174–78.

32. Quaife, *Diary of Polk*, III, 245–46, 262–63; Polk to Pillow, Dec. 19, 1847, PLPB, III, 266–74; Buchanan to Trist, Dec. 21, 1847, Manning, *Diplo. Corres.*, VIII, 218–19; Marcy to Scott, Dec. 24, 1847, *SWLG*, 1. Marcy's requests for information and the replies of each general are in Court of Inquiry FF-300, exhibits 3-8, 10, 22–4, 26.

33. Marcy to W. O. Butler, Jan. 13, 1848, *SWLG*, 3–5; War Dept., GO #2, Jan. 13, 1848, *H. Ex. Doc. 60, 30th Cong., 1st Sess.*, 1043–44; Marcy to Scott, Jan. 13, 1848 (2 letters), *H. Ex. Doc. 56, 30th Cong., 1st Sess.*, 230–35; Marcy to AG, Jan. 13, 1848, *AGLR'48*, M-46. On March 17 Col. W. G. Belknap replaced Col. Butler. Marcy to AG, March 17, 1848, *ibid.*, M-60.

34. HQ Army, Orders #59, Feb. 18, Army of Mexico, Orders #1, Feb. 19, 1848, *Niles*, LXXIV (March 4, 1848), 4; Marcy to Butler, Jan. 25, 1848, *SWLG*, 19–20. Among the reinforcements was an additional battalion of Marines under Maj. John Harris. It was intended for the expedition against the Isthmus of Tehuantepec but arrived in Mexico after the close of fighting and garrisoned Alvarado until sent home. Henderson to Harris, March 1, 1848, *CMCLB*, 363; Perry to W. Lang, May 15, 1848, Matthew C. Perry Collection, CHS. The completion of the Frémont court-martial released a number of its witnesses for duty in Mexico, including Gen. Kearny and Lt. Col. Cooke. Jones to Kearny, to Cooke, Feb. 23, 1848, *AGLS*, XXIV, #410, 411.

35. The Court of Inquiry transcript is in Courts of Inquiry Proceedings FF-300 and is reprinted in *S. Ex. Doc. 65, 30th Cong., 1st Sess.* See also War Dept., GO #40, July 21, 1848, Cushing Papers, Box 170; Polk, Draft of Statement on Court of Inquiry, n.d., Polk Papers; Marcy to Scott, July 14, 24, 1848, *SWMA*, XXVIII, 334, 345.

36. Marcy, Memo . . . Pillow Court-Martial, April 26, 1848, *AGLR'48*, M-194.

37. Scott to Jones, May 1, 1848, *ibid.*, S-360; Hitchcock, *50 Years*, 328.

19: Peace at Last

WHEN SCOTT AGREED to the armistice outside the walls of Mexico City on August 23, 1847 he assumed that Mexican interest in negotiations was genuine. Not only had Santa Anna's agents claimed that the Mexican leader would negotiate after a battle before his capital, but the battles on August 19-20 had been a devastating defeat for Mexican arms. Yet it quickly became evident that Scott and Trist were wrong in their estimate of the situation. The political realities within Mexico City did not permit serious negotiations, if indeed such had ever been Santa Anna's intention.

His hold on the reins was too weak and the pressure for an unyielding stand too strong to permit real negotiations. The result of these pressures can be seen in an interesting document entitled "Points for discussion in the conferences with the commissioners of the U. S." drawn up by the President and his advisers. It insisted that the Americans agree to:

1. meet on neutral ground;
2. drop further claims on the Mexican government;
3. accept a Nueces boundary;
4. lift the blockade;
5. negotiate the status of California north of 26° only;
6. pay for damages caused by the war and by American troops;
7. prohibit slavery in any territory acquired by the United States;
8. a guarantee of the agreement by either European powers or an Inter-American Congress;

9. release of the San Patricio prisoners;
10. keep American troops outside Mexico City; and
11. return all captured vessels and other trophies.

These were, of course, victor's demands and totally unrealistic in the situation even as negotiating points.[1]

Trist's interpretation of the state of affairs within the Mexican government also varied considerably from reality. He expected that Santa Anna would establish a dictatorship in order to ease acceptance of peace. To hasten that imagined tactic, Trist informed the Mexican leader that he was willing to pay the maximum sum authorized in his instructions for the boundary which Polk desired. Moreover, he would pay upon ratification in such a way as to facilitate conversion into cash. Meanwhile, Santa Anna encountered difficulties in even finding negotiators. Three men, including ex-President José Joaquín Herrera, turned down the assignment, although Santa Anna was able eventually to prevail upon Herrera to take the thankless mission. Three other men joined him: General Mora; José Bernardo Couto, a distinguished and respected lawyer; and Miguel Atristáin, a lawyer closely connected with the British commercial community. Their instructions showed what one modern Mexican commentator called "the petulance of Santa Anna, the ignorance of his ministers, and the lack of reality with which they entered the discussions."[2]

The commissioners met for the first time at Atzcapuzalco, about eight miles from Tacubaya, on August 27. There Trist learned to his dismay that the Mexicans were empowered only to transmit his proposals to their government. The American insisted that he was authorized to treat only with commissioners possessing full powers but read a statement of the propositions which he was ready to offer. When the negotiators met the following day, Trist suggested a change of location, so the meetings moved to the Casa Colorado near Tacubaya. Since the house was within the Mexican lines, this was scarcely a wise move when dealing with a government as unrealistic as the Mexican, because it implied that the Americans were suing for peace.

During the twenty-ninth the Mexican cabinet considered the American proposals and the following day Santa Anna discussed them with his generals. Although everyone concurred in granting the Mexican commissioners the plenary power demanded by Trist, a new complication arose. The commissioners refused to accept the powers because even the revised Mexican terms were unreasonable. At this Santa Anna retreated and agreed to allow the negotiators to make any concessions they believed necessary.[3]

With the question of power to negotiate finally settled, the commissioners began serious talks on September 1. The Mexicans offered as a counterproposal terms similar to those suggested by Atocha in January: the Nueces boundary with a neutral ground between it and the Rio Grande; Mexican retention of New Mexico; sale of northern California only, and no transit-right grant in Tehuantepec. Trist countered with an offer to give up Baja California, which he knew the Mexicans were aware was not mandatory, and the transit rights in return for all of Upper California. When it became clear that the Mexicans would not seriously consider giving up territory, he offered on September 2, to extend the armistice forty to forty-five days while he secured an explicit decision on the neutralization proposal. In return the Mexicans agreed to submit the California proposal to their government. It appears certain that neither side expected its government to make the concessions and that both recognized that the negotiations were at a stalemate. On Trist's part, the arrangement was a desperate attempt to keep the negotiations alive.[4]

What turned out to be the final meeting of the commissioners occurred on September 6. The Mexicans arrived late and delivered their *contraproyecto* with a covering letter intended for public consumption. The patently unacceptable proposal called for a boundary line along the Nueces to its source; thence west to New Mexico and along its eastern, northern, and western boundaries to 37° north latitude; thence west to the territory; American payment of all claims of Mexican citizens for war damages; and the restoration of all duties collected by the United States in Mexican ports. In return the Mexicans offered to leave the area between the Nueces and the Rio Grande unsettled. There was no discussion. Both sides recognized that the negotiations had been abrogated and with them the armistice. Scott made the latter definite by denouncing the cease-fire later in the day on the basis of the interference with the supply trains and the strengthening of the fortifications.[5]

The collapse of negotiations coincided with extensive reconsiderations of the peace terms in Washington. On September 4 President Polk decided that if the war continued, the United States should increase the amount of territory it demanded. The cabinet generally agreed that the price to be paid for New Mexico and California be reduced but split widely over the amount of land to be added. Buchanan, with his eyes as always on the 1848 nomination, wished to reduce the price to $15 million and to insist upon the right of passage across Baja California. Secretary of the Treasury Walker and Attorney General Nathan Clifford both favored adding Tamaulipas to the United States and were willing to overrun all of Mexico if she refused to sue for peace after the fall of her capital. Faced with that divergence of advice, Polk postponed a decision.[6]

The news of the armistice arrived on the heels of the indecisive cabinet discussions and displeased Polk. He concluded that Scott should have demanded a prompt decision on Trist's terms and then seized the Mexican capital immediately and levied contributions if the Mexicans rejected them. Polk reasoned correctly that the Mexicans would merely use the time won to reorganize their forces.[7] But Polk did not have to contend with the realities and subtleties of the actual situation.

On September 27 Trist wrote Buchanan that he believed Santa Anna wished to make peace but not upon the terms which the American administration desired.[8] The administration ignored the advice, since it had decided upon a new strategy. Polk concluded that the Mexicans would never come to terms while they believed that the United States was overanxious for peace or too weak or disunited to continue the war. After conferring with Buchanan, Marcy, and Walker, the President took an adamant stand. He ordered Trist home and instructed General Scott to contact the White House if the Mexican government approached him about negotiations. In the meantime the army would continue its efforts to stamp out guerrillas and impose contributions which would force the Mexicans "as far as practicable [to] defray the expenses of the war."[9]

When Polk learned the details of Trist's negotiations, he was appalled. "Mr. Trist had exceeded his instructions and had suggested terms . . . which I could not have approved," he complained in his diary. This brought stronger instructions to the diplomat: If you have completed a treaty bring it with you; if not, suspend negotiations and inform the Mexicans that their proposed terms will be forwarded to the President. In any case, return without delay. Buchanan added a private letter scolding the diplomat for even considering the abandonment of the Rio Grande boundary.[10] Trist did not receive the recall notice, however, until mid-November.

On October 20 Trist wrote Mexican Foreign Minister Luis de la Rosa. The letter purported to be an answer to the last Mexican note before the breakdown of negotiations in September.[11] Trist's attempt to reinstitute negotiations coincided with a rise in pressures within Mexico for peace and the appearance of a growing sentiment among both the natives and foreigners for American annexation of all the country. One manifestation of that sentiment was a November visit to Scott by some Mexican liberals who proposed that he become dictator of Mexico as a step toward annexation. In January other Mexicans saluted the American conquest and the prospects of annexation at a banquet in honor of Scott and his staff.[12]

On the last day of October, Rosa promised to appoint new commissioners. But the Peña regime did not feel sufficiently strong to carry out the promise although the moderate position was strengthened when Congress met in November. On the eleventh the legislators elected General Pedro María Anaya interim president over the Santanista candidate, General Juan N. Almonte. The moderate Anaya promptly named Peña as his foreign minister.[13]

Just as the prospects for peace once again appeared to brighten, events darkened them. On November 16 Trist received the instructions to stop negotiations and return to Washington. Rather than transmit the unwelcome information officially, Trist did so unofficially through Edward Thornton. He coupled it with the suggestion that the Mexicans act quickly. Thornton reported back that Peña was thunderstruck and disappointed but hopeful that Trist would continue the negotiations, since Mexico had now appointed commissioners. They were Couto, Cuevas, Atristáin, and General Manuel Rincón. Nevertheless, Trist on the twenty-fourth regretfully informed Peña that he saw no way to avoid complying with his instructions. The American diplomat forwarded the formal rejection of the Mexican boundary proposals and made plans to leave Mexico City on December 4 or 5.[14]

While Trist awaited the departure of a wagon train for Veracruz, pressures mounted for him to ignore his recall and stay to complete the negotiations. Thornton led the appeal, supported by Mexican peace advocates and apparently also by Scott. All of them believed that a failure to seize the opportunity to negotiate would indefinitely postpone any settlement. It was clear to them that if the new administration plan took effect, the terms acceptable to the United States would be stiffer than those which Trist might accept.[15] During the morning of December 4 Trist, who undoubtedly needed little coaxing, decided to remain:

> Knowing it to be the very last chance, and impressed with the dreadful consequences to our country which cannot fail to attend the loss of that chance I will make a treaty, if it can be done, on the basis of the Bravo, and across by the 32°; giving 15 millions besides the 3 millions cash.

He then sent the welcome news to Thornton.[16]

Trist informed Buchanan of the decision in what must be considered, for physical effort if nothing else, one of the most impressive and gratuitously insulting American public papers ever written. He covered sixty-five large pages with attacks upon the criticism of Scott's armistice, General Gideon J. Pillow, and the government's failure to understand the situation in Mexico. The diplomat justified his remaining by arguing that a treaty could be negotiated then but not later; and his conviction that Mexico would yield no additional territory. Furthermore, he pointed out, the treaty could be disavowed if the administration wished. His stand received the strong support of Thornton, who assured the American that the peace had indeed to be negotiated then if ever.[17]

While the Mexicans debated their response, the new British Minister, Percy W. Doyle, reached Mexico. He firmly but politely informed Peña that the British would intervene only to offer their good offices. Doyle and Thornton also counseled the appointment of commissioners to meet with Trist, a move which Peña hoped to delay until after the meeting of Congress in January. Finally, in late December, he capitulated and agreed to negotiations but issued instructions as unrealistic as those of the summer.

The formal "powers" for the three commissioners reached Mexico City on New Year's Day of 1848 and private meetings started the following day. When the Mexican negotiators demanded foreign arbitration and a European guarantee of the boundary, Trist firmly but diplomatically refused both points. He did the same with a Mexican request that American troops withdraw to within 130 miles of the coast upon signing of the treaty. Trist did accede, however, to a Mexican proposal that the boundary line in New Mexico follow the Gila River and the Alta–Baja California boundary rather than the 32nd Parallel. This produced a heated argument over whether San Diego, which Trist had been specifically instructed to secure, lay north or south of the line. With great care he refuted the Mexican contentions and proved convincingly that the port lay in American territory. Throughout all the meetings Trist maintained his patience and humor, guiding the Mexicans gently into positions acceptable to the United States. It was Trist's finest hour. Yet the negotiations advanced very slowly. When Anaya's term expired on January 8, 1848 before Congress could meet to select a successor, Peña again became interim president. His second tour in office evidenced no greater strength of will than the first. Indeed, he was so thoroughly frightened by an uprising in San Luis Potosí that he demanded the price of a settlement be raised to $30 million in order to provide the money necessary to sustain the government. Trist refused to go beyond half of that.

Even the eternally optimistic Trist had to admit that the negotiations scarcely progressed. On January 29 he tried a new tack. Reminding the Mexican commissioners that their intransigence prevented the signing of a treaty, he announced that the negotiations would cease on February 1 if no agreement had been reached. It produced the desired effect. On January 31 the Mexican commissioners accepted a treaty draft and forwarded it to their superiors in Querétaro for their concurrence. It remained to be seen, however, whether the irresolute Peña and his advisers would accept it. In order to strengthen their resolve, Scott hinted that once the treaty was signed he would protect the government from revolution. Doyle and Thornton added not inconsequential British support for the acceptance while the commissioners themselves added their advice that the terms were as good as could be secured. Faced with such pressure, Peña capitulated. He authorized the commissioners to sign the treaty, which they did at Guadalupe-Hidalgo on February 2.[18]

By the terms of the treaty, Mexico renounced her claims to Texas, California, and New Mexico in return for $15 million and an abandonment of claims antedating the treaty. The boundary ran up the Rio Grande to the southern boundary of New Mexico; followed the southern and western limits of New Mexico to the point nearest the Gila River; from there it ran north to the Gila and followed that stream to the Colorado River. It dropped down the Colorado to the boundary line between Alta and Baja California, which it followed to the Pacific.[19] Trist had secured the boundary demanded by his instructions but little more. The passage rights across the Isthmus of Tehuantepec which had loomed so large in the thinking of Robert Walker and many other Americans in 1847 did not appear in the treaty, since they had already been granted to British speculators. The treaty, in Article XXI, contained provisions for arbitration of future disputes between the two nations. This far-reaching provision apparently grew out of a persistent campaign by American pacifists and marked one of the high points of their nineteenth-century efforts.[20]

Trist forwarded the treaty to Washington as soon as it was signed. As his messenger he chose one of his intimates, James L. Freaner, a correspondent for the New Orleans *Delta*, who signed his reports "Mustang." Since the treaty contained provision for a cessation of hostilities, it remained for the two military forces to arrange the details. The Mexicans, who hoped for a full-fledged armistice rather than a cessation of fighting in the Valley of Mexico, delayed the signing. Finally Generals Ignacio Mora y Villamil and Benito Quitano met on February 22 with the American representatives, Generals Worth and Persifor Smith. The meeting followed the now familiar pattern of extravagant Mexican demands which were rejected by the Americans and an American counterproposal which granted the Mexicans the maximum freedom commensurate with military needs. Such an agreement was finally signed on February 29.[21]

The agreement had provided for a general suspension of hostilities; cessation of advances by either side; free trade between the zones; suspension of the collection of contributions; American noninterference in elections in the occupied areas; collection of Mexican taxes in those regions; and establishment of Mexican police in the American-held zone.[22]

On the same day General Butler authorized a passport permitting Santa Anna to leave the country. When the Mexican leader reached Perote he was entertained by Colonel George W. Hughes and narrowly avoided a serious incident with Colonel John C. Hays and a number of his Texans. Santa Anna reciprocated Hughes's kindness at Encero, and on May 5 he embarked at Antigua on a Spanish brig bound for Jamaica.[23]

The Americans desired to disturb Mexican life as little as possible during the period of waiting. At the time of the Mexican elections on April 2, General Butler restricted American troops to their barracks, and at the end of the month lifted the export ban on gold and silver ingots. When the newly elected Congress met, it elected General Herrera president and he, after some reluctance, patriotically accepted the post in late May.

Upon learning of the reopened negotiations, Polk complained that Trist had become "the perfect tool of Scott." It was mild compared to the explosion which greeted the January 15 arrival of Trist's long, vituperative December 6 essay. Polk called it "the most extraordinary document I have ever heard from a diplomatic representative . . . arrogant, impudent, and very insulting to his Government, and . . . personally offensive to the President. . . . I have never in my life felt so indignant."[24]

Trist's total disregard of his recall left the President in a quandary. What steps should be taken to bring him into line? Should any treaty he might negotiate be accepted? Some of his advisers, notably Senators Lewis Cass and Ambrose Sevier, suggested notifying the Mexicans directly that Trist had been recalled. Polk ignored that advice and settled on a sensible solution. He refused to commit himself in advance of a treaty, preferring to make the decision on the document's merits. He did, however, direct that Scott expel Trist from Mexico City and the army. In the midst of these considerations appeared the now familiar figure of Colonel Atocha. On February 8 Secretary Buchanan reported a letter in which the Colonel suggested he could bribe the Mexican Congress to accept peace. Polk dismissed it with the observation that "Attocha [sic] is a great scoundrel."[25]

Dusk had fallen on Saturday, February 19, when Freaner reached Washington with the copy of the treaty and a covering dispatch from Scott. The following afternoon Polk called the cabinet together for an unusual Sunday session to consider the document. Buchanan and Walker, making common cause for once, recommended rejection. The rest of the group favored acceptance, although all concurred in rejecting a provision which had the effect of validating Mexican land titles in Texas granted after independence. When the cabinet resumed its deliberations on Monday, Polk announced his decision to send the treaty to the Senate, since it conformed in the main to the instructions given Trist in April. He feared, he told his colleagues, the domestic political consequences of rejection, since it would give the Whigs political ammunition. Like Richard Nixon in 1973, he had also to consider the possibility that Congress would not appropriate sufficient funds to force militarily a better settlement. Buchanan's insistence that the territorial settlement was too small strengthened the President's conviction that his Secretary of State was running for the presidential nomination.[26]

Polk sent an advance copy of the treaty to Senator Sevier who, as Chairman of the Foreign Relations Committee, would guide it through the ratification maze. The following day Polk formally submitted the document to the Senate, recommending rejection of the land-titles article and a secret one extending the time during which it could be ratified. The Senate's initial response was strongly negative because of the manner of its negotiation, but Polk reminded the senators they had under consideration the treaty, not its negotiator. Moreover, with a better understanding of the situation in Mexico than he usually displayed, the President advised the senators that it would be impossible to renegotiate the treaty.

Although the administration's opponents chortled audibly at Polk's discomfort in recommending a treaty negotiated against his positive orders, they had little basis on which to attack it. Once the treaty came to be considered on its own merits, its passage was assured. Only the minority "all-of-Mexico" Democrats and the Whigs opposed. As a result, when the final vote was tallied on March 10 the yeas numbered thirty-eight and the nays but fourteen, three votes more than necessary to ratify.[27] At least as far as Trist was concerned, Polk's revenge took a monetary form. He refused to reimburse Trist at all; not until 1871 did the diplomat collect his expenses.

Polk wished to send Louis McLane to Mexico City to handle exchange of ratifications, but Mrs. McLane's precarious health prevented it. The President then turned to Senator Sevier, who delayed his acceptance until March 12. Shortly after accepting, Sevier himself became seriously ill. Since his departure appeared to be delayed for some time, Polk in desperation prevailed upon Attorney General Clifford to serve as Associate Commissioner. The instructions to the two commissioners were to gain Mexican ratification of the treaty as approved by the American Senate. If Mexico refused, however, they could negotiate a new agreement. At the same time General Butler received permission to enter into an armistice or to use his forces as he saw fit to check any preparations to continue the war.[28]

Because of Sevier's illness, Clifford proceeded alone. He landed at Veracruz in early April and reached Mexico City on the eleventh. Sevier, whose recovery was more rapid than expected, joined him four days later. On the seventeenth the two Americans notified Rosa of their arrival, but they had to wait for over a month while the Mexican Congress debated the treaty. At last, in mid-May, common sense prevailed and both houses approved. On May 22 the American diplomats, escorted by a company of dragoons and a company of mounted riflemen under command of the President's brother, Major William H. Polk, rode out to Querétaro. There they exchanged official ratifications on May 30 to bring the war to an end.[29]

On May 19 Butler had alerted Major Osborn Cross, the quartermaster at Veracruz, to the impending ratification of the peace treaty and directed the collection of transports to evacuate the sick and wounded at Jalapa and the seaport. On the twenty-third Butler ordered Persifor Smith to take charge at Veracruz.[30]

The abandonment of outlying posts began even before the exchange of ratifications. The Cuernavaca and Toluca garrisons marched back to Mexico City in May. The Orizaba force in June moved directly to Veracruz. Withdrawal for the main body started on May 27. On June 1 all the General Court-Martial prisoners, including the San Patricios, were released from prison. Most of the Americans turned their faces toward the sea and home with joy, but to some the past sparkled as the future never could. As it set out, the 3d Infantry band saluted those whose hearts had been captured by a Mexican señorita by playing "The Girl I Left Behind Me."[31]

The last American troops in Mexico City, Worth's division, formed in the Grand Plaza in the early morning of June 12. They watched the American flag come down and heard the salutes from a Mexican and Duncan's batteries as the Mexican tricolor rose. The Americans then began their march to the coast accompanied by Peace Commissioner Ambrose H. Sevier. In his baggage Sevier carried the official Mexican ratification of the peace treaty. He did not, however, carry the receipt for the $3 million. The Mexicans were still counting it![32]

The passage of troops through Veracruz was rapid and well handled. In order to protect the health of the men, they were held at Jalapa until just before scheduled to embark. They then moved to a pair of camps at Vergara and entered Veracruz only to board their transport. Because of the limited availability of supplies at Veracruz, most transports could be provisioned only for a short voyage. As a result the bulk of the troops sailed to New Orleans or Pass Christian, Mississippi, where newly erected hospitals awaited the sick and wounded.[33]

General Butler himself embarked for New Orleans on June 20 and the last major unit, Worth's division, completed its outloading on July 15. All that remained of the American army were the Veracruz garrison, a company of dragoons, and the quartermaster's men superintending the movement of the last of the supplies. The dragoons sailed on July 22 and the 1st Artillery ended their garrison duty at Veracruz on August 1. The next day most of the remaining quartermaster's men and horses left for home. The occupation had ended.[34]

NOTES

For key to abbreviations used in Notes, see page xi.

1. Santa Anna *et al.*, "Points for discussion . . . ," Aug. 24, 1847, *S. Ex. Doc. 52, 30th Cong., 1st Sess.,* 314-15.
2. Trist to Buchanan, Aug. 24, Sept. 4, 1847, Manning, *Diplo. Corres.,* VIII, 927-29, 933-40; Herrera to Pacheco, Antonio Fernández Monjardín to Pacheco, Pacheco,

Instructions, Aug. 25, Pacheco to Herrera, Antonio Garay to Pacheco, Aug. 26, 1847, all in *S. Ex. Doc. 52, 30th Cong., 1st Sess.*, 314–21, 325; Smith, *War with Mexico*, II, 135. The comment is from Cabrero, *Diario del Polk*, III, 377n.

3. Pacheco to Trist, Trist to Pacheco, Aug. 26, Trist to Buchanan, Aug. 29, 1847, Manning, *Diplo. Corres.*, VIII, 930–32; Pacheco, Instructions, Aug. 30, to Herrera *et al.*, Aug. 31, 1847, *S. Ex. Doc. 52, 30th Cong., 1st Sess.*, 330–35; Smith, *War with Mexico*, II, 396. The revised Mexican instructions were to insist upon the Nueces boundary but to agree to a neutralized zone on either side; no cession of New Mexico or California, although an American trading factory might be established at San Francisco; no transit concession on the isthmus of Tehuantepec; and an indemnity to repay Mexico for all customs lost as a result of the occupation of her ports.

4. Trist to Buchanan, Sept. 4, 1847, *loc. cit.*; Smith, *War with Mexico*, II, 136–37, 396.

5. Pacheco *et al.*, Instructions, Herrera *et al.*, *Contraproyecto*, Sept. 5, Herrera *et al.* to Trist, Scott to Santa Anna, Scott to Marcy, Sept. 11, 1847, *S. Ex. Doc. 52, 30th Cong., 1st Sess.*, 335–44, 346, 354–56, 359.

6. Quaife, *Diary of Polk*, III, 160–61, 163–65; Edward G. Bourne, "A Proposed Absorption of Mexico in 1847–48," *Annual Report of the American Historical Association for the Year 1899* (Washington, 1900), I, 160.

7. Quaife, *Diary of Polk*, III, 167, 170–72.

8. Trist to Buchanan, Sept. 27, 1847, Manning, *Diplo. Corres.*, VIII, 953–56.

9. Quaife, *Diary of Polk*, III, 185–87; Buchanan to Trist, Oct. 6, 1847, Manning, *Diplo. Corres.*, VIII, 214–16; Marcy to Scott, Oct. 6, 1847, *H. Ex. Doc. 60, 30th Cong., 1st Sess.*, 1006–9.

10. Quaife, *Diary of Polk*, III, 196; Buchanan to Trist, Oct. 25, 1847, Manning, *Diplo. Corres.*, VIII, 217–18; same to same (private), Oct. 25, 1847, Trist Papers, XXVI.

11. Trist to Rosa, Oct. 20, 1847, *S. Ex. Doc. 52, 30th Cong., 1st Sess.*, 214–15.

12. Trist to Buchanan, Oct. 25, 1847, Manning, *Diplo. Corres.*, VIII, 958–64. When the letter was later submitted to Congress the section dealing with annexation was deleted. *S. Ex. Doc. 52, 30th Cong., 1st Sess.*, 205–12; James A. Magner, *Men of Mexico* (Milwaukee, 1942), 342–43.

13. Rosa to Trist, Oct. 31, 1847, Manning, *Diplo. Corres.*, VIII, 971; McCormac, *Polk*, 521–22. It is a commentary on the fluid state of affairs in Mexico that Trist was so certain that the interim government could not for some time develop sufficient support to negotiate that he asked for permission to return home. Trist to Buchanan, Oct. 31, 1847, *ibid.*, 969–70. Peña to Trist, Nov. 22, 1847, *S. Ex. Doc. 52, 30th Cong., 1st Sess.*, 98–99; Brooks, *Complete History*, 576.

14. McCormac, *Polk*, 520; McMaster, *History of the People of the U.S.*, VII, 524; Thornton to Trist, Nov. 22, Trist to Peña, Nov. 24, to Buchanan, Nov. 27, 1847, Manning, *Diplo. Corres.*, VIII, 973n, 980–84; Peña to Trist, Nov. 22, 1847, *S. Ex. Doc. 52, 30th Cong., 1st Sess.*, 98–99; Trist to Thornton, Nov. 24, 1847, Trist Papers, XXVI. Rincón refused the appointment.

15. The additional price for peace that the administration plan would cost was not settled in Washington. The cabinet split over the extent of additional territory to be demanded. Except for Walker none of the cabinet joined the "All of Mexico" forces. Quaife, *Diary of Polk*, III, 215–18, 269–93; Bourne, "Absorption of Mexico," 161–62.

16. Trist to wife, Dec. 4, 1847, Trist Papers, XXVI; to Thornton, Dec. 4, 1847, Manning, *Diplo Corres.*, VIII, 984n–5n. In submitting the text to Congress, Marcy deleted Thornton's name as addressee. *S. Ex. Doc. 52, 30th Cong., 1st Sess.*, 100–2.

17. Trist to Buchanan, Dec. 6, 1847, Manning, *Diplo. Corres.*, VIII, 984-1020; Thornton to Trist, Dec. 11, 1847, Trist Papers, XXVI.

18. The description of the final negotiations is based upon Trist to Buchanan, Jan. 12, 25, 1848, Manning, *Diplo. Corres.*, VIII, 1032-59; Trist, Notes, Trist Papers; Rives, *U.S. and Mexico*, II, 602-13; Graebner, *Empire on the Pacific*, 206-8; Smith, *War with Mexico*, II, 238-40; McCormac, *Polk*, 536-37.

19. *S. Ex. Doc. 52, 30th Cong., 1st Sess.*, 38-66.

20. Merl E. Curti, "Pacifist Propaganda and the Treaty of Guadalupe Hidalgo," *AHR*, XXXIII (April 1928), 596-98.

21. Trist to Buchanan, Feb. 2, 1848, Manning, *Diplo. Corres.*, VIII, 1059-60; Worth and Smith, Memorandum of conversations, Feb. 22 (with continuations to 26th), "Military Convention for the Provisional Suspension of Hostilities," Feb. 29, 1848, Mexican War Collection, CHS. That collection also contains copies of the commissions of the representatives, the Mexican project for an armistice, and the American reply of Feb. 23.

22. Army of Mexico, Orders #18, March 6, 1848, *AGGO*, XLII.

23. Thomas to Twiggs, March 6, 1848, *AMLB*; W. I. Gray, Pass, March 17, 1848, Smith Transcripts, XII, 218; Tilghman to D. Woodruff, April 10, 1848, Lloyd Tilghman Collection, CHS; Callcott, *Santa Anna*, 274-76; Kenly, *Memoirs*, 393-97.

24. Quaife, *Diary of Polk*, III, 283, 300-1.

25. *Ibid.*, 311, 314, 329; Bourne, "Absorption of Mexico," 106.

26. Quaife, *Diary of Polk*, III, 345-50; J. Knox Polk, Memorandum of Cabinet Meeting, Feb. 20, 1848, Polk Papers.

27. Quaife, *Diary of Polk*, III, 35; Polk to Senate, Feb. 23, 1848, Richardson, *Messages and Papers*, V, 2423-24; *S. Ex. Doc. 52, 30th Cong., 1st Sess.*, 4-36; Rives, *U.S. and Mexico*, II, 614-37; Smith, *War with Mexico*, II, 246-48.

28. Quaife, *Diary of Polk*, III, 375, 377-80, 390-91; Clifford to Polk, March 18, 1848, Polk Papers; Polk to Senate, March 18, 1848, Richardson, *Messages and Papers*, V, 2427; Buchanan to Clifford, to Sevier, March 18, to Sevier and Clifford, March 22, 1848, Manning, *Diplo. Corres.*, VIII, 228-35; Marcy to Butler, March 15, 1848, *SWLG'48*, 33-35. On February 23 Buchanan requested the Treasury to authorize Butler to draw the $3 million initial payment under the treaty and on the following day cautioned the General against paying before the Mexicans ratified. Buchanan to Walker, Walker to Butler, Feb. 23, 1848, *S. Ex. Doc. 52, 30th Cong., 1st Sess.*, 108-9; Marcy to Butler, Feb. 24, 1848, *SWLG'48*, 23-24.

29. Clifford to wife, April 13, May 21, 26, 1848, Philip Greely Clifford, *Nathan Clifford Democrat (1803-1881)* (New York, 1922), 173-74, 183, 198; Sevier to Buchanan, April 18, Sevier and Clifford to Rosa, April 17, to Buchanan, May 25, 30, 1848, Manning, *Diplo. Corres.*, VIII, 1079-81, 1086-87; Army of Mexico, Orders #101, May 21, 1848, *AGGO*, XLII; Rives, *U.S. and Mexico*, II, 641-55. Daniel Moreno (ed.), *Manuel Crescencia Rejón Pensamient Politico* (México, 1968), 93-145, reprints Rejón's bitter attack in "Observaciones Sobre los Tratados de Guadalupe."

30. Thomas to Cross, May 19, Thomas to Brooke, May 21, 1848, *AMLB*; Butler to Smith, May 23, 1848, *BLB*. Upon Twiggs's return to the United States in the early spring, Col. Wilson again assumed charge at Veracruz. General Kearny replaced him in April but came down with yellow fever and had to be shifted to command of the 2d Division at Mexico City. Kearny to AG, April 9, 1848, *AGLR'48*, K-108; Thomas to Kearny, April 17, 1848, *AMLB*; same to same, May 6, 1848, Lansing B. Bloom (ed.), "A Group of Kearny Letters," *NMHR*, V (Jan. 1930), 36; Army of Mexico, Orders #103, May 23, 1848, *AGGO*, XLII; Clarke, *Kearny*, 377.

31. Bonham to Thomas, May 26, 1848, Cuernavaca *LB;* Collins, "Journal," 99; Thomas to Worth, to R. E. Lee, May 27, *AMLB*; 2VolDiv, Orders #7, May 31, 1848, *BOB*, 22; Orizaba Dept. Orders #112, Army of Mexico, Orders 116, June 1, 1848, *AGGO*, XLIII, XLII; John Darragh Wilkins, Journal, YWA.

32. Thomas to Worth, June 6, 1848, *AMLB*; Clifford to Buchanan, June 12, 1848, Manning, *Diplo. Corres.*, VIII, 1088; Wilcox, *Mexican War*, 550–52; Wallace, *Worth*, 185. The $3 million was paid as follows:

Army drafts on Washington	$ 900,000.00
Cash	769,650.00
Value of arms sold to Mexican government	87,655.90
Contributions levied on Federal District and assumed by Mexican government	49,712.28
12 drafts on U.S. government sold to L. S. Hargous	1,151,874.16
Premium allowed by Hargous	41,107.66

Clifford to Buchanan, July 2, 1848, *Desp. Mex.*, XIII.

33. Veracruz Dept. Orders #233, June 12, 1848, *V.C. Orders*; War Dept., GO #25, June 8, 1848, *H. Ex. Doc. 1, 30th Cong., 2d Sess.*, 170–73; Marcy to Lawson, March 31, 1848, Thomas Lawson Papers, L.C.; Jones to Twiggs, May 3, 1848, *AGLS*, XXV, #899.

34. Thomas to Kearny, to Worth, June 18, 1848, *AMLB*; 1st Division of Volunteers, Orders #19, June 22, 1848, *BOB*, 12; Worth to AG, June 27, 1848, *AGLR'48*, W-505; Army in Mexico, Orders #11, 1, 23, June 27, July 16, 31, 1848, *AGGO*, XLII, *V.C. Orders*; Maj. T. Swords to Jesup, July 2, 1848, Statement of Embarkation of U.S. Troops from Vera Cruz, Mexico, *H. Ex. Doc. 1, 30th Cong., 2d Sess.*, 192–203; Wilcox, *Mexican War*, 553. Among the troops sent to New Orleans were sixty-two men of Manuel Domínguez's Spy Company and thirty of their dependents. Butler to SW, July 7, 1848, *SWLR'48*, B-314; Brooke to Jones, July 10, 1848, *AGLR'48*, B-726.

Epilogue

❧❧

THE WAR so decisively won by American arms and concluded by
Nicholas P. Trist's unconventional diplomacy has traditionally appeared under a cloud in American history books. It has been described
as the unprovoked despoiling of a sister republic for the sake of a
rapacious American imperialism. Yet the reality was different. James
K. Polk may have been an imperialist but he was not rapacious. The
war developed contrary to his plans because of miscalculations and
the intransigence of his adversary. The peace terms were much less
harsh than those the success of American arms gave Trist the right
to demand. Yet, except for the acquisition of California, the immediate benefits to the United States were largely negative. The
slavery issue, so skillfully handled in the Missouri Compromise, was
reopened by the addition of new territory, as foreshadowed by the
Wilmot Proviso. The fact that the newly acquired territory was
ill-suited to a slave-based economy was less important than the belief
fostered in the North by abolitionists and others that the whole intent of the war was to enlarge the slave-holding area of the country.
Thus the Mexican War played directly into the great sectional confrontation which culminated in the Civil War.

Even if we recognize the detrimental effect of the war, it is difficult
to envision any set of circumstances which would have prevented
an effort to add Mexico's northern regions to the American commonwealth, since they stood in the way of the inexorable movement

westward of the American frontier and the American settlers. While one can postulate conditions under which that movement might have been held in abeyance for a period of time, it would have been impossible to contain the pressure indefinitely. Too many Americans saw their future tied to the opportunities, real or imagined, which stretched before them in the Southwest and the Mexican-controlled portions of the West coast.

According to his Secretary of the Navy, Polk came into the White House with four objectives: settlement of the Oregon question; acquisition of California; reduction of the tariff to a revenue base; and the establishment of an independent Treasury.[1] Even the inclusion of California among the administration's objectives did not determine the precise timing of the conflict. No preordained force set 1845 as the date for the annexation of Texas, although the results of the 1844 elections in the United States indicated that it would occur soon. Even then the annexation need not have brought war had not Polk chosen the arrangement of the Texas boundary as the vehicle to achieve a general settlement with Mexico which included the acquisition of California. Yet a President more attuned to the realities of Mexican politics or less devoted to intrigue might have postponed the final confrontation. In the last analysis Polk's program of graduated pressure defeated his policy of peaceful settlement and forced Mexico into a position from which her myopic leaders believed themselves unable to retreat.

Mexico's leaders bear a large share of the responsibility for the conflict. Many, if not most, used the popular resentment over the fancied *gringo* aggression which they themselves largely created as a stepping-stone to power. Once in power those politicians found themselves captives of that propaganda.[2] Almost alone among the Mexican political leaders José Joaquín Herrera recognized that love of country embraced a reasonable settlement with the giant of the north. Far too many of Mexico's leaders were unprincipled opportunists like Mariano Paredes y Arrillaga, or, like Antonio López de Santa Anna, had difficulty separating opportunism from love of country.

If the war's greatest immediate impact on American political life was to heighten the sectional conflict and the chances for a disruption of the Union, its effects in Mexico were nearly as great. Both the liberals and the conservatives were horrified by the clear lack of patriotism evinced both by the political leaders and by many of the Mexican masses. They sought, with only limited success, means of kindling what nationalistic spark remained. This lack of national spirit helped create the climate of conservative opinion which looked increasingly toward a monarchy as the solution of Mexico's ills.[3] Thus both nations plunged into civil wars less than a decade and a half after their confrontation; civil wars which traced much of their impetus to this earlier clash.

In directing his nation's war effort, Polk held a very tight rein on his military. He established the general strategy of the nation; chose the commanding officers for the different forces; gave much personal attention to supply matters; and used his service secretaries as coordinators. As a result his war leadership exemplified the Hamiltonian concept of unity of the executive power. In the process he allowed the war effort to become as involved in domestic politics as did Lyndon Johnson and Richard Nixon. That caused him too often to evaluate his commanders and their actions in terms of their impact on the coming presidential campaign. It is probably true that the tight control he exercised arose more from necessity than conviction. Polk was a highly partisan politician who questioned the political loyalty of his senior professional military leaders. He was also a commander in chief whose service secretaries (at least in the case of Marcy and Bancroft) were indifferent administrators and exercised only limited control over their services.[4] Considering his lack of training and the paucity of information upon which to make decisions, Polk's general plan of the war was sensible. His grand strategy embraced three objectives: to defend the Rio Grande boundary; to seize California and New Mexico; and to inflict sufficient punishment on the Mexican Army to force a political settlement favorable to the United States. Yet Polk failed to perceive the central factor in Mexican politics—that alienation of any Mexican territory, including Texas, was an unacceptable affront to the Mexican nation. This led him initially to conduct a limited war to "conquer peace." This mistaken belief caused the Monterrey campaign which threw Zachary Taylor's Army of Occupation deep into northern Mexico but could not bring the desired peace. Not until the failure of both his undercover peace moves and the northern campaign did Polk agree to an amphibious campaign against the main seat of Mexican power at Mexico City.

The administration's actions against the undefended peripheral parts of Mexico were more successful. Although the California operations were often opera buffe in execution, they did establish American control, as did General Stephen Kearny's operations in New Mexico. In their distant operations the Americans could be their own strongest enemies. In California the inept actions of Robert F. Stockton and the power struggle between Stockton and Kearny were as dangerous to American interests as the timorous actions of John D. Sloat.

The other naval operations were conducted with quiet competence but without the glare of publicity which would have gained the sea service the popular support it derived from the War of 1812. Unfortunately neither David Conner nor W. Branford Shubrick, the two most competent naval commanders, appealed to the press, nor did Matthew C. Perry despite his later fame in Japan. As a result the Navy had to wait until the fall of New Orleans in the Civil War to gain an admiral.

The nature of the war and the fratricidal relationships between the administration and its senior commanders ensured that few major heroes would emerge from the struggle. Winfield Scott stood far above the others despite the shortcomings of his temperament. No other American general of his generation, and few of any other, could have successfully conducted the Mexico City campaign under similar conditions. Zachary Taylor had a homespun façade which would carry him triumphantly into the White House but evidenced no great military capacity. His greatest strength was an imperturbable serenity in battle, which prevented missteps since he did not change his battle plans if it could be avoided. John Wool proved himself to be a capable administrator and possibly next to Scott the most adept general. That position could be challenged by Kearny, but his record is marred by the unfortunate collision with Stockton in California and the mishandling of the Battle of San Pasqual.

None of the Army's other generals, regular or volunteer, were exceptionally talented, although some like Bennet Riley and James Shields demonstrated capacity as subordinate commanders. Others like Joseph Lane and William J. Worth had unique talents or showed flashes of brilliance but could not develop consistency.

The conflict served as the training ground for many of the officers who would lead the armies of the Civil War. Few of those held even field rank, yet the roster of acting assistant adjutant generals and engineering officers, the two generally recognized intellectually demanding junior-officer assignments, reads like the general-officer list of a decade and a half later: W. T. Sherman, Irwin McDowell, Joseph Hooker, J. H. Carleton, Henry Prince, McClellan, Meade, Mansfield, Emory, Lee, Lorenzo Thomas. Robert E. Lee wrote perhaps the most distinguished record of any of the junior officers; while Bragg acquired more fame in Mexico. If young officers like U. S. Grant, George H. Thomas, and T. J. Jackson won minor recognition for their performance, others who would join them in the hierarchy of

Civil War heroes, like H. W. Halleck and W. T. Sherman, held staff positions which kept them from the battlefield.

The war saw the first utilization of the newly invented electric telegraph. Although its reliability was still limited, it did permit rapid transmission of orders and information between Washington and New York. More important to the individual soldier was the introduction of ether as an anesthetic by Army surgeons in Mexico. It cannot be determined how widely it was used, since it is not mentioned in the reports of the surgeons although newspaper accounts do refer to it and we know that Dr. E. H. Barton used it at Veracruz in the spring of 1847 during the amputation of the leg of a teamster.[5] Other technological innovations were less unusual. Railroads and steamboats were used to a degree heretofore unknown, but both had seen earlier military use.

Like many other American wars, the contest with Mexico played against the background of growing discontent and disillusionment. The failure to produce the expected rapid and bloodless victory which most Americans seem to have anticipated caused many initial supporters to turn against it. The historian has difficulty evaluating the depth of discontent, since those who declaimed loudest received a disproportionate amount of space in the press and therefore have been stressed by later writers. But the press, then as now, undoubtedly did not reflect accurately the thoughts of the public. Nor did the politician declaiming in the halls of Congress or upon the stump in the hinterlands necessarily reflect more than the imagined orientation of the particular group to which the statement was aimed. Nevertheless, it is clear that the politicians increasingly found a negative position on the war was safer than one which supported the administration. Thus the administration faced growing difficulties in securing the appropriations and the men necessary to conduct operations. Equally clear is the probability that had peace terms been offered in circumstances other than the particularly muddled situation which forced the Senate to ratify the treaty as written, it would have been very difficult for the Senate to agree over the proper settlement.

There are many similarities between the War with Mexico and the more recent one in Vietnam. In both instances the United States found itself at war because of miscalculations about the enemy which destroyed the effectiveness of a campaign of gradual escalation. Despite victories in the field, which by conventional standards were staggering, America could not force the opposition to negotiate seriously. When peace in Mexico did come, it resulted from a temporary combination of conditions in Mexico which made a weak interim administration willing to settle lest American demands increase exponentially.

In May 1846 there were only 637 officers and 5,925 enlisted men in the army. During the war, 1,016 officers and 35,009 enlisted men joined the regular army, swelling its ranks to 42,587 men, while an additional 73,532 men appeared on the rolls of the various volunteer units. The following table indicates the losses suffered by the regulars and the volunteers in battle, and more importantly outside of it.

TABLE 2
COMBAT AND NON-COMBAT LOSSES

	REGULARS	VOLUNTEERS	TOTALS
Killed in action	585	607	1,192
Died of wounds	425	104	529
*Disease, etc.**	4,899	6,256	11,155
Wounded in action	2,745	1,357	4,102
Discharged for disability	2,554	7,200	9,754
Deserters	5,331	3,876	9,207

* Includes deaths from disease, accidents, executions, and miscellaneous causes.
SOURCES: *S. Ex. Doc. 36, 30th Cong., 1st Sess.*, 6–7; Scott, *Military Dictionary*, 645–49; Kreidberg and Henry, *History of Military Mobilization*, 78; Heitman, *Historical Register*, II, 282.

While battle deaths amounted to only 1.5 percent of the troops, those from disease and other non-combat causes were nearly 10 percent. Another 8 percent were discharged for disability, either from wounds or illness, while almost as many simply deserted. Nothing illustrates better the difficulties in maintaining the health of the troops under the conditions of the campaign and the state of medical knowledge than these figures. The high incidence of desertion eloquently bespeaks the unwillingness of the late Jacksonian period soldier to serve his nation at personal discomfort. The ranking of self-indulgence over service, despite the loud complaints of contemporary commentators, is not an invention of the overcoddled youth of the 1960s and 1970s.

The war cost the United States about $58 million[6] in direct costs for military operations, plus the $15 million paid to Mexico under the treaty. An additional $64 million[7] went for veterans' pensions and other benefits to the participants, little of it before 1887. Since the

United States acquired 529,017 square miles of land by the Treaty of Guadalupe Hidalgo, the price was forty-eight cents an acre.

The Navy, despite the increased manpower allotment of the 1846 law, actually declined in strength in the first year of the war and rose only slightly thereafter.[8] This resulted from the difficulties of the service recruiting in competition with a booming merchant marine. Because of its limited combat opportunity, the Navy suffered fewer casualties in action and a greater number from illness. The greatest scourges visited on the squadrons, however, were scurvy and yellow fever, which caused few fatalities although they did render large numbers of officers and men incapable of performing even simple duties for varying lengths of time.[9] The Marine Corps strength, on the other hand, rose sharply because of the creation of new units for Mexican service. It numbered forty-two officers and 986 men before the war and rose to a peak of seventy-five officers and 1,757 men in 1847. The officially recognized totals of eleven killed and twenty-eight wounded are a reasonable figure for the service which the Marines saw, although less than the Army average.[10]

Despite the difficulties which the country faced in starting the war with a small army, and the increased responsibilities which peace brought, the President and his advisers concluded that the defense of the enlarged country required no permanent increase in the size of the military. As early as July 6, 1848 President Polk informed Congress that he foresaw no need to enlarge the Army beyond its pre-war size. That day the Adjutant General reported that the Army consisted of 8,866 regulars, of whom only 7,500 were effective. He concluded that 4,383 additional men were needed to bring the force up to its authorized strength of sixty-four privates per company. As a result Congress made no changes in the enlisted strength of the Army when it established procedures for the integration of war-appointed regular officers and an overdue enlargement of the staff corps.[11]

Nor does the lack of a formal veterans' lobbying organization fit into the modern pattern. Not until 1866 did Alexander Kenaday in California establish the Association of Mexican War Veterans. Eight years later, largely because of the great success of the Grand Army of the Republic, the California group became national in scope as the National Association of Mexican War Veterans. Its primary purpose was to gain pensions for its members, but it reached a peak membership of only 5,095 in 1879 and largely ceased operations following the death of Kenaday in 1897.[12]

The conflict with Mexico was the product of the conjunction of American and Mexican national aspirations brought together by the miscalculations of the leaders of both countries. It was fought with doggedness by the soldiers and sailors of each nation under the leadership of both brilliant and inept commanders until the superior strength and leadership of the American invaders overcame the resistance of the defenders, who even then refused to discuss seriously a reasonable political settlement. When peace came it was, in the imperishable words of Philip Hone, "negotiated by an unauthorized agent, with an unacknowledged government, submitted by an accidental president to a dissatisfied Senate . . . ."[13]

NOTES

For key to abbreviations used in Notes, see page xi.

1. Bancroft, "Biographical Sketch of James K. Polk," 25, Bancroft Collection, NYPL.
2. See Gene M. Brack, "Mexican Opinion, American Racism, and the War of 1846," *Western Historical Quarterly*, I (April 1970), 161–74.
3. The impact of the war on Mexican thought is extensively and well discussed in Charles A. Hale, "The War with the United States and the Crisis in Mexican Thought," *The Americas*, XIV (Oct. 1957), 153–74. Equally thought-provoking is Jorge Carrion, "Effectos Psicologiocos de la Guerra de 47 en al Hombre de Mexico," *Cuadernos Americanos*, VII (Jan.–Feb. 1948), 116–32.
4. In particular see the evaluations of Polk as commander in chief in White, *Jacksonians*, 51; Leonard D. White, "Polk," in Ernest R. May (ed.), *The Ultimate Decision* (New York, 1960); and Louis Smith, *Democracy and Military Power* (Chicago, 1951), 42.
5. Smith and Judah, *Chronicles of the Gringos*, 349–50. For account of the difficulties of the medical department and the general lack of facilities see Percy M. Ashburn, *A History of the Medical Department of the United States Army* (Boston, 1929), 58.
6. Excess of wartime appropriations for the War and Navy departments over the average for 1844–45. Bureau of the Census, *Historical Statistics of the United States* (Washington, 1960), 719.
7. *Ibid.*, 739.
8. 1,095 officers, 11,189 men in 1845; 1,053 officers, 10,131 men in 1846; 1,126 officers, 11,193 men in 1847; and 1,041 officers, 11,238 men in 1848. Bureau of the Census, *Historical Statistics*, 737.
9. The navy's casualties have never been determined with accuracy. The officially recognized one man killed and three wounded is too low even for combat losses. It does not take into account deaths due to sickness or accident.
10. Bureau of Census, *Historical Statistics*, 737.
11. *H. Ex. Doc. 69, 30th Cong., 1st Sess.,* 4; Jones to Marcy, July 6, 1848, *H. Ex. Doc. 74, 30th Cong., 1st Sess.,* 2; 9 *U.S. Stat.,* 247–48.
12. Wallace E. Davies, "The Mexican War Veterans as an Organized Group," *Mississippi Valley Historical Review*, XXXV (Sept. 1948), 222–37.
13. Bayard Tuckerman (ed.), *The Diary of Philip Hone* (2 vols., New York, 1910), II, 347.

Bibliography

THIS BIBLIOGRAPHY lists those works which were most useful in the writing of this study. They number perhaps only 50 percent of the titles dealing with the Mexican War. More complete lists can be found in Henry E. Haferkorn, *The War with Mexico* (Washington, 1914); Seymour V. Connor and Odie B. Faulk, *North America Divided, The Mexican War, 1846–1848* (New York, 1971); and Elizabeth R. Snoke, *The Mexican War* (U.S. Army Military History Research Collection, Special Bibliography 7, April 1973).

The basic American materials for any study of the Mexican War are the official records preserved in the National Archives. The largest groups of pertinent material are in Record Groups 45, Office of Naval Records and Library, which contains most of the naval operational orders and reports; 59, Department of State, which includes both diplomatic correspondence and the often highly significant consular reports; 94, Office of the Adjutant General, which not only retained copies of all correspondence with the field commanders but also had custody of the materials gathered or generated by the active commands; and 107, Office of the Secretary of War, containing his correspondence.

Most, but by no means all, important correspondence between the President, Secretaries of State, War, and Navy, and the senior officials in the field found their way into Congressional Documents forming part of the Serial Set. The most useful collections are the appendices to the Annual Reports of the Secretaries of State, War, and Navy and the massive collection of *Mexican War Correspondence (House Executive Document 60, 30th Congress, 1st Session)*. Most of the diplomatic correspondence has been reprinted in William R. Manning, *The Diplomatic Correspondence of the United States, Latin American Affairs, 1831–1860* (21 vols., Washington, 1932–39). Wherever printed copies of documents have been located the citations have been made to that source on the assumption that this would be more useful to the reader who wished access to a full copy.

The Mexican official records are in the custody of the Archivo General de la Nación in Mexico City. In addition, much Mexican material, either original or transcript, is to be found in various other depositories, notably the Gómez Farías, Riva Palacio, and Justin H. Smith Transcript collections in the Latin American Collection of the University of Texas. Some Mexican reports are printed in the *Memoria del Ministerio del Despacho de Guerra y Marina* and the memoirs of Mexican commanders.

Substantial collections of personal papers exist for many of the significant American figures of the war. The most valuable of these are the papers of President Polk, Nicholas P. Trist, and Commodore David Conner. No large collections exist for General Scott, Secretary of the Navy John Y. Mason, or Commodore M. C. Perry, however. Other collections, of varying size and utility, are listed below. The major concentrations of private papers relating to the war exist at the Library of Congress, the Western Americana Collection of Yale University, the Bancroft Library of the University of California at Berkeley, the University of Texas, and the Missouri Historical Society. Other collections, some highly useful, are widely scattered. A large number of letters and diaries of junior officers and enlisted men have been reprinted, a surprising number in the past few years. Here also, wherever possible, citations have been made to the printed rather than the manuscript versions.

Except for Winfield Scott, no major political, military, naval, or diplomatic figure wrote an extended memoir of his activities, although several like General John E. Wool and Commodore Robert F. Stockton commissioned or cooperated in the preparation of works by third parties. Of the numerous memoirs and accounts of the war by junior officers, the most valuable are W. A. Croffut's edition of the diary of Ethan Allen Hitchcock, *Fifty Years in Camp and Field* (New York, 1909), because of Hitchcock's role on Scott's staff, and Raphael Semmes, *Service Afloat and Ashore During the Mexican War* (Cincinnati, 1851), whose author served both in Conner's squadron and with Scott's army. Other memoirs are no less valuable for the more restricted activities which they cover.

For over fifty years the best single study of the war has been Justin H. Smith, *The War with Mexico* (2 vols., New York, 1919) despite numerous challenges to its tone and its concern with the editorial comments of newspapers in an era of low literacy. Smith used nearly every surviving collection of papers, except those of General Wool, and read everything written on the conflict, American or Mexican, up to that time. Moreover, he had fuller access to the Mexican archives than any scholar, American or Mexican, since. The best Mexican study is José María Roa Bárcena, *Recuerdos de la Invasión Norte-Americana (1846–1848)* (3 vols., México, 1947). Other useful, post-Justin Smith studies are Robert Selph Henry, *The Story of the Mexican War* (Indianapolis, 1950), Alfred Hoyt Bill, *Rehearsal for Conflict* (New York, 1947), Otis A. Singletary, *The Mexican War* (Chicago, 1960), and José C. Valades, *Breve Historia de la Guerra con los Estados Unidos* (México, 1947). George Winston Smith and Charles Judah have edited eyewitness accounts of the war into the highly successful *Chronicles of the Gringos* (Albuquerque, 1968).

Most aspects of the war have received monographic treatment either within larger studies or individually in books or articles. In most instances the subject matter will be self-evident in the titles listed below.

I. MANUSCRIPTS

A. Official Records in the National Archives

OFFICE OF THE ADJUTANT GENERAL (RECORD GROUP 94)
  Army in Mexico, Letter Book
  Army of Occupation, Letter Books
  Army of Occupation, Letters Received
  Army of Occupation, Orders
  Army of Occupation, Special Orders
  Army of Occupation & 2d Division Order Book
  Maj. Gen. W. O. Butler, General Orders 1847–48
  Case (AGO) Files
  Col. Thomas Childs, Order Book 1848
  Commanding General, City of Mexico, Letter Book
  Department of Cuernavaca, Letter Book
  General and Special Orders
  Letters to Generals in the Field and to State Governors
  Letters Received
  Letters Sent
  Miscellaneous Letters and Orders, Mexican War
  Papers Captured with General Arista's Baggage
  Department of Matamoros, Orders
  Pension Office (RPO) Case Files
  Brig. Gen. Franklin Pierce, Order Book
  Maj. Gen. G. J. Pillow, Order Books
  Department of Puebla, General and Special Orders 1848
  Department of Tampico, Orders
  Department of Veracruz, Orders 1848
  1st Volunteer Brigade, General and Special Orders 1847
  1st Volunteer Division, Letter Book
  Col. Archibald Yell, Letter Book
UNITED STATES ARMY COMMANDS (RECORD GROUP 98)
  10th Military District, Letters Received
  10th Military District, Letters Sent
OFFICE OF THE JUDGE ADVOCATE GENERAL (RECORD GROUP 153)
  Courts of Inquiry Proceedings
  Courts-Martial Proceedings
UNITED STATES MARINE CORPS (RECORD GROUP 127)
  Commandant, Letter Books
  Orders
OFFICE OF NAVAL RECORDS AND LIBRARY (RECORD GROUP 45)
  Area File
  Commodore David Conner, Letter Book
  Lt. T. A. M. Craven, Journal . . . Cruise of the USS *Dale*
  Mid. J. C. P. DeKrafft, Journal of a Cruise in . . . *Raritan*
  Home Squadron Letters
  Log Books

Log of USS *Cyane*, Wm. Mervine Comdg.
Cdr. J. B. Montgomery, Letter Book
Secretary of the Navy, Executive Letter Books
Secretary of the Navy, Letters from Bureaus
Secretary of the Navy, Letters from Navy Agents
Secretary of the Navy, Letters to Bureaus
Secretary of the Navy, Letters to Navy Agents
Secretary of the Navy, Letters to Officers, Ships of War
Secretary of the Navy, Record of Confidential Letters
Pacific Squadron Letters
Commo. M. C. Perry, Letter Book 1848
NAVY DEPARTMENT (RECORD GROUP 80)
Secretary of the Navy, Letters to Marine Corps Officers
Secretary of the Navy, Marine Corps Letters
DEPARTMENT OF STATE (RECORD GROUP 59)
Despatches from United States Consuls in Mazatlán
Despatches from United States Consuls in Mexico City
Despatches from United States Consuls in Monterrey
Despatches from United States Consuls in Tampico
Despatches from United States Consuls in Veracruz
Diplomatic Despatches from Ministers to Mexico
OFFICE OF THE SECRETARY OF WAR (RECORD GROUP 107)
Confidential and Unofficial Letters Sent
Letters Received
Letters Received, Unregistered Series
Letters Sent, Military Affairs
Letters Sent to the President
Letters to Generals in the Field
Miscellaneous Letters and Orders, Mexican War

B. Personal Papers

BANCROFT LIBRARY, UNIVERSITY OF CALIFORNIA
J. B. Alvarado, Historia de California
William Baldridge, The Days of 1846
H. H. Bancroft Collection
Documentos para la Historia de California . . . Antonio F. Coronel
Documentos para la Historia de California . . . José Matias Moreno
Documentos para la Historia de California . . . Agustín Olvera
Documentos para la Historia de California . . . Thomas Savage
H. W. Halleck, Memorandum . . . Concerning His Expedition
   in Lower California
T. O. Larkin Official Correspondence
T. O. Larkin Papers
J. P. Leesee, Papers of the Bear Flag
CALIFORNIA HISTORICAL SOCIETY
Sloat Documents
CHICAGO HISTORICAL SOCIETY
Gunther Collection

Hardin Family Papers
J. E. Johnston Collection
Mexican War Collection
Harvey Neville, Diary
M. C. Perry Collection
Lloyd Tilghman Collection
W. H. L. Wallace Collection
J. E. Wool Collection
W. J. Worth Collection

HENRY E. HUNTINGTON LIBRARY AND ART GALLERY
Facsimile Collection
Fort Sutter Papers
W. A. Leidesdorff Papers
Miscellaneous Collection

LIBRARY OF CONGRESS
David Conner Papers
Caleb Cushing Papers
A. C. Jackson, Journal of a Cruise ... *Savannah*
T. S. Jesup Papers
Thomas Lawson Papers
W. L. Marcy Papers
Franklin Pierce Papers
J. K. Polk Papers
D. D. Porter Papers
J. L. Saunders Papers
Zachary Taylor Papers
N. P. Trist Papers

LOS ANGELES PUBLIC LIBRARY
R. C. Duvall, Cruise of the U.S. Frigate *Savannah* (photostat)

MARINE CORPS MUSEUM
T. Y. Field Papers
W. A. T. Maddox Papers (photocopies)
Levi Twiggs Papers

MASSACHUSETTS HISTORICAL SOCIETY
George Bancroft Papers

MISSOURI HISTORICAL SOCIETY
J. W. Abert Papers
P. G. T. Beauregard Papers
Adolph Engelmann, Letters to Parents (Typescript)
S. W. Kearny, Letter Book
LaMotte-Coppinger Papers
J. V. Masten Papers
Mexican War Papers
R. H. Miller Papers
C. F. Ruff Papers

NEW YORK HISTORICAL SOCIETY
Electus Backus, Details of the Controversy Between the Regulars and
    Volunteers ... Monterey

Abner Doubleday, From Mexican War to the Rebellion
H. L. Kendrick, Letters
Jay Langdon, Diary
7th New York Volunteers, Order Book
7th New York Volunteers, Regimental Order Book
Papers Captured with General Arista's Baggage
G. J. Pillow Papers
J. D. Stevenson, Letter Book
NEW YORK PUBLIC LIBRARY
George Bancroft Collection
David Conner Papers
Croghan Papers
F. E. Pinto, Diary
NEW YORK STATE LIBRARY
J. E. Wool Papers
PRINCETON UNIVERSITY LIBRARY
W. W. Belknap Papers
R. F. Stockton, Letter Book
RENSSELAER COUNTY HISTORICAL SOCIETY
Griswold-Wool Papers
FRANKLIN D. ROOSEVELT LIBRARY
David Conner Papers
SOCIETY OF CALIFORNIA PIONEERS
H. L. Ford, The Battle of Salinas
UNIVERSITY OF TEXAS ARCHIVES
R. E. Cochran Papers
F. M. Dimond Papers
J. S. Ford Papers
J. P. Gaines, March of the First Regiment of Kentucky Volunteer Cavalry
(typescript)
Robert Hagan, Diary
Henderson Family Papers
J. A. Hendricks Papers
G. W. Kendall Papers
G. W. Morgan Manuscript
J. H. Smith Papers
UNIVERSITY OF TEXAS, LATIN AMERICAN COLLECTION
Valentín Gómez Farías Papers
J. H. Smith Transcripts
UNIVERSITY OF CALIFORNIA, LOS ANGELES, LIBRARY
A. H. Gillespie Papers
UNITED STATES MILITARY ACADEMY LIBRARY
Alden Family Papers
E. B. Alexander Papers
R. L. Baker Papers
P. N. Barbour Journal
Jefferson Davis Papers
James Duncan Papers

Robert Hazlitt Papers
Bennet Riley Papers
WESTERN AMERICANA COLLECTION, YALE UNIVERSITY
Edmund Bradford Papers
David Conner Papers
J. W. Geary Papers
A. C. Jackson, The Conquest of California
Ayuntamiento de Jalapa, Correspondence and Papers
E. A. F. La Vallette Papers
Samuel Lockwood Papers
W. L. Marcy, Drafts and Copies of Letters to Commanders in the Field,
    1846–47
Memoranda of Campaigns in Mexico
Mexican War Letters
Battles of Mexico City
H. J. Moore, Mexican War Diary
E. G. Parrott Papers
J. R. Smith Papers
J. D. Wilkins, Journal
Henry Wilson Papers

II. PRINTED DOCUMENTS

27th Congress, 3d Session. House Document 166. *Message from the President
    . . . in Relation to the Taking Possession of Monterey by Commodore
    Thomas ap Catesby Jones.*

28th Congress, 1st Session. House Executive Document 271. *Message from the
    President . . . Transmitting the Rejected Treaty for the Annexation of the
    Republic of Texas. . . .*

28th Congress, 1st Session. Senate Document 341. *Proceedings of the Senate
    on the Annexation of Texas.*

29th Congress, 1st Session. House Executive Document 194. *Soldiers of the
    Army Shot for Desertion.*

29th Congress, 1st Session. House Executive Document 196. *Message from the
    President . . . Relative to an Invasion and Commencement of Hostilities
    by Mexico.*

29th Congress, 1st Session. House Executive Document 197. *Despatches from
    General Taylor.*

29th Congress, 1st Session. House Executive Document 207. *Official Despatches
    from General Taylor.*

29th Congress, 1st Session. House Executive Document 209. *Reports from
    General Taylor.*

29th Congress, 1st Session. Senate Executive Document 1. *Message from the
    President . . . at the Commencement of the First Session of the 29th
    Congress.*

29th Congress, 1st Session. Senate Document 337. *Message from the President
    . . . Communicating Information of the Existing Relations Between the
    United States and Mexico, and Recommending the Adoption of Measures*

for Repelling the Invasion Committed by the Mexican Forces upon the Territory of the United States.

29th Congress, 1st Session. Senate Document 378. *Message from the President . . . Relative to the Calling of Volunteers . . . Without Legal Authority. . . .*

29th Congress, 1st Session. Senate Document 387. *Message from the President . . . Relative to Call Made by General Gaines for Volunteers. . . .*

29th Congress, 1st Session. Senate Document 388. *Message of the President . . . Relative to the Operations and Recent Engagements on the Mexican Frontier.*

29th Congress, 1st Session. Senate Document 392. *Message from the President . . . Relative to the Mode of Raising Funds for Carrying on the War. . . .*

29th Congress, 1st Session. Senate Document 402. *Report of the Secretary of War . . . in Relation to Calls Made . . . for Volunteers and Militia.*

29th Congress, 1st Session. Senate Document 439. *Report of the Secretary of War . . . Communicating Information as to the Employment of Any Individual . . . to Raise Volunteers. . . .*

29th Congress, 2d Session. House Executive Document 4. *Message from the President . . . at the Commencement of the Second Session of the Twenty-Ninth Congress.*

29th Congress, 2d Session. House Executive Document 19. *Occupation of Mexican Territory.*

29th Congress, 2d Session. House Document 42. *Volunteers Received into the Service of the United States.*

29th Congress, 2d Session. House Executive Document 48. *Volunteers—Terms of Service, &c.*

29th Congress, 2d Session. Senate Document 1. *Message from the President . . . at the Commencement of the Second Session of the Twenty-Ninth Congress.*

29th Congress, 2d Session. Senate Document 4. *Report of the Secretary of War . . . Killed, Wounded, or Missing in the Battles of Palo Alto and Resaca de la Palma.*

29th Congress, 2d Session. Senate Document 43. *Message from the Secretary of the Navy . . . in Relation to the Loss of the United States Brig Somers. . . .*

29th Congress, 2d Session. Senate Document 94. *Report of the Secretary of the Navy . . . in Relation to the Return of the Frigate Cumberland and the Steamer Mississippi. . . .*

29th Congress, 2d Session. Senate Document 107. *Message of the President . . . Relating to Affairs with the Republic of Mexico . . . and the Proceeding of the Senate Thereon. . . .*

30th Congress, 1st Session. House Executive Document 8. *Message from the President . . . at the Commencement of the First Session of the Thirtieth Congress.*

30th Congress, 1st Session. House Executive Document 17. *Correspondence with General Taylor.*

30th Congress, 1st Session. House Executive Document 40. *Propositions for Peace.*

30th Congress, 1st Session. House Executive Document 56. *Correspondence Between the Secretary of War and Generals Scott and Taylor and Between General Scott and Mr. Trist.*

30th Congress, 1st Session. House Executive Document 59. *Correspondence Between the Secretary of War and General Scott.*

30th Congress, 1st Session. House Executive Document 60. *Mexican War Correspondence.*

30th Congress, 1st Session. House Executive Document 62. *Regulars and Volunteers Engaged in the Mexican War.*

30th Congress, 1st Session. House Executive Document 69. *Treaty with Mexico.*

30th Congress, 1st Session. House Executive Document 70. *New Mexico and California.*

30th Congress, 1st Session. House Executive Document 74. *Strength of the Army at the Close of the Mexican War.*

30th Congress, 1st Session. House Report 817. *California Claims.*

30th Congress, 1st Session. Senate Executive Document 1. *Message from the President . . . at the Commencement of the First Session of the Thirtieth Congress.*

30th Congress, 1st Session. Senate Executive Document 14. *Message from the President . . . Relative to Forced Contributions. . . .*

30th Congress, 1st Session. Senate Executive Document 18. *Message from the President . . . Relative to General Taylor's Letter . . . July 20, 1845 . . . and Any Similar Communication from Any Officer. . . .*

30th Congress, 1st Session. Senate Executive Document 19. *Message from the President . . . in Relation to General Orders No. 376, Issued by General Scott.*

30th Congress, 1st Session. Senate Executive Document 20. *Message from the President . . . in Relation to the Negotiations . . . During the Suspension of Hostilities After the Battles of Contreras and Churubusco.*

30th Congress, 1st Session. Senate Executive Document 33. *. . . . Proceedings of the Court-Martial of Colonel Fremont.*

30th Congress, 1st Session. Senate Executive Document 36. *Report of the Secretary of War Showing the Number of Troops in the Service . . . the Killed and Wounded, &c.*

30th Congress, 1st Session. Senate Executive Document 52. *The Treaty Between the United States and Mexico. . . .*

30th Congress, 1st Session. Senate Executive Document 62. *Message from the President . . . Relative to an Alleged Mutiny at Buena Vista, about 15th August 1847.*

30th Congress, 1st Session. Senate Executive Document 65. *. . . . Proceedings of the Two Courts of Inquiry in the Case of Major General Pillow.*

30th Congress, 1st Session. Senate Report 75. *California Claims.*

30th Congress, 2d Session. House Executive Document 1. *Message from the President . . . at the Commencement of the Second Session of the Thirtieth Congress.*

30th Congress, 2d Session. House Executive Document 14. *Military Force in the Mexican War.*

30th Congress, 2d Session. House Executive Document 24. *Numbers, etc., of Persons Employed in the Naval and Marine Service in the Mexican War.*

30th Congress, 2d Session. Senate Executive Document 19. . . . *Map of the Valley of Mexico, by Lieutenants Smith and Hardcastle.*

30th Congress, 2d Session. Senate Executive Document 31. . . . *Commodore Stockton's Despatches.* . . .

31st Congress, 1st Session. Senate Executive Document 17. *California and New Mexico.*

31st Congress, 1st Session. House Executive Document 24. *Military Forces Employed in the Mexican War.*

34th Congress, 3d Session. Senate Executive Document 34. *Message from the President . . . Respecting the Pay and Emoluments of Lieutenant General Scott.*

Census, Bureau of the. *Historical Statistics of the United States, Colonial Times to 1957.* Washington: Department of Commerce, 1960.

Congressional Globe, 29th-30th Congresses.

Dublán, Manuel, and José María Lozano. *Legislación Mexicana o Colección Completa de las Disposiciónes Legislativas Expedidas desde la Independencia de la República.* 6 vols. México: Imprenta del Comercio, 1876–77.

Guerra y Marina, Ministerio de. *Memoria del . . . 11 de Septiembre 1845.* . . . México: n.p., 1845.

————. *Memoria del . . . 9 de Diciembre de 1846.* México: Imprenta de Torres, 1846.

————. *Memoria del . . . 1-2 de Mayo 1849.* México: n.p., 1849.

————. *Reglamento para el Corso de Particulares Contra los Enemigos de la Nación.* México: Imprenta del Aguila, 1846.

————. *Reglamento sobre la Organización del Cuerpo de Artilleria.* México: Imprenta del Aguila, 1846.

Manning, William Ray (ed.). *The Diplomatic Correspondence of the United States, Latin American Affairs.* 21 vols. Washington: Carnegie Endowment for International Peace, 1932–39.

Mexico, Estado de. *La Legistura del . . . a los Habitantes del Mismo.* Toluca: Impreso por Quijána y Gallo, 1847.

Richardson, James D. (ed.). *A Compilation of the Messages and Papers of the Presidents.* 20 vols. New York: Bureau of National Literature, Inc., 1897–1922.

Statutes at Large of the United States. 12 vols. Boston: Little, Brown, 1845–65.

III. NEWSPAPERS

Baltimore *Niles National Register.*
Baltimore *Sun.*
Chihuahua *The Anglo Saxon.*
Mexico City *American Star.*
Monterey *Californian.*
Monterrey *American Pioneer.*
New Orleans *Daily Picayune.*
Puebla *Flag of Freedom.*
Veracruz *American Eagle.*

IV. ACCOUNTS OF PARTICIPANTS

Ames, George Walcott, Jr. (ed.). "A Doctor Comes to California. The Diary of John S. Griffin, Assistant Surgeon with Kearny's Dragoons, 1846–47," *CHSQ*, XXI (Sept.–Dec. 1942), 193–224, 333–38.

—— (ed.). "Gillespie and the Conquest of California," *CHSQ*, XVII (June–Dec. 1938), 123–40, 271–84, 325–50, XVIII (Sept. 1939), 217–28.

Ampudia, Pedro de. *El Ciudadano General Pedro de Ampudia ante el Tribunal Respectable de la Opinión Publica, por los Primeros Sucesos Ocurrides en la Guerra a Que Nos Provaca, Decreta y Sostiene de Gobierno de los Estados Unidos de America*. San Luis Potosí: Imprenta de Gobierno, 1846.

——. *Manifesto del General Ampudia a Sus Conciudadamos*. México: Ignacio Cumplido, 1847.

Anderson, Charles Robert. *Journal of a Cruise to the Pacific Ocean, 1842–1844, in the Frigate United States with Notes on Herman Melville*. Durham: Duke University Press, 1937.

Aztec Club of 1847. *Constitution of . . . and List of Members*. N.p., 1909.

Bailey, Thomas, "Diary of the Mexican War," *Indiana Magazine of History*, XIV (June 1918), 134–47.

Balbontín, Manuel. *La Invasión Americana 1846 a 1847. Apuntes del Subteniente de Artilleria Manuel Balbontín*. México: Gonzalo A. Estera, 1883.

Ballentine, George. *Autobiography of An English Soldier in the United States Army Comprising Observations and Adventures in the States and Mexico.* New York: Stringer & Townsend, 1853.

Barringer, Graham A. (ed.). "The Mexican War Journal of Henry S. Lane," *Indiana Magazine of History*, LIII (Dec. 1957), 383–434.

Basler, Roy P. (ed.). *The Collected Works of Abraham Lincoln*. 8 vols. New Brunswick: Rutgers University Press, 1953.

Belknap, Charles (ed.). "Notes from the Journal of Lieutenant T. A. M. Craven, U.S.N., *U.S.S. Dale* Pacific Squadron, 1846–49," *USNIP*, XIV (March–June 1888), 119–48, 301–36.

[Benham, Henry W.] *Recollections of Mexico and the Battle of Buena Vista, Feb. 22 and 23, 1847*. Boston: n.p., 1871.

Benton, Thomas Hart. *Thirty Years' View: Or, A History of the Working of the American Government for Thirty Years, From 1820 to 1850*. 2 vols., New York: D. Appleton & Co., 1856.

Bieber, Ralph P. (ed.). *Exploring Southwestern Trails 1846–1854*. Glendale: Arthur H. Clark Co., 1938.

—— (ed.). *Journal of a Soldier Under Kearny and Doniphan 1846–1847. George Rutledge Gibson*. Glendale: Arthur H. Clark Co., 1935.

—— (ed.). *Marching With the Army of the West 1846–1848*. Glendale: Arthur H. Clark Co., 1936.

Bigler, Henry W. "Extracts from the Journal of . . . ," *UHQ*, V (April–Oct. 1932), 35–64, 87–112, 134–60.

Blackwood, Emma Jerome (ed.). *To Mexico with Scott. Letters of Captain E. Kirby Smith to His Wife*. Cambridge: Harvard University Press, 1917.

Bliss, Robert S. "The Journal of . . . with the Mormon Battalion," *UHQ*, IV (July–Oct. 1931), 67–96, 110–28.

Bloom, Lansing B. (ed.). "A Group of Kearny Letters," *MNHR*, V (Jan. 1930), 17–37.

Bosh García, Carlos. *Material para la Historia Diplomatica de México (México y los Estados Unidos, 1820–1848)*. México: Escuela Nacional de Ciencias Politicas y Sociales, 1957.

Boucher, Chauncey S., and Robert P. Brooks (eds.). "Correspondence Addressed to John C. Calhoun 1837–1849," *Annual Report of the American Historical Association for the Year 1919*. Washington: Government Printing Office, 1930.

[Bruell, James D.] *Sea Memories: Or, Personal Experiences in the U.S. Navy in Peace and War. By An Old Salt*. Biddeford Pool, Me.: The Author, 1886.

Bryant, Edwin, *What I Saw in California: Being the Journal of a Tour . . . Through California, in the Years 1846, 1847*. New York: D. Appleton & Co., 1848.

Buchanan, A. Russell (ed.). "George Washington Trahern: Texas Cowboy Soldier from Mier to Buena Vista," *SWHQ*, LXXVIII (July 1954), 60–90.

Buhoup, Jonathan W. *Narrative of the Central Division, or, Army of Chihuahua, Commanded by Brigadier General Wool. . . .* Pittsburgh: M. P. Morse, 1847.

Burr, Barbara (ed.). "Letters from Two Wars," *Journal of the Illinois State Historical Society*, XXX (April 1937), 137–58.

Cabrero, Luis (ed.). *Diario del Presidente Polk (1845–1847). Reproducción de Todos los Asientos Relativos a México, Tomados de la Edición Completa de M. M. Quaife con Numerosos Documentos Annexos Relacionados con la Guerra entre México y Estados Unidos*. 2 vols., México: Antigua Libreria Robredo, 1948.

Calderón de la Barca, Fanny. *Life in Mexico. The Letters of. . . .* Garden City: Anchor Books, 1970.

Calvin, Ross (ed.). *Lieutenant Emory Reports: A Reprint of Lieutenant W. H. Emory's Notes of a Military Reconnaissance*. Albuquerque: University of New Mexico Press, 1951.

Carleton, James Henry. *The Battle of Buena Vista with the Operations of the "Army of Occupation" for One Month*. New York: Harper & Bros., 1848.

Carpenter, William C. *Travels and Adventures in Mexico: With the Course of Journeys of Upwards of 2500 Miles. . . .* New York: Harper & Bros., 1851.

Chamberlain, Samuel E. *My Confession*. New York: Harper & Bros., 1956.

Claiborne, J. F. H. *Life and Correspondence of John A. Quitman, Major-General, U.S.A., and Governor of the State of Mississippi*. 2 vols., New York: Harper & Bros, 1860.

Clarke, Dwight L. (ed.). *The Original Journals of Henry Smith Turner with Stephen Watts Kearny to New Mexico and California 1846–1847*. Norman: University of Oklahoma Press, 1966.

Clay, Cassius Marcellus. *The Life of Cassius Marcellus Clay. Memoirs, Writings, and Speeches, Showing His Conduct in The Overthrow of American Slavery, The Salvation of the Union, and the Restoration of the Autonomy of the States.* New York: Negro Universities Press, 1969.

Collins, Maria Clinton (ed.). "Journal of Francis Collins, An Artillery Officer in the Mexican War," *Quarterly Publications of the Historical and Philosophical Society of Ohio,* X (April–July 1915), 37–109.

Colton, Walter. *Deck and Port: Or, Incidents of a Cruise in the United States Frigate Congress to California.* New York: A. S. Barnes & Co., 1850.

———. *Three Years in California.* New York: A. S. Barnes & Co., 1850.

Connelley, William Elsey (ed.). *Doniphan's Expedition and the Conquest of New Mexico and California.* Topeka: n.p., 1907.

Cooke, Philip St. George. *The Conquest of New Mexico and California. An Historical and Personal Narrative.* New York: G. P. Putnam's Sons, 1878.

———. *The Official Journal of Lieutenant Colonel Philip St. George Cooke, From Santa Fe to San Diego, etc.* 30th Congress, Special Session, Senate Document 2.

Croffut, W. A. (ed.). *Fifty Years in Camp and Field. Diary of Major General Ethan Allen Hitchcock U.S.A.* New York: G. P. Putnam's Sons, 1909.

Davis, George T. M. *Autobiography of the Late Col. Geo. T. M. Davis, Captain and Aid-de-Camp Scott's Army of Invasion (Mexico).* New York: n.p., 1891.

Davis, William Heath. *Seventy-Five Years in California.* San Francisco; John Howell, 1929.

Deas, George. "Reminiscences of the Campaign on the Rio Grande," *Historical Magazine,* VII (Jan.–May 1870), 19–22, 99–103, 236–38, 311–16.

Devlin, John S. *The Marine Corps in Mexico; Setting Forth Its Conduct as Established by Testimony Before A General Court Martial . . . For The Trial of First Lieut. John S. Devlin, of The U.S. Marine Corps.* Washington: Lemuel Towers, 1852.

Donnavan, Corydon. *Adventures in Mexico; Experienced During a Captivity of Seven Months.* Boston: George R. Holbrook & Co., 1848.

Doubleday, Rhoda van Bibber Tanner (ed.). *Journal of the Late Brevet Major Philip Norbourne Barbour Captain in the 3rd Regiment, United States Infantry and His Wife Martha Isabella Hopkins Barbour. Written During the War with Mexico 1846.* New York: G. P. Putnam's Sons, 1936.

Downey, Joseph T. *The Cruise of the Portsmouth.* New Haven: Yale University Press, 1958.

Drumm, Stella M. (ed.). *Down the Santa Fe Trail and Into Mexico. The Diary of Susan Shelby Magoffin, 1846–1847.* New Haven: Yale University Press, 1926.

DuPont, Samuel Francis. *Official Despatches and Letters of Rear Admiral DuPont.* Wilmington: Ferris Bros., 1883.

———. "The War with Mexico; the Cruise of the U.S.S. Cyane During the Years 1845–48," *USNIP,* VIII (Sept. 1882), 419–37.

Duvall, Robert Carson. "Extracts from the Log of the U.S. Frigate *Savannah* Kept by . . . ," *CHSQ,* III (July 1924), 105–25.

Edwards, Frank S. *A Campaign in New Mexico with Colonel Doniphan*. Philadelphia: Carey & Hart, 1847.

Emory, William H. *Notes of a Military Reconnaissance from Fort Leavenworth in Missouri, to San Francisco, in California, Including Part of the Arkansas, Del Norte, and Gila Rivers*. 30th Congress, 1st Session, Senate Document 7.

Engelmann, Otto B. (trans. and ed.). "The Second Illinois in the Mexican War. Mexican War Letters of Adolph Engelmann, 1846–1847," *Journal of the Illinois State Historical Society*, XXVI (Jan. 1934), 357–452.

An Eyewitness. "The Capture of Vera Cruz," *The Knickerbocker*, XXX (July 1847), 1–8.

Frémont, John Charles. "The Conquest of California," *The Century Magazine*, XLI (April 1891), 917–27.

——. *Defence of Lieut. Col. J. C. Frémont Before the Military Court Martial, Washington, January, 1848*. Washington: n.p., 1848.

——. *Memoirs of My Life*. 2 vols., Chicago: Belford, Clarke, 1887.

French, Samuel G. *Two Wars: An Autobiography*. Nashville: Confederate Veteran, 1901.

Fulton, Maurice Garland (ed.). *Diary and Letters of Josiah Gregg*. 2 vols., Norman: University of Oklahoma Press, 1941–44.

Furber, George C. *The Twelve Months Volunteer: Or, Journal of A Private in the Tennessee Regiment of Cavalry, in the Campaign, in Mexico, 1846–7*. . . . Cincinnati: J. P. Jones, 1857.

Gallaher, F. M. (ed.). "Official Report of the Battle of Temascalitos (Brazito)," *NMHR*, III (Oct. 1928), 381–89.

[Giddings, Luther]. *Sketches of the Campaign in Northern Mexico by an Officer of the First Regiment of Ohio Volunteers*. New York: George P. Putnam & Co., 1853.

Goetzmann, William F. (ed.). "Our First Foreign War," *American Heritage*, XVII (June 1966), 19–23, 85–99.

Golder, Frank Alfred (ed.). *The March of the Mormon Battalion from Council Bluffs to California. Taken from the Journal of Henry Standage*. New York: The Century Co., 1928.

Gracy, David B., II, and Helen J. Rugeley (eds.). "From the Mississippi to the Pacific: An Englishman in the Mormon Battalion," *Arizona and the West*, VII (Summer 1965), 127–60.

Grant, Ulysses S. *Personal Memoirs of U.S. Grant*. Ed. E. B. Long. Cleveland: World Publishing Co., 1952.

Gudde, Erwin G. (ed.). *Bigler's Chronicle of the West. The Conquest of California, Discovery of Gold, and Mormon Settlement as Reflected in Henry William Bigler's Diaries*. Berkeley: University of California Press, 1962.

Hamilton, Charles S. "Memoirs of the Mexican War," *Wisconsin Magazine of History*, XIV (Sept. 1930), 63–92.

Hamlin, Percy Gatling (ed.). *The Making of a Soldier. Letters of General R. S. Ewell*. Richmond: Whitlet & Sheppardson, 1935.

Hammond, George P. (ed.). *The Larkin Papers*. 8 vols., Berkeley: University of California Press, 1951–62.

Hartman, George W. *A Private's Own Journal Giving an Account of the Battles in Mexico.* . . . Greencastle, Pa.: E. Robinson, 1849.

Hendrickson, Walter B. (ed.). "The Happy Soldier. The Mexican War Letters of John Nevin King," *Journal of the Illinois State Historical Society*, XLIV (Spring–Summer 1953), 13–27, 151–70.

Henry, William S. *Campaign Sketches of the War with Mexico.* New York: Harper & Bros., 1847.

Hinds, Charles F. (ed.). "Mexican War Journal of Leander M. Cox," *Kentucky Historical Society Register*, LV (Jan.–April 1957), 29–52, 213–36, LVI (Jan. 1958), 47–69.

Hobbs, James. *Wild Life in the Far West; Personal Adventures of A Border Mountain Man.* Hartford: Wiley, Waterman, & Eaton, 1872.

Holland, John K. (ed.). "Diary of a Texan Volunteer in the Mexican War," *SWHQ*, XXX (July 1926), 1–33.

Hollingsworth, John McHenry. *Journal of John McHenry Hollingsworth of the First New York Volunteers (Stevenson's Regiment), September 1846–August 1848.* San Francisco: California Historical Society, 1923.

Howe, M. A. DeWolf (ed.). *Home Letters of General Sherman.* New York: Charles Scribner's Sons, 1909.

———. *The Life and Letters of George Bancroft.* 2 vols., New York: Charles Scribner's Sons, 1908.

Hughes, George W. *Memoir Descriptive of the March of a Division of the United States Army, Under the Command of Brigadier General John E. Wool, from San Antonio de Bexar, in Texas, to Saltillo, in Mexico.* 31st Congress, 1st Session, Senate Executive Document 32.

Hughes, John T. *Doniphan's Expedition; Containing an Account of the Conquest of New Mexico: General Kearny's Overland Expedition to California; Doniphan's Campaign Against the Navajos; His Unparalleled March upon Chihuahua and Durango; and the Operations of General Price at Santa Fe.* Cincinnati: J. A. and U. P. James, 1848.

Jackson, Alonzo C. *The Conquest of California.* New York: n.p., 1953.

Jameson, J. Franklin (ed.). "Correspondence of John C. Calhoun," *Annual Report of the American Historical Association for the Year 1899.* Washington: Government Printing Office, 1900.

Johnson, Ludwell H. (ed.). "William Booth Taliaferro's Letters From Mexico, 1847–1848," *Virginia Magazine of History and Biography*, LXXIII (Oct. 1965), 455–73.

Jones, Rebecca M. (ed.). "Extracts from the Life Sketch of Nathaniel V. Jones," *UHQ*, IV (Jan. 1931), 3–23.

Jones, Robert R. (ed.). "The Mexican War Diary of James Lawson Kemper," *Virginia Magazine of History and Biography*, LXXIV (Oct. 1966), 387–428.

Kemble, John Haskell (ed.). "Amphibious Operations in the Gulf of California, 1847–1848," *American Neptune*, V (April 1945), 121–36.

——— (ed.). "Naval Conquest in the Pacific," *CHSQ*, XX (June 1941), 193–234.

Kenly, John R. *Memoirs of a Maryland Volunteer, War with Mexico, in the Years 1846–7–8.* Philadelphia: J. B. Lippincott & Co., 1873.

Law, Robert A. (ed.). "A Letter from Vera Cruz in 1847," *SWHQ*, XVIII (Oct. 1914), 215–18.

Lawton, Eba Anderson (ed.). *An Artillery Officer in the Mexican War 1846–7. Letters of Robert Anderson, Captain 3rd Artillery, U.S.A.* New York: G. P. Putnam's Sons, 1911.

Livingston–Little, D. E. (ed.). *The Mexican War Diary of Thomas D. Tennery.* Norman: University of Oklahoma Press, 1970.

[Lombard, Albert]. *The "High Private" with a Full and Exciting History of the New-York Volunteers, and the "Mysteries and Miseries" of the Mexican War.* New York: n.p., 1848.

Longstreet, James. *From Manassas to Appomattox. Memoirs of the Civil War in America.* Philadelphia: J. B. Lippincott Co., 1908.

Lugo, José del Carmen, "Life of a Rancher," *HSSCP*, XXXII (Sept. 1950), 185–236.

McCall, George A. *Letters from the Frontiers.* Philadelphia: J. B. Lippincott & Co., 1868.

McPherson, John D. "A Controversy of the Mexican War," *The Century Magazine*, LVI (July 1898), 467–68.

McSherry, Richard. *El Punchero; or a Mixed Dish from Mexico Embracing General Scott's Campaign with Sketches of Military Life, in Field and Camp, of the Character of the Country, Manners and Ways of the People, etc.* Philadelphia: Lippincott, Grambo, & Co., 1850.

————. *Essays and Lectures.* Baltimore: Kelly, Piet & Co., 1869.

Mason, Amos Lawrence (ed.). *Memoirs and Correspondence of Charles Steedman, Rear Admiral, United States Navy, with His Autobiography and Private Journals, 1811–1890.* Cambridge: Riverside Press, 1912.

Maury, Dabney Herndon. *Recollections of a Virginian in the Mexican, Indian, and Civil Wars.* New York: Charles Scribner's Sons, 1894.

May, George S. (ed.). "An Iowan in the Mexican War," *Iowa Journal of History*, LIII (April 1955), 167–74.

Meade, George Gordon. *The Life and Letters of George Gordon Meade, Major-General United States Army.* 2 vols., New York: Charles Scribner's Sons, 1913.

Moore, H. Judge. *Scott's Campaign in Mexico from the Rendezvous on the Island of Lobos to the Taking of the City. . . .* Charleston: J. B. Nixon, 1849.

Moore, John Bassett (ed.). *The Works of James Buchanan.* 12 vols., Philadelphia: J. B. Lippincott & Co., 1908–11.

Moore, John Hammond (ed.). "Private Johnson Fights the Mexicans, 1847–1848," *South Carolina Historical Magazine*, LXVII (Oct. 1966), 203–28.

Moreno, Daniel (ed.). *Manuel Crescencio Rejón, Pensamiento Politico.* México: Universidad Nacional Autónoma de México, 1968.

Morrison, George S. "Letter from Mexico by George S. Morrison, A Member of Capt. Albert Pike's Squadron," *Arkansas Historical Quarterly*, XVI (Winter 1957), 398–401.

Myers, William Starr (ed.). *The Mexican War Diary of George B. McClellan.* Princeton. Princeton University Press, 1917.

Nichols, Roy F. (ed.). "The Mystery of the Dallas Papers," *Pennsylvania*

Magazine of History and Biography, LXXIII (July–Oct. 1949), 349–92, 475–517.

"An Officer of the Staff." *A Series of Intercepted Mexican Letters, Captured by the American Guard at Tacubaya, August 22, 1847, Containing Many Interesting Particulars Never Before Published in the U.S. Together with an Introductory Sketch of the Operations of the American Army. Reprinted from the "American Star" Mexico.* N.p., n.d.

Oswandel, J. Jacob. *Notes of the Mexican War 1846–47–48.* Philadelphia: n.p., 1885.

Parker, William Harwar. *Recollections of a Naval Officer, 1841–1865.* New York: Charles Scribner's Sons, 1883.

[Parrodi, Anastasio]. *Memoria Sobre la Evacuación Militar del Puerto de Tampico de Tamaulipas.* San Luis Potosí: n.p., 1848.

Perry, Bliss (ed.). *The Heart of Emerson's Journals.* Boston: Houghton Mifflin Co., 1926.

[Phelps, William D.]. *Fore and Aft; or, Leaves from the Life of an Old Sailor. By "Webfoot."* Boston: Nicholas & Hall, 1871.

The Philadelphia Grays' Collection of Official Reports of Brigadier-General George Cadwalader's Services During the Campaign of 1847 in Mexico. Philadelphia: T. K. & P. G. Collins, 1848.

Pillow, Gideon J. *Defence of Maj. Gen. Pillow Before the Court of Inquiry, Frederick, Maryland, Against the Charges Preferred Against Him by Maj. Gen. Winfield Scott.* N.p., 1848.

Preston, William. *Journal in Mexico, By Lieutenant Colonel William Preston of the Fourth Kentucky Regiment of Volunteers, Dating from November 1, 1847 to May 25, 1848.* Paris, Ky.: n.p., n.d.

Quaife, Milo Milton (ed.). *The Diary of James K. Polk During His Presidency, 1845 to 1849.* 4 vols., Chicago: A. C. McClurg & Co., 1910.

Relacción Histórica de la Segunda Invasión que Hicieron los Americanos en Tabasco, y de la Conducta que Observó en Ella el Comandante General de Aquel Estado D. Domingo Echagaray, Escrita por un Testigo Imparcial y Verídico. Veracruz: J. M. Blanco, 1847.

Revere, Joseph Warren. *Keel and Saddle; A Retrospect of Forty Years of Military and Naval Service.* Boston: J. R. Osgood & Co., 1873.

———. *A Tour of Duty in California. An Account of Principal Events Attending the Conquest of California.* Boston: J. H. Francis, 1849.

Reynolds, John G. *A Conclusive Exculpation of the Marine Corps in Mexico, From the Slanderous Allegations of One of Its Former Officers; With Full Official Copy of the Record of the General Court Martial, Held at Brooklyn. . . .* New York: Stringer & Townsend, 1853.

Richardson, William H. *The Journal of William H. Richardson, A Private Soldier in the Campaign of New and Old Mexico.* New York: William H. Richardson, 1848.

[Robertson, John B.]. *Reminiscences of a Campaign in Mexico By A Member of the "Bloody First."* Nashville: J. York & Co., 1849.

Robinson, Jacob S. *A Journal of the Santa Fe Expedition Under Colonel Doniphan.* Princeton: Princeton University Press, 1932.

Rogers, Fred Blackburn (ed.). *Filings from an Old Saw. Reminiscences of San*

Francisco and California's Conquest by "Filings"—Joseph T. Downey. San Francisco: John Howell, 1956.

———— (ed.). *A Navy Surgeon in California 1846–1847. The Journal of Marius Duvall.* San Francisco: John Howell, 1957.

Rowland, Dunbar (ed.). *Jefferson Davis Constitutionalist. His Letters, Papers, and Speeches.* 10 vols., Jackson: Mississippi Department of Archives and History, 1923.

Ruxton, George Frederick Augustus. *Adventures in Mexico and the Rocky Mountains.* New York: Harper & Bros., 1848.

Samson, William H. (ed.). *Letters of Zachary Taylor from the Battle-Fields of the Mexican War. Reprinted from the Originals in the Collection of Mr. William K. Bixby of St. Louis, Mo.* Rochester: The Genesee Press, 1908.

Sands, Benjamin Franklin. *From Reefer to Rear Admiral. Reminiscences of Nearly Half a Century of Naval Life.* New York: F. A. Stokes Co., 1899.

Santa Anna, Antonio López de. *Detall de las Operaciones Ocurridas en la Defensa de la Capital de la República, Atacada por el Ejército de los Estados-Unidos del Norte en la Año de 1847.* México: Ignacio Cumplido, 1848.

————. *The Eagle. The Autobiography of Santa Anna.* Ed. Ann Fears Crawford. Austin: The Pemberton Press, 1967.

————. *Las Guerras de México con Tejas y los Estados Unidos.* México: Ch. Bouret, 1910.

————. *Mi Historia Militar y Política 1810–1874.* México: Ch. Bouret, 1905.

————. *Parte Oficial del Exmo. Sr. General de División Benemerito de la Patria D. Antonio López de Santa Anna, al Supremo Gobierno, Sobre la Sorpresa, que el General Lanz Intentó Darle en Techuocan la Madrugada del Día 23 de Enero Próximo Pasado, y el Documento que Mismo Parte Menciona.* Orizava: Imprenta de la Amisdad, 1848.

Scammon, E. Parker. "A Chapter in the Mexican War," *Magazine of American History*, XIV (Dec. 1885), 567.

[Scott, John A.] *Encarnacion Prisoners. Comprising an Account of the March of the Kentucky Cavalry from Louisville to the Rio Grande. . . .* Louisville: Prentice & Weissanger, 1848.

Scott, Winfield. *Memoirs of Lieut.-General Scott, LL.D. Written by Himself.* New York: Sheldon & Co., 1864.

Sedgwick, John. *Correspondence of John Sedgwick, Major General.* 2 vols., n.p., 1902.

Semmes, Raphael. *The Campaign of General Scott in the Valley of Mexico.* Cincinnati: Moore & Anderson, 1852.

————. *Service Afloat and Ashore During the Mexican War.* Cincinnati: William H. Moore & Co., 1851.

Simon, John Y. (ed.). *The Papers of Ulysses S. Grant.* 10 vols., Carbondale: Southern Illinois University, 1967–.

Sioussat, St. George L. (ed.). "Polk–Donelson Letters, Letters of James K. Polk and Andrew J. Donelson, 1843–1848," *Tennessee Historical Magazine*, III (March 1917), 51–74.

Smith, George Winston, and Charles Judah (eds.). *Chronicles of the Gringos:*

The U.S. Army in the Mexican War, 1846–1848, Accounts of Eyewitnesses and Combatants. Albuquerque: University of New Mexico Press, 1968.

Smith, Gustavus W. "Company A Engineers in Mexico, 1846–1847," *The Military Engineer,* LVI (Sept.–Oct. 1964), 336–40.

Smith, Isaac. *Reminiscences of a Campaign in Mexico. An Account of the Operations of the Indiana Brigade.* Indianapolis: Chapmans & Spahn, 1848.

Smith, Justin H. (ed.). "Letters of General Antonio López de Santa Anna Relating to the War Between the United States and Mexico, 1846–1848," *Annual Report of the American Historical Association for the Year 1917.* Washington: Government Printing Office, 1920.

Smith, S. Compton. *Chile Con Carne, or The Camp and the Field.* New York: Miller & Curtis, 1857.

Steele, John. "Extracts from the Journal of . . . ," *UHQ,* VI (Jan. 1933), 3–28.

Strode, Hudson (ed.). *Jefferson Davis. Private Letters 1823–1889.* New York: Harcourt, Brace & World, Inc., 1966.

Taylor, Bayard. *Eldorado, or, Adventures in the Path of Empire, Comprising a Voyage to California . . . and Experiences of Mexican Travel.* New York: Alfred A. Knopf, 1949.

Taylor, Fitch W. *The Broad Pennant, or, A Cruise in the United States Flag Ship of the Gulf Squadron, During the Mexican Difficulties. . . .* New York: Leavitt, Trow & Co., 1848.

Thompson, Arthur W. (ed.). "A Massachusetts Mechanic in Florida and Mexico, 1847," *Florida Historical Quarterly,* XXXIII (Oct. 1954), 130–41.

Thorndike, Rachel Sherman (ed.). *The Sherman Letters. Correspondence Between General and Senator Sherman from 1837 to 1891.* New York: Charles Scribner's Sons, 1894.

Tuckerman, Bayard (ed.). *The Diary of Philip Hone, 1828–1851.* 2 vols., New York: Dodd, Mead & Co., 1910.

Tyler, George W. (ed.). "Recollections of the Mexican War, Taken from the Journals of Lieutenant Stephen C. Rowan, U.S. Navy, Executive Officer of the U.S.S. Cyane, Pacific Squadron, 1845–1848," *USNIP,* XIV (Sept. 1888), 530–60.

Valencia, Gabriel. *Detall de los Acciones de los Días 19 y 20 en los Campos de Padierna, y Otros Pormenores Recientemente Comunicados por Personas Fidedignos.* Morelia: Ignacio Arango, 1847.

Wallace, Lew. *An Autobiography.* 2 vols., New York: Harper & Bros., 1906.

Warren, Vida Lockwood (ed.). "Dr. John S. Griffin's Mail, 1846–53," *CHSQ,* XXXIII (June 1954), 97–123.

Weed, Harriet A. (ed.). *Autobiography of Thurlow Weed.* Boston: Houghton, Mifflin & Co., 1883.

Williams, T. Harry (ed.). *With Beauregard in Mexico. The Mexican War Reminiscences of P. G. T. Beauregard.* New York: DeCapo Press, 1969.

Wise, Henry A. *Los Gringos, or, an Inside View of Mexico and California, with Wanderings in Peru, Chili, and Polynesia.* New York: Baker & Scribner, 1849.

Wislizenus, Frederick A. *Memoir of a Tour to Northern Mexico, Connected* with Col. Doniphan's Expedition, in 1846 and 1847. 30th Congress, 1st Session, Senate Miscellaneous Document 26.

Wood, William Maxwell. *Wandering Sketches of People and Things in South America, Polynesia, California, and Other Places Visited During a Cruise on Board of the U.S. Ships Levant, Portsmouth, and Savannah.* Philadelphia: Carey & Hart, 1849.

V. MONOGRAPHS AND SECONDARY SOURCES

Adams, Ephraim Douglas. *British Interests and Activities in Texas 1838–1846.* Baltimore: Johns Hopkins Press, 1910.

———. "English Interest in Annexation of California," *AHR*, XIV (July 1909), 744–63.

Aldrich, M. Almy. *History of the United States Marine Corps.* Boston: Henry L. Shepard & Co., 1875.

Alessio Robles, Vito. *Coahuila y Texas desde la Consumación de la Independencia hasta el Tratado de Paz de Guadalupe Hidalgo.* 2 vols., Mexico: n.p., 1945–46.

[Allen, G. N.]. *Mexican Treacheries and Cruelties. Incidents and Sufferings in the Mexican War . . . By a Volunteer Returned from the War.* Boston: Hall's, 1847.

Alvear Acevedo, Carlos. *La Guerra del 47.* México: Editorial Jus, 1957.

Ames, George Walcott, Jr., "Horse Marines, California, 1846," *CHSQ*, XVIII (March 1939), 72–84.

Anderson, John Q. "Soldier Lore of the War with Mexico," *Western Humanities Review*, XI (Autumn 1951), 321–30.

Armstrong, Andrew. "The Brazito Battlefield," *NMHR*, XXXV (Jan. 1960), 63–74.

Ashburn, Percy N. *A History of the Medical Department of the United States Army.* Boston: Houghton Mifflin Co., 1929.

Babcock, Elkanah. *A War History of the Sixth U.S. Infantry From 1798 to 1903. . . .* Kansas City: Hudson-Kemberly Publishing Co., 1903.

Bancroft, Hubert Howe. *History of Arizona and New Mexico 1530–1888.* San Francisco: The History Co., 1889.

———. *History of California.* 7 vols., San Francisco: The History Co., 1884–90.

———. *History of Mexico.* 6 vols. San Francisco: The History Co., 1883–88.

———. *History of the North Mexican States and Texas.* 2 vols., San Francisco: The History Co., 1884–89.

Barrows, Edward M. *The Great Commodore. The Exploits of Matthew Calbraith Perry.* Indianapolis: Bobbs-Merrill, 1935.

Battles of Mexico: Containing an Authentic Account of All the Battles Fought in That Republic from the Commencement of the War Until the Capture of the City of Mexico. New York: Martin & Ely, 1847.

Bauer, K. Jack. *Surfboats and Horse Marines: U.S. Naval Operations in the Mexican War.* Annapolis: U.S. Naval Institute, 1969.

———. "The U.S. Navy and Texas Independence: A Study in Jacksonian Integrity," *Military Affairs*, XXXIV (April 1970), 44–48.

————. "The Veracruz Expedition of 1847," *Military Affairs*, XX (Fall 1956), 162–69.

[Bayard, Samuel John]. *A Sketch of the Life of Com. Robert F. Stockton. . . .* New York: Derby & Jackson, 1856.

Baylies, Francis. *A Narrative of Major General Wool's Campaign in Mexico, in the Years 1846, 1847 & 1848.* Albany: Little & Co., 1851.

Beach, Moses S. "A Secret Mission to Mexico," *Scribner's Monthly Magazine*, XVIII (May 1879), 136–40.

Beers, Henry Putney. "A History of the U.S. Topographical Engineers 1813–1863," *The Military Engineer*, XXXIV (June–July 1942), 287–91, 348–52.

————. *The Western Military Frontier 1815–1846.* Philadelphia: n.p., 1935.

Bemis, Samuel Flagg (ed.). *The American Secretaries of State and Their Diplomacy.* 17 vols. New York: Alfred A. Knopf, 1927–67.

Bender, A. B. "Frontier Defense in the Territory of New Mexico 1846–1853," *NMHR*, IX (July 1934), 249–72.

————. "Government Explorations in the Territory of New Mexico, 1846–1859," *NMHR*, IX (Jan. 1934), 1–32.

Berruto Ramón, Federico. *En Defensa de Un Soldado Mexicano.* Saltillo: Colección de Escritores Coahuilenses, n.d.

Bill, Alfred Hoyt. *Rehearsal for Conflict.* New York, Alfred A. Knopf, 1947.

Billington, Ray Allen. *The Far Western Frontier 1830–1860.* New York: Harper & Bros., 1956.

Birkhimer, William E. *Historical Sketch of the Organization, Administration, Material and Tactics of the Artillery, United States Army.* New York: Greenwood Press, 1968.

Bishop, Farnham. *Our First War with Mexico.* New York: Charles Scribner's Sons, 1916.

Blaisdell, Lowell L. "The Santangelo Case: A Claim Preceding the Mexican War," *Journal of the West*, XI (April 1972), 248–59.

Bloom, John Porter. "New Mexico as Viewed by Americans, 1846–1849," *NMHR*, XXXIV (July 1959), 165–98.

Bonner, John. "Scott's Battles in Mexico," *Harper's New Monthly Magazine*, XI (Aug. 1855), 311–24.

Bonsal, Stephen. *Edward Fitzgerald Beale, A Pioneer in the Path of Empire 1822–1903*, New York: G. P. Putnam's Sons, 1912.

Bourne, Edward G. "A Proposed Absorption of Mexico in 1847–48," *Annual Report of the American Historical Association . . . . 1899.* Washington: Government Printing Office, 1900.

————. "The United States and Mexico, 1847–1848," *AHR*, V (April 1900), 491–502.

Brack, Gene M. "Mexican Opinion, American Racism, and the War of 1846," *Western Historical Quarterly*, I (April 1970), 161–74.

————. "Mexican Opinion and the Texas Revolution," *SWHQ*, LXXII (Oct. 1968), 170–82.

Brackett, Albert G. *General Lane's Brigade in Central Mexico.* Cincinnati: H. W. Derby & Co., 1854.

————. *History of the United States Cavalry, from the Formation of the*

Federal Government to the 1st of June, 1863. New York: Greenwood Press, 1968.

Bravo Ugarte, José. *Historia de México.* 3 vols., México: Editorial Jus, 1959.

Brent, Robert A. "Mississippi and the Mexican War," *Journal of Mississippi History,* XXXI (Aug. 1969), 202–14.

————. "Nicholas P. Trist and the Treaty of Guadalupe Hidalgo," *SWHQ,* LXXVII (April 1954), 454–74.

Brooke, George M., Jr. "The Vest Pocket War of Commodore Jones," *PHR,* XXXI (Aug. 1962), 217–34.

Brooks, Nathan Covington. *A Complete History of the Mexican War: Its Causes, Conduct, and Consequences: Comprising an Account of the Various Military and Naval Operations, from its Commencement to the Treaty of Peace.* Chicago: Rio Grande Press, 1965.

Brown, Walter Lee. "The Mexican War Experiences of Albert Pike and the 'Mounted Devils' of Arkansas," *Arkansas Historical Quarterly,* XII (Winter 1953), 301–15.

Browne, J. Ross. "Explorations in Lower California," *Harper's New Monthly Magazine,* XXXVII (Oct. 1868), 582–83.

Buley, R. C. "Indiana in the Mexican War," *Indiana Magazine of History,* XV (Sept.–Dec. 1919), 261–326, XVI (March 1920), 48–68.

Bustamante, Carlos María. *Campaña Sin Gloria Tenida en el Recinto de México, Causada por Habes Persistido Don Valentín Gómez Farías, Vice-Presidente de la República Mexicana en Llevan Adelante las Leyes de 11 de Enero y 4 de Februaro de 1847, Llamades de Mauo-Muertas, que Depojan al Clero de Sui Propiedades, con Oposición Caci General de la Nación.* México: Ignacio Cumplido, 1847.

————. *El Nuevo Bernal Díaz del Castillo o Sea, História de la Invasión de los Anglo-Americanos en México.* 2 vols., México: Secretaria de Educación Publíca, 1949.

Callahan, James Morton. *American Foreign Policy in Mexican Relations.* New York: Macmillan, 1932.

Callcott, Wilfrid Hardy. *Church and State in Mexico.* Durham: Duke University Press, 1926.

————. *Santa Anna, The Story of an Enigma Who Once Was Mexico.* Norman: University of Oklahoma Press, 1936.

Camp, Charles L. "Kit Carson in California," *CHSQ,* I (Oct. 1922), 111–51.

Canaday, Dayton W. "Voice of the Volunteer of 1847," *Journal of the Illinois State Historical Society,* XLIV (Autumn 1951), 199–209.

A Captain of Volunteers. *Alta California.* Philadelphia: H. Packer & Co., 1847.

Cardenas de la Peña, Enrique. *Semblanza Marítima del México Independiente y Revolucionario.* 2 vols., México: Secretaria de Marina, 1970.

Carreño, Alberto María. *Jefes del Ejército Méxicano en 1847. Biografías de Generales de División y de Brigada y de Coroneles del Ejército Méxicano por Fines del Año de 1847.* México: Secretaria de Formento, 1914.

Carrion, Jorge. "Efectos Psicologiocos de la Guerra de 47 en el Hombre de México," *Cuadernos Americanos,* VII (Jan.–Feb. 1948), 116–32.

Castañeda, Carlos E., "Relations of General Scott with Santa Anna," *HAHR,* XXIV (Nov. 1949), 455–73.

Castillo Nájera, Francisco. *Invasión Norte-Americana, Efectivos y Estado de los*

Ejércitos Beligerentes, Consideraciones sobre da Compaña. México: n.p., 1947.

Castillo Negrete, Emelio del. *Invasión de los Norte-Americanos en México.* 2 vols., México: n.p., 1890.

Chamberlain, Eugene Keith. "Nicholas Trist and Baja California," *PHR*, XXXII (Feb. 1963), 49–64.

Chambers, William Nisbet. *Old Bullion Benton, Senator from the New West.* Boston: Little, Brown & Co., 1956.

Chase, Lucien B. *History of the Polk Administration.* New York: George P. Putnam, 1850.

Chidsey, Donald Barr. *The War with Mexico.* New York: Crown Publishers, Inc., 1968.

Chitwood, Oliver Perry. *John Tyler Champion of the Old South.* New York: D. Appleton-Century Co., 1939.

Churubusco en la Acción Militar del 20 de Agosto de 1847. México: Museo Histórico de Churubusco, 1947.

Clark, Francis D. *The First Regiment of New York Volunteers Commanded by Col. Jonathan D. Stevenson, in the Mexican War.* New York: Evans, 1882.

Clarke, Dwight L. "Soldiers Under Stephen Watts Kearny," *CHSQ*, XLVI (June 1966), 132–48.

——. *Stephen Watts Kearny Soldier of the West.* Norman: University of Oklahoma Press, 1961.

——. and George Ruhlen. "The Final Roster of the Army of the West, 1846–1847," *CHSQ*, XLIV (March 1964), 37–44.

Cleland, Robert Glass. *A History of California: The American Period.* New York: Macmillan Co., 1922.

Clendenen, Clarence C. *Blood on the Border. The United States Army and the Mexican Irregulars.* New York: Macmillan Co. 1969.

Clifford, Philip Greely. *Nathan Clifford Democrat (1803–1881).* New York: G. P. Putnam's Sons, 1922.

Coakley, Robert W., Paul J. Scheips, and Emma J. Portuondo. *Antiwar and Antimilitary Activities in the United States, 1846–1954.* Washington: Office of the Chief of Military History, 1970.

Coit, Margaret L. *John C. Calhoun. American Portrait.* Cambridge: Houghton Mifflin Co., 1950.

Coleman, Mrs. Chapman. *The Life of John J. Crittenden, with Selections from His Correspondence and Speeches.* 2 vols., Philadelphia: J. B. Lippincott & Co., 1871.

Collins, John R. "The Mexican War: A Study in Fragmentation," *Journal of the West*, XI (April 1972), 225–34.

Complete History of the Late Mexican War, Containing an Authentic Account of All the Battles Fought In That Republic, Including the Treaty of Peace. . . . New York: F. J. Dow & Co., 1850. Reprint of *Battles of Mexico.*

Condon, William H. *The Life of Major-General James Shields. Hero of Three Wars and Senator from Three States.* Chicago: Blakely Printing Co., 1900.

Conner, Philip Syng Physick. *The Home Squadron Under Commodore Con-*

ner in the War with Mexico, Being a Synopsis of His Services. n.p., 1896.

Connor, Seymour V., and Odie B. Faulk. *North America Divided. The Mexican War, 1846–1848.* New York: Oxford University Press, 1971.

Cooper, Susan F. "Rear Admiral William Branford Shubrick," *Harper's New Monthly Magazine,* LIII (Aug. 1878), 400–7.

Cotner, Thomas Ewing. *The Military and Political Career of José Joaquín de Herrera, 1792–1854.* Austin: University of Texas Press, 1949.

——— and Carlos E. Castañeda (eds.). *Essays in Mexican History.* Austin: Institute of Latin American Studies, 1958.

Coughlin, Sister Magdalen. "California Ports: A Key to West Coast Diplomacy, 1820–1845," *Journal of the West,* V (April 1966), 153–72.

Coy, Owen C. *The Battle of San Pasqual. A Report of the California Historical Survey with General Reference to Its Location.* Sacramento: California State Printing Office, 1921.

Cue Cánovas, Agustín. *Historia Social y Económica de México (1821–1854).* México: Editorial F. Trillas, 1963.

Cuevas, Mariano. *Historia de la Nación Mexicana.* México: Editorial Porrua, 1967.

Cunliffe, Marcus. *Soldiers and Civilians. The Martial Spirit in America 1775–1865.* Boston: Little, Brown & Co., 1968.

Curti, Merl E. "Pacifist Propaganda and the Treaty of Guadalupe Hidalgo," *AHR,* XXXIII (April 1928), 596–98.

Cutts, James Madison. *The Conquest of California and New Mexico by the Forces of the United States in the Years 1846 and 1847.* Philadelphia: Carey & Hart, 1847.

Dabb, Jack Autrey. *The Mariano Riva Palacio Archives. A Guide.* Vol. I. Mexico: Editorial Jus, 1967.

Davies, Thomas M., Jr. "Assessments During the Mexican War," *NMHR,* XLI (July 1966), 197–216.

Davies, Wallace E. "The Mexican War Veterans as an Organized Group," *MVHR,* XXXV (Sept. 1948), 221–38.

[Davis, Varina H.] *Jefferson Davis, Ex-President of the Confederate States of America. A Memoir by His Wife.* 2 vols., New York: Belford Co., 1890.

Dawson, Henry B. *Battles of the United States by Land and Sea.* 2 vols., New York: Johnson, Fry & Co., n.d.

De Armond, Louis. "Justo Sierra O'Reilly and Yucatán-United States Relations, 1847–1848," *HAHR,* XXXI (Aug. 1951), 420–36.

DeVoto, Bernard. *The Year of Decision 1846.* Boston: Little, Brown & Co., 1943.

DeWitt, Charles J. "Crusading for Peace in Syracuse During the War with Mexico," *New York History,* XIV (April 1933), 100–12.

Diccionario Porrúa de Historia, Biografía y Geografía de México. México: Editorial Porrúa, 1964.

Dios Bonilla, Juan de. *Historia Marítima de México.* México: Editorial Litorales, 1962.

Dodd, William E. "The West and the War with Mexico," *Illinois State Historical Society Journal,* V (July 1912), 159–72.

Donnelly, Ralph W. "Rocket Batteries of the Civil War," *Military Affairs*, XXV (Summer 1961), 69–93.

Dorris, Jonathan T. "Michael Kelly Lawler: Mexican and Civil War Officer," *Illinois State Historical Society Journal*, XLVIII (Winter 1955), 366–404.

Downey, Fairfax. *Sound of the Guns, The Story of American Artillery from the Ancient and Honorable Company to the Atomic Cannon and Guided Missile*. New York: David McKay Co., 1956.

———. "Tragic Story of the San Patricio Battalion," *American Heritage*, VI (June 1955), 20–23.

Driver, Leo. "Carrillo's Flying Artillery: The Battle of San Pedro," *CHSQ*, XLVIII (Dec. 1969), 335–49.

Drury, Clifford M. "Walter Colton, Chaplain and Alcalde," *CHSQ*, XXXV (June 1956), 97–117.

Duncan, Louis C. "A Medical History of General Zachary Taylor's Army of Occupation in Texas and Mexico, 1845–1847," *Military Surgeon*, XLVIII, 1921), 76–104.

Dufour, Charles L. *The Mexican War, A Compact History 1846–1848*. New York: Hawthorn Books, 1968.

DuPont, Henry A. *Rear Admiral Samuel Francis DuPont, United States Navy, A Biography*. New York: National Americana Society, 1926.

Dupuy, R. Ernest, and Trevor N. Dupuy. *Military Heritage of America*. New York: McGraw-Hill Book Co., 1956.

Dyer, Brainerd. *Zachary Taylor*. Baton Rouge: Louisiana State University Press, 1946.

Ekirch, Arthur A., Jr. *The Civilian and the Military*. New York: Oxford University Press, 1959.

Ellicott, John M. "Comedy and Tragedy in Our Occupation of California," *Marine Corps Gazette*, XXXV (March 1951), 49–53.

———. *The Life of John Ancrum Winslow, Rear Admiral U.S. Navy*. New York: G. P. Putnam's Sons, 1902.

Elliott, Charles Wilson. *Winfield Scott, The Soldier and the Man*. New York: Macmillan Co., 1937.

Ellison, Joseph. "The Struggle for Civil Government in California, 1846–1850," *CHSQ*, X (March–Sept. 1931), 3–26, 129–64, 220–44.

Ellison, William H. "San Juan to Cahuenga: The Experiences of Frémont's Battalion," *PHR*, XXVII (Aug. 1958), 245–61.

Ellsworth, Clayton Sumner. "The American Churches and the Mexican War," *AHR*, XLV (Jan. 1940), 301–46.

Emmons, George Fox. *The Navy of the United States from the Commencement, 1775, to 1853. . . .* Washington: Gideon & Co., 1853.

"An Eyewitness." *Complete History of the Late Mexican War!! Containing an Authentic Account of All the Battles Fought in That Republic to the Close of the War, with a List of the Killed and Wounded; Together with a Brief Sketch of the Lives of Generals Scott and Taylor Including the Treaty of Peace*. New York: F. T. Dow, 1850.

Fakes, Turner J., Jr. "Memphis and the Mexican War," *West Tennessee Historical Society Papers*, II (1948), 119–44.

Falk, Stanley L. "Artillery for a Land Service: Development of a System," *Military Affairs*, XXVIII (Fall 1964), 103–9.

Faulk, Odie B., and Joseph A. Stout (eds.). *The Mexican War, Changing Interpretations*. Chicago: The Swallow Press, 1973.

Feipel, Louis N. "The United States Navy in Mexico, 1821–1914," *USNIP*, XLI (Jan.–Dec. 1915), 33–52, 489–97, 889–903, 1059–72, 1527–34, 1993–2002, XLII (Jan. 1916), 171–82.

Filler, Louis. *The Crusade Against Slavery 1830–1860*. New York: Harper & Row, 1960.

Finke, Detmar H. "Organization and Uniforms of the San Patricio Units of the Mexican Army, 1846–1848," *"Military Collector and Historian*, IX (Summer 1957), 36–38.

Franklin, William B. "The Battle of Buena Vista, February 22–23, 1847," *Military Historical Society of Massachusetts Papers*, XIII (1913), 545–57.

Freeman, Douglas Southall. *R. E. Lee*. 4 vols., New York: Charles Scribner's Sons, 1934.

Frost, John. *Life of Major General Zachary Taylor: With Notices of the War in New Mexico, California, and in South Mexico; and Biographical Sketches of Officers who have Distinguished Themselves in the War with Mexico*. New York: D. Appleton & Co., 1847.

———. *The Mexican War and Its Warriors; Comprising a Complete History of All the Operations of the American Armies in Mexico: With Biographical Sketches and Anecdotes of the Most Distinguished Officers in the Regular Army and Volunteer Force*. New York: H. Mansfield, 1848.

———. *Pictorial History of Mexico and the Mexican War*. Philadelphia: Thorne, Cowperthwait & Co., 1849.

Fry, J. Reese, and Robert T. Conrad. *A Life of Gen. Zachary Taylor Comprising a Narrative of Events Connected with His Professional Career, Derived from Public Documents and Private Correspondence. . . .* Philadelphia: Grigg, Elliott & Co., 1847.

Fuentes Días, Vicente. *La Intervención Norteamericana en México*. México: Nuevo Mundo, 1947.

Fuentes Mares, José. *Santa Anna, Aurora y Ocaso de Un Comediante*. México: Editorial Jus, 1956.

Fuess, Claude M. *The Life of Caleb Cushing*. 2 vols., New York: Harcourt Brace & Co., 1923.

Fuller, John Douglas Pitts. *The Movement for the Acquisition of All Mexico 1846–1848*. New York: Da Capro Press, 1969.

———. "Slavery Propaganda During the Mexican War," *SWHQ*, XXXVIII (April 1935), 235–45.

———. "The Slavery Question and the Movement to Acquire Mexico, 1846–1848," *MVHR*, XXI (June 1934), 31–48.

Fulmore, Z. T. "The Annexation of Texas and the Mexican War," *Quarterly of the Texas State Historical Association*, V (July 1901), 28–48.

Gabriel, Ralph H. "American Experience with Military Government," *AHR*, XLIX (July 1944), 630–43.

Gallatin, Albert. *Peace With Mexico*. New York: Bartlett & Welford, 1847.

Ganoe, William Addleman. *The History of the United States Army*. Ashton, Md.: Eric Lundberg, 1964.

Gaxiola, F. Javier. *La Invasión Norte-Americana en Sinaloa. Revista Historica del Estado, de 1845 a 1849.* 2 vols., México: Antonio Rosas, 1891.

General Scott and His Staff: Comprising Memoirs of Generals Scott, Twiggs, Smith, Quitman, Shields, Pillow, Lane, Cadwalader, Patterson, and Pierce: Colonels Childs, Riley, Harney, and Butler, and Other Distinguished Officers Attached to General Scott's Army . . . Intersperced with Numerous Anecdotes of the Mexican War, and Personal Adventures of the Officers. Philadelphia: Grigg, Ellicott & Co., 1848.

General Taylor and His Staff. . . . Philadelphia: Lippincott, Grambo & Co., 1851.

Gerhard, Peter. "Baja California in the Mexican War," *PHR*, XIV (Nov. 1945), 418–24.

Germain, Dom Aidan Henry. *Catholic Military and Naval Chaplains 1776–1917.* Washington: Catholic University, 1929.

Giffen, Guy J. *California Expedition. Stevenson's Regiment of First New York Volunteers.* Oakland: Biobooks, 1951.

Giffen, Helen S. "The California Battalion's Route to Los Angeles," *Journal of the West*, V (April 1966), 207–14.

Gleason, Duncan. "The Lost Islands of San Pedro," *Sea*, XV (May 1951), 18–19, 41–42.

Goetzmann, William H. *Army Exploration in the American West 1803–1863.* New Haven: Yale University Press, 1959.

———. *Exploration and Empire. The Explorer and the Scientist in the Winning of the American West.* New York: Alfred A. Knopf, 1966.

Going, Charles Buxton. *David Wilmot. Free Soiler.* New York: D. Appleton & Co., 1924.

Goldin, Gurston. "Business Sentiment and the Mexican War with Particular Emphasis on the New York Businessman," *New York History*, XXXIII (Jan. 1952), 54–70.

Goodwin, Cardinal. *John Charles Frémont. An Explanation of His Career.* Stanford: Stanford University Press, 1930.

Gordon, George H. "The Battles of Contreras and Churubusco," *Military Historical Society of Massachusetts Papers*, XIII (1913), 561–98.

———. "The Battles of Molino del Rey and Chapultepec," *Military Historical Society of Massachusetts Papers*, XIII (1913), 601–39.

Graebner, Norman A. *Empire on the Pacific. A Study in American Continental Expansion.* New York: Ronald Press, 1955.

———. "Party Politics and the Trist Mission," *Journal of Southern History*, XIX (May 1953), 137–56.

Griffis, William Elliott. *Matthew Calbraith Perry: A Typical American Naval Officer.* Boston: Houghton Mifflin Co., 1890.

Grivas, Theodore. *Military Governments in California, 1846–1850.* Glendale: Arthur H. Clark Co., 1963.

Guinn, James Miller. *A History of California and an Extended History of Los Angeles and Environs.* 3 vols., Los Angeles: Historic Record Co., 1915.

———. "Siege and Capture of Los Angeles, September 1846," *HSSCP*, III (1893), 47–53.

Haferkorn, Henry E. *The War with Mexico*. Washington: U.S. Engineer School, 1914.

Hale, Charles A. "The War With the United States and the Crisis in Mexican Thought," *The Americas*, XIV (Oct. 1957), 153–74.

Hamilton, Holman. *Zachary Taylor, Soldier of the Republic*. Indianapolis: Bobbs-Merrill, 1941.

Hanighen, Frank C. *Santa Anna. The Napoleon of the West*. New York: Coward-McCann, 1934.

Haun, Cheryl. "The Whig Abolitionists' Attitude Toward the Mexican War," *Journal of the West*, XI (April 1972), 260–72.

Hawgood, John A. (ed.). *First and Last Consul. Thomas Oliver Larkin and the Americanization of California*. San Marino: Huntington Library, 1962.

Hawthorne, Nathaniel. *Life of Franklin Pierce*. Boston: Tichnor, Reed & Fields, 1852.

Haynes, Martin A. *Gen. Scott's Guide in Mexico. A Biographical Sketch of Col. Noah E. Smith*. Lake Village, N.H.: Lake Village Times, 1887.

Headley, Joel T. *The Life of Winfield Scott*. San Francisco: A. Roman & Co., 1861.

Heinl, Robert Debs, Jr. *Soldiers of the Sea. The United States Marine Corps, 1775–1962*. Annapolis: U.S. Naval Institute, 1962.

Heitman, Francis B. *Historical Register and Dictionary of the United States Army, From Its Organization, September 29, 1789, to March 2, 1903*. 2 vols., Urbana: University of Illinois Press, 1965.

Henderson, Alfred J. "A Morgan County Volunteer in the Mexican War," *Journal of the Illinois State Historical Society*, XLI (Dec. 1948), 383–99.

Henry, Robert Selph. *The Story of the Mexican War*. Indianapolis: Bobbs-Merrill Co., 1950.

Heyman, Max L. *Prudent Soldier. A Biography of Major General E. R. S. Canby 1817–1873*. Glendale: Arthur H. Clark Co., 1959.

High, James. "Jones at Monterey," *Journal of the West*, V (April 1966), 173–86.

Hinckley, Ted C. "American Anti-Catholicism During the Mexican War," *PHR*, XXXI (May 1962), 121–38.

Hopkins, G. T. "The San Patricio Battalion in the Mexican War," *U.S. Cavalry Journal*, XXIV (Sept. 1913), 279–84.

Horgan, Paul. *Great River: The Rio Grande in North American History*. 2 vols., New York: Rinehart & Co., 1954.

Howard, Oliver Otis. *General Taylor*. New York: D. Appleton & Co., 1892.

Hoyt, Edwin P. *Zachary Taylor*. Chicago: Reilly & Lee Co., 1966.

Hunt, Aurora. *Major General James Henry Carleton 1814–1873 Western Frontier Dragoon*. Glendale: Arthur H. Clark Co., 1958.

Hunt, Elvid. *History of Fort Leavenworth 1827–1927*. Fort Leavenworth: The General Service Schools Press, 1926.

Hurtado y Nuño, Enrique. "Ataque y Defensa del Puerto de Alvarado," *Revista General de la Armada de México*, III (Aug.–Oct. 1963), 11–18, 37–41.

Hussey, John Adam. "Bear Flag Revolt," *American Heritage*, I (Spring 1950), 24–27.

428 THE MEXICAN WAR, 1846–1848

————. "Commander John B. Montgomery and the Bear Flag Revolt," *USNIP*, LXXV (July 1939), 973–80.

————. "The Origin of the Gillespie Mission," *CHSQ*, XIX (March 1940), 43–58.

Huston, James A. *The Sinews of War: Army Logistics 1775–1953*. Washington: Office of the Chief of Military History, 1966.

Ingersoll, L. D. *A History of the War Department of the United States with Biographical Sketches of the Secretaries*. Washington: Francis B. Mohun, 1879.

Irey, Thomas R. "Soldiering, Suffering, and Dying in the Mexican War," *Journal of the West*, XI (April 1972), 285–98.

Jackson, Helen Hunt. "Echoes in the City of the Angels," *Century Magazine*, XXVII (Dec. 1883), 194–210.

Jay, William. *A Review of the Causes and Consequences of the Mexican War*. Boston: Benjamin B. Mussey & Co., 1849.

Jenkins, John S. *History of the War Between the United States and Mexico, From the Commencement of Hostilities to the Ratification of the Treaty of Peace*. Auburn: Derby & Miller, 1851.

————. *The Life of James Knox Polk Late President of the United States*. Hudson: P. S. Wynkoop, 1850.

Johnson, Allen, and Dumas Malone (eds.). *Dictionary of American Biography*. 20 vols., New York: Charles Scribner's Sons, 1928–36.

Johnson, Kenneth M. "Baja California and the Treaty of Guadalupe Hidalgo," *Journal of the West*, XI (April 1972), 328–47.

Johnson, Lucius W. "Yellow Jack, Master of Strategy," *USNIP*, LXXVI (July 1950), 1075–83.

Johnson, Robert Underwood, and Clarence Clough Buel (eds.). *Battles and Leaders of the Civil War*. 4 vols., New York: The Century Co., 1888.

Johnston, William Preston. *The Life of Gen. Albert Sidney Johnston, Embracing His Service in the Armies of the United States, the Republic of Texas, and the Confederate States*. New York: D. Appleton & Co., 1878.

Jones, Oakah L., Jr. "The Pacific Squadron and the Conquest of California," *Journal of the West*, V (April 1966), 187–202.

————. *Santa Anna*. New York: Twayne Publishers, Inc., 1968.

Karnes, Thomas L. *William Gilpin Western Nationalist*. Austin: University of Texas Press, 1970.

Kearny, Thomas. *General Philip Kearny Battle Soldier of Five Wars*. New York: G. P. Putnam's Sons, 1937.

————. "Kearny and 'Kit' Carson as Interpreted by Stanley Vestal," *NMHR*, V (Jan. 1930), 1–16.

————. "The Mexican War and the Conquest of California," *CHSQ*, VIII (Sept. 1929), 251–61.

Keleher, William A. *Turmoil in New Mexico, 1846–1868*. Santa Fe: The Rydal Press, 1952.

Kelly, Sister M. Margaret Jean. *The Career of Joseph Lane, Frontier Politician*. Washington: Catholic University Press, 1947.

Kelsey, Raynor Wickersham. "The United States Consulate in California," *Publications of the Academy of Pacific Coast History*, I, no. 5.

Kendall, George Wilkins. *The War Between the United States and Mexico . . . with a Description of Each Battle. . . .* New York: D. Appleton Co., 1851.

Klein, Julius. *The Making of the Treaty of Guadaloupe Hidalgo, on February 2, 1848.* Berkeley: The University Press, 1905.

Klein, Philip Shriver. *President James Buchanan A Biography.* University Park: Pennsylvania State University, 1962.

Kohl, Clayton Charles. *Claims as a Cause of the Mexican War.* New York: Graduate School, New York University, 1914.

Kreidberg, Marvin A., and Merton G. Henry. *History of Military Mobilization in the United States Army 1775–1945.* Washington: Department of the Army, 1955.

Kurtz, Wilbur G., Jr. "The First Regiment of Georgia Volunteers in the Mexican War," *Georgia Historical Quarterly,* XXVII (Dec. 1943), 301–23.

Ladd, Horatio O. *The War with Mexico.* New York: Dodd, Mead & Co., 1883.

Lamar, Howard Roberts. *The Far Southwest 1846–1912 A Territorial History.* New Haven: Yale University Press, 1966.

Lambert, Paul F. "The Movement for the Acquisition of all Mexico," *Journal of the West,* XI (April 1972), 317–27.

Lane, William B. "The Regiment of Mounted Riflemen in Mexico," *United Service,* XIV (Oct. 1895), 306–13.

———. "What Our Cavalry in Mexico Did and Did Not Do and Other Things," *United Service,* XV (June 1896), 482–503, XVI (July–Oct. 1896), 14–33, 110–19, 301–13.

Lanier, William D. "The Halls of Montezuma," *USNIP,* LXVII (Oct. 1941), 1385–98.

Lavender, David. *Bent's Fort.* New York: Doubleday & Co., 1954.

———. *Climax at Buena Vista: The American Campaign in Northeastern Mexico.* Philadelphia: J. B. Lippincott Co., 1966.

Lawton, W. T. *Essay on the Literature of the Mexican War.* N.p., n.d.

Lerdo de Tejada, Miguel M. *Apuntes Históricos de la Heróica Ciudad de Veracruz.* 3 vols., México: Vicente García Tores, 1850–58.

Lerwill, Leonard L., *The Personnel Replacement Systems in the U.S. Army.* Washington: Office of the Chief of Military History, 1952.

Lewis, Charles Lee. *Admiral Franklin Buchanan, Fearless Man of Action.* Baltimore: Norman, Remington Co., 1929.

———. *Famous American Marines.* Boston: L. C. Page & Co., 1950.

Lewis, Lloyd. *Captain Sam Grant.* Boston: Little, Brown & Co., 1950.

Lewis, Oscar (ed.). *California in 1846.* San Francisco: Grabhorn Press, 1934.

Lister, Florence C., and Robert H. Lister. *Chihuahua, Storehouse of Storms.* Albuquerque: University of New Mexico Press, 1966.

Livermore, Abiel Abbot. *The War with Mexico Reviewed.* Boston: American Peace Society, 1850.

Lofgren, Charles A. "Force and Diplomacy, 1846–1848," *Military Affairs,* XXXI (Summer 1967), 57–65.

Lott, W. S. "The Landing of the Expedition Against Vera Cruz in 1847,"

Military Service Institution of the United States, XXIV (May 1899), 422-28.

McCormac, Eugene Irving. *James K. Polk. A Political Biography*. New York: Russell & Russell Inc., 1965.

McCornack, Robert B. "The San Patricio Deserters in the Mexican War," *The Americas*, VIII (Oct. 1951), 131-42.

McCoy, Charles A. *Polk and the Presidency*. Austin: University of Texas Press, 1960.

McDonald, Archie P. (ed.). *The Mexican War: Crisis for American Democracy*. Lexington: D. C. Heath & Co., 1969.

McEniry, Sister Blanche Marie. *American Catholics in the War with Mexico*. Washington: Catholic University, 1932.

McKinley, Silas Bent, and Silas Bent. *Old Rough and Ready. The Life and Times of Zachary Taylor*. New York: Vanguard Press, 1946.

McMaster, John Bach. *A History of the People of the United States, From the Revolution to the Civil War*. Vol. VII. *1841-1850*. New York: D. Appleton & Co., 1914.

McNitt, Frank. "Navajo Campaigns and the Occupation of New Mexico, 1847-1848," *NMHR*, XLIII (July 1968), 173-94.

McWhinney, Grady, and Sue McWhinney (eds.). *To Mexico with Taylor and Scott 1845-1847*. Waltham: Blaisdell Publishing Co., 1969.

Mackall, William W. *A Son's Recollections of His Father*. New York: E. P. Dutton & Co., 1930.

Magner, James A. *Men of Mexico*. Milwaukee: Bruce Publishing Co., 1942.

Mahoney, Tom. "50 Hanged and 11 Branded, The Story of the San Patricio Battalion," *Southwest Review*, XXXII (Autumn 1947), 373-76.

Manno, Francis Joseph. "Yucatán en la Guerra Entre México y Estados Unidos," *Revista de la Universidad de Yucatán*, V (July–Aug. 1963), 51-64.

Mansfield, Edward D. *Life of General Winfield Scott*. New York: A. S. Barnes & Co., 1851.

————. *The Mexican War. A History of Its Origins, and a Detailed Account of the Victories which Terminated in the Surrender of the Capital; with the Official Despatches of the Generals*. New York: A. S. Barnes & Co., 1898.

Marti, Werner H. *Messenger of Destiny. The California Adventures, 1846-1847 of Archibald H. Gillespie, U.S. Marine Corps*. San Francisco: John Howell, 1955.

Martínez, Pablo L. *Historia de Baja California*. México: Editorial Baja California, 1956.

May, Ernest R. (ed.). *The Ultimate Decision: The President as Commander in Chief*. New York: George Braziller, 1960.

Meadows, Don. *The American Occupation of La Paz*. Los Angeles: Glen Dawson, 1955.

Meigs, William M. *The Life of Thomas Hart Benton*. Philadelphia: J. B. Lippincott & Co., 1904.

Meissner, Sophie Radford de. *Old Naval Days. Sketches from the Life of*

Rear Admiral William Radford, U.S.N. New York: H. Holt & Co., 1920.

Meriwether, Colyer. *Raphael Semmes.* Philadelphia: George W. Jacobs & Co., 1913.

Merk, Frederick. *Manifest Destiny and Mission in American History. A Reinterpretation.* New York: Alfred A. Knopf, 1963.

——. *The Monroe Doctrine and American Expansionism 1843–1846.* New York: Alfred A. Knopf, 1966.

Mestre Ghigliazza, Manuel. *Invasión Norteamericana en Tabasco (1846–1847), Documentos.* México: Imprenta Universitaria, 1948.

Metcalf, Clyde H. *A History of the United States Marine Corps.* New York: G. P. Putnam's Sons, 1939.

The Mexican War and Its Heroes: Being a Complete History of the Mexican War . . . Together with Numerous Anecdotes of the War, and Personal Adventures of the Officers. 2 vols. in 1, Philadelphia: Lippincott, Grambo & Co., 1850.

Molina, Ignacio. "El Asalto al Castillo de Chapultepec el Día 13 de Septiembre de 1847," *Revista Positiva,* II (Oct. 1, 1902), 444–64.

Montgomery, H. *The Life of Major General Zachary Taylor, Twelfth President of the United States.* Auburn: Derby & Miller, 1854.

Moore, John Bassett. *History and Digest of the International Arbitrations to Which the United States Has Been A Party. . . .* 6 vols., Washington: Government Printing Office, 1898.

Morison, Samuel Eliot. *"Old Bruin" Commodore Matthew Calbraith Perry.* Boston: Little, Brown & Co., 1967.

——, Frederick Merk, and Frank Freidel. *Dissent in Three American Wars.* Cambridge: Harvard University Press, 1970.

Morrison, Chaplin W. *Democratic Politics and Sectionalism: The Wilmot Proviso Controversy.* Chapel Hill: University of North Carolina Press, 1967.

Neasham, Aubrey. "The Raising of the Flag at Monterey, California, July 1846," *CHSQ,* XXV (June 1946), 193–203.

Neeser, Robert Wilden. *Statistical and Chronological History of the United States Navy 1775–1907.* 2 vols., Macmillan Co., 1909.

Nevins, Allan. *Fremont. Pathmaker of the West.* New York: Longmans, Green, & Co., 1955.

Nichols, Edward J. *Towards Gettysburg. A Biography of General John F. Reynolds.* State College: Pennsylvania State University Press, 1958.

——. *Zach Taylor's Little Army.* Garden City: Doubleday & Co., 1963.

Nichols, Roy Franklin. *Franklin Pierce: Young Hickory of the Granite Hills.* Philadelphia: University of Pennsylvania Press, 1931.

——. *The Stakes of Power 1845–1877.* New York: Hill & Wang, 1961.

Nortrup, Jack. "Nicholas Trist's Mission to Mexico: A Reinterpretation," *SWHQ,* LXXI (Jan. 1968), 321–46.

Nye, Russell B. *George Bancroft: Brahmin Rebel.* New York: Alfred A. Knopf, 1944.

Oficial de Infantería, *Campaña Contra los Americanos del Norte. Primera Parte. Relación Histórica de las Cueranta Días que Mandó en Gefe el*

Ejército del Norte el E. Sr. General de División Don Mariano Arista. México: Ignacio Cumplido, 1846.

Olejar, Paul D. "Rockets in Early American Wars," *Military Affairs*, X (Winter 1946), 16–34.

Oliva, Leo E. *Soldiers on the Santa Fe Trail.* Norman: University of Oklahoma Press, 1967.

Owen, Charles H. *The Justice of the Mexican War. A Review of the Causes and Results of the War with a View to Distinguishing Evidence from Opinion and Inference.* New York: G. P. Putnam's Sons, 1908.

Paullin, Charles Oscar. *Paullin's History of Naval Administration, 1775–1911.* Annapolis: U.S. Naval Institute, 1968.

Payne, Darwin. "Camp Life in the Army of Occupation: Corpus Christi, July 1845 to March 1846," *SWHQ*, LXXIII (Jan. 1970), 326–42.

Pelzer, Louis. *Marches of the Dragoons in the Mississippi Valley. An Account of Marches and Activities of the First Regiment United States Dragoons in the Mississippi Valley Between the Years 1833 and 1850.* Iowa City: State Historical Society of Iowa, 1917.

Perry, Oran. *Indiana in the Mexican War.* Indianapolis: William B. Burford, 1908.

Peterson, Charles J. *The American Navy, Being Authentic History of U.S. Navy and Biographical Sketches of American Naval Heroes From the Formation of the Navy to the Close of the Mexican War.* Philadelphia: J. B. Smith & Co., 1858.

Plumb, Robert J. "The Alcalde of Monterrey," *USNIP*, XCV (Jan. 1969), 72–83.

Porter, Valentine Mott. "A History of Battery 'A' of St. Louis," *Missouri Historical Society Collections*, II (March 1905), 1–48.

Price, Glenn W. *Origins of the War with Mexico: The Polk–Stockton Intrigue.* Austin: University of Texas Press, 1967.

Prince, L. Bradford. *Historical Sketches of New Mexico from the Earliest Records to the American Occupation.* New York: Leggatt Bros, 1883.

Quisenberry, Anderson Chenault. *History by Illustration. General Zachary Taylor and the Mexican War.* Frankfort: Kentucky State Historical Society, 1911.

Ramírez, José Fernando. *Mexico During the War with the United States.* Ed. Walter V. Scholes. Trans. Elliott B. Scheer. Columbia: University of Missouri Press, 1950.

Ramsey, Albert C. (trans.). *The Other Side: Or, Notes for the History of the War Between Mexico and the United States.* New York: John Wiley, 1850.

Rea, Robert R. *Sterling Price. The Lee of the West.* Little Rock: Pioneer Press, 1959.

Rea, Vargas (ed.). *Apuntes Históricos Sobre los Acontecimientos Notables de la Guerra Entre México y los Estados Unidos del Norte.* México: Biblioteca Aportación Histórica, 1945.

Read, Benjamin M. *Guerra México-Americana.* Santa Fe: Cia. Impresora del Nuevo Méxicano, 1910.

Reavis, L. U. *The Life and Military Services of Gen. William Selby Harney.* St. Louis: Bryan, Brand & Co., 1878.

Reed, Nelson. *The Caste War of Yucatan.* Stanford: Stanford University Press, 1964.

Reeves, Jesse S. *American Diplomacy Under Tyler and Polk.* Baltimore: Johns Hopkins Press, 1907.

———. "The Treaty of Guadalupe-Hidalgo," *AHR*, X (Jan. 1905), 309–24.

Reid, Samuel C., Jr. *The Scouting Expeditions of McCulloch's Texas Rangers: Or, the Summer and Fall Campaigns of the Army of the United States in Mexico—1846.* . . . Philadelphia: J. W. Bradley, 1860.

Rezneck, Samuel. *Profiles Out of the Past of Troy, New York Since 1789.* Troy: Greater Troy Chamber of Commerce, 1970.

Richman, Irving Berdine. *California Under Spain and Mexico 1535–1847.* Boston: Houghton Mifflin Co., 1911.

Ripley, Roswell Sabine. *War with Mexico.* 2 vols., New York: Harper & Bros., 1899.

Rippy, J. Fred. *Joel R. Poinsett, Versatile American.* New York: Greenwood Press, 1968.

———. *The United States and Mexico.* New York: Alfred A. Knopf, 1926.

Risch, Erna. *Quartermaster Support of the Army. A History of the Corps 1775–1939.* Washington: Quartermaster Historian's Office, 1962.

Riva Palacio, Vicente (ed.). *México a Través de los Siglos.* 6 vols., México: Editorial Cumbre, 1940.

Rivera Cambas, Manuel. *Historia Antigua y Moderna de Jalapa y de las Revoluciones del Estado de Veracruz.* 5 vols., México: Ignacio Cumplido, 1869–71.

Rives, George L. "Mexican Diplomacy on the Eve of War with the United States," *AHR*, XVIII (Jan. 1913), 275–94.

———. *The United States and Mexico 1821–1848.* 2 vols., New York: Charles Scribner's Sons, 1913.

Roa Bárcena, José María. *Recuerdos de la Invasión Norte-Americana (1846–1848).* 3 vols., México: Editorial Porrua, 1947.

Roberts, Brigham Henry. *The Mormon Battalion. Its History and Achievements.* Salt Lake City: The Deseret News, 1919.

Robinson, Fayette. *An Account of the Organization of the Army of the United States; with Biographies of Distinguished Officers of All Grades.* Philadelphia: E. H. Butler & Co., 1848.

———. *Mexico and Her Military Chieftains, From the Revolution of Hidalgo to the Present Time.* Hartford: Silas Andrus & Son, 1848.

Rodenbough, Theodore F. *From Everglades to Cañon with the Second Dragoons . . . 1836–1875.* New York: D. Van Nostrand, 1875.

——— and William L. Haskin (eds.). *The Army of the United States. Historical Sketches of the Staff and Line with Portraits of the Generals-in-Chief.* New York: Merrill & Co., 1896.

Rogers, Fred Blackburn. "Bear Flag Lieutenant," *CHSQ*, XXIX (June–Dec. 1950), 129–38, 261–78, 333–44, XXX (March 1951), 49–66.

———. *Montgomery and the Portsmouth.* San Francisco: John Howell, 1958.

Rogers, Joseph M. *Thomas Hart Benton.* Philadelphia: G. W. Jacobs & Co., 1905.

Romer, Margaret. " 'Lean John' Rides for Help," *Journal of the West*, V (April 1966), 203–6.

Rose, Victor M. *The Life and Services of Gen. Ben McCulloch.* Austin: The Steck Co., 1958.

The Rough and Ready Annual; or Military Souvenir. New York: D. Appleton & Co., 1848.

Royce, Josiah. *California, from the Conquest in 1846 to the Second Vigilance Committee in San Francisco: A Study of American Character.* New York: Alfred A. Knopf, 1948.

————. "Montgomery and Fremont: New Documents on the Bear Flag Affair," *Century Magazine,* XLI (March 1891), 780–83.

Ruhlen, George. "Kearny's Route from the Rio Grande to the Gila," *NMHR,* XXXII (July 1957), 213–30.

Ryan, Daniel J. "Ohio in the Mexican War," *Ohio Archaeological and Historical Quarterly,* XXI (April–July 1912), 277–95.

Sabin, Edward Legrand. *Kit Carson Days 1809–1868. "Adventure in the Path of Empire."* 2 vols., New York: Press of the Pioneers, Inc., 1933.

Sanchez, Lamego, Miguel A. *El Colegio Militar y la Defensa de Chapultepec en Septiembre de 1847.* México: n.p., 1947.

Scheina, Robert L. "The Forgotten Fleet: The Mexican Navy on the Eve of War, 1845," *American Neptune,* XXX (Jan. 1970), 46–55.

————. "Seapower Misused: Mexico at War 1846–8," *Mariner's Mirror,* LVII (1971), 203–214.

Scott, Henry L. *Military Dictionary: Comprising Technical Definitions; Information on Raising and Keeping Troops; Actual Service, Including Make-Shifts and Improved Materiel; and Law, Government, Regulation, and Administration Relating to Land Forces.* New York: Greenwood Press, 1968.

Scott, James Brown (ed.). *Prize Cases Decided in the United States Supreme Court.* 3 vols., Oxford: Oxford University Press, 1923.

Seager, Robert, II. *And Tyler Too. A Biography of John and Julia Gardiner Tyler.* New York: McGraw-Hill Book Co., 1963.

Sears, Louis Martin. *John Slidell.* Durham: Duke University Press, 1925.

————. "Nicholas P. Trist, A Diplomat with Ideals," *MVHR,* XI (June 1924), 85–98.

————. "Slidell's Mission to Mexico," *South Atlantic Quarterly,* XII (Jan. 1913), 12–26.

Sellers, Charles. *James K. Polk Continentalist 1843–1846.* Princeton: Princeton University Press, 1966.

Shenton, James P. *Robert John Walker, A Politician from Jackson to Lincoln.* New York: Columbia University Press, 1961.

Sherman, Edwin A. *The Life of the Late Rear Admiral John Drake Sloat.* . . . Oakland: Carruth & Carruth, 1902.

Sibley, Joel H. *The Shrine of Party, Congressional Voting Behavior, 1841–1852.* Pittsburgh: University of Pittsburgh Press, 1967.

Silver, James W. *Edmund Pendleton Gaines, Frontier General.* Baton Rouge: Louisiana State University Press, 1949.

Singletary, Otis A. *The Mexican War.* Chicago: University of Chicago Press, 1960.

Sioussat, St. George Leakin. "James Buchanan Secretary of State March 5, 1845 to March 6, 1849," in Samuel Flagg Bemis (ed.). *The American*

Secretaries of State and Their Diplomacy, V, New York: Cooper Square Publishers, 1963.

Smiley, David L. *Lion of White Hall. The Life of Cassius M. Clay.* Madison: University of Wisconsin Press, 1962.

Smith, Arthur D. Howden. *Old Fuss and Feathers. The Life and Exploits of Lt.-General Winfield Scott.* New York: Greystone Press, 1937.

Smith, Justin H. "American Rule in Mexico," *AHR*, XXIII (Jan. 1918), 287–302.

———. *The Annexation of Texas.* New York: Barker & Taylor Co., 1911.

———. "La Republica de Rio Grande," *AHR*, XXV (July 1920), 660–75.

———. *The War with Mexico.* 2 vols., New York: Macmillan Co., 1919.

Smith, Louis. *American Democracy and Military Power: A Study of Civil Control of the Military Power in the United States.* Chicago: University of Chicago Press, 1951.

Smith, Ralph A. "Contrabando en la Guerra con Estados Unidos," *Historia Méxicana*, XI (Jan.–March, 1962), 361–81.

Spell, Lota M. "The Anglo-Saxon Press in Mexico, 1846–1848," *AHR*, XXXVIII (Oct. 1932), 20–31.

Spencer, Ivor Debenham. "Overseas War—In 1846!" *Military Affairs*, IX (Winter 1945), 306–13.

———. *The Victor and the Spoils. A Life of William L. Marcy.* Providence: Brown University Press, 1959.

Sprout, Harold and Margaret. *The Rise of American Naval Power 1775–1918.* Princeton: Princeton University Press, 1942.

Stenberg, Richard R. "The Failure of Polk's Mexican War Intrigue of 1845," *PHR*, IV (March 1935), 36–68.

———. "Intrigue for Annexation," *Southwestern Review*, XXV (Jan. 1939), 58–69.

———. "The Motivation of the Wilmot Proviso," *MVHR*, XVIII (March 1932), 535–51.

———. "Polk and Frémont, 1845–1846," *PHR*, VII (June 1938), 211–27.

———. "President Polk and California: Additional Documents," *PHR*, X (June 1941), 217–19.

Stephenson, Nathaniel W. *Texas and the Mexican War: A Chronicle of the Winning of the Southwest.* New Haven: Yale University Press, 1921.

Stevens, Hazard. *The Life of Isaac Ingalls Stevens.* 2 vols., Boston: Houghton Mifflin & Co., 1901.

Stevens, Isaac I. *Campaigns of the Rio Grande and of Mexico.* New York: D. Appleton & Co., 1851.

Strode, Hudson. *Jefferson Davis American Patriot, 1808–1861.* New York: Harcourt, Brace & Co., 1955.

Sumner, Charles. "Report on the War with Mexico," *Old South Leaflets*, VI, no. 132 (1904).

Sydnor, Charles S. *The Development of Southern Sectionalism 1819–1848.* Baton Rouge: Louisiana State University Press, 1948.

Tanner, John Douglas. "Campaigns for Los Angeles—December 29, 1846 to January 10, 1847," *CHSQ*, XLVIII (Sept. 1969), 219–41.

Taylor and His Generals. A Biography of Major General Zachary Taylor;

Sketches of the Lives of Generals Worth, Wool, and Twiggs; with a Full Account of the Various Actions of Their Divisions in Mexico up to the Present Time; Together with a History of the Bombardment of Vera Cruz, and a Sketch of the Life of Major General Winfield Scott. Philadelphia: E. H. Butler & Co., 1847.

Tays, George. "Fremont Had No Secret Instructions," *PHR,* IX (May 1950), 157-71.

Thomas, David Yancey. *A History of Military Government in Newly Acquired Territory of the United States.* New York: Columbia University Press, 1904.

Thorpe, T. B. *Our Army at Monterey.* Philadelphia: Carey & Hart, 1847.

———. *Our Army on the Rio Grande.* Philadelphia: Carey & Hart, 1846.

Tinkcom, Henry Marlin. *John White Geary, Soldier-Statesman, 1819-1873.* Philadelphia: University of Pennsylvania Press, 1940.

Todd, Charles Burr. *The Battles of San Pasqual. A Study.* Pomona: Progress Publishing Co., 1925.

Toro, Alfonso. *Compendia de la Historia de México.* México: Editorial Patria, 1943.

Trens, Manuel B. *Historia de Veracruz.* 4 vols., México, n.p., 1947-50.

Twelfth U.S. Infantry 1798-1919, Its Story—By Its Men. N.p.: Twelfth Infantry, 1919.

Twitchell, Ralph Emerson. *The Conquest of Santa Fe 1846.* Truchas: Tate Gallery, 1967.

———. *The History of the Military Occupation of the Territory of New Mexico from 1846 to 1851 by the Government of the United States.* Denver: Smith-Brooks Co., 1909.

Tyler, Daniel. *A Concise History of the Mormon Battalion in the Mexican War 1846-1847.* N.p., 1881.

———. "Governor Armijo's Moment of Truth," *Journal of the West,* XI (April 1972), 307-16.

Underhill, Reuben L. *From Cowhides to Golden Fleece.* Palo Alto: Stanford University Press, 1946.

Upton, Emory. *The Military Policy of the United States.* New York: Greenwood Press, 1968.

Valades, José C. *Breve Historia de la Guerra con los Estados Unidos.* México: Editorial Patria, 1947.

———. *Historia del Puebla de México.* 2 vols., México: Editores Méxicanos Unidos, 1967.

Van Deusen, Glyndon G. *The Jacksonian Era 1828-1848.* New York: Harper & Bros., 1966.

Vandiver, Frank E. "The Mexican War Experience of Josiah Gorgas," *Journal of Southern History,* XIII (Aug. 1947), 373-94.

———. *Mighty Stonewall.* New York: McGraw-Hill Book Co., 1957.

———. "A Note on Josiah Gorgas in the Mexican War," *Journal of Southern History,* XI (Feb. 1945), 103-6.

Vestal, Stanley. *Kit Carson, The Happy Warrior of the Old West.* Boston: Houghton Mifflin Co., 1928.

Vigil y Robles, Guillermo. *La Invasión de México por los Estados Unidos en los Años de 1846, 1847, y 1848.* México: Tip. E. Correcional, 1923.

Viola, Herman J. "Zachary Taylor and the Indiana Volunteers," *SWHQ,* LXXII (Jan. 1969), 335–46.

Wallace, Edward S. "The Battalion of Saint Patrick in the Mexican War," *Military Affairs,* XIV (Summer 1950), 84–91.

———. "Deserters in the Mexican War," *HAHR,* XV (Aug. 1935), 374–82.

———. *Destiny and Glory.* New York: Coward-McCann, Inc., 1957.

———. "General William Jenkins Worth and Texas," *SWHQ,* LIV (Oct. 1950), 159–68.

———. *General William Jenkins Worth. Monterrey's Forgotten Hero.* Dallas: Southern Methodist University Press, 1953.

———. "The United States Army in Mexico City," *Military Affairs,* XIII (Fall 1949), 158–66.

Wallace, Isabel. *Life and Letters of General W. H. L. Wallace.* Chicago: R. R. Donnelley & Sons Co., 1909.

Wallace, Joseph. *Sketch of the Life and Public Services of Edward D. Baker, United States Senator from Oregon, and Formerly Representative in Congress from Illinois, Who Died Near Leesburg, Va., October 21, A.D. 1861.* Springfield, Ill.: n.p., 1870.

Wallace, Lee A., Jr. "The First Regiment of Virginia Volunteers, 1846–1848," *Virginia Magazine of History and Biography,* LXXVII (Jan. 1969), 46–77.

———. "Raising a Volunteer Regiment for Mexico, 1846–1847," *North Carolina Historical Review,* XXXV (Jan. 1958).

Walton, Brian G. "The Elections for the Thirtieth Congress and the Presidential Candidacy of Zachary Taylor," *Journal of Southern History,* XXXV (May 1969), 186–202.

Webb, Walter Prescott. *The Texas Rangers: A Century of Frontier Defense.* Boston: Houghton Mifflin Co., 1935.

Weigley, Russell F. *History of the United States Army.* New York: Macmillan Co., 1967.

Weinberg, Albert K. *Manifest Destiny: A Study of Nationalist Expansion in American History.* Chicago: Quadrangle Paperbacks, 1963.

Wessels, William L. *Born to Be a Soldier. The Military Career of William Wing Loring of St. Augustine, Florida.* Fort Worth: Texas Christian University Press, 1971.

West, Richard Sedgewick, Jr. *The Second Admiral: A Life of David Dixon Porter, 1813–1891.* New York: Coward-McCann, 1937.

Wharton, Clarence R. *El Presidente. A Sketch of the Life of General Santa Anna.* Austin: Gammel's Book Store, 1924.

White, Leonard D. *The Jacksonians. A Study in Administrative History 1829–1861.* New York: Macmillan Co., 1954.

Wilcox, Cadmus M. *History of the Mexican War.* Washington: Church News Publishing Co., 1892.

Williams, Mary Wilhelmine. "Secessionist Diplomacy of Yucatán," *HAHR,* IX (May 1929), 132–43.

Wiltsee, Ernest A. "The British Vice Consul and the Events of 1846," *CHSQ*, X (June 1931), 99–138.

———. *The Truth About Frémont: An Inquiry.* San Francisco: J. H. Nash, 1936.

Winslow, Arthur. *Francis Winslow. His Forebears and Life. Based Upon Family Records and Correspondence During XXX Years.* Norwood: Plimpton Press, 1935.

Wood, Walter Shea. "The 130th Infantry, Illinois National Guard. A Military History, 1778–1919," *Journal of the Illinois State Historical Society*, XXX (July 1937), 193–255.

Woodward, Arthur. "Juan Flaco's Ride," *HSSCQ*, XIX (Jan. 1937), 22–39.

———. *Lances at San Pascual.* San Francisco: California Historical Society, 1948.

Wormser, Richard. *The Yellowlegs. The Story of the United States Cavalry.* Garden City: Doubleday & Co., 1966.

Wright, Corrine King. "The Conquest of Los Angeles," *HSSCP*, XI (1918), 18–25.

Wright, Marcus J. *General Scott.* New York: D. Appleton & Co., 1897.

Ynsfrán, Pablo Max. *Catálogo de los Manuscriptos del Archivo de Don Valentín Gómez Farías Obrantes en la Universidad de Texas Colección Latinamericana.* México: Editorial Jus, 1968.

Index

Index

Hagner, Lt. Peter V., 322
Halcoma, Pue., 334
Hale, Rep. John P., 359
Hall, Pvt. Willard P., 135
Halleck, Capt. Henry W., 347, 350, 396
Hamer, Brig. Gen. Thomas L., 75
Hamilton, Lt. Fowler, 38
Hammond, Lt. Thomas C., 134, 187–8
Hamtramck, Col. John F., 225, 231
Hannegan, Sen. Edward A., 370
Hardee, Capt. William J., 48
Hardin, Col. John J., 147, 149–50, 210, 216
Hargous, Luis S., 125
Harney, Lt. Col. William S., 146–8, 160, 251, 261, 265, 300, 322, 332
Harris, Maj. John, 377
Haskell, Col. William, 267
Hawkins, Capt. Edgar S., 50, 52
Hays, Col. John C., 93, 272, 330, 334, 385
Hazard, Lt. Samuel F., 117
Heady, Capt. William J., 207
Henderson, Gov. J. Pinckney, 42, 90, 95, 99, 219
Hendley, Capt. Israel R., 140
Hendrie, Daniel D., 227
Henry, Sgt. Thomas, 267
Heredia, Brig. Gen. José A., 154–5
Herndon, Lt. Cdr. W. L., 339
Herrera, Gen. José Joaquín de, 4, 16–17, 21–5, 328, 331, 373, 379, 385, 393
Herrera, Lt. Col. José María, 92
Herrera, Col. Pedro Miguel, 252
Herron, Capt. John, 329
Heywood, Lt. Charles, 347–9
Hidalgo, Col. Claro, 341
Higgins, Mid. Eugene, 171
Hitchcock, Lt. Col. Ethan A., 18, 33, 35, 246, 268, 274, 311–12
Holzinger, Lt. Sebastián, 250
Hone, Philip, 399
Hopping, Brig. Gen. Enos D., 277
Houston, Sam, 7, 10, 272
Howard, George T., 127, 131
Howard, Capt. W. A., 116, 340
Huamantla, Battle of, 331
Hudson, Capt. Thomas B., 151
Huger, Capt. Benjamin, 309, 312, 320
Hughes, Col. George W., 334, 385
Hughes, Bishop John, 85
Hull, Cdr. Joseph B., 167, 344

Hunt, Lt. Henry J., 320
Hunt, Lt. Col. Thomas F., 84, 376
Hunt, Lt. William E., 115, 119
Hunter, Lt. Bushrod, 114
Hunter, Lt. Charles G., 260

Ibarra, Domingo, 284
Independence, 179, 195, 345–6, 357
Independent Treasury, 359, 393
Ingraham, Cdr. Duncan N., 109
Iris, 339
Irvin, Lt. Col. William, 218

Jackson, Seaman Samuel, 115
Jackson, Lt. Thomas J., 316, 319, 395
Jalapa, Ver., 25, 28, 252, 260–1, 268, 272–3, 283, 330, 332–4, 387–8
Jalisco, 201, 332
Jararo, Brig. Gen. José María, 263
Jarauta, Fr. Caledonio Domeco, 273, 330, 334–5
Jarvis, Cdr. Joseph R., 58
Jefferson Barracks, Mo., 57
Jefferson City, Mo., 128, 131
Jesup, Brig. Gen. Thomas S., 36, 84, 205, 239, 259, 272
Jeune Nelly, 257
John Adams, 114, 339
Johnson, Sen. Henry, 8
Johnson, Gov. Isaac, 48, 57
Johnston, Capt. Abraham R., 188
Johnston, Col. Albert Sidney, 87
Johnston, Lt. Col. Joseph E., 241, 314
Jones, Pres. Anson, 9–10
Jones, Brig. Gen. Roger, 6, 32, 48, 150, 220, 237, 328, 398
Jones, Commo. Thomas apCatesby, 13, 164, 350
Jornada del Muerto, N. Mex., 151–2
Juan Manuel, Archbishop of Mexico City, 336
Julia, 193
Juno, 172
Juvera, Brig. Gen. Julián, 211–12, 214–15

Kearny, Capt. Philip, 300
Kearny, Brig. Gen. Stephen W., 74; New Mexico, 127–34, 377, 390, 394–5; California, 128, 135, 137–8, 169, 186–9, 194–5; Frémont, 193–6, 367–8; Baja California, 345